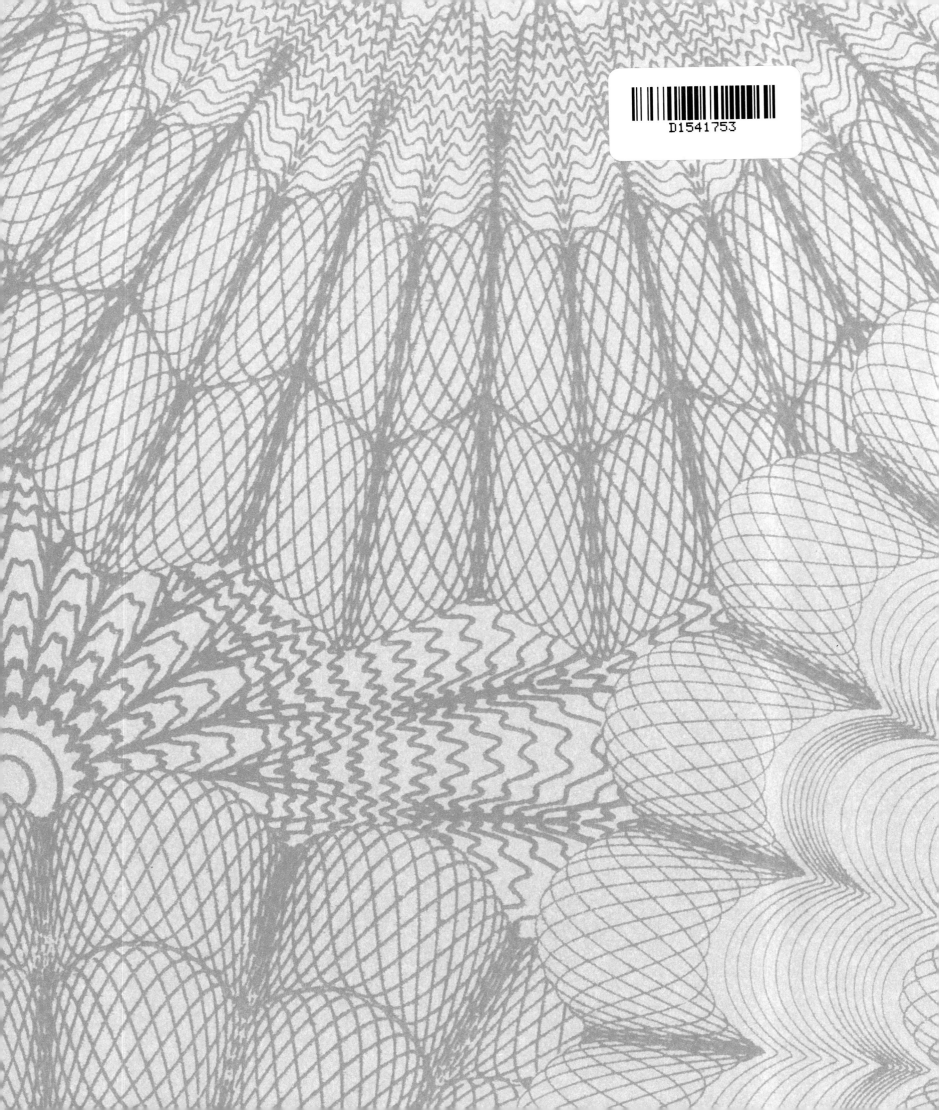

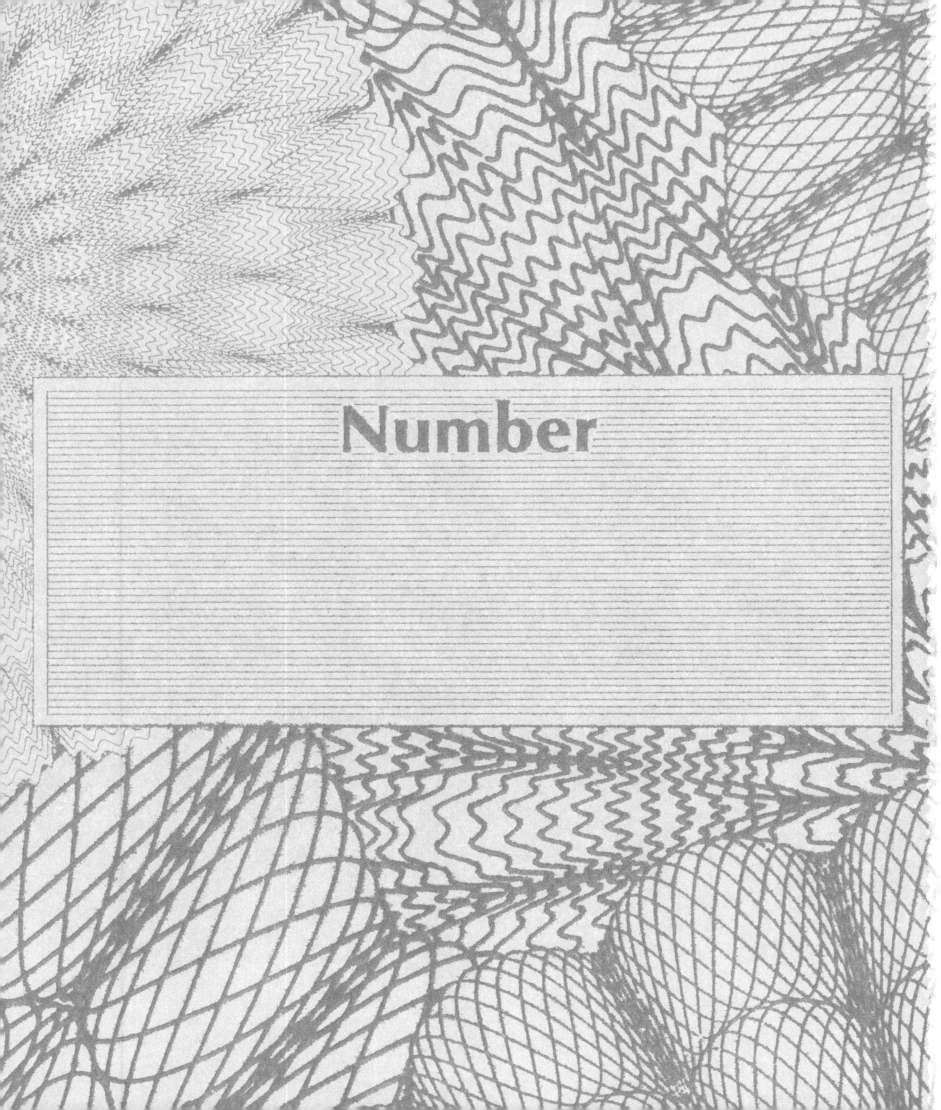

Number

Genealogy of American Finance

Genealogy of American Finance

Robert E. Wright

Richard Sylla

MUSEUM OF AMERICAN FINANCE
48 WALL STREET, NEW YORK CITY

Columbia Business School
Publishing

Genealogy of American Finance

Museum of American Finance
48 Wall Street
New York, NY 10005
www.moaf.org

Columbia University Press
Publishers Since 1893
New York Chichester, West Sussex
cup.columbia.edu

Design: Thumb/Luke Bulman
with Celine Gordon and Camille Sacha Salvador

Library of Congress Cataloging-in-Publication Data

Wright, Robert E. (Robert Eric), 1969–
Sylla, Richard (Richard Sylla), 1940–
  Genealogy of American finance/Robert E. Wright and Richard Sylla.
     pages cm
  Includes bibliographical references and index.
  ISBN 978-0-231-17026-0 (cloth : alk. paper)
1. Banks and banking—United States. 2. Investment banking—United States.
     3. Financial institutions—United States. I. Title.
  HG2491.W75 2015
  332.1'20973—dc23

                    2014027289

Columbia University Press books are printed on permanent and durable acid-free paper.
This book is printed on paper with recycled content. Printed in Canada.

c 10 9 8 7 6 5 4 3 2 1

Contents

The Big 50

Foreword

I was introduced to the leadership of the Museum of American Finance through my friend and television personality, Consuelo Mack, who serves on the Museum's Board of Trustees. During the course of my initial conversation with President David Cowen, I brought up an idea I have had for years, which is to trace the genealogies—or family trees—of the major American financial firms. I have been working in finance for more than 50 years and have witnessed first-hand many dramatic changes in the industry. So many firms that existed when I first began investing are no longer around.

Given that my firm looks for "value" in companies when we invest, I asked David if there was value in this idea. His response was that, indeed, this would be an invaluable research tool. This book is the first output of that discussion.

As the only independent finance museum in the nation, the Museum often fields calls from researchers inquiring about what happened to certain firms or banks—now defunct or acquired. Many times those questions have been difficult to answer. Moreover, the two main regulatory bodies, The Federal Reserve and the FDIC, do not have complete information and are, therefore, also unable to also answer those questions. According to the Museum's exhibit team, an area of the "Banking in America" exhibit featuring an abridged genealogy of the Bank of America was the single largest piece of research that went into any section of the Museum's permanent exhibits. This is largely because more than one hundred years' worth of merger and acquisition data is so difficult to come by.

My conversations with David and the Museum team resulted in my commitment to underwrite a massive research project to compile these family trees and house them in a central location. It has taken well over a year of research—which included hundreds of hours of archival legwork—to compile these genealogies and make them publicly available.

I applaud Professors Wright and Sylla for their research and writing efforts, which have made this project a reality. As a Columbia University MBA, I am pleased to note that my alma mater has enthusiastically embraced this idea as well, and that this beautiful book has been produced by Columbia Business School Publishing.

Now, if the Museum receives a research inquiry about past financial firms, the staff is able to answer where that firm's history fits into the modern financial landscape. Or, better yet, people can access the information themselves via this book or the Museum's website.

This project sheds tremendous light into the dynamic nature of our nation's financial history. One can never completely understand the future without a comprehension of the past. In an easy-to-read and understandable manner, this book gives a narrative history that is accessible to all—from the newcomer working at a bank to the finance professional, from the student to the scholar, from the practitioner to the regulator.

Please enjoy the book, as each chapter will transport you back in time to see the birth and growth of these 50 financial institutions.

—Charles M. Royce
CEO, The Royce Funds

MINNEAPOLIS–45
PARAMUS, NJ–25
PORTLAND, ME–44
BOSTON–40, 41
PROVIDENCE, RI–38
BRIDGEPORT, CT–22
NORWALK, CT–22
BUFFALO–21, 30
DETROIT–1
CHICAGO, RIVERWOODS–33, 18
LIVINGSTON, NJ–13
CLEVELAND–29
NEW YORK CITY–2, 3, 5, 6, 14, 17, 19, 23, 24, 28, 31, 32, 48
RENO–27
SALT LAKE CITY–50
PITTSBURGH–35
DES MOINES–37
COLUMBUS–26
SAN FRANCISCO–12, 46, 49
CINCINNATI–20
WILMINGTON, DE–9
MCLEAN, VA–11
WINSTON-SALEM–7
LOS ANGELES–15
TULSA–10
BIRMINGHAM–39
ATLANTA–42
COLUMBUS–43
DALLAS–16
SAN ANTONIO–47
HOUSTON–8
HONOLULU–4
SAN JUAN, PR–36

#		#		#	
1	Ally Financial	18	Discover Financial	35	PNC Financial Services
2	American Express	19	E*Trade	36	Popular
3	American International Group	20	Fifth Third Bancorp	37	Principal Financial Group
4	BancWest	21	First Niagara	38	RBS-Citizens Financial
5	Bank of America	22	General Electric Capital	39	Regions Financial
6	Bank of New York Mellon	23	Goldman Sachs	40	Santander Holdings USA
7	BB&T	24	HSBC North America	41	State Street
8	BBVA Compass Bancshares	25	Hudson City Bancorp	42	SunTrust Banks
9	BMO Financial	26	Huntington Bancshares	43	Synovus Financial
10	BOK Financial	27	John Deere Capital	44	TD Bank US Holding
11	Capital One Financial	28	JPMorgan Chase	45	U.S. Bancorp
12	Charles Schwab	29	KeyCorp	46	UnionBanCal
13	CIT Group	30	M&T Bank	47	USAA
14	Citigroup	31	Morgan Stanley	48	Utrecht-America Holdings
15	City National	32	New York Community Bancorp	49	Wells Fargo
16	Comerica	33	Northern Trust	50	Zions Bancorporation
17	Deutsche Bank	34	People's United Financial		

Holding Company Location

CANADA
BMO Financial
TD Bank US Holding

FRANCE
BancWest

GERMANY
Deutsche Bank

GREAT BRITAIN
HSBC North America
RBS-Citizens Financial

JAPAN
UnionBanCal

NETHERLANDS
Utrecht-America Holdings

SPAIN
BBVA Compass Bancshares
Popular
Santander Holdings USA

UNITED STATES
Ally Financial
American Express
American International Group
Bank of America
Bank of New York Mellon
BB&T
BOK Financial
Capital One Financial
Charles Schwab
CIT Group
Citigroup
City National
Comerica
Discover Financial
E*Trade
Fifth Third Bancorp
First Niagara
General Electric Capital
Goldman Sachs
Hudson City Bancorp
Huntington Bancshares
John Deere Capital
JPMorgan Chase

KeyCorp
M&T Bank
Morgan Stanley
New York Community Bancorp
Northern Trust
People's United Financial
PNC Financial Services
Principal Financial Group
Regions Financial
State Street
SunTrust Banks
Synovus Financial
U.S. Bancorp
USAA
Wells Fargo
Zions Bancorporation

Industry of Origin

BROKERAGE
Charles Schwab
E*Trade

COMMERCIAL BANKING
BancWest
Bank of America
Bank of New York Mellon
BB&T
BBVA Compass Bancshares
BMO Financial
BOK Financial
Citigroup
City National
Comerica
Deutsche Bank
Fifth Third Bancorp
First Niagara
HSBC North America
Hudson City Bancorp
Huntington Bancshares
KeyCorp
M&T Bank
New York Community Bancorp
Northern Trust
People's United Financial
PNC Financial Services
Popular
RBS-Citizens Financial
Regions Financial
Santander Holdings USA
State Street
SunTrust Banks
Synovus Financial
TD Bank US Holding
U.S. Bancorp
UnionBanCal
Utrecht-America Holdings
Zions Bancorporation

COMMERCIAL BANKING / WATER UTILITY
JPMorgan Chase

CREDIT CARDS
Capital One Financial
Discover Financial

FINANCE
CIT Group

FREIGHT
American Express
Wells Fargo

INSURANCE
American International Group
Principal Financial Group
USAA

INVESTMENT BANKING
Goldman Sachs
Morgan Stanley

MANUFACTURING
Ally Financial
General Electric Capital
John Deere Capital

Assets

JPMorgan Chase	2,400,000,000,000
Bank of America	2,100,000,000,000
Citigroup	1,900,000,000,000
Wells Fargo	1,400,000,000,000
Goldman Sachs	939,000,000,000
Morgan Stanley	803,000,000,000
American International Group	537,000,000,000
General Electric Capital	529,000,000,000
Bank of New York Mellon	360,000,000,000
U.S. Bancorp	353,000,000,000
HSBC North America	322,000,000,000
PNC Financial Services	305,000,000,000
Capital One Financial	297,000,000,000
TD Bank US Holding	229,000,000,000
State Street	227,000,000,000
Principal Financial Group	197,000,000,000
BB&T	183,000,000,000
SunTrust Banks	172,000,000,000
American Express	152,000,000,000
Ally Financial	151,000,000,000
Charles Schwab	136,000,000,000
Fifth Third Bancorp	123,000,000,000
RBS-Citizens Financial	122,500,000,000
USAA	120,000,000,000
Regions Financial	119,000,000,000
BMO Financial	112,000,000,000
UnionBanCal	102,000,000,000
Northern Trust	97,000,000,000
KeyCorp	91,000,000,000
M&T Bank	83,000,000,000
BancWest	80,000,000,000
Santander Holdings USA	79,000,000,000
Discover Financial	75,000,000,000
Deutsche Bank	72,000,000,000
BBVA Compass Bancshares	70,000,000,000
Comerica	63,000,000,000
Huntington Bancshares	56,000,000,000
Zions Bancorporation	55,000,000,000
Utrecht-America Holdings	49,000,000,000
E*Trade	45,000,000,000
CIT Group	44,500,000,000
New York Community Bancorp	44,000,000,000
Hudson City Bancorp	40,000,000,000
First Niagara Financial Group	37,000,000,000
Popular	36,500,000,000
People's United Financial	31,000,000,000
John Deere Capital	30,500,000,000
BOK Financial	28,000,000,000
City National	27,000,000,000
Synovus Financial	26,500,000,000

Earliest Known Ancestor

RBS-Citizens Financial	1727
Wells Fargo	1782
Bank of America	1784
Bank of New York Mellon	1784
State Street	1792
PNC Financial Services	1796
JPMorgan Chase	1799
People's United Financial	1802
KeyCorp	1803
TD Bank US Holding	1803
BB&T	1805
M&T Bank	1806
SunTrust Banks	1811
Citigroup	1812
HSBC North America Holdings	1812
BMO Financial	1817
Regions Financial	1820
First Niagara	1823
Santander Holdings USA	1828
John Deere Capital	1837
New York Community Bancorp	1841
Huntington Bancshares	1846
Fifth Third Bancorp	1847
American Express	1848
BancWest	1848
Popular	1848
Comerica	1849
U.S. Bancorp	1853
American International Group	1853
Hudson City Bancorp	1854
Capital One Financial	1858
UnionBanCal	1864
Goldman Sachs	1869
Deutsche Bank Trust	1870
Zions Bancorporation	1873
General Electric Capital	1878
Principal Financial Group	1879
BBVA Compass Bancshares	1885
Synovus Financial	1887
BOK Financial	1887
Northern Trust	1889
Utrecht-America Holdings	1898
CIT Group	1908
Discover Financial Services	1911
Morgan Stanley	1911
E*Trade Financial	1912
Ally Financial	1919
City National	1920
USAA	1922
Charles Schwab	1971

Portrait of Alexander Hamilton.

Introduction: A Brief History of Banking in America

*Most commercial nations have found it necessary to institute banks,
and they have proved to be the happiest engines that ever were invented
for advancing trade.*
— Alexander Hamilton, 1781

These words are part of a remarkable letter that Alexander Hamilton, future Secretary of the Treasury, wrote to Robert Morris, the nation's foremost financial expert soon to be appointed Superintendent of Finance for the Continental Congress. The Revolutionary War was raging, and later that year Morris would create the first bank ever to exist on these shores, the Bank of North America, to assist in financing the war effort.

Both of these gentlemen understood the power and value of finance; it was the horse to the economy's cart. And within the financial system, the banks were central to the ability to join together savers and users of capital, all in the effort to promote economic growth.

When Hamilton wrote the letter, he was a young aide on General George Washington's staff. Eight years later, in 1789, Washington was elected the first President of the United States; shortly thereafter, an act of Congress created the Treasury Department. Washington rewarded Hamilton with the post of Treasury Secretary, and Hamilton stood at the helm with a firm vision of where to guide the new nation's finances. His plans to encourage growth included the creation of a central bank and reliance on the few banks in existence, like the Bank of North America and the Bank of New York, for loans to the government.

Two hundred twenty-five years have passed since then. While it is clear that banks have been integral to the growth of the American economy, most Americans don't think in those terms, but rather in terms of their interactions with their own banks. And those banks have probably changed hands, name and location in recent decades—possibly several times—owing to a wave of mergers, acquisitions and other restructuring that has led to a continually evolving banking landscape. In the wake of the 2008 financial crisis, many have questioned the impact these changes have had on the economy, the financial markets and the consumers of banking and investment services, and how the various banks and their clients have weathered the recent financial storm.

To that end, this book provides narrative histories of the nation's 50 largest bank holding companies (or BHCs—companies that do nothing except own or hold banks and other financial institutions) through September 2013. It also features illustrated "genealogies" of their lineage, similar to family trees. Some, like Bank of America and Wells Fargo, are household names that have hundreds or thousands of component banks. Others, such as Zions Bancorporation (founded by Brigham Young and owned by the Mormon Church until 1960), are lesser known but have fascinating histories nonetheless. To fully comprehend the history or genealogy of any bank or BHC, a general knowledge of US banking and business organizational history is required.

Before the American Revolution (1775–1783), only a handful of financial companies operated in North America, and most of those were not chartered by the King, Parliament or any colonial legislature. Rather, they operated as sole proprietorships or general partnerships.[1] After the Revolution, and especially after adoption of the Constitution in 1788, financial corporations proliferated. Prior to the US Civil War (1861–1865), most American depository banks and insurers were joint-stock companies (i.e., owned by stockholders) that received their charters (acts of incorporation or articles of association) from their respective state governments. A few joint-stock banks were not incorporated for some or all of their existence, but increasingly, states forced them to obtain charters or exit the banking business. Some insurance companies that issued bearer paper liabilities similar to bank notes were also pressured into desisting or chartering as a bank.[2]

So-called private banks—unincorporated banks organized as sole proprietorships or partnerships—existed throughout American history, but they became increasingly numerous in the antebellum period, especially in states that chartered fewer joint-stock banks than local businesses needed.[3] State legislatures and regulators, however, generally frowned upon them, especially if they issued bank notes, and they enjoined them to exit or incorporate.

By contrast, states encouraged investment banks and securities broker-dealers, both of which became increasingly numerous and prominent over the 19th century, to organize as unincorporated proprietorships or general partnerships. Until the 1960s, the New York Stock Exchange also required member firms to be structured as partnerships.[4] Since then, however, most investment banks, brokerages and other securities firms, beginning with Kidder, Peabody in 1964, have obtained corporate charters and gone public (sold shares to investors).[5]

Many states passed limited partnership laws that allowed businesses to organize with general partners (who ran the company day-to-day and were fully liable for its debts) and limited partners (who were not involved in daily operations or responsible for any sums beyond their invested capital). Most states did not allow commercial banks to form or operate under limited partnership laws, but some, including New York, allowed investment banks to form limited partnerships to help them raise capital.[6]

Four banks received special charters from the national government to act as central banks, or the government's depository, a lender of last resort during financial crises and a regulator of other banks and the money supply. The first three—the Bank of North America (1781–1785, as nominal central bank), the first Bank of the United States (1791–1811) and the second Bank of the United States (1816–1836)—were joint-stock corporations owned in part by the federal government and in part by private investors, including foreigners. Headquartered in Philadelphia, the Bank of North America never really acted as a central bank, and its legal status was muddy because it was chartered by the federal government and by several different states. The bank's home state, Pennsylvania, revoked its charter in 1785 and provided it with a new, less expansive one in 1787.[7]

Both institutions called the Bank of the United States, however, were central banks that handled the government's money, stymied financial panics, regulated state banks by redeeming their notes for specie (gold and silver) and influenced the money supply as best they could under a specie standard. Both were shuttered when their charters expired and were not renewed by the federal government, largely for political reasons.[8] Both banks inspired the creation of state banks, but technically, neither left any corporate progeny.

The nation's fourth central bank, the Federal Reserve System, or "Fed" for short, was created in 1913 by a special federal charter that contained a 20-year sunset clause. The McFadden Act of 1927, however, extended the charter indefinitely, or until repealed by Congress.[9] Technically, the Fed is a joint-stock corporation, but its shares are restricted to member banks only, and its dividends are capped by law, with excess profits credited to the US Treasury. The Fed handles the government's money, regulates the BHCs at the heart of this study, acts as a lender of last resort during crises and implements monetary policy through interest rates and open-market purchases and sales of government bonds.[10]

In the nation's first few decades, all incorporated (hybrid, joint-stock and mutual) banks received special charters, which granted them corporate powers such as perpetual succession, entity shielding, defined liability (whether limited, double, proportional or full) and the right to sue and be sued under a common name and seal. Special charters were costly to incorporators (time, lobbying), legislatures (time, up to three-quarters of legislative sessions) and democratic sensibilities (bribery and other forms of corruption were rife in some states, especially for bank charters). Therefore, beginning in the 1830s, some states passed general incorporation laws that allowed banks to obtain corporate powers by paying a small fee and providing basic information about their officers and capitalization.[11]

Such "free banking," or general incorporation, laws were in place in all states by the end of the 19th century and mandatory in most.[12] In addition, after 1863 joint-stock banks that met certain criteria could opt to obtain a general charter from the national government under the federal free banking law known as the National Banking Act. National banks were national only in the sense that they obtained their charters from the national government; for decades, most could not establish branches across the street, much less across state lines. The option of chartering with state or national governments created the so-called dual banking system that persists to this day.[13]

Like insurers, finance companies—nondepository lenders that focus on consumer, business and/or real estate loans—are also state chartered, with no federal general incorporation option. Some are owned by nonfinancial holding companies, including the major automakers. When owned by BHCs, they fall under the purview of the Fed; otherwise, they are regulated by the state that chartered them and the Federal Trade Commission (FTC) if they operate across state lines.[14]

Trust companies are also state-chartered financial institutions. Strictly speaking, trusts were designed to invest money on behalf of widows, orphans, nonprofit institutions and the like. Practically speaking, they often accepted deposits, made loans and acted much like banks, which complained bitterly about competition from their less regulated financial brethren until they learned to set up trust companies of their own. Many of the largest BHCs today have trust companies lurking in their corporate genealogies and histories, and a few joined the big league rankings by merging with one or more big trust companies.

In addition to commercial banks, several other types of financial institutions have been able to obtain charters under federal general incorporation laws. Building and loans were traditionally state-chartered. As the new savings and loan industry arose from the ashes of the Great Depression, however, a federal S&L charter option was created along with federal deposit insurance and a federal home loan bank that lent to thrifts in need of liquidity.[15] All federal and many state S&Ls were mutuals until 1982, when the Garn-St. Germain Act authorized the formation of federal joint-stock S&Ls.[16]

Credit unions are small, mutual depository institutions authorized to invest in a relatively narrow range of assets. The first credit union in the nation was chartered in New Hampshire in 1908; Massachusetts enacted a general incorporation law for credit unions early the next year. By 1930, 32 states had enacted similar legislation, all of which made clear that credit unions were mutual companies by definition. In 1934 the Roosevelt administration and Congress created a federal chartering option.[17]

A century ago, industrial loan corporations (ILCs) emerged as small, state-chartered joint-stock companies that made uncollateralized loans to the working poor. As recently as 1987, most ILCs were small and offered limited deposit services. In the last few decades, however, regulators in many states permitted ILCs to function essentially as FDIC-insured state-chartered banks, minus only demand deposits.[18] Many were purchased by nonfinancial companies and securities firms to circumvent the Bank Holding Company Act (BHCA) and other regulations. For example, Ally Bank (née General Motors Acceptance Corporation) began its corporate existence as an ILC before converting to a commercial bank charter in 2009. ILC industry assets hit $270.6 billion in 2007, up from just $28.6 billion in 1998.[19]

Credit card "banks" were created by BHCs and established in states, like South Dakota, with no maximum interest rate (a.k.a. usury) laws. They were and are exempted from the BHCA because they are not depository institutions and do not make commercial loans.[20]

Additional technical background follows in the next chapter, which details the structure of various types of holding companies and describes the method behind the madness in the "genealogies" presented in many of the BHC entries that follow. The good news is that the background material allows the entries on individual BHCs, from the leviathan JPMorgan Chase to the relatively tiny Synovus, to be short, pithy and easily digested by anyone who takes the time to peruse the first two chapters.

Notes

1. Kenneth Meier, *The Political Economy of Regulation: The Case of Insurance* (Albany: State University Press of New York, 1988), 49.

2. Robert E. Wright, *Corporation Nation* (Philadelphia: University of Pennsylvania Press, 2014).

3. Richard Sylla, "The Forgotten Private Banker," *The Freeman* (April 1, 1995); Jane Knodell, "The Role of Private Bankers in the US Payments System, 1835–1865," *Financial History Review* 17, 2 (October 2010): 239–62.

4. Jane W. D'Arista, *The Evolution of US Finance Vol. II: Restructuring Institutions and Markets* (Armonk, NY: M.E. Sharpe, 1994), 73.

5. Charles R. Geisst, *The Last Partnerships: Inside the Great Wall Street Money Dynasties* (New York: McGraw–Hill, 2001); Henry Kaufman, *On Money and Markets: A Wall Street Memoir* (New York: McGraw–Hill, 2000), 85–98.

6. Eric Hilt and Katherine O'Banion, "The Limited Partnership in New York, 1822–1858: Partners without Kinship," *Journal of Economic History* 69, 3 (2009): 615–45.

7. Lawrence Lewis, *A History of the Bank of North America, the First Bank Chartered in the United States* (Philadelphia: J. B. Lippincott, 1882).

8. David J. Cowen, *The Origins and Economic Impact of the First Bank of the United States, 1791-1797* (New York: Garland Publishing, 2000); Walter B. Smith,

Federal Reserve Bank building, Washington, DC.

Economic Aspects of the Second Bank of the United States (Cambridge, MA: Harvard University Press, 1953).

9. Allan Meltzer, *A History of the Federal Reserve, Volume I: 1913–1951* (Chicago: University of Chicago Press, 2003), 67, 216–17.

10. Robert E. Wright, *Money and Banking 2.0* (Irvington, NY: Flat World Knowledge, 2011), 177–224.

11. Howard Bodenhorn, "Bank Chartering and Political Corruption in Antebellum New York: Free Banking as Reform," (NBER Working Paper, 2004).

12. Eugene White, "The Political Economy of Banking Regulation, 1864–1933," *Journal of Economic History* 42 (March 1982): 34.

13. White, "The Political Economy of Banking Regulation," 34; Christine E. Blair and Rose M. Kushmeider, "Challenges to the Dual Banking System: The Funding of Bank Supervision," *FDIC Banking Review* 18, 1 (2006), 1–22.

14. D'Arista, *Evolution of US Finance*, 72, 75; *www.fdic.gov/about/contact/ask/other-agencies.html#FTC.*

15. *http://eh.net/encyclopedia/article/mason.savings.loan.industry.us*

16. *www.ots.treas.gov/_files/48035.html*

17. Saule T. Omarova and Margaret E. Tahyar, "That Which We Call a Bank: Revising the History of Bank Holding Company Regulations in the United States," (SSRN Working Paper 1969522, December 2011), 51–55.

18. Robert W. Crowley, ed. *Unique Treatment of GMAC Under TARP* (New York: Nova Science Publishers, 2010), 10–11.

19. Omarova and Tahyar, "That Which We Call a Bank," 38–47.

20. Omarova and Tahyar, "That Which We Call a Bank," 47–50.

Banks, Holding Companies and Corporate Genealogies: Necessary Technical Talk

I n standard American usage, a "bank" is a depository institution, or a business run for the profit of its stockholders and/or customers, that accepts deposits and makes loans. Traditionally, depository institutions came in three main varieties: commercial (always joint-stock, i.e., owned by stockholders; lent to large businesses); community (typically joint-stock; lent to small businesses/consumers); and thrifts, including savings banks (traditionally mutual, i.e., owned by depositors; lent to businesses and homeowners), building and loans/savings and loans (typically mutual until the 1980s; lent to homeowners) and credit unions (invariably mutual; lent to small businesses, consumers and homeowners).

Nondepository institutions also commonly referred to as "banks" were differentiated from depository institutions by adjectives like merchant and investment. Merchant banks traditionally[1] dealt in foreign exchange, while investment banks ruled the securities markets, which is to say the issuance, and via brokerages the subsequent trading, of stocks (corporate equities) and bonds (debt instruments issued by businesses and governments).

All of those types of "banks" still exist, but today it is more accurate to reference commercial, investment or savings *banking activities* rather than commercial, investment or savings *banks* as discrete institutions. That is because most of America's 50 largest and most influential "banks" are now "universal banks" lawfully authorized to provide a wide range of financial services.[2] In other words, they are finance-related holding companies (HCs), or financial corporations that own one or more other financial corporation, as in Figure 1.[3] A few are straight-up bank holding companies (BHCs), or corporations that own one or more commercial banks.[4] As in Figure 2, a BHC may also own other BHCs. It may also own small stakes in nonfinancial companies.[5] A few of the largest "banks" are savings and loan holding companies (SLHCs), or corporations that own one or more savings and loans (S&L) or other SLHCs. Most of the biggest 50 "banks," though, are financial holding companies (FHCs), or BHCs that elect to be treated as financial conglomerates and are approved to operate as such by the Federal Reserve. As in Figure 3, BHCs registered as FHCs can own depository institutions but also insurance companies, securities firms like brokerages, other financial services providers and nonfinancial commodities trading companies (e.g., oil and gas traders).[6] Nine of the 10 largest BHCs are FHCs. (The other, General Electric Capital Corporation [#7], is an SLHC.)

For ease of exposition, this book henceforth will use the term BHC generically to refer to all finance-related holding companies, be they technically BHCs, BHCs registered as FHCs or SLHCs. (The entries on individual "banks" that follow, however, may refer to each institution's exact HC type.) Per the Bank Holding Company Act (BHCA) of 1956, the Federal Reserve serves as the primary regulator of all BHCs,[7] but most issue federally insured deposits and, hence, are also regulated by the Federal Deposit Insurance Corporation (FDIC). State banking authorities or the Office of the Comptroller of the Currency (OCC) may also regulate one or more of a BHC's subsidiaries. Similarly, the appropriate nonbank regulator may functionally regulate a BHC's nonbank subsidiaries. For example, state insurance regulators supervise BHC insurance subsidiaries.[8]

Snapshots of the organizational structures of actual BHCs are reported annually in FR Y-6 *Annual Report of Bank Holding Companies*.[9] Figure 4 reproduces the FR Y-6 of Wisconsin Bank Services for the fiscal year ending December 31, 2012. Readers interested in the current organizational structure of a BHC should consult the National Information Center repository[10] for its latest available FR Y-6, plus its most recent FR Y-*Report of Changes in Organizational Structure*, which must be filed by top-tier (parent) BHCs (BHCs, like Wisconsin Bank Services, Inc., not owned by another BHC) upon any organizational change, from merger or internal reorganization down to merely relocating a branch office.

Corporate Genealogies

This book, by contrast, presents a "genealogy" of the 50 largest BHCs or, in other words, a chronological overview of BHC development and acquisition-driven growth. Unlike an organizational chart, which focuses on the present, a corporate genealogy shows how an organization has changed from its inception to the present by following "lineages" analogous to those genealogists create for "family trees." A corporation is "born" when it obtains a charter or begins business. As it "lives," it may change names, charter type, organizational form or legal status. It may also purchase other businesses, which can be thought of as "adoptions," or merge with them, which can be likened to "marriages."[11] (Although the terms are often used interchangeably in a loose sense, and will be at times in the BHC entries that follow whenever the historical record is unclear, mergers and acquisitions are technically differentiated by financial securities. In a merger, the securities of both the merged companies are exchanged for new securities. In an acquisition, the securities of the target company are bought by the purchasing company, sometimes for cash, sometimes with the purchasing company's own shares.[12])

Finally, a corporation in a sense "dies" when it ceases business, either voluntarily by amalgamation into another corporation or involuntarily as a result of bankruptcy. Scare quotes are used throughout this discussion because the notion of a corporation having a "genealogy" or a "family" is meant only analogically; corporations are legal constructs, not biological entities.

Creating the genealogies that appear in this book was no simple task, as none of the banking system's many regulators has systematically tracked mergers and acquisitions over more than two centuries of US banking history. The two major sources of information were the Federal Reserve and the FDIC, but both provided only partial data and at times conflicting information, such as different dates and interpretations of which bank was the acquirer and which the acquisition. The author resolved discrepancies, when possible, by reference to corporate histories or logic (e.g., a bank has to exist before it can be acquired by another bank). In the absence of third party verification, the Fed's information/interpretation was privileged, a choice that provided consistency, but was ultimately arbitrary. Much of the information on investment bank mergers and acquisitions came from corporate

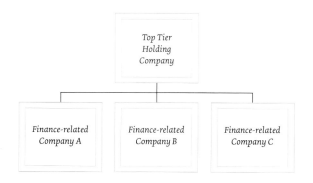

1. *Generic Finance-Related Holding Company Organizational Structure.*

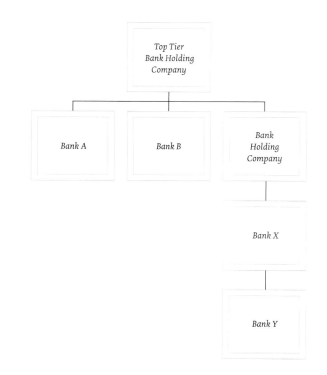

2. *Generic Bank Holding Company Organizational Structure.*

3. *Generic Financial Holding Company Organizational Structure.*

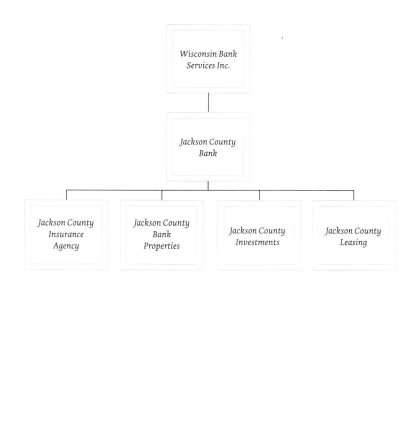

4. *Organizational Chart of Wisconsin Bank Services, 2012.*

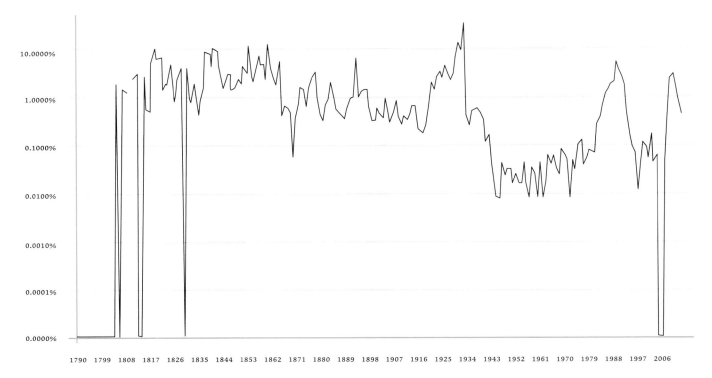

5. *Annual Bank Failure Rates in the United States, 1790–2010.*

histories and verifiable news sources, as they are not included in the Fed or FDIC's data.

Some BHCs—those that have only recently become BHCs or are not rooted in commercial banks—do not have extensive genealogies. Most, however, have acquired so many other banks and financial entities that their genealogies had to be split into two, one for BHCs and one for their core underlying bank or banks, to make them more manageable and easy to read. The largest of the BHCs had too many components to fit in a manageable printed format, so their full genealogies may be found online at www.moaf.org/bankgenealogy.

The Size and Scope of BHCs

Today, most "banks" do not stand alone but rather are subsidiaries of BHCs. Over the last few decades, the total number of BHCs in the United States has been trending downward, but more than 4,000 remain in business and independent.[13] Most BHCs, however, remain relatively small and static. Large BHCs (most of which, again, are technically FHCs), by contrast, have exploded in size and complexity in the last 20-plus years.[14] America's largest BHCs, termed LCFIs (large, complex financial institutions) by scholars, now dwarf the nation's other financial institutions in both size and complexity.

The share of assets controlled by the top 10 BHCs has been trending upwards for the last few decades, from approximately 30% in 1991 to 50% a decade ago.[15] Today, the top 10 own assets valued at over $11 trillion, or roughly three-quarters of the $15 trillion or so in assets owned by the nation's 50 largest BHCs.

For the most part, the largest BHCs have grown to such gargantuan proportions not through organic growth (by doing more business), but through acquisition. Sometimes BHCs maintain the independent brand and balance sheets of their acquisitions, which become subsidiaries in their respective holding companies, for years or even decades. Other times, BHCs immediately absorb the names and balance sheets of their acquisitions, effectively ending the corporate identities of the acquired corporations.[16] Acquisitions listed in the corporate

genealogies that follow, therefore, may or may not appear in a BHC's most recent FR Y-6 organization chart.

The current corporate composition of large BHCs, especially the LCFIs, is extremely complex and grows more so with each new acquisition. In the 1990s, LCFIs each owned hundreds of subsidiaries; they now each own thousands. They also now each operate in 40–80 different countries, up from 20–60 in 1990.[17] LCFIs also tend to be staid. One of the lineages of The Bank of New York Mellon Corporation (#9), for example, traces back to an unincorporated joint-stock bank formed by Alexander Hamilton and other Manhattanites in early 1784.

Exclusions to the Genealogies

Not surprisingly, then, the corporate genealogies of LCFIs are also extremely complex. The task of compiling them would be cost- and time-prohibitive without focusing on core domestic financial operations. Thankfully, hundreds of small, foreign, unusual or otherwise inconsequential subsidiaries can be ignored without limiting our understanding of LCFI development. Foreign subsidiaries tend to be relatively small; about three-quarters of total BHC assets are held in the United States. Also, several of America's largest BHCs are not top-tier HCs, but rather subsidiaries of huge foreign banks like HSBC (#11), RBS (#25) and Santander (#32). The histories of the foreign banks are sketched, necessitating the introduction of foreign currencies including the pound sterling [£], euro [€], Hong Kong dollar [$HK], Canadian pound [£CA] and others, but no attempt has been made to complete the foreign banks' sundry lineages.

Many domestic subsidiaries are also relatively small and unimportant. In 2012, for example, JPMorgan Chase (#1) controlled 3,391 subsidiaries, 2,940 of which were domestically domiciled. Only four of those were commercial banks, and they held 86% of JPMorgan Chase's total assets. Other BHCs, like Goldman Sachs (#5), also have numerous foreign subsidiaries (1,670 of 3,115 total subsidiaries) and/or, like Morgan Stanley (#6), invest mostly in investment banking businesses.[18]

Survival of the Fittest Banks

The entries in this book document the complex origins of America's largest banks throughout history, thereby furthering scholars', policy-makers', voters' and investors' understanding of these important components of the nation's economic well-being. The key business issue at stake in this study regards the characteristics of successful banks.

As shown in Figure 5, American financial history generally has been placid (fewer than 1% of banks failing per year), but at times it has been punctuated by periods of extreme tumult (with over 1% and even over 10% of banks failing in a single year). All told, more than 23,000 banks have gone bankrupt throughout American history.[19] Today's LCFIs are, in a sense, the victors in a 225-year Darwinian struggle for existence.[20] (Even longer for some foreign banks, like RBS-Citizens.) Why these institutions thrived while others faltered is of keen interest to bankers, investors, uninsured bank creditors, regulators and policymakers.

The key policy issue at stake in this study is whether LCFIs should be promoted, left alone, discouraged or outright dismantled. To determine that, policymakers must know the extent to which LCFIs formed and persisted because of their economic efficiency, including economies of scale and scope, and the extent to which they grew and continue to exist because of artificial incentives, like the "Too Big to Fail" policy, which provides LCFIs with inexpensive risk insurance. Policymakers must also grapple with trade-offs, like the extent to which large banks become too big to manage or govern effectively and the social costs created by LCFI mistakes, malfeasance and failures.[21]

The distinction between an "LCFI" and "just another BHC" is not clear and may change over time or depend on observer perspective, so the decision was made to cover herein each of the 50 largest BHCs by assets as of September 30, 2013. Larger BHCs, and those with more available sources, naturally have somewhat longer entries, but each chapter follows the same template:[22]

- the BHC's current name and ticker symbol (where applicable)
- its rank by assets and total dollar value of assets as of September 30, 2013
- the state where it was headquartered at the end of September 2013
- its year of genesis, which is generally the year of charter of its oldest bank
- its corporate "genealogical" chart
- a brief overview of the BHC's history, including iconic or illustrative images from its past
- a list of sources [23]

Notes

1. More recently, the term "merchant banking" has come to be used to describe private equity financing. See Board of Governors of the Federal Reserve System, *Report to the Congress on Financial Holding Companies under the Gramm–Leach–Bliley Act* November 2003, 14–16; Ron Chernow, *The House of Morgan: An American Banking Dynasty and the Rise of Modern Finance* (New York: Grove Press, 1990), 694–95; Edwin J. Perkins, *Wall Street to Main Street: Charles Merrill and Middle-Class Investors* (New York: Cambridge University Press, 1999), 70.
2. D'Arista, *Evolution of US Finance*, 78–83, 189–90.
3. Dafna Abraham, Patricia Selvaggi and James Vickery, "A Structural View of US Bank Holding Companies," *Federal Reserve Bank of New York Economic Policy Review* (July 2012), 65.
4. Omarova and Tahyar, "That Which We Call a Bank," 1.
5. Abraham, Selvaggi and Vickery, "A Structural View," 67.
6. http://www.federalreserve.gov/bankinforeg/fhc.htm; Abraham, Selvaggi and Vickery, "A Structural View," 67.
7. Abraham, Selvaggi and Vickery, "A Structural View," 67.
8. Abraham, Selvaggi and Vickery, "A Structural View," 67.
9. Abraham, Selvaggi and Vickery, "A Structural View," 69.
10. http://www.ffiec.gov/nicpubweb/nicweb/NicHome.aspx
11. Amey Stone and Mike Brewster, *King of Capital: Sandy Weill and the Making of Citigroup* (New York: Wiley, 2002), 243; *Union Bank of Switzerland, 1862, 1912, 1962* (Zurich: Union Bank of Switzerland, 1962), 73.
12. John Spiegel, Alan Gart and Steven Gart, *Banking Redefined: How Superregional Powerhouses Are Reshaping Financial Services* (Chicago: Irwin Professional Publishing, 1996), 63.
13. Abraham, Selvaggi and Vickery, "A Structural View," 66.
14. Abraham, Selvaggi and Vickery, "A Structural View," 65.
15. Abraham, Selvaggi and Vickery, "A Structural View," 66.
16. Ronald A. Wirtz, "Banks Paring Back Their Branches" *Federal Reserve Bank of Minneapolis Fedgazette*, July 2013, 15.
17. Abraham, Selvaggi and Vickery, "A Structural View," 66, 70, 72.
18. Abraham, Selvaggi and Vickery, "A Structural View," 70–72, 80.
19. Robert E. Wright, "Governance and the Success of US Community Banks, 1790–2010: Mutual Savings Banks, Local Commercial Banks, and the Merchants (National) Bank of New Bedford, Massachusetts," *Business History Online* 9 (2011), 1–2.
20. "Institutions, like members of a species, must adapt to the environment or die out." Claude Singer, *U.S. National Bank of Oregon and U.S. Bancorp, 1891–1984* (Portland: U.S. Bancorp, 1984), 14. "In banking's version of survival of the fittest, the stronger banks get stronger by devouring the customers and operations of the weak." Tara Skinner, "The Empiricist Paradox: Fostering Internal Stability While Pursuing Change at Synovus Financial Corp." (MA thesis, Stonier Graduate School of Banking, 1999), 35. "Charles Darwin once said, 'It is not the strongest of the species that survive, nor the most intelligent, but the one most responsive to change.'" Eugene A. Miller, *Comerica Incorporated: Promises Kept, Promises Renewed* (New York: Newcomen Society, 2000), 19.
21. Viral Acharya, Thomas Philippon, Matthew Richardson and Nouriel Roubini, "The Financial Crisis of 2007–2008: Causes and Remedies," in *Restoring Financial Stability: How to Repair a Failed System*, ed. Viral Acharya and Matthew Richardson. (Hoboken: Wiley, 2009), 26–27; Matthew Richardson, Roy C. Smith and Ingo Walter, "Large Banks and the Volcker Rule," in *Regulating Wall Street: The Dodd–Frank Act and the New Architecture of Global Finance*, ed. Viral Acharya et al. (Hoboken: Wiley, 2011), 195.
22. www.ffiec.gov/nicpubweb/nicweb/Top50Form.aspx
23. The histories were constructed from the best available printed sources, both primary (original charters and historical newspaper and magazine articles) and secondary (articles, books, chapters and dissertations). Whenever possible, official corporate histories were triangulated with other sources to ensure a balanced view. Corporate websites, annual reports and the like were used only as a last resort.

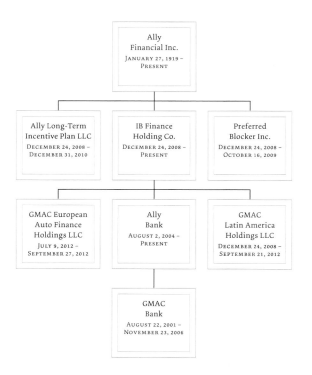

Ally Financial

RANK	HEADQUARTERS	TICKER	ASSETS	EARLIEST KNOWN ANCESTOR	INDUSTRY OF ORIGIN
20	Detroit, MI	ALLY	$151,000,000,000	1919	Manufacturing

Portrait of John J. Raskob, 1905.

Postcard featuring the General Motors building in Detroit, Michigan, 1945.

I f Ally Financial doesn't sound familiar, think GMAC, as in General
Motors Acceptance Corporation, which automobile manufacturer
General Motors (GM) created in 1919 to finance the sale of its cars
and trucks. Mass production techniques had driven down prices,
but not enough for most Americans to purchase their new-fangled
horseless carriages outright. At first, most banks were hesitant to get
into the market, new as they were to consumer credit and new as the
automobile industry then was. Many bankers saw automobiles as lux-
uries, not as a revolution in transportation, and worried that default
rates would be unprofitably high. So GM, led by John J. Raskob and
following the lead of now long-defunct automaker Willys-Overland,
decided to supply the necessary credit to their dealers and customers.
Thus, GMAC was born.

The bankers' fears proved groundless. Even at the height of the
Great Depression, GMAC's loss ratio remained below 1%, owing to
good screening, sufficient collateral (including down payments) and
the high use value most owners placed on their automobiles, which no
longer were just for Sunday jaunts.

From early in its history, especially under the leadership of John J.
Schumann Jr. (1929–1954), GMAC was a stickler for carefully aligning
the incentives of GM, automobile owners and dealers. The company
insisted that dealers share some of the risk in cases of default to
ensure that they screened loan applicants carefully. It encouraged
sufficient down payments and reasonable contract lengths, which
of course were related to the quality of the cars its parent sold. It also
endeavored to stay profitable while keeping down interest costs for
borrowers, which induced more sales and reduced defaults. A policy of
"honesty and square dealing" was its solution to that tricky trade-off.
For a long time the strategy worked, although the company was sub-
jected to federal scrutiny at times regarding the way finance charges
were advertised and the contractual relationship between GMAC and
GM dealers.

Between 1919 and 1963, GMAC, while still a subsidiary of GM,
financed 43 million new cars through dealers and 46 million cars (21
million new and 25 million used) directly for consumers. By 1960 the

company claimed almost 20% of the new automobile credit market,
even though it supported only GM dealers and their customers. That
meant about $4 billion in retail credit and $9 billion in wholesale
credit at a time when a billion dollars was a lot of money. The subsidiary also operated in Canada and a number of other foreign countries.

GMAC eventually also offered insurance to both dealers and
consumers. General Exchange Insurance Corporation, another GM
subsidiary charged with providing automobile owners with collision
insurance, was later replaced by Motors Insurance Corporation and
made a subsidiary of GMAC. The change made sense, as collision
insurance helped to maintain the value of the physical collateral back-
ing GMAC's installment credit business.

In the mid-1980s, around the time it financed its 100 millionth
vehicle, GMAC expanded the scope of its business to diversify its risks
out of the automobile sector and to earn greater profits for its parent.
It started with home mortgages, buying Colonial Mortgage from
Philadelphia National Bank. The company also engaged in marine
financing and investment services; it later expanded into general
commercial loans and made several international moves as well.

In November 2006 GM sold 51% of GMAC to a consortium of investors led by Cerberus Capital Management. In addition to earning $14
billion for GM, the deal allowed GMAC to retain close ties to its former
parent, but to borrow on better terms than available to it as a captive
of the auto giant, which had been facing declining market share and
reduced margins for years. In early 2009, it would need a large federal
government bailout to avoid bankruptcy.

By the time the subprime crisis struck in 2007, GMAC owned three
major businesses: automotive finance, insurance and mortgage (with
Residential Capital, or "ResCap," a global real estate finance business).
GMAC also owned GMAC Bank, which was chartered as an industrial
loan company. Not surprisingly, along with most of the rest of the
mortgage industry, ResCap, and hence its parent, began to suffer
losses in 2007 — $7.9 billion by the end of the first quarter of 2008. By
late 2008 GMAC's core automotive financing business had also been
hit by the economic downturn.

General Motors Corporation stock certificate, 1955.

The company was experiencing such considerable financial difficulty that the Federal Reserve quickly approved its application to become a BHC in order to gain access to emergency Fed funding—but only on the condition that it raise $7 billion in new equity capital. Shareholders put up $2 billion of that, and the Treasury contributed the other $5 billion from the Troubled Asset Relief Program (TARP). When so-called stress tests revealed that more capital was necessary, the Treasury purchased an additional $12 billion or so of preferred (nonvoting) shares after investors showed they were uninterested in putting more cash into the company.

The justification for the capital infusions was not that GMAC itself was "too big to fail," but that GM was, and that GM—including its network of dealers—needed GMAC as much in 2009 as it did when it created the company 90 years earlier. In 2009 GMAC also began providing financing for Chrysler dealers and customers, as well as for a downsized GM, rendering it even more crucial to economic recovery in the eyes of government officials.

That same year, GMAC Bank rebranded as Ally Bank, and in 2010 GMAC, the BHC, rebranded itself Ally Financial. Finally freed from exclusive ties to GM, it began to search for profitable new niches by aggressively establishing preferred financing relationships with RV manufacturers Thor Industries and Forest River, as well as auto manufacturers Fiat, Maserati North America and Mitsubishi.

Unlike GM and Chrysler, Ally Financial was never put into bankruptcy by the Treasury, so its stockholders, including Cerberus, were essentially bailed out as well. This contributed to the perception that the Treasury provided Ally with special treatment. By 2010 all three major parts of Ally Financial's business—GMAC, ResCap and Ally Bank—were again profitable, thanks in part to trouble at Toyota and strong overseas growth in China, Brazil and the UK. Stabilization of home and mortgage values in the United States and Europe also helped considerably, allowing ResCap to sell its European mortgage portfolio at well above its carrying value.

By the end of 2013, Ally had sold off the majority of its international assets, exited its mortgage operations and repaid the Treasury over $6 billion. In April 2014, Ally completed its initial public offering and had returned approximately $17.8 billion to the Treasury, which is about $700 million more than was originally invested in the company.

Sources

Bair, Sheila. *Bull by the Horns: Fighting to Save Main Street from Wall Street and Wall Street from Itself.* New York: Free Press, 2012, 172, 175–77.

Congressional Oversight Panel.*An Update on TARP Support for the Domestic Automotive Industry.* January 13, 2011.

Crowley, Robert W., ed. *Unique Treatment of GMAC Under TARP.* New York: Nova Science Publishers, Inc., 2010.

Mattera, Philip. *World Class Business: A Guide to the Most Powerful Global Corporations.* New York: Holt, 1992, 311–23.

Sloan, Alfred P., Jr. *My Years with General Motors.*Edited by John McDonald and Catharine Stevens. Garden City, NY: Doubleday, 1964.

Bob Peck Chevrolet dealership in Arlington, Virginia, 2006.

Automobiles parked on the roof of a Buick Sales and Service building, 1925.

In this spectacular motorcar display salon of unique design General Motors proudly presents an array of the latest models of CHEVROLET, PONTIAC, OLDSMOBILE, BUICK, LA SALLE and CADILLAC.

Back cover of General Motors' "Futurama" booklet from the company's exhibit and ride at the 1939 World's Fair. The image shows GM's latest models.

GENERAL MOTORS ACCEPTANCE CORPORATION

TWENTY-TWO YEAR 4½% DEBENTURE DUE 1985

DUE NOVEMBER 1, 1985

GENERAL MOTORS ACCEPTANCE CORPORATION, a corporation duly organized and existing under the laws of the State of New York (herein referred to as the "Company"), for value received, hereby promises to pay to

or registered assigns at the office or agency of the Company in the Borough of Manhattan, The City of New York, the principal sum of

DOLLARS

on November 1, 1985, in such coin or currency of the United States of America as at the time of payment shall be legal tender for the payment of public and private debts, and to pay interest on said principal sum at the rate of 4½% per annum at the office or agency of the Company in the Borough of Manhattan, The City of New York, in like coin or currency from the first interest payment date to which interest on the Debentures has been paid preceding the date hereof (unless the date hereof is an interest payment date to which interest on the Debentures has been paid, in which case from the date hereof, or unless the date hereof is prior to May 1, 1964, in which case from November 1, 1963), semi-annually on May 1 and November 1 of each year, until payment of said principal sum has been made or duly provided for.

This Debenture is one of a duly authorized issue of debentures of the Company, designated as its Twenty-Two Year 4½% Debentures Due 1985 (herein referred to as the "Debentures"), of an aggregate principal amount of $150,000,000, issued under and pursuant to an indenture dated November 1, 1963 (herein referred to as the "Indenture"), duly executed and delivered by the Company to Morgan Guaranty Trust Company of New York, Trustee. Reference is hereby made to the Indenture and all indentures supplemental thereto for a description of the rights, limitations of rights, obligations, duties and immunities thereunder of the Trustee, the Company and the holders of the Debentures and coupons.

In case an Event of Default, as defined in the Indenture, shall have occurred and be continuing, the principal hereof may be declared, and upon such declaration shall become, due and payable in the manner, with the effect, and subject to the conditions, provided in the Indenture.

The Indenture contains provisions permitting the Company and the Trustee, with the consent of the holders of not less than 66⅔% in aggregate principal amount of the Debentures at the time outstanding, evidenced as in the Indenture provided, to execute supplemental indentures adding any provisions to or changing in any manner or eliminating any of the provisions of the Indenture or any supplemental indenture or modifying in any manner the rights of the holders of the Debentures and coupons; provided, however, that no such supplemental indenture shall (i) extend the fixed maturity of any Debentures, or reduce the principal amount thereof, or reduce the rate or extend the time of payment of interest thereon, without the consent of the holder of each Debenture so affected, or (ii) reduce the aforesaid percentage of Debentures, the consent of the holders of which is required for any such supplemental indenture, without the consent of the holders of all Debentures then outstanding.

No reference herein to the Indenture and no provision of this Debenture or of the Indenture shall alter or impair the obligation of the Company, which is absolute and unconditional, to pay the principal of (and premium, if any) and interest on this Debenture at the place, at the respective times, at the rate, and in the currency, herein prescribed.

The Debentures are issuable as coupon Debentures, registrable as to principal, in the denomination of $1,000, and as registered Debentures without coupons in the denominations of $1,000 and any multiple of $1,000 authorized by the Company. Coupon Debentures and registered Debentures without coupons, and the several authorized denominations thereof, are interchangeable in equal aggregate principal amounts at the office or agency of the Company in the Borough of Manhattan, The City of New York, and in the manner and subject to the limitations provided in the Indenture without charge except for any tax or other governmental charge imposed in connection therewith.

The Debentures may not be redeemed before November 1, 1971, except as stated below. On and after that date and prior to maturity the Company may, at its option, redeem the Debentures, either as a whole or from time to time in part, upon not less than 30 days' notice, at their principal amount plus the following redemption premiums (expressed in percentages of principal amount) if redeemed during the twelve months period beginning November 1 in each of the following years:

Year	Redemption Premium	Year	Redemption Premium
1971	2.00%	1976	1.00%
1972	1.80	1977	0.80
1973	1.60	1978	0.60
1974	1.40	1979	0.40
1975	1.20	1980	0.20

and thereafter at their principal amount without premium, together in each case with interest accrued to the date fixed for redemption. Under certain circumstances of declining retail receivables specified in the Indenture, the Debentures may be redeemed at any time in the manner provided above at their principal amount plus the following redemption premiums (expressed in percentages of principal amount) if redeemed during the twelve months period beginning November 1 in each of the following years:

Year	Redemption Premium	Year	Redemption Premium
1963	2.000%	1967	1.500%
1964	1.875	1968	1.375
1965	1.750	1969	1.250
1966	1.625	1970	1.125

and thereafter at their principal amount plus one-half the applicable redemption premium referred to in the next preceding table; or the redemption may be at their principal amount without premium; together in each case with interest accrued to the date fixed for redemption; all upon the conditions set forth and as more fully provided in the Indenture.

This Debenture is transferable by the registered holder hereof or by his attorney duly authorized in writing at the office or agency of the Company in the Borough of Manhattan, The City of New York, but only in the manner and subject to the limitations provided in the Indenture without charge except for any tax or other governmental charge imposed in connection therewith, and upon surrender of this Debenture. Upon any such transfer a new registered Debenture or Debentures without coupons, of authorized denominations, for an equal aggregate principal amount will be issued to the transferee in exchange therefor.

The Company, the Trustee, any paying agent and any Debenture registrar may deem and treat the registered holder hereof as the absolute owner of this Debenture (whether or not this Debenture shall be overdue and notwithstanding any notation of ownership or other writing hereon made by anyone other than the Company or any Debenture registrar), for the purpose of receiving payment hereof or on account hereof and interest due hereon and for all other purposes, and neither the Company nor the Trustee nor any paying agent nor any Debenture registrar shall be affected by any notice to the contrary.

No recourse under or upon any obligation, covenant or agreement contained in the Indenture or in any indenture supplemental thereto, or in any Debenture or coupon, or because of any indebtedness evidenced thereby, shall be had against any incorporator, or against any past, present or future stockholder, officer or director, as such, of the Company or of any successor corporation, either directly or through the Company or any successor corporation, under any rule of law, statute or constitutional provision or by the enforcement of any assessment or by any legal or equitable proceeding or otherwise, all such liability being expressly waived and released by the acceptance of this Debenture and as part of the consideration for its issuance.

This Debenture shall not be valid or become obligatory for any purpose until the certificate of authentication hereon shall have been signed by the Trustee under the Indenture.

IN WITNESS WHEREOF, General Motors Acceptance Corporation has caused this Debenture to be signed manually or by facsimile by its President or one of its Executive Vice Presidents or one of its Vice Presidents and by its Treasurer or one of its Assistant Treasurers or its Secretary or one of its Assistant Secretaries, and has caused a facsimile of its corporate seal to be affixed hereunto or imprinted hereon.

Dated

General Motors Acceptance Corporation,

BY

SPECIMEN

EXECUTIVE VICE PRESIDENT

SPECIMEN

TREASURER

TRUSTEE'S CERTIFICATE OF AUTHENTICATION

This is one of the Debentures described in the within-mentioned Indenture.

MORGAN GUARANTY TRUST COMPANY OF NEW YORK,
AS TRUSTEE,

BY

AUTHORIZED OFFICER

GENERAL MOTORS ACCEPTANCE CORPORATION
CORPORATE
1919
SEAL
NEW YORK

General Motors Acceptance Corporation specimen bond certificate, 1963.

General Motors Corporation stock certificate, 1955.

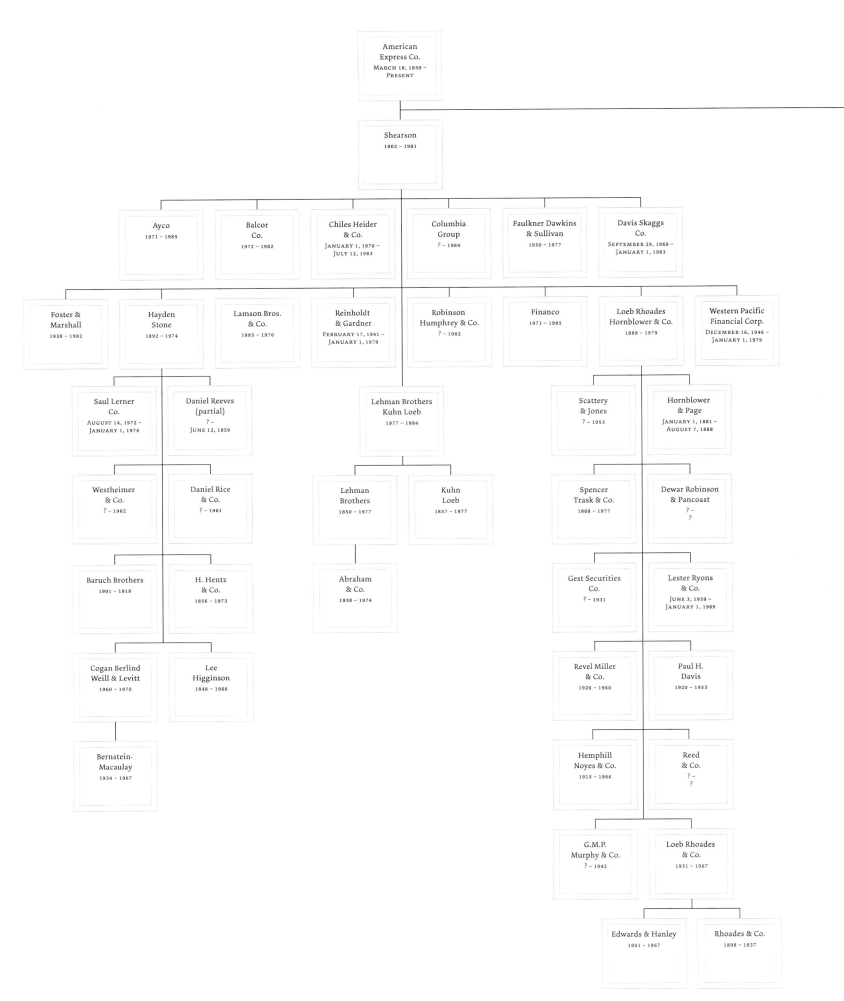

American Express Co.
MARCH 18, 1850 –
PRESENT

Shearson
1902 – 1981

Ayco
1971 – 1985

Balcor
Co.
1972 – 1982

Chiles Heider
& Co.
JANUARY 1, 1970 –
JULY 12, 1983

Columbia
Group
? – 1984

Faulkner Dawkins
& Sullivan
1950 – 1977

Davis Skaggs
Co.
SEPTEMBER 29, 1969 –
JANUARY 1, 1983

Foster &
Marshall
1938 – 1982

Hayden
Stone
1892 – 1974

Lamson Bros.
& Co.
1885 – 1976

Reinholdt
& Gardner
FEBRUARY 17, 1941 –
JANUARY 1, 1979

Robinson
Humphrey & Co.
? – 1982

Financo
1971 – 1985

Loeb Rhoades
Hornblower & Co.
1888 – 1979

Western Pacific
Financial Corp.
DECEMBER 16, 1946 –
JANUARY 1, 1979

Saul Lerner
Co.
AUGUST 14, 1972 –
JANUARY 1, 1974

Daniel Reeves
(partial)
? –
JUNE 12, 1959

Lehman Brothers
Kuhn Loeb
1977 – 1984

Scattery
& Jones
? – 1953

Hornblower
& Page
JANUARY 1, 1881 –
AUGUST 7, 1888

Westheimer
& Co.
? – 1962

Daniel Rice
& Co.
? – 1961

Lehman
Brothers
1850 – 1977

Kuhn
Loeb
1857 – 1977

Spencer
Trask & Co.
1868 – 1977

Dewar Robinson
& Pancoast
? –
?

Baruch Brothers
1901 – 1918

H. Hentz
& Co.
1856 – 1973

Abraham
& Co.
1938 – 1974

Gest Securities
Co.
? – 1931

Lester Ryons
& Co.
JUNE 3, 1959 –
JANUARY 1, 1969

Cogan Berlind
Weill & Levitt
1960 – 1970

Lee
Higginson
1848 – 1966

Revel Miller
& Co.
1926 – 1960

Paul H.
Davis
1920 – 1953

Bernstein-
Macaulay
1934 – 1967

Hemphill
Noyes & Co.
1915 – 1966

Reed
& Co.
? –
?

G.M.P.
Murphy & Co.
? – 1942

Loeb Rhoades
& Co.
1931 – 1967

Edwards & Hanley
1951 – 1967

Rhoades & Co.
1898 – 1937

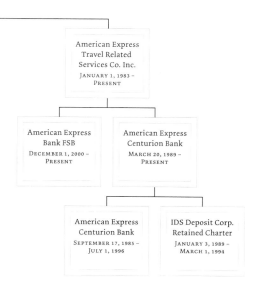

American Express Travel Related Services Co. Inc.
JANUARY 1, 1983 – PRESENT

American Express Bank FSB
DECEMBER 1, 2000 – PRESENT

American Express Centurion Bank
MARCH 20, 1989 – PRESENT

American Express Centurion Bank
SEPTEMBER 17, 1985 – JULY 1, 1996

IDS Deposit Corp. Retained Charter
JANUARY 3, 1989 – MARCH 1, 1994

American Express

RANK	HEADQUARTERS	TICKER	ASSETS	EARLIEST KNOWN ANCESTOR	INDUSTRY OF ORIGIN
19	New York, NY	AXP	$152,000,000,000	1848	Freight

Employees of the American Express Company. Corner of Hudson, Jay and Staples Streets, New York City, June 21, 1858.

Night scene on the New York Central Railroad, American Express's special express train, 1884.

American Express possesses a brand identity for integrity forged over its long, varied history. It was formed out of a meeting of the owners of several small express companies — businesses that quickly shipped mail and other goods — that took place in Buffalo in 1850. Established by experienced express men, including Henry Wells and William G. Fargo, American Express concentrated first and foremost on providing quality service ("courtesy," as Wells put it) and strict punctuality. The company's founders also realized that a large network was more valuable to their potential customers than a small one, so soon after their agglomeration into American Express, they purchased the Buffalo and Canadian Express Company and forged connections to America's rapidly growing "Old Northwest" (the region now called the Midwest). In its first four months, American Express paid a whopping 10% dividend.

Two years after founding American Express, Fargo and Wells wanted to push to California to get in on the business of shipping east the $60 million a year in new gold that gushed forth from the state's streams and mines. When other directors voted down the proposal, the duo established Wells, Fargo and Company (#4). Rather than competing, the two companies worked in tandem, with Wells in the West and American in the East.

American Express continued to thrive, though it occasionally suffered losses as a result of shipwrecks and frauds. In 1855, for example, its agent in Dubuque, Iowa, accepted what was represented as $50,000 in gold for shipment to the US Treasury in New York. When the package was opened in New York, however, it contained only lead bullets. The company made good on the $50,000 and learned from its mistake.

Perhaps the best thing would have been for American Express to distribute the bullets to its drivers, who received gold watches if they successfully defended their cargo from the sundry brigands who roamed even east of the Mississippi. This precedent was set after driver John Kenny took a six-inch knife to the face but still managed to apprehend a would-be robber.

With high risks came high rewards. From $150,000 at its inception, the unincorporated company's capitalization rose to $750,000 by 1854, and vigorous expansion in all directions continued as customers came to believe that the company was the most responsible in the world. By 1862 American Express had 890 offices, 1,500 employees and over 9,200 miles of routes earning about three cents per mile daily.

After the Civil War, the company faced a major challenge from a new company, the Merchants Union Express. Formed in 1867 and capitalized at $20 million, Merchants Union sought to drive American Express out of business in a year-long rate battle. From $100,000 a month in profits, American Express started running monthly losses up to a quarter-million dollars. The company gave worse than it got, however, as Merchants Union lost $7 million before agreeing to merge. Despite their contentious past, the new company — the American Merchants Union Express Company — got on surprisingly well and capitalized at $18 million. Wells retired, and Fargo took over the new company, which reverted to calling itself the American Express Company in 1873.

When Fargo died in 1881, his younger brother, James Congdell "J.C." Fargo, took over and led the company for the next 35 years. It was J.C. who first began the company's transformation into the American Express we know today, developing the American Express Money Order — with significant help from employees like Marcellus Fleming Berry and William E. Brown, the men who actually implemented J.C.'s orders and created an ingenious money transfer form that protected the company from fraud. The company's money order soon out-competed the postal money order because it could be purchased in many more locations, including railroad stations and drugstores.

Later, after J.C. had difficulty raising cash with traditional letters of credit while vacationing in Europe, he ordered Berry to develop something better. "If the president of American Express has that sort of trouble, just think what ordinary travelers face. Something has got to be done about it," he said. After several months of ruminating, Berry created the American Express Travelers Cheque, an instrument that was almost as liquid as cash, but relatively safe from theft because of its dual signature feature, which required the owner to sign the instrument upon receipt and when tendering it, as a form of identification.

To get vendors worldwide to accept the new means of payment, the company guaranteed that no one who cashed one of its travelers checks would suffer a loss so long as they did so in good faith and with reasonable care, i.e., that they checked to make sure the signatures matched and were not in cahoots with forgers and crooks. By 1913 sales of the new financial instrument hit $32 million. By the 1920s American Express Travelers Cheques were allegedly preferred to gold in locations as remote as the Sahara Desert.

In 1895 American Express established a beachhead in Europe by opening an office in Paris. Others soon followed in London, Liverpool,

American Express trucks transporting gold shipped by Great Britain to New York City for safekeeping during World War I, 1915.

Hamburg, Bremen and Le Havre. By 1900 the "European invasion" was even more widespread but far from complete, as each new country required adaptations. In Paris, for instance, the American Express office became an informal travelers' aid society and post office, while in Italy, rampant crime forced the company to put armed guards aboard its train cars to protect the cheese and olive oil its customers shipped. Every office handled travelers checks, of course, as well as foreign exchange and financial securities.

When World War I erupted, the international payments system collapsed, leaving 150,000 Americans stranded in Europe without funds. Those American Express workers not mobilized for war toiled 18 hours a day to see that their customers received the money they were due. The company also helped get customers home on overcrowded ships that just weeks before had been luxury ocean liners. In Rotterdam, where money disappeared overnight, the American Express office issued small denomination notes, payable to the bearer on demand. The notes were technically illegal, but the company's reputation was such that they circulated at par. In early August, nine New York banks, the US Navy and American Express teamed up to ship $10 million in gold to Europe to help relieve the distress. News that the battleship *Tennessee* was en route to Europe was enough to stem the panic and get credit flowing again.

World War I also had a major impact on the company. When America entered the war, it nationalized the express industry, including American Express's domestic express routes and the physical infrastructure that made them run, along with the express business assets of Wells Fargo, Adams and other delivery companies. Wells Fargo used the opportunity to leave the domestic express business altogether, and it sold its Mexican and Canadian businesses to American Express in 1920. Adams Express became an investment trust.

For its part, American Express ramped up the financial side of its business—its travelers checks, money orders and foreign remittances (a good business, as many Americans sent money to their relatives in Europe every month). It also beefed up its travel department, which did a brisk business after the war finally ended. Just two-and-a-half months after the Armistice, it ran a full cruise to the Caribbean. In October 1919 it ran its first escorted tour to Europe. In 1922 came its first true world cruise.

American Express grew in the 1920s, but not too quickly. It got burned during the postwar recession holding shipments, including most infamously 50,000 glass eyes that no one could or would pay for. Reflecting on the losses suffered, Frederick Small, president after 1923, said the company should "stick to our knitting" and did so. It used the ebullient economy of the 1920s to improve its efficiency, especially in the back office, where it greatly improved the accounting and auditing systems core to its far-flung financial operations. It also enhanced its crime detection and prevention units. Under the leadership of Del Richer, the company's inspectors department became so efficient that the best criminals would not touch its checks. Small-time crooks who found its checks in their possession often turned them in to the nearest office rather than face Richer's wrath.

American Express had become a lean, mean financial machine, so in 1929 Chase National Bank (now part of #1), via its subsidiary Chase Securities Corporation, purchased a controlling interest in the company. When the government shut down the banks in March 1933 (the so-called bank holiday), "American Express," in the words of its early historian, "stood like a granite cliff in the financial whirlwind . . . completely solvent." During the bank runs preceding the holiday, the same panicky depositors who pulled millions out of their banks gave it to American Express.

Not a bank in the formal sense nor—with $10 million in legal tender in a vault in New York—financially distressed, the government allowed American Express to remain open during the holiday. Every day it shipped out $1–$2 million in cash from its vault to its offices across the nation. People who demanded thousands of dollars in travelers checks cashed immediately changed their minds when the company's clerks cheerfully accepted them and began to count out the money. Then people holding currency rushed to convert their cash, which could be stolen, into travelers checks. The outflow of tender became an inflow.

Regulators forced Chase to divest American Express after the passage of the Securities Exchange Act of 1934, so it spun off Chase Securities, which became Amerex Holding Corporation. American Express was its major asset. On its own once again, American Express survived the rest of the Depression and World War II. During the latter, business boomed unexpectedly as armed forces personnel and itinerant industrial workers and their families used travelers checks to transport their money across the nation and both theaters of war. After the war, the company worked hard to reestablish its network of offices across Europe and Asia Pacific, often as a result of the US marines, sailors and soldiers who desperately required its financial services.

At its centenary, American Express operated in 29 countries and employed 5,500 people worldwide. Its headquarters in New York occupied over 130,000 square feet and housed 2,500 of those employees, as well as countless pieces of information about travel conditions, passenger fares, freight rates and customs duties. The company's business was built on its reputation for quality service.

As Small said, clients had "to be serviced all the way"; the company's unofficial motto was "American Express can do anything." From inviting a lonely, elderly traveler to Christmas dinner, to delivering cash to distressed travelers in the Himalayas by military helicopter, American Express employees have over the years provided legendary customer service, while never neglecting quotidian transactions.

The company grew with the American economy in the 1950s, and in 1958 it introduced its famous charge card. Despite steep losses its first few years, "Amex" cards eventually superseded travelers checks in terms of both profits and visibility. In the 1960s American Express reorganized, computerized, decentralized and rebranded itself as "the company for people who travel." Every year it opened dozens of new overseas offices.

Then scandal rocked the company. One of its subsidiaries vouched for the inventories of soybean oil in the tank farm of Allied Crude Vegetable Oil Refining Corporation in Bayonne, New Jersey, so that company could use the oil as collateral for bank loans. When Allied suddenly folded in November 1963 because of derivatives trading losses, its tanks contained only 80 million pounds of soybean oil, not the 1.4 billion pounds that American Express had guaranteed (rather naively, as it exceeded the inventory of the entire country, according to the US Census Bureau). On the hook for $150 million, or about 15% of its total assets, American Express's stock plummeted on rumors of its own impending bankruptcy. Instead of trying to renege on the claim and in the process hurt its cash cow—the travelers check business—the company stepped up and paid Allied's creditors some $60 million, further strengthening its already strong reputation for honoring its obligations.

American Express had owned a bank briefly during the Great Depression and had long toyed with the idea of establishing another because many of its overseas offices found it necessary to acquire banking licenses anyway. In 1968 it finally formed what one chronicler called "an odd duck," a bank headquartered in New York that did business only overseas because of restrictive US banking regulations. It began doing business slowly in out-of-the-way places like Karachi, Pakistan and US military bases in West Germany and Japan. In the 1970s the bank grew quickly—too quickly it turned out—under Dick Bliss, a Bankers Trust (now part of Deutsche Bank #34) veteran.

Ex-GE executive Bob Smith changed that after careful review of the bank's operations in 1982 revealed it lacked strategic focus. Smith took de facto control of the bank, shifting the bank's focus to private banking (providing financial services for wealthy clients), which in 1983 triggered a merger with Trade Development Bank (TDB). A major private bank established by Edmond Safra in 1960 and headquartered in Geneva, Switzerland, TDB grew on the motto that "when you give Safra your money, you get your money back, plus interest. Guaranteed." One of Safra's analysts warned against the merger, but Safra proceeded anyway. The two institutions never meshed well; American Express sold TDB to a Swiss company for $1 billion in 1990. Meanwhile, the bank continued to struggle, largely because of its exposure to sovereign debt defaults by several less-developed countries, but Smith slowly turned it around.

American Express regained its financial footing for a time by becoming an acquisitions machine and the third most widely recognized corporate name in America, behind only Coca-Cola and McDonald's. It achieved this visibility thanks to several major marketing pushes that expanded on the company's earlier and highly successful "Do You Know Me?" and "Don't Leave Home Without It" campaigns. The first, a print campaign called "Portraits" launched in 1987, consisted of a series of single shots of celebrities in everyday garb and poses, along with the number of years they had been an Amex cardholder and the tag line "Membership has its privileges." The ads featured actors Candice Bergen, John Cleese and Jessica Tandy; NHL star Wayne Gretzky; politician Tip O'Neill; and singers Amy Grant and Luciano Pavarotti. The campaign was so successful that it was brought to television by actor Paul Newman in a 1990 Super Bowl ad.

The second campaign consisted of a series of some 30 advertisements that began in the early 1990s featuring popular comedian Jerry Seinfeld. The spots targeted a broader, younger audience who feared that Amex cards were not widely accepted where they shopped. In one ad, Seinfeld used his card to buy his way off a desert island, while in others he purchased gasoline and even single stamps using his Amex card.

Rapid growth and a strong brand masked a series of problems, however. During the recession of 1990–1991, merchants staged the "Boston Fee Party" to protest the company's high commissions (3%–5%), and six months later the company's Optima card faced the highest customer default rate in credit card history to date.

American Merchants Union Express Company proof stock certificate, ca. 1873. Note that "Merchants Union" is crossed out to reflect the name change back to simply "American Express Company" in 1873.

Much greater trouble was in store for American Express after it entered the securities business. In 1981 the company purchased Shearson Loeb Rhodes, one of the largest American securities firms. The company's CEO, Sanford "Sandy" Weill, had built the investment bank through mergers during the 1960s and 1970s by following the strategy of buying big troubled firms, adopting their brands, slashing costs and closing or selling underperforming businesses. Weill became president of the company in 1983, a position he held for two years. In 1984 the acquisitions continued, as the venerable investment banking and trading firm of Lehman Brothers Kuhn Loeb was added, itself the product of the amalgamation of storied investment banks Lehman Brothers and Kuhn Loeb in 1977. The combination was called Shearson Lehman Brothers, and it faced serious difficulties, losing $900 million in 1990 alone.

Eventually Moody's downgraded $7 billion of the company's debt. CEO James D. Robinson tried to sell the company to GE Capital (#8), but CEO Jack Welch did not bite. Nor did Robert Allen at AT&T. In 1993 American Express sold much of Shearson to Primerica, which Weill had run since 1988. The sale was part of the company's 1993 turnaround effort, which included ousting Robinson in favor of Harvey Golub, whose Investor Diversified Services (IDS) division, which employed

7,500 financial planners who sold everything from annuities to life insurance, went gangbusters under his leadership in the late 1980s.

While Brian Kleinberg got the Optima card back on track, Golub slashed expenses at TRS (Travel Related Services, which included credit cards) by cutting 4,800 workers. He slowed the merchants' revolt by cutting average charges on Amex card purchases from 3.3% to 2.9%, while Steven Grant provided merchants with better service, including ways of increasing customer loyalty. Golub also refocused the company on TRS by disgorging some magazine publishing, stock brokering and insurance businesses while rebuilding "respect" for the American Express brand. The stock price rebounded strongly as a result of those moves. With almost 43 million cardholders and earnings at record levels, American Express in 1997 quietly sought a merger with Citi (#3) from a position of strength, but again no deal was struck.

By the early 21st century it was again hard to leave home without American Express. With 2,200 locations in 160 countries, it was the world's largest travel agency and owned more than 60 credit cards, including cards issued in China, Russia and Eastern Europe. It also still owned several magazines (*Departures*, *Food & Wine* and *Travel & Leisure* among them) and an online bank. It spun off its investment advising business, Ameriprise Financial, in 2005 and sold its tax division to

American Express stock certificate signed by Henry Wells as president, William Fargo as secretary and Alex Holland as treasurer, issued 1865.

H&R Block. Thanks to a successful lawsuit in 2004, American Express was able to partner with more banks, those previously prevented by Visa and MasterCard from issuing American Express cards. Its Amex card came to be used in almost a quarter of all credit card transactions in the United States.

Throughout the first decade of the new millennium, American Express was feted by *Fortune* magazine as one of the "100 Best Companies to Work For," one of "America's Most Admired" companies and one of the world's top 25 brands. Like most large BHCs, however, the company got caught up in the subprime mortgage crisis. In 2007 it began allowing clients to place monthly mortgage payments on their credit cards in exchange for rewards points. But its transgressions were minor compared to those of other major BHCs; by 2010 its earnings per share had rebounded to $3.35, six cents above its 2007 high, and legendary investor Warren Buffett touted its stock.

Sources

"American Express and Primerica: The Comeback Kid and the Hare." *The Economist*, October 2, 1993, 88–89.

Buffett, Mary and David Clark. *The Warren Buffett Stock Portfolio: Warren Buffett Stock Picks: Why and When He Is Investing in Them.* New York: Scribner, 2011, 49–60.

Burrough, Bryan. *Vendetta: American Express and the Smearing of Edmond Safra.* New York: HarperCollins, 1992.

"Catch Up." *The Economist*, April 26, 1997, 71–72.

Friedman, Jon and John Meehan. *House of Cards: Inside the Troubled Empire of American Express.* New York: Putnam, 1992.

Garmhausen, Stephen. "American Express Shuffles Longtime Card Exec to Ailing Discount Brokerage." *American Banker*, August 25, 1997.

Grant, Steven. "American Express Company: Make Membership a Privilege." *Customer Service: Extraordinary Results at Southwest Airlines, Charles Schwab, Lands' End, American Express, Staples, and USAA*, edited by Fred Wiersema, 120–43. New York: HarperBusiness, 1998.

Grossman, Peter Z. *American Express: The Unofficial History of the People Who Built the Great Financial Empire.* New York: Crown, 1987.

Haig, Matt. *Brand Royalty: How the World's Top 100 Brands Thrive and Survive.* Philadelphia: Kogan Page, 2004, 18–20, 291–93.

Hatch, Alden. *American Express: A Century of Service.* Garden City, NY: Doubleday, 1950.

McDonald, Duff. *Last Man Standing: The Ascent of Jamie Dimon and JPMorgan Chase.* New York: Simon and Schuster, 2009.

Riggs, Thomas, ed. *Encyclopedia of Major Marketing Campaigns.* Farmington, MI: Gale Group, 2000, 44–50.

Wetfeet. *25 Top Financial Services Firms.* San Francisco: Wetfeet. 2008, 12–14.

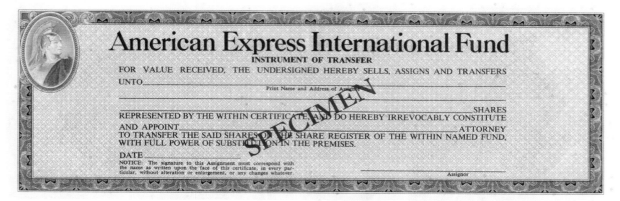

American Express International Fund specimen instrument of transfer.

American Express International Fund specimen stock certificate.

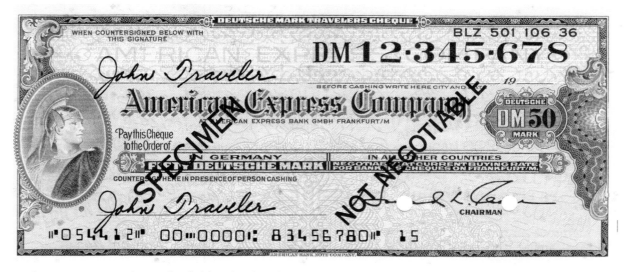

American Express Company specimen traveler's check for 50 deutsche marks.

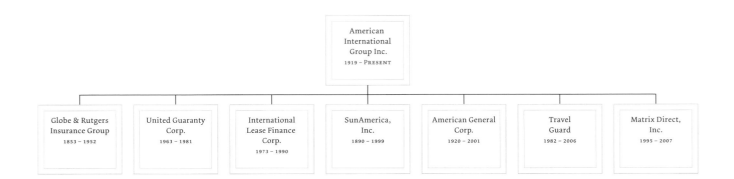

American International Group

RANK	HEADQUARTERS	TICKER	ASSETS	EARLIEST KNOWN ANCESTOR	INDUSTRY OF ORIGIN
7	New York, NY	AIG	$537,000,000,000	1853	Insurance

"Native Quarter," Shanghai, ca. 1910-1915.

The headlines on September 16, 2008, shocked most Americans. The US government had seized control of American International Group (AIG), one the world's largest insurance companies. AIG became symbolic of the financial crisis—incredible amounts of risk-taking without proper controls, a staggering $182 billion government bailout and corporate bonuses that led to public outrage and protest. Yet under the leadership of Robert Benmosche, who took the helm in August 2009, the firm not only paid back the $182 billion but returned another $22 billion to the government as well. This story of one of the most remarkable turnarounds in American financial history is little known, as is the firm's nearly 100-year history.

AIG traces its roots to 1919, when American entrepreneur Cornelius Vander Starr, a 27-year-old entrepreneur from California, started a general insurance agency, American Asiatic Underwriters, in Shanghai, China. Starr hired bright and talented local people to fill his two-room office, and the agency became known as a company willing and able to provide coverage for diverse risks. A longtime colleague described Starr in those early years as quiet and unassuming, yet with the ability to sell anybody anything.

By the late 1920s Starr had expanded his enterprise throughout Southeast Asia. In 1926 he opened his first office in the United States—American International Underwriters Corporation (AIU)—in New York and in 1939 moved his headquarters from Shanghai to New York City. The move was in response to Japanese military expansion, communist insurrections and other events. To his credit, Starr was a pioneer in New York when it came to equal employment opportunity, hiring people he believed would help his company regardless of their race or nationality, and rapidly promoting only the best. That included many non-Americans and people from modest, even humble, backgrounds. He gave everyone from executives to kitchen staff substantial equity stakes in his companies, and they responded as economists predicted they would. They worked tirelessly, often 12 hours a day, six days a week.

In the late 1930s, Starr also focused on opportunities in the Latin American market, which was growing steadily and offset the decline in business from Asia during World War II.

After the war, AIU entered Japan and Germany to provide insurance for American military personnel. The company helped fill a void in Europe, providing capacity needed by recovering European industries. The 1950s were a time of tremendous expansion for AIU, with the company establishing operations in all the key insurance markets of Western Europe, as well as the Middle East and Africa. In 1952 Starr began to focus on the American market by acquiring Globe & Rutgers Fire Insurance Company. By the end of the decade, Starr's general and life insurance organization included an extensive network of agents and offices in more than 75 countries.

As the company expanded through large swathes of the globe, Starr gave his key employees much leeway to run underwriting agencies as they saw fit and to adapt them to local market circumstances. Pirate insurance, for example, made little sense in France but was a key offering in Indonesia in the 1920s. One thing Starr insisted upon was the proper pricing of risk: premiums had to cover the likelihood of loss and expenses. By treading where others feared to go, Starr enjoyed considerable pricing power, a soft monopoly according to AIG chronicler Roddy Boyd. He also developed an exceptional claims unit, the first in Asia to use forensic science to defend against fraud.

In 1960 Starr hired Maurice R. "Hank" Greenberg to develop an international accident and health business. Two years later, Greenberg transformed one of Starr's US holdings — an agency company that faced severe competition from larger insurers. Greenberg successfully refocused the business on selling insurance through independent brokers rather than agents. In 1967 AIG was incorporated as a unifying umbrella organization for most of Starr's general and life insurance businesses. In 1968, shortly before his death, Starr named Greenberg his successor. The company went public in 1969.

From a small, privately held yet far-flung empire that was not highly profitable, Greenberg forged a global giant. Because of its international focus, AIG under Greenberg largely avoided the asbestos and environmental liability claims that ruined many of its competitors, allowing the company to gain market share during "hard" markets (periods of high premiums and high underwriting standards). The company was also market savvy and had a knack for cheaply reinsuring at just the right moment. That is not to say that AIG did not assume risks, but it often avoided the big hits that ruined so many of its competitors. Its large size, Greenberg boasted, allowed it to take risks that others could not, and that maintained its soft monopoly in many niche markets. For example, AIG underwrote such esoteric risks as kidnapping, Texas ostrich farms and directors and officers insurance. When it could not develop a product internally, it often acquired a company that had already done so.

Under Greenberg, the organization continued to be known for innovative coverages and a willingness to take on diverse risks. In the mid-1970s, for instance, one AIG subsidiary took the lead in underwriting satellite launches. Another AIG company provided transmission interruption coverage in 1974 for the broadcast of "Rumble in the Jungle," a historic boxing championship fight. And in the early 1980s AIG provided nonappearance and cancellation insurance for the Academy Awards.

During the 1980s AIG developed new sources of income through diverse investments, including the acquisition of mortgage insurer United Guaranty Corporation (which it still owns today). In 1987 it established Financial Products, which focused on derivatives and structured finance markets.

Throughout the 1990s and the early 2000s AIG continued expanding in strategic markets. In 1992 the company returned to China when it received the first foreign insurance license granted in over 40 years by the Chinese government. Within the US, AIG entered the retirement savings market through its acquisition of SunAmerica, Inc. in 1999 and, two years later, acquired American General Corporation, a leading domestic life insurance and annuities provider.

In 1998 Dearborn Financial ranked AIG the 86th best stock to own in America on the basis of its geographical and sectional diversification. It offered policies in about 130 countries, including China and Russia, and derived 50% of its total revenue from outside the United States. About a third of its revenue came from life insurance, 56% from property and casualty insurance and 11% from various other financial

services. About 33,000 employees worldwide generated those revenues, which grew fast enough to generate a 594% increase in the company's stock price over the previous decade.

In late 2004 and early 2005 AIG became embroiled in a series of investigations by the US Securities and Exchange Commission, the US Justice Department and the New York State Attorney General's office. Greenberg left AIG in March 2005, and longtime AIG executive Martin J. Sullivan succeeded him as CEO. Shortly after, AIG restated its financial position and issued a reduction in book value of $2.7 billion. About a year later AIG and the New York State Attorney General's office agreed to a settlement in which AIG would pay a fine of $1.6 billion.

At the beginning of 2008 AIG was, according to *Forbes*, the 18th largest public company in the world (including nonfinancial companies), and it was a component of the Dow Jones Industrial Average (DJIA) with a double-A credit rating. By the end of that year, after several credit downgrades that dried up its sources of funding, AIG was a ward of the federal government. It was removed from the DJIA, and its size was indeterminable because many of its assets, including various derivatives like mortgage-backed securities and credit default swaps, were unable to be properly marked to market, given market conditions.

By then AIG was doing business in 130 countries through 176 foreign financial services companies (including insurers and other financial services firms) and 71 US insurance companies. The latter were regulated by state insurance commissioners coordinated nationally by the National Association of Insurance Commissioners (NAIC) on the basis of state of domicile and type of insurance (life and annuities, commercial lines or personal lines). For the most part, AIG's insurance subsidiaries were healthy. But AIG Financial Products (AIGFP), a London-based subsidiary established in the late 1980s by Howard Sosin, was not.

Sosin, dubbed the "Dr. Strangelove of Derivatives" by the *Wall Street Journal*, made huge profits by developing advanced derivative products, but he was forced out in 1993 so that Greenberg could exert more control over such an important profit center. Greenberg warned the unit's new leader, Tom Savage, about jeopardizing AIG's triple-A credit rating. Savage's successor, Joe Cassano, was also convinced that AIGFP could generate huge, virtually riskless profits in the credit default swap business.

The result, as Federal Reserve Chairman Ben Bernanke put it, was that AIGFP "made huge numbers of irresponsible bets" on credit default swaps. Contrary to its risk models, it eventually lost most of those bets — and to the world's largest and most troubled financial institutions! Billions evaporated virtually overnight, and the AIG HC could not lawfully tap into its insurance subsidiaries for backup capital, so it quickly ran out of cash once its credit dried up.

The impending bankruptcy of the AIG HC threatened the solvency of many other already shaky financial institutions, and hence the entire financial system. Therefore, directly bailing out the AIG holding company with taxpayer money was a way to indirectly bail out the system. As Bernanke said, "We're not doing this to bail out AIG or their shareholders, certainly. We're doing this to protect our financial system and to avoid a much more severe crisis in our global economy. . . . We really had no choice."

Hundreds of millions to several billion dollars were paid to AIG to make whole contracts with JPMorgan Chase (#1), Merrill Lynch/Bank of America (#2), Wachovia/Wells Fargo (#4), Goldman Sachs (#5), Morgan Stanley (#6), HSBC (#11), RBS-Citizens (#25), BMO (#26), Santander (#32), Deutsche Bank (#34) and a slew of foreign megabanks, like Société Générale and Calyon. Those payments kept AIG and others afloat, but what really incensed Americans and President Barack Obama were the

American International Group specimen stock certificate.

huge bonuses that AIG/US taxpayers paid in 2009 to employees, and in particular to AIGFP employees.

When AIG hired Robert Benmosche in 2009, few thought anyone could turn the company around. Many members of Congress scoffed when he predicted in May 2010 that the taxpayers would be repaid in full. Benmosche believed that when people are given the freedom to act — and they exercise that freedom — it is surprising what can happen. And he knew that all the while AIG's insurance units continued to protect, and profitably at that, the income and property of millions of people worldwide. Benmosche was also raising capital by selling stakes in many of the units, especially those overseas like Nan Shan Life.

By late 2012 the firm had repaid its TARP money, along with $22 billion in interest. A thank you ad in December 2012 read, "We promised to repay America in full. We promised to deliver a profit to America. We're proud to have kept both promises." It was an incredible turnaround, the likes of which had not been seen before in American business. As AIG looks toward its 100th anniversary in 2019, the company is focused on demonstrating that what it has accomplished up until now is sustainable well into the future.

Sources

Ario, Joel. "AIG's Impact on the Global Economy: Before, During and After Federal Intervention." In *The AIG Debacle: Global Impact and the Need for Government Intervention,* edited by Peter A. Wayland, 1–12. New York: Nova Science Publishers, Inc., 2010.

Boyd, Roddy. *Fatal Risk: A Cautionary Take of AIG's Corporate Suicide.* Hoboken, NJ: Wiley, 2011.

Clark, Rodney. "Testimony of Rodney Clark, Managing Director, Ratings Services, Standard & Poor's Financial Services." In *The AIG Debacle: Global Impact and the Need for Government Intervention,* edited by Peter A. Wayland, 15–21. New York: Nova Science Publishers, 2010.

Liddy, Edward M. "Testimony of Edward M. Liddy, Chairman and Chief Executive Officer, American International Group (AIG) Before the House Financial Services Committee." In *The AIG Debacle: Global Impact and the Need for Government Intervention,* edited by Peter A. Wayland, 27–53. New York: Nova Science Publishers, 2010.

McLean, Bethany and Joe Nocera. *All The Devils Are Here: The Hidden History of the Financial Crisis.* New York: Penguin, 2010, 69–81, 187–203.

Spencer, Andrew. *Tower of Thieves: AIG.* New York: Brick Tower Press, 2009.

Walden, Gene. *The 100 Best Stocks to Own in America* 5th ed. Chicago: Dearborn Financial Publishing, 1998, 309–311.

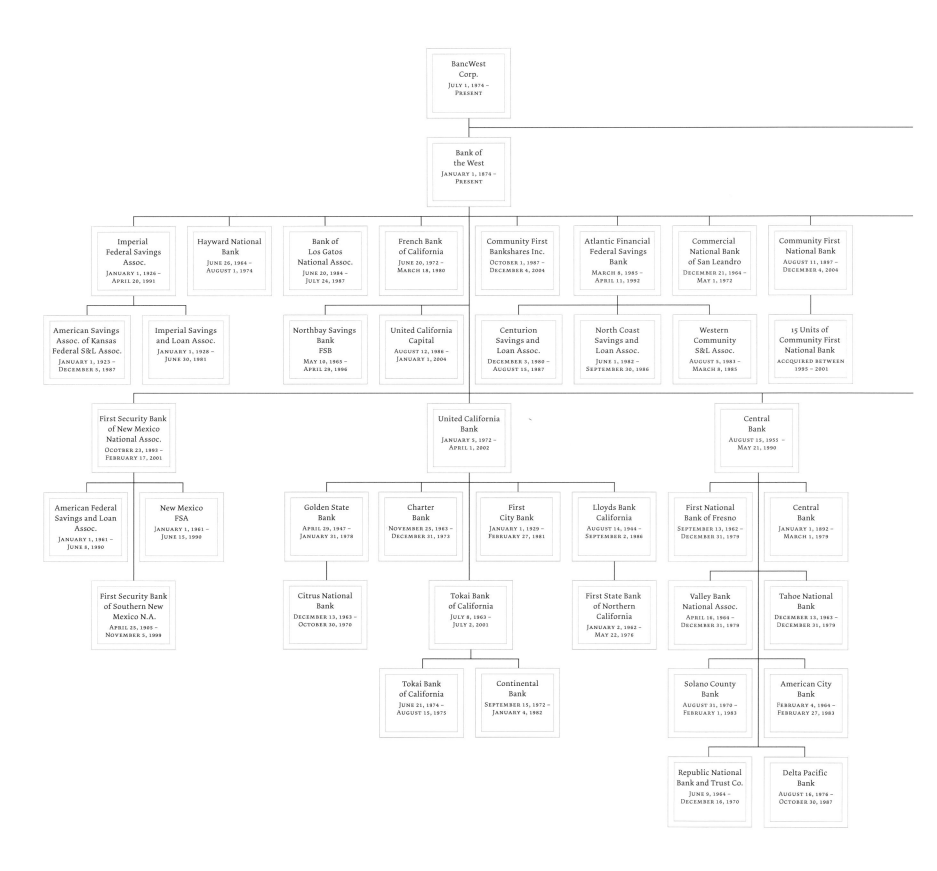

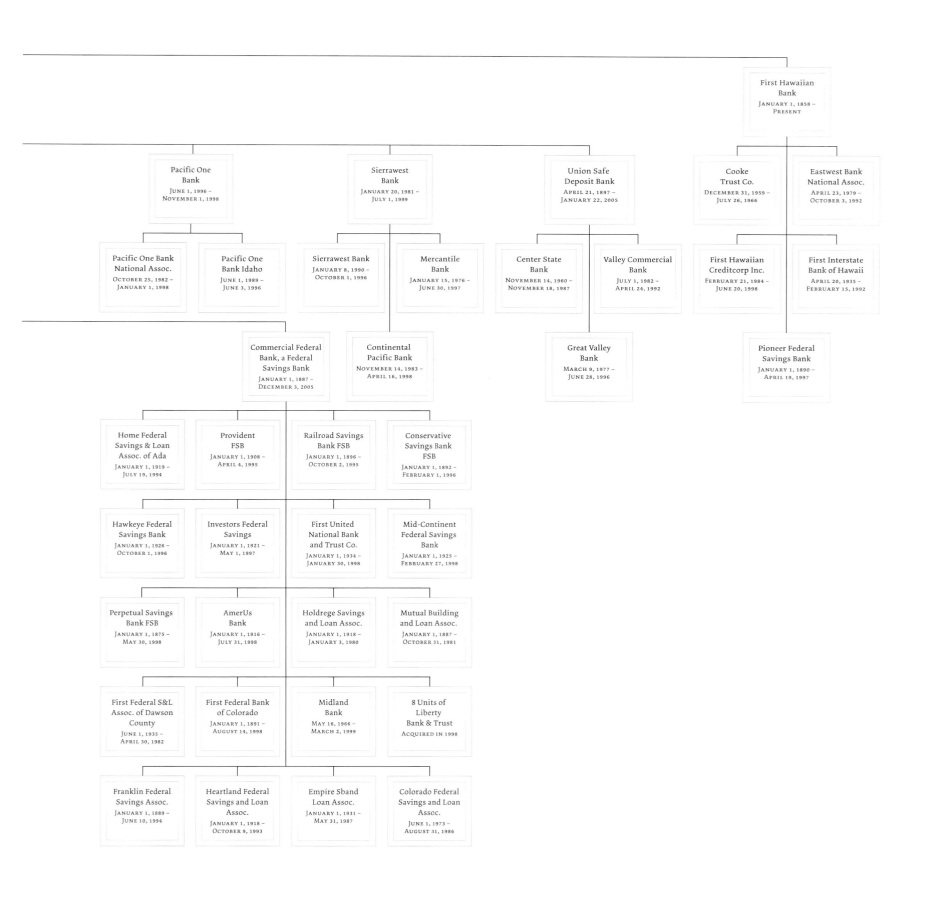

First Hawaiian Bank
JANUARY 1, 1858 –
PRESENT

Pacific One Bank
JUNE 1, 1996 –
NOVEMBER 1, 1998

Sierrawest Bank
JANUARY 20, 1981 –
JULY 1, 1999

Union Safe Deposit Bank
APRIL 21, 1897 –
JANUARY 22, 2005

Cooke Trust Co.
DECEMBER 31, 1959 –
JULY 26, 1966

Eastwest Bank National Assoc.
APRIL 23, 1979 –
OCTOBER 3, 1992

Pacific One Bank National Assoc.
OCTOBER 25, 1982 –
JANUARY 1, 1998

Pacific One Bank Idaho
JUNE 1, 1989 –
JUNE 3, 1996

Sierrawest Bank
JANUARY 8, 1990 –
OCTOBER 1, 1996

Mercantile Bank
JANUARY 15, 1976 –
JUNE 30, 1997

Center State Bank
NOVEMBER 14, 1960 –
NOVEMBER 18, 1987

Valley Commercial Bank
JULY 1, 1982 –
APRIL 24, 1992

First Hawaiian Creditcorp Inc.
FEBRUARY 21, 1984 –
JUNE 20, 1998

First Interstate Bank of Hawaii
APRIL 20, 1935 –
FEBRUARY 15, 1992

Commercial Federal Bank, a Federal Savings Bank
JANUARY 1, 1887 –
DECEMBER 3, 2005

Continental Pacific Bank
NOVEMBER 14, 1983 –
APRIL 16, 1998

Great Valley Bank
MARCH 9, 1977 –
JUNE 28, 1996

Pioneer Federal Savings Bank
JANUARY 1, 1890 –
APRIL 19, 1997

Home Federal Savings & Loan Assoc. of Ada
JANUARY 1, 1919 –
JULY 19, 1994

Provident FSB
JANUARY 1, 1908 –
APRIL 4, 1995

Railroad Savings Bank FSB
JANUARY 1, 1896 –
OCTOBER 2, 1995

Conservative Savings Bank FSB
JANUARY 1, 1892 –
FEBRUARY 1, 1996

Hawkeye Federal Savings Bank
JANUARY 1, 1926 –
OCTOBER 1, 1996

Investors Federal Savings
JANUARY 1, 1921 –
MAY 1, 1997

First United National Bank and Trust Co.
JANUARY 1, 1934 –
JANUARY 30, 1998

Mid-Continent Federal Savings Bank
JANUARY 1, 1925 –
FEBRUARY 27, 1998

Perpetual Savings Bank FSB
JANUARY 1, 1875 –
MAY 30, 1998

AmerUs Bank
JANUARY 1, 1916 –
JULY 31, 1998

Holdrege Savings and Loan Assoc.
JANUARY 1, 1918 –
JANUARY 3, 1980

Mutual Building and Loan Assoc.
JANUARY 1, 1887 –
OCTOBER 31, 1981

First Federal S&L Assoc. of Dawson County
JUNE 1, 1935 –
APRIL 30, 1982

First Federal Bank of Colorado
JANUARY 1, 1891 –
AUGUST 14, 1998

Midland Bank
MAY 16, 1966 –
MARCH 2, 1999

8 Units of Liberty Bank & Trust
ACQUIRED IN 1998

Franklin Federal Savings Assoc.
JANUARY 1, 1889 –
JUNE 10, 1994

Heartland Federal Savings and Loan Assoc.
JANUARY 1, 1918 –
OCTOBER 9, 1993

Empire Sband Loan Assoc.
JANUARY 1, 1931 –
MAY 31, 1987

Colorado Federal Savings and Loan Assoc.
JUNE 1, 1973 –
AUGUST 31, 1986

BancWest

Bank *(abridged)*

RANK	HEADQUARTERS	TICKER	ASSETS	EARLIEST KNOWN ANCESTOR	INDUSTRY OF ORIGIN
31	**Honolulu, HI**	**BWE**	**$80,000,000,000**	**1848**	**Commercial Banking**

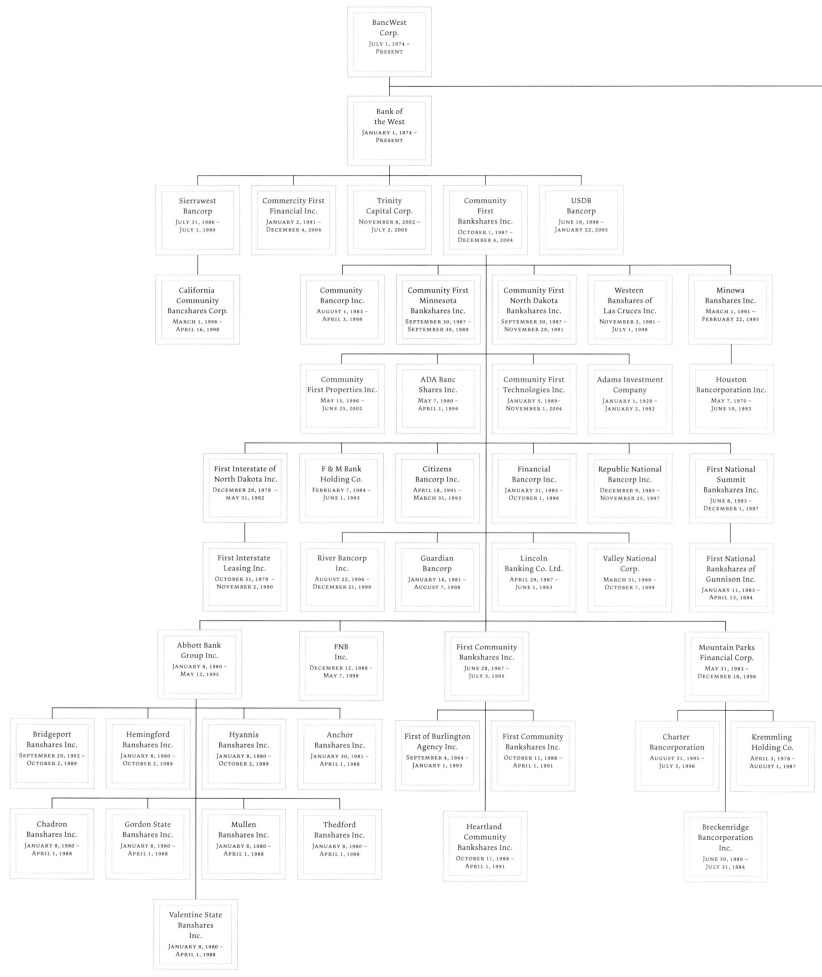

BancWest Corp.
JULY 1, 1974 –
PRESENT

Bank of the West
JANUARY 1, 1874 –
PRESENT

Sierrawest Bancorp
JULY 31, 1986 –
JULY 1, 1999

Commercity First Financial Inc.
JANUARY 2, 1991 –
DECEMBER 4, 2004

Trinity Capital Corp.
NOVEMBER 8, 2002 –
JULY 2, 2005

Community First Bankshares Inc.
OCTOBER 1, 1987 –
DECEMBER 4, 2004

USDB Bancorp
JUNE 19, 1998 –
JANUARY 22, 2005

California Community Bancshares Corp.
MARCH 1, 1996 –
APRIL 16, 1998

Community Bancorp Inc.
AUGUST 1, 1983 –
APRIL 3, 1998

Community First Minnesota Bankshares Inc.
SEPTEMBER 30, 1987 –
SEPTEMBER 30, 1989

Community First North Dakota Bankshares Inc.
SEPTEMBER 30, 1987 –
NOVEMBER 29, 1991

Western Banshares of Las Cruces Inc.
NOVEMBER 2, 1981 –
JULY 1, 1998

Minowa Banshares Inc.
MARCH 1, 1991 –
FEBRUARY 22, 1995

Community First Properties Inc.
MAY 15, 1996 –
JUNE 25, 2002

ADA Banc Shares Inc.
MAY 7, 1980 –
APRIL 1, 1994

Community First Technologies Inc.
JANUARY 5, 1989–
NOVEMBER 1, 2004

Adams Investment Company
JANUARY 1, 1929 –
JANUARY 2, 1992

Houston Bancorporation Inc.
MAY 7, 1970 –
JUNE 10, 1993

First Interstate of North Dakota Inc.
DECEMBER 28, 1978 –
MAY 31, 1992

F & M Bank Holding Co.
FEBRUARY 7, 1984 –
JUNE 1, 1993

Citizens Bancorp Inc.
APRIL 18, 1991 –
MARCH 31, 1993

Financial Bancorp Inc.
JANUARY 31, 1985 –
OCTOBER 1, 1996

Republic National Bancorp Inc.
DECEMBER 9, 1985 –
NOVEMBER 25, 1997

First National Summit Bankshares Inc.
JUNE 8, 1993 –
DECEMBER 1, 1997

First Interstate Leasing Inc.
OCTOBER 31, 1979 –
NOVEMBER 2, 1990

River Bancorp Inc.
AUGUST 22, 1996 –
DECEMBER 21, 1999

Guardian Bancorp
JANUARY 16, 1981 –
AUGUST 7, 1998

Lincoln Banking Co. Ltd.
APRIL 29, 1987 –
JUNE 1, 1993

Valley National Corp.
MARCH 31, 1999 –
OCTOBER 7, 1999

First National Bankshares of Gunnison Inc.
JANUARY 11, 1983 –
APRIL 13, 1994

Abbott Bank Group Inc.
JANUARY 8, 1980 –
MAY 12, 1995

FNB Inc.
DECEMBER 12, 1988 –
MAY 7, 1998

First Community Bankshares Inc.
JUNE 28, 1967 –
JULY 3, 1995

Mountain Parks Financial Corp.
MAY 31, 1983 –
DECEMBER 18, 1996

Bridgeport Banshares Inc.
SEPTEMBER 20, 1982 –
OCTOBER 2, 1989

Hemingford Banshares Inc.
JANUARY 8, 1980 –
OCTOBER 2, 1989

Hyannis Banshares Inc.
JANUARY 8, 1980 –
OCTOBER 2, 1989

Anchor Banshares Inc.
JANUARY 30, 1981 –
APRIL 1, 1988

First of Burlington Agency Inc.
SEPTEMBER 4, 1964 –
JANUARY 1, 1993

First Community Bankshares Inc.
OCTOBER 11, 1988 –
APRIL 1, 1991

Charter Bancorporation
AUGUST 31, 1995 –
JULY 3, 1996

Kremmling Holding Co.
APRIL 3, 1978 –
AUGUST 1, 1987

Chadron Banshares Inc.
JANUARY 8, 1980 –
APRIL 1, 1988

Gordon State Banshares Inc.
JANUARY 8, 1980 –
APRIL 1, 1988

Mullen Banshares Inc.
JANUARY 8, 1980 –
APRIL 1, 1988

Thedford Banshares Inc.
JANUARY 8, 1980 –
APRIL 1, 1988

Heartland Community Bankshares Inc.
OCTOBER 11, 1988 –
APRIL 1, 1991

Breckenridge Bancorporation Inc.
JUNE 30, 1980 –
JULY 31, 1984

Valentine State Banshares Inc.
JANUARY 8, 1980 –
APRIL 1, 1988

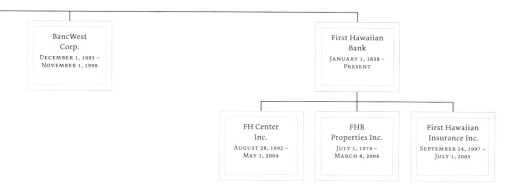

BancWest Corp.	First Hawaiian Bank
DECEMBER 1, 1995 – NOVEMBER 1, 1998	JANUARY 1, 1858 – PRESENT

FH Center Inc.	FHB Properties Inc.	First Hawaiian Insurance Inc.
AUGUST 28, 1992 – MAY 1, 2004	JULY 1, 1974 – MARCH 8, 2004	SEPTEMBER 24, 1997 – JULY 1, 2005

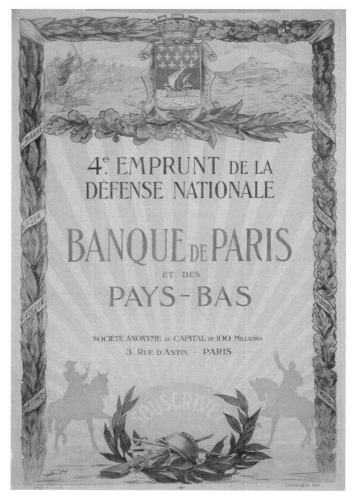

Banque de Paris et des Pays-Bas poster for the 4ᵗʰ National Defense Loan, 1918.

Banque de Paris et des Pays-Bas poster for the National Loan, 1920.

BancWest Corporation is the US holding company of BNP Paribas, the French giant created by the 2000 merger of Paribas and Banque Nationale de Paris (BNP). Paribas began operations in 1872 as Banque de Paris et des Pays-Bas (Bank of Paris and the Netherlands). That bank was the result of the merger of two French investment banks, Banque de Crédit et de Dépôt des Pays-Bas, which was formed in 1863 at the impetus of the Bischoffsheim *haute banque* (elite merchant bank specializing in financing international trade), and the Banque de Paris, which was founded in 1869 in opposition to the Rothschilds's *haute banque*. Banque de Paris et des Pays-Bas had a capital of FR125 million, and its first major act was to help the French government pay reparations incurred by its loss in the Franco-Prussian War of 1870–1871.

Until the Great War, the bank battled Rothschilds's interests, other competitors, financial instability and explosive increases in the volume of business by developing what its historian called the "Paribas system." The system was an extensive network of foreign offices loosely controlled from Paris and three concentric circles of alliances with other banks, including Crédit Lyonnais and Barings in the inner circle; banks in Austro-Hungary, Italy and Scandinavia in the middle circle; and banks in the Balkans, Russia and Spain in the outermost ring. It also forged loose relationships with banks in Africa, Asia and the New World.

The bank used those connections to underwrite and distribute securities—from sovereign and municipal bonds to common stocks—and to trade portfolios of financial assets. Imperial Russia was one of its most important foreign clients; the bank and its network helped to finance the trans-Siberian railway in the 1890s, and it led a huge issue of FR2 billion in 1906. It also financed private industry, including privately owned transportation infrastructure, utilities and manufacturing companies. Between 1900 and 1913, the bank's assets soared from FR278 million to FR782 million (gold), FR159 million of which were investments it traded on its own account. Its stock price also soared, from FR500 in 1872 to FR900 in 1905 to FR1,336 per share in 1913, indicating rising profitability as well as sheer size.

Both world wars and the monetary instability and depression sandwiched in between the wars were trying times for Paribas. The Great War's western front devastated the French countryside and an entire generation of Frenchmen. In the 1920s, when many US banks recovered during the economic boom, the bank suffered huge losses on assets denominated in German marks and other currencies that suffered from hyperinflation. Because France clung tenaciously to the gold standard until 1936, the Great Depression hit it longer and harder than most other nations. And during World War II, the Nazis occupied northern France and turned the south over to its puppet Vichy regime. By 1952 the bank's share price, which had been sliding for decades, sank to an all-time low of FR39 (gold).

After liberation, the institution's two main assets were its brand and the human capital of its remaining 1,500 or so employees. Under the leadership of Jean Reyre from 1948 until 1969, it first concentrated on rebuilding its domestic business, avoiding nationalization by the French government. It also allowed its inner circle to act more independently and eventually to morph into subsidiaries of the French holding company, Financière de Paris et des Pay-Bas (which was

Scene on a pineapple plantation with harvested pineapples, Hawaii, ca. 1910-1925. BancWest's two major properties were Bank of the West and First Hawaiian Bank.

renamed Paribas, a portmanteau of Paris and Bas, in 1982).

In 1960 the bank established an office in New York and began underwriting securities there the following year. It established a similar presence in London, which remained important globally, in 1964. Neither office initially showed much in the way of profits, but they signaled the bank's determination to once again become a world player. Profits came in the 1970s, as did expansion into Africa, Canada, Japan, Latin America and southern Europe. In 1986 *International Financing Review* named Paribas "International Bank of the Year."

By 1980 the investment banking side of Paribas employed 3,000 people, and by 1990 some 9,000 people. Including two major acquisitions—Compagnie Bancaire (a group of consumer and mortgage finance companies founded in 1959 that the bank purchased a controlling interest in over a period of years) and a commercial bank, Crédit du Nord (which the bank merged with Banque de l'Union Parisienne in 1974 before absorbing the combined entity)—it employed 30,000 people by 1990. Assets, which were FR31.1 million in 1972, hit FR347 million in 1982 and FR1 billion in 1991.

BHC Groupe Paribas attributed its success to its culture of caution and its size. As its historian explained, "despite the failures and despite the mistakes that have been made, caution has always prevailed. Whenever the bank set off in new directions, it did so fully aware of what these new directions implied." Most importantly, the bank grew strategically instead of haphazardly. "Although size does not have the same degree of importance for a *banque d'affaires* group, such as Paribas, as for more traditional commercial banks," explained Jacques de Fouchier (chairman from 1970–1978 and 1981–1982) in 1992, "it can

provide stability and credibility in the international context which should not be underestimated."

In August 1999, however, Banque Nationale de Paris (BNP) acquired Paribas for $13 billion in a hostile action. Paribas had not been completely oblivious to the threat, which was exacerbated by multiple management shake-ups, a trading scandal and rollercoaster profitability.

BNP traces its corporate origins to the formation of Comptoir d'Escompte in 1848. The bank ran into serious trouble in 1889, when it needed a bailout from a consortium of French banks, which established its remaining husk as depository institution Comptoir National d'Escompte de Paris (CNEP). While its predecessor had restricted itself to Paris and a few foreign cities, CNEP opened branches in numerous French provinces. By 1920 it had 223 branches. Controlled by the German government after the fall of France in 1940, and by the French government after 1946, CNEP grew slowly but steadily.

BNP's second main progenitor, Banque Nationale de Crédit, formed in 1913. It grew extremely rapidly through acquisitions and new branch formation. By the end of the Great War it was already France's fourth largest bank. It merged with one of its sponsors, Banque Francaise pour le Commerce et l'Industrie, in 1920, and had to be reorganized, as Banque Nationale plour le Commerce et l'Industrie (BNCI), in 1932. It, too, was nationalized by the French government after World War II, but it continued to grow quickly, especially outside of France.

In 1966 BNCI and CNEP merged. The latter supplied a large network of branches in France, while the former boasted the largest network of foreign branches of any French bank. BNP continued BNCI's precedent,

$1 Hawaii silver certificate.

establishing branches or offices in Cairo, Chicago, Manila, Moscow, San Francisco, Seoul, Tehran, Tokyo, Toronto, Vancouver and other important cities around the globe. Although both of its progenitors had given up investment banking after forced reorganizations, BNP reentered the business via its Banexi capital unit. When it acquired Paribas in 1999, BNP had about 2,000 branches in France, which accounted for 40% of its total revenues. Its international offices spanned 76 countries.

BancWest's two major properties were Bank of the West and First Hawaiian Bank, the largest and oldest bank in America's 50th state. The latter's origins lay in Bishop & Co., which Charles Bishop and William Aldrich formed as a private bank under the laws of the Kingdom of Hawaii in 1858 as an outgrowth of their whaling ship provisioning business. The favorable reputations and unlimited liability of both partners won praise from the press and considerable business, almost $4,800 in deposits on the first day alone. The bank quickly forged connections with the most important Hawaiian business, political and professional leaders, as well as foreign banks and the Bank of California (now part of #27). Bishop himself became a member of Hawaii's House of Nobles and its Privy Council. The former was a lifetime appointment, and he served on the latter until 1892. He was also Minister of Foreign Affairs for a time, so the bank's interests were amply represented in the islands' constitutional monarchy.

Hawaii's whaling economy collapsed in 1860–1861 as the Civil War erupted, and increasingly expensive whale oil gave way to Pennsylvania "rock oil." By the 1870s the Hawaiian economy had successfully shifted emphasis to agriculture, especially cane sugar, rice and coffee. The bank evolved too, serving as an agent for the Pacific Insurance Company of San Francisco and the Manhattan Life Insurance Company of New York.

In 1875 Bishop & Co. faced a minor run when word reached Honolulu that its correspondent, the Bank of California, had suspended payments. When cashier Samuel Mills Damon happily paid out a large sum and proved willing to accommodate as many others as wanted their deposits back, the run ended and the deposits returned. The bank was able to do this because it was making a fortune financing sugar cane plantations, the combined acreage of which increased from 12,000 in 1874 to 125,000 in 1898.

At first it dealt with plantation owners directly, but later it lent mostly to agencies that combined several sources of funding to supply agribusinesses with various types of short-, medium- and long-term financing. It also financed rice farmers who enjoyed modest success exporting to California, but whose main function was to feed the Chinese working on the sugar plantations. In 1884, a second bank, owned by California sugar magnate Claus Spreckels, opened for business. This was Bishop & Co.'s first direct competitor.

In 1895, a year after Hawaii became a Republic, Bishop sold the bank to Damon for $800,000 so that he could take a position in the Bank of California. Damon was too busy to run the bank himself, so he admitted others, including his son, Samuel Edward Damon, into partnership.

In 1898 the islands became a US territory, which necessitated changing its laws to conform to American standards. That required splitting the bank's business into three parts—trust, banking and insurance—in 1905. But new rules also brought new hope that business could be safely conducted in Hawaii. This led to increased investment from James Dole (the canned pineapple king) and others, which increased the bank's business.

US military spending at Pearl Harbor and elsewhere also quickened the pace of the island's economy. The bank grew along with the local economy, establishing a branch in the growing agricultural town of Hilo in 1910. Three collection offices soon followed, as did a branch at Waimea on the west side of Kauai in 1911. In the boom days of the Great War, two more branches opened on the north shore of Oahu.

Damon left because of ill health in 1914, and five years later the bank incorporated for the first time. Capitalized at $12.5 million and with deposits of about $17 million, it changed its name to the Bank of Bishop & Company, Limited. It purchased Spreckel's Bank of Honolulu in 1920, and three years later it added a new branch in Kona on the west side of the island of Hawaii. Others followed as business demanded. In 1929 the bank became Bishop First National Bank of Honolulu owing to a five-way merger with First National Bank of Hawaii, First American Savings Bank, Army National Bank of Schofield Barracks and the Baldwin Bank, Limited. Thanks to the merger, the bank showed almost $31.5 million of deposits on its books at the end of 1930, up from $17 million a decade prior. Due to branching restrictions, it had to form an HC called Bishop Company, Limited.

The Great Depression did not strike Hawaii with as much force as it did the mainland because bumper crops and military spending made up for reduced prices. The bank's deposits dropped only a few percent before rebounding, and it survived the bank holiday on its 75th anniversary in 1933. Later that year, branching restrictions were lifted, and the bank changed its name to the Bishop National Bank of Hawaii at Honolulu in order to comply with the national bank naming standards then in force.

The territorial government declared martial law right after the Japanese attack on Pearl Harbor and other US military bases in Hawaii. It remained in effect for the next four years and allowed the government to limit the amount of cash any individual or business could have on hand to low levels for fear it would fall into Japanese hands in the event of a successful invasion. Adding to the turmoil, the Alien Property Custodian seized, shuttered and liquidated three of Hawaii's seven banks because they were owned by Japanese interests. In June 1942 the government issued currency stamped "Hawaii," rendering the notes worthless should the enemy seize them. After the initial shock of the Japanese attack wore off, the economy of Hawaii grew rapidly during the war fueled by high prices and unprecedented levels of military spending. Deposits at the bank jumped from $54.4 million at the end of 1940 to $276.3 million at the end of 1945, a figure not matched again until 1960.

Postwar Hawaii was littered with the detritus of war, but the conflict had made the people and economy less insular. Many servicemen and women who passed through the islands during the war wanted to return to enjoy the weather and beaches under less stressful circumstances, and many natives who left the islands to fight became interested in the broader world. In 1956 the bank changed its name again, to Bishop National Bank of Hawaii. Statehood came in 1959, as did regular commercial jet airliner service and a big jump in tourism. The following year, the bank again switched monikers, this time to First National Bank of Hawaii.

As the economy of Hawaii changed, becoming less dependent on agriculture, so too did the bank, which updated its back office technology in the 1950s in order to keep up with an increased number of transactions. The first computer arrived in 1963, and by 1968 the data processing department employed 120 people. In 1965 the state finally allowed banks to engage in the trust business, and soon after the bank snapped up Cooke Trust Company, Limited, which had been founded in 1935.

In 1969 the bank converted to a state charter and became First Hawaiian Bank with deposits of some $500 million. In 1974 it became the subsidiary of one-bank HC First Hawaiian, Inc. That change allowed the bank to buy the troubled Hawaii Thrift and Loan in 1975, which helped to boost its deposits over the $1 billion mark the following year. In 1978 Hawaii Thrift entered the consumer loan business in Japan, and by 1983 it had opened 20 offices there. Organic growth was also achieved by expanding the bank's branch network and enlarging some of its branches. By 1982 First Hawaiian's deposits exceeded $2 billion.

The other major piece of BancWest, Bank of the West, began operations in 1874 as the Farmers National Gold Bank. It changed its name to the First National Bank of San Jose in 1880. In the 1970s it changed its name to Bank of the West and established a holding company called BancWest. BNP bought a controlling stake in the institution in 1979 and made it the "platform for its US ambitions," as a journalist put it in 2001, because BancWest was "regarded as having one of the best managements in US banking."

In 1989 BancWest bought 46 branches from Central Banking System for $54 million. Four years later, it relieved Citicorp of 15 of its unwanted branches in northern California. In 1997 it bought Essex Credit Corp. of Connecticut, and the following year BancWest merged with First Hawaiian. At the time of the merger, the latter had assets of $8.15 billion and over 100 branches in Hawaii, Idaho, Oregon and Washington. The former had assets of $5.8 billion and 105 branches in northern and central California.

The merger diluted BNP Paribas's ownership stake in BancWest to 45%, but in 2001 it purchased the rest of the BHC's shares. Later that year, the bank bought United California Bank from the Japanese banking group UFJ for $2.4 billion. By 2007 BNP Paribas employed almost 142,000 people in some 2,200 offices in 85 countries. Its three core businesses were retail banking, asset management (including insurance) and investment banking.

BNP Paribas prided itself on being a "prudent" institution, so it suffered little in the 2008 financial crisis, reporting earnings in the first quarter of 2009 that were well above analyst expectations. The subsequent Eurozone crisis, especially the fear of a sovereign debt default by Greece, eventually put the bank, and France's other big banks, in a tizzy. "We can no longer borrow dollars. US money-market funds are not lending to us anymore," an executive at BNP Paribas told the *Wall Street Journal* in September 2011.

Eventual stabilization of the crisis put the bank back on track. As late as the third quarter of 2013, the *Wall Street Journal* reported that it was "soldiering on as others falter," with financial results that were "solid if unspectacular."

Sources

"Bank of the West Acquisition." *American Banker*, August 21, 1997, 2.

"Bank of the West to Buy Citi Branches." *American Banker*, April 23, 1993, 2.

"BNP Paribas Pays $2.4bn for UFJ's California Bank." *FT.com*, December 10, 2001.

Bussière, Eric. *Paribas, Europe and the World, 1872–1992.* Antwerp: Gonds Mercator, 1992.

De Quillacq, Leslie. "Paribas CEO Quits in Wake of BNP Hostile Bid's Success." *American Banker*, August 26, 1999, 18.

Hardy, Quentin. "First Hawaiian Agrees to Merge with BancWest." *Wall Street Journal*, May 29, 1998, A4.

Joesting, Edward. *Tides of Commerce.* Honolulu: First Hawaiian, Inc., 1983.

Kamm, Thomas. "Shakeout of French Banks Picks Up Steam: Société Générale to Acquire Paribas Retail-Bank Unit." *Wall Street Journal*, January 10, 1997, A8.

Lecaussin, Nicolas. "The Trouble With French Banks; A BNP Paribas Executive Makes His Concerns Known." *Wall Street Journal Online*, September 13, 2011.

Loosvelt, Derek, et al. *The Vault Guide to the Top 50 Banking Employers: 2008 Edition.* New York: Vault, 2007, 220–23.

Mandaro, Laura. "In Brief: BNP Paribas Buys Rest of BancWest." *American Banker*, December 21, 2001, 20.

Peaple, Andrew. "BNP Paribas's Interesting Lack of Drama; French Bank Delivers Solid if Unspectacular Earnings, Unlike Its European Peers." *Wall Street Journal Online*, October 31, 2013.

Sheldon, Annamarie. "Banque Nationale de Paris & Paribas." In *Cases in Corporate Acquisitions, Buyouts, Mergers, & Takeovers*, edited by Kelly Hill, 134–39. Boston: Gale Group, 1999.

Smith, Emmanuelle. "BNP Paribas at Forefront of Bank Gains." *FT.com*, May 6, 2009.

Zuckerman, Sam. "Bank of the West Buying Central's 46 Branches." *American Banker*, October 9, 1989, 2.

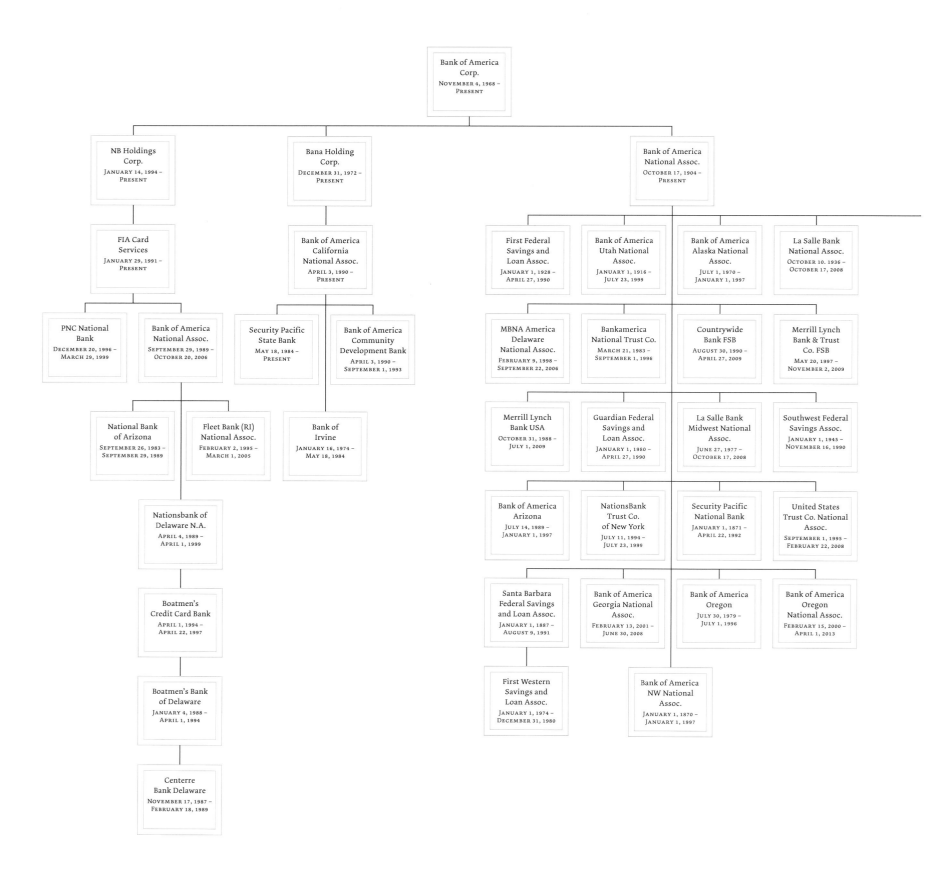

Bank of America Corp.
NOVEMBER 4, 1968 –
PRESENT

NB Holdings Corp.
JANUARY 14, 1994 –
PRESENT

Bana Holding Corp.
DECEMBER 31, 1972 –
PRESENT

Bank of America National Assoc.
OCTOBER 17, 1904 –
PRESENT

FIA Card Services
JANUARY 29, 1991 –
PRESENT

Bank of America California National Assoc.
APRIL 3, 1990 –
PRESENT

First Federal Savings and Loan Assoc.
JANUARY 1, 1928 –
APRIL 27, 1990

Bank of America Utah National Assoc.
JANUARY 1, 1916 –
JULY 23, 1999

Bank of America Alaska National Assoc.
JULY 1, 1970 –
JANUARY 1, 1997

La Salle Bank National Assoc.
OCTOBER 10. 1936 –
OCTOBER 17, 2008

PNC National Bank
DECEMBER 20, 1996 –
MARCH 29, 1999

Bank of America National Assoc.
SEPTEMBER 29, 1989 –
OCTOBER 20, 2006

Security Pacific State Bank
MAY 18, 1984 –
PRESENT

Bank of America Community Development Bank
APRIL 3, 1990 –
SEPTEMBER 1, 1993

MBNA America Delaware National Assoc.
FEBRUARY 9, 1998 –
SEPTEMBER 22, 2006

Bankamerica National Trust Co.
MARCH 21, 1983 –
SEPTEMBER 1, 1996

Countrywide Bank FSB
AUGUST 30, 1990 –
APRIL 27, 2009

Merrill Lynch Bank & Trust Co. FSB
MAY 20, 1997 –
NOVEMBER 2, 2009

National Bank of Arizona
SEPTEMBER 26, 1983 –
SEPTEMBER 29, 1989

Fleet Bank (RI) National Assoc.
FEBRUARY 2, 1995 –
MARCH 1, 2005

Bank of Irvine
JANUARY 16, 1974 –
MAY 18, 1984

Merrill Lynch Bank USA
OCTOBER 31, 1988 –
JULY 1, 2009

Guardian Federal Savings and Loan Assoc.
JANUARY 1, 1980 –
APRIL 27, 1990

La Salle Bank Midwest National Assoc.
JUNE 27, 1977 –
OCTOBER 17, 2008

Southwest Federal Savings Assoc.
JANUARY 1, 1945 –
NOVEMBER 16, 1990

Nationsbank of Delaware N.A.
APRIL 4, 1989 –
APRIL 1, 1999

Bank of America Arizona
JULY 14, 1989 –
JANUARY 1, 1997

NationsBank Trust Co. of New York
JULY 11, 1994 –
JULY 23, 1999

Security Pacific National Bank
JANUARY 1, 1871 –
APRIL 22, 1992

United States Trust Co. National Assoc.
SEPTEMBER 1, 1995 –
FEBRUARY 22, 2008

Boatmen's Credit Card Bank
APRIL 1, 1994 –
APRIL 22, 1997

Santa Barbara Federal Savings and Loan Assoc.
JANUARY 1, 1887 –
AUGUST 9, 1991

Bank of America Georgia National Assoc.
FEBRUARY 13, 2001 –
JUNE 30, 2008

Bank of America Oregon
JULY 30, 1979 –
JULY 1, 1996

Bank of America Oregon National Assoc.
FEBRUARY 15, 2000 –
APRIL 1, 2013

Boatmen's Bank of Delaware
JANUARY 4, 1988 –
APRIL 1, 1994

First Western Savings and Loan Assoc.
JANUARY 1, 1974 –
DECEMBER 31, 1980

Bank of America NW National Assoc.
JANUARY 1, 1870 –
JANUARY 1, 1997

Centerre Bank Delaware
NOVEMBER 17, 1987 –
FEBRUARY 18, 1989

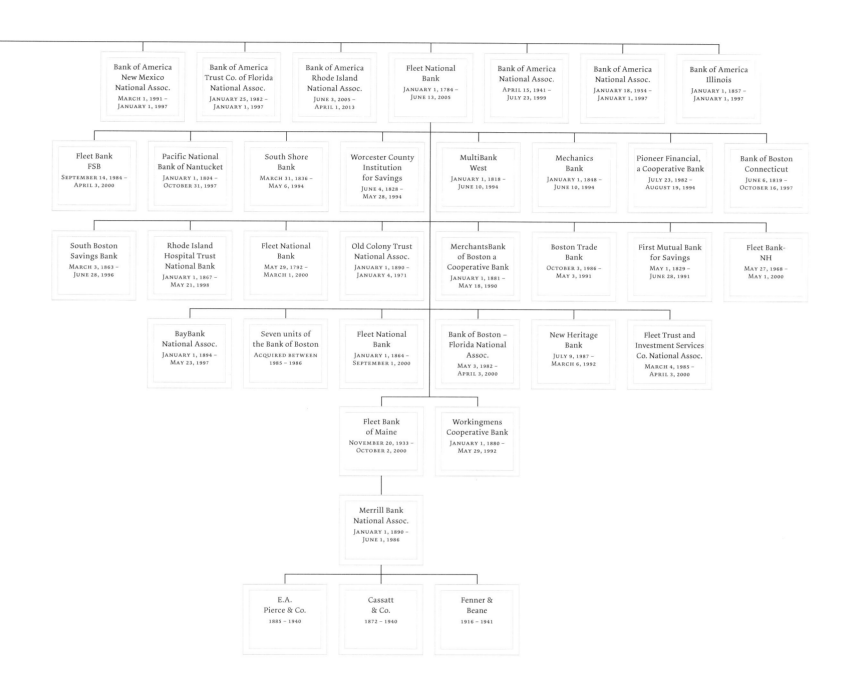

Bank of America

Bank *(abridged)*

Rank	Headquarters	Ticker	Assets	Earliest Known Ancestor	Industry of Origin
2	**Charlotte, NC**	**BAC**	**$2,100,000,000,000**	**1784**	**Commercial Banking**

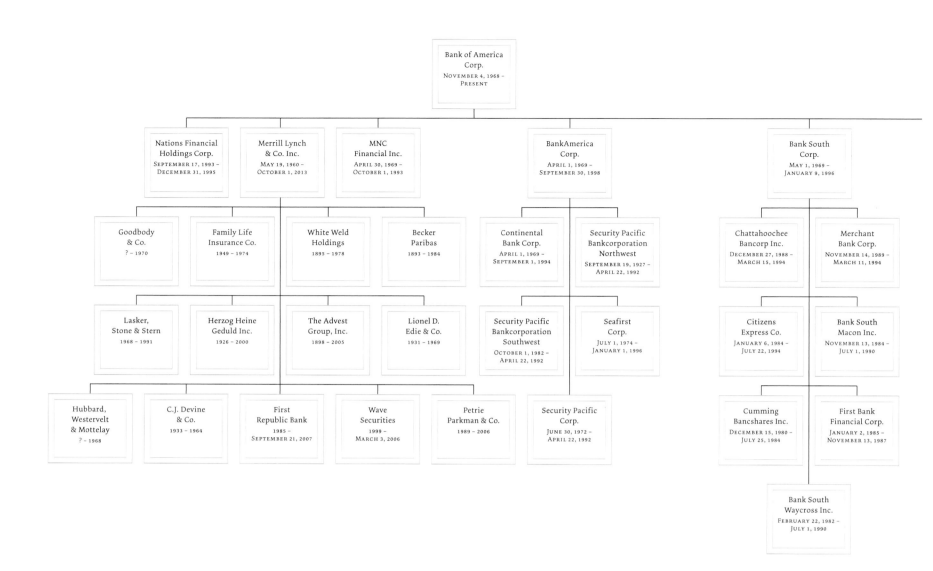

Bank of America Corp.
NOVEMBER 4, 1968 –
PRESENT

Nations Financial Holdings Corp.
SEPTEMBER 17, 1993 –
DECEMBER 31, 1995

Merrill Lynch & Co. Inc.
MAY 19, 1960 –
OCTOBER 1, 2013

MNC Financial Inc.
APRIL 30, 1969 –
OCTOBER 1, 1993

BankAmerica Corp.
APRIL 1, 1969 –
SEPTEMBER 30, 1998

Bank South Corp.
MAY 1, 1969 –
JANUARY 9, 1996

Goodbody & Co.
? – 1970

Family Life Insurance Co.
1949 – 1974

White Weld Holdings
1895 – 1978

Becker Paribas
1893 – 1984

Continental Bank Corp.
APRIL 1, 1969 –
SEPTEMBER 1, 1994

Security Pacific Bankcorporation Northwest
SEPTEMBER 19, 1927 –
APRIL 22, 1992

Chattahoochee Bancorp Inc.
DECEMBER 27, 1988 –
MARCH 15, 1994

Merchant Bank Corp.
NOVEMBER 14, 1989 –
MARCH 11, 1994

Lasker, Stone & Stern
1968 – 1991

Herzog Heine Geduld Inc.
1926 – 2000

The Advest Group, Inc.
1898 – 2005

Lionel D. Edie & Co.
1931 – 1969

Security Pacific Bankcorporation Southwest
OCTOBER 1, 1982 –
APRIL 22, 1992

Seafirst Corp.
JULY 1, 1974 –
JANUARY 1, 1996

Citizens Express Co.
JANUARY 6, 1984 –
JULY 22, 1994

Bank South Macon Inc.
NOVEMBER 13, 1984 –
JULY 1, 1990

Hubbard, Westervelt & Mottelay
? – 1968

C.J. Devine & Co.
1933 – 1964

First Republic Bank
1985 –
SEPTEMBER 21, 2007

Wave Securities
1999 –
MARCH 3, 2006

Petrie Parkman & Co.
1989 – 2006

Security Pacific Corp.
JUNE 30, 1972 –
APRIL 22, 1992

Cumming Bancshares Inc.
DECEMBER 15, 1980 –
JULY 25, 1984

First Bank Financial Corp.
JANUARY 2, 1985 –
NOVEMBER 13, 1987

Bank South Waycross Inc.
FEBRUARY 22, 1982 –
JULY 1, 1990

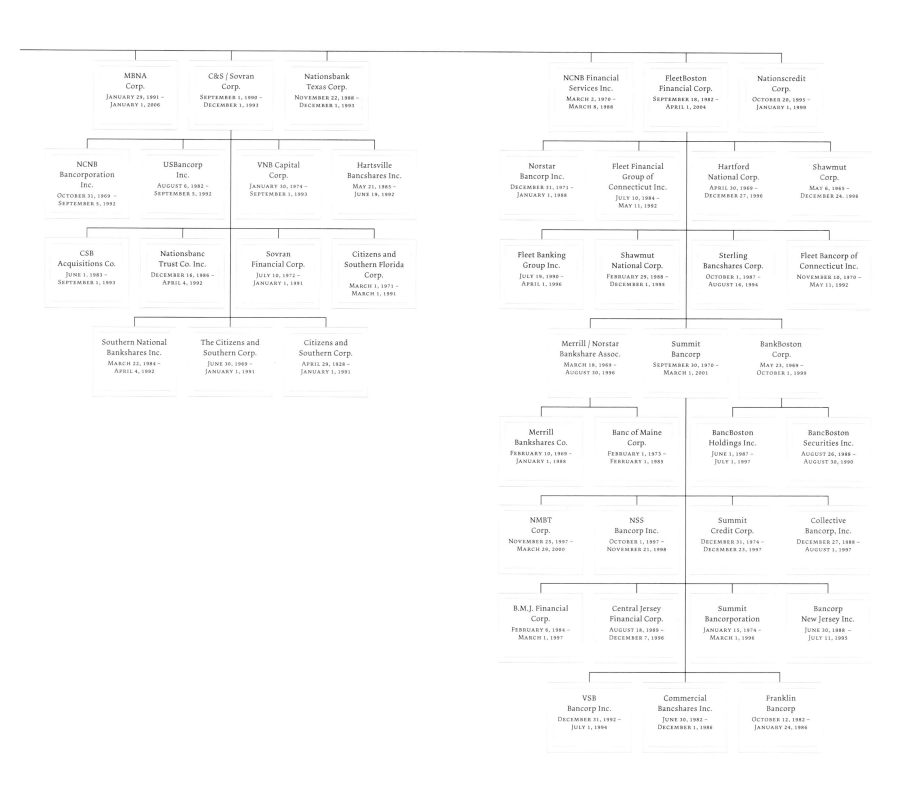

Bank of America

Holding Company *(abridged)*

Today's Bank of America (BoA) was formed when a North Carolina bank called NationsBank acquired the old Bank of America (B of A), a California bank, in 1998. NationsBank assumed the Bank of America name (and ticker symbol), presumably because it had more cachet. But the old Bank of America certainly has a more interesting history.

When the founder of the Bank of America, Amadeo P. Giannini, died in 1949, employees in all 520 or so of B of A's branches mourned while they continued to service customers. After all, Giannini's son, Mario, had been running the bank day-to-day since 1936, while Giannini's spirit still guided the rest of its top leadership. His daughter, Claire, took his spot on the board, so the bank continued the Giannini way, spotting trends before its competitors and capitalizing on them. "Aim to put yourself in a position to do something the other fellow can't do," Giannini had urged his colleagues.

Giannini's genius explains how the bank, founded in 1904 as the Bank of Italy and headquartered in San Francisco, survived the big earthquake of 1906 and subsequent banking panic. It also turned a tidy profit in the wake of those catastrophes by lending when no one else would, or could. Brilliant banking also saved the institution during the Great Depression, when wave after wave of bank failures nearly broke the nation.

It was early in those dark days that Giannini consolidated his holdings to create the nation's third largest bank, which he christened the Bank of America after an old but tiny Manhattan bank. He had acquired the bank, and lost it soon after, in a failed bid to create a truly nationwide bank through a holding company called Transamerica. Giannini almost lost control of Transamerica to Wall Streeters, but he regained his grip by winning a thrilling fight to control the votes of stockholders. Working through the prevailing prejudices and legal restrictions against interstate branching proved impossible, however. So Bank of America, which was a national trust and savings association, remained largely a California institution after the Federal Reserve forced its separation from Transamerica in 1957 after a 20-year battle.

Nevertheless, by 1945 the B of A was big enough for its name and was hailed the largest in the world. It had over $5 billion in assets, representing 60% of Californians' savings, and more than five million individual accountholders. It dominated the banking system of the world's seventh largest economy, America's 31st state, on the credo that "serving the needs of others is the only legitimate business in the world."

Due to its large size, the bank often led the industry in technological innovation and adoption, as when it automated check processing and introduced electronic recording machine accounting in the 1950s. Automation cut costs significantly and created economies of scale that the bank tapped by growing ever larger. The number of branches increased from 617 in 1957 to 871 in 1964. By 1967 it had more than 7.12 million accounts, compared to its California competitors with just 1.78 million at Crocker Citizens (now part of Wells Fargo) and 1.45 million at Wells Fargo (#4). The following year, the BankAmerica BHC was formed so the institution could acquire nonbanking subsidiaries.

The bank's founding Giannini spirit, however, could not last forever. Over time, Giannini's brother, both sons and key supporters like Russell G. Smith wavered before moving on or passing away, as Mario did in 1952. Only his daughter, Claire Hoffman, carried on, and hers was but one female voice on a male-dominated board. She became a nonvoting emeritus director in 1970 and resigned from that post in March 1985.

The bank had continued to grow and innovate, but in the process worried that it was losing touch with its customers. To become more efficient, it resorted to using numbers pumped into static formulas to decide who got loans and who didn't. This turned out to be a mistake, which the bank soon paid for, as its credit rating plummeted from triple-A to BAA-3 in just a few years.

In May 1987 Bank of America was in crisis after three years of staggering losses. It had successfully fought off a takeover bid by First Interstate of Los Angeles the previous year, but then Citibank (#3) wrote off $2.5 billion worth of distressed Brazilian government debt. The market looked to B of A, which was also exposed to Brazil, to do likewise, but it was short of capital and in no condition to take another big loss. Financiers scrambled, girding themselves for a global financial crisis, while rumors swirled that regulators were prepared to pounce. B of A stock, which had been at $32 just a few years before, sank below $8. The bank, however, was already on its way back to profitability.

Several years earlier, board member Charles Schwab (founder of #21) stepped in with a plan to turn around the bank's fortunes by stopping dividends, cutting employment, trimming expenses (like the corporate jet) and raising new capital. The gigantic institution could not turn as quickly as the entrepreneurial Schwab advised, but a compromise was struck and progress was made. Executives who had underperformed were allowed graceful exits and were replaced by seasoned veterans from Citibank, Wells Fargo and American Express (#19). Expenses were reduced, and all of the bank's bad loans greater than $1 million came under intense scrutiny.

The bank sold Charles Schwab, and Schwab resigned from the board. Former leader Tom Clausen returned to the bank's presidency, which restored some confidence and accelerated the badly needed reforms. By the end of 1988, the B of A had experienced what one analyst called the "greatest recovery ever witnessed in the US banking industry." Dividends were reinstated, and by the early 1990s the profits were pouring in so quickly that the bank could expend nearly $5 billion acquiring banks in Arizona, Hawaii, Nevada, Oregon, Washington and California, where it purchased Security Pacific for $4.5 billion in 1991. More than 10,000 people lost their jobs, but the deals again made B of A the largest bank in the nation, if only in terms of market capitalization and number of branches.

By the end of 1994 B of A was the nation's second largest BHC, with assets of $215 billion and 36 million customer accounts. It dominated much of the western United States, including Alaska and Hawaii, and via its acquisition of Continental Bank Corp. it had a foothold in Illinois. It also operated 61 branches and offices in 36 foreign countries.

About that time, the bank embarked on a broad-based effort to make itself a good corporate citizen. That included what one author described as "community reinvestment, philanthropy, environmental responsibility, affirmative action, accommodations for people with disabilities" and even emergency response capabilities in the communities it served. It supported the Americans with Disabilities Act of 1991, for example, and strove to not only comply with its letter, but also its spirit in its interactions with both customers and employees. A decade after its turnaround, however, the bank would exist only in name, swallowed up by NationsBank, which emerged from the relaxation of interstate branching restrictions in the Southeast.

NationsBank began operations in Charlotte, North Carolina, as Commercial National Bank in 1874. In 1958, in an attempt to keep pace with Wachovia (now part of #4), Commercial National merged with American Trust Company (née Southern States Trust Co., chartered 1901) to become American Commercial Bank. It changed its name to North Carolina National Bank (NCNB) two years later, after merging with Security National, which was also eager to compete with Wachovia.

Portrait of Amadeo P. Giannini, founder of the Bank of Italy, ca. 1910-1930.

Bank of America Victory bond ad, San Francisco, 1943.

Security National formed after the 1933 bank holiday permanently closed every bank in Greensboro, North Carolina. Jefferson Standard Life Insurance Company, local textile mills and their employees found making deposits 15 miles away and getting loans in New York City inconvenient, so they teamed up with the Reconstruction Finance Corporation to form a new bank, which they gave a safe-sounding name. Despite the arrival of competitors, Security dominated the Greensboro banking market, but it maintained conservative lending practices owing to the depressing circumstances of its birth.

NCNB's president, Addison Reese, wanted to create a statewide bank, and he set about it by purchasing a bank in Iredell County, just north of Charlotte, and First National Bank in Winston-Salem before the end of 1961. That brought the total number of offices to 40, spread nicely throughout the larger towns and cities in the center part of the state. Only Asheville in the west and Fayetteville in the east remained unconquered, but the bank entered the foothills the following year by purchasing the Bank of North Wilkesboro. Later in 1962, it also acquired the Bank of Wilmington, which had begun its corporate existence as the Bank of Cape Fear in 1804.

By the end of 1963 NCNB's assets reached nearly $654 million, and it was computerizing to keep up with the business generated by 58 branches spread over 11 counties. By 1967, after more mergers, NCNB was almost a billion-dollar bank and nipping at Wachovia's heels. But Addison made clear that the bank did not "want to be the biggest, just the best," so he initiated an executive training program to create more layers of talent throughout the organization. The program accepted just five trainees annually, but one year it made an exception for Hugh McColl and was later glad that it did. The ambitious, young ex-Marine put 60,000 miles on his Volkswagen in his first five years at the bank

working for the correspondent banking department. He would rise to become president several decades later.

In 1966 NCNB beat out Wachovia to become Bank of America's unofficial North Carolina franchisee for its new credit card network, the BankAmericard system (now Visa). About the same time, NCNB began to keep better records on loans, electronically, in a new computer system. That allowed it to track how much business loan officers did, as well as how their loans subsequently performed. In 1968 the bank established NCNB Corp. and reorganized under it as a one-bank holding company.

The move allowed the bank to own nonbank subsidiaries, such as finance companies, mortgage lenders and insurance agencies, which it promptly did. It also began to sell commercial paper when deposits proved inadequate to fund all the loans it thought proper to make. By the mid-1970s only about a quarter of the bank's portfolio was covered by deposits; the rest came from the money market. Thanks to such aggressive moves, NCNB had surpassed Wachovia to become North Carolina's largest bank by the time Reese retired at the end of 1973. The lead, however, went back and forth over the next several years.

By then McColl was one of a hungry cadre of young executives eager to expand on Reese's impressive legacy. Acquisitions continued but became increasingly difficult, as Wachovia and First Union (now part of #4) competed for the dwindling supply of smaller banks available for purchase. The 1970s brought other problems as well, including stagflation, high nominal interest rates and the first significant bank failures since the Great Depression.

NCNB suffered when a credit crunch dried up the market for its commercial paper. As soon as analysts realized what happened, its stock price dropped from a high of $39.75 to just over $23. Two overseas offices established in 1971 and 1972 in Nassau and London saved the day by raising $40 million on Independence Day 1974. But its credit evaporated again a week later when the Israel-British Bank of London failed, defaulting on the $3 million it owed NCNB. In desperation, the bank turned to the institutions where it had open lines of credit. One of those banks, Bank of America, doubled its credit limit from $10 to $20 million. With additional help from Chemical Bank (now part of #1) and Citicorp (#3), NCNB survived the crisis and got back to basics, like making good loans and not betting the bank on interest rate fluctuations.

Healed by time, the bank was ready to begin expanding again. Having exhausted its opportunities in North Carolina, in 1979 it pushed the state government to permit regional branching. At first stymied by entrenched interests and the disinterest of Wachovia and First Union, the idea slowly gained traction, especially as the attraction of markets like rapidly growing but underbanked Florida waxed stronger.

Instead of waiting for regulatory reform, however, the bank found a legal loophole that allowed it to purchase the tiny but troubled First National Bank of Lake City, about an hour west of Jacksonville. In 1982, while making its last major acquisition in North Carolina, the Bank of North Carolina, NCNB expanded its beachhead in Florida while jealous competitors pushed for a regional branching compact, which was finally put into place in 1984 and upheld the following year by the US Supreme Court.

McColl became the bank's president and CEO in September 1983, and more acquisitions soon followed. By the time the Florida market opened to most of its rivals, NCNB had already doubled in size and built a huge, lighthouse-like building in Tampa. "Everywhere my airplane lands," McColl boasted, "bank stocks go up" in anticipation of a buyout.

After the Supreme Court upheld the regional interstate branching compact, the bank moved aggressively into Georgia and South Carolina. It lost First Atlanta to Wachovia, but in July 1985 it signed with a smaller Atlanta bank called Southern National Bank, as well as with the $4 billion Bankers Trust of South Carolina. Those deals put NCNB over the $20 billion asset mark, made it the first BHC with banks in three southeastern states and put it decisively ahead of Wachovia. By 1987 NCNB had infiltrated six fast-growing southern states and was the largest bank in the Southeast, with First Union close behind.

The following year, with help from a favorable IRS tax ruling, the bank invaded Texas by taking over the failed First Republic. The FDIC favored its bid over those of Citicorp and Wells Fargo because strength of management, and not size, was the determining factor. NCNB executives "were really ready to move and had their game plan in order," FDIC director C.C. Hope explained. After the First Republic acquisition, the bank continued to take over failed Texas thrifts.

On the first day of 1992, after another long chain of mergers including C&S/Sovran (which was the troubled spawn of a 1989 merger between Citizens and Southern Corporation of Atlanta and Sovran Financial Corporation of Norfolk, Virginia), NCNB changed its name to NationsBank. After the C&S merger, McColl, by then chairman, immediately cut 6,000 workers and numerous redundant branches. Even after the cuts, NationsBank was still America's third largest bank, with assets of $119 billion, 59,000 workers and some 2,000 branches.

More acquisitions followed, and by the end of 1994 NationsBank remained the nation's third largest BHC, with assets of about $170 billion. At that time, it operated 1,929 branches in nine states and Washington, DC, as well as 288 consumer finance offices in 34 states. The largest BHC in the Southeast, NationsBank was also one of the country's 10 largest credit card issuers. By the end of 1995, its

ATM network was, at 2,900, the second largest in the nation, behind only Bank of America and its 5,600 ATMs.

But McColl wanted more. He pushed so hard for the Riegle-Neal branching law, passed in 1994, that some claimed it should have been called the "Hugh McColl Act." He used the new legislation to make the bank the "dominant financial institution from Baltimore to Miami" and then the "preeminent financial institution" in the nation. The bank acquired Barnett Bank and others before taking out its longtime ally, Bank of America, in 1998. For a few years, McColl ran the new BoA, helping it to become "America's bank" before he bowed out in 2001, after receiving a "Banker of the Year Award" from *American Banker*.

In 2004, under the leadership of Ken Lewis, BoA became the second largest bank in the world when it purchased FleetBoston, which traced its origins to the Bank of Boston (chartered 1784), for $47 billion. BoA bought credit card giant MBNA in January 2006 for $34 billion. The following year, it purchased US Trust from Charles Schwab (#21). By 2008 Bank of America employed more than 200,000 people and operated almost 5,700 branches in 30 states and Washington, DC, as well as another 300 or so offices internationally. It also had more than 54 million debit and credit cardholders, making it the nation's largest issuer of plastic. The bank held 9.7% of all domestic deposits, which was such a large amount that it began to encourage some depositors to leave so that it could make additional acquisitions. (Regulations prohibited any bank from holding more than 10% of total domestic deposits as the result of a merger.)

By temperament, BoA was still a domestic bank, with some Giannini still in its culture. Its investment banking arm, Banc of America Securities, was considered "solid, but not as prestigious" as Goldman (#5) and Morgan (#6). In January 2008 it purchased Countrywide, an originator that had once dominated the subprime mortgage market, for $4 billion on the heels of the $21 billion purchase of LaSalle Bank of Chicago. (The Countrywide purchase would prove to be a disaster during the 2008 financial crisis as the housing bubble burst. Its CEO, Angelo Mozilo, agreed to pay $67.5 million in fines and accepted a lifetime ban from serving as an officer or director of any public company.)

After every major merger, Bank of America quickly cut thousands, and in some cases tens of thousands, of jobs. Although considered by some to be one of the best companies to work for because of its liberal compensation packages (which included cash bonuses for employees who made less than $100,000 per year), many senior-level employees said they felt they were paid well below market averages.

After appearing to be in good shape at first, the bank suffered severely as the financial crisis deepened. Under pressure from the government, it purchased giant Merrill Lynch, a storied investment firm that was teetering on failure because of massive mortgage exposure. The Merrill story began in 1914 with founder Charles Merrill (1885–1956), who was soon after joined in partnership by Edmund C. Lynch (1885–1938). The company excelled at first, both in underwriting new securities issues and providing retail brokerage services, but it slumbered through the Great Depression while Merrill made millions as a grocery chain store magnate.

In 1940, however, Merrill returned to Wall Street to revivify his creation, which grew rapidly in the postwar decades as increasing numbers of Americans sought to sock away money in stocks. "The interests of our customers must come first," Merrill stressed, so he put his brokers on salary instead of commission to discourage them from needlessly churning customer accounts. He also invested heavily in broker training. Those and other innovations allowed the company

Bank of America building in San Francisco, 1943.

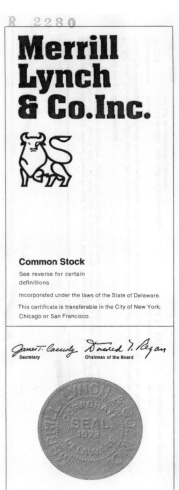

Merrill Lynch & Co. Inc. specimen stock certificate.

to grow its retail business. Its underwriting business also picked up speed, as the company soared from 42nd in the league tables in 1942 to seventh a decade later.

Merrill Lynch grew to mythic proportions in the second half of the 20th century, and its large and inimitable sales force became known as "The Herd." But after it went public, switching from a partnership to a joint-stock corporation, it began to take on increasing amounts of risk, particularly under the leadership of E. Stanley O'Neal, who became CEO in 2002. When "The Herd" began to falter in late 2007, Goldman Sachs and New York Stock Exchange alum John Thain took over the helm at Merrill.

Soon after acquiring Merrill Lynch, which was laden with toxic mortgage derivatives, BoA decided it had paid too much for it, so Lewis approached the government for aid. After threats and counter-threats, its request was eventually granted. All told, BoA received $45 billion of taxpayer money, some $30 billion of which covered Merrill Lynch's losses, including $3 billion for its 2008 bonuses. BoA dividends were cut to a penny per share, and the bank's share price sank below $5, from $50 as recently as 2007.

In January 2009 Lewis replaced Thain with Brian Moynihan, a holdover from Fleet. Lewis, who had been named "Banker of the Year" in 2001 and 2008 by *American Banker*, was ousted from the chairmanship in April 2009. That September he resigned as CEO, and the newly reconfigured board replaced him with Moynihan. Meanwhile, Merrill Lynch turned in big trading profits that kept the bank afloat during the post panic recession.

For years after the panic, the bank shed jobs, branches and assets in an attempt, led by Moynihan, to return itself to profitability by becoming leaner and more efficient. Fallout from the crisis continued, however, and as recently as the fourth quarter of 2013, it was still suffering from problems related to the subprime mortgage crisis, particularly Countrywide mortgage securitizations.

Sources

Bair, Sheila. *Bull by the Horns: Fighting to Save Main Street from Wall Street and Wall Street from Itself.* New York: Free Press, 2012, 114, 126–28.

Covington, Howard E., Jr. and Marion A. Ellis. *The Story of NationsBank: Changing the Face of American Banking.* Chapel Hill: University of North Carolina Press, 1993.

Douglas, Danielle. "Bank of America Says U.S. May File Civil Lawsuit." *Washington Post.* October 31, 2013, A14.

Farrell, Greg. *Crash of the Titans: Greed, Hubris, the Fall of Merrill Lynch, and the Near Collapse of Bank of America.* New York: Crown Business, 2010.

Fitzpatrick, Dan. "Bank of America Ramps Up Job Cuts." *Wall Street Journal.* September 20, 2012, A1.

Johnson, Moira. *Roller Coaster: The Bank of America and the Future of American Banking.* New York: Ticknor & Fields, 1990.

Loosvelt, Derek, et al. *The Vault Guide to the Top 50 Banking Employers: 2008 Edition.* New York: Vault, 2007, 126–31.

McKenney, James, Duncan Copeland and Richard Mason. *Waves of Change: Business Evolution Through Information Technology.* Boston: Harvard Business School Press, 1995, 41–95.

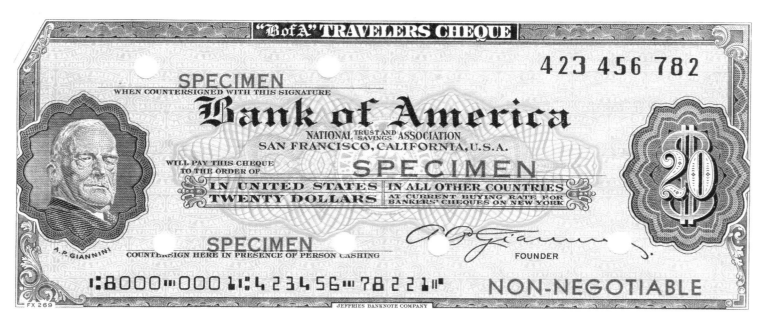

Bank of America specimen traveler's check for $20. The portrait on the left features founder Amadeo P. Giannini.

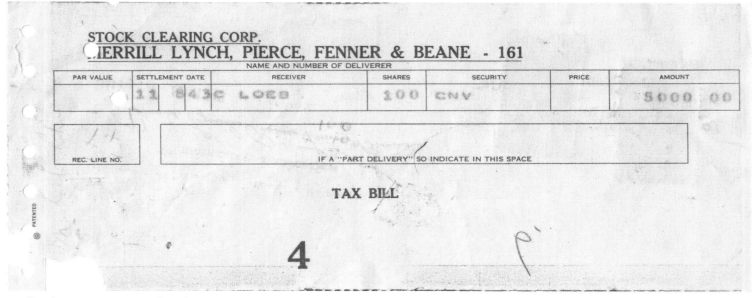

Merrill Lynch, Pierce, Fenner & Beane stock transfer receipt, 1943.

McLean, Bethany and Joe Nocera. *All The Devils Are Here: The Hidden History of the Financial Crisis*. New York: Penguin, 2010, 163–67.

Perkins, Edwin J. *Wall Street to Main Street: Charles Merrill and Middle-Class Investors*. New York: Cambridge University Press, 1999.

Smith, Roy. *Comeback: The Restoration of American Banking Power in the New World Economy*. Boston: Harvard Business School Press, 1993, 63–65.

Spechler, Jay W. *Reasonable Accommodation: Profitable Compliance with the Americans with Disabilities Act*. Delray Beach, FL: St. Lucie Press, 1996, 27–44.

Spiegel, John, Alan Gart, and Steven Gart. *Banking Redefined: How Superregional Powerhouses Are Reshaping Financial Services*. Chicago: Irwin Professional Publishing, 1996, 199–222, 401–19.

Wetfeet. *25 Top Financial Services Firms*. San Francisco: Wetfeet. 2008, 15–17.

Yockey, Ross. *McColl: The Man with America's Money*. Atlanta: Longstreet, 1999.
    Merrill Lynch & Co. Inc. specimen stock certificate.

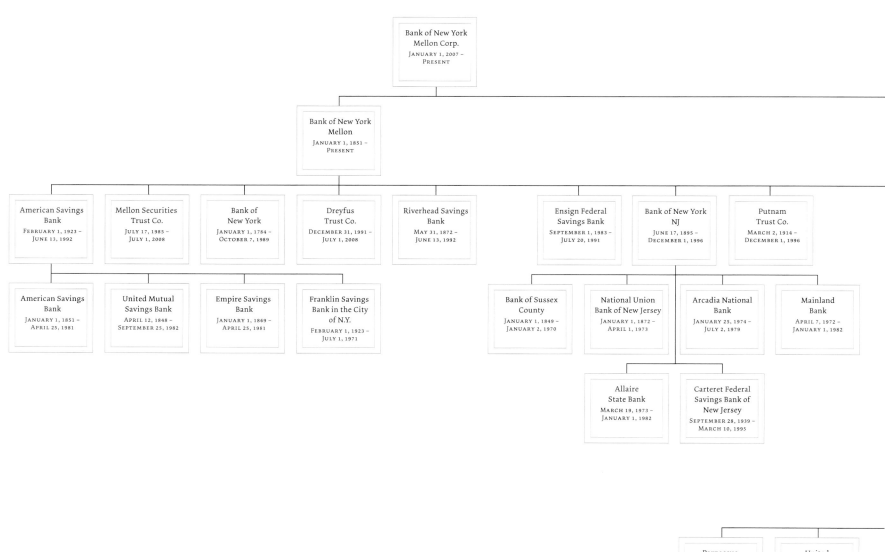

Bank of New York Mellon Corp.
JANUARY 1, 2007 – PRESENT

Bank of New York Mellon
JANUARY 1, 1851 – PRESENT

American Savings Bank
FEBRUARY 1, 1923 – JUNE 13, 1992

Mellon Securities Trust Co.
JULY 17, 1985 – JULY 1, 2008

Bank of New York
JANUARY 1, 1784 – OCTOBER 7, 1989

Dreyfus Trust Co.
DECEMBER 31, 1991 – JULY 1, 2008

Riverhead Savings Bank
MAY 31, 1872 – JUNE 13, 1992

Ensign Federal Savings Bank
SEPTEMBER 1, 1983 – JULY 20, 1991

Bank of New York NJ
JUNE 17, 1895 – DECEMBER 1, 1996

Putnam Trust Co.
MARCH 2, 1914 – DECEMBER 1, 1996

American Savings Bank
JANUARY 1, 1851 – APRIL 25, 1981

United Mutual Savings Bank
APRIL 12, 1848 – SEPTEMBER 25, 1982

Empire Savings Bank
JANUARY 1, 1869 – APRIL 25, 1981

Franklin Savings Bank in the City of N.Y.
FEBRUARY 1, 1923 – JULY 1, 1971

Bank of Sussex County
JANUARY 1, 1849 – JANUARY 2, 1970

National Union Bank of New Jersey
JANUARY 1, 1872 – APRIL 1, 1973

Arcadia National Bank
JANUARY 25, 1974 – JULY 2, 1979

Mainland Bank
APRIL 7, 1972 – JANUARY 1, 1982

Allaire State Bank
MARCH 19, 1973 – JANUARY 1, 1982

Carteret Federal Savings Bank of New Jersey
SEPTEMBER 28, 1939 – MARCH 10, 1995

Parnassus National Bank
JANUARY 1, 1934 – AUGUST 26, 1951

United Penn Bank
FEBRUARY 13, 1868 – DECEMBER 31, 1991

Citizens Bank of Tunkhannock
OCTOBER 15, 1902 – DECEMBER 7, 1970

First National Bank of Meshoppen
JUNE 15, 1900 – DECEMBER 30, 1972

Berwick Bank
JANUARY 1, 1903 – APRIL 1, 1973

Miners Bank and Trust Co. of West Hazleton, Pa.
MAY 13, 1913 – OCTOBER 4, 1974

Security Bank and Trust Co.
AUGUST 2, 1909 – JUNE 1, 1985

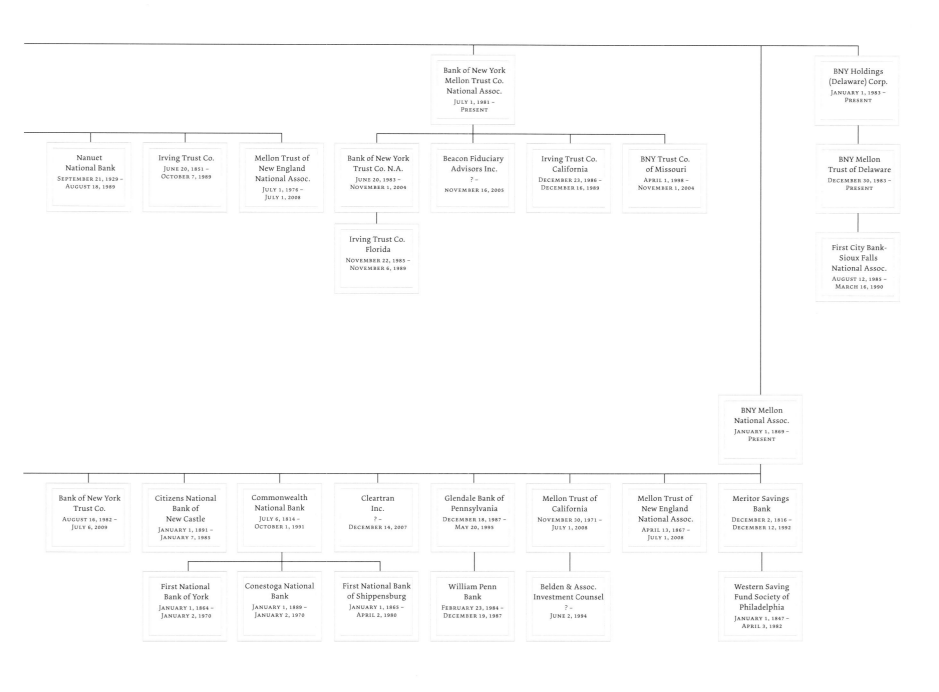

Bank of New York Mellon

Bank *(abridged)*

RANK	HEADQUARTERS	TICKER	ASSETS	EARLIEST KNOWN ANCESTOR	INDUSTRY OF ORIGIN
9	**New York, NY**	**BK**	**$360,000,000,000**	**1784**	**Commercial Banking**

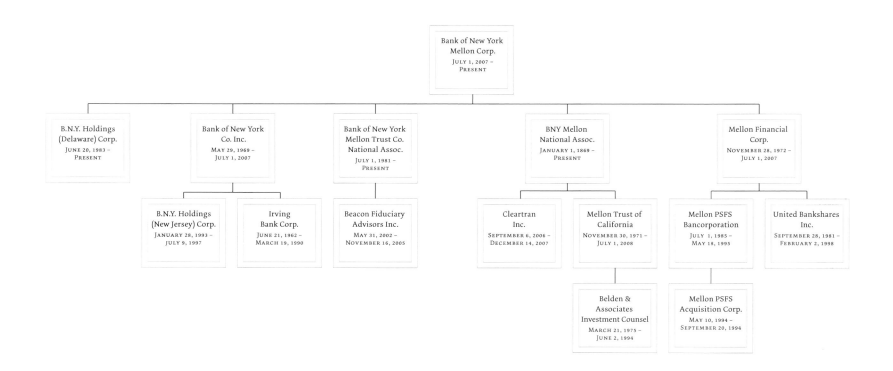

Bank of New York Mellon

Holding Company *(abridged)*

Portrait of Alexander Hamilton, published by The Knapp Co., ca. 1896.

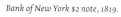

Bank of New York $2 note, 1819.

Not many banks can claim they were founded by Alexander Hamilton, America's first Treasury Secretary, but The Bank of New York Mellon (BONY) is one of them. In 1784 the great financial statesman drafted the bank's original articles of association and skillfully guided William Seton, its cashier, through the nation's first financial panic in 1792. After finally receiving a charter from the state in 1791, BONY, which was originally capitalized at $900,000, thrived by discounting the commercial paper of Manhattan merchants and other businesses.

While banks broke all around it in the 1810s through the 1930s, the BONY stood not only firm but tall, bolstered by its conservative image and quality banking practices. After a succession of presidents of short tenure, the bank found stability in Matthew Clarkson. Clarkson's reign began in 1804, soon after the Louisiana Purchase, and ended in 1825, after the economy settled down from the shocks incurred during the War of 1812 and the Panic of 1819. He was succeeded by Charles Wilkes, who had also provided stability by serving as cashier from 1794 until assuming the presidency, which he held until 1832. In 1830 Wilkes and three BONY directors helped to form the New York Life Insurance and Trust Company (NYLITC). President John Oothout led the BONY from 1843, just as the economy was emerging from the recession induced by the Panic of 1837, to 1858, just as it recovered from the Panic of 1857.

At the end of the Civil War, BONY took up a national charter and became the National Bank of New York. After the war, it grew along with New York's often buoyant economy, regularly declaring semi-annual dividends of 5%. When its centennial rolled around, it noted that it had missed only one dividend payment, in 1837, because it had been legally compelled to do so. Even this one missed payment was addressed the following year, when a special two-times payment was made. Assets hit $23.3 million in June 1878 and $28.2 million at the beginning of 1894.

Early in the 20th century BONY continued its tradition of safe growth, aided, as its historian Allan Nevins pointed out, by the "marked economy of its management and the staunch loyalty of its employees. Expenses were kept at a very moderate level; there were no swollen salaries, no large disbursements for advertising." During the Great War, BONY bought $37.7 million of Liberty and Victory bonds at issuance. It also bought over $46 million of shorter-term Treasury debt

for itself and its customers, paid dividends that totaled 26% annually and added largely to its surplus.

The BONY was well respected on Wall Street for its banking prowess, but it was relatively small and generally unknown by consumers, so its board looked for merger opportunities. It finally found a suitable one in 1922, with NYLITC, the institution it had helped establish 92 years earlier. Once called by a prominent European banker "the Gibraltar of American trust companies," NYLITC had been run conservatively but brilliantly by just two men, David Thompson and Henry Parish, in the 70 years from 1846 until 1916.

As part of the merger with NYLITC, the BONY again took a state charter, upped its capitalization to $4 million and styled itself the Bank of New York and Trust Company. Headed by NYLITC's former president, Edwin G. Merrill, from the merger until 1931, the new BONY had assets of over $100 million, some of which it invested in a new building at the corner of William and Wall Streets in Lower Manhattan. (The structure survives to this day, and the bottom floors and the stunning former main banking hall, replete with eight murals depicting Manhattan's economic history, have been the home of the Museum of American Finance since January 2008.)

Led by John C. Traphagen from 1931 until 1948, BONY survived the Great Depression with as much ease as it had weathered so many earlier financial storms. Deposits poured into the bank, as they did other banks with reputations for liquidity and probity, as panicked depositors fled sinking banks for the BONY's safe harbor. The bank prepared to aid its foundering comrades until the government interceded instead with its Reconstruction Finance Corporation. It also weathered the war years with ease. In 1948 the bank, which had dropped "and Trust Company" from its name in 1938, merged again, this time with Fifth Avenue Bank, another relatively small but conservatively managed institution that did a large trust business. The move gave BONY two strategically located midtown branches and another $2 million of capital. It dropped "and Fifth Avenue Bank" from its name in 1952. A decade later, the bank employed more than 1,300 people.

In the 1960s BONY engaged in several mergers and acquisitions with other New York City banks, including Empire Trust in 1966. In 1968 the bank, the assets of which had recently exceeded $1 billion, formed a holding company in preparation for a buying spree that included

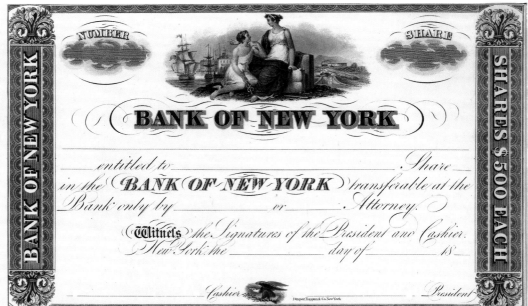

Bank of New York specimen stock certificate.

several upstate banks from White Plains to Buffalo. The biggest prize was County Trust Company of White Plains, which had assets of almost $845 million and extensive expertise in retail banking. By the end of 1969 BONY had 81 branches in 50 communities statewide, except Long Island, the lucrative market of which it did not penetrate until its purchase of Valley National in 1971. More acquisitions followed, and all were merged into the BONY in 1976, following relaxation of New York's restrictive branching laws. The bank remained state chartered, but it was a member of the Federal Reserve and the FDIC.

In 1980 BONY became a $10 billion bank by acquiring the Empire National Bank of Newburgh, which had assets of $500 million and 38 branches near the Hudson River between Manhattan and Albany. That same year it also formed a reinsurance subsidiary and a leasing company, and it acquired two mortgage banks. The following year it formed the Bank of New York Trust Company. In 1982 J. Carter Bacot became chairman, and under his leadership the bank underwent dramatic changes, including the sale of its upstate branches. Bacot's BONY also made larger loans and came to loan decisions more quickly by focusing on the utilities, oil and gas, securities and commercial industries. BONY, which boasted assets of $12 billion by its bicentennial, also began to specialize in processing securities brokers' daily transactions.

The biggest change came in 1987, when the bank acquired North American Bancorp and Bacot started a year-long war that ended with the hostile takeover of Irving Trust, the first hostile takeover of a bank allowed by regulators. When the dust settled in 1988, BONY was the nation's 14th largest BHC. Despite selling off several Irving Trust subsidiaries upstate, it had assets of $39 billion in December 1991 because at the same time it made acquisitions, including Bankers Trust's (now part of #34) factoring business.

In 1992 BONY purchased six branches from American Savings Bank, three branches from Riverhead Savings and 62 branches of Barclays Bank of New York, including $1.8 billion of its assets. It merged with National Community Bank of Rutherford, New Jersey, and acquired two more factoring businesses, those of the Bank of Boston and the Canadian Financial Corporation, the following year. In 1994 and 1995 the bank continued buying. Aside from Putnam Trust in Connecticut, most of the acquisitions involved parts of other banks' businesses rather than entire institutions. Such purchases were easier to swallow

than full acquisitions and kept the bank focused, well-capitalized and lean, with an overhead/efficiency ratio below 50%.

By the early 1990s Bacot and President Thomas A. Renyi were considered by SunTrust CFO John Spiegel to be "one of the finest" management teams in the industry. Spiegel also lauded the bank's culture for being "customer-driven, highly productive [and] shareholder-conscious." Much of its business was wholesale, i.e., between the bank and other major financial institutions, but BONY also had a significant retail presence — 385 branches, or more than all its competitors except Chemical Bank (now part of #1) — throughout downstate New York and the northern half of New Jersey.

After the Irving Trust merger, BONY continued to grow. In 1994 it boasted assets of almost $49 billion, but it slipped to the 16th spot in the BHC rankings, in part because its foreign operations, which included 25 branches from Brazil to China to Turkey to the UK, dropped from 37% of total revenues in 1991 to just 8.1% in 1994. Almost 40% of its income that year was fee-based, and another 22% came from its six million credit cardholders.

The bank's credit card business was highly profitable because BONY was able to obtain funds at a lower cost than its competitors. That enabled it to offer cardholders low rates and to hand pick the best of them, which led to one of the lowest default rates in the industry. Low interest costs also allowed the bank to spend more on marketing, including sending offers to 90 million customers in 1994 alone. Thanks to its low interest, its response rate was four times the industry average.

By the end of 2006 BONY had 22,900 employees working in 1,600 offices in 33 countries worldwide. *Fortune* ranked it one of America's "Most Admired" companies that year, and many found the institution "friendly and relaxed," especially for employees who stuck it out for two or more years. The bank's conservative nature and disinclination to take on big risks also meant that it survived the 2008 financial crisis relatively unscathed.

It helped that in 2007 BONY merged with Mellon Financial Corporation, another conservatively managed diversified financial services company with a bank (albeit based in Pittsburgh rather than New York) at its core. Called the "JP Morgan of the Alleghenies," Mellon, like BONY, usually generated over half of its revenues from fees, engaged

Union Trust Company of Pittsburgh, 1923.

Girard Trust Company Building in Philadephia, 1918.

extensively in wholesale banking and generally enjoyed a low loss ratio on its loans. Traditionally, it was also well-capitalized and conservatively run, all the way back to its founding by Irish immigrant Thomas Mellon in 1869.

The company, called T. Mellon & Sons', grew organically along with Pittsburgh by bankrolling Henry Clay Frick and other budding industrialists and steering clear of the banking panics of 1873 and 1893 by maintaining the liquidity of most assets. In 1882 Thomas turned ownership of the bank over to his son, Andrew, then only 26 years old. Almost immediately, Andrew purchased the Union Insurance Company, and four years later he helped organize Fidelity Title and Trust. Andrew made his brother, Richard, a full partner in 1887, when Richard returned after running a bank in Bismarck, Dakota Territory (now the capital of North Dakota), for some time. Working closely together, the brothers made important loans to companies, including Alcoa, Carborundum and Gulf Oil, that would later become giants. Energy, engines, plate glass, railways and steel constituted its milieu.

In 1889 Fidelity's leaders, including Andrew, founded a second trust company, which was known as Union Trust Company of Pittsburgh (after an 1892 name change). After a slow start as an appendage to Fidelity, Union Trust also grew into an important Pittsburgh financial institution, even after Andrew resigned the presidency in 1894. In 1902 it acquired Citizens National Bank, which had been chartered in 1853, and established the Union Savings Bank, which offered innovative "banking by mail" services. In 1918 it bought the City Deposit Bank and Trust Company, which had been chartered in 1866. It bought the Farmers Deposit National Bank the next year.

In addition to deposit banking and trust services, Union also engaged in investment banking activities. With growth came profitability: Union Trust's stock value rose from $60 in 1909 to a whopping $21,500 in 1929. Even during the Depression it paid dividends of 200%, and its assets continued to grow, almost topping $366 million by the end of the third quarter of 1939, because it was one of the few banks that depositors knew was safe.

Meanwhile, the Mellon boys rechartered their bank as Mellon National Bank in 1902. With a paid-in capital of $2 million and assets of $24 million, it quickly established a reputation for growth through acquisition by buying the Pittsburgh National Bank of Commerce,

which had been organized in 1864. In 1905 it entered the travelers check business, which in addition to generating profits spread its brand across the globe. Perhaps seeking to emulate American Express (#19), it also dabbled with a travel agency in the 1910s.

When, in 1921, Andrew began his 11-year tenure as Treasury Secretary under Presidents Coolidge, Harding and Hoover, Richard took over control of the bank and did an admirable job of it. Capital hit $7.5 million in 1922, and two years later assets topped $136.5 million, just as the bank moved into a much-needed new office.

In 1929 Richard established a sort of early BHC called the Mellbank Corporation to consolidate and manage his stockholdings in about 20 Pittsburgh-area banks. With Mellon support, they all survived the Depression, during which Mellon National Bank grew in size and reputation as deposits poured into it because it was the safest thing going. Soon after Richard's death in December 1933, control of Mellon fell to his son, Richard King Mellon (R.K.), who had started at the bank as a messenger in 1919. In 1935, as a result of Glass-Steagall's restrictions, R.K. formed Mellon Securities Corporation to engage in investment banking activities like underwriting and distributing equities and bonds. Andrew later served as director of Mellon Securities, which in 1946 merged with First Boston.

In 1944 Mellon Bank owned assets valued at a then whopping $617 million, but two years later R.K. merged it with Union Trust anyway, forming Mellon National Bank and Trust Company in the process. The combined institution boasted assets of over $1.1 billion and soon controlled one-third of all trust assets in Pennsylvania. Shortly after, Mellon officially acquired some two dozen smaller banks in the Pittsburgh area, most associated with Mellbank, as Pennsylvania slowly revoked its branching restrictions. In 1950 Farmers Deposit National Bank (née Pittsburgh Saving Fund Company, chartered in 1832), which had long been in the Mellons' orbit, was also officially acquired, lifting the bank's assets to over $1.7 billion. Two years later, Mellon began building a branch network. By 1969 it operated almost 100 branches, almost half of which were de novo, in six western Pennsylvania counties.

R.K. moved from the presidency to chairman of the board in 1946 and held the latter post until 1967. Due to his considerate, gentle manner, his underlings always said they worked "with" him, rather than

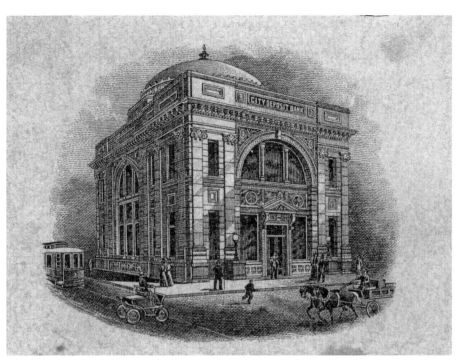

The City Deposit Bank of Pittsburgh.

"for" him. By 1969 Mellon National Bank and Trust had assets exceeding $4.5 billion. It ranked as the ninth most highly capitalized bank in the nation and had the fifth largest trust business by assets. In 1972 the bank chartered a BHC in Pennsylvania and continued its entrance into the mortgage and consumer finance businesses through acquisition. It also formed a life insurance subsidiary and expanded tentatively overseas. In the early 1980s, after Pennsylvania further relaxed its branching restrictions, Mellon acquired numerous banks throughout the state, including Girard, the second largest bank in Philadelphia. It also purchased another Philadelphia landmark institution, the Philadelphia Savings Fund Society (PSFS), which was established in 1816 and was once the largest savings bank in the nation.

Mellon stumbled in 1987, when it recorded the first loss in its history as a result of charge-offs on loans to, and in, less-developed countries, as well as to Texas oil companies and on Philadelphia real estate. The bank responded by replacing its chairman, shuttering 20 foreign branches and hiring Frank Cahouet, the man who turned around Crocker Bank before its sale to Wells Fargo (#4).

Cahouet cut 10% of the staff, froze the salaries of the rest and established a "bad bank" to hold Mellon's nonperforming assets. He then went out and purchased the investment companies Boston Company and Dreyfus and continued to upgrade the Bank's IT in a successful effort to drive down its efficiency ratio from 67% in 1993 to 63% by the first half of 1995. By 1996 bank consultant Steven Gart noted that "a merger of equals with Bank of New York . . . cannot be ruled out." He was right, although it took over a decade for that marriage to occur.

The combined BNY-Mellon operated in 37 different countries and had more than 40,000 employees, more than $1 trillion under management and more than $20 trillion under custody or administration. It also serviced over $11 trillion in debt for corporate clients. It dealt mostly with other corporations, not directly with individuals, but as author Mary Buffett, former daughter-in-law of Warren Buffett, put it: "that mutual fund that you have invested money in more than likely banks with BNY-Mellon."

The bank restructured its investment securities portfolio during the third quarter of 2009, with the associated write-down triggering a loss for the quarter and full year. The bank quickly reverted to form, in part because the US Treasury tapped it to act as the master custodian for the TARP bailout funds. In 2010 Warren Buffett began to add BNY-Mellon shares to his storied investment portfolio, and the following year its net earnings stopped just shy of $2.5 billion.

Sources

"Attorney General Announces Bank of New York Mellon Lost Personal Information of 135,000 More Residents." *U.S. Fed News Service*, September 2, 2008.

"Bank of New York Settles U.S. Probe." *Wall Street Journal*, November 9, 2005, C4.

Block, Alan A. and Constance A. Weaver. *All Is Clouded by Desire: Global Banking, Money Laundering, and International Organized Crime.* New York: Praeger, 2004.

Buffett, Mary and David Clark. *The Warren Buffett Stock Portfolio: Warren Buffett Stock Picks: Why and When He Is Investing in Them.* New York: Scribner, 2011, 61–68.

Loosvelt, Derek, et al. *The Vault Guide to the Top 50 Banking Employers: 2008 Edition.* New York: Vault, 2007, 224–27.

McCullough, C. Max. *One Hundred Years of Banking: The History of Mellon National Bank and Trust Company.* Pittsburgh: Herbick & Held, 1969.

Mellon National Bank: A Brief Historical Sketch of the Bank, Beginning With Its Founding by Thomas Mellon in 1869. Pittsburgh: Mellon National Bank, 1944.

Nevins, Allan. *History of the Bank of New York and Trust Company, 1784 to 1934.* New York: Bank of New York, 1934.

Parmet, Herbert S. *200 Years of Looking Ahead: Commemorating the Bicentennial of the Founding of The Bank of New York.* New York: Bank of New York, 1984.

Smith, Roy. *Comeback: The Restoration of American Banking Power in the New World Economy.* Boston: Harvard Business School Press, 1993, 72–73.

Spiegel, John, Alan Gart and Steven Gart. *Banking Redefined: How Superregional Powerhouses Are Reshaping Financial Services.* Chicago: Irwin Professional Publishing, 1996, 345–59, 383–97.

"State Street Says It Is Not Like Bank of New York Mellon." *Wall Street & Technology Online*, April 6, 2012.

Wright, Robert E. *Origins of Commercial Banking in America, 1750–1800.* Lanham, MD: Rowman and Littlefield, 2001.

Wright, Robert E. and David Cowen. *Financial Founding Fathers: The Men Who Made America Rich.* Chicago: University of Chicago Press, 2006.

The Bank of New York building at 48 Wall Street in New York City, ca. 1922.

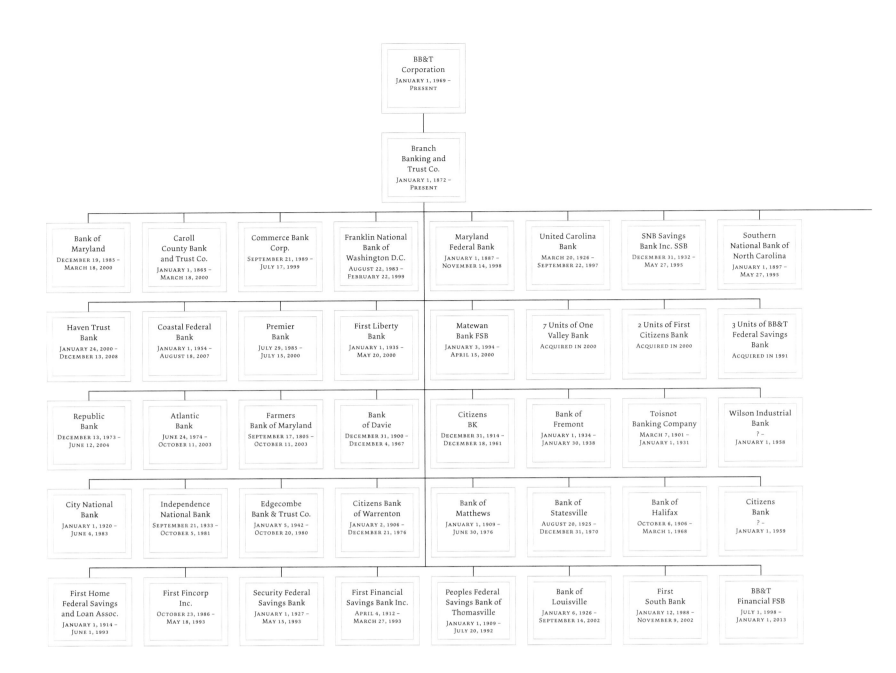

BB&T Corporation							
JANUARY 1, 1969 – PRESENT							

Branch Banking and Trust Co.							
JANUARY 1, 1872 – PRESENT							

Bank of Maryland	Caroll County Bank and Trust Co.	Commerce Bank Corp.	Franklin National Bank of Washington D.C.	Maryland Federal Bank	United Carolina Bank	SNB Savings Bank Inc. SSB	Southern National Bank of North Carolina
DECEMBER 19, 1985 – MARCH 18, 2000	JANUARY 1, 1865 – MARCH 18, 2000	SEPTEMBER 21, 1989 – JULY 17, 1999	AUGUST 22, 1983 – FEBRUARY 22, 1999	JANUARY 1, 1887 – NOVEMBER 14, 1998	MARCH 20, 1926 – SEPTEMBER 22, 1997	DECEMBER 31, 1932 – MAY 27, 1995	JANUARY 1, 1897 – MAY 27, 1995
Haven Trust Bank	Coastal Federal Bank	Premier Bank	First Liberty Bank	Matewan Bank FSB	7 Units of One Valley Bank	2 Units of First Citizens Bank	3 Units of BB&T Federal Savings Bank
JANUARY 24, 2000 – DECEMBER 13, 2008	JANUARY 1, 1954 – AUGUST 18, 2007	JULY 29, 1985 – JULY 15, 2000	JANUARY 1, 1935 – MAY 20, 2000	JANUARY 3, 1994 – APRIL 15, 2000	ACQUIRED IN 2000	ACQUIRED IN 2000	ACQUIRED IN 1991
Republic Bank	Atlantic Bank	Farmers Bank of Maryland	Bank of Davie	Citizens BK	Bank of Fremont	Toisnot Banking Company	Wilson Industrial Bank
DECEMBER 13, 1973 – JUNE 12, 2004	JUNE 24, 1974 – OCTOBER 11, 2003	SEPTEMBER 17, 1805 – OCTOBER 11, 2003	DECEMBER 31, 1900 – DECEMBER 4, 1967	DECEMBER 31, 1914 – DECEMBER 18, 1961	JANUARY 1, 1934 – JANUARY 30, 1938	MARCH 7, 1901 – JANUARY 1, 1931	? – JANUARY 1, 1958
City National Bank	Independence National Bank	Edgecombe Bank & Trust Co.	Citizens Bank of Warrenton	Bank of Matthews	Bank of Statesville	Bank of Halifax	Citizens Bank
JANUARY 1, 1920 – JUNE 4, 1983	SEPTEMBER 21, 1933 – OCTOBER 5, 1981	JANUARY 5, 1942 – OCTOBER 20, 1980	JANUARY 2, 1906 – DECEMBER 21, 1976	JANUARY 1, 1909 – JUNE 30, 1976	AUGUST 20, 1925 – DECEMBER 31, 1970	OCTOBER 6, 1906 – MARCH 1, 1968	? – JANUARY 1, 1959
First Home Federal Savings and Loan Assoc.	First Fincorp Inc.	Security Federal Savings Bank	First Financial Savings Bank Inc.	Peoples Federal Savings Bank of Thomasville	Bank of Louisville	First South Bank	BB&T Financial FSB
JANUARY 1, 1914 – JUNE 1, 1993	OCTOBER 23, 1986 – MAY 18, 1993	JANUARY 1, 1927 – MAY 15, 1993	APRIL 4, 1912 – MARCH 27, 1993	JANUARY 1, 1909 – JULY 20, 1992	JANUARY 6, 1926 – SEPTEMBER 14, 2002	JANUARY 12, 1988 – NOVEMBER 9, 2002	JULY 1, 1998 – JANUARY 1, 2013

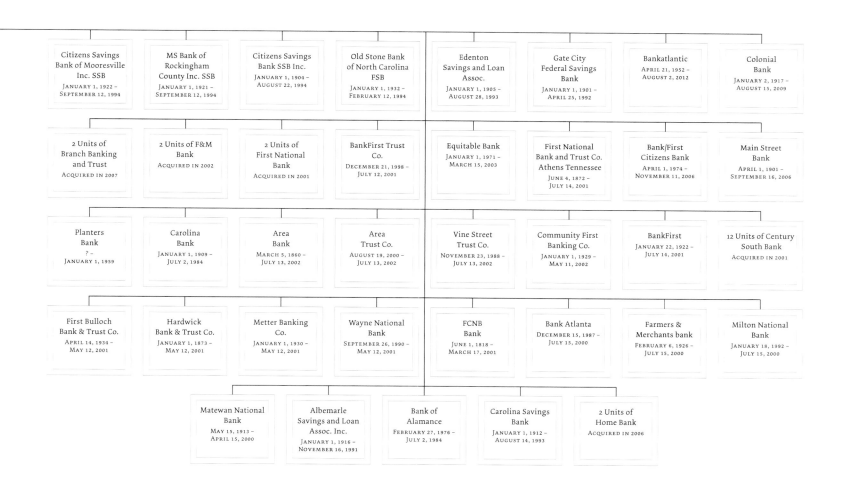

| Citizens Savings Bank of Mooresville Inc. SSB | MS Bank of Rockingham County Inc. SSB | Citizens Savings Bank SSB Inc. | Old Stone Bank of North Carolina FSB | Edenton Savings and Loan Assoc. | Gate City Federal Savings Bank | Bankatlantic | Colonial Bank |
| JANUARY 1, 1922 – SEPTEMBER 12, 1994 | JANUARY 1, 1921 – SEPTEMBER 12, 1994 | JANUARY 1, 1904 – AUGUST 22, 1994 | JANUARY 1, 1932 – FEBRUARY 12, 1994 | JANUARY 1, 1905 – AUGUST 28, 1993 | JANUARY 1, 1901 – APRIL 25, 1992 | APRIL 21, 1952 – AUGUST 2, 2012 | JANUARY 2, 1917 – AUGUST 15, 2009 |

| 2 Units of Branch Banking and Trust | 2 Units of F&M Bank | 2 Units of First National Bank | BankFirst Trust Co. | Equitable Bank | First National Bank and Trust Co. Athens Tennessee | Bank/First Citizens Bank | Main Street Bank |
| ACQUIRED IN 2007 | ACQUIRED IN 2002 | ACQUIRED IN 2001 | DECEMBER 21, 1998 – JULY 12, 2001 | JANUARY 1, 1971 – MARCH 15, 2003 | JUNE 4, 1872 – JULY 14, 2001 | APRIL 1, 1974 – NOVEMBER 11, 2006 | APRIL 1, 1901 – SEPTEMBER 16, 2006 |

| Planters Bank | Carolina Bank | Area Bank | Area Trust Co. | Vine Street Trust Co. | Community First Banking Co. | BankFirst | 12 Units of Century South Bank |
| ? – JANUARY 1, 1959 | JANUARY 1, 1909 – JULY 2, 1984 | MARCH 5, 1860 – JULY 13, 2002 | AUGUST 19, 2000 – JULY 13, 2002 | NOVEMBER 23, 1988 – JULY 13, 2002 | JANUARY 1, 1929 – MAY 11, 2002 | JANUARY 22, 1922 – JULY 14, 2001 | ACQUIRED IN 2001 |

| First Bulloch Bank & Trust Co. | Hardwick Bank & Trust Co. | Metter Banking Co. | Wayne National Bank | FCNB Bank | Bank Atlanta | Farmers & Merchants bank | Milton National Bank |
| APRIL 14, 1934 – MAY 12, 2001 | JANUARY 1, 1873 – MAY 12, 2001 | JANUARY 1, 1930 – MAY 12, 2001 | SEPTEMBER 26, 1990 – MAY 12, 2001 | JUNE 1, 1818 – MARCH 17, 2001 | DECEMBER 15, 1987 – JULY 15, 2000 | FEBRUARY 6, 1926 – JULY 15, 2000 | JANUARY 18, 1992 – JULY 15, 2000 |

| Matewan National Bank | Albemarle Savings and Loan Assoc. Inc. | Bank of Alamance | Carolina Savings Bank | 2 Units of Home Bank |
| MAY 15, 1913 – APRIL 15, 2000 | JANUARY 1, 1916 – NOVEMBER 16, 1991 | FEBRUARY 27, 1976 – JULY 2, 1984 | JANUARY 1, 1912 – AUGUST 14, 1993 | ACQUIRED IN 2006 |

BB&T

Bank *(abridged)*

RANK	HEADQUARTERS	TICKER	ASSETS	EARLIEST KNOWN ANCESTOR	INDUSTRY OF ORIGIN
17	Winston Salem, NC	BBT	$183,000,000,000	1805	Commercial Banking

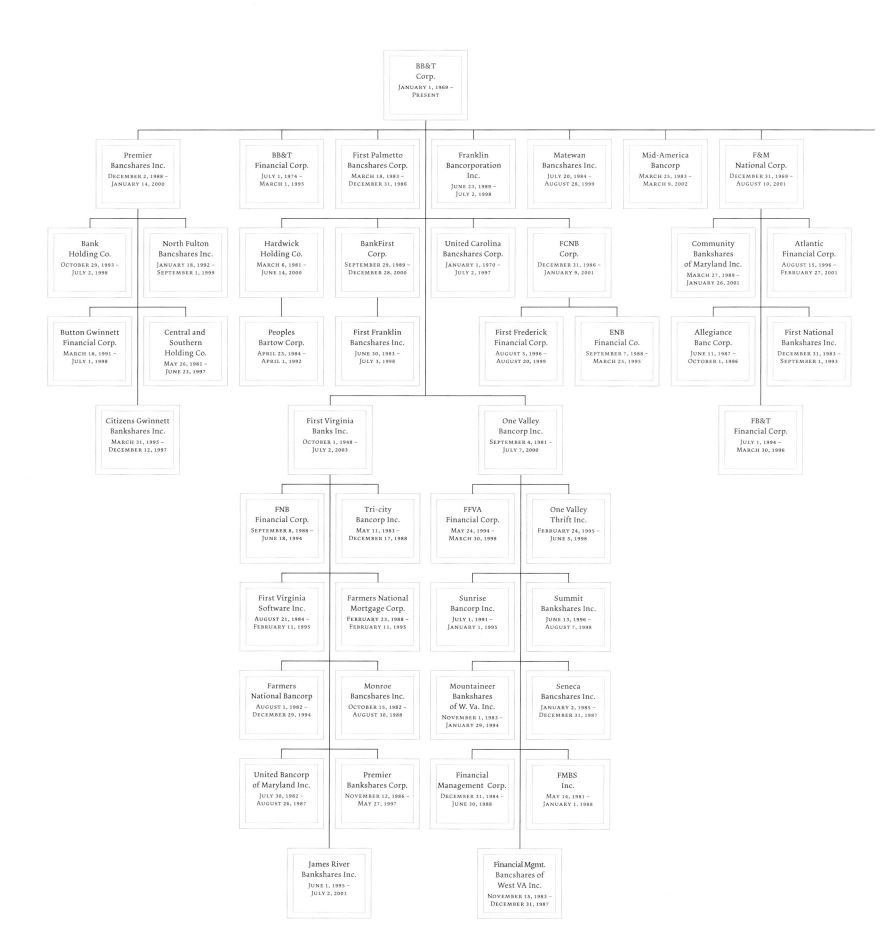

BB&T Corp.
JANUARY 1, 1969 – PRESENT

Premier Bancshares Inc.
DECEMBER 2, 1988 – JANUARY 14, 2000

BB&T Financial Corp.
JULY 1, 1974 – MARCH 1, 1995

First Palmetto Bancshares Corp.
MARCH 18, 1983 – DECEMBER 31, 1986

Franklin Bancorporation Inc.
JUNE 23, 1989 – JULY 2, 1998

Matewan Bancshares Inc.
JULY 20, 1984 – AUGUST 28, 1999

Mid-America Bancorp
MARCH 25, 1983 – MARCH 9, 2002

F&M National Corp.
DECEMBER 31, 1969 – AUGUST 10, 2001

Bank Holding Co.
OCTOBER 29, 1993 – JULY 2, 1998

North Fulton Bancshares Inc.
JANUARY 18, 1992 – SEPTEMBER 1, 1999

Hardwick Holding Co.
MARCH 6, 1981 – JUNE 14, 2000

BankFirst Corp.
SEPTEMBER 29, 1989 – DECEMBER 28, 2000

United Carolina Bancshares Corp.
JANUARY 1, 1970 – JULY 2, 1997

FCNB Corp.
DECEMBER 31, 1986 – JANUARY 9, 2001

Community Bankshares of Maryland Inc.
MARCH 27, 1989 – JANUARY 26, 2001

Atlantic Financial Corp.
AUGUST 15, 1996 – FEBRUARY 27, 2001

Button Gwinnett Financial Corp.
MARCH 18, 1991 – JULY 1, 1998

Central and Southern Holding Co.
MAY 26, 1981 – JUNE 23, 1997

Peoples Bartow Corp.
APRIL 23, 1984 – APRIL 1, 1992

First Franklin Bancshares Inc.
JUNE 30, 1983 – JULY 3, 1998

First Frederick Financial Corp.
AUGUST 5, 1996 – AUGUST 20, 1999

ENB Financial Co.
SEPTEMBER 7, 1988 – MARCH 25, 1995

Allegiance Banc Corp.
JUNE 11, 1987 – OCTOBER 1, 1996

First National Bankshares Inc.
DECEMBER 31, 1983 – SEPTEMBER 1, 1993

Citizens Gwinnett Bankshares Inc.
MARCH 31, 1995 – DECEMBER 12, 1997

First Virginia Banks Inc.
OCTOBER 1, 1948 – JULY 2, 2003

One Valley Bancorp Inc.
SEPTEMBER 4, 1981 – JULY 7, 2000

FB&T Financial Corp.
JULY 1, 1994 – MARCH 30, 1996

FNB Financial Corp.
SEPTEMBER 8, 1988 – JUNE 18, 1994

Tri-city Bancorp Inc.
MAY 11, 1983 – DECEMBER 17, 1988

FFVA Financial Corp.
MAY 24, 1994 – MARCH 30, 1998

One Valley Thrift Inc.
FEBRUARY 24, 1995 – JUNE 5, 1998

First Virginia Software Inc.
AUGUST 21, 1984 – FEBRUARY 11, 1995

Farmers National Mortgage Corp.
FEBRUARY 23, 1988 – FEBRUARY 11, 1995

Sunrise Bancorp Inc.
JULY 1, 1991 – JANUARY 1, 1995

Summit Bankshares Inc.
JUNE 13, 1996 – AUGUST 7, 1998

Farmers National Bancorp
AUGUST 1, 1982 – DECEMBER 29, 1994

Monroe Bancshares Inc.
OCTOBER 15, 1982 – AUGUST 30, 1988

Mountaineer Bankshares of W. Va. Inc.
NOVEMBER 1, 1983 – JANUARY 29, 1994

Seneca Bancshares Inc.
JANUARY 2, 1985 – DECEMBER 31, 1987

United Bancorp of Maryland Inc.
JULY 30, 1982 – AUGUST 26, 1987

Premier Bankshares Corp.
NOVEMBER 12, 1986 – MAY 27, 1997

Financial Management Corp.
DECEMBER 31, 1984 – JUNE 30, 1988

FMBS Inc.
MAY 14, 1981 – JANUARY 1. 1988

James River Bankshares Inc.
JUNE 1, 1995 – JULY 2, 2001

Financial Mgmt. Bancshares of West VA Inc.
NOVEMBER 15, 1983 – DECEMBER 31, 1987

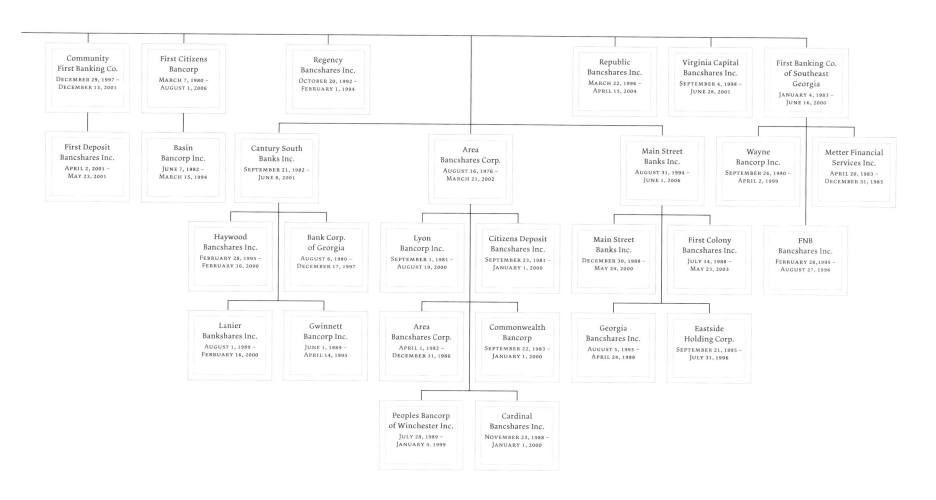

Community First Banking Co.
DECEMBER 29, 1997 –
DECEMBER 13, 2001

First Citizens Bancorp
MARCH 7, 1980 –
AUGUST 1, 2006

Regency Bancshares Inc.
OCTOBER 20, 1992 –
FEBRUARY 1, 1994

Republic Bancshares Inc.
MARCH 22, 1996 –
APRIL 15, 2004

Virginia Capital Bancshares Inc.
SEPTEMBER 4, 1998 –
JUNE 28, 2001

First Banking Co. of Southeast Georgia
JANUARY 4, 1983 –
JUNE 16, 2000

First Deposit Bancshares Inc.
APRIL 2, 2001 –
MAY 23, 2001

Basin Bancorp Inc.
JUNE 7, 1982 –
MARCH 15, 1994

Cantury South Banks Inc.
SEPTEMBER 21, 1982 –
JUNE 8, 2001

Area Bancshares Corp.
AUGUST 16, 1976 –
MARCH 21, 2002

Main Street Banks Inc.
AUGUST 31, 1994 –
JUNE 1, 2006

Wayne Bancorp Inc.
SEPTEMBER 26, 1990 –
APRIL 2, 1999

Metter Financial Services Inc.
APRIL 20, 1983 –
DECEMBER 31, 1985

Haywood Bancshares Inc.
FEBRUARY 28, 1995 –
FEBRUARY 16, 2000

Bank Corp. of Georgia
AUGUST 6, 1980 –
DECEMBER 17, 1997

Lyon Bancorp Inc.
SEPTEMBER 1, 1981 –
AUGUST 19, 2000

Citizens Deposit Bancshares Inc.
SEPTEMBER 23, 1981 –
JANUARY 1, 2000

Main Street Banks Inc.
DECEMBER 30, 1988 –
MAY 24, 2000

First Colony Bancshares Inc.
JULY 14, 1988 –
MAY 23, 2003

FNB Bancshares Inc.
FEBRUARY 28,1995 –
AUGUST 27, 1996

Lanier Bankshares Inc.
AUGUST 1, 1989 –
FEBRUARY 16, 2000

Gwinnett Bancorp Inc.
JUNE 1, 1989 –
APRIL 14, 1995

Area Bancshares Corp.
APRIL 1, 1982 –
DECEMBER 31, 1986

Commonwealth Bancorp
SEPTEMBER 22, 1983 –
JANUARY 1, 2000

Georgia Bancshares Inc.
AUGUST 5, 1995 –
APRIL 24, 1999

Eastside Holding Corp.
SEPTEMBER 21, 1995 –
JULY 31, 1996

Peoples Bancorp of Winchester Inc.
JULY 28, 1989 –
JANUARY 4. 1999

Cardinal Bancshares Inc.
NOVEMBER 23, 1988 –
JANUARY 1, 2000

BB&T

Holding Company *(abridged)*

Map of Wilson, North Carolina, 1908. The Branch Banking Co. building is second from the left in the top row.

Justice, integrity and stewardship are so ingrained in the corporate culture of this BHC that longtime CEO John A. Allison said his mission, and that of his executive team, was to help clients, employees, communities and shareholders to achieve their goals and thus "make the world a better place to live." His team believed they deserved to earn only in proportion to their ability to help others achieve their goals and not simply by virtue of running a large, complex organization.

BB&T arose from the ashes of Old Dixie. The Civil War did more than destroy physical and human capital; it wrecked the South's financial markets, including most of its banks. Many attempts to fill the void in the immediate postwar years failed. In 1872 former Confederate soldiers Alpheus Branch and Thomas Jefferson Hadley opened a private bank, Branch and Hadley, in the emerging market town of Wilson, North Carolina. Unlike other early efforts, it was able to stick, probably because of Branch's extensive business connections, which included the Wilson Cotton Mills and the Wilmington and Weldon Railroad.

Branch bought out Hadley in 1887 for $81,000 and continued to operate the private bank even as he obtained a state banking charter in 1889. The name of the chartered institution changed several times but settled as the Branch Banking Company in 1893, the year Branch died. In 1900 the chartered bank bought out the private one, uniting the two concerns.

In 1897 the other main lineage of BB&T began when Angus Wilton McLean and other businessmen in Lumberton, 90 miles southeast of

Wilson, formed the Bank of Lumberton. Like Branch, McLean busied himself with a variety of concerns, including a law practice, a railroad, a land development company and three cotton mills. While serving as state governor or Undersecretary of the US Treasury, McLean made certain that his bank's customers were well served by taking the overnight train to Fayetteville every Thursday evening, working in the bank Friday and Saturday, and attending church Sunday morning before commuting by train back to Washington or Raleigh. Under such close supervision, the bank thrived making agricultural and business loans until McLean's death in 1935.

When regulators questioned the bank's ability to withstand a sustained run on its deposits in 1930, McLean retorted that his bank was "so fortified with cash and quickly marketable securities that I cannot see any possibility of its closing." Its cash reserves amounted to enough to repay two-thirds of its depositors, and another 20% of its deposits were held by the bank's directors "and their interests, and these would not be withdrawn under any circumstances," McLean noted. He borrowed and conspicuously displayed $1 million in cash just to be sure; no run occurred on his bank while other banks in Robeson County and elsewhere fell like dominoes. The bank's employees and officers all took pay cuts too, though its business increased dramatically as the customers of failed banks flocked to it.

When McLean died, more than 10,000 people attended his funeral in Lumberton. Albert White, the businessman and politician who was

Portrait of Angus Wilton McLean.

Branch Banking Company advertisements from the Wilson Times, *December 20, 1912.*

the bank's vice president, subsequently took over. He continued to run the institution in a conservative fashion, which is not surprising given that at least one of its founders, Henry B. Jennings, was still on the board. White died in 1941, succeeded by his son-in-law Russell Beam, a local doctor, who allowed the cashier and the board to make the banking decisions. He died in 1946 and was replaced by Morris Cobb, who had joined the bank as cashier in 1918 and, not surprisingly, continued the bank's traditions until he was appointed chairman of the board in 1955. The move made room for Hector MacLean (not a typo, Hector's preference), McLean's youngest son.

Under MacLean, the bank began to show signs of ambition while maintaining its traditional focus on service and sound banking practices. It opened a drive-in location in 1957, for example, and also began financing automobile purchases. MacLean worried that the bank was tied too closely to tobacco fortunes, and after decades of attempting to persuade local farmers to diversify their crop mix, he decided that geographical expansion was necessary to diversify the bank's loan portfolio.

The first change came in 1959, when he changed the bank's name to Southern National Bank and established a de novo branch in Laurinburg. After the acquisition of the small, agriculture-centered Bank of Rowland in 1964, a wave of acquisitions began that did not dissipate until the union with BB&T in 1995. The bank spread throughout North Carolina in the 1970s and into South Carolina in the 1980s.

During MacLean's 35 years of service, which ended in 1990, the bank's assets grew from $11 million to $3.3 billion, with 148 branches spread over both Carolinas. By 1995, under MacLean's handpicked successor, Glenn Orr, Southern National ran 230 branches in 118 cities.

Meanwhile, back in Wilson, Branch opened a trust department in 1907, the first in the state, and in 1913 changed its name to Branch Banking and Trust (BB&T) to reflect the new department's growing importance to the business. The bank flirted with the idea of switching to a national banking charter following the Panic of 1907, but it decided against the move and remained a state-chartered bank through 2013. It thrived on the ethic of President Jacob Cecil Hales, who argued that "courtesy, consideration, kindness and accommodation rightly distributed pay good interest in the long run."

The bank actually ran an advertisement in 1915 stating "that business will succeed best which most completely embodies friendship and brotherhood." Half a decade later, the bank was lauded as a "sterling financial institution" that ranked highly "not only among Southern banks, but of those of the entire nation."

Unlike its seven competitors in Wilson, Branch Bank and Trust survived the Great Depression, in some measure because of its still modest branch system, which spread out its risks a bit, and a subsidiary called the Branch Investment Company that soaked up its bad mortgages. Also, during a crucial run in late December 1931, the US Post Office surreptitiously redeposited monies that individuals withdrew from

WILSON OFFICE—OFFICERS AND DIRECTORS
(Reading from left to right)

Front Row W. A. FINCH   F. N. BRIDGERS   D. S. BOYKIN   H. D. BATEMAN   A. H. ANDERSON   F. L. CARR   DR. C. E. MOORE
           Director   Director   Director   President & Director Chairman & Director Director   Director

Back Row   J. T. CHEATHAM   C. L. HARDY   E. B. CROW Jr.   S. W. ANDERSON   G. F. WATSON Jr.   J. J. LANE   H. P. LANE   C. S. LAWRENCE   H. W. CARR
           Director   Director   Trust Officer   Director   Director   Director   Director   Vice President, Cashier Director
                                                                                                                                & Director

BB&T Board of Directors, 1930.

the bank to deposit in the purportedly safer Postal Savings system. Those funds, and deliberately slow service, kept the bank alive until a Brink's truck, alleged to contain $1 million, arrived. The conspicuous, if somewhat dangerous, display of cash worked. Deposits began to flow back into the bank, the assets of which increased from about $6.4 million during the run to almost $13.8 million by the end of 1933. Part of that growth was funded by preferred stock sold to the Reconstruction Finance Corporation, a New Deal bailout vehicle, and invested in government bonds.

Branch Bank and Trust grew by leaps and bounds during World War II, its assets nearly doubling in 1941 alone, in part as a result of a thriving correspondent banking business. By the early 1950s, half of the bank's deposits were those of other banks, making it truly a "banker's bank." The postwar era was also good for the US economy, North Carolina's tobacco producers and the bank. By 1951 its total assets sat just shy of $125 million, and its branch network had expanded to 17. In 1958 the bank acquired the Wilson Industrial Bank and in 1959 the Planters Bank.

In the 1960s the bank continued growing organically and via acquisitions, picking up the Bank of Davie in 1967 and the Bank of Halifax in 1968. It also entered the credit card business, but the bank remained centered. In 1973, after the acquisition of the Bank of Statesville in 1970, President John Lafayette Satchwell told stockholders that the bank wanted "no part of hasty construction, bigness just for the sake of bigness, growth with no sense of direction, but rather we subscribe to the idea of growth by virtue of excellence." A revamped management development program, run by young Charlotte native John Allison, saw to that.

In 1974 the bank created and made itself a subsidiary of Branch Corporation, a one-bank holding company. Mergers proceeded apace: Bank of Matthews in mid-1976, Citizens Bank of Warrenton in late 1976, Edgecombe Bank and Trust in 1980 and Independence National Bank in 1981. All were relatively small but strategic. The Independence deal, for example, increased the bank's exposure to the industrial sector. The mergers added $383 million in assets, but that was less than the bank's organic growth over the period.

After the US Supreme Court upheld the right of states to form reciprocal interstate banking agreements in 1985, the bank soon moved into South Carolina with the 1987 acquisition of Community Bancorporation of Greenville. It also continued expanding in North Carolina through acquisitions, the establishment of de novo branches and an agreement to put branches in Kroger supermarkets.

Allison was named president of the bank in 1987. He changed the company's name to BB&T Financial Corporation the next year and took over when chairman and CEO L. Vincent Lowe Jr. died of a massive heart attack in 1989. Lowe was the second of the bank's top executives to pass away suddenly from a heart attack that decade. Allison's heart held out during a remarkable period of change and growth for the bank, during which it acquired numerous troubled thrift institutions and expanded into insurance, automobile finance and venture capital. When Allison took over, BB&T owned $4.5 billion in assets and operated 191 offices in 105 locations in both Carolinas. When he left, BB&T had assets of $136.5 billion, and its national asset ranking had jumped from 96th to 14th. More importantly, the bank, which Allison pledged to make "the best of the best," was also a higher quality institution, in the nation's top 10% in terms of profitability, efficiency and credit quality.

The key move was the merger with Southern. Allison and Orr struck a merger agreement in 1994 because both feared they would be eaten up by a larger, insatiable northern or western bank if they did not. The new bank took the name BB&T to save on signage costs, but the headquarters went to Southern National's digs in Winston-Salem. Orr agreed to retire, putting Allison firmly in charge of the new bank from the beginning. The new bank's board and top management team was divided between the two institutions.

To smooth transitions, the bank set up a "buddy system," whereby experienced staffers helped to orient newbies to the company's processes. Only 5% of the workforce was cut and, with its career transitions program, the bank helped them find new jobs. The merger was completed in May 1995, and a year later it had created more than $800 million in additional shareholder value. Not surprisingly, the media praised it as a model way for mergers of equals to proceed.

Other, smaller deals, like the acquisition of Atlanta's Main Street Banks in 2006, continued. Between 1989 and 2007, the bank bought more than 60 community banks and thrifts, 85 insurers and 34 nonbank financial services businesses. By 2007 BB&T employed almost 30,000 people in nearly 1,500 offices, mostly in the Southeast and Mid-Atlantic regions. It offered numerous nonbanking services through its subsidiaries, including insurance, insurance premium financing, insurance software and hardware provision, leasing services, consumer finance, wholesale mortgage lending to brokers, auto and small equipment financing and employee benefits consulting. Presidents in charge of its 33 "regions" kept bureaucratic red tape to a minimum.

BB&T avoided the bulk of the subprime derivatives mess that caused the 2008 financial crisis, but like everyone else was unsure what the future would bring given the instability caused by the failure of icons like Bear Stearns, Lehman Brothers, AIG, Fannie Mae and Freddie Mac. Fearful of losing another big company and desirous of making its bailouts appear profitable for taxpayers, the government forced it to participate in TARP. The bank passed its stress test with flying colors and entirely repaid the government's investment, with dividends, in June 2009. It was one of the first institutions to do so.

Allison turned over leadership to Kelly King in 2009, the same year BB&T purchased Colonial Bank of Alabama, its biggest acquisition to date, with FDIC assistance. Colonial was one of the many victims of the 2008 financial crisis, and BB&T was able to pick up its $20 billion of deposits because it emerged from the crisis in relatively good shape. Although it purchased One Valley in 2000 and First Virginia in 2003, unlike other big BHCs it didn't dive into businesses it didn't understand. Instead, it invested in technology, websites and smart phone apps with features that its customers wanted and that saved the bank on back office expenses. It also invested in sports marketing, including its first NASCAR sponsorship.

Sources

Allison, John A. *The Financial Crisis and the Free Market Cure: Why Pure Capitalism Is the World Economy's Only Hope.* New York: McGraw-Hill, 2013.

Bass, Vidette and Ken Hamrick. *BB&T: A Tradition with a Future.* 6th ed. 1990.

Building on Our Values: A History of BB&T Corporation. 9th ed. 1999.

Johnson, Clint. *Service None Better: The History of Southern National Bank.* 1997.

Loosvelt, Derek, et al. *The Vault Guide to the Top 50 Banking Employers: 2008 Edition.* New York: Vault, 2007, 305–9.

Our Account: A History of BB&T. 10th ed. 2012.

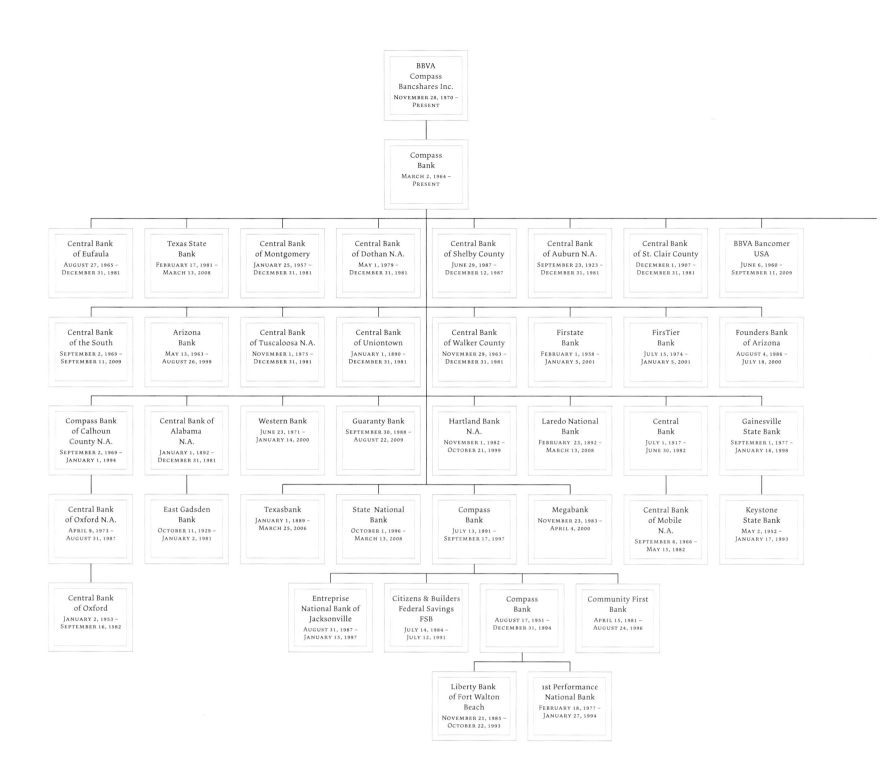

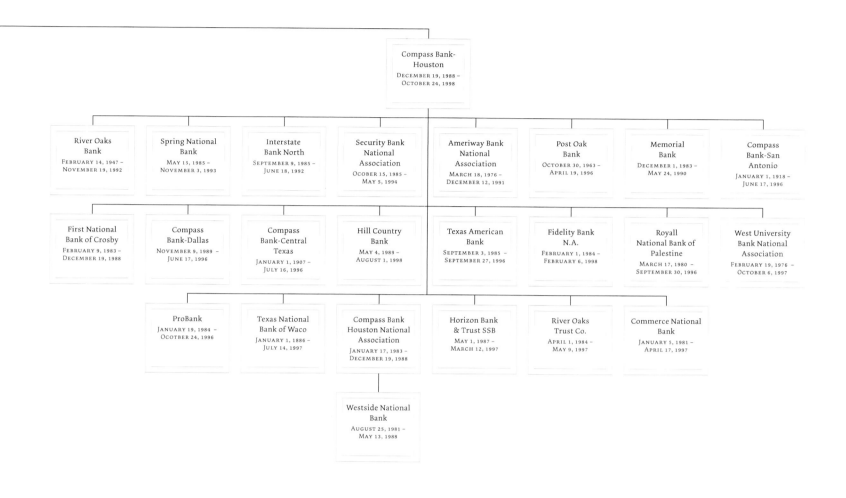

Compass Bank-Houston
DECEMBER 19, 1988 –
OCTOBER 24, 1998

River Oaks Bank
FEBRUARY 14, 1947 –
NOVEMBER 19, 1992

Spring National Bank
MAY 15, 1985 –
NOVEMBER 3, 1993

Interstate Bank North
SEPTEMBER 9, 1985 –
JUNE 18, 1992

Security Bank National Association
OCOBER 15, 1985 –
MAY 5, 1994

Ameriway Bank National Association
MARCH 18, 1976 –
DECEMBER 12, 1991

Post Oak Bank
OCTOBER 30, 1963 –
APRIL 19, 1996

Memorial Bank
DECEMBER 1, 1983 –
MAY 24, 1990

Compass Bank-San Antonio
JANUARY 1, 1918 –
JUNE 17, 1996

First National Bank of Crosby
FEBRUARY 9, 1983 –
DECEMBER 19, 1988

Compass Bank-Dallas
NOVEMBER 9, 1989 –
JUNE 17, 1996

Compass Bank-Central Texas
JANUARY 1, 1907 –
JULY 16, 1996

Hill Country Bank
MAY 4, 1989 –
AUGUST 1, 1998

Texas American Bank
SEPTEMBER 3, 1985 –
SEPTEMBER 27, 1996

Fidelity Bank N.A.
FEBRUARY 1, 1984 –
FEBRUARY 6, 1998

Royall National Bank of Palestine
MARCH 17, 1980 –
SEPTEMBER 30, 1996

West University Bank National Association
FEBRUARY 19, 1976 –
OCTOBER 6, 1997

ProBank
JANUARY 19, 1984 –
OCOTBER 24, 1996

Texas National Bank of Waco
JANUARY 1, 1886 –
JULY 14, 1997

Compass Bank Houston National Association
JANUARY 17, 1983 –
DECEMBER 19, 1988

Horizon Bank & Trust SSB
MAY 1, 1987 –
MARCH 12, 1997

River Oaks Trust Co.
APRIL 1, 1984 –
MAY 9, 1997

Commerce National Bank
JANUARY 5, 1981 –
APRIL 17, 1997

Westside National Bank
AUGUST 25, 1981 –
MAY 13, 1988

BBVA Compass Bancshares

Bank *(abridged)*

RANK	HEADQUARTERS	TICKER	ASSETS	EARLIEST KNOWN ANCESTOR	INDUSTRY OF ORIGIN
35	**Houston, TX**	**BBVA**	**$70,000,000,000**	**1885**	**Commercial Banking**

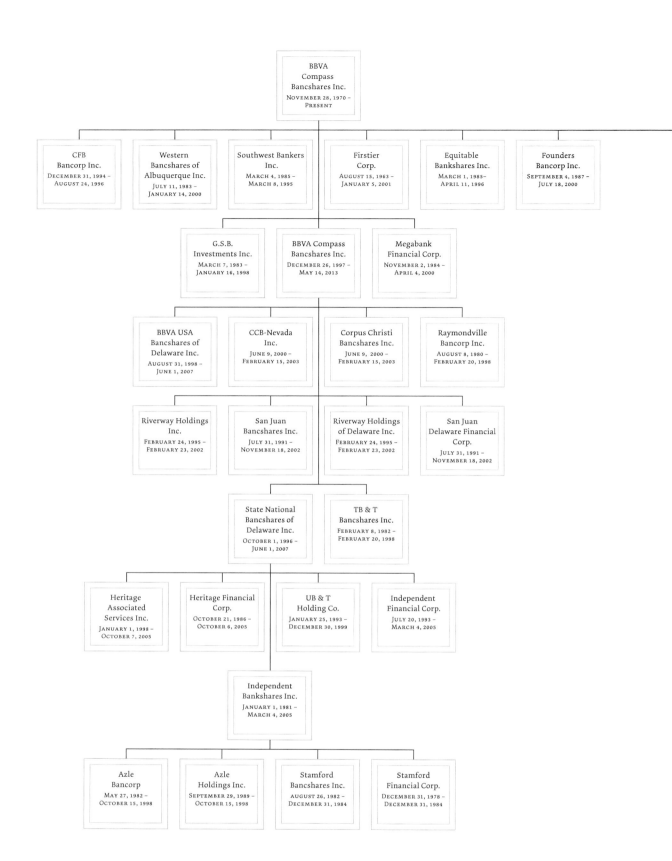

BBVA Compass Bancshares Inc.
NOVEMBER 28, 1970 – PRESENT

CFB Bancorp Inc.
DECEMBER 31, 1994 – AUGUST 24, 1996

Western Bancshares of Albuquerque Inc.
JULY 11, 1983 – JANUARY 14, 2000

Southwest Bankers Inc.
MARCH 4, 1985 – MARCH 8, 1995

Firstier Corp.
AUGUST 15, 1963 – JANUARY 5, 2001

Equitable Bankshares Inc.
MARCH 1, 1985 – APRIL 11, 1996

Founders Bancorp Inc.
SEPTEMBER 4, 1987 – JULY 18, 2000

G.S.B. Investments Inc.
MARCH 7, 1983 – JANUARY 16, 1998

BBVA Compass Bancshares Inc.
DECEMBER 26, 1997 – MAY 14, 2013

Megabank Financial Corp.
NOVEMBER 2, 1984 – APRIL 4, 2000

BBVA USA Bancshares of Delaware Inc.
AUGUST 31, 1998 – JUNE 1, 2007

CCB-Nevada Inc.
JUNE 9, 2000 – FEBRUARY 15, 2003

Corpus Christi Bancshares Inc.
JUNE 9, 2000 – FEBRUARY 15, 2003

Raymondville Bancorp Inc.
AUGUST 8, 1980 – FEBRUARY 20, 1998

Riverway Holdings Inc.
FEBRUARY 24, 1995 – FEBRUARY 23, 2002

San Juan Bancshares Inc.
JULY 31, 1991 – NOVEMBER 18, 2002

Riverway Holdings of Delaware Inc.
FEBRUARY 24, 1995 – FEBRUARY 23, 2002

San Juan Delaware Financial Corp.
JULY 31, 1991 – NOVEMBER 18, 2002

State National Bancshares of Delaware Inc.
OCTOBER 1, 1996 – JUNE 1, 2007

TB & T Bancshares Inc.
FEBRUARY 8, 1982 – FEBRUARY 20, 1998

Heritage Associated Services Inc.
JANUARY 1, 1998 – OCTOBER 7, 2005

Heritage Financial Corp.
OCTOBER 21, 1986 – OCTOBER 6, 2005

UB & T Holding Co.
JANUARY 25, 1993 – DECEMBER 30, 1999

Independent Financial Corp.
JULY 20, 1993 – MARCH 4, 2005

Independent Bankshares Inc.
JANUARY 1, 1981 – MARCH 4, 2005

Azle Bancorp
MAY 27, 1982 – OCTOBER 15, 1998

Azle Holdings Inc.
SEPTEMBER 29, 1989 – OCTOBER 15, 1998

Stamford Bancshares Inc.
AUGUST 26, 1982 – DECEMBER 31, 1984

Stamford Financial Corp.
DECEMBER 31, 1978 – DECEMBER 31, 1984

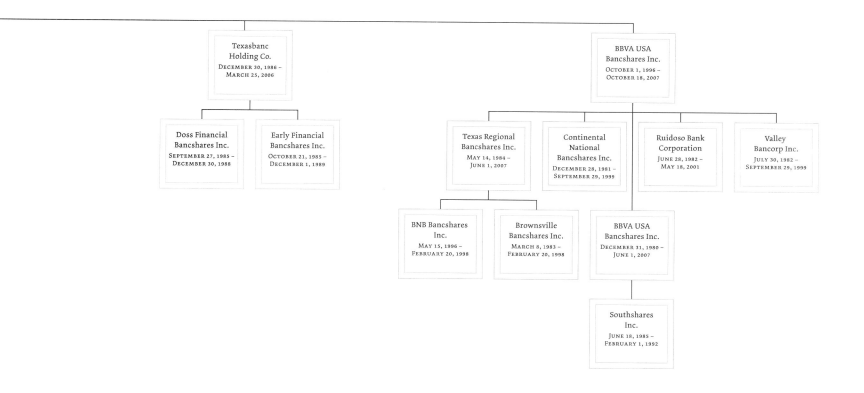

BBVA Compass Bancshares   Holding Company *(abridged)*

Banco del Bilbao note for 100 Spanish reales.

BVA Compass is the holding company of Banco Bilbao Vizcaya Argentaria (BBVA), Spain's second largest bank behind Santander (#32). It was formed from the mergers of Argentaria, Banco Bilbao, Banco de Vizcaya, Banco Exterior de España, Caja Postal de Ahorros and some minor entities in the late 1980s and 1990s, as part of a wave of mergers triggered by deregulation of the Spanish banking system. From that period emerged only the biggest and/or most profitable banks. Each new acquisition brought with it numerous problems and leadership clashes, but rapid growth was seen as essential to continued existence, so buying continued. It was interrupted only when rivals—like Santander—swooped in and outbid the bank, as it did with troubled Banesto.

BBVA's managers responded to higher levels of competition in Spanish banking by innovating, globalizing and paying more attention to customers who were newly empowered by the Internet and a wider range of choices. Overseas expansion, mostly into Mexico but also into South America's relatively rich southern cone, was meant to diversify risk by increasing the geographical spread of its assets. It also sought to position itself strategically for growth in Latin America's population and economies, all while minimizing costs because of shared language, culture and banking products.

A shift in emphasis away from retail and toward wholesale banking had a similar intent. In addition to seeking out new, strategic growth areas, BBVA's managers looked for continuous improvements in day-to-day operations, much like the Japanese automobile manufacturers' *kaizen* movement. The basics were just as important to the bank's success, they believed, as more complex strategies. This was evident in the bank's low level of nonperforming loans through 2006.

Like Santander, BBVA invested heavily and intelligently in IT systems that freed up workers to stimulate top line growth. Many acquisitions were driven by the desire of the acquired company to tap the bank's superior customer information system, which since the 1990s has been customer-focused, rather than product-focused. Good IT also made it possible to adapt products to new countries and markets relatively quickly and cheaply. Buoyed by solid economic growth in Spain and consistent profitability, BBVA was the world's 36th largest bank in 2006, with assets of almost $463 billion. BBVA also moved tentatively into the United States, basically by following the expanding Hispanic market. By 2006 its American properties consisted of five businesses: 1) three Texas banks (Laredo National, Texas Regional and State National); 2) a California bank called BBVA Bancomer that catered to first generation Spanish-speaking immigrants; 3) BBVA Puerto Rico, which was active in mortgages and consumer finance; 4) a US-Mexico money transfer specialist called Bancomer Transfer; and 5) BBVA Finanzia USA, which specialized in consumer finance and credit cards. In its boldest move to date, BBVA added Compass, a bank with $34 billion in assets headquartered in Birmingham, Alabama, to its US portfolio in 2007.

Compass was formed in 1963 as the Central Bank and Trust by Hugh Daniel, a civic leader and co-owner of a major interstate construction company who wanted a bank that operated on Saturdays; Schuyler Baker, an ambitious attorney; and Harry Brock, a young executive at Exchange Security Bank (now part of #25). They decided to establish a new bank because at the time, two banks—First National Bank of Birmingham and Birmingham Trust National Bank—held 90% of the banking deposits in Birmingham.

Even as racial violence exploded—ripping the city apart and making potential investors skittish—Baker, Brock and Daniel forged ahead with their plans. The key was to fashion an old-style board of directors, people who owned significant stakes in the institution and actively promoted its interests. Big stockholders would also have to keep big deposits and promote the bank in their business networks. Stock options (10 years, 50,000 shares, $2 strike) incentivized Brock, who was brought in as CEO in early 1964; Daniel became chairman of the board.

Despite Birmingham's many troubles, $1 million in stock was quickly oversubscribed. To get their allotments, larger shareholders were told they would have to keep deposits 10 times larger than their stock investment. The plan worked. When the books closed, 565 subscribers promised to do business with the bank. Deposits also poured in from Daniel Construction Company workers who desperately needed Saturday banking hours. After the first day of business, March 2, 1964, the bank was already a $4 million institution.

Baker and the other founders said they chose the name Central Bank because "C" stood for "customer." By concentrating on customers' needs, Brock realized, the bank could take business away from the city's bigger banks, even if Birmingham's growth stagnated. And that

National currency issued by the First National Bank of Birmingham.

is exactly what it did, with a lot of help from its board of directors and biggest shareholders. At the end of 1964, deposits were just shy of $14 million. By the middle of 1968, they stood at just under $73 million, and assets were at almost $81.7 million. By then 7% of the Birmingham market belonged to Central, which was ready to make a bold move. It initiated a hostile takeover of State National Bank, which was Alabama's third largest bank with branches in 12 northern counties. It was two-and-a-half times Central's size.

State National began its existence in 1892 as the Merchants Bank of Florence. It moved to Decatur in 1906 and changed its name to Tennessee Valley Bank (TVB) in 1908. Unlike most Alabama banks of that era, TVB was interested in branching. It had established 15 branches across eight counties by 1911, when the state outlawed branching outside of city or county boundaries. TVB's branches, however, were "grandfathered" along with several other branching banks, but all the others had failed by the end of the Great Depression. TVB became insolvent too, but it reorganized in 1934 with its branching rights intact. It also retained its branches when it converted to a national banking charter and became State National in 1939. It subsequently

established the right to move its branches at will, giving it a power no other bank in the state possessed, but which Brock coveted because he understood its potential power.

The Central-State merger caused a legal riot, as 107 Alabama banks petitioned to block it, and disgruntled stockholders filed lawsuits. The bank lost the case three times and then tried to form a BHC that would own both banks. Its bigger competitors, however, moved to block that maneuver by introducing legislation that would have stripped State National of its unique branching powers. Central fought back hard, portraying in cartoons the big banks as bullies crying to their mommies for protection from the skinny kid down the block. What won the day was not public opinion but the powerful House speaker Rankin Fite, who assigned the bill to a committee that he controlled. "We had to defeat that bill," Brock later observed. They did so by letting it rot in committee. The governor, a director in a small bank competing with State National, spoke out against branch banking but did little to fight Fite. The bill came up to a vote in a state senate committee but lost five to four, perhaps as a result of quiet help from Frank Plummer, who in another year would create First Alabama

Tennessee Valley Bank slip, 1914.

Bancshares, a forerunner of Regions (#24).

The BHC finally became a reality in December 1971. Called Central Bancshares of the South after 1973, it added Citizens Bank of Eufaula, Deposit National Bank of Mobile County, First National Bank of Auburn, Peoples Bank and Trust and Planters and Merchants Bank of Uniontown to its group in 1972. The following year it added First State Bank of Oxford, and in 1974 the Sumiton Bank in Walker County. Bank of Springville was claimed in 1978, and de novo banks were formed in Tuscaloosa and Dothan in 1975 and 1979, respectively. It bought the $80 million Baldwin County Bank and the $27.5 million First City National Bank of Oxford in 1981, but it did not acquire another bank until 1987 (although it did acquire eight branches divested by a competitor in 1985).

These were all relatively small purchases, mostly of banks in distress; in 1981, only 22.75% of its assets were owned by the new acquisitions. Other new Alabama BHCs moved more quickly to acquire banks, so Central slipped to number four in the state by 1973 and remained small throughout the 1970s and 1980s. Of the state's 12 largest markets, Central led in only one—Decatur—home of State National. At the end of 1986, its $3.8 billion in assets were still eclipsed by three other Alabama BHCs.

Nevertheless, Central was profitable. Good interest rate spreads and fee income, combined with solid expense and tax management, kept the bank in the black with return on assets generally around 1% and return on equity in the double digits every year except 1981, when it dipped to 8.6%. That year, though, relaxation of branching restrictions finally allowed Central to formally merge with State National and the BHC's other subsidiaries.

In 1987 Central bought a troubled bank near Houston, mainly so it could enter the Houston market. Brock told Central Bancshares aficionados that "Central should never be intimidated by larger financial institutions. Our success against them is well-documented. The Central organization is built to survive and endure if we always strive to give our customers a better deal than our competitors do."

Brock was referring to the bank's entrepreneurial focus and strong customer service ethic. He realized that "you have to serve the people so that as they become more successful, you'll be more successful, too." So, rather than conform to the standards set by other banks, it stayed open during a rare Alabama snowstorm in 1985. But that was in the days of relationship banking, when most borrowers and depositors had one bank and stuck with it through thick and thin. As transaction banking became more common, Central, which changed its name to Compass in 2000, found it needed to grow quickly or get bought up. The latter was its fate, at the hands of a foreign bank not noted for its entrepreneurial ways.

Ultimately, however, BBVA's cautious nature had a major upside. "They've been one of the clear winners of this crisis," a banking analyst at BPI in Portugal told *Wall Street Journal* reporters in August 2009. BBVA got through the 2008 financial crisis well enough to send its CEO and chairman, Francisco Gonzalez, on a discreet early 2009 visit to FDIC Chairman Sheila Bair to inform her that his bank was interested in making "tactical" acquisitions in southern and southwestern states. It made several purchases, including Guaranty of Texas.

By 2012, however, BBVA's profits and stock price were down, and ING downgraded its stock from "buy" to "hold." In 2013 BBVA Compass began to offer its customers four new checking account options, including one with personalized debit cards and a free one for "Every Day Heroes": law enforcement, healthcare workers, teachers and active and retired military personnel. It shrank its branch network by 21, however, including 16 in Texas, reducing its footprint to 688, most of which were located in seven Sunbelt states.

Sources

Catan, Thomas and Christopher Bjork. "Spain's BBVA Plots Its Rise in the US." *Wall Street Journal*, August 18, 2009, C1.

Cumming, Chris. "BBVA Compass Closes 18 Branches, with Three More to Follow." *American Banker*, June 26, 2013.

Davis, Paul. "BBVA Compass Sets New Path After Guaranty Deal." *American Banker*, March 26, 2010.

Gamble, Richard H. *A Competitive Spirit: The Story of Central Bank of the South.* Birmingham, AL: Birmingham Printing and Publishing, 1987.

Kase, Kimio and Tanguy Jacopin. *CEOs as Leaders and Strategy Designers: Explaining the Success of Spanish Banks.* New York: Palgrave Macmillan, 2008.

Mulligan, Mark. "BBVA Emerges from Santander's Shadow." *FT.com*, August 24, 2009.

Robinson, Duncan. "Spanish Stocks Hit as BBVA Downgraded." *FT.com*, March 12, 2012.

Todd, Sarah. "BBVA Compass Introduces Four New Checking Options." *American Banker*, October 9, 2013.

Wright, Robert E. *Corporation Nation.* Philadelphia: University of Pennsylvania Press, 2014.

First National Bank, Birmingham, Alabama, ca. 1906.

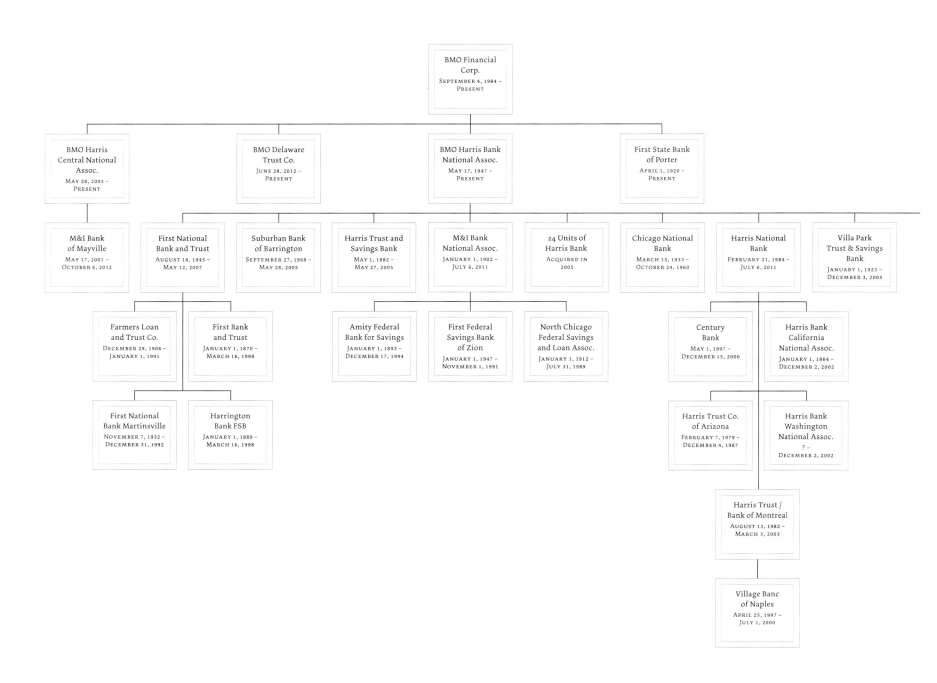

BMO Financial Corp.
SEPTEMBER 4, 1984 – PRESENT

BMO Harris Central National Assoc.
MAY 28, 2005 – PRESENT

BMO Delaware Trust Co.
JUNE 28, 2012 – PRESENT

BMO Harris Bank National Assoc.
MAY 17, 1947 – PRESENT

First State Bank of Porter
APRIL 1, 1920 – PRESENT

M&I Bank of Mayville
MAY 17, 2001 – OCTOBER 6, 2012

First National Bank and Trust
AUGUST 18, 1945 – MAY 12, 2007

Suburban Bank of Barrington
SEPTEMBER 27, 1968 – MAY 28, 2005

Harris Trust and Savings Bank
MAY 1, 1882 – MAY 27, 2005

M&I Bank National Assoc.
JANUARY 1, 1902 – JULY 6, 2011

24 Units of Harris Bank
ACQUIRED IN 2005

Chicago National Bank
MARCH 15, 1933 – OCTOBER 24, 1960

Harris National Bank
FEBRUARY 21, 1984 – JULY 6, 2011

Villa Park Trust & Savings Bank
JANUARY 1, 1923 – DECEMBER 3, 2005

Farmers Loan and Trust Co.
DECEMBER 29, 1906 – JANUARY 1, 1991

First Bank and Trust
JANUARY 1, 1870 – MARCH 16, 1998

Amity Federal Bank for Savings
JANUARY 1, 1893 – DECEMBER 17, 1994

First Federal Savings Bank of Zion
JANUARY 1, 1947 – NOVEMBER 1, 1991

North Chicago Federal Savings and Loan Assoc.
JANUARY 1, 1912 – JULY 31, 1989

Century Bank
MAY 1, 1997 – DECEMBER 15, 2000

Harris Bank California National Assoc.
JANUARY 1, 1864 – DECEMBER 2, 2002

First National Bank Martinsville
NOVEMBER 7, 1932 – DECEMBER 31, 1992

Harrington Bank FSB
JANUARY 1, 1889 – MARCH 16, 1998

Harris Trust Co. of Arizona
FEBRUARY 7, 1979 – DECEMBER 4, 1987

Harris Bank Washington National Assoc.
? – DECEMBER 2, 2002

Harris Trust / Bank of Montreal
AUGUST 13, 1982 – MARCH 3, 2003

Village Banc of Naples
APRIL 25, 1997 – JULY 1, 2000

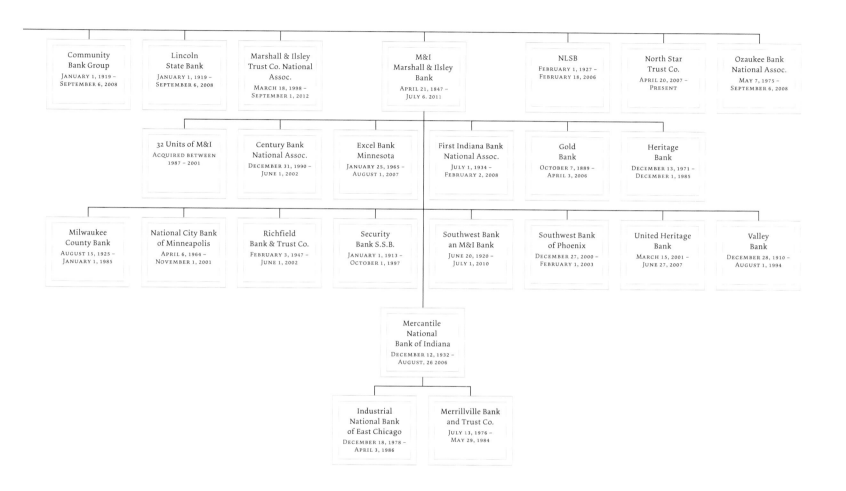

Community Bank Group JANUARY 1, 1919 – SEPTEMBER 6, 2008	Lincoln State Bank JANUARY 1, 1919 – SEPTEMBER 6, 2008	Marshall & Ilsley Trust Co. National Assoc. MARCH 18, 1998 – SEPTEMBER 1, 2012	M&I Marshall & Ilsley Bank APRIL 21, 1847 – JULY 6. 2011	NLSB FEBRUARY 1, 1927 – FEBRUARY 18, 2006	North Star Trust Co. APRIL 20, 2007 – PRESENT	Ozaukee Bank National Assoc. MAY 7, 1975 – SEPTEMBER 6, 2008

32 Units of M&I ACQUIRED BETWEEN 1987 – 2001	Century Bank National Assoc. DECEMBER 31, 1990 – JUNE 1, 2002	Excel Bank Minnesota JANUARY 25, 1965 – AUGUST 1, 2007	First Indiana Bank National Assoc. JULY 1, 1934 – FEBRUARY 2, 2008	Gold Bank OCTOBER 7, 1889 – APRIL 3, 2006	Heritage Bank DECEMBER 13, 1971 – DECEMBER 1, 1985

Milwaukee County Bank AUGUST 15, 1925 – JANUARY 1, 1985	National City Bank of Minneapolis APRIL 6, 1964 – NOVEMBER 1, 2001	Richfield Bank & Trust Co. FEBRUARY 3, 1947 – JUNE 1, 2002	Security Bank S.S.B. JANUARY 1, 1913 – OCTOBER 1, 1997	Southwest Bank an M&I Bank JUNE 20, 1920 – JULY 1, 2010	Southwest Bank of Phoenix DECEMBER 27, 2000 – FEBRUARY 1, 2003	United Heritage Bank MARCH 15, 2001 – JUNE 27, 2007

Valley Bank DECEMBER 28, 1910 – AUGUST 1, 1994

Mercantile National Bank of Indiana DECEMBER 12, 1932 – AUGUST, 26 2006

Industrial National Bank of East Chicago DECEMBER 18, 1978 – APRIL 3, 1986	Merrillville Bank and Trust Co. JULY 13, 1976 – MAY 29, 1984

BMO Financial

Bank *(abridged)*

RANK	HEADQUARTERS	TICKER	ASSETS	EARLIEST KNOWN ANCESTOR	INDUSTRY OF ORIGIN
26	**Wilmington, DE**	**BMO**	**$112,000,000,000**	**1817**	**Commercial Banking**

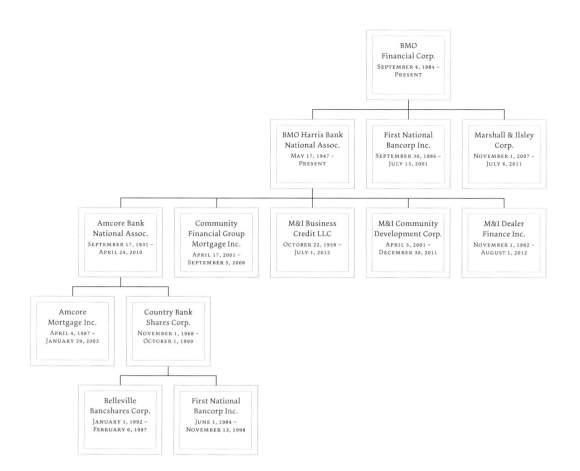

BMO Financial Holding Company *(abridged)*

Donald A. Smith driving in the final iron spike of the Canadian Pacific Railway at Craigellachie, British Columbia, west of the Eagle Pass, November 7, 1885.

BMO Financial is the American wing of Canada's storied Bank of Montreal, the core of BMO Financial Group, now headquartered in Toronto. Nine Montreal merchants formed the Bank of Montreal in 1817 to supply Canadians with credit, but also cash (bank notes and deposits) that would not flee the country as readily as gold and silver coins. Initially capitalized at $1 million (£CA250,000) and staffed by seven employees, the bank was owned and operated not by French-speaking Quebecois but by Scots, who had quite the reputation for banking prowess back then.

The bank, which received a royal charter in 1822, soon established branches but dealt mostly with Anglos, like brewer John Molson, an original stockholder who also became its president. In addition to supplying its communities with domestic media of exchange, the bank made loans to businesses and large projects, like the canal built around the Lachine Rapids. It also provided currency exchange within Canada — which was not yet a unified nation with a single currency — and between Montreal, New York and London.

During the US Civil War and following the independence and confederation of Canada in the 1860s and 1870s, the Bank of Montreal under the leadership of E.H. King grew quickly and profitably. It did this in part by cementing its relationship to the provincial, national and imperial governments; in part by attracting US deposits and other business; and in part by out competing numerous new rivals, many of which ended up as Bank of Montreal branches.

Even during the recession that followed the Panic of 1873, it was able to pay dividends that averaged nearly 12%. Its expansion slowed, however, until the great boom on the western plains in the early 1880s temporarily raised land prices in Winnipeg above those of Toronto and Montreal. The opening of the Canadian Pacific Railway in 1886 revived Canada's amazing growth story, and the bank's as well. Panics and wars, always of foreign origin, interceded thereafter but never hurt the economy for long. The bank stood by to acquire the pieces of any smaller banks that failed along the way. By 1900 it had 48 branches "at important or promising points" throughout the country. Boosters referred to it as "The Greatest Bank in America" because its $CA12 million in paid-up capital was the largest of any bank on the continent.

Just five years later, the bank had 100 branches, thanks to its acquisition of the People's Bank of Halifax and the Ontario Bank. In its centenary history, the Bank of Montreal was described as "the oldest bank in British North America and one of the largest in the British Empire." Indeed, with a paid-up capital of $CA16 million and deposits in excess of $CA300 million, before the end of the Great War the bank was one of Canada's "Big Six." Together, the Big Six banks accounted for over 95% of Canada's total banking market. Between 1917 and 1920, the bank's branch count exploded from 182 to 319, thanks in large part to the acquisition of the Bank of British North America. In 1920 it moved overseas in a big way by purchasing a 60% stake in the Colonial Bank, which operated largely in the West Indies and West Africa.

When the war and postwar commodities boom went bust in 1920, wheat prices plummeted from $CA2.85 to $CA1.80 a bushel on the Winnipeg Grain Exchange. Wages dipped 15%, unemployment hit 6% and labor unrest cost the economy 3.4 million work days. The bank also came under fire from discontents, but its leaders retorted that it had "maintained to the limit of prudence" its "policy of carrying deserving customers in difficult times." Its war profits, some said, had gone to employee bonuses and strengthening the bank's capital cushion. But the Bank of Montreal pushed on, picking up the Merchants Bank of Canada in 1921. Established in 1861, Merchants had over 400 branches spread from the Maritimes in the east to Vancouver Island in the west. About one in six were shuttered soon after the acquisition. The Merchants Bank had made some dangerously large loans, but its total assets of $CA190 million, a capital and surplus of almost $CA20 million and a strong dividend record more than compensated.

With the Merchants Bank acquisition, Canada was down to just 17 increasingly large chartered banks, raising the specter of a "money trust" controlling the nation's finances. In public hearings, the Bank of Montreal suggested that farmers who wanted long-term mortgages should create mutual corporations for that purpose and not endanger the country's entire credit structure. In 1925, however, the bank merged with Molsons Bank (which had been chartered in 1855, though it had been in business long before that), mostly to help barley and other grain farmers who supplied Molson breweries and distilleries. It paid 12% dividends until the bust of 1920, when it found itself overextended. Always on friendly terms with the Bank of Montreal, Molsons Bank naturally turned to it for relief.

In the latter half of the 1920s, the Canadian economy boomed due in part to a flood of American physical and financial capital. The Bank of Montreal went along for the ride, adding $CA1 million to surplus in 1927 while paying the usual 12% dividend and an additional 2% bonus. When the stock market broke in 1929, therefore, the bank, which by then had an authorized capital of $CA50 million and assets of nearly $CA1 billion, was in a strong financial position made stronger by its early realization that "the rise in prices cannot go on forever and . . . there is a well-defined limit to bank loans on stocks."

The bank's assets shrank 20% away from the billion mark because commercial borrowing plummeted as the Depression deepened in the early 1930s. It remained profitable, however, paying the usual 12% dividend without strain or accounting legerdemain, by shifting its resources into long-term government bonds and cutting its branch network back from 669 in 1929 to 567 by 1934. It also shuttered its branches in Mexico and Paris and sold its stake in Colonial (since renamed Barclays after several mergers).

Although unemployment and want increased substantially during the Great Depression, Canada suffered no bank runs, failures or holidays. (Unlike bank failures, branch closings imposed no losses on note holders or depositors, although it did make banking less convenient for those who resided near shuttered branches.) Nevertheless, in 1934 the country finally formed a central bank, the Bank of Canada. Thus ended the Bank of Montreal's close connection to the government in Ottawa, as well as its right to issue notes.

The Bank of Montreal did not reel from the losses, however, because the Canadian economy was already rebounding from the depths of the

Depression and would soon flourish during World War II, the Korean War and the long and unprecedented prosperity of the 1950s and 1960s. The bank's assets finally hit the billion mark in 1939. They reached $CA2 billion a decade later and $CA3 billion nine years after that. The number of branches also rebounded after declining to 468 in 1943 because of the war, and grew annually from between nine and 49 branches. The thousandth branch opened in 1966 in Sussex, New Brunswick, by which time the bank had more than three million customers, 8,000 employees and assets over $CA5 billion. Its $CA10 par value shares traded for $CA56 each in 1967.

After the war, the Bank of Montreal expanded overseas again, via a joint partnership called the Bank of London and Montreal, Limited (BOLAM). By the end of 1966 BOLAM had 37 offices in 10 Latin American nations. South of the border, BMO had enjoyed a small US presence since the 1920s with a subsidiary called the "Bank of Montreal (San Francisco)" or, after 1962, "Bank of Montreal (California)." It also had a branch in Chicago that it closed in 1952 after it ran afoul of Illinois's branching restrictions. And, of course, it had operations in New York, especially in the Eurodollar market. The Bank of Montreal was not the first in Canada to install computers, but in 1963 it became the first to introduce integrated check clearing and ledger posting operations.

Canada's banking system remained stable through it all, with the Big Six competing strongly, but not fiercely, with each other. In the 1980s, however, deregulation shook the old establishment by allowing banks to expand into new areas of finance, including insurance, investment banking and trust services. The Big Six felt compelled to oblige lest they be overshadowed, and eventually acquired, by the emerging megabanks in the United States, Britain and continental Europe.

By 1990 BMO was struggling to adapt to the rapidly changing financial scene in Canada, the United States and many other countries. Although its finances remained fundamentally sound, it posted a loss and morale plummeted. According to James Logan, an employee in BMO's electronic banking services department, the bank had to transform itself "away from a traditional, patriarchal bureaucracy and toward a culture of learning" in order to survive.

Central to its transformation was a long-term strategic plan called Vision 2002. Among other reforms, Vision 2002 established the Institute for Learning (IFL), a $CA50 million residential learning facility that opened in 1994. The IFL tripled the bank's existing training and education programs and extended them with a flexible, competency-based framework for skill development. In other words, BMO began to invest heavily and intelligently in its human capital, especially the thinking capacity of its employees, so that it could respond to challenges more quickly and with greater flexibility and innovation. Vision 2002 and the IFL paid off. By the late 1990s BMO had more than 34,000 employees spread over numerous branches throughout Canada and BMO's sundry subsidiaries. It controlled more than $CA200 billion in assets, including Harris Bank in the midwestern United States and a 16% interest in Mexico's then second largest bank, Group Financiero Bancomer.

BMO stumbled in 1998, however, when it agreed to a merger with Royal Bank of Canada, the largest of the Big Six, before obtaining the necessary clearance. Minister of Finance Paul Martin and Prime Minister Jean Chrétien quickly blocked the deal.

In 2006 BMO Capital Markets, a subsidiary that offered a full range of wholesale banking services, including advice, brokerage, research, risk management and trading, had 26 offices across the globe, including one in Chicago and another in New York. The US offices focused on the middle of the market, corporations with $CA250 million to $CA1 billion in sales. It was known for "good research" and occasionally

THE · MOLSONS · BANK

THE·MOLSONS·BANK

Molsons Bank branch in Thunder Bay, Ontario.

landed a big name client, but it generally did not make much of a showing in the investment banking league tables. The culture was friendly, meritocratic and team-oriented, insiders claimed, with "big egos" as rare as a Canadian suntan beach. With Harris Bank still not much of a property, BMO in 2010 paid $4.1 billion for Marshall & Ilsley of Milwaukee (M&I), which gave it 688 US branches. This was a big boost, but only half that of rival TD Bank (#14).

Sources

Centenary of the Bank of Montreal, 1817–1917. Montreal: Bank of Montreal, 1917.

Denison, Merrill. *Canada's First Bank: A History of the Bank of Montreal* 2 vols. Montreal: McClelland and Stewart, 1966.

Logan, James. "Cultivating Competence to Sustain Competitive Advantage: The Bank of Montreal." In *The Bases of Competence: Skills for Lifelong Learning and Employability*, edited by Frederick T. Evers, James C. Rush, and Iris Berdow, 229–38. San Francisco: Jossey-Bass, 1998.

Loosvelt, Derek, et al. *The Vault Guide to the Top 50 Banking Employers: 2008 Edition*. New York: Vault, 2007, 310–14.

Oxley, J. Macdonald. "The Greatest Bank in America." *The Canadian Magazine* 16, 2 (December 1900): 99–112.

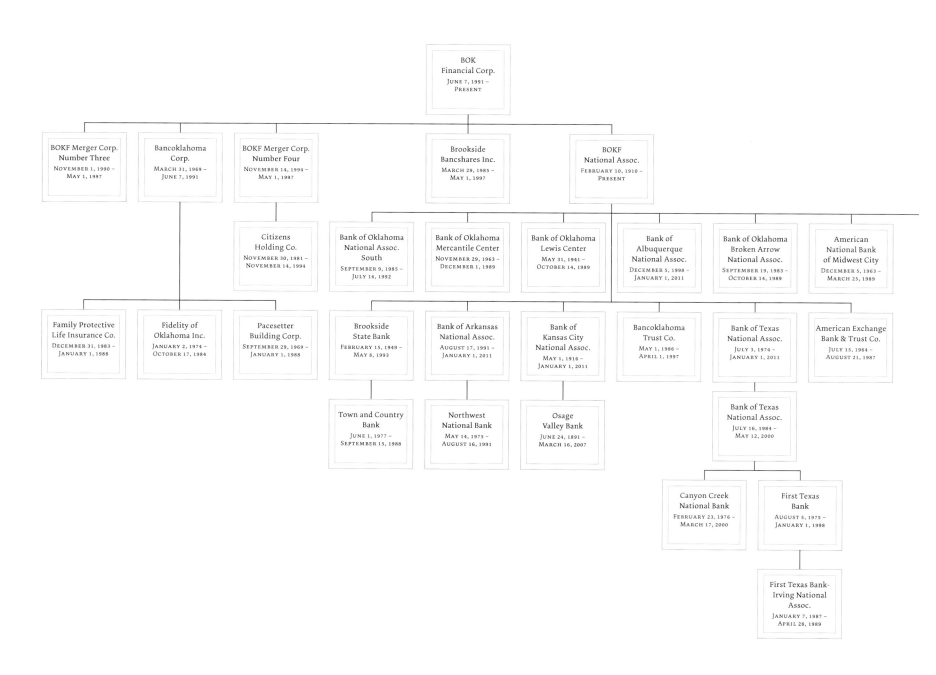

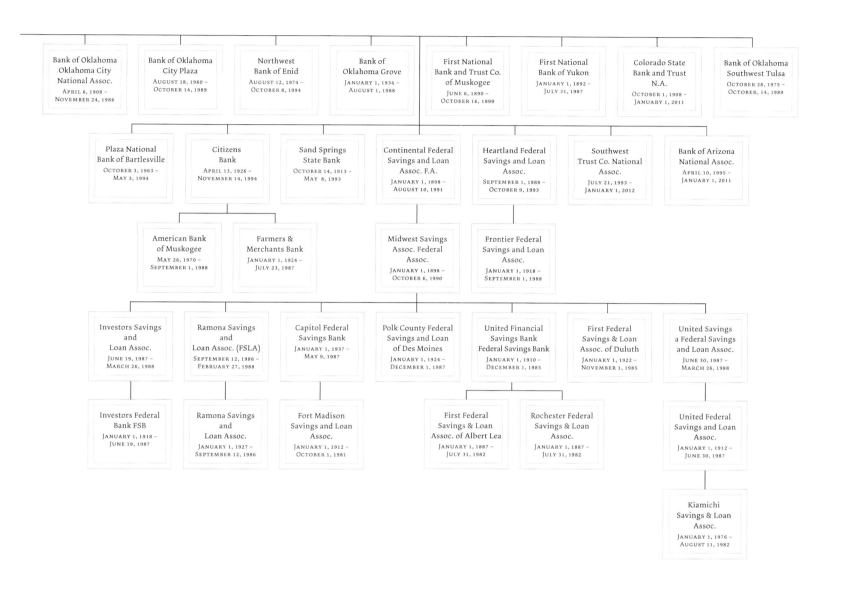

BOK Financial

RANK	HEADQUARTERS	TICKER	ASSETS	EARLIEST KNOWN ANCESTOR	INDUSTRY OF ORIGIN
48	Tulsa, OK	BOK	$28,000,000,000	1887	Commercial Banking

While it may sound like a Southeast Asian bank, BOK is actually the BHC of the Bank of Oklahoma. The bank, which came into being in 1910 as the Exchange National Bank of Tulsa, was initially forged from the remnants of the failed Farmers National Bank. It thrived as the "leading oil bank" in the country, but one of its early investors and president, Harry F. Sinclair, was implicated in the Teapot Dome Scandal and served six months for jury tampering. During the Great Depression, the bank needed a cash infusion from several Tulsa oil magnates to stay afloat, but it had to reorganize in 1933 anyway (as the National Bank of Tulsa) with the aid of $4 million from the Reconstruction Finance Corporation.

The bank changed its name to the Bank of Oklahoma in 1975 and thrived as oil prices soared. But by 1986 it was experiencing credit quality difficulties as a result of a prolonged slump in oil prices and bad loans it picked up in its 1984 acquisition of Fidelity Bank of Oklahoma City. "By planning on the basis of a worst case on each loan," Chairman Gerald R. Marshall told a local newspaper in May 1986, "we feel our chances are that Bank of Oklahoma not only will survive, but will make money in the future." Later that year the bank was granted a rare "open bank" assistance package by the FDIC, which enabled it to remain open under the same leadership instead of going into receivership. In 1990 Tulsa oilman George B. Kaiser bought out the FDIC's stake in the bank for $61 million.

Under Kaiser, the bank expanded aggressively into growing markets near Oklahoma. By 1991 it was again profitable and lauded as an example of how "the entrepreneurial spirit is alive and well in banking." But Kaiser kept pushing, buying the 19 branches of Sooner Federal in 1992, as well as numerous other acquisitions. The following year it returned to the credit card business, which it had sold to Norwest (now part of #4) in 1988 to raise capital. It also began expanding organically with de novo branch openings and new products like mutual funds.

The bank moved into Arkansas in 1994 by purchasing Citizens Holding of Muskogee, which had acquired a failed three-branch Arkansas bank in 1991. In 1996 its CEO, Stanley Lybarger, announced that the bank was looking for a merger of equals, or a slew of small prey, in order to dilute Kaiser's 79% stake in the institution. Only the latter came to pass. By 1997, when it acquired the First Texas Bank of Dallas, an institution owned by African Americans including legendary country and western singer Charlie Pride, BOK had assets of $5 billion.

By 2007 BOK Financial had branch networks in nine states including Arizona, Arkansas, Colorado, Kansas and Utah, and Moody's upgraded its credit rating to A-1 Stable Outlook from A-3 on the strength of 17 straight years of record earnings. The bank remained cautious, however, cutting a few hundred jobs and warning that 2008 would be difficult for banks. It also scaled back on acquisitions and de novo branch formation, which had hit 15 in 2007. BOK suffered little during the ensuing fiasco because it had relatively little to no exposure to credit cards, commercial real estate, home equity or subprime mortgage loans. It also operated in states little affected by the housing bubble.

In May 2009 Lybarger somewhat ironically told an audience at the University of Tulsa that weak financial institutions should have been allowed to fail and not been bailed out by taxpayers. Not surprisingly, BOK was one of the few big banks not to accept TARP funds. By early 2010, as the economy improved somewhat, the bank was ready to resume its disciplined growth and record profit streak.

"Through all of this," Lybarger said in 2012, "BOK Financial remained focused and proactive. While competition retrenched, in many ways we continued to invest and expand. We moved forward with a clear strategy for success, despite the substantial challenges posed by the new regulatory environment and slow economic recovery." Lybarger, who began in the bank's management training program in 1974, relinquished control of BOK at the end of 2013. A $10,000 investment in the bank in 1991, after it emerged from the FDIC's control, was worth about $170,000 by early 2013.

Sources

"Bank of Oklahoma Ratings Upgraded." *Oklahoma City Journal Record*, March 13, 2007, 1.

Caliendo, Heather. "BOK Financial President: Bailouts Will Increase Duration of Recession." *Oklahoma City Journal Record*, May 13, 2009.

"Company Watch: Bank of Oklahoma: A Lesson in Lifesaving." *Financial World* 160, 19 (September 17, 1991): 16.

Chase, Brett. "BOK Financial on the Lookout for a Partner or Small Prey." *American Banker*, May 8, 1996, 5.

Davis, Kirby Lee. "Lybarger Leaving His Mark: Tulsa-Based BOK Financial Executive to Step Down." *Oklahoma City Journal Record*, April 30, 2013.

———. "Okla.-Based BOK Financial Foresees Slower, More Cautious Growth." *Oklahoma City Journal Record*, February 12, 2008, 1.

———. "Okla.-based BOK Financial Seeks to Renew Record Run." *Oklahoma City Journal Record*, April 27, 2010.

———. "Tulsa-based BOK Financial Outlines Growth Model Behind Its Industry-Leading Performance." *Oklahoma City Journal Record*, April 24, 2012.

"Defends Sinclair as a 'Wronged Man': Former Senator Owen, in a Pamphlet, Calls Oil Operator a Victim of Circumstances." *The New York Times*, April 2, 1930, 14.

Gite, Lloyd. "The 'Pride' of Dallas No More: First Texas Bank of Dallas Sold to BOK Financial." *Black Enterprise* 27, 12 (July 1997): 20.

Henriques, Diana B. "Did Kaiser or FDIC Get Lucky on Bank of Oklahoma Sale?" *Oklahoma City Journal Record*, November 13, 1990.

Kepfield, Mindy. "Bank of Oklahoma Enters Arkansas Through Merger." *Oklahoma City Journal Record*, November 15, 1994.

Nichols, Max. "Bank of Oklahoma Used 'Worst Case' Scenario to Assess Loans." *Oklahoma City Journal Record*, May 10, 1986.

"Oklahoma Banks Closed: State Concern Forced to the Wall by Failure of National Bank." *The New York Times*, December 15, 1909, 9.

"R.F.C. Has Subscribed $4,000,000 in Stock, Matching $4,000,000." *The New York Times*, April 25, 1933, 27.

"R. P. Brewer Dies; New York Banker Succumbs to Long Illness in Tulsa, Okla., Where He Had Won Success." *The New York Times*, June 15, 1933, 17.

Stewart, Jackie. "Profits Up, Stocks Down at BOK Financial." *American Banker*, February 2, 2012.

Titus, Nancy Raiden. "Acquisition Fits Bank of Oklahoma's Aggressive Growth." *Oklahoma City Journal Record*, August 12, 1992.

———. "Bank of Oklahoma Returns to Credit Card Business." *Oklahoma City Journal Record*, July 17, 1993.

4A-H301

Postcard featuring the National Bank of Tulsa building.

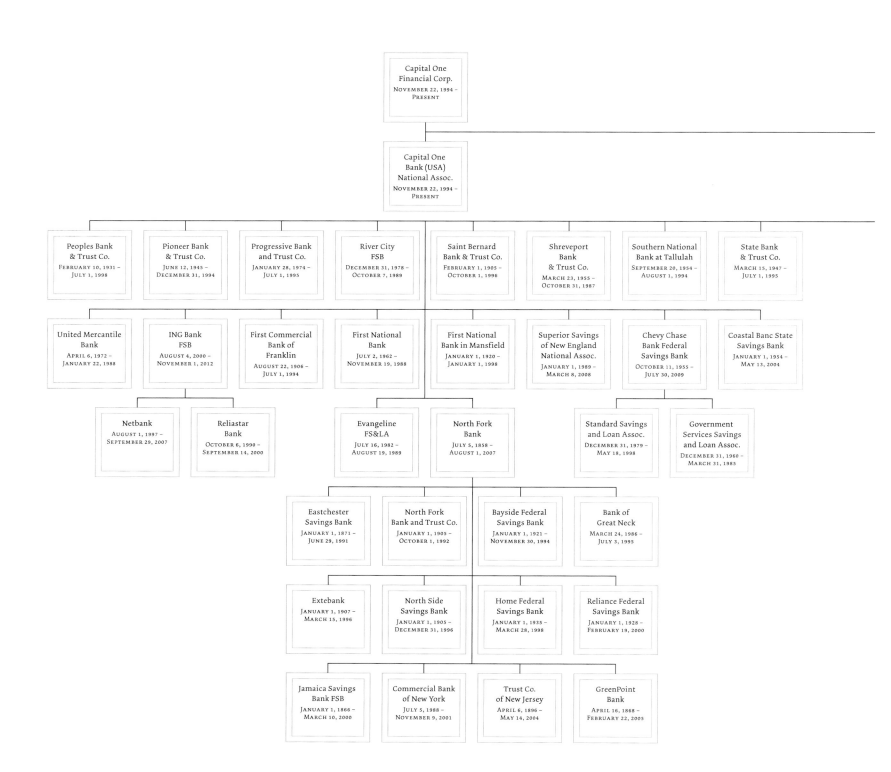

Capital One
Financial Corp.
NOVEMBER 22, 1994 –
PRESENT

Capital One
Bank (USA)
National Assoc.
NOVEMBER 22, 1994 –
PRESENT

Peoples Bank
& Trust Co.
FEBRUARY 10, 1931 –
JULY 1, 1998

Pioneer Bank
& Trust Co.
JUNE 12, 1945 –
DECEMBER 31, 1994

Progressive Bank
and Trust Co.
JANUARY 28, 1974 –
JULY 1, 1995

River City
FSB
DECEMBER 31, 1978 –
OCTOBER 7, 1989

Saint Bernard
Bank & Trust Co.
FEBRUARY 1, 1905 –
OCTOBER 1, 1996

Shreveport
Bank
& Trust Co.
MARCH 23, 1955 –
OCTOBER 31, 1987

Southern National
Bank at Tallulah
SEPTEMBER 20, 1954 –
AUGUST 1, 1994

State Bank
& Trust Co.
MARCH 15, 1947 –
JULY 1, 1995

United Mercantile
Bank
APRIL 6, 1972 –
JANUARY 22, 1988

ING Bank
FSB
AUGUST 4, 2000 –
NOVEMBER 1, 2012

First Commercial
Bank of
Franklin
AUGUST 22, 1906 –
JULY 1, 1994

First National
Bank
JULY 2, 1962 –
NOVEMBER 19, 1988

First National
Bank in Mansfield
JANUARY 1, 1920 –
JANUARY 1, 1998

Superior Savings
of New England
National Assoc.
JANUARY 1, 1989 –
MARCH 8, 2008

Chevy Chase
Bank Federal
Savings Bank
OCTOBER 11, 1955 –
JULY 30, 2009

Coastal Banc State
Savings Bank
JANUARY 1, 1954 –
MAY 13, 2004

Netbank
AUGUST 1, 1997 –
SEPTEMBER 29, 2007

Reliastar
Bank
OCTOBER 6, 1990 –
SEPTEMBER 14, 2000

Evangeline
FS&LA
JULY 16, 1982 –
AUGUST 19, 1989

North Fork
Bank
JULY 5, 1858 –
AUGUST 1, 2007

Standard Savings
and Loan Assoc.
DECEMBER 31, 1979 –
MAY 18, 1998

Government
Services Savings
and Loan Assoc.
DECEMBER 31, 1960 –
MARCH 31, 1985

Eastchester
Savings Bank
JANUARY 1, 1871 –
JUNE 29, 1991

North Fork
Bank and Trust Co.
JANUARY 1, 1905 –
OCTOBER 1, 1992

Bayside Federal
Savings Bank
JANUARY 1, 1921 –
NOVEMBER 30, 1994

Bank of
Great Neck
MARCH 24, 1986 –
JULY 3, 1995

Extebank
JANUARY 1, 1907 –
MARCH 15, 1996

North Side
Savings Bank
JANUARY 1, 1905 –
DECEMBER 31, 1996

Home Federal
Savings Bank
JANUARY 1, 1935 –
MARCH 28, 1998

Reliance Federal
Savings Bank
JANUARY 1, 1928 –
FEBRUARY 19, 2000

Jamaica Savings
Bank FSB
JANUARY 1, 1866 –
MARCH 10, 2000

Commercial Bank
of New York
JULY 5, 1988 –
NOVEMBER 9, 2001

Trust Co.
of New Jersey
APRIL 6, 1896 –
MAY 14, 2004

GreenPoint
Bank
APRIL 16, 1868 –
FEBRUARY 22, 2005

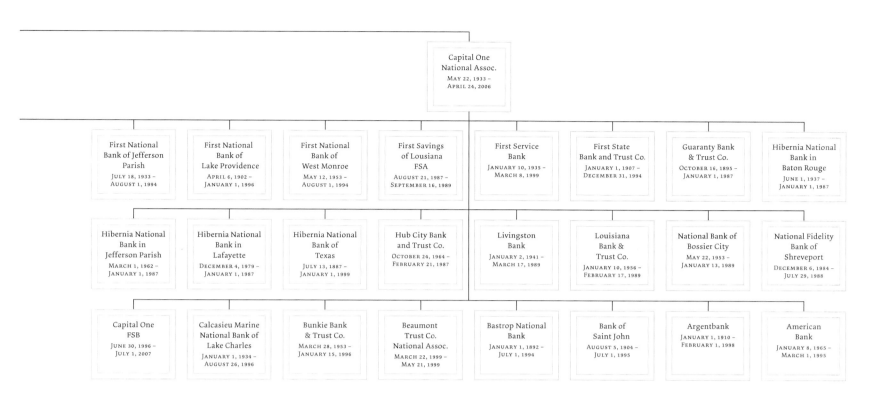

Capital One Financial

Bank *(abridged)*

RANK	HEADQUARTERS	TICKER	ASSETS	EARLIEST KNOWN ANCESTOR	INDUSTRY OF ORIGIN
13	McLean, VA	COF	$297,000,000,000	1858	Credit Cards

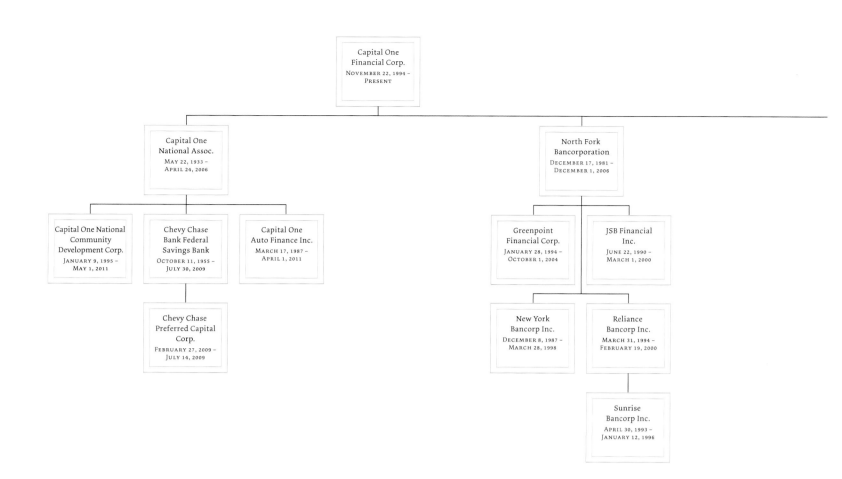

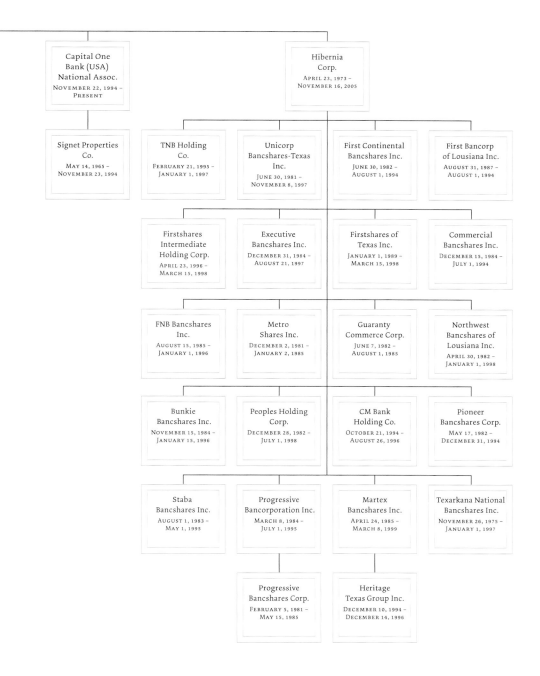

Capital One Bank (USA) National Assoc.
NOVEMBER 22, 1994 – PRESENT

Hibernia Corp.
APRIL 23, 1973 – NOVEMBER 16, 2005

Signet Properties Co.
MAY 14, 1965 – NOVEMBER 23, 1994

TNB Holding Co.
FEBRUARY 21, 1995 – JANUARY 1, 1997

Unicorp Bancshares-Texas Inc.
JUNE 30, 1981 – NOVEMBER 8, 1997

First Continental Bancshares Inc.
JUNE 30, 1982 – AUGUST 1, 1994

First Bancorp of Lousiana Inc.
AUGUST 31, 1987 – AUGUST 1, 1994

Firstshares Intermediate Holding Corp.
APRIL 23, 1996 – MARCH 15, 1998

Executive Bancshares Inc.
DECEMBER 31, 1984 – AUGUST 21, 1997

Firstshares of Texas Inc.
JANUARY 1, 1989 – MARCH 15, 1998

Commercial Bancshares Inc.
DECEMBER 15, 1984 – JULY 1, 1994

FNB Bancshares Inc.
AUGUST 15, 1985 – JANUARY 1, 1996

Metro Shares Inc.
DECEMBER 2, 1981 – JANUARY 2, 1985

Guaranty Commerce Corp.
JUNE 7, 1982 – AUGUST 1, 1985

Northwest Bancshares of Lousiana Inc.
APRIL 30, 1982 – JANUARY 1, 1998

Bunkie Bancshares Inc.
NOVEMBER 15, 1984 – JANUARY 15, 1996

Peoples Holding Corp.
DECEMBER 28, 1982 – JULY 1, 1998

CM Bank Holding Co.
OCTOBER 21, 1994 – AUGUST 26, 1996

Pioneer Bancshares Corp.
MAY 17, 1982 – DECEMBER 31, 1994

Staba Bancshares Inc.
AUGUST 1, 1983 – MAY 1, 1995

Progressive Bancorporation Inc.
MARCH 8, 1984 – JULY 1, 1995

Martex Bancshares Inc.
APRIL 24, 1985 – MARCH 8, 1999

Texarkana National Bancshares Inc.
NOVEMBER 26, 1975 – JANUARY 1, 1997

Progressive Bancshares Corp.
FEBRUARY 5, 1981 – MAY 15, 1985

Heritage Texas Group Inc.
DECEMBER 10, 1994 – DECEMBER 14, 1996

Capital One Financial

Holding Company *(abridged)*

Hibernia Bank Building, New Orleans, La.

Postcard featuring the Hibernia National Bank building in New Orleans.

Postcard featuring a photograph of the North Fork Bank building, ca. 1949.

Capital One is a credit card issuer most famous for a series of television advertisements in which sundry barbarians behaving poorly ask, "What's in your wallet?" In Capital One's wallet were some tremendous assets: 50 million credit cardholders, mortgage services, auto and healthcare finance, some consumer banking and a short but solid history of innovation. In addition to its disconcertingly unique TV commercials, over the years Capital One's diverse, hard-working, creative employees have identified and exploited many new market niches for plastic credit, including prepaid cards, subprime cards and cards for people with special interests and affiliations. Its stock price reflected its precocity, increasing more than 1,000% between its IPO and the market crash that began in March 2000 (over which span the S&P grew about 300%).

According to Harvard Business School research associate Christopher H. Paige, Capital One achieved early success because of its information-based strategy, or IBS, which allowed it to cheaply deliver to its customers a seeming oxymoron: "mass customization." CEO Richard Fairbank summarized the strategy as "the right product to the right customer at the right time for the right price." Working as a consultant to a major bank in the 1980s, Fairbank realized that most credit card issuers were unfamiliar with the ability to use increasingly inexpensive computer technology to tailor their products precisely to individual needs. In 1998 he found Signet (now part of #4), a small regional bank based in Richmond, Virginia, willing to give his ideas a try. Disaster preceded success, as Signet's charge-off rate increased from 2%, one of the credit card industry's best, to 6%, one of its worst. More troubling, Signet's mortgage portfolio suffered big losses that almost killed the bank.

In 1991, however, Fairbank hit pay dirt by introducing the balance transfer, an easy mechanism for debt-ridden consumers to consolidate their credit card debt. Luring customers in with a low "teaser" rate, Signet's customer base grew so fast that at one point in 1992 it hired 100 people in a week simply to handle balance transfers. Signet's stock exploded; it was the best performer on the NYSE until Signet spun off Capital One, which by then produced two-thirds of Signet's total revenue, in a $1.1 billion IPO in 1994. (Three years later, Signet joined First Union for $3.3 billion.) Fairbank became chairman and CEO.

Fairbank and COO Nigel Morris were all about constructing and testing scientific models used to assess creditworthiness and product offerings. A culture of science and testing became critical to the bank and extended even to the point of allowing employees to criticize the CEO when the data did not support his pet projects.

Postcard showing the safe deposit department of the Hibernia National Bank in New Orleans, Louisiana.

Capital One was economically astute, too, realizing that people who accepted their offers straight away were the worst risks (because of adverse selection) and adapted its marketing strategies accordingly. To figure out which strategies to pursue, it conducted controlled experiments, with sample sizes ranging from 1,000 to 50,000, to test competing hypotheses without risking much capital. Such experiments were not unusual events; the company performed 36,000 tests in 1999 alone. From the results of such experiments, Capital One could keep the most profitable customers by instantaneously offering them superior terms when they called to cancel while allowing less profitable customers to leave if they did not like their current terms.

Capital One's experiments also allowed it to make rapid decisions about which innovations worked and which did not. "Often, when competitors are getting into products," Fairbanks once bragged, "we are getting out." Such rapid responsiveness required a new type of organization, one in which IT personnel, marketers and customer service representatives (CSRs) worked closely with each other in real time. Cross-functional teams continuously formed and disbanded as circumstances dictated. Rapid response also required massive investment in new technology and training, including training for in-house programmers that cost $100 million in 1997 alone. By the time the Y2K threat loomed, Capital One had 23 terabytes of proprietary data, or about 40 single-spaced pages per American.

Capital One also experimented with its own CSRs so that it could tailor their incentive plans and training. That gave it one of the lowest turnover rates in the industry and also allowed its computers to route customers to the CSRs best equipped to help them. Not surprisingly, the company was also a careful recruiter. "Most companies spend 2% of their time recruiting and half their time managing their recruiting mistakes," Fairbank claimed, but Capital One did "the exact opposite." Through 1997, Morris or Fairbank individually interviewed every candidate for business analyst. When the pace of hiring grew more frantic in 1998, they met with candidates in groups of two or three and actively sought management consulting firm types, not bankers. But even here they relied on quantitative measures, including standardized tests taken by previous applicants, to help them find the best matches.

From its inception, Capital One envisioned itself as an information company, not a credit card issuer. Its credit card experience translated most easily to the credit card businesses of other countries, and it first entered the UK in 1996, and then expanded to Canada, France, South Africa and elsewhere. It also early considered auto insurance, but ultimately did not make a move because the industry was so competitive. State regulators also proved nettlesome for a company that prided itself on innovation. "We don't like any business," Fairchild explained, "where regulation inhibits the freedom to test and mass-customize."

Capital One also did not like what it saw in auto finance, where dealers had first crack at customers, leaving only the undesirable crumbs behind. Nevertheless, in 1998 Capital One decided to test the waters by purchasing Summit Acceptance Corporation, a subprime auto financing company that operated in 26 states. Analysts expressed concerns, but it worked well enough that a few years later Capital One bought the superprime online automobile finance lender PeopleFirst Inc. Three years after that, in 2004, it acquired Onyx Acceptance Corp., a California-based prime and near-prime auto lender.

In 1999 Capital One realized that innovative as it was, others were also coming up with creative ideas. It, therefore, established North Hill Ventures, a venture capital arm designed to help start-ups doing "things at the edges that Capital One would normally do." Early in the new millennium, Capital One bought some traditional banks, like Hibernia of New Orleans and North Fork, a bank with $60 billion of assets and operations in New York, New Jersey and Connecticut, to fund its credit card operations with cheap bank deposits. Although purchased soon after Hurricane Katrina, Hibernia burnished the company's earnings, which were down as a result of a rise in credit card charge-offs associated with the pending change in federal personal bankruptcy laws. The North Fork acquisition brought with it exposure to the home mortgage market, something that worried Capital One even in early 2006 when the deal was struck. Analysts, however, noted that the move greatly diversified the company's revenue base and did not add much to expenses, as North Fork's efficiency ratio was an amazing 41.17%. In 2005 Capital One was ranked number one in the *InformationWeek* 500, and with little wonder as its financials surged ever upward. In 2006 Fairbank won the "Banker of the Year" award from *American Banker*.

The company, which in 2007 operated about 720 branches in Louisiana, the Northeast and Texas, felt bloated, so it cut 2,000 of its 33,000 employees as part of a $700 million restructuring. Later in the year it eliminated another 1,900 jobs when it shuttered GreenPoint Mortgage Funding, which had come to it as part of the North Fork deal. By the end of 2007 both its stock price and credit rating had sunk. Its relatively light exposure to the mortgage market, however, saved the company during the 2008 financial crisis and the ensuing recession. It incurred losses, but nothing compared to the biggest LCFIs. It was in good enough shape to buy Chevy Chase Bank of Maryland and its 244 branches in the Washington, DC, area for $520 million in December 2008.

Capital One received $3.57 billion in TARP funds, which it promptly repaid after passing regulatory "stress tests," but bears and poor financials kept its stock price down well into 2010. As Fairbank told the *Wall Street Journal*, a "striking" lack of demand for credit persisted as consumers played it safe in the wake of the worst financial disaster since the Great Depression.

By 2011 profits were again on the rise, and the company was again in acquisition mode, purchasing Internet bank ING Direct USA and HSBC's (#11) $30 billion US credit card business. The ING deal attracted considerable attention from regulators, who finally consented. The company also took a hard look at E*Trade (#40), but ultimately decided to pass. The HSBC deal brought Capital One into Sioux Falls, South Dakota, the credit card mecca of the country, where it quickly doubled its workforce. In 2013, with credit card loan growth flat, the company announced a $1 billion stock buy-back plan while also buying Beech Street Capital, an upstart multifamily (apartment building) mortgage lender that caught its attention.

Sources

Barba, Robert. "Capital One to Go Slow in Absorbing Niche Lender Beech." *American Banker*, August 20, 2013.

Bergquist, Erick. "Big Players Stepping Up Activity in Auto Loans; Capital One, HBOS. Act as Credit Outlook Improves in Segment." *American Banker*, September 23, 2004, 1.

"Capital One to Buy HSBC Unit." *Investor's Business Daily*, August 11, 2001, A2.

Davis, Paul. "Capital One Chief Named 2006 Banker of the Year." *American Banker*, September 26, 2006, 2.

———. "Capital One's 'Endgame' Acquisition." *American Banker*, March 14, 2006, 1.

———. "Capital One Shuts GreenPoint, Citing Mortgage Turmoil." *American Banker*, August 21, 2007, 20.

Eavis, Peter. "The Warning Shot from Capital One." *Wall Street Journal Online*, January 24, 2010.

Fitzpatrick, Dan. "Capital One to Acquire Chevy Chase Bank." *Wall Street Journal*, December 4, 2008, C10.

Gilford, Sam. "Capital One Brings 400 New Jobs to South Dakota." *Targeted News Service*, May 2, 2012.

Hansell, Saul. "First Union Is Set to Buy Signet Bank." *The New York Times*, July 21, 1997.

Heath, Thomas. "Capital One to Cut Staff by 6%: Layoffs to Reduce Operating Expenses $700 Million." *Washington Post*, June 28, 2007, D4.

Lee, W.A. "In Focus: Will Auto Loan Pitch Work for Capital One?" *American Banker*, March 15, 2002, 1.

Marlin, Steven. "What's In Capital One's Wallet?" *InformationWeek*, September 19, 2005, 45–47, 49.

Merle, Ranae. "Capital One to Acquire ING Arm." *Washington Post*, June 17, 2011, A14.

O'Hara, Terence. "Hibernia Helped Capital One Profit Grow: McLean Parent Expects New Orleans Bank to Feel Effects of Hurricanes for Years." *Washington Post*, January 20, 2006, D4.

Paige, Christopher H. "Capital One Financial Corporation." Harvard Business School Case 9–700–124. Revised May 2, 2001.

Philbin, Brett, Matthias Rieker and Gina Chon. "How E*Trade Irked Citadel: Capital One Talks Fizzled, Upsetting the Hedge Fund." *Wall Street Journal*, July 20, 2011, B2.

Rieker, Matthias. "Capital One Avoided a Big Mess." *Wall Street Journal*, September 10, 2008, B5.

Wetfeet. *25 Top Financial Services Firms*. San Francisco: Wetfeet. 2008, 25–27.

North Fork Bancorporation stock certificate.

CAPITAL STOCK

SEE REVERSE FOR
CERTAIN DEFINITIONS

SEE REVERSE FOR LEGEND

SHARES

INCORPORATED UNDER THE LAWS
OF THE STATE OF DELAWARE

NORTH FORK BANCORPORATION, INC.

IES THAT

CUSIP 659424 10 5

ER OF

SHARES OF THE CAPITAL STOCK OF THE PAR VALUE OF $2.50 EACH OF

Fork Bancorporation, Inc. transferable on the books of the Company in person or by
n surrender of this certificate properly endorsed.
ertificate is not valid unless countersigned and registered by the Transfer Agent and Registrar.
s the seal of the Company and the signatures of its duly authorized officers.

REGISTERED:
**CHICAGO TRUST COMPANY
OF NEW YORK**

TRANSFER AGENT
AND REGISTRAR

AUTHORIZED OFFICER

NORTH FORK BANCORPORATION, INC.
INCORPORATED
1980
DELAWARE

PRESIDENT

SECRETARY

Charles Schwab
Corp.
JANUARY 11, 1983 –
PRESENT

Charles Schwab
Bank
APRIL 28, 2003 –
PRESENT

Charles Schwab

RANK	HEADQUARTERS	TICKER	ASSETS	EARLIEST KNOWN ANCESTOR	INDUSTRY OF ORIGIN
21	San Francisco, CA	SCHW	$136,000,000,000	1971	Brokerage

Entrepreneur Charles "Chuck" Schwab in an early Schwab office.

At the time of writing, inveterate entrepreneur Charles "Chuck" Schwab, the person (hereafter simply Schwab), owned 13% of Charles Schwab, the corporation, making this big BHC one of the few with a founder still playing an owner's role. The firm's origins date back to 1971, when it was called First Commander Corp. and Schwab shared ownership with a number of partners. In 1973, with those partners bought out, Schwab renamed the company Charles Schwab & Co., Inc. and at age 36 began to build the business on the belief that investors should make their own financial decisions on the basis of objective, unbiased information, not expensive and potentially conflicted advice from alleged experts. As he described it in his first book, *How to Be Your Own Stockbroker*, "Today any investor can be truly independent—independent of unfair, bloated commissions and of the self-serving broker whose 'advice' is tainted."

Schwab understood that many people were not mere savers, as most bankers thought of them, but investors. And he believed that millions more would benefit by being investors. As he said then, "I knew exactly who my customers would be; I was one of them! If I hadn't started my own discount brokerage firm, I would have become some other discounter's best customer." His company thrived because of it. It also thrived because it thought of itself broadly as being in the business of helping investors to improve their financial lives. That enabled it to adapt to changing market circumstances. David Pottruck, co-CEO with Schwab from 1998 to 2003, told strategy professor Gary Hamel that "We're addicted to change." Over its more than 40-year history, Charles Schwab has continued to evolve along with changes in the markets, changes in technology and changes in the types of products and

services it can provide to meet its clients' goals and the ever-changing needs of investors.

In 1975, when the SEC deregulated commissions, Schwab invented the discount brokerage industry by undercutting the big fees exacted by traditional brokers like Merrill Lynch (now part of Bank of America [#2]) and PaineWebber (now part of the Swiss bank UBS). Revenues grew from $4.6 million in 1977 to $126.5 million in 1983. Bank of America (#2) bought the company in 1983, but ultimately sold it back to Schwab and his management team in 1987 as part of its famous late-1980s turnaround. The episode did not materially injure the company, which in 1984 controlled 20% of the discount brokerage business. In fact its independence—Charles Schwab went public in 1987 just a few months after buying itself back from BofA—gave it the flexibility and freedom to grow dramatically. By 1988 it had 40% of the market and revenues of $392 million. Thanks to up-to-date technology and cost controls, revenues led to profits, which drove the company's market capitalization from $152 million in 1987 to over $1.2 billion by the end of 1991 to almost $6 billion by 1996.

Charles Schwab grew, in part, by attracting the business of investors like John Davis, who felt that his broker treated him as a "sales target" and a way to pad his commission account, rather than as a customer with needs that ought to be addressed. Davis moved his money into five different mutual funds, but he found all of the paperwork overwhelming. He eventually switched to Charles Schwab's OneSource, a sort of supermarket of more than 1,000 different mutual funds that the company launched in July 1992. Davis's friend had used the service, which made the funds available to consumers without "loads" or transaction fees, successfully for five years and insisted that Davis give it a try. He complied and was happy he did. "I now get one statement" instead of seven, he told the authors of *The Profit Zone*. "The service is better and my costs are lower—on everything."

Like his friend who insisted that he try Charles Schwab, Davis began to press others to sign up. By the late 1990s the company was generating 100,000 new, unsolicited accounts per month, much of it owing to satisfied customers like Davis spreading the word. With OneSource, Charles Schwab effectively became a facilitator that linked investors to mutual fund companies. This became a profitable business for the company.

Charles Schwab also grew by partnering with independent financial planners and registered investment advisors, small companies that helped people to make better financial decisions. The planners and advisors brought business to Charles Schwab, and the company gave planners good investments to present to their clients plus back office support, which helped the planners keep costs down while leaving something for themselves. Schwab's "genial" and "trustworthy" face, which was plastered throughout the company's advertising, also helped to attract business by letting people believe that Chuck himself stood behind his services.

While folks like John Davis were happy with the company's service, wealthier investors, already accustomed to exacting personal attention, were less impressed. So in 1994 Charles Schwab began to provide larger customers, those who traded frequently or kept six figure plus accounts, with more personalized, 24/7 service. By 1999 it had enrolled more than 750,000 customers into this "Signature Services" program.

About the same time, it slashed online commissions to draw Internet traders away from E*Trade (#40) and other upstart rivals of its completely online e.Schwab service, which it launched in 1995 after the company learned "there were more computers being sold in the United States than television sets." The commission reduction worked, garnering the company almost a million new customers and increasing total commission revenues. Despite its aggressive move online, the extensive network of branches (more than 270) that the company had built continued to play a major role in its business, and especially helped to attract neophyte investors and others who wished to feel close to their money, even if they mostly traded online. Charles Schwab became, in other words, one of the first "click-and-mortar" companies.

Due to such adaptability, the company's top and bottom lines grew at an astonishing pace. It soon left its initial rival, Quick & Reilly (now part of Bank of America [#2]), in the dust, and in December 1998 its market capitalization exceeded that of Merrill Lynch. All of this resulted from a laser focus on customers' needs, not financial metrics like profits or share price. "If we do right by the customer," Bob Duste, CEO of Schwab Europe, told Hamel, "profitability will take care of itself." Like other top executives, Duste moved up quickly because he was an innovator. He moved the company into the telecom revolution by pushing VoiceBroker and TeleBroker services in 1989 that allowed customers to get stock quotations and execute trades by phone. But just as importantly, Duste understood the company's mission, which ultimately was to make the world a better place.

To remind himself of the importance of this mission, Schwab personally served soup to senior citizens at a Salvation Army kitchen once a month. If only they had saved, he thought. He wondered why Charles Schwab hadn't helped them to do so. Such thinking led, in 1996, to discount term life insurance, so the death of a breadwinner would not lead to destitution. Horror stories of elderly people forced to continue laboring for their daily bread moved Schwab in 1997 to

author *Charles Schwab's Guide to Financial Independence: Simple Solutions for Busy People*. The book, which provided readers with patient, objective advice (it gave more space to Schwab's wife Helen's investment club than it did to the company), became a bestseller. Schwab donated all of the proceeds to charity through The Charles Schwab Corporation Foundation.

The corporate culture at Charles Schwab was an entrepreneur's dream. According to one observer, the company enjoyed "an endless stream of young, talented people who they turn the keys over to and let them go to work." It was an atmosphere where honest mistakes were tolerated. Not surprisingly, mistakes were made, several of them sizeable. But by tolerating mistakes, Charles Schwab attracted innovators and, just as importantly, retained 94% of them annually.

By the late 1990s Charles Schwab was led by Schwab and co-CEO David Pottruck who, like Chuck, sought to nurture strong customer service values—"fairness, empathy and responsiveness," as Pottruck put it—and turn them into profits. Its compensation system was not based on generating trades, as with most brokerages, but rather was a salary plus system that provided bonuses to salespeople for attracting and keeping assets in the company and for generating customer goodwill as measured by random surveys. Similarly, the bonuses of customer service representatives were tied to how much business a client did with the company in the six months after filing a complaint compared to the previous six months. "More than half the customers we talk to," Pottruck claimed, "actually do more business with us after we have serviced their complaint."

By the end of the 1990s, Charles Schwab had more than 18,000 employees and controlled about 10% of Americans' mutual fund assets. But it wasn't done yet. Beginning in the late 1990s, Charles Schwab began to offer its clients professional investment advice, as well as investment product research and market data. In doing so it assiduously avoided conflicts of interest that soon bedeviled other brokerages. It also stretched into the institutional investor and wealthy individual investor markets after the turn of the century with the acquisition of SoundView Technology Group, a stock-research firm for institutional investors, and US Trust.

Its revenues still largely fueled by trading commissions, Charles Schwab was hurt by the bear market of the early 2000s, when trading volumes slumped off their tech boom highs. It laid off a third of its workforce between 2000 and 2003, but profits continued to sag, inducing the company's board to ask Schwab himself to reassume the CEO position in 2004. He refocused the company on its core business of individual investors, independent IRAs and 401(k) plans by selling SoundView to UBS in 2004 and US Trust to Bank of America (#2) in 2007.

By all measures the turnaround was a success, and the *San Francisco Chronicle* named Schwab "CEO of the Year" in 2008. That same year, Schwab turned the company over to Walter Bettinger II. Bettinger, a long-time Schwab executive since the firm he founded at age 22, the Hampton's Company, was purchased by Schwab in 1995, shared Chuck's entrepreneurial approach and passion for the long view and what he called a "through clients' eyes strategy." Together, they continued to move the firm from being one that focused on transactions such as stock and mutual fund trades, to a relationship-based firm that provided investment guidance. What once was a company known for inexpensive trades had become a firm where half its clients' assets were managed through a fee-based relationship.

During and after the 2008 financial crisis, unlike many peers that were beset with financial struggles and restructuring, the company's relatively straightforward business model and careful capital

Charles Schwab, 2012.

management helped it to survive and thrive. Charles Schwab was one of the few major financial firms that did not require or take federal TARP funding during the crisis. Despite the challenges of the period, the company was able invest in the business and grow its pool of clients and client assets each year. From the beginning of 2009 through 2012, Charles Schwab grew client assets by $529 billion compared to growth of $320 billion by its four main publicly traded competitors combined: Ameritrade, BofA-Merrill, E*Trade and Morgan Stanley.

The up-and-down ride continued through 2013 because of sustained low interest rates, which dissuaded saving, and repeated US and European government fiscal difficulties that increased investor perceptions of risk. For Charles Schwab, the business challenges resulted in impacts to financial results, depressing earnings for the period, but the company's turnaround that began in 2005 continued as it brought in hundreds of billions in new client assets and thousands of new client accounts.

In 2009, arguably the depths of the crisis, the company added almost one million new client accounts while maintaining a healthy balance sheet and delivering significant improvements to client services and products. By the end of the third quarter of 2012, as the crisis was fading, Charles Schwab had 8.7 million active brokerage accounts and 844,000 banking accounts, up 3% and 10%, respectively, from a year earlier. By the end of 2013 the company passed $2 trillion in client assets under management, making it one of the top investment services firms in the world, while maintaining its focus on client-focused innovation and disruption. As John Kador described it in his *Charles Schwab: How One Company Beat Wall Street and Reinvented the Brokerage Industry*, "Schwab continues to liberate the world of personal finance, and we are all, rich and poor, better off for it."

Sources

Charles Schwab Corporation Annual Report. San Francisco, 1987–2013.

Hamel, Gary. *Leading the Revolution*. Boston: Harvard Business School Press, 2000.

Kador, John. *Charles Schwab: How One Company Beat Wall Street and Reinvented the Brokerage Industry*. Hoboken, NJ: Wiley, 2000, 1.

Mariotti, Steve, Tony Towle and Debra DeSalvo. *The Young Entrepreneur's Guide to Starting and Running a Business*. New York: Random House, 1996, 116–17.

Philbin, Brett. "Charles Schwab Profit Drops 20%." *Wall Street Journal Online*, April 16, 2012.

———. "Global Finance: Charles Schwab Profit Rises 12%" *Wall Street Journal*, October 16, 2012, C3.

Pottruck, David S. "Charles Schwab & Company, Inc.: Invest in Trust." In *Customer Service: Extraordinary Results at Southwest Airlines, Charles Schwab, Lands' End, American Express, Staples, and USAA*, edited by Fred Wiersema, 39–78. New York: HarperBusiness, 1998.

Pottruck, David S. and Terry Pearce. *Clicks and Mortar: Passion Drive Growth in an Internet Driven World*. San Francisco: Jossey-Bass, 2000.

Rieker, Matthias. "Global Finance: Charles Schwab Is Okay After Heart Surgery." *Wall Street Journal*, December 28, 2010.

Schwab, Charles. *Charles Schwab's Guide to Financial Independence: Simple Solutions for Busy People*. New York: Crown, 1997.

———. *How to Be Your Own Stockbroker*. New York: Dell, 1984.

Slywotzky, Adrian, David Morrison and Bob Andelman. *The Profit Zone: How Strategic Business Design Will Lead You to Tomorrow's Profits*. New York: Times Business, 1997, 153–74.

Wetfeet. *25 Top Financial Services Firms*. San Francisco: Wetfeet. 2008, 28–30.

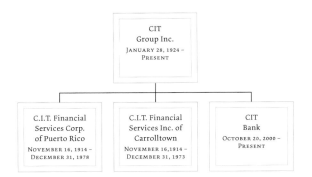

CIT Group

RANK	HEADQUARTERS	TICKER	ASSETS	EARLIEST KNOWN ANCESTOR	INDUSTRY OF ORIGIN
41	Livingston, NJ	CIT	$44,500,000,000	1908	Finance

Studebaker car, 1922.

CIT Group traces its roots to 1908. Initially chartered in St. Louis and the brainchild of 36-year-old merchant Henry Ittleson, Commercial Credit and Investment Company, immediately called CCI Co. for short, purchased business accounts receivable at a discount. CCI did not have a banking charter because it did not need one, as it did not accept deposits. Instead it loaned its own capital, as well as money it borrowed from investors and banks. Its first clients were companies like Providence Jewelry Company, Mound City Chair Company, Delmar Manufacturing, Shumate Razor, Big Muddy River Construction Coal Company and Monsanto Chemical Works.

This business was fairly lucrative and relatively safe because the borrowers, which were all substantial businesses, pledged both collateral and their general credit for repayment. Most of CCI's first customers were based in the St. Louis region, but soon it began lending on the receivables of more distant corporations, like Dow Chemical of Michigan. By the eve of the Great War, most of its borrowers were located far from St. Louis, along an arc stretching from the Rocky Mountains to the Atlantic Ocean.

The company also shifted emphasis away from manufacturers and wholesalers and toward retailers, who were also responsible for repaying the loans whether their customers paid them for their merchandise or not. In that era, decades before charge cards, retailers sold all sorts of consumer goods, including buggies, pianos, bicycles, firearms and furniture "on time." Losses to the company on such business were rare and small, so it stopped buying credit insurance and ate any defaults itself.

Due to his company's increasingly national focus, Ittleson decided to move CCI and Co.'s headquarters to New York City in 1915. It was an easy move for a finance company, but one that would have been nearly impossible for a bank at that time. As part of the move, the company reorganized as a "Massachusetts trust" to minimize its tax bill. It also changed its name to Commercial Investment Trust, which was eventually shortened to CIT. Also in 1915 the company began to enter into factoring arrangements whereby it took on the responsibility and risk of collection. Finally, it received a $250,000 line of credit from Goldman, Sachs & Company (#5), which it used to enter the automobile finance business in a major way through an exclusive deal with Studebaker of South Bend, Indiana. Terms were stringent at first — one-third down and the rest due in eight monthly payments — but that put people behind the wheel more easily than the earlier cash-only policy.

The following year, CIT opened an account with the Canadian Bank of Commerce in Toronto, presumably to finance Studebaker sales north of the border, which were then substantial. World War I cut into auto sales on both sides of the border but helped the company in other ways, for example, by allowing it to sell a machine tool it had repossessed to arms manufacturer Victor Browning.

After the war, automobile sales boomed as roads improved and cars became cheaper and more reliable. GM responded by establishing its own financing unit, GMAC (#20); CIT responded by ending its exclusive contract with Studebaker and playing the field, which then included almost 90 manufacturers with such exotic names as Brewster, Dixie Flyer, Essex, Hudson, Meteor, Packard, Willys-Knight and Pierce-Arrow. It hired Arthur Dietz, one of the few people in the country with much experience in the line, to run the business. The young man tirelessly traversed the continent signing up both top-notch dealers and even a few manufacturers, like Nash Motors. Thanks to Dietz and rapid acceptance of installment buying, CIT ran second in automobile financing volume behind only GMAC during the heady 1920s.

But local competition from the numerous small finance companies that sprouted up during the decade — between 1,600 and 1,700 by 1925 — was intense and drove down both interest and other charges and credit terms (minimum down payments dropped and length of

1939 advertisement for Universal Credit Company.

Univeral Credit Company 1939 pocket calendar.

repayment increased). CIT bought up some of its smaller rivals, like the Mercantile Acceptance Company of Chicago in 1922, but missed the opportunity to buy others, which fell to the rival Commercial Credit Company.

CIT and Commercial Credit discussed merging in late 1925, but Ittleson decided instead to purchase United Dominions Trust Limited in Great Britain. CIT sold most of its stake in United Dominions in April 1928, but in the meantime turned a nice profit. To help its customers to trade with Germany, CIT established Commercial Investment Trust Aktien-Gesellschaft (CITAG) in 1926. It opened small operations in Mexico and Denmark the following year and purchased a substantial interest in a French finance company in 1928. Over the next two years, it set up offices or agents in eight Latin American countries, the rest of Europe, South Africa, India, Australia and New Zealand, most of which came along with the acquisition of Motor Dealers Credit Corporation for $5 million from Studebaker.

After taking some big losses in Florida in 1926, Ittleson tightened lending parameters. Past due accounts dropped to just .33% within a year, but volume also suffered. It responded by buying the factoring firm Peierls, Buhler in August 1928. Urged on by a new executive that came as part of the Peierls deal, in early 1929 CIT bought the nation's oldest and most prestigious factoring firm, Fredk, Vietor & Achelis, Inc. The two firms were merged under the Commercial Factors Corporation and became a CIT subsidiary. CIT, however, directly integrated its next acquisition, Equipment Finance Corporation, which it bought in May 1929 for $2 million.

Ittleson had not seen the approaching storm and, in fact, he claimed in his 1929 annual report to stockholders that "we are now in an era of worldwide industrial and financial development." Shortly after, CIT merged cotton factor Ridley, Watts & Company with its Commercial Factors subsidiary. It also decided to finally go public by selling 125,000 shares of common stock and 400,000 shares of preferred stock in the middle of October 1929. The offering went off without a hitch, but the price of its common stock, which peaked at $76, plummeted with the rest of the market. Just two weeks later it closed at $38, and it eventually sank to $28 before rallying and closing out the year at $39.25.

CIT suffered along with everyone else during the Great Depression, but owing to the nature of its business it was never in serious trouble. In 1933 *Fortune* claimed that few companies "have better withstood the more searching test of the Depression." Unlike a factor, CIT could

National Surety Company name plaque.

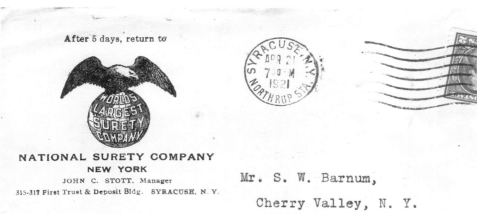

National Surety Company advertising envelope, 1921.

contract business relatively painlessly, and unlike a bank, it did not face the prospect of a run by depositors. Automobile loan defaults ticked upward but remained below 1% per year. Profits shrank along with the volume of loans on the balance sheet, but the company remained well "in the black," though it did scale back its international commitments to Canada.

It used the downturn to buy factoring companies, like Schefer, Scharamm & Vogel and L. Erstein & Bros., both in 1930, on the cheap. It also bought some of its own shares—a few for as little as $24.50. In 1931 it acquired two more factoring companies, Morton H. Meinhard & Company and Greeff & Company, and merged them into a new subsidiary, Meinhard-Greeff & Co., Inc., to maintain their strong brand identities. The following year, William Iselin & Co., the nation's oldest and second largest factor, fell to CIT, which it made a third factoring subsidiary.

During the bank holiday, the government allowed CIT to stay open. Although its own bank accounts were frozen, the company began to accumulate large sums as people made cash payments. It stuffed the money into a safe and hired two armed guards to cover it until the money was lent out to major clients desperate for cash to

make payroll. "From this action," the company's chronicler claimed, "CIT derived much good will that lasted for years. A number of companies wrote letters of appreciation to Ittleson." Just two months later, CIT purchased Henry Ford's finance company, Universal Credit, for $15.5 million, a sum that Ford historians later labeled "a terrible mistake on Ford's part."

Over the next few years, CIT's volume of business and stock price surged, the latter from a low of $18.50 to a high of $91.50 in November 1936. Both allowed the company to grow even more, as with its creation in 1935 of its Equipment Acceptance Corporation subsidiary, which financed the purchase of home appliances covered under the new FHA insurance program. It soon had 50% of the national market. CIT maintained its dominance for the rest of the decade before leaving the market entirely because of the increase in FHA red tape.

In 1936 CIT purchased for just over $10 million a distressed underwriter of fidelity, burglary, plate glass and other insurance called National Surety, as well as another factoring firm, Bachmann, Emmerich & Company. Two years later, it bought a tiny insurance company, Service Fire Insurance Company of New York, and built it into a business that could insure all of the automobiles it financed. In 1939 it

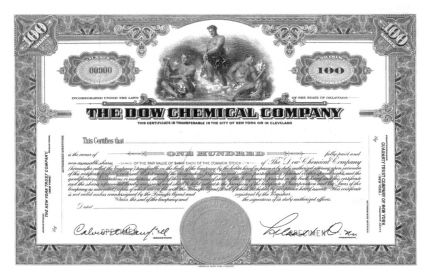

Dow Chemical specimen stock certificate.

First National Bank in Yonkers stock certificate, 1955.

bought Michigan Bank to help it enter the consumer finance business. Further movement, however, had to await the end of World War II, during which the federal government imposed tight credit controls in an effort to minimize inflationary pressures and direct resources to the military effort. By then Michigan Bank did not look so appealing, so CIT sold it in 1950.

During the war, the company retrenched and officially changed the name of its industrial finance subsidiary to CIT Financial Incorporated to avoid the wrath of New York regulators, who had come to consider all trusts as banks. Growth resumed, with net income soaring from $7.3 million in 1947 to $30.8 million in 1950, when credit controls were again enacted in response to the Korean War. Ittleson died in 1948, but his son, Henry Ittleson Jr., and his executive team were more than ready to take over.

The company established Patriot Life Insurance Company in 1953 to provide credit life insurance to its consumer borrowers. About the same time, it decided to sell National Surety, which had produced more losses and headaches than profits until the sale netted $5 million. In 1958 it also bought Picker X-Ray Corporation and North American Accident Insurance Company, which despite its name was a life insurer based in Chicago. Its name suitably changed in 1960, it ended the need to hang on to the much smaller Patriot Life, which was sold in 1966. Throughout it all, net income continued upward, increasing from $34.8 million in 1953 to $42.5 million in 1959.

From 1960 until 1970, Walter Lundell was president of CIT (and Arthur Dietz was board chairman). During his time in office, net income increased to $62.6 million, and receivables purchased increased from $4.62 to $6.03 billion. Earnings per share increased, motivating a stock split in 1961 and increasing share prices. One of Lundell's first deals was Unifinanz A.G., a joint venture with American Express (#19) launched in 1960 that conducted a general financing business throughout Western Europe. CIT bought out its partner's half in 1963 and in 1967 sold off a German unit and liquidated the British one. Also in 1960 Lundell formed CIT Leasing, which leased all sorts of industrial equipment, except motor vehicles. Unlike Unifinanz, CIT Leasing did well, innovating and expanding rapidly into commercial transport aircraft, locomotives, marine cargo containers, construction equipment and many other income-producing physical assets.

In 1965 Lundell bought Meadow Brook National Bank, a leading bank in the suburbs of New York City, especially Long Island. The move was possible because the Bank Holding Company Act (BHCA) of 1956 had forbidden nonbanks to own major stakes in two or more banks, but allowed them to control one bank regardless of size. With 66 branches and assets of $869 million, Meadow Brook was the nation's 45th largest bank at the end of 1964. It traced its lineage to the First National Bank of Merrick, which was chartered in 1924. Initially capitalized at $25,000, it failed during the Great Depression but was resuscitated by the Reconstruction Finance Corporation.

From those modest beginnings, a behemoth grew through multiple acquisitions, including the First National Bank and Trust of Freeport and the Bank of Huntington (of New York, not to be confused with #37). As the bank grew, the name was changed to Meadow Brook in deference to Long Island's original name. With a big bank on its balance sheet, CIT became so attractive that in 1968 Xerox Corporation gave serious public consideration to buying it, but the deal fell through. Bankers watched closely, and many bigger or more aggressive players, including NCNB (now part of #2) and Wachovia (now part of #4), quickly emulated CIT by forming one-bank holding companies.

Meadow Brook continued its acquisitive ways under CIT's aegis, buying in 1967 the Bank of North America of New York, which had been chartered as an industrial bank in 1924 and had assets of more than $400 million and 16 branches. In 1969 the National Bank of North America (the bank's name after the merger) purchased Trade Bank and Trust Company, a sizable institution founded in 1922, and First National Bank of Yonkers. By 1970 the bank had assets of $2.2 billion. Revision of the BHCA that year tightened the one-bank HC loophole, but CIT successfully lobbied for a grandfather clause that allowed it to keep its bank.

Lundell's moves were part of a trend that continued in the 1970s to get CIT out of wholesale and retail automobile finance and into other more lucrative and less volatile lines of business, especially consumer loans. The move hurt Service Fire Insurance and North American Company for Life and Health, but they adjusted. In 1973 net profits increased to $89.1 million, and Standard & Poor's increased the company's credit rating from A to AA. Henry Ittleson Jr. died that year, too, but his son, Anthony, remained with the company as a vice president and a director of the National Bank of North America. By 1980, however,

Monsanto Company debenture certificate, 1977.

the company had fallen to the Radio Corporation of America (RCA, now part of General Electric, the owner of #8).

RCA and CIT did not hit it off, so Manufacturers Hanover (MH, now part of #1) bought control of CIT for $1.5 billion in 1984. It struggled at times because of intense competition, but by the end of the decade CIT had about 2,500 employees spread across 50 offices throughout the country. In 1990 MH sold its stake to Japan's Dai-Ichi Kangyo Bank, which by 1996 owned 80% of CIT. The Japanese bank slowly reduced its stake until it hit 27% in 2001, when Tyco International bought CIT for $9 billion. Tyco soon became embroiled in corporate scandals, and it spun off CIT in 2002 after it could not find a corporate buyer.

After finally regaining its independence, CIT grew rapidly by acquiring units from Barclays Bank, GE (#8), HSBC (#11) and CitiCapital (part of #3). In early 2007, before the subprime crisis really exploded, Vault considered the CIT Group to be "a healthy global commercial and consumer finance company" that operated across 30 industries in 50 nations on every major inhabited landmass on earth except Africa. Its five main businesses were corporate finance (leasing and advisory services), trade finance (factoring), transportation finance (banking and other financial services to the aerospace, defense and rail industries), vendor finance (for manufacturers and intermediaries like Dell Computers) and collateralized and government guaranteed consumer and small business loans, including home mortgages, SBA loans and student loans. CIT's customers, therefore, ranged from individuals and small businesses to the world's biggest companies. In fact, it did business with 800 of the *Fortune* 1,000 companies and managed over $74 billion in assets.

But significant problems were in store. Like many other companies, CIT's downturn came when it increased its assets by 77% from 2004 to 2008 with significant participation in the commercial real estate and subprime mortgage markets. These assets became toxic, and

the company needed $2.3 billion in TARP funds to remain alive. CIT declared bankruptcy in November 2009, but quickly reemerged. By May 2013 regulators officially released it from enforcement action as its new CEO, John Thain (previously of Merrill Lynch), brought it back to profitability and a tier one capital ratio over 16%.

Sources

Bair, Sheila. *Bull by the Horns: Fighting to Save Main Street from Wall Street and Wall Street from Itself*. New York: Free Press, 2012, 178–80.

Covington, Howard E., Jr. and Marion A. Ellis. *The Story of NationsBank: Changing the Face of American Banking*. Chapel Hill: University of North Carolina Press, 1993, 86–88.

Cumming, Chris. "CIT Group Freed from Fed Order." *American Banker*, May 31, 2013.

Deogun, Nikhil, Stephen Lipin and Mark Maremont. "Tyco to Acquire CIT for About $9 Billion: Expansion Into New Field Of Commercial Finance To Aid Sale of Products." *Wall Street Journal*, March 13, 2001, A3.

Forde, John P. "Hanover Struggles to Lift Profits at Ailing CIT Group Finance Unit." *American Banker*, November 17, 1987, 1.

Loosvelt, Derek, et al. *The Vault Guide to the Top Financial Services Employers: 2008 Edition*. New York: Vault, 2007, 88–93.

Noble, Christopher. "Tyco to Buy CIT Group for $9.2 Billion in Stock, Cash Deal." *Los Angeles Times*, March 14, 2001, C3.

O'Connor, Colleen Marie. "Tyco Regroups, Plans Mega-IPO for CIT." *The IPO Reporter*, April 29, 2002, 1.

Sesit, Michael R. and Michele Manges. "Manufacturers Hanover's Sale of Stake in CIT to Help Shore Up Balance Sheet." *Wall Street Journal*, January 2, 1990, A4.

Wilson, William L. *Full Faith and Credit: The Story of CIT Financial Corporation, 1908-1975*. New York: Random House, 1976.

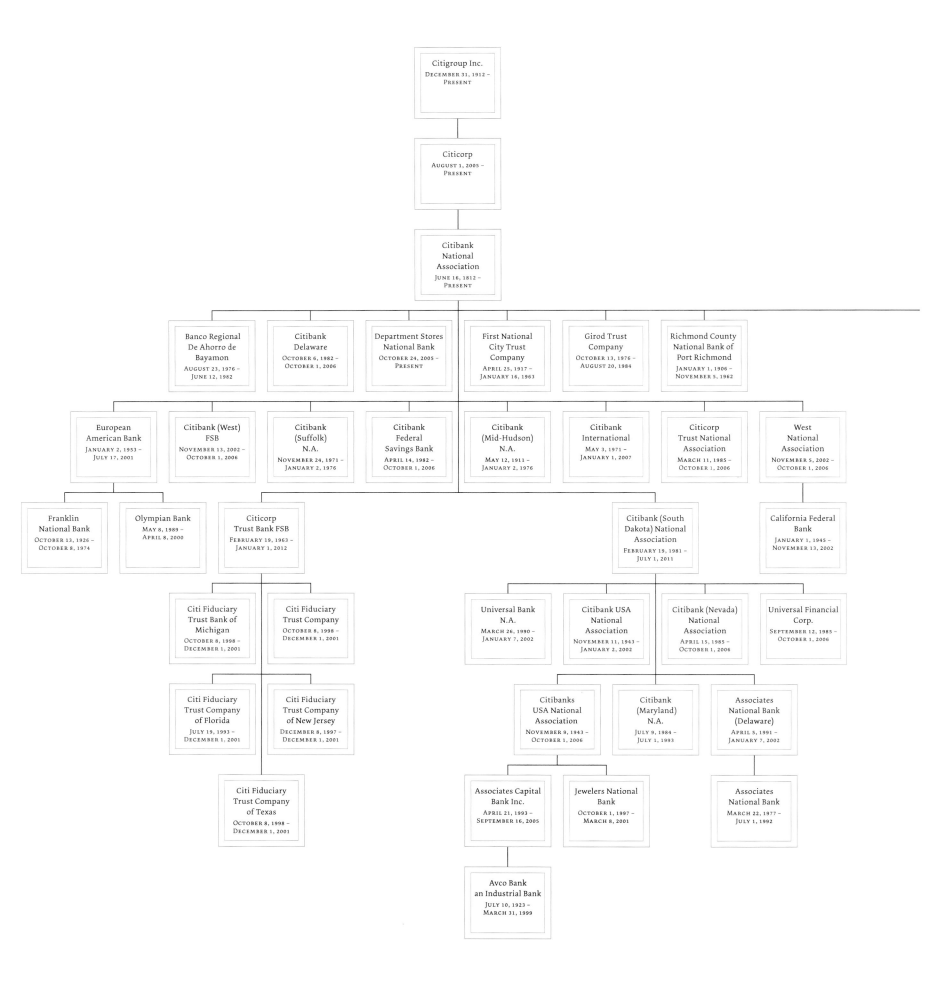

Citigroup Inc.
DECEMBER 31, 1912 –
PRESENT

Citicorp
AUGUST 1, 2005 –
PRESENT

Citibank National Association
JUNE 16, 1812 –
PRESENT

Banco Regional De Ahorro de Bayamon
AUGUST 23, 1976 –
JUNE 12, 1982

Citibank Delaware
OCTOBER 6, 1982 –
OCTOBER 1, 2006

Department Stores National Bank
OCTOBER 24, 2005 –
PRESENT

First National City Trust Company
APRIL 25, 1917 –
JANUARY 16, 1963

Girod Trust Company
OCTOBER 13, 1976 –
AUGUST 20, 1984

Richmond County National Bank of Port Richmond
JANUARY 1, 1906 –
NOVEMBER 5, 1962

European American Bank
JANUARY 2, 1953 –
JULY 17, 2001

Citibank (West) FSB
NOVEMBER 13, 2002 –
OCTOBER 1, 2006

Citibank (Suffolk) N.A.
NOVEMBER 24, 1971 –
JANUARY 2, 1976

Citibank Federal Savings Bank
APRIL 14, 1982 –
OCTOBER 1, 2006

Citibank (Mid-Hudson) N.A.
MAY 12, 1911 –
JANUARY 2, 1976

Citibank International
MAY 3, 1971 –
JANUARY 1, 2007

Citicorp Trust National Association
MARCH 11, 1985 –
OCTOBER 1, 2006

West National Association
NOVEMBER 5, 2002 –
OCTOBER 1, 2006

Franklin National Bank
OCTOBER 13, 1926 –
OCTOBER 8, 1974

Olympian Bank
MAY 8, 1989 –
APRIL 8, 2000

Citicorp Trust Bank FSB
FEBRUARY 19, 1963 –
JANUARY 1, 2012

Citibank (South Dakota) National Association
FEBRUARY 19, 1981 –
JULY 1, 2011

California Federal Bank
JANUARY 1, 1945 –
NOVEMBER 13, 2002

Citi Fiduciary Trust Bank of Michigan
OCTOBER 8, 1998 –
DECEMBER 1, 2001

Citi Fiduciary Trust Company
OCTOBER 8, 1998 –
DECEMBER 1, 2001

Universal Bank N.A.
MARCH 26, 1990 –
JANUARY 7, 2002

Citibank USA National Association
NOVEMBER 11, 1943 –
JANUARY 2, 2002

Citibank (Nevada) National Association
APRIL 15, 1985 –
OCTOBER 1, 2006

Universal Financial Corp.
SEPTEMBER 12, 1985 –
OCTOBER 1, 2006

Citi Fiduciary Trust Company of Florida
JULY 19, 1993 –
DECEMBER 1, 2001

Citi Fiduciary Trust Company of New Jersey
DECEMBER 8, 1997 –
DECEMBER 1, 2001

Citibanks USA National Association
NOVEMBER 9, 1943 –
OCTOBER 1, 2006

Citibank (Maryland) N.A.
JULY 9, 1984 –
JULY 1, 1993

Associates National Bank (Delaware)
APRIL 5, 1991 –
JANUARY 7, 2002

Citi Fiduciary Trust Company of Texas
OCTOBER 8, 1998 –
DECEMBER 1, 2001

Associates Capital Bank Inc.
APRIL 21, 1993 –
SEPTEMBER 16, 2005

Jewelers National Bank
OCTOBER 1, 1997 –
MARCH 8, 2001

Associates National Bank
MARCH 22, 1977 –
JULY 1, 1992

Avco Bank an Industrial Bank
JULY 10, 1923 –
MARCH 31, 1999

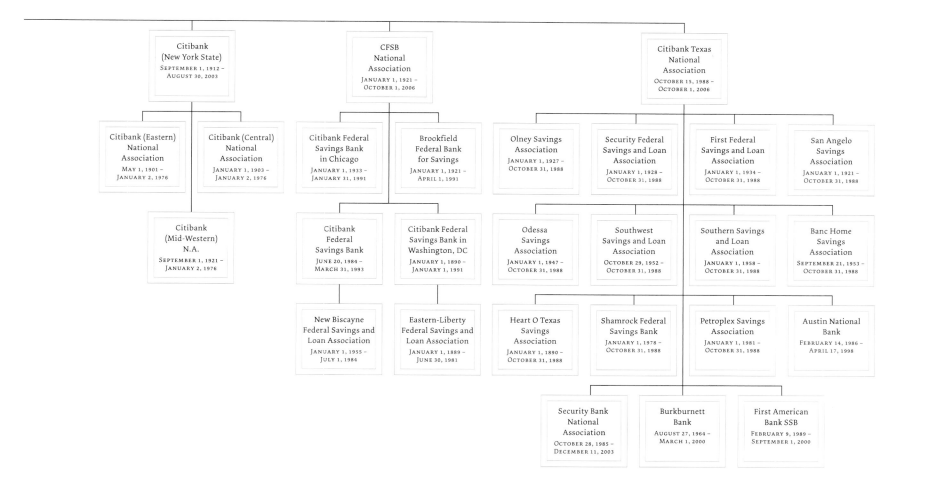

Citibank (New York State)
September 1, 1912 –
August 30, 2003

CFSB National Association
January 1, 1921 –
October 1, 2006

Citibank Texas National Association
October 15, 1988 –
October 1, 2006

Citibank (Eastern) National Association
May 1, 1901 –
January 2, 1976

Citibank (Central) National Association
January 1, 1903 –
January 2, 1976

Citibank Federal Savings Bank in Chicago
January 1, 1933 –
January 31, 1991

Brookfield Federal Bank for Savings
January 1, 1921 –
April 1, 1991

Olney Savings Association
January 1, 1927 –
October 31, 1988

Security Federal Savings and Loan Association
January 1, 1928 –
October 31, 1988

First Federal Savings and Loan Association
January 1, 1934 –
October 31, 1988

San Angelo Savings Association
January 1, 1921 –
October 31, 1988

Citibank (Mid-Western) N.A.
September 1, 1921 –
January 2, 1976

Citibank Federal Savings Bank
June 20, 1984 –
March 31, 1993

Citibank Federal Savings Bank in Washington, DC
January 1, 1890 –
January 1, 1991

Odessa Savings Association
January 1, 1947 –
October 31, 1988

Southwest Savings and Loan Association
October 29, 1952 –
October 31, 1988

Southern Savings and Loan Association
January 1, 1958 –
October 31, 1988

Banc Home Savings Association
September 21, 1953 –
October 31, 1988

New Biscayne Federal Savings and Loan Association
January 1, 1955 –
July 1, 1984

Eastern-Liberty Federal Savings and Loan Association
January 1, 1889 –
June 30, 1981

Heart O Texas Savings Association
January 1, 1890 –
October 31, 1988

Shamrock Federal Savings Bank
January 1, 1978 –
October 31, 1988

Petroplex Savings Association
January 1, 1981 –
October 31, 1988

Austin National Bank
February 14, 1986 –
April 17, 1998

Security Bank National Association
October 28, 1985 –
December 11, 2003

Burkburnett Bank
August 27, 1964 –
March 1, 2000

First American Bank SSB
February 9, 1989 –
September 1, 2000

Citigroup

Bank *(abridged)*

RANK	HEADQUARTERS	TICKER	ASSETS	EARLIEST KNOWN ANCESTOR	INDUSTRY OF ORIGIN
3	**New York, NY**	**C**	**$1,900,000,000,000**	**1812**	**Commercial Banking**

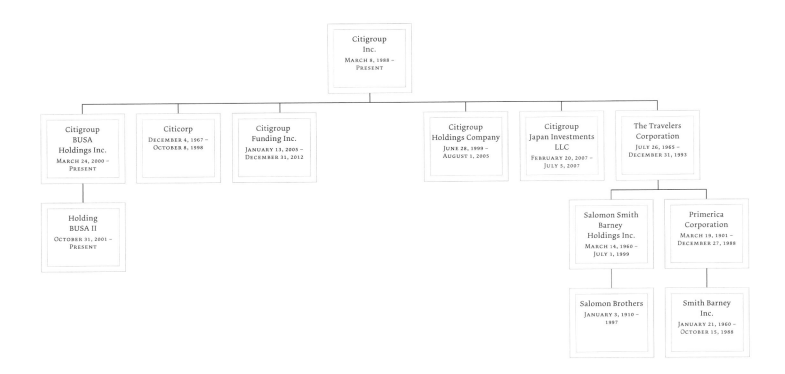

Citigroup Inc.
March 8, 1988 – Present

Citigroup BUSA Holdings Inc.
March 24, 2000 – Present

Holding BUSA II
October 31, 2001 – Present

Citicorp
December 4, 1967 – October 8, 1998

Citigroup Funding Inc.
January 13, 2005 – December 31, 2012

Citigroup Holdings Company
June 28, 1999 – August 1, 2005

Citigroup Japan Investments LLC
February 20, 2007 – July 5, 2007

The Travelers Corporation
July 26, 1965 – December 31, 1993

Salomon Smith Barney Holdings Inc.
March 14, 1960 – July 1, 1999

Primerica Corporation
March 19, 1901 – December 27, 1988

Salomon Brothers
January 3, 1910 – 1997

Smith Barney Inc.
January 21, 1960 – October 15, 1988

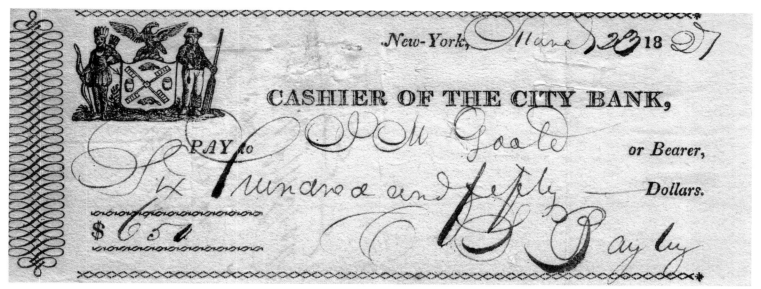

Early check drawn on the cashier of the City Bank for $650, dated June 23, 1827.

Citi began life in Manhattan in 1812 as the City Bank of New York. Capitalized at $2 million with shares of $50 par value, the bank paid a $120,000 bonus into New York State's common school fund in exchange for its charter. Its stock nevertheless traded above par by the end of its first year, in part no doubt because of the outbreak of the War of 1812 and the high yields on government bonds the war engendered. The bank's stock price plummeted after the war, allowing merchant Charles Lawton to purchase a majority of the shares in 1825, which he sold to members of the board of directors. Over the next several decades, the bank's stock price fluctuated, following the vagaries of the city's boom-and-bust economy.

By the late 1830s, however, the bank was clearly struggling, as its stock price sagged and then sagged some more instead of rebounding smartly as it had in the past. It dropped from a high of 124% of par in January 1837 to a banking panic low of 55% of par in May of that same year. That is when capitalist John Jacob Astor and his associate, Moses Taylor, stabilized the bank with purchases. By the end of the year, the City Bank's stock was again heading toward 120% of par. It consistently stayed above par, often well above par, throughout the antebellum period.

In 1865 City Bank switched from a New York free banking charter, forced on it when its special charter expired in 1852, to a national charter. It did so ostensibly because national regulations, which required a minimum reserve of cash and capped the size of loans, signaled safety. The bank, which changed its name to National City Bank of New York, remained relatively diminutive, however, until James Stillman took over as president in 1891.

Stillman tied the bank to John D. Rockefeller's Standard Oil empire and developed other corporate clients as well. By 1912 National City was a financial institution for big businesses — especially those engaged in international trade — and the federal government. It was by then the biggest bank in the United States, thanks in part to its large clients and in part to the formation of National City Company, its investment banking affiliate formed in 1911. Within days, the NCC bought majority interests in several small banks and took minority positions in large banks and trust companies in Boston, Indianapolis, Kansas City, New York, Philadelphia and Washington, DC.

National City Company transformed the bank from a large but branchless unit bank into a behemoth with national aspirations. Its actions, therefore, aroused the ire of competitors, politicians eager for reelection and many others who feared large concentrations of financial power. Under political pressure, National City Bank soon divested its domestic bank holdings, but it kept, and then expanded, its foreign and investment banking interests. The former included a wildly successful branch established in Buenos Aires in 1914, and branches set up in Rio de Janeiro in 1915 and in Bahia, Brazil; Santiago, Cuba; and Valparaiso, Chile in 1916. By 1929 the bank had branches in more than 20 countries in Latin America, Europe and Asia.

National City Company's investment banking interests had begun developing early in the 20th century, and by the Great War it was renowned for its ability to sell large quantities of bonds to investors large and small. That ability, which was magnified by its purchase of N. Wetmore Halsey's investment banking network in 1916, made the bank indispensable during the war, when first foreign and then American governments needed to sell an unprecedented volume of bonds.

By 1919 National City Company had securities sales offices in 51 cities. Its sales approach was largely educational (i.e., "This is what bonds are and what they can do for you and your family"), and its research staff approved some bonds as investments. Only in 1927 did National City Company begin to pitch a few common stocks it thought worthy investments. In one advertisement from the era, a National City Company banker and his young, well-dressed client loom over a cityscape with the banker's long arm pointing to a suitable opportunity. Its extensive and efficient distribution network gave the company ample power to place large securities issues, giving its underwriters the leg up on issuance deals. Other major investment banks often asked the company to participate in deals with their established clients while the company vigorously pursued the business of new issuers. It originated more than 3,200 of the 50,300 or so securities (government and corporate) issued in the United States during the 1920s and participated in another 7,500 deals.

After a few bumpy years following the Great War — during which the bank lost its Petrograd branch to the Bolsheviks, Stillman passed away and the bank experienced losses as a result of the collapse of the Cuban sugar market — a bond broker and National City Company president named Charles E. Mitchell took control of National City Bank. Mitchell was committed to bringing financial opportunity to the person on the street and soon righted the bank by clearing its books of nonperforming loans, repaying its debt to the Federal Reserve and improving back office operations including accounting and auditing procedures. After passage of the McFadden Act in 1927, Mitchell opened almost two score retail branches in New York City and acquired the Farmers' Loan and Trust Company in 1929. Two years later, the bank purchased Bank of America's 32-branch network in New York, a transaction that gave it the largest retail network in the city.

Like many banks, however, the National City Bank ran into considerable difficulty during the Great Depression because of bad loans and other problems. Its assets dropped from over $2 billion in 1929 and 1930 to just $1.5 billion in 1933 and 1934. But National City faced added pressure because Mitchell invested heavily in the bank's own stock and was suspected of trying to avoid paying taxes. In the process he personally fell deeply in debt to J.P. Morgan (#1). Though acquitted of wrongdoing, Mitchell had to resign from the bank and ended up paying over $1.1 million in back taxes and penalties. Meanwhile, passage of the Glass-Steagall Act meant that National City Company had to be dismantled and its securities business liquidated.

After World War II, National City Bank took advantage of America's new position as world superpower to expand its domestic and international commercial banking operations. It grew, largely organically and in fits and starts, from assets of $4.8 billion in 1945 to $6 billion in 1954. In 1955 it resumed rapid acquisitive growth by merging with First National Bank, after which it became known as First National City Bank (FNCB). FNCB's assets grew from $6.9 billion in 1955 to $23.5 billion in 1970. Between 1960 and 1970, the number of FNCB's foreign branches also increased rapidly, jumping from 50 to 157. The bank also moved into the Eurodollar market, credit card issuance and the residential mortgage business. To facilitate such diversification, FNCB formed a one-bank holding company in 1968, which bank officials said was "part of an attempt to broaden the range of financial services which it could offer to meet what we perceived as unfilled marketplace needs." The HC changed its name to Citicorp in 1974, and FNCB became Citibank in 1976.

In the early 1970s Citibank found itself embattled with consumer advocate Ralph Nader after one of Nader's study groups attacked the bank in a report and subsequent book. Citibank provided the authors with "masses of information" in the hopes of receiving a "searching . . . critical outside appraisal." Instead, the bank felt that the authors "selected only those pieces which fit the indictment they were preparing."

A short book rebutting Nader's charges "point-by-point" soon appeared and provided a treasure trove of information about the bank's operations in this period. It revealed, for instance, that in the early 1970s Citibank made many more personal loans, and actually more loans to lower income individuals, than any other bank in New York. Even more importantly, however, it revealed the thinking of its top executives, including its famed CEO Walter Wriston. "Citibank is not immune to errors in judgment and in practice," Wriston conceded in the rebuttal's introduction, "but we never stop trying to correct them." As the result of recommendations made by unbiased outside consultants, he pointed out, improvements had been made in personal loan collection procedures, noise was reduced in work areas and loan forms were simplified, among numerous other reforms.

Wriston had taken the helm at the bank in 1967, and he did well at first. By the late 1970s, however, Citibank was in deep trouble because of its credit card business. Many of its credit cardholders couldn't or wouldn't repay their balances, and it cost a small fortune to operate a high volume business out of Manhattan. Even worse, because of the Federal Reserve's stringent monetary policies and New York State's usury law (interest rate cap), the bank was actually paying more for its funds than it could lawfully charge its borrowers. It reacted by moving its credit card operations to Sioux Falls, South Dakota, where good workers were plentiful, costs were far less than Manhattan and the bank could charge its cardholders the interest rate the market would bear.

Those and other reforms righted the ship once again. In 1982 Citicorp began to expand nationally by taking over ailing S&Ls like Fidelity Savings of San Francisco. That year, Citicorp was rebuffed by regulators when it tried to enter into the insurance business via South Dakota and a perceived loophole in the Bank Holding Company Act (BHCA) of 1956. Credit card issuance, however, continued apace: the company had 31 million credit cards in 18 million households by 1991. When Wriston retired in 1984, succeeded by John Reed, Citicorp's stock price closed at $17.31, well above the $6.75 opening price that had greeted Wriston on his first day on the job 17 years earlier.

By the late 1980s Citicorp had eight million customers in 40 countries in addition to its 24 million US customers. But its expansion and diversification came at a cost. Citicorp took a $3 billion charge on its sovereign debt portfolio in 1987, and other losses also mounted. In 1991 it had assets of $217 billion, revenues of $14.8 billion and 86,000 employees, but it ran at a loss of almost half a billion dollars.

Under Reed, Citicorp turned it around in the 1990s by cutting costs, increasing high margin retail business, selling off noncore businesses and raising new equity. By 1995 its earnings had rebounded to $3.5 billion, the most ever for any American bank, and its stock was up almost 20%. By 1997 it had a presence in 98 countries and was the world's biggest credit card issuer, with 64 million pieces of plastic in use. It aimed to have a billion customers worldwide by 2010.

To reach that goal, Citi decided in 1998 to create a brand as widely known as Disney or Pepsi, and that meant creating a financial superstore. Its merger with Travelers Group—in the process forming a new BHC called Citigroup—followed. (Through at least 2013, Citibank referred to the main banking subsidiary while Citigroup referred to the holding company, which engaged in investment banking, brokerage, financial planning, asset management, store branded credit cards and a range of other financial services. Often the entire entity was simply called Citi.) Although hailed by some as the deal of the century, the merger created numerous difficulties.

In 2000 Travelers Group's CEO Sanford "Sandy" Weill took full control of Citi and promptly terminated many of Reed's projects, which included more than 50 academic studies of the bank that could have provided unparalleled insight into its culture, operations and industry. Weill had built the modern Travelers Group from scraps beginning in 1986, a year after resigning from the presidency of American Express (#19), when, with help from Jamie Dimon (later CEO of JPMC [#1]), he took control of Commercial Credit, a struggling consumer finance company based in Maryland. Weill turned that company around sufficiently in two years for it to buy Primerica Corp., which included the brokerage Smith Barney. He and his team quickly turned Primerica around, cutting more than 370 jobs at headquarters and over $50 million in expenses. Then they took on a portion—16 branch offices and 500 brokers—of the teetering junk bond empire of Drexel Burnham Lambert, which finally went bankrupt in February 1990.

In 1992 a rejuvenated Primerica took a big stake in Travelers, an insurance company founded in 1864 that had gotten severely burned in the mortgage market. Before taking the rest of Travelers the next year, Primerica bought the Shearson (brokerage) part of Shearson Lehman from American Express (#19), which spun off the ill-fated Lehman Brothers investment bank. (Weill himself had forged Shearson in the 1970s and sold it to American Express in 1981.)

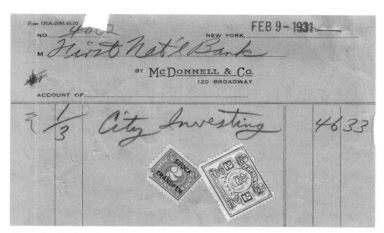

First National Bank stock transfer receipt, 1931.

A 1974 Citicard.

In 1997, by then operating as Travelers Group and boasting assets in excess of $100 billion, Weill's company bought the brash, storied investment bank Salomon Brothers, the longtime home of the brilliant economic analyst Henry Kaufman (the "Dr. Doom" of the 1970s–1980s) and the subject of Michael Lewis's 1989 bestseller *Liar's Poker*, for $9 billion. By merging the firm with Smith Barney Shearson, the 11,400 brokers nipped at the heels of Merrill Lynch (now part of #2) and its 13,000 brokers.

The Citicorp-Travelers Group merger was one of the biggest corporate deals in history but cost Weill his leading lieutenant, Dimon, who was forced out after a month. After Dimon's departure, Citi shares dropped 2%, analysts downgraded it to "hold" from "buy" and many Salomon Smith Barney traders and brokers left the company. Under Weill, however, Citi continued to expand internationally, buying Mexico's Banamex in 2001. It soon decided, though, that its financial superstore strategy was not as profitable as expected.

As the ever-witty *Economist* put it, "rather than cross-sell, the different bits of Citi and Travelers have got cross with each other." The next year, Citi spun off Travelers's property insurance businesses. Three years later, it sold off Travelers's life insurance and annuities businesses to MetLife, but it kept Travelers's investment banking companies, including Salomon Smith Barney. Citi also sold its asset management business to Legg Mason and rolled up all its securities properties into Citi Markets and Banking, which by the eve of the 2008 financial crisis had established itself as one of Wall Street's "bulge bracket" investment banks atop many of the most important investment banking league tables.

By 2002 it appeared that Weill had done well and that Citi was too well-diversified and too well-managed to encounter further financial difficulties. Citigroup was the first US bank to attain over $1 trillion in assets and had more than 7,500 branches and offices worldwide, including some 3,000 in the United States and Canada, staffed by more than 327,000 employees. Citi looked to be in great shape in 2005, but profits were down in 2006. Weill was succeeded by Charles O. Prince, who concentrated on improvements in training and communications, enhanced focus on talent and leadership, balanced performance appraisals and compensation and strengthened controls.

By 2008 Citibank was in poor condition as a result of its exposure to subprime mortgages and their sundry derivatives, as well as what FDIC Chairman Sheila Bair called its "weak management, high levels of leverage and excessive risk-taking." As the bank's condition worsened, it began to rapidly lose its uninsured, overseas funding base, and it needed a large bailout when the crisis hit. Under CEO Vikram Pandit, Citi was shored up in three ways: FDIC debt guarantees, hundreds of billions of dollars of emergency Federal Reserve loans and $45 billion in capital from TARP funds. In 2012 the bank's depressed stock price rebounded 30% with a turnover in leadership, but problems remained with legacy mortgage lawsuits and the need for more capital. In total, the US Treasury netted a cumulative profit for taxpayers of $12 billion as a result of its investment in Citi.

In early 2014 CEO Mike Corbat recognized his company's many challenges and said he was optimistic about the future of one of the most storied names in American banking history. In a letter to his colleagues, Corbat stated that "Citi is firmly on a path to being regarded as an indisputably strong and safe financial institution."

Sources

Bair, Sheila. *Bull by the Horns: Fighting to Save Main Street from Wall Street and Wall Street from Itself.* New York: Free Press, 2012, 95–105, 113–27, 165–74.

Citibank. *Citibank, Nader and the Facts.* New York: Citibank, 1974.

Cleveland, Harold van B. and Thomas Huertas. *Citibank, 1812–1970.* Cambridge, MA: Harvard University Press, 1985.

Galbraith, John Kenneth. *The Great Crash, 1929.* Boston: Houghton Mifflin, 1954.

Kaufman, Henry. *On Money and Markets: A Wall Street Memoir.* New York: McGraw-Hill, 2000, 86–111.

Leinsdorf, David and Donald Etra. *Citibank: Ralph Nader's Study Group Report on First National City Bank.* New York: Grossman, 1973.

Loosvelt, Derek, et al. *The Vault Guide to the Top 50 Banking Employers: 2008 Edition.* New York: Vault, 2007, 76–81, 120–25.

Mattera, Philip. *World Class Business: A Guide to the Most Powerful Global Corporations.* New York: Holt, 1992, 151–59.

McDonald, Duff. *Last Man Standing: The Ascent of Jamie Dimon and JPMorgan Chase.* New York: Simon and Schuster, 2009.

Morgenson, Gretchen and Joshua Rosner. *Reckless Endangerment: How Outsized Ambition, Greed, and Corruption Led to Economic Armageddon.* New York: Times Books, 2011, 43–45, 235–37.

Smith, Roy. *Comeback: The Restoration of American Banking Power in the New World Economy.* Boston: Harvard Business School Press, 1993, 67.

Starr, Peter. *200 Years Citi: Celebrating the Past, Defining the Future.* New York: Citigroup, 2012, 241–242.

Stone, Amey and Mike Brewster. *King of Capital: Sandy Weill and the Making of Citigroup.* New York: Wiley, 2002.

"Underneath the Headlines: Citigroup." *The Economist Online*, October 17, 2013.

Wetfeet. *25 Top Financial Services Firms.* San Francisco: Wetfeet. 2008, 31–34.

Zweig, Phillip L. *Wriston: Walter Wriston, Citibank, and the Rise and Fall of American Financial Supremacy.* New York: Crown, 1995.

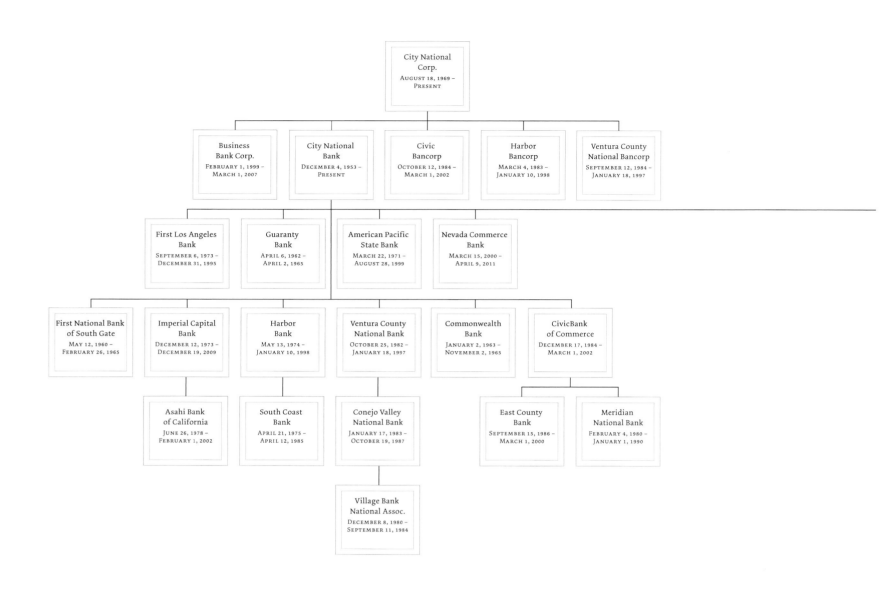

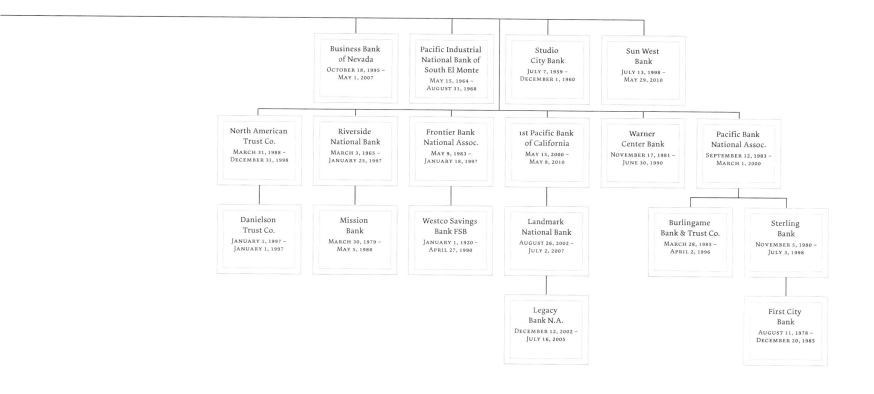

City National

RANK	HEADQUARTERS	TICKER	ASSETS	EARLIEST KNOWN ANCESTOR	INDUSTRY OF ORIGIN
49	Los Angeles, CA	CYN	$27,000,000,000	1920	Commercial Banking

Hollywood sign in Los Angeles, California, 2012.

City National has been called the "bank to the stars" because it was established by a small group of Beverly Hills entrepreneurs and initially catered to the entertainment and real estate industries. It was headquartered in Beverly Hills, a small but uber posh community, until 2009, when it relocated to Los Angeles (which entirely surrounds Beverly Hills). The bank also established branches in Manhattan and Nashville so it could cater to the stars of Broadway theatre and the Grand Ole Opry. Nevertheless, despite some high-profile customers like actor and entrepreneur Paul Newman, most of its business was middle market and conservatively underwritten.

Aided by its wealthy clientele, the bank grew quickly at first, achieving assets of $66 million in 1958, just four years after opening for business. It became a BHC in 1969, and shares began to trade over the counter the following year. Assets hit $1 billion in 1978 on strong organic growth fueled by de novo branches in Torrance, Encino, Newport Beach, San Diego and elsewhere. The bank's shares began trading on the New York Stock Exchange in 1990, and California opened itself to East Coast bankers in 1991.

However, City National proved too profitable for any of the big banks to buy, even after it suffered major losses in 1992, when the Office of the Comptroller of the Currency forced it to raise $65 million in new capital, improve its loan officer training and adopt a new business plan. The changes were made, branches were culled, directors infused $10 million of their own money, California's economy improved and the bank's fortunes soon turned around. Analysts upgraded their stock recommendations from "sell" to "hold" in June 1993. Its rights offering that month was oversubscribed, and in 1994 it began a long stretch of profitability.

In 1995 the bank had 16 branches and assets of $3.3 billion. That year it made its first substantial acquisition, buying the troubled First Los Angeles Bank from San Paulo Holding Company of Turin, Italy for $84 million. The deal was one of the bank's first acquisitions of any size. It bought a bank in 1964 but then stayed out of the game entirely until purchasing Warner Center Bank in 1989. "Buying banks is not normal for us," City National CFO J.F. Schulte told reporters in 1989.

But that changed in 1995, and by the end of 2013 it had made 19 more acquisitions. These included the Pacific Bank, which had offices in eight California counties between San Diego and San Francisco, and Civic Bancorp, which doubled the bank's presence in the Oakland market.

In 1998 the bank declared a 20% stock dividend. In other words, it gave shareholders an additional share for every five they owned. "Obviously when you declare this kind of dividend," Schulte told reporters, "you have high expectations. . . . We are going to have an excellent year."

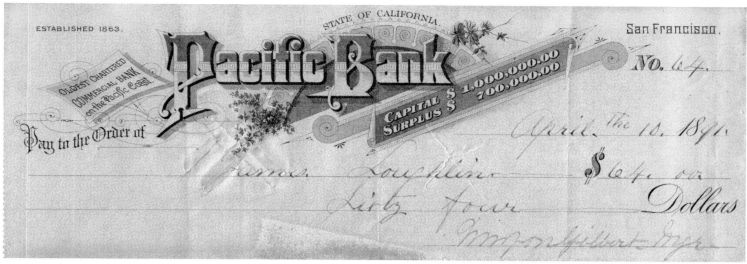

Pacific Bank check, 1891.

At the time, seven out of 10 of the bank's borrowers had variable interest rate loans tied to the prime rate, which was on the rise, but the bank did not have to increase rates on deposits in order to retain them, so its spread increased and went right to the bottom line.

In 2001, when the bank had assets of $10 billion plus another $18 billion under management or administration (up from $14.2 billion after its 1998 acquisition of North American Trust of San Diego), it updated its logo and brand identity and launched a series of online products, including Online Foreign Exchange and Online Letters of Credit. The following year, having established a reputation for having "one of the cleanest balance sheets in the industry," it set up an office in New York, its first outside of California. It also made the *Forbes* "Super 500" list for the first time in 2002, and in addition to its acquisitions, it continued to open de novo branches, including three in Orange County and one in downtown Los Angeles in 2005, when it became a financial holding company.

In 2007 the bank had more than $15 billion in total assets and was ranked in the top 10 on *Bank Director* magazine's annual performance scorecard for the third consecutive year. The magazine was not off mark, as City National sailed through the 2008 financial crisis largely unscathed. Like many other solidly managed banks in the bottom half of the "Big 50," it accepted TARP funds but used them to buy failed or failing banks (e.g., Imperial Capital in late 2009). It repaid the $400 million quickly.

Awards continued to pour in, as did revenues, which topped $1 billion for the first time in 2010, fueled by continued acquisitions and the formation of additional new branches in New York City, Los Angeles and elsewhere. In 2011 City National celebrated its 19th consecutive year of profitability, and it remained strong and independent through 2013.

Sources

Berry, Kate. "City National Propelled by Loan Growth, Expense Management." *American Banker*, April 22, 2013.

"Calif.'s City National to Buy Trust Firm." *American Banker*, September 29, 1998, 12.

Carson, Teresa. "The Search for Profitability: City National's Goldsmith: Glitzy or Gritty, Loans Get Personal Touch." *American Banker*, October 21, 1990, 31.

"City National Offering Is Oversubscribed." *American Banker*, June 8, 1993, 2.

"Company History: Nearly 60 Years of Service and Success." Accessed December 6, 2013. *https://www.cnb.com/about/company-history.asp*.

Curtis, Janice. "City National Bank Sets First Acquisition Since Deal in 1964." *Los Angeles Business Journal*, November 27, 1989, 9.

Fajt, Melissa. "City National Finishes Repaying TARP Funds." *American Banker*, March 5, 2010, 5.

——— . "City National in Deal, Still to Repay TARP." *American Banker*, December 22, 2009, 4.

"In Brief: City National of Calif. Adopts Poison Pill Plan." *American Banker*, March 5, 1997, 26.

Kristof, Kathy M. "City National Declares 20 Percent Stock Payment." *Los Angeles Business Journal*, September 5, 1988, 7.

Kuehner-Hebert, Katie. "Even at City National, Credit Quality an Issue." *American Banker*, October 25, 2002, 1.

Matthews, Gordon. "City National Upgrade Hints at Calif. Rebound." *American Banker*, June 3, 1993, 20.

Mullen, Liz. "City National Corp., CU Bancorp Both Make Profitable Recoveries from Bad Times." *Los Angeles Business Journal*, April 18, 1994, 9.

——— . "City National Mounts Effort to Assuage Regulator Fear." *Los Angeles Business Journal*, November 30, 1992, 5.

Rhoads, Christopher. "City National, Bank of the Stars, Buying Ailing Neighbor for $82M." *American Banker*, August 21, 1995, 12.

Zuckerman, Sam. "Calif.'s City National Shutting 6 Branches." *American Banker*, November 24, 1993, 6.

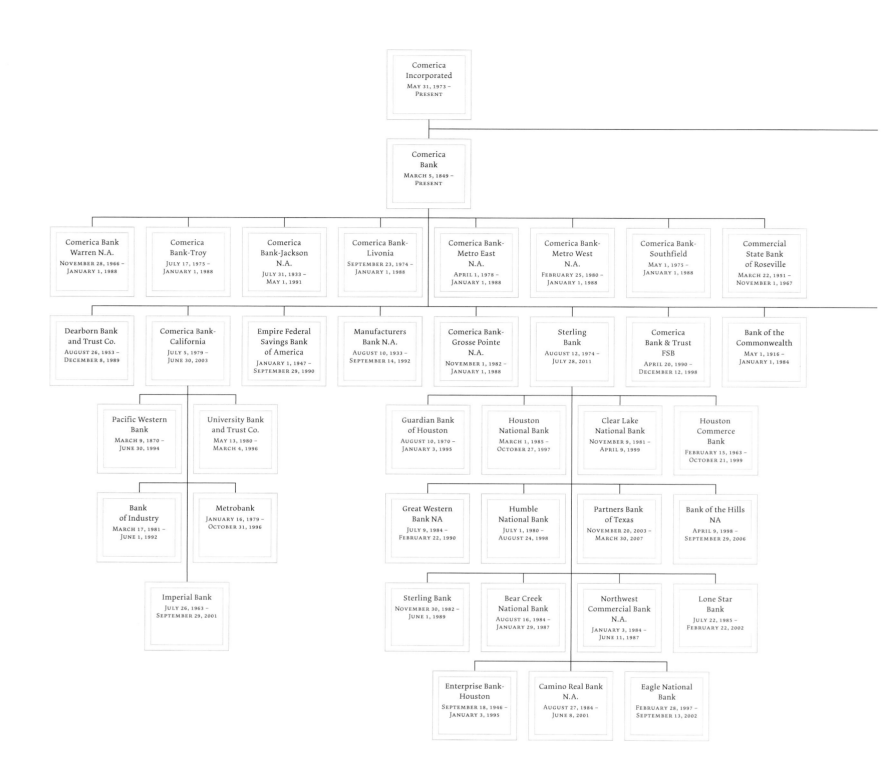

Comerica
Incorporated
MAY 31, 1973 –
PRESENT

Comerica
Bank
MARCH 5, 1849 –
PRESENT

Comerica Bank
Warren N.A.
NOVEMBER 28, 1966 –
JANUARY 1, 1988

Comerica
Bank-Troy
JULY 17, 1975 –
JANUARY 1, 1988

Comerica
Bank-Jackson
N.A.
JULY 31, 1933 –
MAY 1, 1991

Comerica Bank-
Livonia
SEPTEMBER 23, 1974 –
JANUARY 1, 1988

Comerica Bank-
Metro East
N.A.
APRIL 1, 1978 –
JANUARY 1, 1988

Comerica Bank-
Metro West
N.A.
FEBRUARY 25, 1980 –
JANUARY 1, 1988

Comerica Bank-
Southfield
MAY 1, 1975 –
JANUARY 1, 1988

Commercial
State Bank
of Roseville
MARCH 22, 1951 –
NOVEMBER 1, 1967

Dearborn Bank
and Trust Co.
AUGUST 26, 1953 –
DECEMBER 8, 1989

Comerica Bank-
California
JULY 5, 1979 –
JUNE 30, 2003

Empire Federal
Savings Bank
of America
JANUARY 1, 1947 –
SEPTEMBER 29, 1990

Manufacturers
Bank N.A.
AUGUST 10, 1933 –
SEPTEMBER 14, 1992

Comerica Bank-
Grosse Pointe
N.A.
NOVEMBER 1, 1982 –
JANUARY 1, 1988

Sterling
Bank
AUGUST 12, 1974 –
JULY 28, 2011

Comerica
Bank & Trust
FSB
APRIL 20, 1990 –
DECEMBER 12, 1998

Bank of the
Commonwealth
MAY 1, 1916 –
JANUARY 1, 1984

Pacific Western
Bank
MARCH 9, 1870 –
JUNE 30, 1994

University Bank
and Trust Co.
MAY 13, 1980 –
MARCH 4, 1996

Guardian Bank
of Houston
AUGUST 10, 1970 –
JANUARY 3, 1995

Houston
National Bank
MARCH 1, 1985 –
OCTOBER 27, 1997

Clear Lake
National Bank
NOVEMBER 9, 1981 –
APRIL 9, 1999

Houston
Commerce
Bank
FEBRUARY 15, 1963 –
OCTOBER 21, 1999

Bank
of Industry
MARCH 17, 1981 –
JUNE 1, 1992

Metrobank
JANUARY 16, 1979 –
OCTOBER 31, 1996

Great Western
Bank NA
JULY 9, 1984 –
FEBRUARY 22, 1990

Humble
National Bank
JULY 1, 1980 –
AUGUST 24, 1998

Partners Bank
of Texas
NOVEMBER 20, 2003 –
MARCH 30, 2007

Bank of the Hills
NA
APRIL 9, 1998 –
SEPTEMBER 29, 2006

Imperial Bank
JULY 26, 1963 –
SEPTEMBER 29, 2001

Sterling Bank
NOVEMBER 30, 1982 –
JUNE 1, 1989

Bear Creek
National Bank
AUGUST 16, 1984 –
JANUARY 29, 1987

Northwest
Commercial Bank
N.A.
JANUARY 3, 1984 –
JUNE 11, 1987

Lone Star
Bank
JULY 22, 1985 –
FEBRUARY 22, 2002

Enterprise Bank-
Houston
SEPTEMBER 18, 1946 –
JANUARY 3, 1995

Camino Real Bank
N.A.
AUGUST 27, 1984 –
JUNE 8, 2001

Eagle National
Bank
FEBRUARY 28, 1997 –
SEPTEMBER 13, 2002

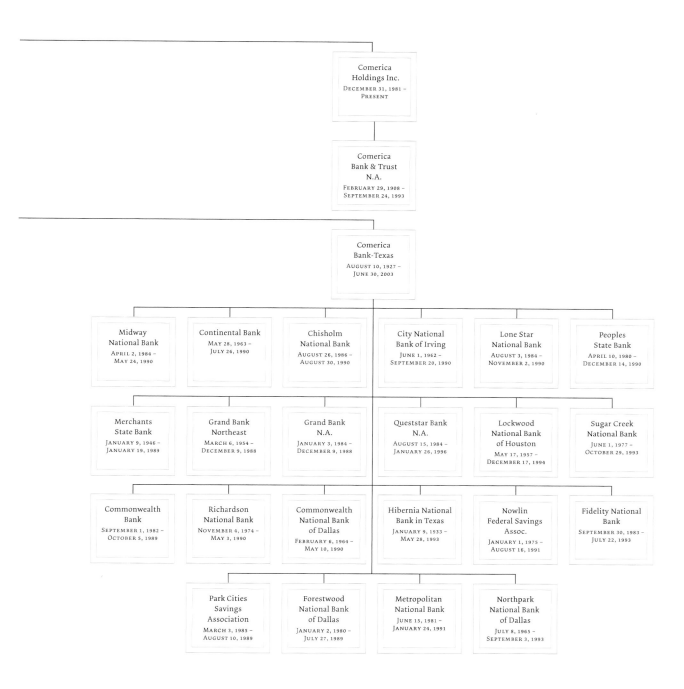

Comerica Holdings Inc.
DECEMBER 31, 1981 –
PRESENT

Comerica Bank & Trust N.A.
FEBRUARY 29, 1908 –
SEPTEMBER 24, 1993

Comerica Bank-Texas
AUGUST 10, 1927 –
JUNE 30, 2003

Midway National Bank
APRIL 2, 1984 –
MAY 24, 1990

Continental Bank
MAY 28, 1963 –
JULY 26, 1990

Chisholm National Bank
AUGUST 26, 1986 –
AUGUST 30, 1990

City National Bank of Irving
JUNE 1, 1962 –
SEPTEMBER 20, 1990

Lone Star National Bank
AUGUST 3, 1984 –
NOVEMBER 2, 1990

Peoples State Bank
APRIL 10, 1980 –
DECEMBER 14, 1990

Merchants State Bank
JANUARY 9, 1946 –
JANUARY 19, 1989

Grand Bank Northeast
MARCH 6, 1954 –
DECEMBER 9, 1988

Grand Bank N.A.
JANUARY 3, 1984 –
DECEMBER 9, 1988

Queststar Bank N.A.
AUGUST 15, 1984 –
JANUARY 26, 1996

Lockwood National Bank of Houston
MAY 17, 1957 –
DECEMBER 17, 1994

Sugar Creek National Bank
JUNE 1, 1977 –
OCTOBER 29, 1993

Commonwealth Bank
SEPTEMBER 1, 1982 –
OCTOBER 5, 1989

Richardson National Bank
NOVEMBER 4, 1974 –
MAY 3, 1990

Commonwealth National Bank of Dallas
FEBRUARY 6, 1964 –
MAY 10, 1990

Hibernia National Bank in Texas
JANUARY 9, 1933 –
MAY 28, 1993

Nowlin Federal Savings Assoc.
JANUARY 1, 1975 –
AUGUST 16, 1991

Fidelity National Bank
SEPTEMBER 30, 1983 –
JULY 22, 1993

Park Cities Savings Association
MARCH 3, 1985 –
AUGUST 10, 1989

Forestwood National Bank of Dallas
JANUARY 2, 1980 –
JULY 27, 1989

Metropolitan National Bank
JUNE 15, 1981 –
JANUARY 24, 1991

Northpark National Bank of Dallas
JULY 8, 1965 –
SEPTEMBER 3, 1993

Comerica

Bank *(abridged)*

RANK	HEADQUARTERS	TICKER	ASSETS	EARLIEST KNOWN ANCESTOR	INDUSTRY OF ORIGIN
36	Dallas, TX	CMA	$63,000,000,000	1849	Commercial Banking

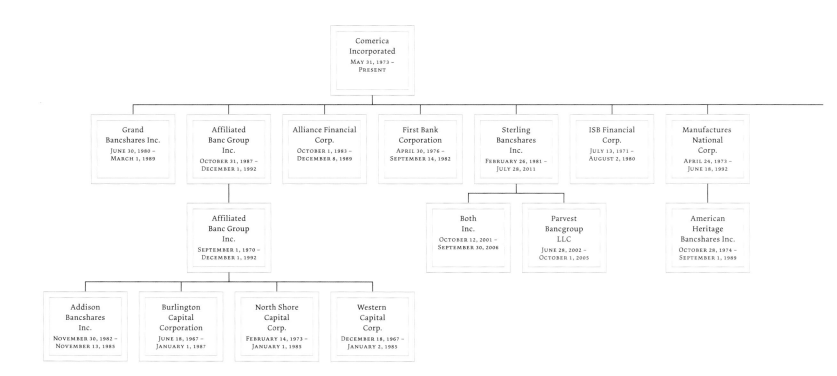

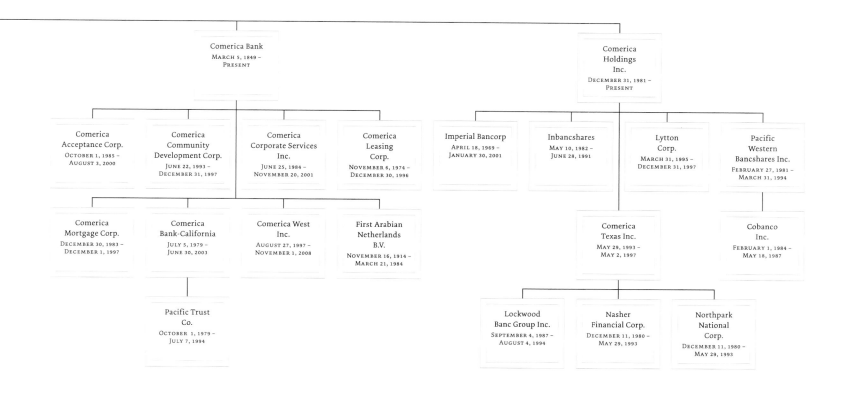

Comerica Bank
MARCH 5, 1849 –
PRESENT

Comerica Holdings Inc.
DECEMBER 31, 1981 –
PRESENT

Comerica Acceptance Corp.
OCTOBER 1, 1985 –
AUGUST 3, 2000

Comerica Community Development Corp.
JUNE 22, 1993 –
DECEMBER 31, 1997

Comerica Corporate Services Inc.
JUNE 25, 1984 –
NOVEMBER 20, 2001

Comerica Leasing Corp.
NOVEMBER 6, 1974 –
DECEMBER 30, 1996

Imperial Bancorp
APRIL 18, 1969 –
JANUARY 30, 2001

Inbancshares
MAY 10, 1982 –
JUNE 28, 1991

Lytton Corp.
MARCH 31, 1995 –
DECEMBER 31, 1997

Pacific Western Bancshares Inc.
FEBRUARY 27, 1981 –
MARCH 31, 1994

Comerica Mortgage Corp.
DECEMBER 30, 1983 –
DECEMBER 1, 1997

Comerica Bank-California
JULY 5, 1979 –
JUNE 30, 2003

Comerica West Inc.
AUGUST 27, 1997 –
NOVEMBER 1, 2008

First Arabian Netherlands B.V.
NOVEMBER 16, 1914 –
MARCH 21, 1984

Comerica Texas Inc.
MAY 29, 1993 –
MAY 2, 1997

Cobanco Inc.
FEBRUARY 1, 1984 –
MAY 18, 1987

Pacific Trust Co.
OCTOBER 1, 1979 –
JULY 7, 1994

Lockwood Banc Group Inc.
SEPTEMBER 4, 1987 –
AUGUST 4, 1994

Nasher Financial Corp.
DECEMBER 11, 1980 –
MAY 29, 1993

Northpark National Corp.
DECEMBER 11, 1980 –
MAY 29, 1993

Comerica

Holding Company *(abridged)*

The Detroit skyline, ca. 1910-1930.

omerica began its corporate existence in Michigan in 1849 as the Detroit Savings Fund Institute (DSFI), a mutual savings bank. Headed by Elon Farnsworth, who one contemporary described as "clear-headed, prudent, of sound judgment, inflexible in the discharge of his duties, straightforward and above reproach," the DSFI was charged with restoring confidence in Michigan's financial system, which had recently been racked by the failure of multiple banks.

Managed by conservative trustees bent on providing interest-bearing savings accounts for the city's poor, the institute grew slowly, escaping the clutches of the Panic of 1857 only through Farnsworth's diligence. At the outbreak of the Civil War, deposits were only about $200,000. The institute continued to grow slowly but surely, its deposits finally reaching $1 million in 1870. The following year, it demutualized and changed its name to the Detroit Savings Bank. The bank remained small enough that it continued to keep its records in 19th century-style ledgers until 1934, when it finally switched to machine-posted ledger cards. The lone typewriter was under control of the president's secretary, who reportedly guarded it jealously from clerks and tellers.

After the bank holiday in 1933, the bank's deposits soared from $10 to $27 million in just a few months as people took cash out of safe deposit boxes, from under their mattresses and out of shaky institutions and deposited it in the bank. It was a sure sign that the public

trusted it more than the institutions around it. The stress of adding more than 36,000 new customers in such a short period using the bank's primitive systems was said to have contributed to the heart attack of one of the bank's clerks. (By the 1950s, in contrast, the bank was at the forefront of bank processing technology by offering "lockboxes," facilities for collecting, crediting and depositing customer checks on behalf of its corporate customers. In the 1990s it became one of the first to store checks electronically.)

In 1936 the bank changed its name to the Detroit Bank. The following year, it stopped training tellers on the job and began offering formal classes. The bank, like most other Depression survivors, thrived during and after World War II. In addition to a few acquisitions, like its 1952 purchase of United States Savings Bank, it formed de novo branches in emerging areas of the city. It established a branch at the corner of Mack and Hillcrest in 1950, for example, a time when the area still had open country, a barn and an asparagus patch. The first manager had to assure area construction workers that their muddy boots were welcome at the branch anytime.

In 1955 the bank became the Detroit Bank and Trust Company, after acquiring Detroit Trust Company, which was famous for having a three story high, 350-ton steel vault thought to be the country's largest. That year and the next it also bought Industrial National Bank, Detroit Wabeek Bank and Trust Company, Birmingham National and Ferndale

National. In the process it became a $1 billion bank. It also continued to grow organically, in part by expanding into lucrative consumer installment, auto, boat and home equity loans, and in part by helping small businesses to thrive. In 1960, for example, Fred Howard started an auto salvage business with a $1,000 loan from the bank, which he used to buy parts that he quickly resold for $1,200. Years later, Howard asked for $25,000 to expand his business. The branch manager demurred, suggesting that $50,000 was more appropriate. Soon, the company was shipping parts as far away as China, and $50,000 was a drop in the bucket.

In 1973 the bank established a BHC called Detroitbank Corporation, and in 1979 it entered the Florida market under a trust charter. Three years later, Detroitbank changed its name to Comerica Incorporated to reflect the company's broader range of activities. Comerica acquired Bank of the Commonwealth, another storied Detroit bank, in 1983. In 1989 it began opening branches in supermarkets, primarily Krogers. A decade later it had 34 of them in Michigan and three in Texas. Comerica opened a loan office in Texas in 1987 and followed up the next year by purchasing Grand Bancshares, the first of 21 acquisitions in the Lone Star state over the next decade or so. By 2000 Dallas-based Comerica Bank-Texas had assets of $3.8 billion and 49 offices in Austin, Forth Worth and Houston.

Comerica moved into California in 1983 with a lone employee in San Jose calling on auto dealers. Within a year, it was financing consumer purchases at 300-plus California dealerships and soon after was financing dealer inventories as well. Later, it began buying up California banks, including Plaza Commerce Bancorp. By 2000 Comerica Bank-California had 30 branches across the Bay Area, Santa Cruz, Los Angeles and San Diego and was experiencing growth as rapid as that of the technology companies it financed. By then the Comerica BHC also had operations in Canada, Colorado, Hong Kong, Illinois, Indiana, Mexico, Nevada, New York, Ohio and Tennessee.

In 1992 Comerica and Manufacturers National Corporation, the HC of Manufacturers National Bank of Detroit, joined in a "merger of equals." Founded by Edsel B. Ford (Henry's son) in 1933, Manufacturers National thrived by concentrating on mid-to-large-sized corporate lending and acquiring banks in key locations like Dearborn and Highland Park. Its close relationship with Ford continued after the merger, which was successful because, as CEO Eugene Miller put it, the two banks were "for the most part, culturally compatible and . . . fit together strategically." The merger eliminated 60 branches and 1,800 jobs, but the new institution was more efficient and better managed than either of the predecessors had been. "All in all," Miller claimed, bank consolidation was "a healthy phenomenon."

By 2000, thanks in large part to nearly 60 mergers and acquisitions over the previous quarter century, Comerica's $39 billion in assets made it the 24th largest BHC in the country, a *Fortune* 500 company and one of the top 200 banking companies in the world. It employed 11,000 people and operated 335 branches and 770 ATMs. Miller attributed the bank's success to its people: "the people we select, the training we provide and the culture that permeates" the organization, "a culture of trust, teamwork and tenacity." Not surprisingly, the bank was named one of the 10 best places to work in the Detroit area by *Crain's* in 1999. But Miller also believed the bank would have to continue to grow if it was to survive because the United States was overbanked, with one bank or credit union for every 10,000 people, versus one for every 1.5 million people in Japan and Canada. "There simply are not enough customers to keep all, or even most, US banks in business," he said.

For Miller, CEO stood not for Chief Executive Officer but for "Customers, Employees and Owners." But the "C" could just as well

have stood for "Community." Like many of the smaller members of the "Big 50," Comerica tried to do well by doing good. Hundreds of its employees donated thousands of hours annually to assist worthy causes like the United Negro College Fund and the Detroit Public Library, and by providing tax preparation services for low-income families. In Texas, Comerica employees helped revitalize Dallas's historic Tenth Street. In California, the bank lent to small businesses that could not obtain conventional financing. In Florida, it donated computers and tutoring to people living in a low-income housing project. And in Detroit, it led the financing of new and expanding businesses in the city's 18.35 square mile Empowerment Zone, a federal program designed to renew bleak neighborhoods via tax breaks.

Unlike many large banks, which struggled to meet the criteria laid out in the Community Reinvestment Act, Comerica received "outstanding" ratings from the Federal Reserve Bank of Chicago several years in the latter half of the 1990s. The Michigan Minority Business Development Council also honored the bank for its role in developing minority businesses. But in the end, not even a large bank could save the Motor City.

How did a bank that had long branded itself as "The Oldest Bank in Michigan," and that had its name emblazoned on the stadium the Detroit Tigers played in, wind up being headquartered in Dallas? In March 2007 it simply announced that it was moving. Detroit, which had been challenged by depopulation and economic depression for years, went bankrupt in 2013. The bank's leadership saw the automobile wreck coming and struck out for the Lone Star state.

By the time the move was announced, Comerica had about 500 offices, 10,800 employees and assets of $58 billion. The employees reported being "treated with a good deal of respect" by managers, who they described as "very open and supportive." Unlike at some big banks, what counted was what employees accomplished while at work, not how many hours of "face time" they logged. Salaries, bonuses and perks, however, were small compared to those paid to employees of some of the LCFIs.

Comerica weathered the 2008 financial crisis better than most of its peers because it carefully structured its loans, especially larger corporate ones, a trait that it maintained through 2013, even as it faced "very, very aggressive" competition from banks that had finally recuperated from the mess five years earlier. Loan volume, however, continued to grow.

"We have very strong relationships with some large national builders that are giving us some good volume," Vice Chairman Lars Anderson told reporters. "In addition . . . we're in some good growth markets like Texas, where the housing market continues to expand and we expect to gain more of the purchase volumes." Cost-cutting measures also helped the bank to maintain profitability.

Sources

Cumming, Chris. "Cost-Cutting Measures Boost Comerica's Profit." *American Banker*, April 17, 2013.

Kline, Alan. "Comerica Taps Brakes on Corporate Banking." *American Banker*, July 17, 2013.

Loosvelt, Derek, et al. *The Vault Guide to the Top 50 Banking Employers: 2008 Edition.* New York: Vault Inc., 2007, 322–26.

Luedtke, Eleanor. *Promises Kept: The Story of Comerica.* Detroit: Comerica Incorporated, 1999.

Miller, Eugene A. *Comerica Incorporated: Promises Kept, Promises Renewed.* New York: Newcomen Society, 2000.

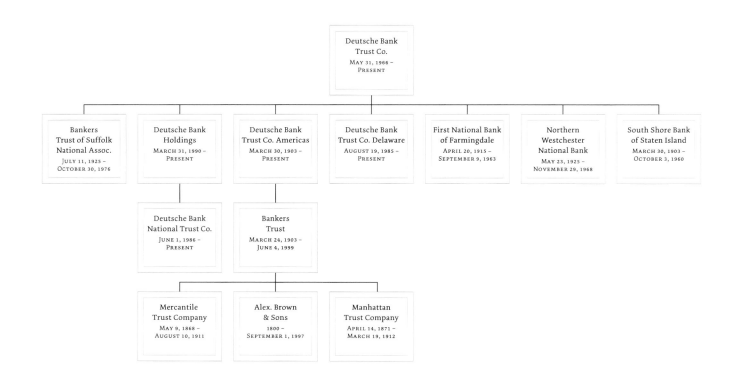

Deutsche Bank

RANK	HEADQUARTERS	TICKER	ASSETS	EARLIEST KNOWN ANCESTOR	INDUSTRY OF ORIGIN
34	New York, NY	DB	$72,000,000,000	1870	Commercial Banking

Mule hauling equipment on track near Aleppo during construction of the German Baghdad Railway, ca. 1900-1910.

Lower Manhattan skyline, ca. 1912. The Bankers Trust skyscraper is visible on the right.

Deutsche Bank AG, the top-tier holding company of the US-based BHC featured here, is one of the largest banks in the world. Deutsche, as it has been known in the English-speaking world, was formed in 1870, just before Germany unified for the first time. Initially headquartered in Berlin, it soon established branches in major port cities including Bremen, Hamburg and London. During the financial crisis of the mid-1870s, it bought up weaker institutions and established itself as one of Germany's leading banks.

Starting in the 1880s, it opened branches in Frankfurt, Munich, Dresden and Leipzig. As a universal bank, Deutsche was also heavily involved in the securities markets and had the heft to finance major projects both at home and abroad, including electric power projects, municipal lighting systems, railways (like the Istanbul to Baghdad or the Northern Pacific in the United States) and bond and stock issues by industrial giants such as Krupp, AEG, Siemens and Bayer. Storied management guru Peter Drucker credited its leader, Georg Siemens, with creating the modern precepts of top-level executive management.

By 1896 Deutsche was Germany's biggest bank. By 1914 a German newspaper celebrated it as the "greatest bank in the world," thanks to its acquisition that year of Bergisch Märkische Bank, which added 38 branches to Deutsche's domestic network of 14. Despite Germany's defeat in the Great War, a revolution in 1919 and a nasty bout of hyperinflation in 1922–1923, Deutsche managed to grow its network to 173 branches by the end of 1926 under the leadership of Oscar Wassermann. In 1929, after reducing its work force from 37,000 (in November 1923) to 13,200, Deutsche remained Germany's largest bank by merging with its longtime rival, Disconto-Gesellschaft. The combined behemoth had 800,000 accounts, 289 full branches spread across the country and 77 smaller urban branches. It survived the pan-European banking crisis of 1931 in relatively good shape.

Soon after Hitler came to power in 1933, the bank supported the Nazi regime. As time went on, the bank, probably having little choice, became further embedded with the Nazis. Deutsche, from a combination of external and internal pressures, first began to remove its Jewish directors and employees, including Wassermann, to comply with Hitler's "aryanization" program (the forced sale of Jewish-owned businesses to gentiles), and then assisted Hitler's henchmen in expropriating millions of marks from Jewish bank accounts and gold in favor of the German Treasury. But the bankers themselves were not immune to the wrath of the Nazis, as two of its directors were executed in 1943, allegedly for making anti-Nazi remarks.

After the war, the Allies broke up Germany's "Great Banks." They split Deutsche into 10 pieces, but proponents of universal banking argued vehemently that the parts were worth less than the whole because banking was subject to considerable economies of scale and brand goodwill. In the 1950s the Allies, now more worried about Soviet communism than a return of Nazism, relented, first by allowing the 10 pieces to merge into three and then, in 1957, by allowing the bank to completely reunify.

Headquartered in Frankfurt because much of Berlin was under Soviet control, Deutsche Bank quickly rebuilt its domestic retail and international operations, growing along with the increasingly prosperous German economy. Istanbul, Cairo, Beirut, Teheran, Tokyo and various points in South America constituted the bank's earliest postwar foreign forays. In the 1960s and 1970s, the bank also expanded its equity investments in German companies and soon held board seats in more than 100 of its largest corporations. Unlike in the prewar era, however, Deutsche also worked extensively with "Mittelstand," Germany's often export-oriented small- and medium-sized companies. The productivity of its workers skyrocketed in the 1970s and 1980s as the bank invested in electronic processing, personal computers, ATMs, fax machines and the other high-tech tools of the computer and telecom revolutions.

Deutsche successfully acquired banks in Britain, Italy and Spain, but America was a different matter. This was due in part to America's large size and in part to its multilayered raft of regulations, many of which prevented universal-style banking. From its inception, Deutsche had paid close attention to the United States, marketed vast sums of its government and corporate securities in Europe and served as a conduit through which technology and human capital flowed between the two nations. However, it managed to do so for nearly a century without establishing any corporate units in America.

That began to change in the late 1960s when Deutsche joined with three other European banks to take over two related Belgian bank subsidiaries operating in New York, established an investment bank subsidiary (Deutsche Bank Capital Corporation, née Atlantic Capital) in 1971, a branch in Manhattan in 1979 and a finance company (Deutsche

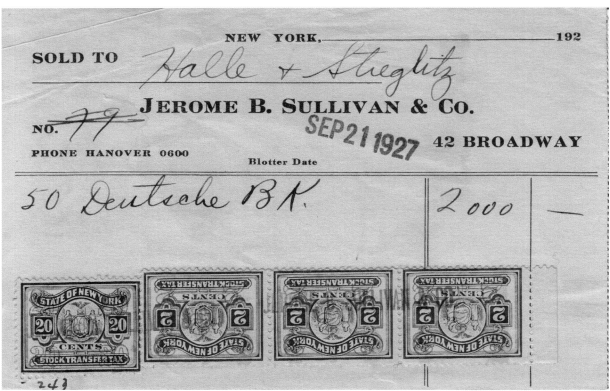

Benjamin Strong, Jr., ca. 1910-1915.

Stamp bill from Jerome B. Sullivan & Co. with stock transfer tax stamps for 50 shares of Deutsche Bank sold to Halle & Stieglitz for $2,000 on September 21, 1927.

Credit Corporation) in Illinois in 1982. By the mid-1990s Deutsche Credit had a large US network from which it lent money to consumers, leased assets to businesses and factored their receivables and financed international trade. The former Belgian banks, which united in 1978 under the name European American Bancorp (EAB), also grew quickly, with assets jumping from around $220 million in 1968 to $1.7 billion by 1973. In the late 1970s EAB bought Franklin National Bank, a distressed retail bank with about 100 branches, mostly on Long Island. But the real conduit into the American market, especially Wall Street, would prove to be the New York branch and, to a lesser extent, the branches established in Chicago and Los Angeles in 1982. Deutsche sold its stake in EAB to its Dutch partners in 1988 to concentrate its efforts on its understaffed branches.

In the late 1980s back in Europe, Deutsche was the largest of Germany's six biggest universal banks, or *grossbanken*, which aggregated 35% of the banking sector's total assets. It nevertheless remained restless, so it created an insurance subsidiary to challenge Allianz, then Europe's leading insurer. It also purchased storied British securities firm Morgan Grenfell for $1.7 billion. At that time, Deutsche strove to make its traditionally conservative corporate culture more aggressive so it could become a top global investment bank and the leading European universal bank.

After the second German unification, which brought communist East and democratic West back together in 1990, Deutsche put its new attitude to the test and beat many US banks in the scramble to acquire East German businesses. The short-term payoff was impressive: in 1991 Deutsche had assets of almost $300 billion (449 billion deutsche marks, up from 257 billion in 1986), revenues of $28 billion, net income of $930 million, 71,400 employees and more than 230,000 corporate customers.

In 1990 Deutsche managed nine German IPOs and led 74 offerings of additional equity. Its overseas investment bank affiliates, which included Morgan Grenfell, McLean McCarthy of Canada and Bain & Company of Australia, were also involved in numerous securities

offerings and merger deals. By 1990 the bank had 77 foreign offices. By the mid-1990s almost a third of its workforce lived outside of Germany. By then the bank's assets had grown to $350 billion, and it had several million retail customers, making it the ninth largest bank in the world and the trendsetter in Germany. "All eyes in European banking," Goldman Sachs partner Roy Smith noted in 1993, "follow Deutsche Bank closely."

Deutsche needed to make a big move, and America, which was rapidly growing its economy and shrinking its financial regulatory structure, was the place to be. Following other European banks, like Credit Suisse and UBS, Deutsche moved aggressively into the US market in the 1990s, culminating in 1999 with the acquisition of Bankers Trust for $9.7 billion.

Several leading New York banks established Bankers Trust in 1903 to offer the trust services (such as estates) that they could not legally engage in themselves until 1914. Led by Benjamin Strong, later head of the Federal Reserve Bank of New York, and other prominent bankers, Bankers Trust grew to be the eighth largest commercial bank in the United States by its 50th birthday with some 4,000 employees, 17 offices and $2 billion in assets. Bankers Trust continued its growth in the 1950s and 1960s by swallowing up numerous smaller banks and expanding aggressively overseas, where it met fewer regulations than at home. By 1962 it was the eighth largest bank in the world with 7,000 employees and $3.2 billion in deposits.

Bankers Trust struggled in the 1970s, as competitive pressures and huge losses in real estate lending took its toll, but Charles Sanford turned the bank around in the 1980s. He did so in part by attracting clever people and rewarding them for creating innovative products. Sanford also developed a new metric—risk-adjusted return on capital—that helped guide the bank's decision making. By 1993 Bankers Trust was again highly profitable and well respected among its peers; the following year it was named the best derivatives bank in a poll taken by Greenwich Equity. From then until the merger, the bank's

Deutsche Bank towers in Frankfurt, Germany, 2013.

fortunes and stock price were extremely volatile as the bank became embroiled in controversies and lawsuits stemming from its sales of derivative products. The share price ranged from a low of $50 per share in 1995 to a high of $133 in 1997 before plummeting again in 1998.

At the time of the Bankers Trust merger, Deutsche had more than 75,000 employees worldwide compared to Bankers Trust's 15,000. Over the next few years, Deutsche quietly purged many former Bankers Trust employees. Postmerger profits were at first quite thin, as Deutsche sloughed off some of its German identity for tax and innovative purposes. In October 2001, less than a month after terrorists destroyed the World Trade Center, Deutsche listed on the New York Stock Exchange. Because of that listing, and the extraordinary support it gave to New York City after the attacks, many came to see the bank as an "American" institution.

In 2001 investment activities accounted for 80% of the bank's pretax earnings, up from 55% the year before. Four years later, 71% of its pretax profits stemmed from investment banking, which returned 30% on equity, far more than the rest of the bank's businesses. That year, US operations, which included more than 600 legal entities (many of which were operated under a BHC called Taunus that it restructured in 2012 to conform to Dodd-Frank), accounted for about one-third of the bank's profits. Nevertheless, Deutsche scaled back in 2005, laying off all but about 2,100 of the remaining Bankers Trust employees in the process. In 2006 it acquired minority stakes in Chinese and Mexican lenders, opened branches in India and raised its global reach to about 73 countries.

It also followed other banks into the mortgage business, buying Chapel Funding, a California-based mortgage originator, in 2006, and MortgageIT for $429 million the next year. By 2007 Deutsche had net income of almost $8 billion and more than 78,000 employees in over 1,800 offices spread across 76 countries.

The bank made few headlines during the 2008 financial crisis, and they were mostly positive ones noting that it appeared not to need fresh infusions of capital. Its stock was battered, but not as much as many of its competitors. Its tier one capital was 10%, well above most of its peers. Deutsche did not require government assistance, however, and by early 2009 was "back in the black."

Sources

Drucker, Peter. *Management: Tasks, Responsibilities, Practices.* New York: Harper & Row, 1973, 605–9.

James, Harold. *The Deutsche Bank and the Nazi Economic War Against the Jews.* New York: Cambridge University Press, 2001.

Kobrak, Christopher. *Banking on Global Markets: Deutsche Bank and the United States, 1870 to the Present.* New York: Cambridge University Press, 2008.

Loosvelt, Derek, et al. *The Vault Guide to the Top 50 Banking Employers: 2008 Edition.* New York: Vault, 2007, 108–13.

Mattera, Philip. *World Class Business: A Guide to the Most Powerful Global Corporations.* New York: Holt, 1992, 200–5.

Moss, David A. "The Deutsche Bank." In *Creating Modern Capitalism: How Entrepreneurs, Companies, and Countries Triumphed in Three Industrial Revolutions,* edited by Thomas McCraw, 227–63. Cambridge, MA: Harvard University Press, 1995.

Partnoy, Frank. *Fiasco: The Inside Story of a Wall Street Trader.* New York: W. W. Norton & Company, 1997, 33.

Patterson, Scott and Serena Ng. "Deutsche Bank Fallen Trader Left Behind $1.8 Billion Hole." *Wall Street Journal,* February 6, 2009, A1.

Smith, Roy C. *Comeback: The Restoration of American Banking Power in the New World Economy.* Boston: Harvard Business School Press, 1993, 169–76.

Steinberg, Jonathan. *The Deutsche Bank and Its Gold Transactions During the Second World War.* Munich: Verlag C. H. Beck 1999.

Wetfeet. *25 Top Financial Services Firms.* San Francisco: Wetfeet. 2008, 39–42.

Wilson, James. "Deutsche Bank Back in Black." *FT.com,* April 28, 2009.

———. "Deutsche Bank May Yet Need Fresh Capital." *FT.com,* October 28, 2008.

Discover
Financial Services
MARCH 13, 2009 –
PRESENT

Bank of
New Castle
AUGUST 18, 1989 –
PRESENT

Discover
Bank
AUGUST 30, 1911 –
PRESENT

Discover Financial

RANK	HEADQUARTERS	TICKER	ASSETS	EARLIEST KNOWN ANCESTOR	INDUSTRY OF ORIGIN
33	Riverwoods, IL	DFS	$75,000,000,000	1911	Credit Cards

SEARS, ROEBUCK & CO.

WE SELL EVERYTHING BY MAIL ORDER ONLY. YOUR MONEY WILL BE PROMPTLY RETURNED FOR ANY GOODS
NOT PERFECTLY SATISFACTORY AND WE WILL PAY FREIGHT OR EXPRESS CHARGES BOTH WAYS

A 7944.

OUR 40 ACRE NEW HOME - THE LARGEST MERCANTILE PLANT IN THE WORLD

BOUNDARIES: KEDZIE AVE HARVARD ST. CENTRAL PARK AVE. AND CHICAGO TERMINAL TRANSFER R.R.

CABLE ADDRESS: SUPPLY CHICAGO.
DIRECT WIRE WITH WESTERN UNION.
AND POSTAL TELEGRAPH CO'S.
LONG DISTANCE PHONE KEDZIE 2500
WITH PRIVATE EXCHANGE TO ALL DEPARTMENTS.

OUR MAMMOTH CATALOGUE CONTAINS OVER
100.000 ILLUSTRATIONS AND QUOTATIONS MAILED
TO ANY ADDRESS FREE ON APPLICATION. THIS BIG
BOOK NAMES THE LOWEST PRICES ON EVERYTHING
WRITE FOR IT TODAY. WE CAN SAVE YOU MONEY
ON ANYTHING YOU WANT TO BUY.

REFERENCE BY SPECIAL PERMISSION.
FIRST NATIONAL BANK CHICAGO.
CORN EXCHANGE NAT'L BANK CHICAGO.
NATIONAL CITY BANK NEW YORK.
NATIONAL SHAWMUT BANK BOSTON.

Sears, Roebuck & Co. letterhead, 1907.

Discover began life as a subsidiary of the retail department store giant Sears, Roebuck and Company. From humble beginnings as a mail order catalog company in 1893, Sears grew quickly and soon expanded into lending and insurance. In 1911 it began sending goods to customers on credit. Sears Finance Corporation began lending money for home modernization in 1934. The following year, Sears launched a merchandise and services charge card that was honored at its growing network of stores. By 1956 installment and credit sales accounted for 41% of all sales.

By the mid-1970s some three-quarters of credit sales were made via the charge card, which was a "revolving" credit line with minimum monthly payments. Sears financed most of its consumer credit itself or through banks like National City Bank of New York (now #3) until the establishment of Sears Roebuck Acceptance Corporation (SRAC), which was modeled after GMAC (now Ally Financial [#20]). SRAC made $12 million in profits in 1977 but, more importantly, maintained the store's competitiveness by facilitating sales.

Sears also entered the insurance market in 1931, when it launched Allstate Insurance, an automobile insurer that sold policies via mail. By selling directly to its large consumer base without having to pay commissions to an agent, Sears kept premiums low and customers happy. To grow, though, it had to become licensed in each state and sell through exclusive agents, salespeople in Sears stores who sold only Allstate policies. By 1945 it had 327,000 policies in force, and by the 1950s Americans were becoming familiar with the slogan, "You're in good hands with Allstate." The company also expanded into personal liability, life and health insurance and began to reinsure the policies of failed insurers like National Life Insurance Company.

In 1981 Sears bought real estate company Coldwell, Banker & Company and brokerage Dean Witter Reynolds. In 1985 the company continued to offer a traditional charge card good only at its stores, but its nonbank financial company—the Dean Witter subsidiary Greenwood Trust—launched a new credit card network, called Discover, to compete with Visa, Mastercard and American Express.

Before its launch that fall, Sears's sales personnel induced thousands of US businesses to accept the new card at point of sale.

Although Sears was a competitor to many of them, Discover charged lower fees to participating merchants than other card networks did and offered access to what reporter Stephen Weiner called "an immense new customer base." Credit cardholders were enticed by annual fee waivers and an innovative rewards program that allowed accumulated "points" to be applied toward balances, and not just goods, as with other cards at the time.

By mid-1986 Sears had issued 4.7 million Discover cards, but only two in five cardholders had actually used their cards. By the following year it had established a new subsidiary, Discover Credit, to run the business, which had outstripped the ability of Greenwood Trust to fund with deposits. Sears continued to lose money, however, because its 22 million cardholders owed Discover only $168 per card, compared to $504 and $510 for Visa and Mastercard, respectively. Over time, however, use increased, as did profits and Discover's profile. In 1993, as the cash poured in, Sears spun off Dean Witter and its subsidiaries into Dean Witter, Discover & Company. It also spun off Allstate that year in a concerted effort to refocus on its core business, retailing consumer goods.

Profits were good most years, even if defaults sometimes hurt the bottom line. But in 1997, when the company merged with Morgan Stanley, analysts questioned whether a credit card network was a good fit for an investment bank. At the time of the merger, when Discover had about 40 million cardholders and a network of two million merchants, bank consultant James Shanahan estimated it was worth between $5 and $10 billion as a stand-alone company. Dean Witter CEO Philip Purcell, however, claimed that "credit cards are a very important component to us and will continue to be."

Morgan Stanley's president, John Mack, said he saw an opportunity to market more sophisticated financial services to the company's cardholders. Some analysts, like James Accomando, agreed, telling *Card News* that there was a "great opportunity for cross selling" investment products to Discover's working- and middle-class cardholders and credit cards to Morgan Stanley's well-heeled wealthy and corporate customers.

Under new ownership, Discover suffered losses (and its name was dropped from Morgan Stanley's official name), but Purcell and Mack were committed. They re-hauled the business in 1998 by ousting its president, renaming the unit Discover Financial Services (dropping NOVUS, the name of the *network*, which had been added in 1993), suing American Express over trademark infringement on the phrase "cash back," beefing up advertising, issuing platinum cards and entering the European market via partnership in Maosco Limited, the creators of Mondex smart cards.

In the early 2000s Morgan Stanley, led by former Dean Witter boss Purcell, continued to allow Discover Financial to innovate even though it remained in fourth place behind its traditional rivals and ahead of only Diners Club (then owned by #3) in the rankings because only two in five of its 46 million cardholders actively used its plastic. In 2004, when Discover entered the debit card business by purchasing Pulse EFT, an electronic network previously owned by 4,100 banks, speculation grew that a sale or spin-off was in the offing. Bank of America (#2), American Express (#19) and HSBC (#11) were all identified as potential buyers of the division, the value of which was estimated at $8 to $11 billion in 2005. However, Purcell pursued the spin-off path instead, and by the time of his departure from Morgan Stanley in early 2006, Discover's profits had improved.

By the end of 2006 the storied investment bank announced the spin-off Purcell had initiated. Discover Financial went public in July 2007, though its shares soon moved below their $28.50 issue price and temporarily stabilized at around $25. Shares thereafter sank until takeover rumors sent them back up to $18. They dropped again with profits in early 2008, as the financial crisis and recession began to take their toll. At the same time, however, the company bought Diners Club from Citigroup for $165 million in an attempt to expand its merchant network, which 20 years on still lagged behind those of its bigger rivals. In October, as the financial crisis reached its crescendo, Discover won a $2.75 billion settlement for unfair business practices perpetrated by those same rivals.

Despite that timely infusion of cash, in December 2008 Discover converted into a BHC, sought federal bailout money and eventually received $1.2 billion, a relatively paltry sum that it repaid in 2010. It still owned Greenwood, which had grown into a $33 billion bank, but CEO David Nelms believed that participating at the parent level maximized the company's overall liquidity. This had become a problem during the crisis when it found it could no longer securitize (package and sell off) its credit card loans, but rather had to carry them on its balance sheet. It made the moves out of caution—unlike many other card issuers, it had worried about the housing bubble and cut back credit limits for cardholders with multiple mortgages—just as it reduced headcount from its payroll and cut dividends as precautionary measures in 2009.

By late 2013 Discover Financial appeared to have moved past its problems, even though its cards were still accepted at far fewer locations than its larger rivals. Its share price was north of $50 on low default rates, strong organic growth ($50 billion in outstanding balances, or sixth just behind Capital One), innovative products like student loans and installment home equity loans (but not to subprime borrowers). The new products also brought diversification, reducing credit card interest income to 80% of revenues from 95% in 2012. It also attracted considerable deposits via mail and the Internet by offering competitive interest rates, which it could afford to do because it did not have an extensive branch network to support.

Sources

Aspan, Maria. "Discover Sees Chance to Buy, Build." *American Banker*, October 29, 2008, 1.

Breitkopf, David. "Discover Upgraded; Stock Price Reacts." *American Banker*, July 12, 2007, 7.

"Dean Witter, Discover & Co." *The New York Times*, July 19, 1996, D19.

Fickenscher, Lisa. "To Some, Discover Suddenly Looks Out of Place." *American Banker*, February 6, 1997, 13.

Hough, Jack. "Discover the Company Behind the Card." *Barron's*, November 4, 2013, 2.

_____. "Finding Gold in Discover Financial." *Wall Street Journal*, November 10, 2013, 2.

"Impact of Discover's Merger Under Debate." *Card News*, February 17, 1997, 4–5.

Kuykendall, Lavonne and Isabelle Lindenmayer. "Report: Morgan Stanley Set to Put Discover Up for Sale." *American Banker*, April 5, 2005, 7.

Loosvelt, Derek, et al. *The Vault Guide to the Top 50 Banking Employers: 2008 Edition.* New York: Vault Inc., 2007, 51.

Martinez, Arthur C. and Charles Madigan. *The Hard Road to the Softer Side: Lessons from the Transformation of Sears.* New York: Crown Business, 2001.

"NOVUS Bows to Discover." *Consumer Trends* 35, 11 (November 1998): 6.

Sidel, Robin and Ann Davis. "Discover Seeks a Rediscovery; Pioneering Morgan Stanley Unit Moves Into Debit-Card Business, Seeks to Motivate Cardholders." *Wall Street Journal*, November 26, 2004, C1.

Silver-Greenberg, Jessica. "Discover: Credit Where Credit Is Due." *BusinessWeek*, February 23, 2009, 56.

Terris, Harry. "Discover Seeks Treasury Funds and Holding Company Status." *American Banker*, December 19, 2008, 8.

_____. "Discover Taps Diners Club as Diversifier." *American Banker*, April 8, 2008, 1.

Wade, Will. "Takeover Talk Lifts Discover." *American Banker*, October 29, 2007, 7.

"Warm Welcome for Discover Card." *American Banker*, December 29, 1986, 8.

Weil, Gordon L. *Sears, Roebuck, U.S.A.: The Great American Catalog Store and How It Grew.* New York: Stein and Day, 1977.

Weiner, Stephen. "Sears's Discover Passes a Hurdle to Introduction: Many Stores Plan to Accept Credit Card, but Some at Test Site Are Balking." *Wall Street Journal*, August 5, 1985, 1.

Weinstein, Lisabeth. "Discover Lags MasterCard, Visa in Usage: Sears' Figures Gain, But Gap Remains." *American Banker*, April 4, 1988, 7.

_____. "New Sears Subsidiary Will Fund Discover Card." *American Banker*, April 10, 1987, 3.

Weinstein, Lisabeth and Mike Weinstein. "Sears Roebuck Calls New Universal Credit Card 'Discover'; Company Plans to Join a National Teller Machine Network." *American Banker*, April 25, 1985, 3.

Wighton, David. "Morgan Stanley to Spin Off Discover." *FT.com*, December 19, 2006.

Zweig, Phillip L. *Wriston: Walter Wriston, Citibank, and the Rise and Fall of American Financial Supremacy.* New York: Crown, 1995, 358, 724.

Interior of a Sears Roebuck store in Syracuse, New York, 1941.

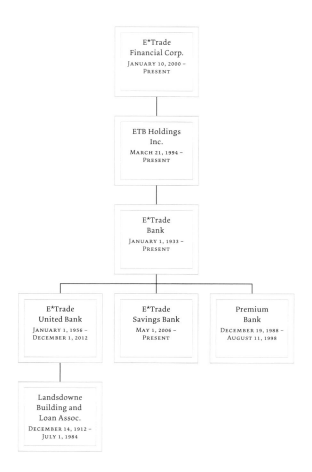

E*Trade

RANK	HEADQUARTERS	TICKER	ASSETS	EARLIEST KNOWN ANCESTOR	INDUSTRY OF ORIGIN
40	**New York, NY**	**EFTC**	**$45,000,000,000**	**1912**	**Brokerage**

Wallet featuring the E*Trade logo.

E*Trade annual report, 1997.

E*Trade is probably most famous for its talking baby capitalist commercials, which debuted during Super Bowl XLII in 2008. That "baby" eventually accumulated 12,000 Facebook fans and 3,000 Twitter followers. E*Trade is itself young, but as the major success of its branding effort has shown, the online discount brokerage is far from immature. This is probably because it was the brainchild of World War II hero and Colorado rancher-turned-inventor Bill Porter.

Porter developed the E*Trade software that a Silicon Valley firm named TradePlus Inc. launched in the early days of the World Wide Web. It entered the market aggressively by pricing at $19.95 per trade, far below rival Charles Schwab (#21), but "many investors" chose Schwab anyway "because of its better-known name." So in its first few years, TradePlus Inc. outspent traditional rivals, including Merrill Lynch and Smith Barney, in an urgent bid to win consumer confidence and market share.

The gambit eventually paid off. Although some users struggled with old browser software, dated computers and slow dial-up Internet access, those who made it to the company's website were usually pleased. "E*Trade's got a pretty good portfolio system—quick and easy to use," wrote journalist and early E*Trade adopter Edward Baker in 1996. "Its greatest asset is that it is responsive to the stock trades you actually make (though, of course, only the ones you make through E*Trade). Every time you buy or sell a security, your E*Trade portfolio adds or subtracts the security and adds or deducts the cash value from your account balance. And the news feature is actually helpful in making investment decisions." He also lauded its customer service center.

The company, which went public at $10.50 per share in August 1996, knew that good technology and good customer service would spell good returns for its investors. Early on, however, it had some difficulty: long wait times for the call center and the threat of a class action lawsuit. Increased name recognition, combined with an explosion of interest in online trading and ever-lower trading fees, helped the company over the rough spots. By the end of 1996 transactions were growing 10% per month, and its average client traded far more frequently—25 times per year—than the average brick and mortar brokerage client did. Early security fears were never realized, as hackers were kept at bay until a successful "denial of service" attack in February 2000.

Like other successful Internet firms, however, E*Trade by 1997 was on the lookout for new revenue sources. It found them in new markets like Australia, Canada and New Zealand and in new alliances with

AOL, Yahoo! and other web portals. By 1999 E*Trade was swamped by "day traders," people who attempted to earn a living by buying and selling stocks, often of technology companies like E*Trade itself. The volume was so enticing that the company offered $150 to anyone who switched to it from the Discover Brokerage unit (now part of #33) of Morgan Stanley Dean Witter (#6).

That November, the company, which was the second largest Internet broker in the nation, tried to buy the thrift Telebanc Financial Corp. Regulators balked because Softbank, a Japanese company, owned 26% of E*Trade, and foreign corporations were not allowed to own more than 25% of a US thrift. The deal went through in January 2000, however, and E*Trade doubled down on banking a few months later by purchasing a network of 8,500 ATMs, making it the third largest ATM operator in the nation behind American Express (#19) and Bank of America (#2). The move was designed to attract yet more deposits to Telebanc, which was the first online-only bank to hit $3 billion in deposits.

During the 2000 Super Bowl, E*Trade spent big bucks and made fun of itself for doing so: "We just wasted two million bucks. What are you doing with your money?" ran the caption after an ad featuring two men, a monkey and the song "La Cucaracha." Another spot, one with a man hospitalized for having "money coming out the wazoo," was a big hit.

The momentum built up by the ad campaign was soon dissipated, however, by the collapse of the tech stock bubble in March. Lower trading volumes and vigorous competition, on both the price of trades and how quickly they would be executed, took their toll. By September 2004 the company guaranteed execution in two seconds or less, or it would refund the fee. By that time, E*Trade had 3.5 million clients and on an average day completed more than 100,000 trades, most of which were completed in less than one second. In early 2007 E*Trade launched a new global trading platform that allowed American investors to easily trade stocks on exchanges in Canada, France, Germany, Hong Kong, Japan and the UK.

In late 2006 rumors swirled that Charles Schwab would use the $3.3 billion in cash that Bank of America paid for its US Trust business to buy E*Trade. Nothing came of the talk, but E*Trade received a big capital infusion from hedge fund Citadel Investment Group in early 2008 owing to losses suffered by its mortgage arm, which like so many others got caught with its fingers in the subprime pie. Interestingly, though, the company's trading arm, which included a variety of derivatives as well as stocks and bonds, actually thrived during and after the financial crisis as existing clients sold off stocks for safer investments and new clients joined the fold.

In 2010 more consolidation rumors swirled, about a link-up with Charles Schwab or TD Ameritrade (part of #14), as another round of competition reduced trading costs to $7.99 per trade for active clients. By 2012 the company was still independent but in the red again. It rebounded, however, in 2013.

Sources

Adubato, Steve. *You Are the Brand.* New Brunswick, NJ: Rutgers University Press, 2011, 154–57.

Anthes, Gary H. "ETrade Beats Clock." *Computerworld,* September 27, 2004, 27–28.

Avery, Helen. "Hedge Fund Strategies: Credit Funds Continue to Sink." *Euromoney.* March 2008, 42.

Baker, Edward H. "Where Am I?" *Financial World,* September 16, 1996, 76.

Bort, Julie. "Investor Power!" *Computerworld,* October 14, 1996, 129.

Braden, Carole. "The 2009 Gold Pacifier Awards." *BabyTalk* 74, 4 (May 2009): 46–48, 50.

"California: ETrade Says Merger with Telebanc Challenged by US Thrift Regulations." *Los Angeles Times,* November 24, 1999, 2.

Carey, Theresa W. "The Envelope, Please." *Barron's,* February 26, 2007, 41.

———. "Making It Click." *Barron's,* March 17, 2008, 37–38.

———. "Market Misery Sends Investors Online." *Barron's,* March 9, 2009, 33.

———. "Online Brokers Eye One Another." *Barron's,* November 15, 2010, 38.

Cariaga, Vance. "ETrade Financial Eyes Return to Profit Growth." *Investor's Business Daily,* July 23, 2013.

Constantinides, Efthymios. "Strategies for Suviving the Internet Meltdown: The Case of Two Internet Incumbents." *Management Decision* 42, 1 (2004): 89–107.

Crain, Rance. "E-Trade's Utton on Relevance, Ad Intuition and Talking Babies." *Advertising Age,* April 20, 2009, 13.

"E*Trade Cuts Fees in Challenge to Rival." *The New York Times,* September 8, 2004, C6.

Fitzgerald, Kate. "Retail Brokerages." *Better Investing* 60, 4 (December 2010): 34–36.

Markman, Jon D. "Wall Street, California: Newest Trick of the Trade; Price War Erupts Among Brokers on the Internet." *Los Angeles Times,* October 29, 1996, 1.

McGeehan, Patrick. "Latest Lure on the Web: Free Trades." *Journal Record,* November 15, 1999, 1.

Pottruck, David S. and Terry Pearce. *Clicks and Mortar: Passion Drive Growth in an Internet Driven World.* San Francisco: Jossey-Bass, 2000.

Sapp, Geneva and Jennifer Jones. "E-Business Service Denied." *InfoWorld,* February 14, 2000, 1, 14.

Shales, Tom. "The Battle of Atlanta, as Fought on Madison Avenue." *Washington Post,* January 31, 2000, C1.

Stein, Benjamin J. "Life Goes On." *American Spectator* 33, 3 (April 2000): 44–49.

Trombly, Maria. "ETrade Makes Move from Clicks to Bricks." *Computerworld,* March 20, 2000, 4.

Wagner, Mitch. "Schwab Woos On-line Home Traders." *Computerworld,* January 8, 1996, 20.

White, Ben. "US Trust Sale Could Fuel Brokerage Deals." *FT.com,* November 21, 2006, 1.

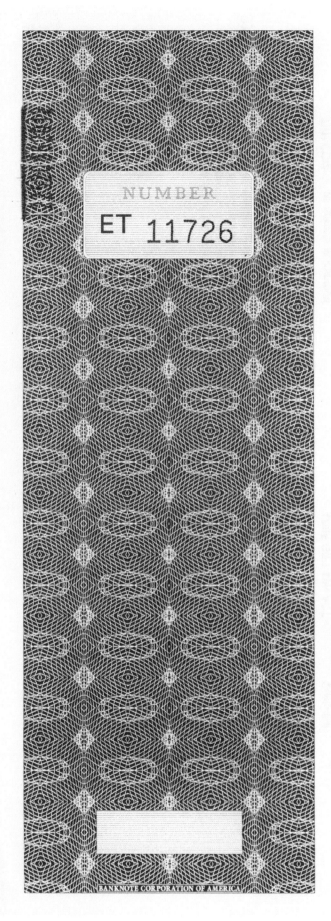

*E*Trade stock certificate printed by the Banknote Corporation of America and dated August 20, 2001.*

08410

COMMON STOCK

SHARES

********1***

ED UNDER THE LAWS OF THE STATE OF DELAWARE

CUSIP 269246 10 4

SE FOR CERTAIN DEFINITIONS AND A STATEMENT AS TO THE RIGHTS, PREFERENCES, PRIVILEGES AND RESTRICTIONS OF SHARES

IIS CERTIFIES THAT

********1*******
*********1******
**********1*****
***********1****
************1***
*************1**

DTC-0226-T2246000075

TREASUREDSTOCKS COM

]42

ONE

THE RECORD HOLDER OF

E*TRADE Group, Inc.

MAY 30
1996

DELAWARE

FULLY PAID AND NON-ASSESSABLE SHARES OF THE COMMON STOCK PAR VALUE OF $0.01 PER SHARE OF

E*TRADE GROUP, INC.

ferable on the books of the Corporation by the holder hereof in person or by duly authorized attorney upon surrender of this Certificate properly

endorsed. This Certificate is not valid until countersigned and registered by the Transfer Agent and Registrar.

WITNESS the facsimile seal of the Corporation and the facsimile signatures of its duly authorized officers.

J:

SEPTEMBER 05, 2002

064 0000523 FAST

TREASURER

PRESIDENT AND CEO

CHAIRMAN OF THE BOARD

BY

COUNTERSIGNED AND REGISTERED:
AMERICAN STOCK TRANSFER & TRUST COMPANY

TRANSFER AGENT AND REGISTRAR

AUTHORIZED SIGNATURE

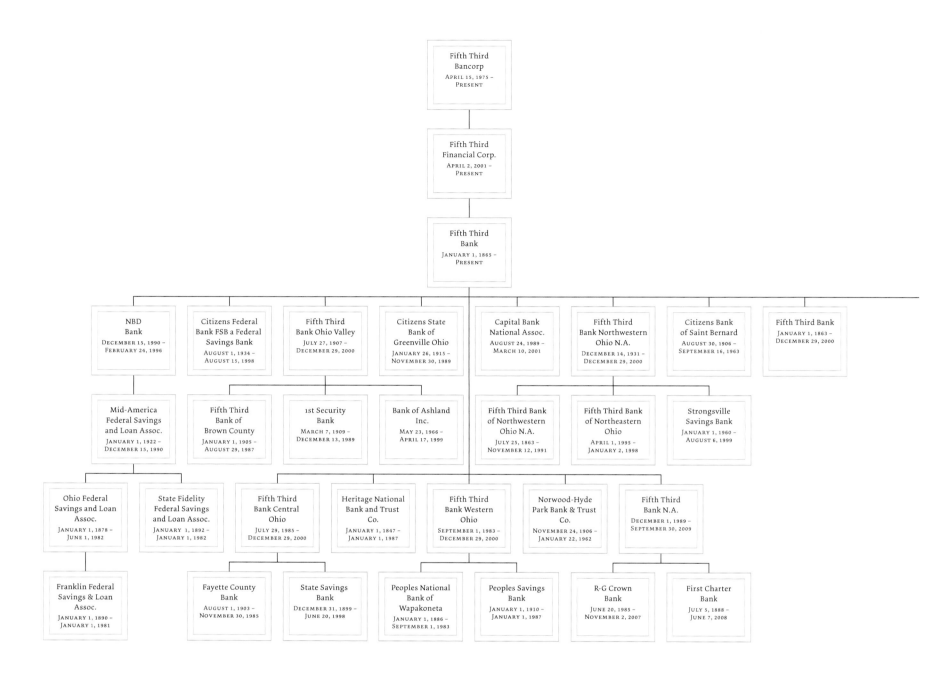

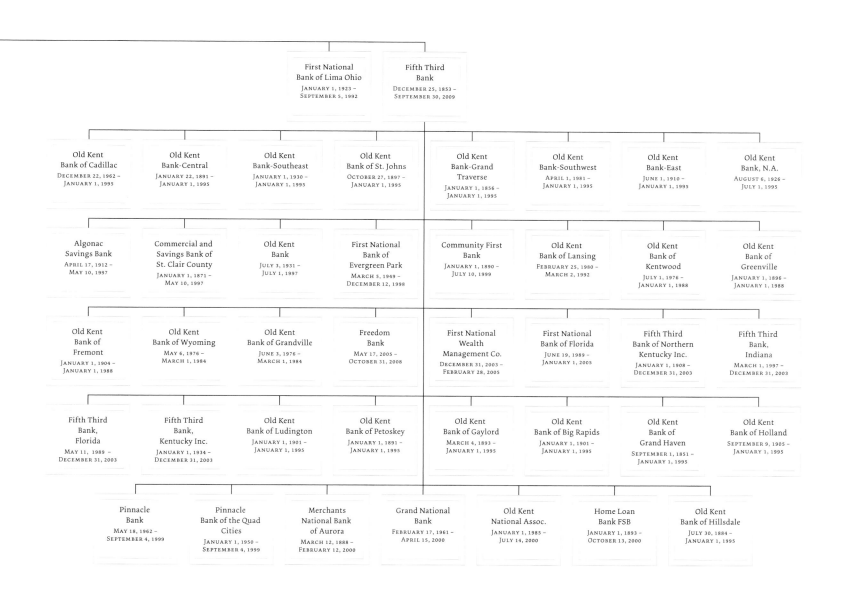

First National
Bank of Lima Ohio
JANUARY 1, 1923 –
SEPTEMBER 5, 1992

Fifth Third
Bank
DECEMBER 25, 1853 –
SEPTEMBER 30, 2009

Old Kent
Bank of Cadillac
DECEMBER 22, 1962 –
JANUARY 1, 1995

Old Kent
Bank-Central
JANUARY 22, 1891 –
JANUARY 1, 1995

Old Kent
Bank-Southeast
JANUARY 1, 1930 –
JANUARY 1, 1995

Old Kent
Bank of St. Johns
OCTOBER 27, 1897 –
JANUARY 1, 1995

Old Kent
Bank-Grand
Traverse
JANUARY 1, 1856 –
JANUARY 1, 1995

Old Kent
Bank-Southwest
APRIL 1, 1981 –
JANUARY 1, 1995

Old Kent
Bank-East
JUNE 1, 1910 –
JANUARY 1, 1995

Old Kent
Bank, N.A.
AUGUST 6, 1926 –
JULY 1, 1995

Algonac
Savings Bank
APRIL 17, 1912 –
MAY 10, 1997

Commercial and
Savings Bank of
St. Clair County
JANUARY 1, 1871 –
MAY 10, 1997

Old Kent
Bank
JULY 3, 1931 –
JULY 1, 1997

First National
Bank of
Evergreen Park
MARCH 5, 1949 –
DECEMBER 12, 1998

Community First
Bank
JANUARY 1, 1890 –
JULY 10, 1999

Old Kent
Bank of Lansing
FEBRUARY 25, 1980 –
MARCH 2, 1992

Old Kent
Bank of
Kentwood
JULY 1, 1976 –
JANUARY 1, 1988

Old Kent
Bank of
Greenville
JANUARY 1, 1896 –
JANUARY 1, 1988

Old Kent
Bank of
Fremont
JANUARY 1, 1904 –
JANUARY 1, 1988

Old Kent
Bank of Wyoming
MAY 6, 1976 –
MARCH 1, 1984

Old Kent
Bank of Grandville
JUNE 3, 1976 –
MARCH 1, 1984

Freedom
Bank
MAY 17, 2005 –
OCTOBER 31, 2008

First National
Wealth
Management Co.
DECEMBER 31, 2003 –
FEBRUARY 28, 2005

First National
Bank of Florida
JUNE 19, 1989 –
JANUARY 1, 2005

Fifth Third
Bank of Northern
Kentucky Inc.
JANUARY 1, 1908 –
DECEMBER 31, 2003

Fifth Third
Bank,
Indiana
MARCH 1, 1997 –
DECEMBER 31, 2003

Fifth Third
Bank,
Florida
MAY 11, 1989 –
DECEMBER 31, 2003

Fifth Third
Bank,
Kentucky Inc.
JANUARY 1, 1934 –
DECEMBER 31, 2003

Old Kent
Bank of Ludington
JANUARY 1, 1901 –
JANUARY 1, 1995

Old Kent
Bank of Petoskey
JANUARY 1, 1891 –
JANUARY 1, 1995

Old Kent
Bank of Gaylord
MARCH 4, 1893 –
JANUARY 1, 1995

Old Kent
Bank of Big Rapids
JANUARY 1, 1901 –
JANUARY 1, 1995

Old Kent
Bank of
Grand Haven
SEPTEMBER 1, 1851 –
JANUARY 1, 1995

Old Kent
Bank of Holland
SEPTEMBER 9, 1905 –
JANUARY 1, 1995

Pinnacle
Bank
MAY 18, 1962 –
SEPTEMBER 4, 1999

Pinnacle
Bank of the Quad
Cities
JANUARY 1, 1950 –
SEPTEMBER 4, 1999

Merchants
National Bank
of Aurora
MARCH 12, 1888 –
FEBRUARY 12, 2000

Grand National
Bank
FEBRUARY 17, 1961 –
APRIL 15, 2000

Old Kent
National Assoc.
JANUARY 1, 1985 –
JULY 14, 2000

Home Loan
Bank FSB
JANUARY 1, 1893 –
OCTOBER 13, 2000

Old Kent
Bank of Hillsdale
JULY 30, 1884 –
JANUARY 1, 1995

Fifth Third Bancorp

Bank *(abridged)*

RANK	HEADQUARTERS	TICKER	ASSETS	EARLIEST KNOWN ANCESTOR	INDUSTRY OF ORIGIN
22	Cincinnati, OH	FITB	$123,000,000,000	1847	Commercial Banking

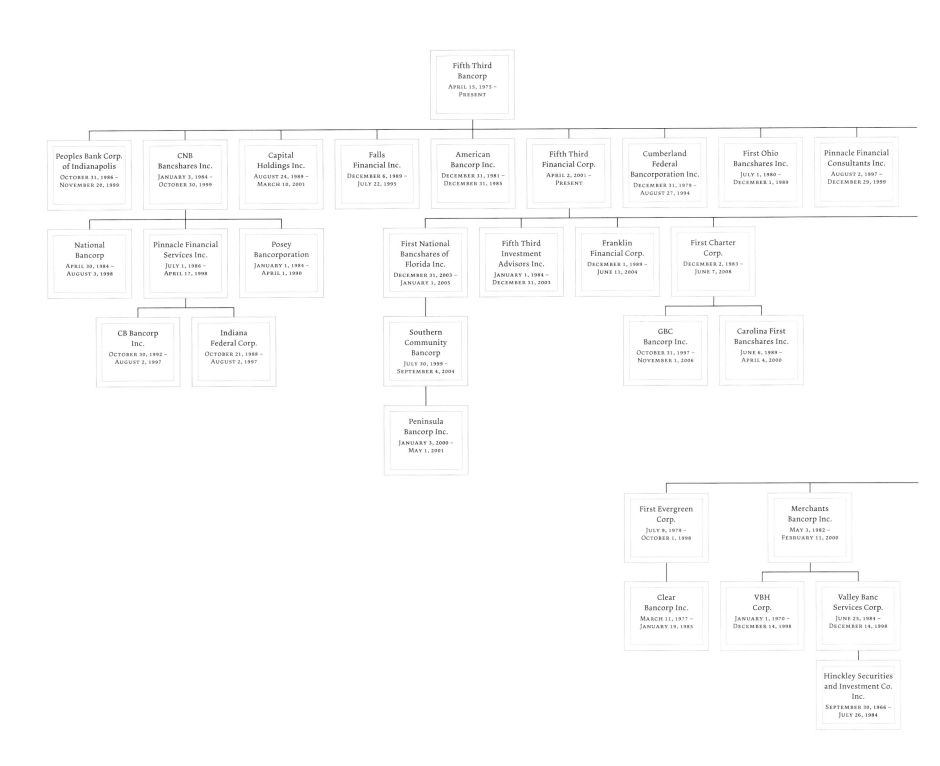

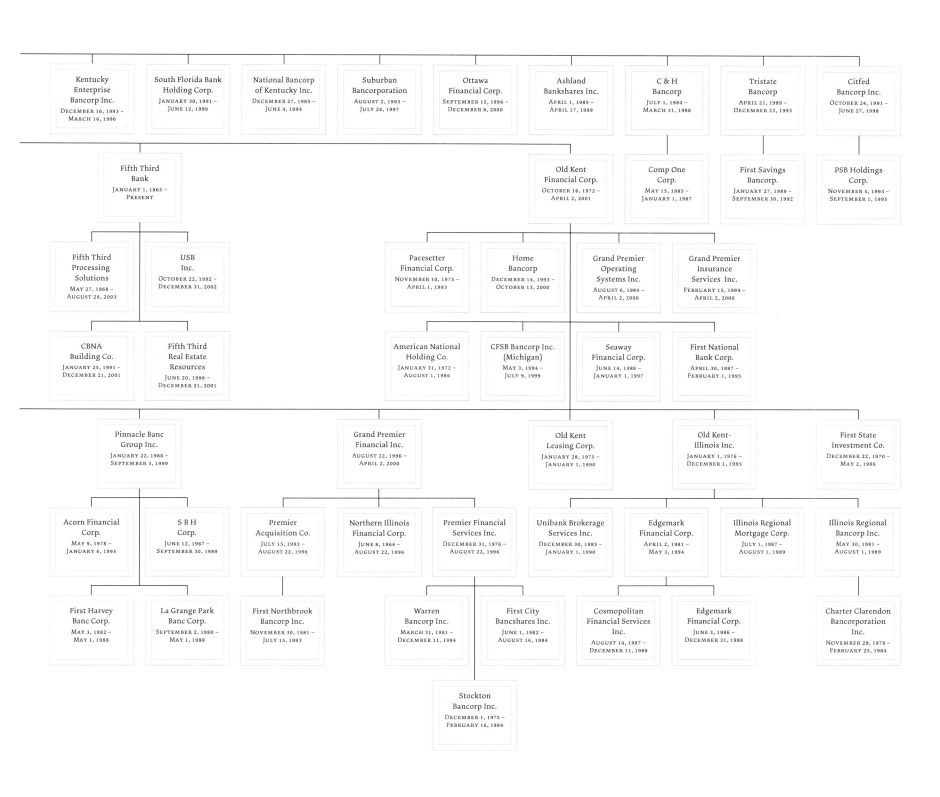

Kentucky Enterprise Bancorp Inc.
DECEMBER 16, 1993 – MARCH 16, 1996

South Florida Bank Holding Corp.
JANUARY 30, 1991 – JUNE 12, 1999

National Bancorp of Kentucky Inc.
DECEMBER 27, 1985 – JUNE 4, 1994

Suburban Bancorporation
AUGUST 2, 1993 – JULY 26, 1997

Ottawa Financial Corp.
SEPTEMBER 15, 1994 – DECEMBER 8, 2000

Ashland Bankshares Inc.
APRIL 1, 1985 – APRIL 17, 1999

C & H Bancorp
JULY 1, 1984 – MARCH 31, 1988

Tristate Bancorp
APRIL 21, 1989 – DECEMBER 23, 1993

Citfed Bancorp Inc.
OCTOBER 24, 1991 – JUNE 27, 1998

Fifth Third Bank
JANUARY 1, 1865 – PRESENT

Old Kent Financial Corp.
OCTOBER 16, 1972 – APRIL 2, 2001

Comp One Corp.
MAY 15, 1985 – JANUARY 1, 1987

First Savings Bancorp.
JANUARY 27, 1989 – SEPTEMBER 30, 1992

PSB Holdings Corp.
NOVEMBER 5, 1993 – SEPTEMBER 1, 1995

Fifth Third Processing Solutions
MAY 27, 1968 – AUGUST 29, 2003

USB Inc.
OCTOBER 22, 1992 – DECEMBER 31, 2002

Pacesetter Financial Corp.
NOVEMBER 10, 1975 – APRIL 1, 1983

Home Bancorp
DECEMBER 14, 1993 – OCTOBER 13, 2000

Grand Premier Operating Systems Inc.
AUGUST 6, 1984 – APRIL 2, 2000

Grand Premier Insurance Services Inc.
FEBRUARY 15, 1984 – APRIL 2, 2000

CBNA Building Co.
JANUARY 25, 1991 – DECEMBER 21, 2001

Fifth Third Real Estate Resources
JUNE 20, 1998 – DECEMBER 21, 2001

American National Holding Co.
JANUARY 31, 1972 – AUGUST 1, 1986

CFSB Bancorp Inc. (Michigan)
MAY 3, 1994 – JULY 9, 1999

Seaway Financial Corp.
JUNE 14, 1988 – JANUARY 1, 1997

First National Bank Corp.
APRIL 30, 1987 – FEBRUARY 1, 1995

Pinnacle Banc Group Inc.
JANUARY 22, 1980 – SEPTEMBER 3, 1999

Grand Premier Financial Inc.
AUGUST 22, 1996 – APRIL 2, 2000

Old Kent Leasing Corp.
JANUARY 28, 1975 – JANUARY 1, 1990

Old Kent-Illinois Inc.
JANUARY 1, 1976 – DECEMBER 1, 1995

First State Investment Co.
DECEMBER 22, 1970 – MAY 2, 1986

Acorn Financial Corp.
MAY 9, 1978 – JANUARY 6, 1995

S B H Corp.
JUNE 12, 1967 – SEPTEMBER 30, 1989

Premier Acquisition Co.
JULY 15, 1993 – AUGUST 22, 1996

Northern Illinois Financial Corp.
JUNE 8, 1964 – AUGUST 22, 1996

Premier Financial Services Inc.
DECEMBER 31, 1976 – AUGUST 22, 1996

Unibank Brokerage Services Inc.
DECEMBER 30, 1985 – JANUARY 1, 1990

Edgemark Financial Corp.
APRIL 2, 1981 – MAY 3, 1994

Illinois Regional Mortgage Corp.
JULY 1, 1987 – AUGUST 1, 1989

Illinois Regional Bancorp Inc.
MAY 30, 1981 – AUGUST 1, 1989

First Harvey Banc Corp.
MAY 3, 1982 – MAY 1, 1988

La Grange Park Banc Corp.
SEPTEMBER 2, 1980 – MAY 1, 1988

First Northbrook Bancorp Inc.
NOVEMBER 30, 1981 – JULY 15, 1993

Warren Bancorp Inc.
MARCH 31, 1981 – DECEMBER 11, 1984

First City Bancshares Inc.
JUNE 1, 1982 – AUGUST 16, 1984

Cosmopolitan Financial Services Inc.
AUGUST 14, 1987 – DECEMBER 31, 1988

Edgemark Financial Corp.
JUNE 3, 1986 – DECEMBER 31, 1988

Charter Clarendon Bancorporation Inc.
NOVEMBER 29, 1976 – FEBRUARY 25, 1984

Stockton Bancorp Inc.
DECEMBER 1, 1975 – FEBRUARY 16, 1984

Fifth Third Bancorp

Holding Company *(abridged)*

Fifth Third Bank has three major lineages: that of the Bank of the Ohio Valley, which formed in 1858 and was purchased by the Third National Bank of Cincinnati in 1871; that of the Fifth National Bank (née Queen City Bank) formed in 1888; and that of the Union Savings Bank and Trust formed in 1890. By 1927 the three were united under the name Fifth Third Union Trust, which changed its name to Fifth Third Bank in 1969. Although Third National was lauded in the 1870s as one of the nation's best-managed banks (a recognition it received again in the 1980s), the Panic of 1907 precipitated the merger of the Third National with the Fifth National. Several years later, in 1910, the new bank's capital hit $3 million upon the acquisition of American National Bank and S. Kuhn & Sons. It added the Market National Bank in 1918.

The bank was long affiliated with the Union Savings Bank and Trust (later the Union Trust Company) in a chain arrangement. The two banks formally united in 1927, creating a bank with assets of about $93 million. It emerged from the bank holiday of 1933 strong enough to buy the troubled Cosmopolitan Bank and Trust, which added another eight branches in Cincinnati.

Additional mergers and organic growth followed World War II, forcing it to move to an electronic data processing system in 1960. More organic growth came in the 1960s thanks to advertising campaigns, the addition of evening hours at eight branches and the publicity generated when astronaut and former Fifth Third director Neil Armstrong landed on the moon. Growth reversed in the late 1960s, however, as Regulation Q, which limited to 6% the amount that banks could pay on savings deposit rates, and Ohio's usury law, which capped bank loan rates at 8%, squeezed the bank's margins and induced depositors to look for other investment outlets.

In the 1970s, after the liquidity crunch of the late 1960s dissipated, the bank began advertising heavily again, this time with Cincinnati Reds catcher and future Hall of Famer Johnny Bench proclaiming that Fifth Third was "the only bank you'll ever need," a slogan that lasted for decades. To continue its growth outside of Hamilton County, the bank formed a BHC in 1975 and soon spread into the surrounding counties, all north of the Ohio River because of interstate branching restrictions. To provide customers with additional access points, the bank introduced an ATM network in 1977 that a third of its customers used in its first year, a very high usage rate at the time, and also began to open branches in supermarkets.

In the 1980s the bank began cross-selling its products more intensively by training and incentivizing all employees to do so (e.g., $15 for referring an approved credit card applicant). By 1991 Fifth Third Bancorp was an 11-bank HC with a capital of almost $900 million and more than 225 offices in 38 counties spread across three states (Ohio, Kentucky and Indiana). The bank's leadership attributed its success to its history and culture, specifically to an evolutionary process whereby banks like Fifth Third with conservative lending and investment policies survived crises and absorbed weaker institutions. "Safety, shareholder return and customer" was its mantra throughout all the ups and downs: the Civil War, the Great War, the Great Depression, World War II and the Savings & Loan Crisis. Those same three values saw the bank through the subprime mortgage crisis and the 2008 financial crisis as well.

Outsiders criticized Fifth Third Bank for holding capital in excess of 10% and for being a "boring bank" that quaintly listened to its customers' needs and then satisfied them in a cost-effective manner. Its stockholders, who saw dividends increase 22 times in just 16 years, did not find that boring at all. In fact, in 1998 Dearborn Financial rated it the 15th best company in the country to own, calling it a "company you can bank on." The bank, it reported, had a "reputation for quick response to credit problems, high credit standards, a strong sales culture and strict cost control measures" that allowed it to post 23 consecutive years of record earnings. At that time, the bank had about 6,400 employees and 15,000 shareholders.

Growth continued apace, even as the bank ranked for a number of years at the very top of *Fortune's* annual ranking of "Most Admired Companies in America" in the superregional bank category. By 2007 the bank sat just shy of $100 billion in assets and had more than 21,000 employees in 1,169 offices in Florida, Indiana, Illinois, Kentucky, Michigan, Missouri, Ohio, Pennsylvania, Tennessee, Virginia and West Virginia.

While the bank said its goal was to get "better at what we do," its execution was generally among the best in the business as a result of what Chief Investment Officer E. Keith Kirtz called "the disciplined approach of our team members" and an excellent training program. Moreover, many considered upper management to be "excellent" and the sales culture "exciting and motivating."

Despite significant executive changeover in 2006–2007, the bank survived the 2008 financial crisis in good enough condition to purchase Freedom Bank, a small failed Florida bank formed in 2005, in late October. It still needed $3.4 billion in TARP funds, however, which it repaid in early 2011, one of the last big banks to do so, on surging profits and lower loan losses.

The turnaround was aided by the addition, in June 2010, of former FDIC Chairman William Isaac to the top management team. Upon accepting the chairmanship, Isaac said his job was to move the bank from crisis mode to healthy growth. He did not want to create another megabank, however, telling the *Wall Street Journal* that "Banks such as Fifth Third are more important than ever," and that he hoped the nation would not experience "massive consolidation continuing in the industry. I think we need institutions like Fifth Third to be strong and growing and prospering in different regions in the country. . . . Banks generally should try to get back to the basics and focus on deposits, loans, strong balance sheets."

In 2013, despite regulatory pressure, Isaac defended the bank's right to make payday loans, which it called deposit advances, and its CEO, Kevin Kabat, argued that social media was better than regulators at keeping bankers honest.

Sources

Bater, Jeff and John Kell. "With Fifth Third Out, Banks Have Repaid 99% of TARP." *Wall Street Journal Online*, March 16, 2011.

Buenger, Clement L. *Fifth Third Bank: "The Only Bank You'll Ever Need."* New York: Newcomen Society, 1991.

"Fifth Third Bank Assumes All Deposits of Freedom Bank." *U.S. Fed News Service*, October 31, 2008.

Kline, Alan. "Fifth Third CEO: Social Media Keeping Banks Honest." *American Banker*, September 24, 2013.

Loosvelt, Derek, et al. *The Vault Guide to the Top 50 Banking Employers: 2008 Edition.* New York: Vault, 2007, 334–37.

Rieker, Matthias. "FDIC Veteran Digs in at Fifth Third; 'Time to Rebuild the House,' Says New Chairman Mr. Isaac; Prominent Post for Critic of Bank Reform." *Wall Street Journal Online*, June 7, 2010.

Walden, Gene. *The 100 Best Stocks to Own in America* 5th ed. Chicago: Dearborn Financial, 1998, 54–57.

American Bank Note Company print of a Bank of the Ohio Valley $3 note.

Third National Bank of Cincinnati specimen stock certificate.

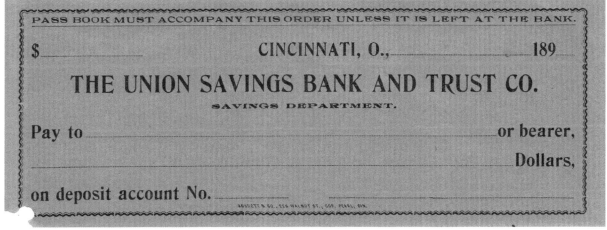

Union Savings Bank and Trust Company check.

STATEMENT OF CONDITION
THIRD NATIONAL BANK, CINCINNATI, O.

DECEMBER 31st, 1883.

___

ASSETS:

Loans and Discounts,		$3,438,545.80
Banking House,		60,000.00
CASH RESOURCES:		
United States 4% Bonds, par value,	$1,716,150.00	
Other Bonds,	69,000.00	
Bond Premiums,	226,950.23	
Due from Approved Reserve Agents,	463,902.64	
Due from Banks and Bankers,	263,129.58	
Cash on hand,	628,813.16	
Due from United States Treasurer,	62,010.00	3,429,955.61
		$6,928,501.41

LIABILITIES:

Capital Stock paid in,	$1,600,000.00
Surplus Fund,	160,000,00
Other Undivided Profits,	8,129.40
Circulating Notes Received from Comptroller,	1,240,200.00
Dividends Unpaid,	48,000.00
Deposits,	3,872,172.01
	$6,928,501.41

Third National Bank financial statement, 1883.

American National Bank building in Washington, DC, ca. 1910-1920.

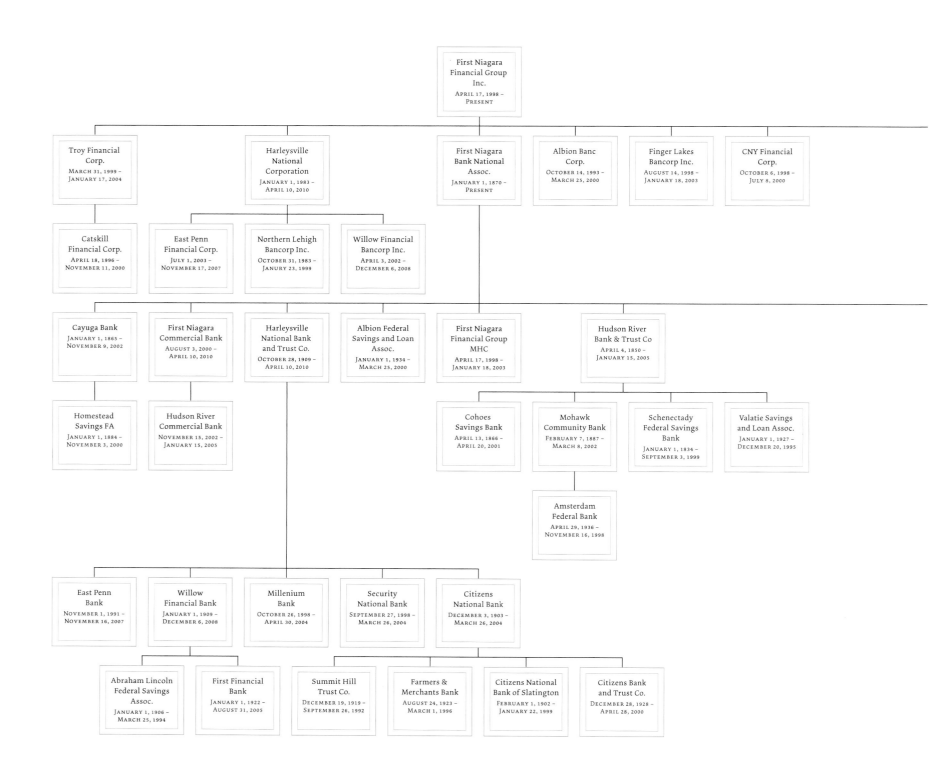

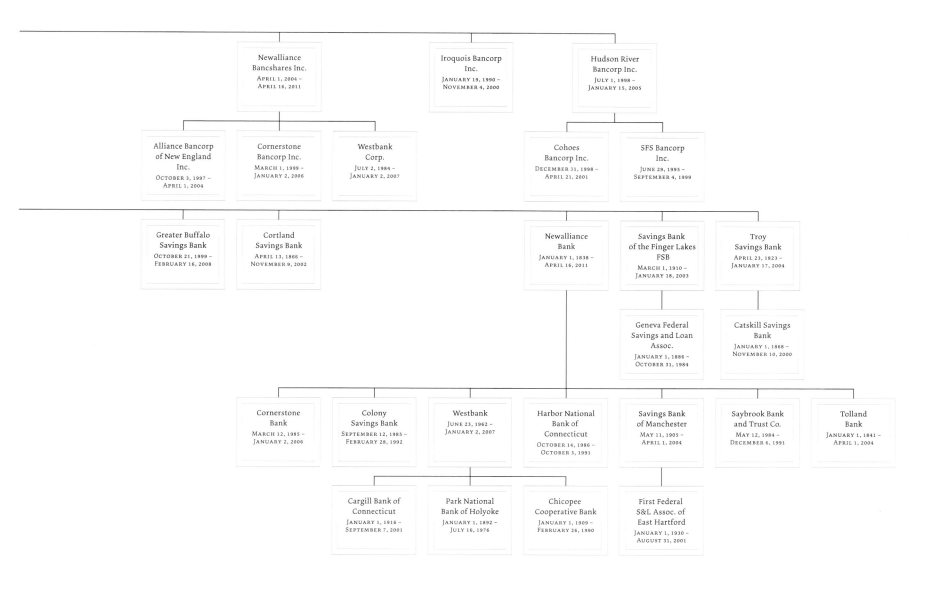

First Niagara

RANK	HEADQUARTERS	TICKER	ASSETS	EARLIEST KNOWN ANCESTOR	INDUSTRY OF ORIGIN
44	Buffalo, NY	FNFG	$37,000,000,000	1823	Commercial Banking

Farmers and Mechanics Savings Bank check, dated 1908.

Panorama of Buffalo Harbor, New York, ca. 1925.

First Niagara began its corporate existence as Farmers and Mechanics' Savings Bank, a mutual savings bank chartered in Lockport, New York, about 30 miles northeast of Buffalo, on May 11, 1870. Little is known of its early years because there are no publicly available copies of its published history, *On the Eve of a New Half-Century Commemorating the Fiftieth Anniversary of an Institution: 1870–1920*, although the bank clearly weathered the Great Depression despite suffering mortgage defaults in Brooklyn. Its president during those hard years, Charles H. Wendell, began with the bank as a bookkeeper in 1889. After that, the second entry in the bank's list of "historical dates" was in 1967, when it changed its name to Lockport Savings Bank. In subsequent years, it opened a handful of branches in western New York towns like Medina, Batavia and Ransomville.

After the collapse of Buffalo's most important thrifts, Empire of America and Goldome, in 1990 and 1991, respectively, the bank began to spread more aggressively from its base in Niagara, Orleans and Genesee counties into Erie County. CEO William Swan, who came to the bank from M&T (#30), believed in organic growth, so instead of making acquisitions, the bank established de novo branches while modernizing its human resources, management and risk systems. At the end of 1991, Lockport Savings was the nation's 273rd largest thrift, with deposits of almost $628 million. Branches launched in several supermarkets in 1993 helped both sides of the balance sheet. In 1997 assets topped $1 billion, branches numbered 15, employees numbered almost 400 and Swan gave an impassioned defense of mutuality, calling it among the most "misunderstood and maligned forms of banking."

Yet the very next year, Swan and his bank could not resist the wave of demutualization sweeping the industry, beginning a demutualization process completed in 2003. Also in 1998, it formed an HC called Niagara Bancorp and entered the risk management business by acquiring Warren-Hoffman Associates, an insurance brokerage. Two years later, in 2000, it changed its name to First Niagara Financial Group because Swan thought that Lockport Savings was "a little bit confining." The bank also expanded its presence in the Rochester area and began buying up small banks and financial services companies. Thereafter, de novo branch formation and acquisitions continued at a frenzied pace even through Swan's death in August 2003 and the 2008 financial crisis.

In 2009, while competitors languished nearly insolvent, CEO John Koelmel kept looking at his bank's balance sheet and a picture of a basketball hoop in his office captioned "You'll always miss 100% of the shots you don't take." Both chided him to make deal after deal, which, bolstered by $184 million in TARP funds (quickly repaid) and $1 billion in new equity, the bank did by acquiring 57 National City/PNC (#12) branches in western Pennsylvania, moving aggressively into southeastern Pennsylvania with the purchase of Harleysville National and relocating its headquarters to Buffalo.

Many lauded the deals, which contained protections for First Niagara if the loan portfolios of the acquired branches and banks further deteriorated. "A lot of healthy institutions looking for institutions that haven't failed yet are looking at [the bank's deals] as one way of mitigating risk," consultant Rick Childs told *American Banker* in December 2009.

Analysts and employees also lauded Koelmel's fun-loving yet analytically disciplined style. "Instead of coming out from the side of a stage with a three-piece suit on and talking to employees, he'll come running down the aisle in a motorcycle outfit or football uniform," a fellow executive told reporter Matthew de Paula. "Employees love it." Yet Washington attorney John Gorman noted that Koelmel was

Interior of the Farmers and Mechanics' Savings Bank, ca. 1910.

Sketch of the Farmers and Mechanics' Savings Bank building located at 116 Main Street, Lockport, New York.

a tough negotiator, telling de Paula that he had seen Koelmel "walk from the table, only to have a deal brought back to him on better terms for the company."

First Niagara became a national bank in 2010, and the following year it acquired 195 HSBC (#11) branches in New York and Connecticut. By 2012, however, it was clear that the bank was having difficulty digesting its acquisitions. Rating agencies saw some problems, ranking it in the B range (not bad, but not great either), and its stock price fell even while the broader S&P bank index moved upward. The board ousted Koelmel in March 2013 because the consensus was that he had expanded too aggressively and that a pause was needed.

Indeed, First Niagara had achieved Swan's decade-old plan to make the bank a smaller version of Citigroup (#3), as it was involved in insurance, investment services, auto lending and leasing, benefit consulting, wealth management and mortgages, as well as traditional retail banking activities. By 2013 it operated approximately 420 branches in New York, Connecticut, Massachusetts and Pennsylvania, and its 6,000 employees serviced about one million customers.

Its competitive advantage, it claimed in its 2013 corporate summary, lay in the quality and experience of its executive leadership and its expert, localized credit decision-making structure. But it still had a big heart, claiming that its "shared passion and unparalleled teamwork are focused on making a positive and lasting difference in the communities where we live and work."

Sources

Agosta, Veronica. "Niagara of Buffalo Aiming for Citigroup-Style Diversity." *American Banker*, April 7, 2000, 6.

"Bank Sells in Brooklyn." *The New York Times*, June 8, 1939, 51.

Barba, Robert. "Too Many Deals, Bad Timing Doomed John Koelmel at First Niagara." *American Banker*, March 21, 2013.

Benford, Robert D. "The College Sports Reform Movement: Reframing the 'Edutainment' Industry." *Sociological Quarterly* 48, 1 (Winter 2007): 14.

"Charles H. Wendell." *The New York Times*, March 29, 1945, 20.

De Guzman, Charina. "Sold on Supermarket Branches, NY State Thrift to Open a Second." *American Banker*, October 15, 1993, 7.

De Paula, Matthew. "First Niagara CEO Is Not One to Stay on the Sidelines." *American Banker*, December 7, 2009, A8.

First Niagara Financial Group. "The First Niagara Story." Unpublished PowerPoint, 2013.

———. "Historical Dates." Unpublished spreadsheet, 2013.

———. "Second Quarter Corporate Summary: Facts, Figures and Community Impact." Buffalo, NY: First Niagara Financial Group, 2013.

Hartley, Tom. "Lockport Savings Builds Empire." *Buffalo Business First*, April 21, 1997.

Kline, Alan. "Thrift IPOs Average 52.5% Jump in First Day." *American Banker*, May 1, 1998, 6.

Peters, Andy. "First Niagara Hiring Lenders as It Looks for Permanent CEO." *American Banker*, July 22, 2013.

Provost, Taran. "Expanding NY Bank Renames Subsidiary." *American Banker*, January 20, 2000, 6.

Sullivan, Joanna. "Heartfelt Chorus of Support for the Fading Mutual Thrift." *American Banker*, April 30, 1997, 5.

"Top 300 U.S. Thrift Institutions in Deposits." *American Banker*, May 14, 1992, 10.

"Upstate Bank Sells Brooklyn Dwelling." *The New York Times*, July 8, 1939, 31.

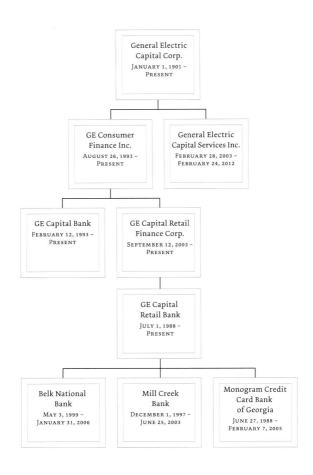

General Electric Capital

RANK	HEADQUARTERS	TICKER	ASSETS	EARLIEST KNOWN ANCESTOR	INDUSTRY OF ORIGIN
8	Norwalk, CT	GEC	$529,000,000,000	1878	Manufacturing

The total capacity of the steam turbine generators produced by the General Electric Company is equal to the working power of 170 million men. More and more the hard tasks of life are being transferred from human shoulders to the iron shoulders of machines.

A monument to courage

This machine is a Curtis Steam Turbine Generator. Many called it a "piece of folly" in 1903. It was the largest turbine generator ever built up to that time.

Today General Electric Company builds steam turbine generators ten times as big as this pioneer; and the "piece of folly" is preserved as a monument to courage.

GENERAL ELECTRIC

General Electric steam turbine generator advertisement, ca. 1909.

Another $2,003.10 coffee break
G-E communications know-how could've prevented

Ten cents for the coffee. Three dollars in wages. And $2,000 in lost business. All because he wasn't reached in time. In time to service a customer.

Communication would've prevented it. Communication speeds business. And General Electric speeds communication.

For instance, a G-E two-way mobile radio system instantly reaches those people who spend more time behind a wheel than behind a desk. Reaches them when they're needed.

Or take the G-E personal paging system. It instantly reaches those inside people who aren't always near a phone. Reaches them quietly and privately.

And a G-E microwave system instantly transmits messages and computer data between plants. Speeds it over long distances.

When communication is counted on for so much, it has to be good. That's why companies going for electronic business communication, go for General Electric.

G-E was in on the communications business from the beginning. It's the world's largest electronics manufacturer. The world's largest electrical equipment manufacturer. That's where it gets its communications know-how.

For these same reasons, G-E also receives R & D assignments. From business. Industry. Government. Companies large and small. For all of them, new methods of communication are constantly being developed.

Through General Electric communications know-how.

Look into it. Contact the G-E communications consultant listed in the Yellow Pages under "Radio Communications." Or write: General Electric Company, Communication Products Dept., Section 3216-10, Lynchburg, Virginia.

Communications for Business
Mobile Radio · Paging Systems · Microwave

GENERAL ELECTRIC

General Electric communications advertisement from U.S. News & World Report, 1966.

General Electric Capital Corporation (GE Capital) is a subsidiary of the industrial conglomerate General Electric (GE), which formed from a merger of Edison General Electric and Thomson-Houston in 1892. GE soon became an industrial giant in a dizzying array of businesses in both the United States and abroad. GE formed the subsidiary as General Electric Credit Corporation (GE Credit) in 1932 and for decades operated it much like GM ran GMAC (now Ally Financial [#20]), except it helped customers to finance GE refrigerators instead of GM automobiles. Only later did the subsidiary expand into automobile financing, aircraft leasing, pet insurance, private-label credit cards and just about everything else under the financial sun.

In 1978 GE Credit earned just $67 million on $5 billion in assets. Jack Welch described it as a "popcorn stand," meaning a side business of little consequence, but he recognized its potential to generate a significant amount of cash. "I fell in love with the idea of melding the discipline and the cash flows from manufacturing with financial ingenuity to build a great business," he explained. So after Welch became CEO in 1981, GE Credit bulked up by convincing GE's best and brightest to join it.

As late as 1982, Welch "stewed and stewed over a $90 million" transaction, the purchase of American Mortgage Insurance from Baldwin United. Double-digit annual growth, however, soon rendered such sums insignificant. Beginning in 1984, GE Credit became what Welch called "an acquisition machine," plunging into leasing, reinsurance and—with the purchase of an 80% stake in Kidder, Peabody—investment banking. The diversification spree prompted the name change to GE Capital in 1987.

By 1991 financial services accounted for 26% of GE's revenues but, thanks to $340 million in losses incurred by a single bond trader at Kidder, Peabody, not as high a percent of GE's profits. In 1994 GE sold Kidder, Peabody for $670 million and a 24% stake in broker PaineWebber. Soon after, UBS paid $10.8 billion for PaineWebber, earning GE $2 billion. Welch was thrilled that the company had turned a bum deal into a modestly successful one, but the episode helped to remind him and the rest of GE Capital of Benjamin Franklin's admonition that you don't really earn any interest if you never collect the principal.

In the 1990s GE Capital completed more than 400 deals involving over $200 billion. By 1995 it owned the country's largest noncaptive US auto lessor, GE Auto Financial Services, as well as its largest mortgage insurance and reinsurance companies. By then its assets had grown to $186 billion as it bought on average 30 insurance, credit card processing and other financial companies each year.

"We fought like hell over a lot of deals," Welch later recalled, especially two giant deals in Japan, the financial system of which lay in tatters after several asset bubbles burst in the late 1980s. After years of due diligence, GE Capital ended up owning big pieces of the Japanese life insurance and short-term consumer loan markets. The latter deal even earned the praises of storied investor Warren Buffett. "If you weren't there," he reportedly told Welch, "I would have taken that one."

During the dotcom boom, several GE Capital traders wanted an equity stake in the deals they were investing GE money in. Welch, however, explained: "There is only one equity currency in GE, and that is GE stock." His rationale was Buffett-esque: "Everyone's life raft is tied to the same boat." If GE went down, then everybody in GE, including the traders in GE Capital, should go down with it. Although a common sense decision, it took some courage for Welch to buck conventional wisdom, especially when it came to GE Capital, which Welch himself called "the growth engine."

Between 1980 and 2000, GE Credit/Capital grew from $11 billion invested in 10 lines of business, all in North America, to $370 billion invested in 24 lines of business spread across 48 countries. By the latter year, GE Capital accounted for about 40% of GE's profits, in large part because its managers did not think about market share. Rather, they thought about creating entirely new markets that the company would naturally dominate, at least at first.

GE Capital sent its executives across the world looking for opportunities in any business allowed by its expansive charter, which was basically anything outside of manufacturing or broadcasting. Their strategy meetings were called "dreaming sessions" and were supposed to be inquisitive and even fun. Nobody was allowed to discuss rate of return or other profit-related numbers. Each session ended with the formulation of hypotheses that were then field-tested. Operational meetings, by contrast, were very businesslike and filled with concrete numbers because business decisions arose from them. In those meetings, some 20 executives with over 400 years of combined business experience put presenters through their paces, outright rejected 10% of the proposals and sent another 20% back to the drawing board.

Searching for new businesses helped to diversify the subsidiary's risks: in 1977, GE Credit was involved in half a dozen lines of domestic finance, but by 2001 GE Capital had its fingers in 28 different financial businesses across the globe. Its constant innovation seemed risky to some outsiders, but deals subject to such careful screening usually worked out. In 1998, for example, in the midst of the Asian currency crisis, it made good money on a partnership with Goldman Sachs (#5) to buy Thai auto loan paper at 45 cents on the dollar. The deal required the company to hire and train 1,000 additional workers in just a few months, but Mark Norbom, the executive in charge, got it done.

Its confidence bolstered, GE Capital went on to make several other troubled asset deals in Asia, "all of which panned out well for GE and the local economies," Welch later said. Similarly, when buying banks in Eastern Europe after the fall of the Berlin Wall, GE was careful not to buy substandard allied businesses, like appliance distribution companies teeming with notorious Russian-made televisions and the like.

Moreover, GE Capital usually began each new venture only in a small way. Welch called it walking before running, or tiptoeing into the water instead of diving in. As one insider explained to strategy professor Gary Hamel, "we do hundreds of acquisitions. But it's very unusual for us to do a big transaction" because it generally carried "big risks." When an investment went south, GE Capital usually did not write it off as a loss and move on, as most BHCs do. Rather it "took it over and ran it" because, as Welch explained, "we had the operational capability that let us stick with a tough asset." In 1989, for example, GE Capital paid too much for its acquisition of Patrick Media from famous dealmaker John Kluge. Billboard use hit rock bottom, but instead of writing off $650 million, GE Capital rebuilt the business and made a modest gain on its sale in 1995.

Like other parts of GE, GE Capital implemented the company's legendary Six Sigma program for increasing quality and efficiency. A Six Sigma team noted that mortgage customers could not get through to the company's customer service representatives almost one-quarter of the time they called 41 of the company's 42 call centers. One center, though, had an almost perfect pick-up record. The team analyzed the successful center and cloned its process flows, equipment, physical layout and staff incentives. "Customers who once found us inaccessible nearly one-quarter of the time," Welch beamed, "now had a 99.9% chance of getting a GE person on the first try."

"The company," Welch claimed, "was always careful about the bets it made in financial services." That goes a long way toward explaining GE Capital's experience during the 2008 financial crisis. In September, investors hammered GE's stock on fears that its promiscuous finance arm had gotten itself into trouble along with the rest of its peers. That spurred talk of spinning off the unit as a BHC eligible for emergency Federal Reserve loans. CEO Jeffrey Immelt decided instead to pursue the less radical alternative of shrinking the finance unit, losses at which caused GE in February 2009 to cut its stock dividend for the first time since the Great Depression.

By mid-2010, however, GE Capital was getting back to its old self, but with more cash and better financial ratios. "Our GE Capital franchise is starting to snap back," Immelt told *Investor's Business Daily*. By the end of 2012 it was again paying a dividend to its parent and making acquisitions, including MetLife's bank. In July 2013 federal regulators branded GE Capital as "systemically important," meaning that they would step up scrutiny of its operations and capital cushion.

Sources

Alloway, Tracy. "AIG and GE Capital Branded 'Systemically Important'." *FT.com*, July 9, 2013.

Cain, Patrick. "Turnaround in GE Capital Arm Helping Parent." *Investor's Business Daily*, May 21, 2010, B3.

Cox, Rob, Lauren Silva and Richard Beales. "Gloomy What-Ifs from GE Capital." *The New York Times*, September 23, 2008, C2.

Guerrera, Francesco and Justin Baer. "GE Capital's Downsizing Welcome." *FT.com*, December 3, 2008.

Hamel, Gary. *Leading the Revolution*. Boston: Harvard Business School Press, 2000.

Mattera, Philip. *World Class Business: A Guide to the Most Powerful Global Corporations*. New York: Holt, 1992, 297–310.

Postal, Arthur D. "MetLife to Sell Bank to GE Capital." *LifeHealthPro*, November 16, 2012.

Slywotzky, Adrian, David Morrison and Bob Andelman. *The Profit Zone: How Strategic Business Design Will Lead You to Tomorrow's Profits*. New York: Times Business, 1997, 85–87.

Welch, Jack and John A. Byrne. *Jack: Straight from the Gut*. New York: Warner Books, 2001.

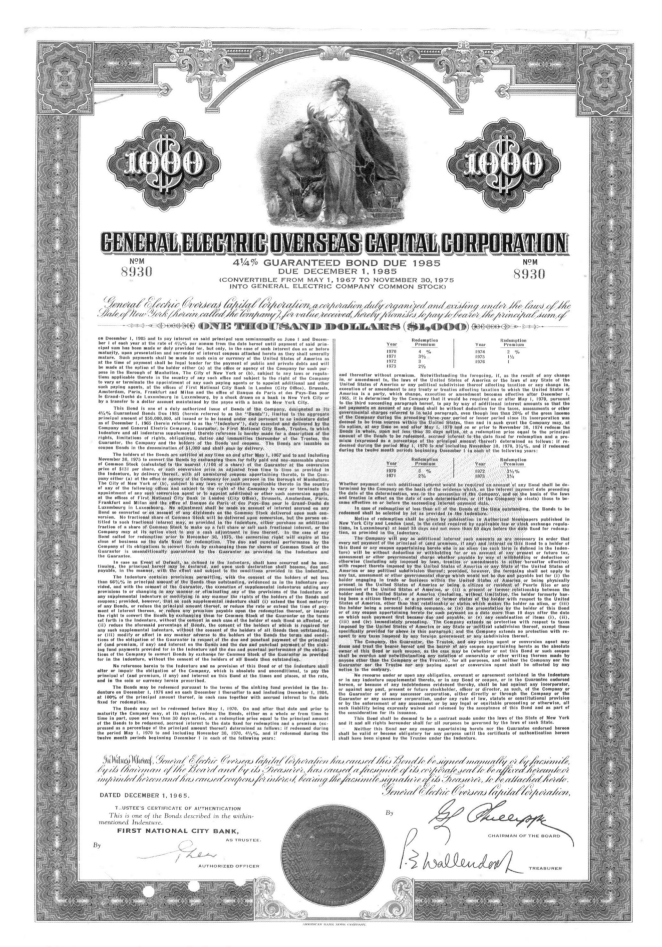

General Electric Overseas Capital Corporation bond certificate, 1965.

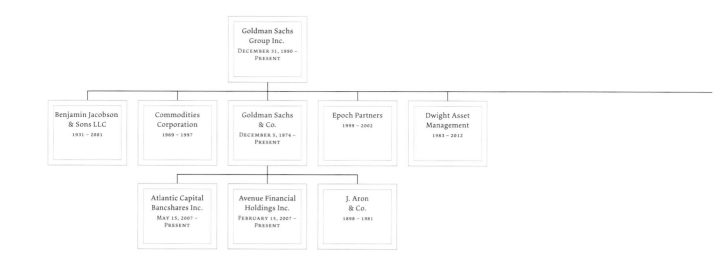

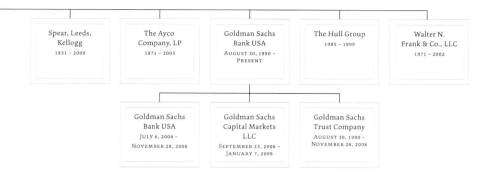

Spear, Leeds, Kellogg
1931 – 2000

The Ayco Company, LP
1971 – 2003

Goldman Sachs Bank USA
AUGUST 30, 1990 – PRESENT

The Hull Group
1985 – 1999

Walter N. Frank & Co., LLC
1971 – 2002

Goldman Sachs Bank USA
JULY 6, 2004 – NOVEMBER 28, 2008

Goldman Sachs Capital Markets LLC
SEPTEMBER 23, 2008 – JANUARY 7, 2009

Goldman Sachs Trust Company
AUGUST 30, 1990 – NOVEMBER 28, 2008

Goldman Sachs

RANK	HEADQUARTERS	TICKER	ASSETS	EARLIEST KNOWN ANCESTOR	INDUSTRY OF ORIGIN
5	New York, NY	GSF	$939,000,000,000	1869	Investment Banking

A brokerage house receives an order to buy ten shares of Goldman Sachs

Magagine cartoon depicting a brokerage house receiving an order to buy 10 shares of Goldman Sachs as papers fly and people cheer and dance.

B.F. Goodrich Rubber Company advertisement from The Literary Digest, *1925.*

Goldman Sachs traces its roots to 1869, when founder Marcus Goldman began arbitraging the promissory notes of leather merchants and jewelers along Maiden Lane in Manhattan. In 1884 Goldman asked his son-in-law, Sam Sachs, to join him in partnership, essentially jilting his own son Henry, who had been clerking since dropping out of Harvard, ostensibly owing to his poor eyesight. As M. Goldman & Sachs expanded, Henry took a job as a traveling salesman. He finally became a partner in the company, by then called Goldman Sachs & Co., in 1894.

In its first half-century, all of the company's partners were members of the intermarried families and ran the firm conservatively. The company bought a seat on the New York Stock Exchange for $15,000 in 1896, when its offices were home to five partners, 10 clerks and six messengers. In 1900 Marcus finally stepped aside and elevated Henry, who liked to trade railroad bonds, to full partner, while Sam, now the senior partner, visited Europe to expand the company's currency trading.

After Marcus died in 1904, Henry was promoted to co-senior partner, and old animosities and jealousies between him and Sam erupted. According to family historian June Breton Fisher, "the two were unable to communicate without ending their meetings in storm clouds of frustrated wrath." The interpersonal difficulties, however, did not prevent the company from joining Lehman to take Sears & Roebuck public in 1904, or doing other important deals with May Department

Stores, F. W. Woolworth Company, B.F. Goodrich Company, Studebaker Corporation and other major companies. But at the end of 1917, with the duo's relationship further strained by differences of opinion regarding America's entry into the Great War, the pro-German Henry resigned. He never spoke to Sam again, and the families broke off social ties for almost a century.

Over the years, even after losing Henry Goldman, the company innovated in the institutional investor, IPO and mergers and acquisition markets. Not all of its innovations, however, turned out well. In December 1928 Goldman, Sachs, prompted by co-chairman Waddill Catchings, established an investment trust, a vehicle that allowed investors to buy into numerous companies at once and to do so with higher levels of leverage (borrowing) than they could have pulled off individually. Called Goldman Sachs Trading Corporation, it grew quickly through an IPO and a merger with another investment trust, the Financial and Industrial Securities Corporation. Enamored of its apparent success, the company decided to create two more investment trusts — Shenandoah and Blue Ridge — and allow Goldman Sachs Trading to acquire Pacific American Associates, yet another trust. The timing was poor, and all three crashed along with the stock market in 1929. By 1932 shares in Goldman Sachs Trading could be had for $1.75, well short of their issue price of $100. The others suffered similar fates but largely left the parent, which had divested most of the poorest investments before the crash, unscathed.

In 1930 Sidney Weinberg replaced Catchings as co-chairman. A short man with a serious lifelong Brooklyn accent, Weinberg turned out to be just the man for the job. He began his 62-year career at the company as assistant porter, a position so low that he was *promoted* to office boy. Paul Sachs (Sam's son) really launched his career, however, by giving him $25 to take a finance course at New York University and promoting him to the mailroom. Weinberg soon streamlined the operation and was put in charge. After a stint in the Navy during the Great War, he persevered until he reached the top of the company. Rather than try to buck the depressed economy of the 1930s or the Second World War (the cause of which he helped as vice chairman of the War Production Board), Weinberg positioned Goldman Sachs to thrive when the markets again swung upward, as they finally did in the 1950s. Then the company began to land big deals, like Ford's IPO in 1956.

Weinberg was still in charge when John Whitehead joined the company in October 1947. A Haverford graduate, Whitehead was a survivor of the Dog Red sector of Omaha Beach on D-Day. (Readers conversant with military history will be *very* impressed with the latter. Other readers should think of the opening scene in *Saving Private Ryan*.) Goldman, Sachs & Co. still dealt in commercial paper, traded securities (mostly bonds) and participated in securities issues.

Whitehead joined six other fellows in an old squash court ventilated only by a tiny porthole that left the court/office broiling in the summer and nippy in the winter. When Whitehead tried to work in a cotton seersucker suit one mid-summer day, Walter Sachs (Sam's grandson) sent him home to change into the company's woolen "uniform." Due to those experiences, Whitehead, who advanced quickly because of his Harvard Business School degree, work ethic and dexterous use of a slide rule, relaxed the dress code a little when he took over as co-chairman of the company in 1976.

Weinberg, dubbed "Mr. Wall Street" by the press, had impressed on Whitehead and other Goldmanites that investment banking was a matter of personal relationships, of friendship even. That meant listening closely to what clients needed and providing solutions that worked for *them*, not for the bank. In fact, during most of its history as a partnership, Goldman Sachs was the good kind of "greedy," willing to give up short-term profits in exchange for cementing long-term relationships that would yield higher profits in the future.

Partners had most of their net worth tied up in the company and, hence, were unwilling to "bet the bank" by taking high short-term risks, lest they lose their deferred bonuses and retirement benefits. So, for example, Whitehead had to wait until he became a partner before he could receive permission to try out an innovation called the "New Business Department" (NBD) that employed salesmen to call on clients in their offices. Up to that time, investment bankers held court in their Manhattan offices, like eastern potentates.

The NBD soon brought in more cash than it cost to run, so it caught on and was later called Investment Banking Services. Growth followed, but even when Mr. Wall Street's obituary made the front page of *The New York Times* in 1969 — four decades after the Great Crash — Goldman Sachs was not the juggernaut of Wall Street. The company's employees were encouraged to work hard and smart but eschew flashy assets and braggadocio. Executives were to play by the same rules, so their offices were not palatial and their furnishings were a bit shabby. The company refused to work with corporate "raiders" because it did not believe that doing so would be in the best interest of its clients.

Despite a few hiccups, such as the 1970 bankruptcy of its commercial-paper client Penn Central, the company's "good" behavior continued as it grew into the envy of Wall Street, and the world, in the 1970s,

1980s and 1990s. Step one was aggressive overseas expansion, beyond the small office in Toronto and into London, continental Europe, Japan and Hong Kong. The company used its expertise in commercial paper (as late as the 1960s it handled half of the US commercial paper market, some $200 million *per day*) and historical reputation as entering wedges. By the end of its international push in the 1990s it was, according to Whitehead, the world's first truly global investment bank in the sense that it did more than service its American clients with overseas projects; it competed with foreign investment banks for *their* domestic business. Step two was revamping the company's internal accounting and budgeting procedures to provide partners and managers with incentives to increase revenues and cut expenses in realistic ways.

Even before he became co-chairman with John Weinberg, Sidney's son, Whitehead feared the company was growing so fast that its Weinbergian culture was in danger of dissolving, so he promulgated Goldman's 14 core business principles. Number one was "our clients' interests always come first." Number two was that reputation was "the most difficult . . . asset . . . to restore." Goldman remained humble even as its future co-chairman, Robert Rubin, in 1981 pushed the company into acquiring rough-and-tumble commodities trader J. Aron — which used the word counterparty instead of customer or client — and into hiring Fischer Black so that it could enter the derivatives game. A million dollars was a big bonus to cap a banner year; most of the partners' equity remained at work in the company, forcing them to take a conservative, long-term perspective that made a virtual religion of the 14 core principles. But those days wouldn't last forever.

After considering for three decades the idea of going public, the company finally pulled the trigger in May 1999. Principle number three, added after the company's IPO, promised that "significant employee stock ownership aligns the interests of our employees and our shareholders." That turned out to be untrue, just as Whitehead had initially feared. Instead of holding a stake in what they hoped would be a long-term enterprise, former Goldman partners suddenly owned shares, very liquid stakes that would lose value if the company did not meet short-term earnings expectations. Executives no longer had to wait until retirement to cash out, and the partners were no longer personally liable for the company's debts. Under the new incentives and external pressures, Goldman slowly but surely transmogrified from an investment bank that engaged in some proprietary trading into a trading company that did a little investment banking on the side. Revenues ballooned from $16 billion in 2003 to almost $38 billion in 2006.

As 2008 dawned, the company's nearly 27,000 employees — ensconced in global financial centers like Frankfurt, Hong Kong, London, New York and Tokyo — worked hard and smart with other people who they believed to be "truly the best and brightest." Revenues poured into all three major divisions: asset management, mergers and acquisitions, and proprietary trading. It dominated the banking league tables by being among the top two or three in most major categories, including completed US mergers and acquisitions and global equity offerings.

Profits were usually very high, and much was paid back to employees in the form of high salaries and huge annual bonuses. That compensation structure, however, encouraged high levels of risk-taking and increased reliance on proprietary trading, which put the company's capital at risk. Instead of believing its own unrealistic risk models as some of its competitors did, however, the company religiously marked to market and also employed leaders who understood the businesses it was engaged in. It still took on a lot of risk, but as the 2008 financial crisis unfolded, it was able to off-load some of that risk onto clients. In one deal, for example, it increased buyer confidence in the securities it was selling by disclosing that it owned a large number of them without disclosing it also had an equally large short position. So if the security tanked, as it later did, Goldman Sachs would lose nothing.

Similarly, the company covered much of its exposure to the subprime meltdown with the "big short," the bet it made against US home values in late 2006 that garnered it some $4 billion when the housing and related financial markets began to crash. It later paid $550 million in fines and disgorgements to the SEC, after admitting that its marketing materials on the deal, which did not mention that it saw the housing crash coming, had "contained incomplete information." The transactions, journalist Roddy Boyd noted, were the sorts of deals "that Goldman was famous for *not* doing. . . . The pressures of being a public company," he argued, "conspired to fog Goldman's common sense."

Even with its adroit last-minute hedging maneuvers, Goldman Sachs still needed government money to stay afloat at the height of the 2008 financial crisis, and the company became a BHC to obtain emergency loans from the Federal Reserve. It also took TARP money and got a big infusion of cash from Warren Buffett, who rightly calculated that Goldman was too savvy a firm not to rebound and become a market leader once again. Its stock price, which hit $165 in September 2008, dropped to $47.41, an all-time low, by Thanksgiving. However, by 2009 the company's CEO, Lloyd Blankfein, was named "Person of the Year" by the *Financial Times*. Goldman's profits soared to $13.2 billion, its stock price rebounded to above $190 per share and its TARP money was repaid.

Sources

Boyd, Roddy. *Fatal Risk: A Cautionary Tale of AIG's Corporate Suicide*. Hoboken, NJ: Wiley, 2011.

Cohan, William D. *Money and Power: How Goldman Sachs Came to Rule the World*. New York: Doubleday, 2011.

Ellis, Charles D. *The Partnership: The Making of Goldman Sachs*. New York: Penguin, 2008.

Endlich, Lisa. *Goldman Sachs: The Culture of Success*. New York: Touchstone, 1999.

Fisher, June Breton. *When Money Was in Fashion: Henry Goldman, Goldman Sachs, and the Founding of Wall Street*. New York: Palgrave Macmillan, 2010.

Galbraith, John Kenneth. *The Great Crash, 1929*. Boston: Houghton Mifflin, 1954.

Loosvelt, Derek, et al. *The Vault Guide to the Top 50 Banking Employers: 2008 Edition*. New York: Vault, 2007, 38–43.

Mandis, Steven G. *What Happened to Goldman Sachs: An Insider's Story of Organizational Drift and Its Unintended Consequences*. Boston: Harvard Business Review Press, 2013.

McLean, Bethany and Joe Nocera. *All The Devils Are Here: The Hidden History of the Financial Crisis*. New York: Penguin, 2010, 98–100, 151–59, 274–84.

Wetfeet. *25 Top Financial Services Firms*. San Francisco: Wetfeet. 2008, 46–49.

Whitehead, John C. *A Life in Leadership: From D-Day to Ground Zero, An Autobiography*. New York: Basic Books, 2005.

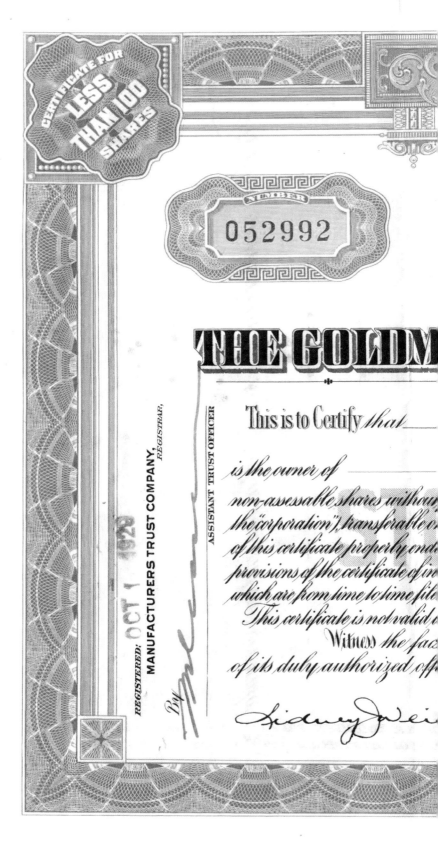

Goldman Sachs Trading Corporation stock certificate, 1929.

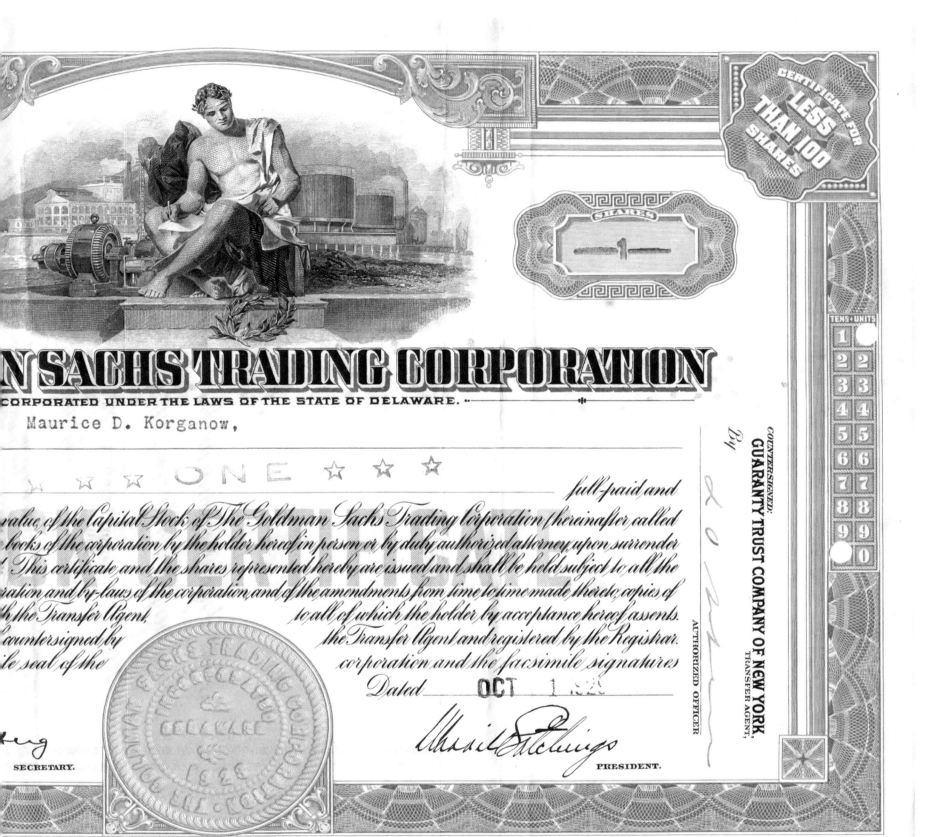

N SACHS TRADING CORPORATION

CORPORATED UNDER THE LAWS OF THE STATE OF DELAWARE.

Maurice D. Korganow,

☆ ☆ ONE ☆ ☆ ☆ ☆

value of the Capital Stock of The Goldman Sachs Trading Corporation (hereinafter called
books of the corporation by the holder hereof in person or by duly authorized attorney, upon surrender
This certificate and the shares represented hereby are issued and shall be held subject to all the
ration and by-laws of the corporation, and of the amendments from time to time made thereto, copies of
the Transfer Agent,   to all of which the holder by acceptance hereof assents.
countersigned by   the Transfer Agent and registered by the Registrar.
le seal of the   corporation and the facsimile signatures

Dated   OCT   1

full-paid and

COUNTERSIGNED:
GUARANTY TRUST COMPANY OF NEW YORK,
TRANSFER AGENT,

By

AUTHORIZED OFFICER

SECRETARY.

PRESIDENT.

AMERICAN BANK NOTE COMPANY.

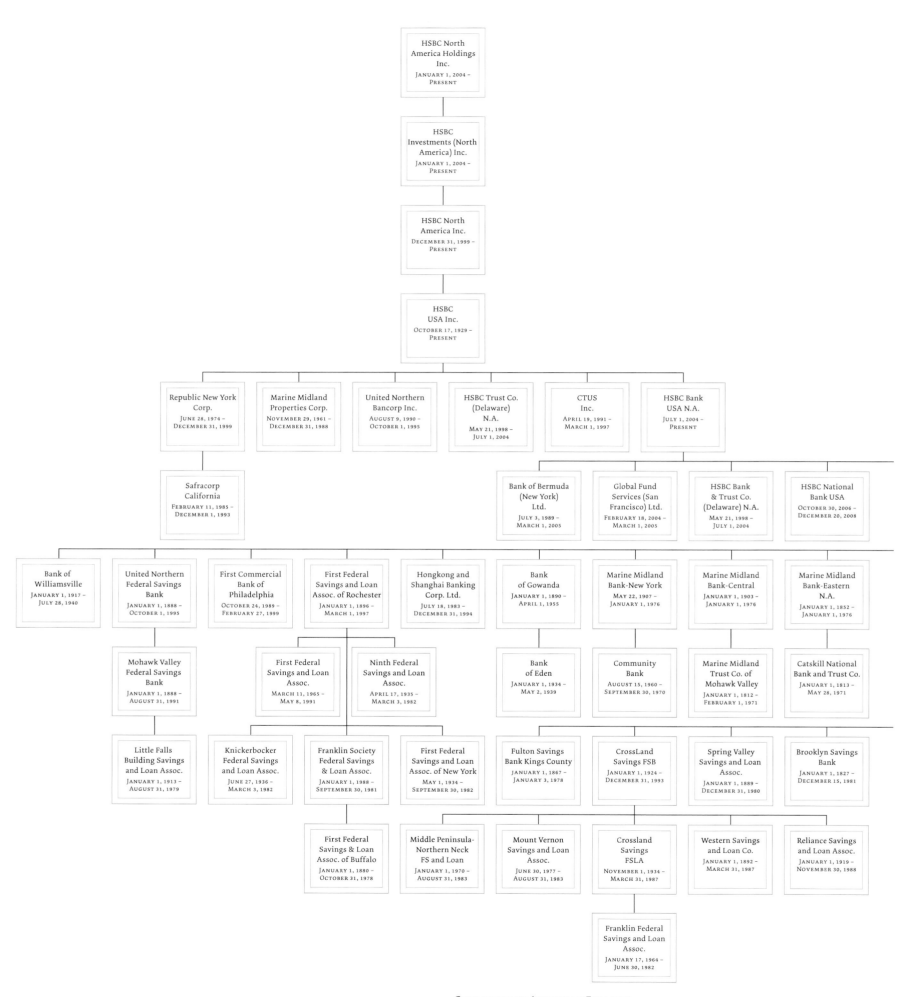

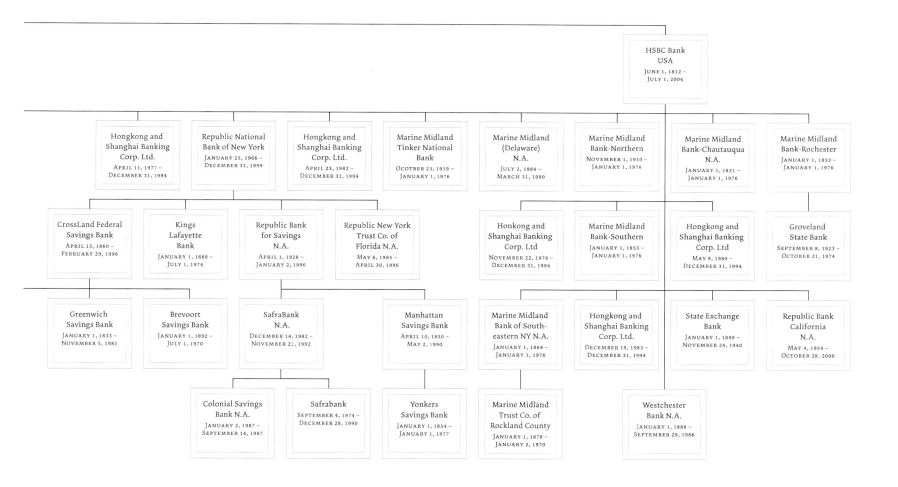

HSBC Bank
USA
JUNE 1, 1812 –
JULY 1, 2004

Hongkong and
Shanghai Banking
Corp. Ltd.
APRIL 11, 1977 –
DECEMBER 31, 1994

Republic National
Bank of New York
JANUARY 25, 1966 –
DECEMBER 31, 1999

Hongkong and
Shanghai Banking
Corp. Ltd.
APRIL 23, 1982 –
DECEMBER 31, 1994

Marine Midland
Tinker National
Bank
OCOTBER 23, 1919 –
JANUARY 1, 1976

Marine Midland
(Delaware)
N.A.
JULY 2, 1984 –
MARCH 31, 1990

Marine Midland
Bank-Northern
NOVEMBER 1, 1910 –
JANUARY 1, 1976

Marine Midland
Bank-Chautauqua
N.A.
JANUARY 1, 1831 –
JANUARY 1, 1976

Marine Midland
Bank-Rochester
JANUARY 1, 1853 –
JANUARY 1, 1976

CrossLand Federal
Savings Bank
APRIL 13, 1860 –
FEBRUARY 29, 1996

Kings
Lafayette
Bank
JANUARY 1, 1889 –
JULY 1, 1974

Republic Bank
for Savings
N.A.
APRIL 1, 1928 –
JANUARY 2, 1996

Republic New York
Trust Co. of
Florida N.A.
MAY 6, 1985 –
APRIL 30, 1996

Honkong and
Shanghai Banking
Corp. Ltd
NOVEMBER 22, 1976 –
DECEMBER 31, 1994

Marine Midland
Bank-Southern
JANUARY 1, 1853 –
JANUARY 1, 1976

Hongkong and
Shanghai Banking
Corp. Ltd
MAY 9, 1980 –
DECEMBER 31, 1994

Groveland
State Bank
SEPTEMBER 8, 1923 –
OCTOBER 21, 1974

Greenwich
Savings Bank
JANUARY 1, 1833 –
NOVEMBER 5, 1981

Brevoort
Savings Bank
JANUARY 1, 1892 –
JULY 1, 1970

SafraBank
N.A.
DECEMBER 14, 1982 –
NOVEMBER 21, 1992

Manhattan
Savings Bank
APRIL 10, 1850 –
MAY 2, 1990

Marine Midland
Bank of South-
eastern NY N.A.
JANUARY 1, 1864 –
JANUARY 1, 1976

Hongkong and
Shanghai Banking
Corp. Ltd.
DECEMBER 19, 1983 –
DECEMBER 31, 1994

State Exchange
Bank
JANUARY 1, 1899 –
NOVEMBER 24, 1940

Republic Bank
California
N.A.
MAY 4, 1984 –
OCTOBER 28, 2000

Colonial Savings
Bank N.A.
JANUARY 2, 1987 –
SEPTEMBER 14, 1987

Safrabank
SEPTEMBER 4, 1974 –
DECEMBER 28, 1990

Yonkers
Savings Bank
JANUARY 1, 1854 –
JANUARY 1, 1977

Marine Midland
Trust Co. of
Rockland County
JANUARY 1, 1878 –
JANUARY 2, 1970

Westchester
Bank N.A.
JANUARY 1, 1888 –
SEPTEMBER 29, 1986

HSBC North America

RANK	HEADQUARTERS	TICKER	ASSETS	EARLIEST KNOWN ANCESTOR	INDUSTRY OF ORIGIN
11	New York, NY	HSBC	$322,000,000,000	1812	Commercial Banking

Chinese staff of the Hong Kong head office in front of the bank premises in 1928.

Back office staff of Midland Bank in York, England, 1928.

As its name suggests, this entity is the holding company for the US operations of a foreign bank, HSBC, headquartered in London. The bank began its existence in 1865 as a joint-stock corporation styled The Hongkong and Shanghai Banking Company (later, Corporation). Established by a broad spectrum of Hong Kong interests, including American and Indian trading houses as well as European and British firms, it offered from its inception a full range of banking products supported by the directors' numerous business connections. Incorporated and headquartered in Hong Kong, it lent to businesses and also the Chinese government, at interest rates as high as 14% and with loans collateralized by customs duties.

Like many 19th century banks, HSBC issued paper notes that the populace used as money, a lucrative business that also helped to bolster the Chinese financial system. The bank also attracted a considerable volume of deposits, including those made by high-ranking government officials, which allowed it to double in size every decade. By the late 19th century HSBC was the largest foreign bank in China and, when necessary, it supported the Chinese banking system by lending to distressed native banks and the imperial government.

By 1930 total deposits at HSBC stood at over HK$925 million, but its unchallenged position had begun to erode after the May Thirtieth Movement of 1925–1926, a major populist backlash against foreign imperialist institutions, especially British ones. In addition to boycotting British-made products, Chinese protestors redeemed HSBC bank notes and withdrew deposits, while Chinese staff members walked off the job. By August 1925 HSBC's note circulation had been cut almost in half. Loans to the Chinese government were also curtailed because of the disruption.

As a result, HSBC focused more of its efforts on Hong Kong, without neglecting the Chinese mainland, particularly Shanghai. As a British colony, Hong Kong was much more stable than the mainland, which since the 1910s had often degenerated into civil war and warlordism. By the mid-1930s the bank knew, in the words of British envoy to China Sir Frederick Leith-Ross, that it was "regarded with considerable mistrust by the Chinese. It is considered in Chinese Government circles that [foreign] banks have deliberately accentuated Chinese difficulties." Nevertheless, in 1939 HSBC tried to stabilize the new Chinese currency, which reeled after the Japanese invasion of 1937, and was able to do so until early 1940. Thereafter, however, China suffered from a hyperinflation that impeded its war effort and ultimately helped to bring the Communist Mao Zedong to power.

HSBC's strong corporate culture, which was centered on executives' shared training in London, helped it to survive such travails. Due to a cultural disdain for committees, for example, HSBC gave its loan officers full discretion up to certain lending limits, over which they passed applications up the chain. That procedure generally allowed it to process loan requests within 24 hours decades before most other banks considered such a fast turnaround even possible, much less desirable.

HSBC started to become acquisitive in 1959 with its purchase of the British Bank of the Middle East and the Mercantile Bank, but it generally allowed its subsidiaries to keep their names and brand identities. In 1980, for example, it acquired a controlling interest (and the whole company in 1987) in Buffalo's Marine Midland, which had been established as the Marine Trust Company in 1850. The bank had long been a fixture in western New York, but it was not renamed HSBC until 1999, even though HSBC bankers had to come in and turn its American partner around in the late 1980s.

In 1992 HSBC Holdings, then a minor subsidiary registered in the UK and headquartered in London, purchased Britain's Midland Bank and its former parent, Hongkong Bank. It also established a BHC in the United States that became a major profit center and the 11th biggest

Hong Kong and Shanghai Banking Corporation $10 note (back) issued March 31, 1981.

bank in America. Despite the Anglo-American coup, Hongkong Bank's corporate culture long remained strong. John Bond, CEO of HSBC from 1993 until 1998, said the bank's strengths continued to be its "strong capital position, sound liquidity, asset quality, good expense control, centrally developed, cost-effective technology, short lines of communication, customer orientation, long-term careers and international teamwork," the very traits that had made Hongkong Bank such a formidable force in coastal China.

By the end of the first decade of the new millennium, however, the old corporate culture was suffering growing pains with untoward results, just as the bank's historian, Frank King, had warned.

In 2002 HSBC continued its move into Latin America, begun in Brazil and Argentina in 1997, with the purchase of a majority stake in Grupo Financiero Bital of Mexico. The next year it bought, for $14.2 billion, US consumer finance and credit card issuer Household International, and the bank acquired an interest in the Chinese life insurance market by the end of 2005. By 2007 HSBC employed 280,000 people in more than 10,000 offices in 82 nations worldwide. It called itself "the world's local bank," but no local bank was as big; at $75.9 billion, its 2006 *revenue* exceeded the *assets* of all but the 32 largest US BHCs in 2013.

Corrective actions taken in 2007 enabled HSBC to weather the 2008 financial crisis, despite having significant subprime mortgage exposure from its purchase of Household International. By 2010 the bank was one of the largest financial institutions in the world, with some 8,500 offices in 86 nations in Europe, Hong Kong, Asia, Africa and Latin America, as well as North America. It also boasted more than 100 million customers and about 220,000 shareholders from 119 countries and territories.

HSBC said it was interested in the long-term and, hence, focused on a strong capital base, strict cost controls, good governance and the development of long-term relationships with its customers. It also developed a sustainability program and argued that lenders must assess the social and environmental consequences of their borrowers' actions because damage caused by borrowers could impact their ability to repay their loans. In addition, it created a special Group Reputational Risk Committee that oversaw existing and potential reputational risks to the bank and its public image.

Nevertheless, the bank—like many others in recent years—has had to deal with several scandals ranging from money laundering to tax evasion. In 2012 it paid $1.92 billion to US authorities because it laundered at least $881 million of Mexican and Colombian drug money between 2006 and 2010.

"We accept responsibility for our past mistakes," HSBC chief Stuart Gulliver stated in late 2012. "We have said we are profoundly sorry for them, and we do so again. The HSBC of today is a fundamentally different organization from the one that made those mistakes."

Sources

Aspan, Maria. "HSBC's $1.9B Money-Laundering Penance Puts Industry on Notice." *American Banker*, December 12, 2012, 2.

Bhimani, Alnoor and Kazbi Soonawalla. "Sustainability and Organizational Connectivity at HSBC." In *Accounting for Sustainability: Practical Insights*, edited by Anthony Hopwood, Jeffrey Unerman, and Jessica Fries, 173–90. London: Earthscan, 2010.

Fontanella-Khan, James. "Belgian Police Raid HSBC Clients' Homes Amid Tax Probe." *FT.com*, October 15, 2013.

Horesh, Niv. *Shanghai's Bund and Beyond: British Banks, Banknote Issuance, and Monetary Policy in China, 1842–1937*. New Haven, CT: Yale University Press, 2009.

Ji, Zhaojin. *A History of Modern Shanghai Banking: The Rise and Decline of China's Finance Capitalism*. Armonk, NY: M.E. Sharpe, 2003, 45–50.

King, Frank. "Does the Corporation's History Matter? Hongkong Bank/HSBC Holdings: A Case Study." In *Business History and Business Culture*, edited by Andrew Godley and Oliver M. Westall, 116–37. New York: Manchester University Press, 1996.

King, Frank. *History of the Hongkong and Shanghai Banking Corporation* 4 vols. New York: Cambridge University Press, 1987.

Loosvelt, Derek, et al. *The Vault Guide to the Top 50 Banking Employers: 2008 Edition*. New York: Vault, 2007, 152–55.

HSBC bank notes.

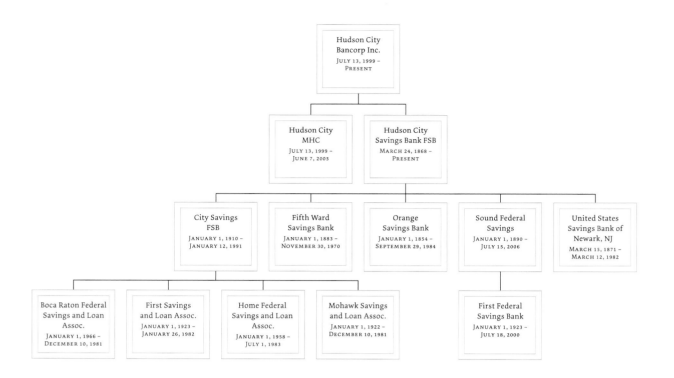

Hudson City Bancorp

RANK	HEADQUARTERS	TICKER	ASSETS	EARLIEST KNOWN ANCESTOR	INDUSTRY OF ORIGIN
43	Paramus, NJ	HCBK	$40,000,000,000	1854	Commercial Banking

Main office of the Hudson City Savings Bank, 1892.

Hudson City Savings Bank, 1895.

Hudson City Bancorp began operations as a mutual savings bank in the city of Hudson, New Jersey, in 1868. The Hudson City Savings Bank, as it was styled, lasted longer than the town of Hudson, which in 1870 merged with Bergen and Jersey to form Jersey City. The bank grew along with northern New Jersey, offering 5% to its depositors. Assets exceeded $1 million by 1899, when its long-serving first (and third) president, Garret D. Van Reipen, retired. The bank sailed through the Panic of 1907 and by 1909 boasted assets of almost $2 million. The Great War also had little effect on the institution, except to shift much of its growing portfolio into Victory bonds.

By the time the Great Depression struck, Hudson City Bank had a surplus and reserve over $663,000 and two offices, both in Jersey City. It remained open during the downturn and even increased its reserves to $779,000 as assets grew to over $11 million. It also grew during World War II, helping to soak up wages that workers could not use to buy rationed consumption goods, and assets exceeded $26 million in 1949, after a third Jersey City office opened.

After the war, New Jersey's population grew twice as fast as the national average, largely as a result of net migration into the state, which offered plenty of good jobs and affordable houses in new suburbs like Clark, Edison, Livingston, Paramus and Parsippany. By 1959 the bank had four Jersey City offices and originated $25 million worth of FHA, veterans and conventional mortgages.

By 1969 New Jersey had loosened its branching restrictions and the bank, which by then had assets of about $142 million, took advantage of the regulatory change by establishing a de novo branch in Waldwick in Bergen County. Over the next decade, CEO Kenneth L. Birchby moved aggressively into 12 counties with 43 new offices. He also moved the bank's headquarters from Jersey City to Paramus, in Bergen County, which suffered less from the depopulation and decrease in economic activity that had decimated other New Jersey cities like Atlantic City, Camden, Hoboken, Newark and Trenton, as well as Jersey City. Some of those cities began to rebound in the 1980s, however, and Leonard Gudelski, who became the bank's president in 1981, saw ample room for continued growth, acquiring the United States Savings Bank in 1982 and the Orange Savings Bank, which had eight offices and $513 million in assets, two years later.

By 1992 Hudson City had not only survived the S&L crisis, but *Money* magazine ranked it one of the safest banks in New Jersey. By that time the bank operated 69 offices throughout the state, its assets had increased to $4.3 billion, and its reserve stood at $475 million, or 12.15%

of deposits. In 1994 the bank's management decided to demutualize the institution in order, as *The New York Times* reported, to better "compete against larger banks." Before its plans to hold the largest mutual savings bank IPO in history came to fruition, however, the bank's board "unanimously voted to cancel plans to go public."

In 1997, when the bank had assets of $6.7 billion and about 75 branches spread over 13 New Jersey counties, Ronald E. Hermance replaced Gudelski as president, but the latter, who had become CEO in 1989, stayed on as CEO and board chairman.

Two years later, the bank created a mutual BHC instead of fully demutualizing. Although many predicted the bank's share price would not climb very fast from its $10 offering price, it jumped by 65% in just over a year on the back of a strategy analysts called "dull" but "successful."

Despite the change in its ownership structure, Hudson City's investment philosophy remained very conservative. In its 125th anniversary history, the bank assured readers that "we won't even consider highly leveraged or speculative bonds [and that] there are no junk bonds in Hudson City's portfolio."

In 2000, after the conversion, Gudelski assured depositors and investors that "We are not flashy. . . . We do not trade securities, our fee income is nominal and we do not have a venture capital arm. With us, day in and day out it is interest received minus interest expense." About 95% of the bank's $8.89 billion portfolio was then invested in residential mortgages, and its efficiency ratio, at 30.8%, was one of the lowest in the nation among thrifts.

In 2002, a year after Hermance replaced Gudelski as CEO, Hudson City's strategy remained that of a traditional thrift — originate and hold mortgages, 70% of which were fixed rate with maturities of 15 to 30 years — even as droves of borrowers refinanced older, higher-rate mortgages at lower rates. Janney Montgomery Scott analyst Rick Weiss told *American Banker* that Hudson City was unusual in that it retained the mortgages it originated rather than securitizing and selling them. "Hudson City," he said, was "about the purest thrift out there." Its profits came from cost controls, cheap deposits and credit quality, not complex banking.

The following year, the bank converted its New Jersey charter into a federal thrift charter in order to cut its regulatory costs by reducing the number of regulators it had to please. In the process it became an SLHC. "I don't think there was a day we didn't have a regulator on board here," Hermance told *American Banker*. "We'd just barely get done

Hudson City Savings Bank, ca. 1950.

with one exam when somebody else was coming in. That cost us a lot of money."

The move also helped the bank to branch across state lines, into downstate New York, and to fully demutualize, which was completed in June 2005, when its assets stood at over $21 billion. "We know how to grow organically," Hermance told reporters, signaling that the bank would continue with its planned de novo branch expansion.

Hudson City did so, but in 2006 it also made its first acquisition, of Sound Federal Bancorp of White Plains, New York. It was a cash deal and, hence, did not dilute the value of the bank's shares. With assets of $28 billion, the bank barely felt the $265 million deal, which added 14 branches, 130 employees and $1.1 billion of "pristine" assets. Founded in 1891, Sound was as sound as its name suggested and sold out simply because it was too small to get its ROE much above 3%.

Hermance was not caught by the housing bubble or subprime mortgage fad, nor was he deterred by negative analysts who considered the bank stodgy. "Many people pooh-pooh the thrift model," he explained, "but here is the thing: I don't think that customer has gone away — the customer who shops for the highest rate on deposits and the lowest mortgage rate."

He was right. Although some of its mortgages went bad during the debacle, the bank sailed through the difficulties of 2007 and 2008 because as defaults mounted so too did deposits as Americans responded to the crisis by cutting consumption and increasing savings. Aided by 125 branches and assets of $54 billion, the bank invested the deposits in its core business, jumbo mortgages on the best credit risks. By 2010 the bank, which was described as one of the healthiest regional banks in the country, was aggressively expanding its loan book.

Such success brought much attention to the bank, which in August 2012 was bought by M&T (#30) for about $3.7 billion. Regulators disliked the activities of some of M&T's recently acquired subsidiaries, however, so the deal was still pending at the end of 2013.

Sources

Alloway, Tracy. "M&T Bank Buys Hudson City for $3.7bn." *FT.com*, August 27, 2012.

Andrejczak, Matt. "NJ's Hudson City Had Trouble Finding Takers in $529M Initial Offering." *American Banker*, July 12, 1999, 7.

Barba, Robert. "Who Would Buy Hudson City If Sale to M&T Fell Through?" *American Banker*, August 26, 2013.

Fontana, Dominick. "Hudson City, Jersey Thrift, Taps Hermance as President." *American Banker*, January 24, 1997, 5.

"Hudson City Savings Bank Plans Initial Public Offering." *The New York Times*, February 17, 1994, D4.

"Hudson City Savings Cancels Plans to Go Public." *The New York Times*, June 30, 1994, D5.

Linder, Craig. "NJ's Hudson City Seeks Switch to OTS." *American Banker*, October 22, 2003, 4.

Monks, Matthew. "4Q Results: M&T, Hudson City Buck Lending Trends." *American Banker*, January 21, 2010, 12.

———. "Hudson City: Deposits Trump Bad Loan Growth." *American Banker*, March 19, 2009, 2.

"New Jersey Bank Commissioner Backs Hudson City-Orange Savings Merger." *American Banker*, January 1, 1982, 2.

New Jersey, the Nation and Hudson City Savings Bank. Peekskill, NY: Fitzgerald & Co., 1993.

Reosti, John. "A Plain-Vanilla Strategy Still First Choice at Hudson City." *American Banker*, November 7, 2002, 1.

———. "At Hudson City of N.J., Simplicity Is Prosperity: Vanilla Works as Other Thrifts Change Flavor." *American Banker*, August 2, 2000, 1.

———. "Cash-Flush Hudson City Eyes Multistate Expansion." *American Banker*, June 17, 2005, 1.

———. "CEO at Hudson City in N.J. to Step Down." *American Banker*, February 12, 2000, 24.

———. "Hudson City Finds a Taker; Clincher: Sound Federal Agrees to Take Cash." *American Banker*, February 10, 2006, 1.

Rieker, Matthias. "Against the Tide, Hudson City Builds Debt." *American Banker*, December 14, 2006, 20.

"Woman Banker Guilty." *The New York Times*, July 2, 1948, 23.

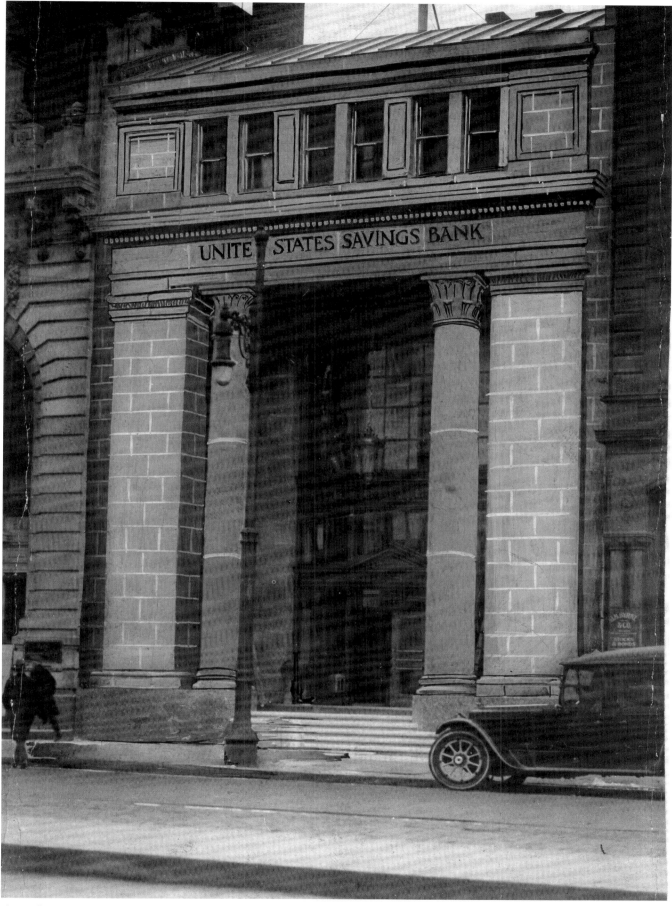

The United States Savings Bank building in Newark, New Jersey, 1920. Image has been hand edited by the Newark Evening Post, *a common pratice to show buildings that were undergoing renovations.*

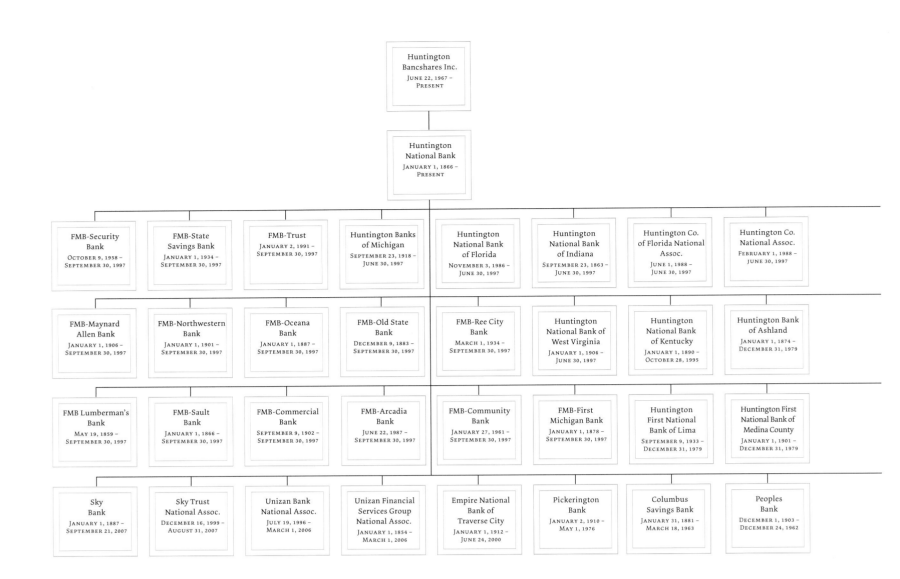

| Huntington Bancshares Inc. | | | | | | | |
| JUNE 22, 1967 – PRESENT | | | | | | | |

| Huntington National Bank | | | | | | | |
| JANUARY 1, 1866 – PRESENT | | | | | | | |

FMB-Security Bank	FMB-State Savings Bank	FMB-Trust	Huntington Banks of Michigan	Huntington National Bank of Florida	Huntington National Bank of Indiana	Huntington Co. of Florida National Assoc.	Huntington Co. National Assoc.
OCTOBER 9, 1958 – SEPTEMBER 30, 1997	JANUARY 1, 1934 – SEPTEMBER 30, 1997	JANUARY 2, 1991 – SEPTEMBER 30, 1997	SEPTEMBER 23, 1918 – JUNE 30, 1997	NOVEMBER 3, 1986 – JUNE 30, 1997	SEPTEMBER 23, 1863 – JUNE 30, 1997	JUNE 1, 1988 – JUNE 30, 1997	FEBRUARY 1, 1988 – JUNE 30, 1997
FMB-Maynard Allen Bank	FMB-Northwestern Bank	FMB-Oceana Bank	FMB-Old State Bank	FMB-Ree City Bank	Huntington National Bank of West Virginia	Huntington National Bank of Kentucky	Huntington Bank of Ashland
JANUARY 1, 1906 – SEPTEMBER 30, 1997	JANUARY 1, 1901 – SEPTEMBER 30, 1997	JANUARY 1, 1887 – SEPTEMBER 30, 1997	DECEMBER 9, 1883 – SEPTEMBER 30, 1997	MARCH 1, 1934 – SEPTEMBER 30, 1997	JANUARY 1, 1906 – JUNE 30, 1997	JANUARY 1, 1890 – OCTOBER 28, 1995	JANUARY 1, 1874 – DECEMBER 31, 1979
FMB Lumberman's Bank	FMB-Sault Bank	FMB-Commercial Bank	FMB-Arcadia Bank	FMB-Community Bank	FMB-First Michigan Bank	Huntington First National Bank of Lima	Huntington First National Bank of Medina County
MAY 19, 1859 – SEPTEMBER 30, 1997	JANUARY 1, 1866 – SEPTEMBER 30, 1997	SEPTEMBER 9, 1902 – SEPTEMBER 30, 1997	JUNE 22, 1987 – SEPTEMBER 30, 1997	JANUARY 27, 1961 – SEPTEMBER 30, 1997	JANUARY 1, 1878 – SEPTEMBER 30, 1997	SEPTEMBER 9, 1933 – DECEMBER 31, 1979	JANUARY 1, 1901 – DECEMBER 31, 1979
Sky Bank	Sky Trust National Assoc.	Unizan Bank National Assoc.	Unizan Financial Services Group National Assoc.	Empire National Bank of Traverse City	Pickerington Bank	Columbus Savings Bank	Peoples Bank
JANUARY 1, 1887 – SEPTEMBER 21, 2007	DECEMBER 16, 1999 – AUGUST 31, 2007	JULY 19, 1996 – MARCH 1, 2006	JANUARY 1, 1854 – MARCH 1, 2006	JANUARY 1, 1912 – JUNE 24, 2000	JANUARY 2, 1910 – MAY 1, 1976	JANUARY 31, 1881 – MARCH 18, 1963	DECEMBER 1, 1903 – DECEMBER 24, 1962

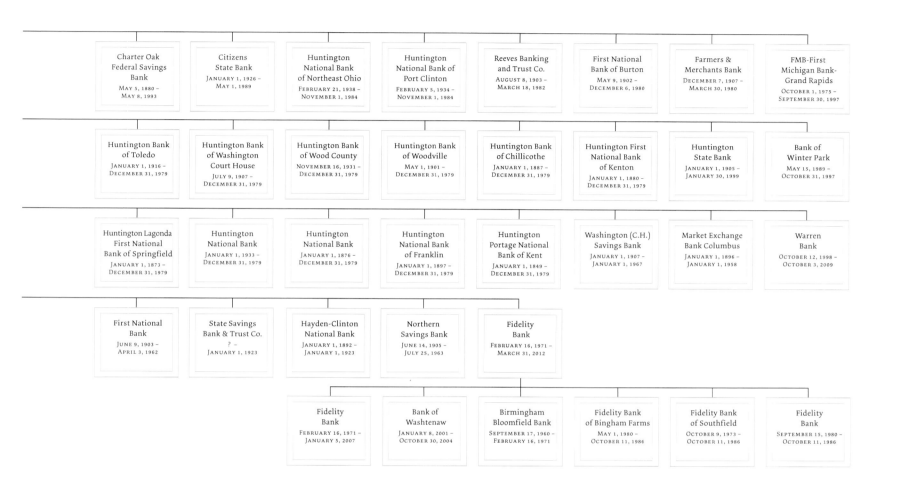

Charter Oak Federal Savings Bank MAY 5, 1880 – MAY 8, 1993	Citizens State Bank JANUARY 1, 1926 – MAY 1, 1989	Huntington National Bank of Northeast Ohio FEBRUARY 21, 1938 – NOVEMBER 1, 1984	Huntington National Bank of Port Clinton FEBRUARY 5, 1934 – NOVEMBER 1, 1984	Reeves Banking and Trust Co. AUGUST 8, 1903 – MARCH 18, 1982	First National Bank of Burton MAY 9, 1902 – DECEMBER 6, 1980	Farmers & Merchants Bank DECEMBER 7, 1907 – MARCH 30, 1980	FMB-First Michigan Bank-Grand Rapids OCTOBER 1, 1975 – SEPTEMBER 30, 1997
Huntington Bank of Toledo JANUARY 1, 1916 – DECEMBER 31, 1979	Huntington Bank of Washington Court House JULY 9, 1907 – DECEMBER 31, 1979	Huntington Bank of Wood County NOVEMBER 16, 1931 – DECEMBER 31, 1979	Huntington Bank of Woodville MAY 1, 1901 – DECEMBER 31, 1979	Huntington Bank of Chillicothe JANUARY 1, 1887 – DECEMBER 31, 1979	Huntington First National Bank of Kenton JANUARY 1, 1880 – DECEMBER 31, 1979	Huntington State Bank JANUARY 1, 1905 – JANUARY 30, 1999	Bank of Winter Park MAY 15, 1989 – OCTOBER 31, 1997
Huntington Lagonda First National Bank of Springfield JANUARY 1, 1873 – DECEMBER 31, 1979	Huntington National Bank JANUARY 1, 1933 – DECEMBER 31, 1979	Huntington National Bank JANUARY 1, 1876 – DECEMBER 31, 1979	Huntington National Bank of Franklin JANUARY 1, 1897 – DECEMBER 31, 1979	Huntington Portage National Bank of Kent JANUARY 1, 1849 – DECEMBER 31, 1979	Washington (C.H.) Savings Bank JANUARY 1, 1907 – JANUARY 1, 1967	Market Exchange Bank Columbus JANUARY 1, 1896 – JANUARY 1, 1958	Warren Bank OCTOBER 12, 1998 – OCTOBER 3, 2009
First National Bank JUNE 9, 1903 – APRIL 3, 1962	State Savings Bank & Trust Co. ? – JANUARY 1, 1923	Hayden-Clinton National Bank JANUARY 1, 1892 – JANUARY 1, 1923	Northern Savings Bank JUNE 14, 1905 – JULY 25, 1963	Fidelity Bank FEBRUARY 16, 1971 – MARCH 31, 2012			

Fidelity Bank FEBRUARY 16, 1971 – JANUARY 5, 2007	Bank of Washtenaw JANUARY 8, 2001 – OCTOBER 30, 2004	Birmingham Bloomfield Bank SEPTEMBER 17, 1960 – FEBRUARY 16, 1971	Fidelity Bank of Bingham Farms MAY 1, 1980 – OCTOBER 11, 1986	Fidelity Bank of Southfield OCTOBER 9, 1973 – OCTOBER 11, 1986	Fidelity Bank SEPTEMBER 15, 1980 – OCTOBER 11, 1986

Huntington Bancshares

Bank *(abridged)*

RANK	HEADQUARTERS	TICKER	ASSETS	EARLIEST KNOWN ANCESTOR	INDUSTRY OF ORIGIN
37	Columbus, OH	HBAN	$56,000,000,000	1846	Commercial Banking

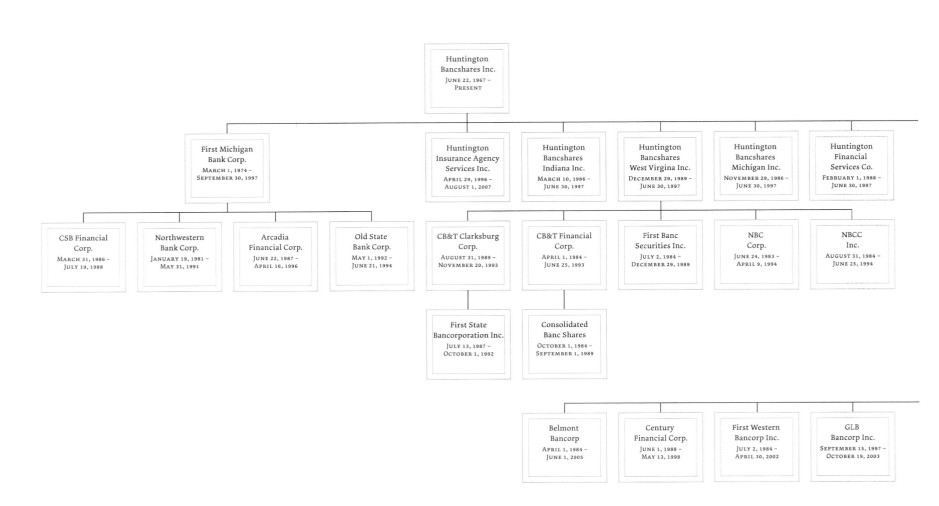

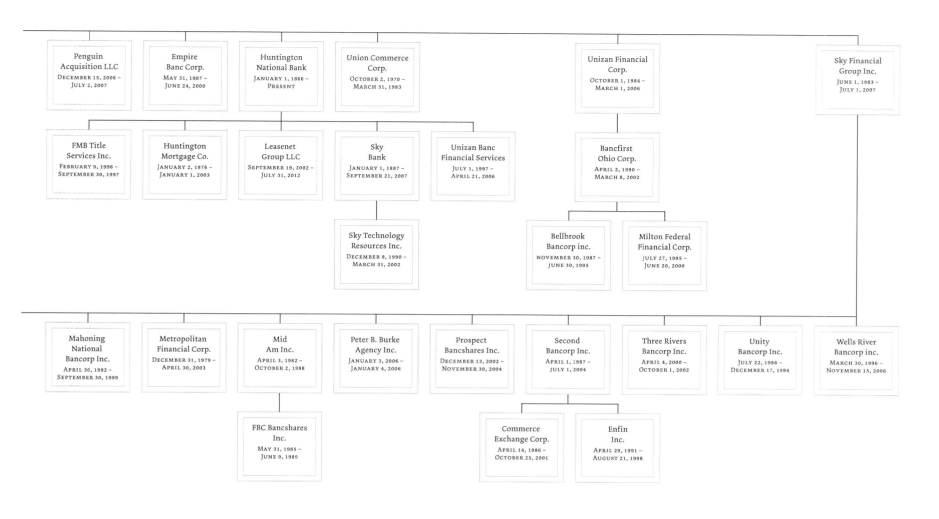

Penguin Acquisition LLC	Empire Banc Corp.	Huntington National Bank	Union Commerce Corp.		Unizan Financial Corp.		Sky Financial Group Inc.
DECEMBER 15, 2006 – JULY 2, 2007	MAY 31, 1987 – JUNE 24, 2000	JANUARY 1, 1866 – PRESENT	OCTOBER 2, 1970 – MARCH 31, 1983		OCTOBER 1, 1984 – MARCH 1, 2006		JUNE 1, 1983 – JULY 1, 2007

FMB Title Services Inc.	Huntington Mortgage Co.	Leasenet Group LLC	Sky Bank	Unizan Banc Financial Services	Bancfirst Ohio Corp.
FEBRUARY 9, 1996 – SEPTEMBER 30, 1997	JANUARY 2, 1976 – JANUARY 1, 2003	SEPTEMBER 19, 2002 – JULY 31, 2012	JANUARY 1, 1887 – SEPTEMBER 21, 2007	JULY 1, 1997 – APRIL 21, 2006	APRIL 2, 1990 – MARCH 8, 2002

Sky Technology Resources Inc.
DECEMBER 9, 1990 – MARCH 31, 2002

Bellbrook Bancorp inc.	Milton Federal Financial Corp.
NOVEMBER 30, 1987 – JUNE 30, 1995	JULY 27, 1995 – JUNE 20, 2000

Mahoning National Bancorp Inc.	Metropolitan Financial Corp.	Mid Am Inc.	Peter B. Burke Agency Inc.	Prospect Bancshares Inc.	Second Bancorp Inc.	Three Rivers Bancorp Inc.	Unity Bancorp Inc.	Wells River Bancorp inc.
APRIL 30, 1992 – SEPTEMBER 30, 1999	DECEMBER 31, 1979 – APRIL 30, 2003	APRIL 3, 1982 – OCTOBER 2, 1998	JANUARY 3, 2006 – JANUARY 4, 2006	DECEMBER 13, 2002 – NOVEMBER 30, 2004	APRIL 1, 1987 – JULY 1, 2004	APRIL 4, 2000 – OCTOBER 1, 2002	JULY 22, 1986 – DECEMBER 17, 1994	MARCH 30, 1996 – NOVEMBER 15, 2006

FBC Bancshares Inc.
MAY 31, 1985 – JUNE 9, 1989

Commerce Exchange Corp.	Enfin Inc.
APRIL 14, 1986 – OCTOBER 25, 2001	APRIL 29, 1991 – AUGUST 21, 1998

Huntington Bancshares   Holding Company *(abridged)*

W. G. Phillips, Eng.

Pelatiah Webster Huntington.

David W. Deshler.

If a major bank in Columbus, Ohio, sounds far-fetched, you must not know much about Columbus, which has long fostered a thriving financial community. Pelatiah Webster Huntington was named after early American political economist Pelatiah Webster (1726–1795). The son of a banker and born in Norwich, Connecticut, in 1836, Huntington moved to Columbus in 1853 after a stint on a whaler. He married and in 1866 joined his father-in-law, David W. Deshler, to form P.W. Huntington and Company, an unincorporated private banking house. After Deshler died, Huntington became the sole owner until 1892, when he began admitting his sons into partnership.

In 1905 Huntington and his sons decided to obtain a national banking charter so their bank could issue more deposits with which to fund loans. The institution weathered the Panic of 1907 and a local banking crisis in 1911–1912 during which three competitors went out of business. This was largely because of its conservative lending practices, as well as the public confidence in Huntington himself, who over his long career had been actively engaged in the region's burgeoning financial, transportation, utilities and industrial sectors.

After Huntington's death in 1918, the bank continued to thrive under the leadership of his son Francis, who was also active in Columbus's economic development. In 1923 the bank began acquiring other banks, including State Savings Bank and Hayden-Clinton

National Bank. Established in 1819, State Savings had purchased Capitol Trust in 1911. Hayden had started in 1866 as Hayden, Hutcheson and converted to a national charter in 1891 with Huntington as president. It eventually merged with the Clinton National Bank, which had been established in 1897, and the Deshler Bank, which had been founded in 1879 and became a national bank in 1891.

After Francis died in 1928, another of Huntington's sons, Theodore, took control of the bank. Imbued with his father's conservative banking principles, Theodore was able to steer the bank through the desperate early years of the Great Depression. His younger brother, B.G., replaced him in 1932. Thus, B.G. was in charge during the Roosevelt administration's imposed bank holiday in March 1933, as well as the subsequent changes in banking regulation and the establishment of the FDIC. During this time, Huntington Bank became one of the largest correspondent banks, or "banker's banks," in the nation while also continuing to service retail customers.

When B.G. moved to board chairman in 1949, John E. Stevenson, who came to the bank with the Hayden-Clinton acquisition, took over as president. He was the first non-Huntington to run the bank's day-to-day operations. Stevenson became CEO in 1958 and began buying up banks in order to establish a branch network; prior to this it had operated as a unit bank. Columbus and its suburbs grew by leaps and bounds after World War II, and Huntington had to expand to maintain its retail market share.

By 1962 the greater Columbus metropolitan area was the second largest in the state, and by 1980 it had surpassed a declining Cleveland for the top spot. Stephenson also invested in new products, including installment and mortgage loans, and sent junior officers to the Stonier Graduate School of Banking at Rutgers University at the bank's expense.

Clair Fultz succeeded Stephenson as CEO in 1963; Stephenson left the board in 1967 after six decades of banking experience. By 1966 Huntington had 15 offices throughout Franklin County, which included Columbus and its suburbs, and eight divisions. In just eight years, assets had doubled, and the number of accounts soared, necessitating more delegation of authority from the top than the bank had hitherto experienced. But Ohio banking law limited its growth by preventing the bank from owning branches across the county line. In 1966, therefore, it established a BHC called Huntington Bancshares. A flurry of acquisitions throughout the state soon followed.

By 1979 Huntington's assets exceeded $2.5 billion, up from about $400 million in 1966, and its 15 subsidiary banks had 97 branches. That year, the subsidiaries merged into one entity, the Huntington National Bank, which became a subsidiary of the BHC. More mergers followed, but under Fultz Huntington it was not just growing, it was developing and innovating. In 1966, for example, it established an office in the Cayman Islands that was "very important to many of the bank's corporate and correspondent bank customers," presumably for tax and regulatory reasons. In 1972 the bank opened the first fully automated banking office open 24/7, and a few years later it began a mortgage company that soon became the largest construction lender in Central Ohio, and a corporate leasing company.

In 1982 Huntington was Ohio's fourth largest BHC, with assets over $5 billion and 176 branches in 94 cities. Two years later, *Fortune* magazine recognized it as the 14th most profitable of America's 100 largest BHCs and the most profitable of the six largest Ohio BHCs. Acquisitions continued apace thereafter, from small ones like Reliance Bank of Melbourne, Florida, in 1995, to medium-sized purchases like the First Michigan Bank, which had assets of over $900 million when it was acquired in 1997.

It also continued to innovate, introducing in 1994 a high-tech branch with only one employee but multiple ATMs and kiosks where customers could deposit checks, withdraw money or obtain advice via video teleconference. Hundreds of bankers from around the world flocked to Columbus to see the marvel firsthand. Huntington National also pushed in new directions to obtain more big business loans in its Cleveland market, where it was perceived as too small to meet the needs of larger corporations. At a cost of $77,821, its 1995 "Take a Closer Look" campaign generated over $150 million in new loans.

By the end of 1995 Huntington had $20 billion in assets and more than 350 offices in a dozen states. The following year, it became the first Ohio-chartered state bank to obtain approval to sell life and health insurance, through its Huntington Life Insurance Agency subsidiary. But trouble lay not far ahead as the bank, which was very centralized with all decisions coming from Columbus, increasingly found itself outmaneuvered by community banks and outgunned by regional and national behemoths.

In 2001, after profits plummeted 22% in 2000, Huntington scaled back to concentrate on the Midwest by selling its Florida banking network, which included 141 branches, to SunTrust (#18) for $705 million. New management, in the form of former Bank One (now part of #1) executive Thomas E. Hoaglin and replacement of 20 of its other top 24 executives, had turned the regional bank around by 2004.

In addition to exiting Florida, Hoaglin scaled back auto loans from 33% to 24% of the bank's lending portfolio and improved credit quality. He also devolved much responsibility on regional vice presidents. "It is not that we are a high-performing bank, but our numbers are much better," he said in an interview with *American Banker*.

Hoaglin disclaimed rumors that the bank was ready to sell out, and in late 2006 he set about to prove it by merging with Sky Financial Group in a $3.29 billion deal that increased the number of the bank's branches to more than 700, its ATMs to 1,384 and its deposits to $38 billion. But the deal turned sour because of Sky's exposure to a subprime commercial lender, which the bank paid dearly for in the ensuing crisis.

Although its shares were battered down to almost nothing, the bank survived the 2008 financial crisis with the help of $1.4 billion in TARP funds. To save $100 million in expenses, it slashed its 2008 bonuses and other incentives for all employees, including $11.5 million slated for Hoaglin, who was forced into retirement.

In a vote of confidence for the bank, CEO Stephen Steinour, three other executives and 10 directors bought $1.58 million of its shares in April 2009. As a condition of employment, Steinour promised to invest his entire salary of $1 million per year in the bank's shares. By the end of 2010 the danger had passed, as profits returned and TARP funds were repaid. In 2013 Steinour put the bank back into growth mode by purchasing the 15-branch, $800-million asset Fidelity, a failed bank based in Dearborn, Michigan.

Sources

Benoit, David and Matt Jaremsky. "Lower Provisions Boost Banks: Huntington and PNC Cut Credit-Loss Reserves, Helping Their Results." *Wall Street Journal*, January 21, 2011, C2.

Budkie, James E. "Huntington's Automated Branch Bank." *AT&T Technology* 10, 4 (Winter 1995/Spring 1996): 8.

Carrns, Ann. "Huntington, Sky to Merge Banks." *Wall Street Journal*, December 21, 2006, C4.

"Customers Take Closer Look at Huntington Bank." *Direct Marketing* 58, 7 (November 1995): 24.

Dvorak, Phred. "How Bank Bailout Cost Mr. Hoaglin: Huntington CEO Took Home $1.3 Million; Non-TARP Rival Got $9.2 Million." *Wall Street Journal*, March 23, 2009, C6.

Fultz, Clair E. *Huntington: A Family and a Bank*. Columbus, OH: Huntington Bancshares Inc., 1985.

"Huntington Bancshares, Inc.: Bank-Holding Concern Plans to Acquire Bank in Florida." *Wall Street Journal*, December 27, 1994, C11.

"Huntington Bancshares Incorporated; Huntington Bank Eliminates 2008 Incentives Across the Board." *Science Letter*, February 17, 2009, 3,628.

"Huntington to Buy First Michigan Bank." *The New York Times*, May 6, 1997, 2.

Mollenkamp, Carrick and Evan Perez. "SunTrust Banks to Pay $705 Million for Huntington's Florida Business." *Wall Street Journal*, September 26, 2001, A4.

Monks, Matthew. "Failed Bank Deal Gives Huntington Consolidation Cred." *American Banker*, April 3, 2012.

Reynolds, David J. "Huntington Executives Put Money in the Bank." *Wall Street Journal*, April 29, 2009, C5.

Sundaramoorthy, Geeta. "Huntington's Turnaround: At This Midtier, Shades of Old Bank One." *American Banker*, June 1, 2004, 1.

West, Diane. "Ohio Huntington Bank Unit Approved to Sell Life Ins." *National Underwriter*, June 3, 1996, 45.

John Deere
Capital Corp.
JULY 6, 2000 –
PRESENT

John Deere
Bank S.A.
JULY 21, 2011 –
PRESENT

John Deere
Financial FSB
DECEMBER 24, 2000 –
PRESENT

John Deere Capital

RANK	HEADQUARTERS	TICKER	ASSETS	EARLIEST KNOWN ANCESTOR	INDUSTRY OF ORIGIN
47	Reno, NV	Not listed	$30,500,000,000	1837	Manufacturing

John Deere blacksmith shop, Marthasville, Missouri.

Deere & Company headquarters, Moline, Illinois, ca. 1956-1965.

John Deere Capital Corporation is the spawn of John Deere Credit Company, which itself came from Deere & Company, the famous manufacturer of tractors and other agricultural equipment based in the quad city region of Illinois. The manufacturing component of the company began operations in 1837 as a sole proprietorship owned by blacksmith-turned-manufacturer John Deere, who invented a steel plow tough enough to cut clean furrows through virgin prairie. He built 10 plows in 1839, and 100 by 1842. The following year, he took Leonard Andrus into partnership. By 1849 the company's 16 workers were manufacturing more than 2,100 plows annually. Deere bought out his partners in 1852 and regularly changed the company's name for the next 16 years until the business finally formally incorporated, under its present name, in 1868. Deere and his son Charles, who had run the company since 1858, owned 60% of the stock.

In 1874 the company sold more than 50,000 plows. The following year, employee Gilpin Moore developed the Gilpin Sulky Plow, which became one of the company's most successful products in the 19th century and won a prestigious international award in 1878. Deere and Mansur, formed in 1877 to make corn planters, merged with Deere & Company in 1910. By 1889 the company had factories in five locations: Kansas City, Minneapolis, Omaha, San Francisco and St. Louis. Sales hit $2 million for the first time in the fiscal year 1899–1900. In 1918 the company finally entered the tractor business by purchasing Waterloo Boy. It sold only 5,634 units that year compared to Ford's 34,000 Fordson tractors. The following year it crushed a strike, which allowed it to avoid unionization until after World War II. By 1930 Deere & Company and International Harvester dominated most major categories in the agricultural equipment industry.

In 1931 Deere & Company bailed out a bank, People's Savings of Moline, where it and many of its employees kept $1.29 million on deposit to cover embezzlement losses. When that bank failed two years later, Deere established and took a 90% stake in the Moline National Bank. During the Great Depression, the company also aided many of its farmer-customers, even as its own sales plunged below $9 million. The ploy won customer loyalty, and the lull caused by the Depression freed up resources that led to the development of two new tractors, the Model A and Model B, that became the most popular tractors in the company's history and remained in production until 1952.

During World War II, Deere converted to the production of military tractors and other war materiel. Deere & Company allowed unionization in 1945 but thrived in the postwar era anyway. One hundred of its shares increased in price from $3,462 in 1955 to $25,995 in 1981, a hefty return when combined with the $14,771 of dividends paid along the way.

Deere surpassed International Harvester in 1963 as the world's largest producer of industrial tractors and equipment and ventured into the consumer market with products like lawn mowers and snow blowers. Sales exceeded $1 billion for the first time in 1966 and $2 billion in 1973, on the heels of the "Nothing Runs Like a Deere" advertising campaign launched in 1971. In the 1970s the company branched into industrial equipment as well with construction, snow removal, forestry and other nonagricultural commercial machinery. By 1979 annual sales topped $5 billion as the company's payroll peaked at 65,392 employees.

Much like General Motors, the parent of GMAC (now Ally Bank [#20]), and GE (#8), Deere & Company found it easier to sell its products to dealers and ultimately to customers if it offered them financing and insurance. It did so directly at first, but during the Depression and other downturns it found having large accounts receivable on its balance sheet inconvenient. So in 1958 it began to establish wholly owned financial subsidiaries including John Deere Credit Company (US), John Deere Finance Limited (Canada), Banco John Deere, S.A. (Brazil), John Deere Credit Oy (Finland), John Deere Leasing Company (US) and several insurance entities. The subsidiaries were stand-alone entities in that their balance sheets were not consolidated with that of the parent manufacturing company, but rather appeared only as investments that produced income or losses.

During the recession of the early 1980s, the financial subsidiaries remained profitable while the parent's fortunes, which were so good in the 1970s, sank, though not as far as those of its competitors, Massey-Ferguson and International Harvester. Large, rapid interest rate fluctuations and other issues, however, concerned regulators, customers and dealers, who pressed for a more complete separation of the manufacturing parent from its financial children. By 1989, however, concerns faded as sales, profits and dividends rebounded, and the company acquired Funk Manufacturing. More domestic acquisitions, international investment and product diversification aided growth in the 1990s, when net earnings topped $1 billion for the first time. Not every move, however, was a success. In 1994, for example, Deere bought Homelite, a manufacturer of lower-end outdoor hand-held power equipment, including weed trimmers and chain saws. The brand lost hundreds of millions of dollars before the company dumped it in 2001.

In the early 1990s John Deere Credit Company (JDC) began to offer its financial expertise to other manufacturers, including Coachman, a maker of recreational vehicles. Coachman dealers found it much easier to arrange customer financing through JDC than the myriad banks and finance companies that they traditionally contended against. Outboard Marine Corporation soon signed on as well. JDC soon discovered, however, that RVs and boats, and the people who buy them, were much different from Deere equipment and farmers. For one, repossessing geographically mobile consumer toys was much harder than finding the giant green combine on a farmer's back 40. By the end of the decade JDC had exited the barely profitable new business. It continued to be profitable overall, however, generating almost $1.2 billion in earnings in 2004 alone.

John Deere Health also tried to stretch in the 1990s. Since 1985, it had managed healthcare costs for Deere and other companies in Deere communities. In the face of a tangle of state regulations, it ran a loss in 1997 and retreated back to the four states where the company maintained a large employee base or previous profitable connections: Illinois, Iowa, Tennessee and Virginia.

John Deere Capital Corporation (JDCap), a wholly owned subsidiary of JDC (which in turn was a wholly owned subsidiary of Deere & Company), became a savings and loan holding company in 2000. This was not your father's S&L, unless your father was a farmer. According to a 2008 securities prospectus, JDCap was "principally engaged in providing and administering financing for retail purchases of new equipment manufactured by Deere & Company's agricultural equipment, commercial and consumer equipment, and construction and forestry divisions and used equipment taken in trade." In 2013 it employed about 1,500 people, about the same number it had in 2008, in several nations, but primarily in the United States, Australia and New Zealand. Its emphasis remained financing dealer and customer purchases and lease agreements.

In 2006 CEO Robert W. Lane was named "CEO of the Year" by *Industry Week*, and *Fortune* listed Deere among the 50 most admired companies in 2011. The following year, Thomson Reuters named the company to its "100 Global Innovators" list, as it set records for net revenues ($36.2 billion) and income ($3.1 billion).

Sources

Broehl, Wayne G., Jr. *John Deere's Company: A History of Deere & Company and Its Times.* New York: Doubleday, 1984.

"John Deere Earns Recognition as Top 100 Global Innovator." *Targeted News Service,* December 4, 2012.

John Deere. "Timeline." *www.deere.com/wps/dcom/en_INT/our_company/about_us/ history/timeline/timeline.page.* Accessed December 17, 2013.

John Deere Capital Corporation. *Prospectus: U.S. $1,500,000,000 JDCC CoreNotes,* May 7, 2008.

Magree, David. *The John Deere Way: Performance That Endures.* Hoboken, NJ: Wiley, 2005.

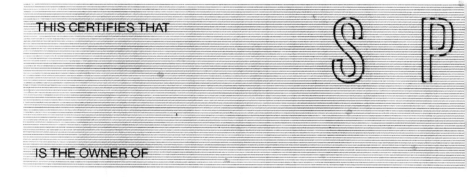

COMMON STOCK
$1 PAR VALUE

THIS CERTIFIES THAT

IS THE OWNER OF

fully paid and non assessable shares of the common
of this certificate properly endorsed. This certificate is not
Witness the si

DATED:
COUNTERSIGNED:
CONTINENTAL ILLINOIS NATIONAL BANK
AND TRUST COMPANY OF CHICAGO
TRANSFER AGENT
BY
AUTHORIZED SIGNATURE

SECRETARY

Deere & Company specimen stock certificate.

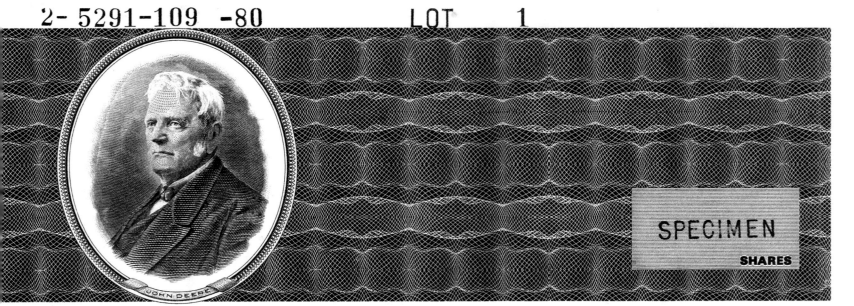

SPECIMEN

SHARES

~RE & COMPANY

INCORPORATED UNDER THE LAWS OF THE STATE OF DELAWARE

THIS CERTIFICATE IS TRANSFERABLE IN
THE CITY OF NEW YORK OR IN CHICAGO

CUSIP 244199 10 5

SEE REVERSE FOR CERTAIN DEFINITIONS

~ECIMEN

~k of Deere & Company transferable in person or by duly authorized attorney upon surrender

~less countersigned by a Transfer Agent and registered by a Registrar

~tures of the duly authorized officers of the Company.

REGISTERED:
THE FIRST NATIONAL BANK OF CHICAGO
REGISTRAR
BY
AUTHORIZED SIGNATURE

William A. Hewitt

CHAIRMAN

AMERICAN BANK NOTE COMPANY.

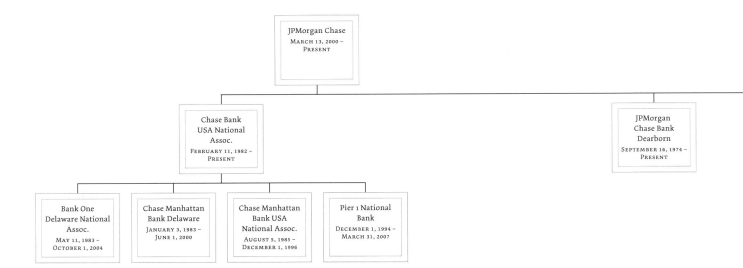

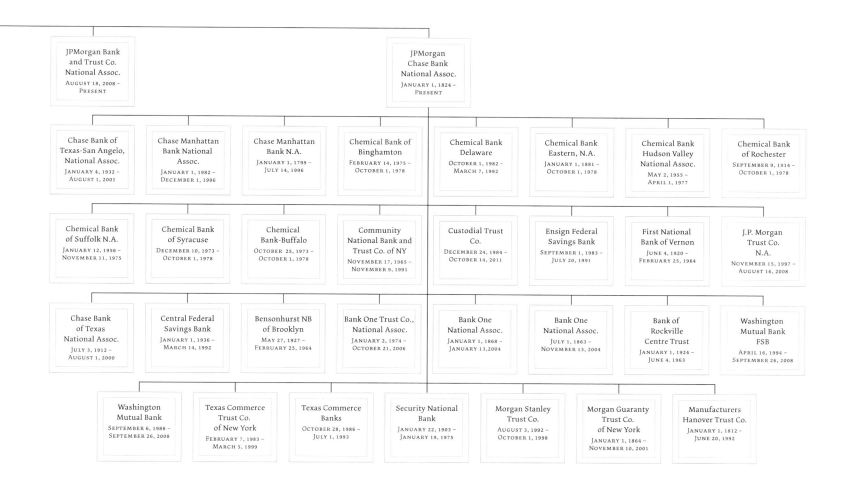

JPMorgan Chase

Bank *(abridged)*

RANK	HEADQUARTERS	TICKER	ASSETS	EARLIEST KNOWN ANCESTOR	INDUSTRY OF ORIGIN
1	New York, NY	JPM	$2,400,000,000,000	1799	Bank / Water Utility

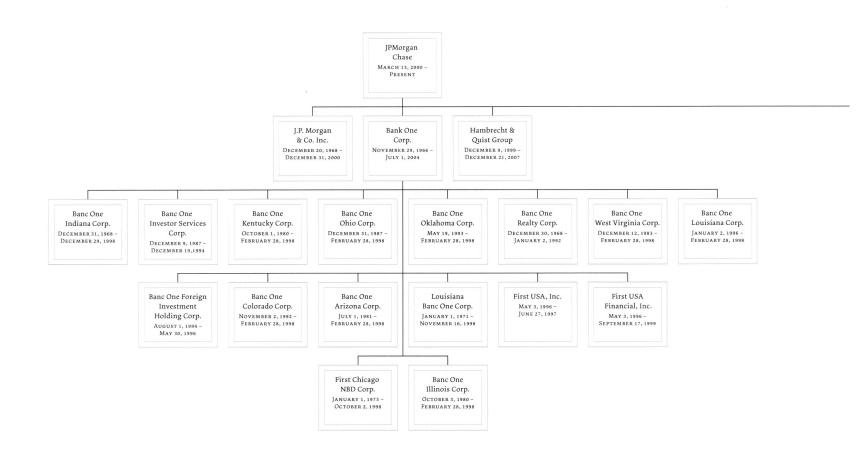

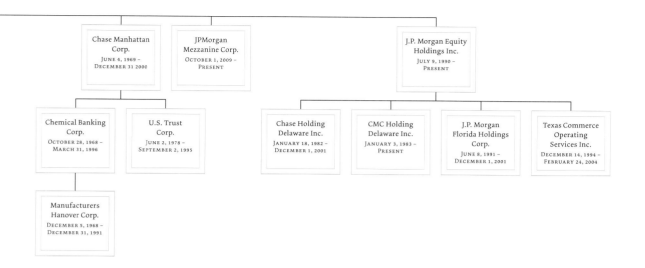

Chase Manhattan Corp.
JUNE 4, 1969 –
DECEMBER 31 2000

JPMorgan Mezzanine Corp.
OCTOBER 1, 2009 –
PRESENT

J.P. Morgan Equity Holdings Inc.
JULY 9, 1990 –
PRESENT

Chemical Banking Corp.
OCTOBER 28, 1968 –
MARCH 31, 1996

U.S. Trust Corp.
JUNE 2, 1978 –
SEPTEMBER 2, 1995

Chase Holding Delaware Inc.
JANUARY 18, 1982 –
DECEMBER 1, 2001

CMC Holding Delaware Inc.
JANUARY 3, 1983 –
PRESENT

J.P. Morgan Florida Holdings Corp.
JUNE 8, 1991 –
DECEMBER 1, 2001

Texas Commerce Operating Services Inc.
DECEMBER 14, 1994 –
FEBRUARY 24, 2004

Manufacturers Hanover Corp.
DECEMBER 5, 1968 –
DECEMBER 31, 1991

JPMorgan Chase

Holding Company *(abridged)*

Like many of the other companies at the top of the BHC asset list, JPMorgan Chase (JPMC) is a new institution forged from merger after merger over the last few decades. It is essentially three storied megabanks combined: investment bank-cum-commercial bank JP Morgan and commercial banks Chase Manhattan and Bank One.

The oldest of the three lineages was Chase Manhattan, itself the result of the merger of Chase National and the Manhattan Company. The latter began life as a water utility with banking powers formed by Aaron Burr and many other prominent New York merchants, politicians and military heroes in 1799. Its history as a water utility was short-lived and uninspired and, as was the case with Wells Fargo (#4) and other dual-industry companies, banking and finance proved more lucrative and slowly came to dominate the company's capital and interests. In 1842 the new High Bridge Aqueduct, part of the Croton Water System, put the water division out of business.

The state and city of New York had both bought shares in the Manhattan Company, ostensibly to help underwrite the costs of its water utility, but held onto their shares well into the 20th century. The bank consequently had friends in high places, like City Hall and Albany, which may explain why it was one of the few early New York banks allowed to establish branches. It shuttered both of them, which were located in Utica and Poughkeepsie, in 1819 after a decade of difficulties. Nevertheless, except for a few years in the troubled 1840s, Manhattan Bank stock generally traded well above par on the strength of the company's dividend record.

The Manhattan Bank joined the Federal Reserve System in 1917 and acquired the Bank of the Metropolis in 1918 and the Bank of Long Island in 1920. That year, the Manhattan Bank also acquired the Merchants Bank, which began operations under the aegis of Alexander Hamilton in 1803. The combined entity had a capital and surplus in excess of $20 million, assets exceeding $200 million and more than a dozen branches, most of them in Queens. The two companies shared digs on Wall Street directly adjacent to one another for over a century, so physically speaking their merger required only the tearing down of a partition wall. But the deeper irony of the merger was not lost on contemporaries: Burr killed Hamilton in a duel, and over a century later Burr's bank killed Hamilton's bank.

Manhattan Bank's eventual merger partner, Chase National Bank, began operations in New York in 1877. John Thompson, its 75-year-old founder, a publisher of *Thompson's Bank Note Reporter* and a banker who according to the *New York Sun* "amassed an immense fortune" by pursuing "an old-fashioned, conservative line of banking," named the bank after his friend and former Treasury Secretary Salmon P. Chase. Chase quickly became a correspondent bank, or "banker's bank," and thanks to its large deposits, also the bank of large industrial borrowers.

By 1884 its capital and surplus exceeded $500,000, and deposits were over $6 million. Just three years later, capital had increased to $900,000 and deposits exceeded $8.5 million. When former New York Banking Department Superintendent, United States Bank Examiner and Comptroller of the Currency Alonzo Barton Hepburn joined Chase in 1899, it employed almost 100 people, including five executives, and boasted $2 million in capital and surplus and $43.6 million in deposits. Hepburn became president in 1904, when deposits sat at almost $53 million with $2.8 million in undivided profits. The institution had such a strong balance sheet that the Panic of 1907 barely phased it. By 1915, when Hepburn published his *History of Currency in the United States*, Chase had deposits over $135 million and over $14 million in capital, surplus and undivided profits.

During the Great War, Chase—led by Albert Wiggin, who helped to form Bankers Trust (now part of #34) in 1903 and succeeded Hepburn

as president in 1911—began to attract considerable deposits from overseas, with over $100 million in 1916 alone. In 1917 Chase established an affiliate, Chase Securities Corporation, to underwrite and distribute corporate and government securities. By 1918 deposits exceeded $333 million, and employees numbered nearly 600.

In 1919 Chase moved into the trust business. By 1922 it was the second largest national bank, with capital, surplus and profits over $40 million, deposits of almost $360 million and seven branches. Its management, however, remained far from content. In the 1920s, for the first time in its history, Chase began to buy other banks. It acquired or merged with five banks, including Metropolitan and Mechanics and Metals National, and after passage of the McFadden Act in 1927 it established de novo branches and obtained others through mergers. By the end of 1929 it had 27 branches and assets of $1.7 billion, making it the third largest bank in the city after National City (#3) and Guaranty Trust (now part of #1). The following year it took the top spot by merging with Equitable Trust.

Chase Securities also expanded rapidly in the 1920s, ending the decade with 27 offices throughout the United States, as well as offices in Berlin, London, Paris, Rome and Warsaw. It started 1930 with a bang, too, acquiring Harris Forbes of Chicago, which came with 35 sales offices in the United States and Canada. The bank liquidated the company in 1933, however, to comply with Glass-Steagall. As part of the liquidation, in 1934 the bank spun off American Express (#19), which Chase Securities had acquired in 1929.

Chase lost over a third of its capital during the Great Depression and accepted a $50 million injection of capital from the Reconstruction Finance Corporation in the form of preferred stock. It repurchased the preferred stock within three years, however, as it rebounded thanks to innovations like amortized term loans and organic deposit growth following the 1933 bank holiday. According to Winthrop Aldrich, Wiggin's successor, the bank "gave its full strength and energy to the prosecution" of World War II, including more than one-fourth of its employees (48 of whom were killed in action) and $8.3 billion in loans (5.3% of the total borrowed by the US government), more than any other institution. During the war, the bank's assets jumped from $3.8 to over $6 billion. By 1945 it was the nation's largest commercial bank, with assets exceeding $6 billion and $300 million in capital. While it shrank back to $4.6 billion in assets by 1948 despite aggressive overseas branch expansion, its merger with the Manhattan Bank in 1955 brought assets to $7.5 billion.

Chase had pursued the Manhattan Bank since 1951 because it wanted to tap its reputation as well as its extensive branch network in Queens, which by 1954 had grown to 57. Legal difficulties prevented the marriage until 1955, when John McCloy, Aldrich's successor, was able to make the deal stick by adopting the Manhattan's 1799 charter (which imposed few restrictions on the organization) and by serving as co-CEO with Manhattan's top executive, J. Stewart Baker. The Manhattan Bank's acquisition of the Bronx County Trust Company just 10 days prior to the merger added only $71 million in deposits but nine additional offices in an area of the city that neither Chase nor Manhattan had yet penetrated.

Passage of the BHCA and the merger act kept Chase Manhattan from continuing to grow through major mergers, so it concentrated on smaller acquisitions and organic growth. It bought the Staten Island National Bank and Trust in 1957 and the Clinton Trust in 1959. By 1960 the bank's assets had hit $9.3 billion, funded by deposits of $8.1 billion channeled through a network of 105 branches, up from 96 at the time of the big merger five years previously. The 1960 Omnibus Banking Act opened up the entire state to BHCs, but only with the approval of

Portrait of financier J.P. Morgan.

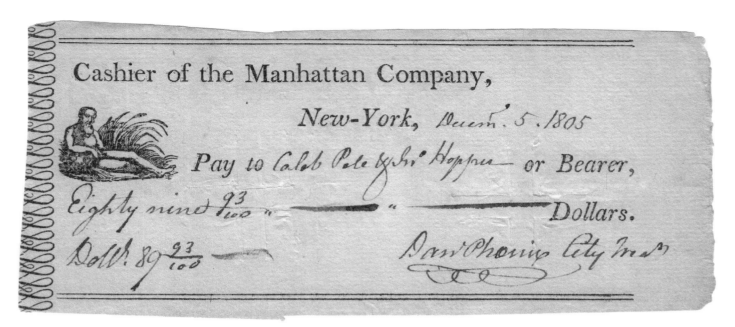

Check drawn on the Manhattan Company by city treasurer Daniel Phoenix, dated December 5, 1805.

regulators. Chase quickly applied for approval of four de novo branches in Nassau and Westchester counties, but only two were approved.

While the bank battled regulators to expand its branch network, it launched a bank charge card system called the Chase Manhattan Charge Plan (CMCP). Volume hit about $25 million by 1960, but owing to high credit losses the CMCP looked like a dog, especially compared to Bank of America's (now part of #2) system. So the bank sold the operation to Uni-Serve, which spruced it up and sold it to former Chase subsidiary American Express, which sold it back to the bank in 1968. After its growth again stalled, Chase converted the cards to the BankAmericard system in 1972.

Two Edge Act corporations — a joint venture called American Overseas Finance Corporation and Chase International Investment Corporation (née Chase Bank) — helped the bank do business overseas, as did its network of overseas branches, which it beefed up in the 1960s to include much of the developing world as well as the big, industrialized economies. Also in the 1960s, David Rockefeller succeeded McCloy as president, and the bank experienced rapid change in its source of funds, its technology and its organizational form. To grow domestically with more flexibility, the bank in 1965 relinquished its 1799 charter for a national charter. Negotiable certificates of deposit replaced traditional retail deposits as its major liability, even as the number of branches increased to 143 by 1968. Despite hitting regulatory snags when it attempted to move into markets upstate, its assets jumped from $10.1 billion in 1960 to $22.2 billion in 1969.

The bank established a one-bank BHC, Chase Manhattan Corporation, in mid-1969, just in time to face the many travails of the 1970s. These included record levels of inflation and exchange rate volatility, as well as loan losses. The BHC soon launched into the factoring, leasing and mortgage businesses via acquisitions. When the BHCA of 1970 removed the distinction between one- and multi-bank HCs by placing both under the authority of the Federal Reserve, and New York State phased in branching reforms over a period of five years, Chase Manhattan began to acquire and set up de novo bank subsidiaries upstate and on Long Island. By 1975 it had 261 branches statewide.

Although finally able to branch throughout the state without regulatory approval starting in 1976, the bank was stopped from expanding nationally when the Fed twice denied its bid for Dial Financing Corporation, a consumer finance company. Headquartered in Des Moines, Iowa, Dial had 461 offices in 33 states, but mostly in the Midwest and West, and accounted for only 2% of the total consumer finance loan market. Apparently, the Fed was concerned about the bank's condition, which deteriorated in 1975 and 1976 as a result of major losses suffered in the depressed real estate market. International expansion, by contrast, continued unabated until few major countries remained outside the bank's ken. Moreover, asset and capital growth continued, with the former increasing from $30.7 billion in 1972 to $45.6 billion in 1976, and the latter from $1.1 to $1.667 billion over the same period. Nevertheless, the bank appeared on the US "Problem List" in 1976, along with rival Citibank (#3). New York City's financial problems in 1975 did not help matters.

The bank turned matters around in 1977, increasing its earnings four-fold by 1981 by focusing on credit quality, country-risk analysis on its substantial book of foreign loans, increased revenue from fees, foreign exchange trading earnings and cost cutting. To get around New York's usury law, which crimped its increasingly important credit card business, it established a Delaware subsidiary in 1982. It also improved its culture, hiring practices and standards and incentive compensation. After a recession-induced burp in 1982, the bank surged again in the mid-1980s, acquiring the Rochester-based Lincoln First in 1984, which expanded the Chase branching network to 331, and six thrifts in Ohio the next year. Acquisitions in other states soon followed. Between 1976 and 1985, assets almost doubled to about $88 billion, and capital increased over two-and-a-half times to almost $4.5 billion. But not even a rapidly growing bank like Chase Manhattan could maintain its independence in the increasingly deregulated US banking industry, marrying J.P. Morgan in 2000 and placing its storied name in front of its own.

J.P. Morgan was perhaps the most famous name in all of American finance. Founded by J. Pierpont Morgan (1837–1913) in 1895, the company traced its roots to J.S. Morgan and Company, which had been established in London by J. Pierpont's father Junius (1813–1890) in 1864, and Drexel, Morgan & Company, a partnership between J. Pierpont and Philadelphia financier Anthony Drexel (1826–1893) founded in 1871. Like most investment banks of the era, J.P. Morgan was organized as a partnership. Unlike most investment banks of the era, it was essentially an informal holding company for London's J.S. Morgan (later Morgan, Grenfell, now part of #34), Morgan, Harjes of Paris and Philadelphia's Drexel & Co.

Between 1895 and 1934, J.P. Morgan originated 1,240 securities issues and was involved in more than 1,800 deals. Half of its issuers were railroads, and almost two in five were manufacturing companies. Over that same span, more than 2,300 economic entities, ranging from commercial banks like National City (#3) to wealthy individuals like John D. Rockefeller, Sr., participated in its syndicates, which raised over $11 billion from investors. Morgan and his partners ensured that most of the securities issued by their clients remained investment grade because they placed one or more of their number on the issuers' board of directors. That led to large cross holdings of corporate stocks and so-called interlocking directorates that appeared to outsiders as proof that the nation's economy was controlled by Morgan and his men. When a banking panic occurred in 1907, there was no central bank to assist. Morgan pledged much of his own money and convinced other bankers to do the same, allowing the alarm to pass. But his prominent role in the fight to stop the Panic of 1907 further exacerbated fears that a few men—like Morgan—controlled the financial system.

The House of Morgan, as the HC was informally known, grew so large and influential that its eponymous founder was hauled before Congress in December 1912 to testify about his role in creating and running the so-called Money Trust, a supposed monopoly of financial capital thought by some, including incoming President Woodrow Wilson, to dictate the course of American industrial development. During those hearings, called Pujo after the Louisiana representative who chaired the House Committee on Banking and Currency, Morgan claimed to neither possess nor covet the "vast power" that he was said to command. People followed his advice, he argued, because they trusted his integrity and judgment. To condemn a man for possessing such qualities, he said, was anathema to most Americans.

Morgan died the following March and was succeeded by his son Jack (J.P. Morgan Jr., 1867–1943), who cut back on the company's stockholdings and, after passage of the Clayton Antitrust Act in 1914, its role on corporate boards. Apparently, not everyone was convinced that the purported power of the nation's "gentlemen bankers" had been sufficiently curbed because in 1915 a pistol- and dynamite-wielding assassin marched into one of Jack's estates and managed to shoot Jack while being subdued. Then, in 1920, a large bomb ripped through the company's Wall Street offices. One Morgan employee died and several others were badly injured by flying glass, but none of the partners were harmed except for Jack's son, Junius S., who was slightly wounded. The blast wrecked offices with windows facing Wall Street, but left the solid stone edifice at 23 Wall Street with nothing but minor pock marks (still visible in 2014).

During the Depression, as the House of Morgan's assets plunged from over $700 million to just $425 million and its net worth dropped just as fast, Jack told the US Senate during the Pecora Hearings much the same story his father had related during the Pujo probe: Morgan and his partners had some financial resources to be sure, but their influence stemmed from "the respect and esteem of the community." Most observers, however, focused on revelations that Jack and other Morgan partners had paid no federal income taxes in 1930, 1931 or 1932. Their deductions for stock losses were legitimate but nonetheless galling to most Americans.

Shortly thereafter, legislation in the Glass-Steagall Act forced Morgan to decide if it was to be a commercial or investment bank. Facing the moribund securities markets of the Depression and the new securities laws promulgated by the Roosevelt administration, most

partners chose the former; the several who did not formed Morgan Stanley (#6). All of the partners probably hoped to one day reunite the companies and reconstitute the House of Morgan, and the companies at first worked together extremely closely, both physically and in business dealings.

But the two companies slowly began to grow apart, as in 1940 when Jack took J.P. Morgan public in part to protect its already depleted capital as senior partners retired or passed on. Jack himself died just three years later, replaced by longtime partner Thomas W. Lamont, who, upon his death in 1948, gave way to Russell Leffingwell. As the Depression morphed into World War II, the bank also severed formal ties with Drexel and Morgan Grenfell.

After the war, J.P. Morgan entered what historian Ron Chernow called "The Casino Age," five decades of increasingly intense, increasingly global competition during which Wall Street bankers slowly lost much of their power and panache as they morphed from being stewards of capital to salesmen. The days of relationship banking, or long-term business relationships between banks and their clients paid for with compensatory balances (large sums left on deposit by clients), were over. Profit on individual transactions came to take precedence over maintaining long-term client satisfaction. Gentleman banking disappeared, and growth, often for growth's sake, became the order of the day.

J.P. Morgan fought those changes at first, retaining its wholesale, private banking model, while National City (#3) and Chase (now part of #1) went retail, raking in consumer deposits in shopping malls and supermarkets. By the mid-1950s Chairman Henry Alexander looked at a big target and merged his bank with Guaranty Trust. Although the trust company was four times J.P. Morgan's size, the merged entity called itself Morgan Guaranty. After the merger was completed in 1960, the bank controlled over $4 billion in deposits, making it the fourth largest bank in the country after National City, Chase Manhattan and Bank of America (#2). It had 10,000 corporate accounts and was the bank of 97 of the nation's 100 largest companies.

In 1969 Morgan Guaranty made itself the subsidiary of a one-bank holding company called J.P. Morgan and Company. Although discussions to recreate the House of Morgan under its umbrella fell through in 1973, the BHC soon became a diversified financial conglomerate. Thereafter, J.P. Morgan, Morgan Stanley and Morgan Grenfell began to compete vigorously, invading each other's markets, territories and clients wherever regulators would allow. In the 1970s J.P. Morgan and other big banks attracted the deposits of Saudis grown rich on oil and oil embargoes.

In 1996 Chemical Bank bought Chase Manhattan and took Chase's name as its own. Chemical Bank had become the nation's second biggest bank in 1991 when it merged with Manufacturers Hanover (long called "Manny Hanny"), itself the product of the 1961 merger of Manufacturers Trust and Hanover Bank. Chemical Bank began operations in Manhattan in 1824 as the New York Chemical Manufacturing Company and was capitalized at $500,000. In addition to manufacturing chemicals (pharmaceuticals), the company, which was initially led by erstwhile grocer Baltus Melick, lent largely to "respectable mechanics" and other proto-industrialists. Melick resigned in favor of John Mason in 1831, and the following year the company—which counted author James Fenimore Cooper and Chancellor James Kent among its stockholders—began to concentrate its efforts on banking.

Mason was well known for his charm, business acumen and lending from his personal fortune when a worthy applicant in need could not be accommodated by the company. The change in personnel and strategy worked as the company's stock increased from a low of $86 in April

1831 to a high of $116.75 by November 1832, when its assets were about $1 million. The stock price vacillated with the vagaries of the antebellum economy, but the good standing of the company's notes, which were generally counted as "good as gold," ensured the price trended upward, hitting $260 in early 1853 when its assets were around $2 million. By 1875, bolstered by dividends ranging from 24%–60% per year on par value, its stock price hit $1,500. By that time the institution had long since given up producing chemicals and taken charters first under New York's free banking law and then the National Banking Act.

The rule of Chemical National Bank under George C. ("Papa") Williams, president from 1878 to 1903, was "that every employee, from the humblest clerk to the highest official, shall be courteous to everyone." By 1895 Chemical, christened the "Olympus of Broadway," paid dividends of 150% and each of its shares cost $4,900, then the record for "the highest-priced stock of any large financial institution in the world." In 1907 it reduced its dividend to 15% by increasing its capital; on the eve of the Great War, its assets stood at $40 million and its capital and surplus at $9 million.

By 1920, on the eve of its merger with Citizens National, Chemical's stock sold for around $590 per share on the strength of a surplus exceeding $7 million and a deposit base in excess of $80 million. Four years later, Chemical celebrated its 100th anniversary by highlighting how business practices had changed over the previous century and by reminding depositors that it had been nicknamed "Old Bullion" for its uncanny ability to remain open long after other banks had suspended specie payments. Aided by almost $1 million in Colombian gold, Chemical stayed strong during the Great Depression, though the bank found it necessary to acquire its own ill-timed security affiliate, Chemical Securities Corporation. By the end of 1938 Chemical boasted deposits in excess of half a billion dollars, a capital of $20 million and a surplus of $45 million.

For most of the 20th century, Chemical's existence was similar to that of the nation's other money center commercial banks. Like other big banks, it innovated when and how it could, for example, by paying interest on certain accounts for the first time in 1917 and by offering loans to the parents of college students beginning in 1961. It grew not so much through acquisition, though it did occasionally purchase other institutions (for example, Corn Exchange Bank Trust Company in 1954 and Bensonhurst National Bank of Brooklyn and First National Bank of Mt. Vernon in 1963), as by virtue of it being a major player in a major market and by accepting deposits from banks, other companies and governments located throughout the country. It was long a fiscal agent for the state government of Tennessee, for example, and offered it a $5 million loan in 1930 to stave off a potential run on its resources as a banking panic rocked Nashville. Due to branching restrictions, however, Chemical could not establish a physical statewide presence, much less a national one, until branching restrictions began to loosen, finding it easier to establish overseas branches via its Edge Act subsidiary than to establish branches across the Hudson River in New Jersey. By 1966 Chemical ranked fourth in deposits in New York City and sixth in deposits in its foreign branches.

In 1968 Chemical formed a one-bank holding company that allowed the $9 billion institution to diversify into nonbanking financial services. The move almost backfired, however, by opening up the bank to a hostile takeover attempt by an upstart computer leasing company named Leasco Data Processing Equipment Corporation. Chemical fought off the move and over the next decade used its BHC to consolidate Chemical Bank-branded and controlled banks throughout New York State.

In late 1986, before it made its first major interstate move by acquiring Texas Commerce, the consolidated Chemical had assets of $56 billion, making it the nation's seventh largest bank. In the late 1980s, with its assets increased to about $75 billion as a result of the Texas deal, the bank fought hard to maintain its middle market presence by lending to tri-state companies with annual sales of $5 million to $250 million and names like ABC Carpet, Reliable Automatic Sprinkler Company and Feuer Leather Corporation. In 1987 Chemical banked about 40% of those companies, but competitors, who were losing business to big corporations that increasingly borrowed directly from investors in the commercial paper and bond markets, began to encroach. Some analysts worried that Chemical had staked too much of its future on the notoriously volatile middle market segment, but others, including James J. McDermott, an analyst at Keefe, Bruyette & Woods, thought the Bank enjoyed a "strong strategic vision." McDermott proved prescient, though he could hardly have foreseen the aggressive acquisition and rebranding strategy that in a decade turned Chemical, shorn of its original name, into JPMC and the country's largest bank.

The final big bank to join the JPMC empire was Bank One. Based in Chicago, it was the nation's sixth largest commercial bank in 2004 when JPMC acquired it in a $58 billion deal. Bank One had formed in 1998 from the merger of First Chicago NBD, itself the result of a 1995 merger between First Chicago and NBD (formerly the National Bank of Detroit), and Banc One of Columbus, which formed from the merger of City National Bank of Columbus and Trust and Farmers Saving and Trust in 1968.

Begun by John H. McCoy as City National Bank of Columbus in 1934, the institution became a BHC called First Banc Group of Ohio in 1967. Over the next 20 or so years, it acquired more than six score banks, first in Ohio and later across five states. By 1994 Banc One had assets of $89 billion and had recently been feted by *Fortune* as America's second most admired bank. Its CEO, John McCoy, had recently been crowned "Banker of the Year" by *American Banker*. Over the previous decade, the bank had achieved the second highest return on equity and the highest return on assets among the nation's largest 25 banks. Its 48,000 employees operated 69 banks, 14,000 branches and 1,900 ATMs in 12 states.

When First Chicago and NBD merged in 1995, they created the seventh largest BHC in the nation, with assets of approximately $120 billion and more than 750 branches. First Chicago had opened for business as the Battle of Gettysburg raged over 600 miles to the east. It merged with Union National in 1900 and Metropolitan National two years later to raise its assets to over $100 million.

It soared during the Great War and the Roaring Twenties and was strong enough during the Great Depression to purchase the Foreman State Bank and First Union Trust and Savings. It began to expand internationally in the late 1960s, and in 1980 it became the first American bank in post-Mao China. First Chicago Corporation, its BHC, formed in 1969 but ran into difficulties during the 1970s because of bad loans and management issues. Over the 1980s and up until its merger, it rebounded only to fall back on several occasions.

NBD had begun life in 1972 as National Detroit Corp., a style it shortened to the initials of its main bank subsidiary, National Bank of Detroit, in 1981. It had 20 bank subsidiaries and 646 branches in Florida, Illinois, Indiana, Michigan and Ohio at the time of its merger. It also had a "stellar reputation for consistent profitability."

After most of the merger dust settled in 2006, William B. Harrison Jr.'s four-decade career at JPMC ended, and Jamie Dimon became chairman and CEO of JPMC. The longtime protégé of Sandy Weill ousted shortly after the merger of Travelers and Citi (#3) in 1998, Dimon had become CEO of Bank One in early 2000, shortly after it became apparent

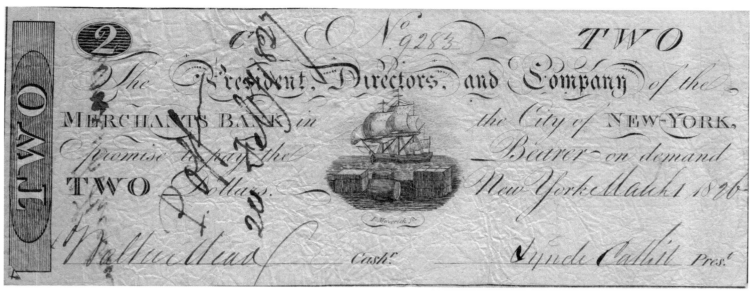

$2 bank note from the Merchants Bank, 1826.

that the big merger between Banc One and First Chicago NBD was failing. Bank One had grown quickly by allowing acquired banks to maintain their independence.

First Chicago and NBD were still not completely integrated yet either, and the former had a reputation for poor customer service. In addition, the cultures in Chicago and Columbus completely clashed. Unable to cope with the situation, McCoy was ousted by his own board, which appointed interim leadership while it searched for somebody who knew how to make big mergers work. Dimon was on everybody's short list. He did so well turning around the badly managed bank that he was promised the top spot at JPMC after two years.

JPMC ran its consumer and small-to-middle business operations under the Chase brand and its wholesale and investment banking businesses under the JPMorgan brand. By 2007 the investment bank alone employed 20,000 people in 50 countries and was divided into various industry groups such as energy, financial institutions, government, health care, technology and transportation. With 174,360 employees working in 2,300 offices worldwide, Chase, which included the company's credit card, home finance, small business, insurance and commercial real estate businesses, dwarfed the JPMorgan wing, but analysts such as Vault Guide considered it a less prestigious place to work.

JPMC experienced considerable "growing pains" in the first decade of the 21st century because its culture and computer systems did not mesh well with those of Chase or Bank One. It also had to pay billions in settlements as a result of its involvement in the Enron and WorldCom fiascos. In 2005 it had to renovate its network of 3,000 plus branches in 17 states. By 2007, however, it was expanding internationally while hauling in record profits. It also basked in the glow of various awards, including a "Top 10 Family Friendly Company" by *Working Mother* and ninth place in *BusinessWeek*'s "Best Places to Launch a Career" rankings. Others also told undergraduates that JPMC was the right place to build a long and lucrative career.

That may still prove correct, but the bank, like the entire financial system, hit a speed bump in 2008. The year began propitiously with the purchase of troubled investment bank Bear Stearns for what many considered a bargain-basement price of $2 per share and the Fed's assumption of its most toxic assets. (The price was later raised to $10 per share.) Bear Stearns, after all, had been a Wall Street icon since 1923, when Joseph Bear, Robert Stearns and Harold Mayer partnered to form

a brokerage that expanded into bonds, investment banking and international finance in the 1930s and 1940s. The partnership went public in 1985 and was involved in some major IPOs in the 1990s, including that of Lucent Technology. Just before its demise, it had $2 billion in net income and 15,000 employees in 30 offices worldwide.

JPMC also bought Washington Mutual (WaMu), a deeply troubled thrift, for $1.9 billion, while its holding company, WMI, filed for bankruptcy and sued the FDIC for what it considered an unjustified seizure and low sale price. WaMu began life as the Washington National Building and Loan Association in 1889 and enjoyed quiet but unspectacular success until it demutualized completely in 1983. As a joint-stock company it had grown rapidly through acquisitions, and in June 2008 it boasted assets in excess of $300 billion, almost 2,300 branches and more than 43,000 employees. Its huge position in option adjustable rate mortgages, a form of subprime mortgage, doomed it by inducing a major run on its deposits in mid-September 2008.

Because it was a less aggressive trader than many of its peers, and also more focused on long-term growth, JPMC itself enjoyed a relatively low risk position when the subprime mortgage crisis turned ugly in September 2008. Unlike the CEOs of most other LCFIs, Dimon had prepped his bank for crisis. But when Henry Paulson asked him to reconstitute the House of Morgan by merging with Morgan Stanley (#6) *at no cost*, Dimon demurred. Not even J. Pierpont himself could have saved the entire US financial system by assuming the balance sheets of its largest and most troubled companies.

Instead of chasing more deals, Dimon did the same thing he had done after taking the reins at Bank One—he cut dividends in order to increase capital. The fact that JPMC's stock *rallied* after the announcement showed how much confidence investors had in Dimon. Bear Stearns and WaMu proved difficult enough to digest without adding Morgan Stanley, which may well have choked JPMC to death. The company had also been settling many lawsuits, often legacies from previous acquisitions.

In 2012 JPMC made headlines when its so-called London Whale Trades cost the bank $6.2 billion, but for the year the bank was still highly profitable with over $21 billion in net income. And that has been the consistent story under Dimon's leadership—JPMC is widely viewed as a market leader with steady and dependable returns for its shareholders.

Sources

Bair, Sheila. *Bull by the Horns: Fighting to Save Main Street from Wall Street and Wall Street from Itself*. New York: Free Press, 2012, 74–75, 90–94.

"Bank 100 Years Old Today: Chemical National, Known as 'Old Bullion,' Celebrates." *The New York Times*, July 30, 1924.

"Bank Statements: Chemical Bank and Trust Company." *The New York Times*, July 1, 1938, 33.

Berg, Eric N. "A Market Where Chemical Is King." *The New York Times*, January 11, 1987, F1.

Chase National Bank of the City of New York, 1877–1922. New York: The Chase National Bank, 1922.

"Chemical Bank Mergers Gain." *The New York Times*, November 7, 1963, 57.

"Chemical Bank to Absorb Citizens." *The New York Times*, March 19, 1920, 20.

"Chemical Bank Unit Is to Be Absorbed." *The New York Times*, December 17, 1932, 27.

"Chemical National Bank of New York to Pay Interest on Bank Deposits." *Bankers Magazine* (June 1917): 665–666.

Chernow, Ron. *The House of Morgan: An American Banking Dynasty and the Rise of Modern Finance*. New York: Grove Press, 1990.

"College Loan Plan Set: Chemical Bank Starts New Program to Aid Parents." *The New York Times*, March 22, 1961, 51.

"Colombian Gold for Chemical Bank." *The New York Times*, March 7, 1931, 34.

Early New York and the Bank of the Manhattan Company, 1799–1920. New York: Bank of the Manhattan Company, 1920.

"Ex-Loan Officer Indicted in Chemical Bank Fraud." *The New York Times*, March 3, 1977, 37.

Gage, Beverly. *The Day Wall Street Exploded: A Story of America in its First Age of Terror*. New York: Oxford University Press, 2009.

Hayes, Thomas C. "Profile/Marc J. Shapiro; This Banker May Be Too Big for Texas." *The New York Times*, July 11, 1993.

Heinemann, H. Erich. "Chemical Bank Sets Overseas Expansion." *The New York Times*, January 15, 1966, 31.

Hershey, Robert D., Jr. "Chemical Bank in Holding Deal: Joins Diversification Trend of Major Institutions." *The New York Times*, October 25, 1968, 65.

History of the Chemical Bank, 1823–1913. New York: Privately Printed, 1913.

Hylton, Richard D. "The Bank Merger; 'Manny Hanny': A Name for History Books." *The New York Times*, July 16, 1991.

Loosvelt, Derek, et al. *The Vault Guide to the Top 50 Banking Employers: 2008 Edition*. New York: Vault, 2007, 62–69, 102–107, 114–19.

McDonald, Duff. *Last Man Standing: The Ascent of Jamie Dimon and JPMorgan Chase*. New York: Simon and Schuster, 2009.

Metz, Robert. "Marketplace: Leasco Eying Chemical Bank." *The New York Times*, February 6, 1969, 52.

Moore, Michael J., Dakin Campbell and Laura Marcinek. "Wall Street Exhales as Volcker Rule Seen Sparing Market-Making." *Bloomberg Online*, December 20, 2013.

"Nashville Bank Sustains Long Run." *The New York Times*, November 15, 1930, 16.

"New Status Cleared for Chemical Bank." *The New York Times*, November 30, 1968, 67.

Pak, Susie J. *Gentleman Bankers: The World of J. P. Morgan*. Cambridge, MA: Harvard University Press, 2013.

Spiegel, John, Alan Gart and Steven Gart. *Banking Redefined: How Superregional Powerhouses Are Reshaping Financial Services*. Chicago: Irwin Professional Publishing, 1996, 97–135.

Stone, Amey and Mike Brewster. *King of Capital: Sandy Weill and the Making of Citigroup*. New York: Wiley, 2002.

Wetfeet. *25 Top Financial Services Firms*. San Francisco: Wetfeet. 2008, 54–57.

Wilson, John D. *The Chase: The Chase Manhattan Bank, N.A., 1945–1985*. Boston: Harvard Business School Press, 1986.

Wright, Robert E. "Artisans, Banks, Credit, and the Election of 1800." *Pennsylvania Magazine of History and Biography* 122, 3 (July 1998): 211–39.

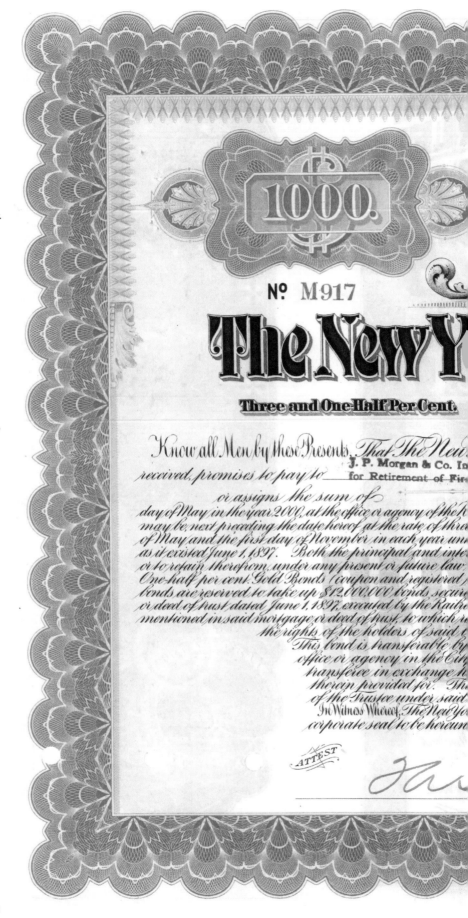

New York and Harlem Railroad bond certificate issued to JP Morgan & Co., Trustee, 1956.

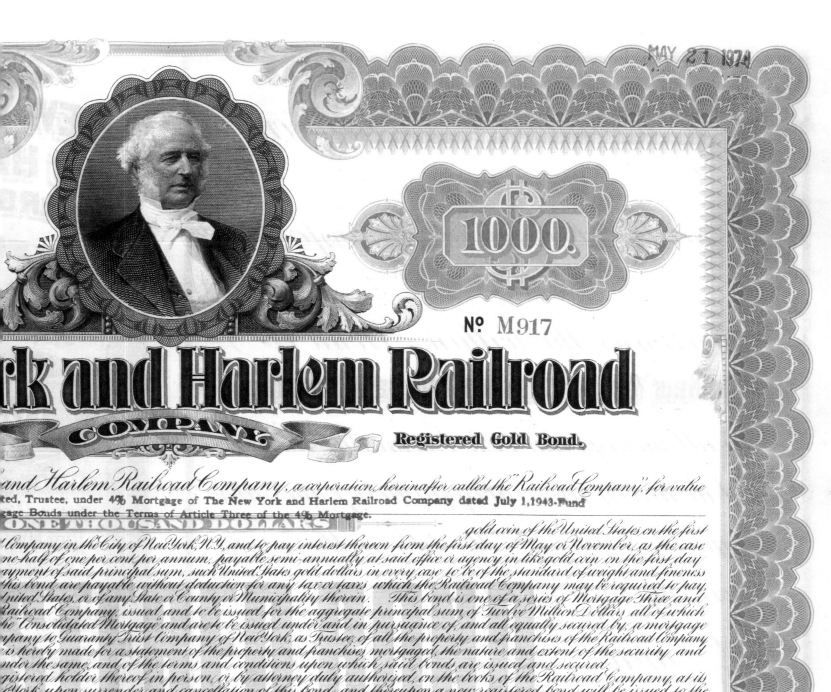

MAY 21 1974

No. M917

rk and Harlem Railroad
COMPANY.

Registered Gold Bond.

$1000.

and Harlem Railroad Company, a corporation, hereinafter called the "Railroad Company," for value

ted, Trustee, under 4% Mortgage of The New York and Harlem Railroad Company dated July 1, 1943. Fund

gage Bonds under the Terms of Article Three of the 4% Mortgage.

ONE THOUSAND DOLLARS gold coin of the United States on the first

Company in the City of New York, N.Y., and to pay interest thereon from the first day of May or November, as the case

ne-half of one per cent per annum, payable semi-annually at said office or agency in like gold coin, on the first day

yment of said principal sum, such United States gold dollars in every case to be of the standard of weight and fineness

his bond are payable without deduction for any tax or taxes which the Railroad Company may be required to pay

nited States, or of any State or County or Municipality therein. This bond is one of a series of Mortgage Three and

Railroad Company, issued and to be issued for the aggregate principal sum of Twelve Million Dollars, all of which

he "Consolidated Mortgage" and are to be issued under and in pursuance of, and all equally secured by, a mortgage

pany to Guaranty Trust Company of New York, as Trustee, of all the property and franchises of the Railroad Company

is hereby made for a statement of the property and franchises mortgaged, the nature and extent of the security, and

nder the same, and of the terms and conditions upon which said bonds are issued and secured.

istered holder thereof in person, or by attorney duly authorized, on the books of the Railroad Company, at its

York, upon surrender and cancellation of this bond; and thereupon a new registered bond will be issued to the

s provided in said mortgage or deed of trust, and on payment, if the Railroad Company shall so require, of the charge

shall not become obligatory for any purpose until it shall have been authenticated by the certificate hereon endorsed

ge or deed of trust.

Harlem Railroad Company has caused these presents to be signed by its President or one of its Vice Presidents, and its

xt, and to be attested by its Secretary or Assistant Secretary this _____4TH_____ day of _____MAY, 1956_____

The New York and Harlem Railroad Company

By

Assistant SECRETARY.   Vice PRESIDENT.

UNITED STATES OF AMERICA

AMERICAN BANK NOTE COMPANY, NEW YORK.

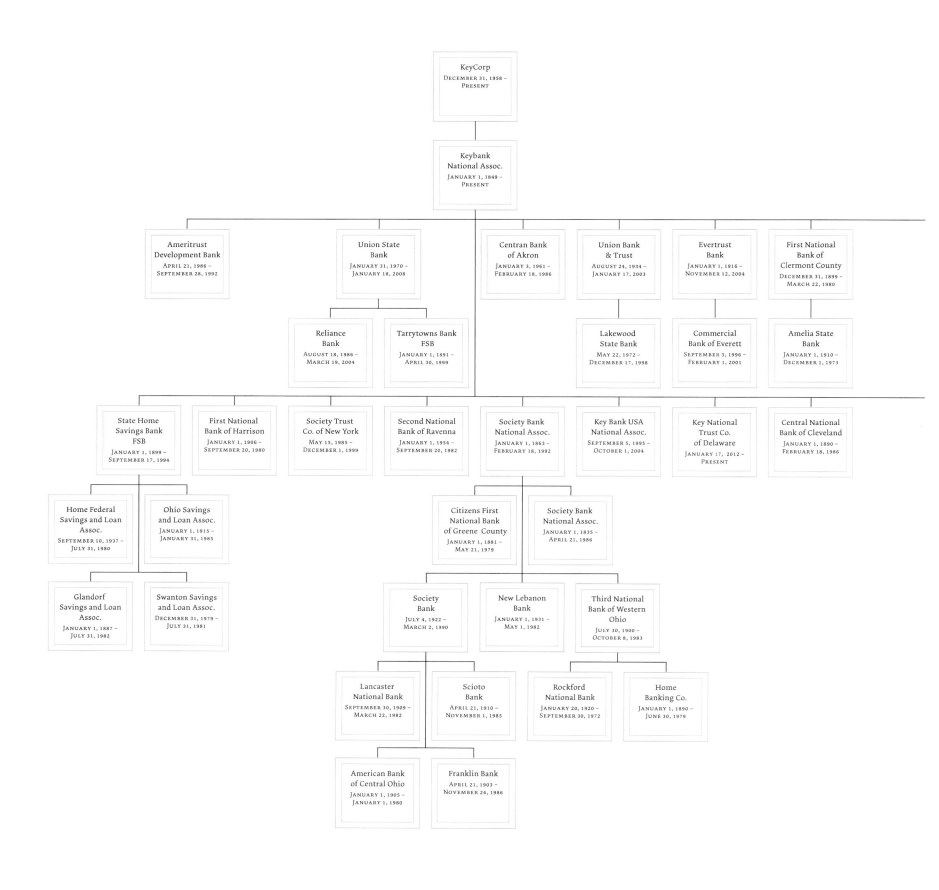

KeyCorp

Bank *(abridged)*

RANK	HEADQUARTERS	TICKER	ASSETS	EARLIEST KNOWN ANCESTOR	INDUSTRY OF ORIGIN
29	**Cleveland, OH**	**KEY**	**$91,000,000,000**	**1803**	**Commercial Banking**

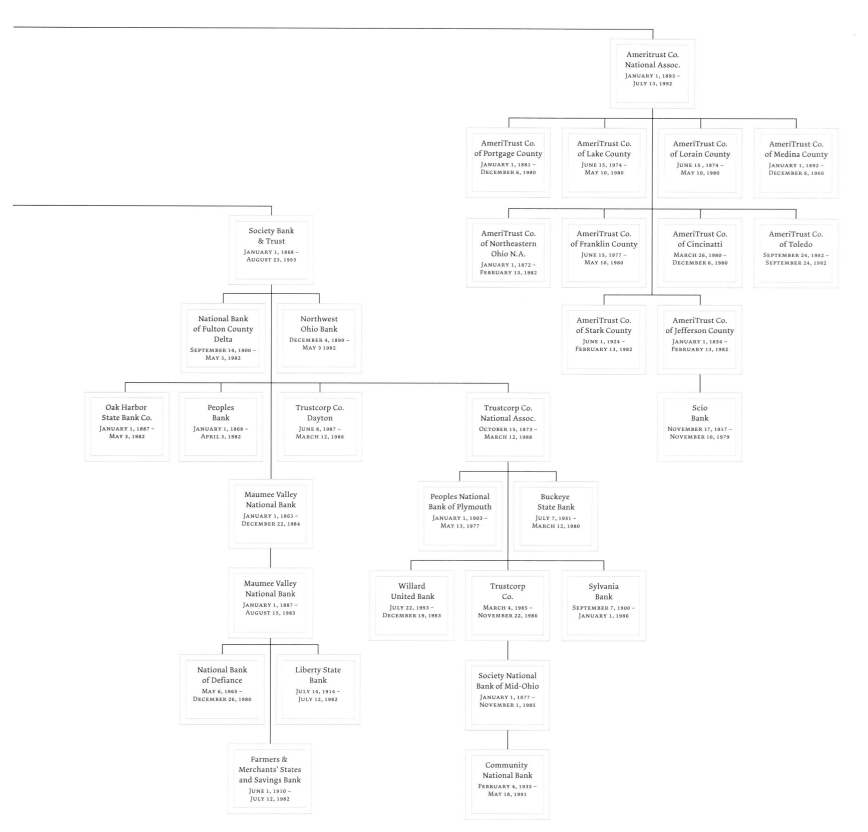

Ameritrust Co.
National Assoc.
JANUARY 1, 1893 –
JULY 13, 1992

AmeriTrust Co.
of Portage County
JANUARY 1, 1881 –
DECEMBER 6, 1980

AmeriTrust Co.
of Lake County
JUNE 15, 1974 –
MAY 10, 1980

AmeriTrust Co.
of Lorain County
JUNE 15, 1974 –
MAY 10, 1980

AmeriTrust Co.
of Medina County
JANUARY 1, 1892 –
DECEMBER 6, 1980

Society Bank
& Trust
JANUARY 1, 1868 –
AUGUST 23, 1993

AmeriTrust Co.
of Northeastern
Ohio N.A.
JANUARY 1, 1872 –
FEBRUARY 13, 1982

AmeriTrust Co.
of Franklin County
JUNE 15, 1977 –
MAY 10, 1980

AmeriTrust Co.
of Cincinatti
MARCH 26, 1980 –
DECEMBER 6, 1980

AmeriTrust Co.
of Toledo
SEPTEMBER 24, 1982 –
SEPTEMBER 24, 1982

National Bank
of Fulton County
Delta
SEPTEMBER 14, 1900 –
MAY 3, 1982

Northwest
Ohio Bank
DECEMBER 4, 1899 –
MAY 3 1982

AmeriTrust Co.
of Stark County
JUNE 1, 1924 –
FEBRUARY 13, 1982

AmeriTrust Co.
of Jefferson County
JANUARY 1, 1854 –
FEBRUARY 13, 1982

Oak Harbor
State Bank Co.
JANUARY 1, 1887 –
MAY 3, 1982

Peoples
Bank
JANUARY 1, 1868 –
APRIL 5, 1982

Trustcorp Co.
Dayton
JUNE 8, 1987 –
MARCH 12, 1988

Trustcorp Co.
National Assoc.
OCTOBER 15, 1873 –
MARCH 12, 1988

Scio
Bank
NOVEMBER 17, 1917 –
NOVEMBER 10, 1979

Maumee Valley
National Bank
JANUARY 1, 1863 –
DECEMBER 22, 1984

Peoples National
Bank of Plymouth
JANUARY 1, 1903 –
MAY 13, 1977

Buckeye
State Bank
JULY 7, 1951 –
MARCH 12, 1980

Maumee Valley
National Bank
JANUARY 1, 1887 –
AUGUST 15, 1983

Willard
United Bank
JULY 22, 1993 –
DECEMBER 19, 1983

Trustcorp
Co.
MARCH 4, 1985 –
NOVEMBER 22, 1986

Sylvania
Bank
SEPTEMBER 7, 1900 –
JANUARY 1, 1986

National Bank
of Defiance
MAY 6, 1965 –
DECEMBER 26, 1980

Liberty State
Bank
JULY 14, 1914 –
JULY 12, 1982

Society National
Bank of Mid-Ohio
JANUARY 1, 1877 –
NOVEMBER 1, 1985

Farmers &
Merchants' States
and Savings Bank
JUNE 1, 1910 –
JULY 12, 1982

Community
National Bank
FEBRUARY 4, 1935 –
MAY 18, 1991

THE BIG 50: KEYCORP

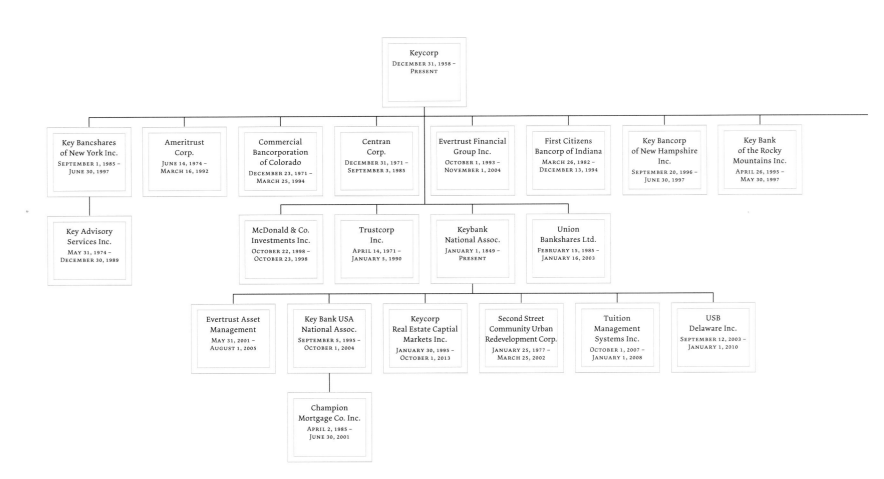

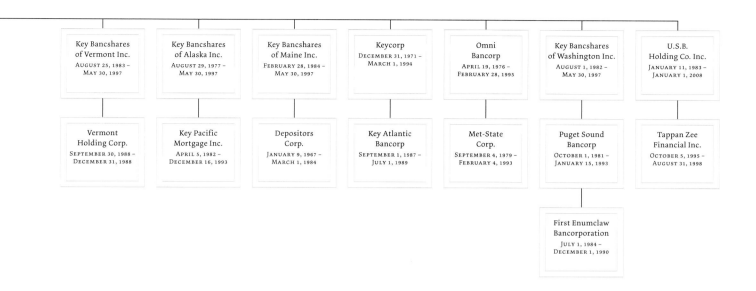

KeyCorp

Holding Company *(abridged)*

Specimen bank check of the Albany City National Bank, payable at the National Shawmut Bank of Boston, early 1900s. The portrait is of Erastus Corning, longtime president of the bank, who died in 1872.

KeyCorp traces its lineage to the Commercial Bank of Albany, which received a commercial banking charter from the state of New York in April 1825, after the political minions of future US President Martin Van Buren rejected its initial charter application in 1824. Incorporated by more than a dozen prominent men and authorized to raise up to $300,000 in capital, in shares of $20 par each, the bank held an IPO that was a rousing success with over $1.5 million subscribed. The ensuing, highly politicized squabble over who was entitled to own stock delayed the bank's opening for over a year. However, it did not stop its rapid initial growth, which was bolstered in 1831 when the state government began depositing some of its funds in the bank. The bank's motto, "Fortiter, Fideliter, Feliciter," meant courage, faith and courtesy.

The Commercial Bank of Albany navigated the Panic of 1837 in such good form that its reputation for financial strength waxed strong. The bank also survived an 1845 hiccup caused by a criminal teller who decided to help himself to the till. The loss caused the revocation of a 4% semiannual dividend payment. In 1847 its initial charter and an extension expired, so the bank chartered under the state's 1838 free banking law. In 1862 the bank lent the state an uncollateralized emergency $3.5 million so it could pay bonuses to soldiers desperately needed to defend Washington, DC, from an encroaching Confederate Army. In 1865 it converted to a national bank and changed its name to the National Commercial Bank of Albany.

In 1901 the bank greatly increased its balance sheet by acquiring the Merchants National Bank of Albany and the Albany City National Bank. The following year, it helped form the Union Trust Company of Albany. Less regulated than commercial banks, Union Trust grew quickly. It acquired the Park Bank in 1902, and in March 1920, after regulatory reforms were enacted, it converted to a commercial banking charter. National Commercial merged with it two months later to form the National Commercial Bank and Trust Company of Albany. Thanks to a long succession of quality leadership, it survived the Great Depression and even remained quasi-open during the 1933 bank holiday so that its corporate customers and the state government could meet payroll. (In 1965 it again helped the state make payroll by offering interest free loans to state employees victimized by a legislative deadlock.) It even sent cash by airplane and state police escort.

The bank breached the $100 million in assets mark in June 1941. During the tenure of President Frank Wells McCabe, which lasted from 1955 until 1963, the bank increased its branch network from 15 to 34, initiated a profit sharing plan, expanded employee educational programs and added many new services. Assets at McCabe's exit had reached $445 million. McCabe's successor, Lester Herzog, grew the bank to more than 60 branches in 13 counties and over $800 million in assets. Herzog also created a mobile branch that traveled to remote areas on a fixed schedule and responded to emergencies like Hurricane Agnes, which wreaked havoc in New York's Southern Tier in 1972. Most importantly, however, Herzog established the HC that would later be called KeyCorp.

The motive for the HC was to circumvent New York's branching restrictions, which prevented banks in the state, whether chartered by the state or the federal government, from acquiring banks outside of its home district, one of nine delineated by regulators. After the Federal Reserve denied the applications of several ambitious HCs, it agreed in 1971 to the formation of the First Commercial Banks, Inc. (FCBI, née Heartland Central NY Corp.), which was composed of National Commercial and the much smaller First Trust and Deposit Company of Syracuse. The transaction made FCBI a billion dollar bank, but more importantly it opened the door to even faster growth. In 1972 FCBI scrutinized nearly every small bank in upstate New York as a possible takeover target and threw in some finance companies for good measure. It agreed to merge with one of the finance companies, but regulators nixed the deal. The acquisition of Kingston Trust was approved, however, and took effect in 1972, raising the HC's assets to $1.54 billion and its branch network to 101.

Those and subsequent acquisitions taught FCBI executives many important, but not too costly, lessons. Kingston Trust, for example, had some fraudulent loans in its mortgage portfolio that ended up costing the jobs of five executives and a $300,000 charge, so FCBI began to look at the books more carefully before pulling the trigger on merger deals. Another early acquisition, Homer National Bank, brought with it Richard Mott, who would later play a major role in Key Bank's development. Oysterman's Bank of Sayville, Long Island, took almost a year to acquire because of inexperience on the part of both regulators and the bank, but future deals went through much more quickly. In the mid-1970s FCBI also moved into credit life insurance and financial advising.

FCBI's earnings stumbled slightly in 1973 but grew steadily over the next 14 years, thanks in part to inflation and acquisitions. By the end of 1976 the bank had $1.63 billion in assets and a record return on equity of 13.56%. Almost 2,400 full- and part-time employees staffed the bank's 117 branches, which stretched from Long Island to central New York. More mergers followed, but so too did organic growth from the

First National Bank of Fairbanks, ca. 1900-1915.

development of the Key Lease Plan, an innovative automobile leasing scheme, in 1977. That same year, the HC removed several of its subsidiaries from the Federal Reserve's oversight in order to reduce their reserve requirements and free up more funds for loans. In 1979 FCBI rebranded itself as Key Banks Inc., acquired Genesee Valley National Bank and Trust and folded that tiny bank into Key Bank of Central New York. It also made five other acquisitions that year. It allowed some subsidiaries to keep their original names but added the phrase "A Key Bank Subsidiary" to their signage, letterhead and marketing materials.

In the early 1980s Key Bank's CEO championed a program to improve the recruitment of minority male employees. A decade and a half later, the bank had more than 60 diversity-related programs for its employees and a Multicultural Division with the stated goals to build a workforce that reflected the communities the bank serviced and to "identify and prepare talented females and minorities for upper management positions." The program paid off: minority representation at the VP level and above increased from 19 in 1990 to 63 in 1995, while over that same period the number of women at the executive level jumped from 63 to 410.

By the early 1980s the BHC owned six banks and five nonbanks, including a credit card issuer called Keycard, had $2.5 billion in assets, just over 3,000 employees and 173 branches. It responded to the economic troubles of the era (high, volatile interest rates and high inflation) by going on a buying binge, including the purchase of some of Bankers Trust's (now part of Deutsche Bank [#34]) branches in Binghamton, Buffalo, Jamestown and Rochester. By then the bank had expanded throughout upstate New York.

Key Bank competed well on the basis of quality, but in downstate New York, New York City and Long Island, banks competed largely on price. Instead of trying to compete with the big banks downstate, Key Bank began to branch across state lines, which was made possible by 1982 legislation that opened New York to the banks of any state that reciprocated by allowing New York banks into their state. Maine had

a similar law on its books, so Key Bank acquired Depositors and Canal Bank, which as Maine's largest bank added 88 branches and assets of $973 million to the rapidly growing Key empire. It was by far the largest acquisition in the bank's history up to that time.

Depositors Trust had formed in 1933, in the wake of the bank holiday. It was an acquisitions hound, too, and by 1964 had deposits of $111 million. It formed a BHC, Depositors Corporation, in 1966, and the following year it purchased Liberty National Bank in Ellsworth and the Newport Trust Company, which triggered a name change for the bank to Depositors Trust of Bangor in 1969. More mergers followed, motivating another name change, to Depositors Trust Company of Eastern Maine, in 1979.

In 1982 Depositors Corporation (the BHC) purchased Canal Corporation, owner of the Canal National Bank of Portland. Like Key Bank's corporate ancestor, Canal had been chartered in 1825 and opened in 1826, and had been capitalized at $300,000. The Depositors deal, which for various legal and tax reasons was not completed until early 1984, rendered Key Bank big enough to obtain a listing on the New York Stock Exchange. Meanwhile, the bank expanded into the trust business in Florida and automobile lease financing in seven major cities (including three in Florida and one in Texas).

By the end of 1983 the bank had $3.1 billion in assets and more than 3,700 employees, but its growth was far from over. In May of the following year it purchased 26 branches put on the block by the Bank of New York (#9). It also added a slew of independent banks to its family later that year and formed Key Mortgage Funding and Key Financial Services too. With further expansion into New England blocked by new laws and old antipathies, Key Bank found only one more outlet available to quench its urge to merge — Alaska, aptly nicknamed "The Last Frontier." In October 1984 Key Bank leapt across the continent and purchased Alaska Pacific Bancorporation, a BHC that traced its roots back to 1905 and the establishment of the First National Bank of Fairbanks. The transaction was completed in 1985. Wall Street shuddered at the

Society National Bank building in Cleveland, Ohio, 1965.

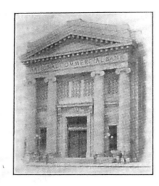

𝕿𝖍𝖊
National Commercial Bank
of Albany, New York

CAPITAL	SURPLUS	DEPOSITS
$500,000	**$1,150,000**	**$15,000,000**

OFFICERS

ROBERT C. PRUYN, President.   EDWARD J. HUSSEY, Cashier
GRANGE SARD, Vice-Pres.   HUGH N. KIRKLAND, Asst. Cashier
CHARLES H. SABIN, Vice-Pres.   WALTER W. BATCHELDER, Auditor

We solicit your New York State and New England items

The National Commercial Bank of Albany advertisement showing a snapshot of its balance sheet.

deal, but investors did not realize that, owing to a variety of fortuitous circumstances, it would give KeyCorp (the BHC's name as of August 1985) entree into Oregon and eventually the entire Northwest.

By the end of 1986 KeyCorp had one of the most geographically diverse loan portfolios in the country. When low oil prices hurt its Alaskan banks, larger profits in New York made up for it. When New England real estate hit the skids, Oregon did well. Although it suffered a decline in earnings in 1987, as did most banks, its complete lack of exposure to foreign loans made its decline short and shallow. More than 400 branches, 8,000 employees and $9.1 billion in assets spread across the "snow belt" proved a stable platform for yet more growth over the next decade, including the federally assisted takeover of numerous troubled institutions like Buffalo's Goldome Savings Bank in 1991. KeyCorp also bought up numerous promising but inexpensive banks in growing, underbanked areas of western states including Colorado, Idaho, Utah and Wyoming.

"America's neighborhood bank," as KeyCorp called itself, also did some streamlining. The bank's efficiency ratio reached the pretty outrageous level of 71.5% in 1987, but branch consolidation and other reforms reduced it to 64% by 1990. In the end, though, it wasn't enough to maintain the bank's independence. In October 1993 it merged with the Society Corporation of Cleveland because Society brought to the table a host of strong products, and Key Bank had a huge retail network (by then about 800 branches), in which to sell them. Consequently, the KeyCorp name remained, but its corporate headquarters moved to Cleveland. The combined bank had 1,300 branches in 22 states and assets of $58 billion, ranking it the nation's 10th largest BHC.

At the time of the merger with KeyCorp, Society concentrated mostly on commercial lending and operated 437 branches in Ohio, Indiana and Michigan. Nonbank subsidiaries provided insurance sales services, reinsurance, securities brokerage, trust services, mortgage banking services and even venture capital services.

In 1995 the new KeyCorp sold off its relatively unremunerative mortgage servicing book to NationsBank (now part of #2), but it continued growing anyway. By 1996 KeyCorp had assets of $66.8 billion and 30,000 employees in branches and affiliated offices spread over 25 states. President Robert Gillespie credited the bank's success to its acquisition prowess, as well as good cost controls, credit management, technology utilization, customer service and marketing skills. He argued that the bank remained customer, and not product, focused. The bank won a gold medal from *Teleprofessional* magazine, for example, for the way it integrated several geographically separated customer call centers into one "virtual" call center.

By 2000 KeyCorp employed more than 22,000 people, owned assets worth $87 billion and enjoyed revenues of almost $8.5 billion. It was by then a multiline financial services company with subsidiaries that provided a wide range of investment management, banking, consumer finance and investment banking products to individuals, corporations and institutional investors. But its stock price, which hit $15.69 in March 2000, and low employee morale made it a potential takeover target. Management responded in a major way, allowing KeyCorp to sail through the 2008 financial crisis because of its new enterprise risk management system. By 2007 KeyCorp had slimmed down to fewer than 20,000 workers in 947 locations across 13 states and had about

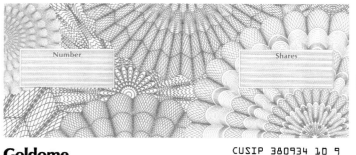

Common Stock

Goldome
Incorporated under the laws of the State of New York

CUSIP 380934 10 9
SEE REVERSE FOR CERTAIN DEFINITIONS

This certifies that

is the owner of

fully paid and nonassessable shares, par value $1 per share, of the Common Stock of Goldome (the "Bank") transferable on the books of the Bank in person or by duly authorized attorney upon surrender of this Certificate properly endorsed. The Common Stock represented by this Certificate is nonwithdrawable capital which is not of an insurable type and is not insured by the Federal Deposit Insurance Corporation. This Certificate is not valid until countersigned and registered by the Transfer Agent and Registrar. Witness the seal of the Bank and the signatures of its duly authorized officers.

Countersigned and Registered:
Manufacturers Hanover Trust Company,
Transfer Agent and Registrar (New York)

Dated

By

Authorized Officer

Vice President and Corporate Secretary

Chairman of the Board

Goldome specimen stock certificate.

2,200 ATMs, the 11th largest network in the country. More importantly, by then it had a firm grasp, perhaps the best in the business, of its risk profile, leading it to sell off its Champion Mortgage subsidiary in 2006 for a small loss.

Instead of a fragmented view of the five major types of risks it faced (credit, market, operational, technological and compliance), KeyCorp consolidated them under a single executive it initially called the Risk Czar (now the Chief Risk Officer or CRO). One of the CRO's main responsibilities was to allocate capital among the bank's businesses to help executives decide where they needed to expand, contract or pay more careful attention. With their bonuses tied to risk as well as return, KeyCorp executives had incentives to increase efficiencies, not just bet the bank. Proper capital allocation, the bank's leaders also believed, helped to decrease its overall earnings volatility. Instead of just value at risk (VAR), perhaps the risk model most commonly used by financial corporations, KeyCorp's risk czar also used probability of default and loss given default models. The CRO did not stand alone, but rather chaired a "risk council" that met periodically according to need and included the bank's chairman, CEO and a number of other senior executives.

KeyCorp also trained employees to help them to build a broad risk perspective and developed a philosophy that "everybody owns the risk." That initiative was part of the bank's larger management philosophy, called "corporate performance management," initiated by Henry Meyer when he became CEO in February 2001. Goal one was to become more "intimate" with customers so that their needs, strictly financial of course, could be better met. The next goal was to become "the most

admired financial institution" in KeyCorp's markets. Executives that would not buy in or could not deliver were replaced, and emphasis was placed on finding candidates that would behave in an "ethical" manner toward both employees and clients. With persistent effort and ongoing measuring and tracking of results, Meyer was able to transform the company's culture from one of "just another bank" to one of service excellence and continuous improvement.

Sources

Brown, Albert J. "A Brief History of KeyCorp." Albany, NY: typescript, 1995.

Chicago Area Partnerships. *Pathways and Progress: Corporate Best Practices to Shatter the Glass Ceiling.* Chicago: Women Employed, 1996, 33–34.

Herzog, Lester W. *150 Years of Service and Leadership: The Story of National Commercial Bank and Trust Company.* New York: Newcomen Society, 1975.

Loosvelt, Derek, et al. *The Vault Guide to the Top 50 Banking Employers: 2008 Edition.* New York: Vault, 2007, 348–82.

Miccolis, Jerry A., Kevin Hively and Brian W. Merkley. *Enterprise Risk Management: Trends and Emerging Practices.* Altamonte Springs, FL: Institute of Internal Auditors Research Foundation, 2001, 95–100.

Paladino, Bob. *Five Key Principles of Corporate Performance Management.* Hoboken, NJ: Wiley, 2007, 77–80, 145–51, 238–45.

Society for Savings. *A Brief History of the Society for Savings in the City of Cleveland.* Cleveland: Society for Savings, 1909.

Spiegel, John, Alan Gart and Steven Gart. *Banking Redefined: How Superregional Powerhouses Are Reshaping Financial Services.* Chicago: Irwin Professional Publishing, 1996, 137–57.

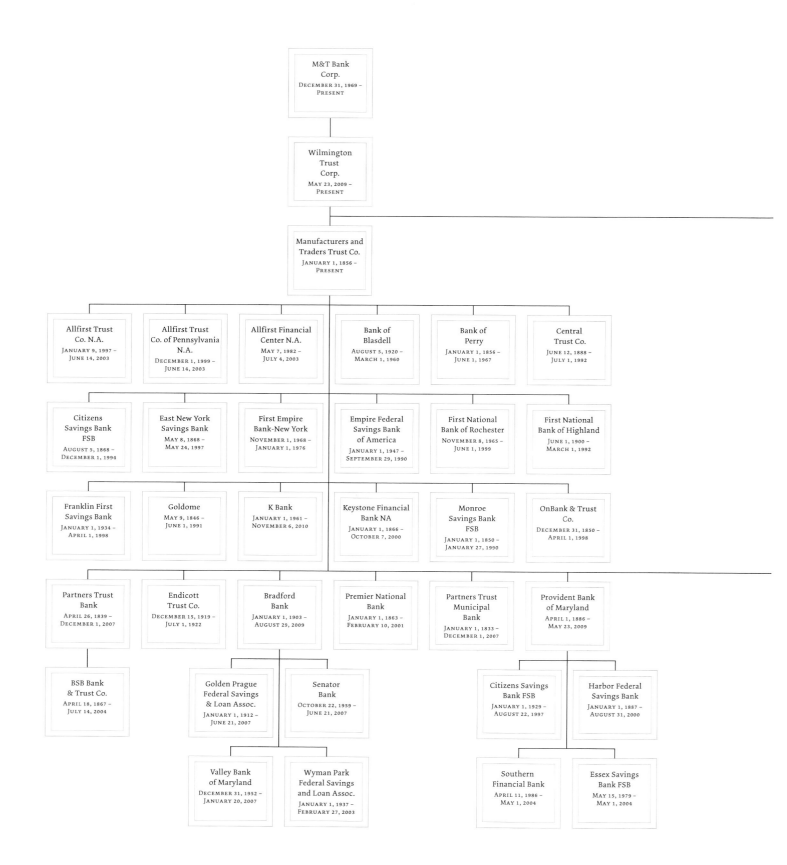

M&T Bank Corp.
DECEMBER 31, 1969 – PRESENT

Wilmington Trust Corp.
MAY 23, 2009 – PRESENT

Manufacturers and Traders Trust Co.
JANUARY 1, 1856 – PRESENT

Allfirst Trust Co. N.A.
JANUARY 9, 1997 – JUNE 14, 2003

Allfirst Trust Co. of Pennsylvania N.A.
DECEMBER 1, 1999 – JUNE 14, 2003

Allfirst Financial Center N.A.
MAY 7, 1982 – JULY 4, 2003

Bank of Blasdell
AUGUST 5, 1920 – MARCH 1, 1960

Bank of Perry
JANUARY 1, 1856 – JUNE 1, 1967

Central Trust Co.
JUNE 12, 1888 – JULY 1, 1992

Citizens Savings Bank FSB
AUGUST 5, 1868 – DECEMBER 1, 1994

East New York Savings Bank
MAY 8, 1868 – MAY 24, 1997

First Empire Bank-New York
NOVEMBER 1, 1968 – JANUARY 1, 1976

Empire Federal Savings Bank of America
JANUARY 1, 1947 – SEPTEMBER 29, 1990

First National Bank of Rochester
NOVEMBER 8, 1965 – JUNE 1, 1999

First National Bank of Highland
JUNE 1, 1900 – MARCH 1, 1992

Franklin First Savings Bank
JANUARY 1, 1934 – APRIL 1, 1998

Goldome
MAY 9, 1846 – JUNE 1, 1991

K Bank
JANUARY 1, 1961 – NOVEMBER 6, 2010

Keystone Financial Bank NA
JANUARY 1, 1866 – OCTOBER 7, 2000

Monroe Savings Bank FSB
JANUARY 1, 1850 – JANUARY 27, 1990

OnBank & Trust Co.
DECEMBER 31, 1850 – APRIL 1, 1998

Partners Trust Bank
APRIL 26, 1839 – DECEMBER 1, 2007

Endicott Trust Co.
DECEMBER 15, 1919 – JULY 1, 1922

Bradford Bank
JANUARY 1, 1903 – AUGUST 29, 2009

Premier National Bank
JANUARY 1, 1863 – FEBRUARY 10, 2001

Partners Trust Municipal Bank
JANUARY 1, 1833 – DECEMBER 1, 2007

Provident Bank of Maryland
APRIL 1, 1886 – MAY 23, 2009

BSB Bank & Trust Co.
APRIL 18, 1867 – JULY 14, 2004

Golden Prague Federal Savings & Loan Assoc.
JANUARY 1, 1912 – JUNE 21, 2007

Senator Bank
OCTOBER 22, 1959 – JUNE 21, 2007

Citizens Savings Bank FSB
JANUARY 1, 1929 – AUGUST 22, 1997

Harbor Federal Savings Bank
JANUARY 1, 1887 – AUGUST 31, 2000

Valley Bank of Maryland
DECEMBER 31, 1952 – JANUARY 20, 2007

Wyman Park Federal Savings and Loan Assoc.
JANUARY 1, 1937 – FEBRUARY 27, 2003

Southern Financial Bank
APRIL 11, 1986 – MAY 1, 2004

Essex Savings Bank FSB
MAY 15, 1979 – MAY 1, 2004

Wilmington Trust
N.A.
OCTOBER 2, 1995 –
PRESENT

M&T Trust
Co. of Delaware
JULY 1, 2003 –
JULY 1, 2011

Wilmington
Trust N.A.
JUNE 11, 1994 –
JULY 1, 2011

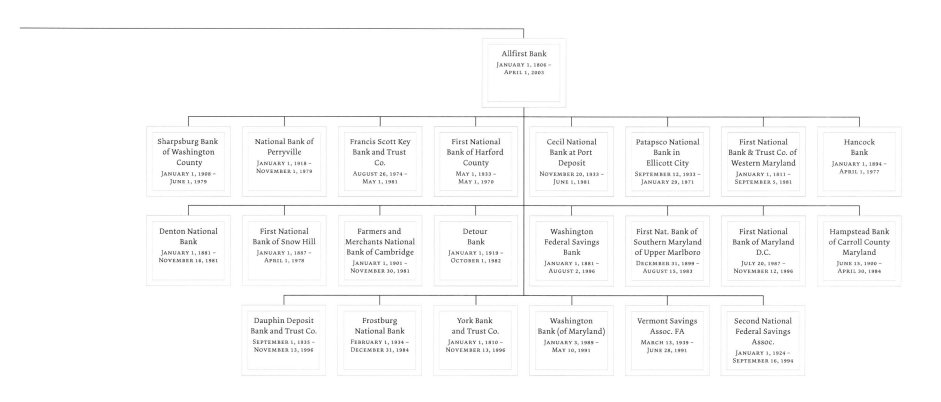

Allfirst Bank
JANUARY 1, 1806 –
APRIL 1, 2003

Sharpsburg Bank
of Washington
County
JANUARY 1, 1908 –
JUNE 1, 1979

National Bank of
Perryville
JANUARY 1, 1918 –
NOVEMBER 1, 1979

Francis Scott Key
Bank and Trust
Co.
AUGUST 26, 1974 –
MAY 1, 1981

First National
Bank of Harford
County
MAY 1, 1933 –
MAY 1, 1970

Cecil National
Bank at Port
Deposit
NOVEMBER 20, 1933 –
JUNE 1, 1981

Patapsco National
Bank in
Ellicott City
SEPTEMBER 12, 1933 –
JANUARY 29, 1971

First National
Bank & Trust Co. of
Western Maryland
JANUARY 1, 1811 –
SEPTEMBER 5, 1981

Hancock
Bank
JANUARY 1, 1894 –
APRIL 1, 1977

Denton National
Bank
JANUARY 1, 1881 –
NOVEMBER 16, 1981

First National
Bank of Snow Hill
JANUARY 1, 1887 –
APRIL 1, 1978

Farmers and
Merchants National
Bank of Cambridge
JANUARY 1, 1901 –
NOVEMBER 30, 1981

Detour
Bank
JANUARY 1, 1919 –
OCTOBER 1, 1982

Washington
Federal Savings
Bank
JANUARY 1, 1881 –
AUGUST 2, 1996

First Nat. Bank of
Southern Maryland
of Upper Marlboro
DECEMBER 31, 1899 –
AUGUST 15, 1983

First National
Bank of Maryland
D.C.
JULY 20, 1987 –
NOVEMBER 12, 1996

Hampstead Bank
of Carroll County
Maryland
JUNE 15, 1900 –
APRIL 30, 1984

Dauphin Deposit
Bank and Trust Co.
SEPTEMBER 1, 1835 –
NOVEMBER 13, 1996

Frostburg
National Bank
FEBRUARY 1, 1934 –
DECEMBER 31, 1984

York Bank
and Trust Co.
JANUARY 1, 1810 –
NOVEMBER 13, 1996

Washington
Bank (of Maryland)
JANUARY 3, 1989 –
MAY 10, 1991

Vermont Savings
Assoc. FA
MARCH 13, 1939 –
JUNE 28, 1991

Second National
Federal Savings
Assoc.
JANUARY 1, 1924 –
SEPTEMBER 16, 1994

M&T Bank

Bank *(abridged)*

RANK	HEADQUARTERS	TICKER	ASSETS	EARLIEST KNOWN ANCESTOR	INDUSTRY OF ORIGIN
30	**Buffalo, NY**	**MTB**	**$83,000,000,000**	**1806**	**Commercial Banking**

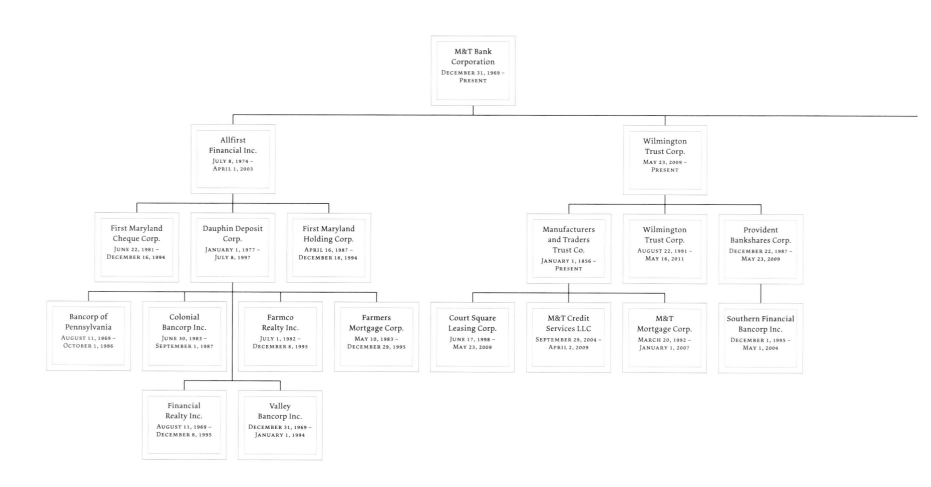

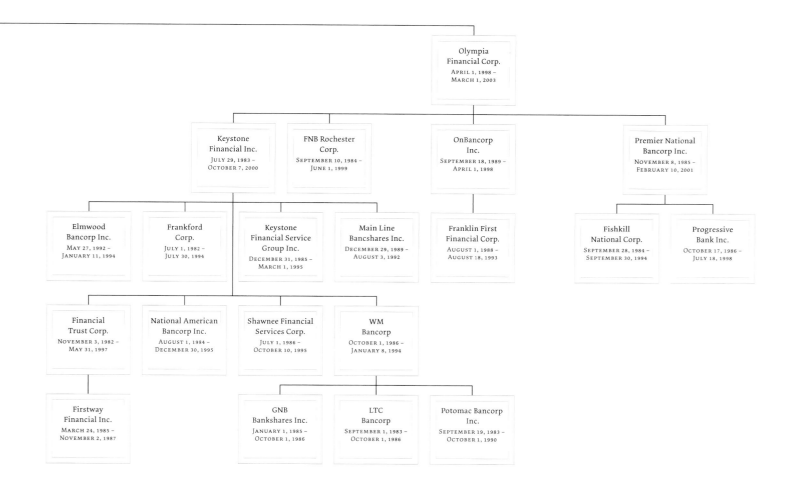

M&T Bank

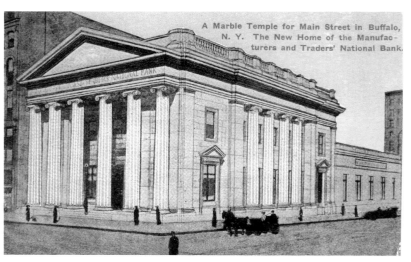

A Marble Temple for Main Street in Buffalo, N. Y. The New Home of the Manufacturers and Traders' National Bank.

Along the Niagara River, Buffalo, New York, ca. 1905.

Manufacturers and Traders National Bank building postcard.

Buffalo, New York, in 1856 was a bustling commercial port, home to about 75,000 souls whose livelihoods were tied closely to Erie—the lake, the canal and the railroad. There were, and still are, farmers in the vicinity, and their custom was important to the city. But were it not for manufacturing and trading activities, Buffalo would have been a mere small town, and not an important city. That year, more than 8,000 vessels cleared her port, and Buffalo's 2,000 or so shipbuilders launched 47 vessels of a total tonnage over 20,000. Almost $181 million worth of goods moved through the city via the three Eries. Many of the city's manufacturers, like Buffalo Iron & Nail Company, were still small, but they were thriving. With the proper aid, observers believed, they were likely to grow and prosper. For those reasons, Henry Martin, Stephen Van Rensselaer Watson, Pascal Paoli Pratt, Sidney Shepard and the other founders of the city's 16th bank called it the Manufacturers and Traders.

Martin, who led the bank from its founding until 1885, was described by a later president as an able banker and interesting character. He quickly induced investors to pay up the bank's initial $200,000 capital and soon after to contribute an additional $300,000, "so great is the confidence felt in the institution," according to an early newspaper account.

The 145 original stockholders—including the son of former President Millard Fillmore (a longtime Buffalo resident)—were rewarded in January 1857 when the bank paid its first dividend. It survived the panic that struck later that year and also the Civil War, and in 1869 it increased its capital to $900,000. Pratt took over for Martin in 1885 and served until his death in 1901. The following year, the bank again increased its capital (to $1 million), converted to a national charter and changed its name to the Manufacturers and Traders National Bank.

In 1915 Harry T. Ramsdell, who had started as a messenger in the bank at age 17, became its president. When Ramsdell came to the bank, it had 10 employees and assets of $2 million. Upon his death in 1934, the bank had assets of $106 million and many more employees. Ramsdell was responsible for much of that growth. The year after he assumed the presidency, the bank bought the Third National Bank of Buffalo (chartered in 1865) and doubled its capital to $2 million. Feeling its power in the 1920s, the bank built several new branches in Buffalo in the classic Roman style. By 1930 it had 16 branches throughout the city.

In 1925 the bank merged with the Fidelity Trust and Guaranty Company of Buffalo, which had been established in 1893 by what the bank's chronicler called "a group of prominent Buffalo businessmen closely identified with Manufacturers and Traders Bank." Capitalized initially at $500,000, Fidelity Trust aggressively attacked its market and

was soon returning tremendous profits. In 1901, for example, it returned 21.5% to stockholders, including $60,000 in the form of dividends and $47,726.97 in the form of additional surplus. By its 10th anniversary its accumulated surplus hit $600,000, or 120% of its capital. From 1910 until 1915, Fidelity Trust shared the same president as the bank, Robert L. Fryer, but it remained a separate legal entity. In the early 1920s, under the leadership of Lewis G. Harriman, Fidelity financed many important projects, including the Bear Mountain-Hudson River Bridge and the Peace Bridge over the Niagara River. By 1925 the trust had assets of $35 million, and Harriman was itching to join the merger wave sweeping over the city's banking industry. He, therefore, created a syndicate of directors and business leaders, including future Secretary of Defense James V. Forrestal, which bought controlling interests in both institutions and merged them under the name Manufacturers and Traders Trust Company.

Just 18 months later, in 1927, Harriman, who now headed the bank, was at it again, acquiring the Peoples Bank of Buffalo. Incorporated in 1889 and initially capitalized at $300,000, the Peoples Bank had done business with some of Buffalo's most prominent businessmen, including Wilson S. Bissell (postmaster general under President Grover Cleveland, Buffalo's former mayor), Charles W. Goodyear, Robert W. Pomeroy and many others, before being swallowed up. The combined entity, which styled itself the Manufacturers and Traders-Peoples Trust Company, had assets in excess of $134 million.

Despite its success, the bank remained sober—literally and figuratively—as Prohibition was on. That was a good thing because its deposits plummeted from $125 million in 1930 to just $70 million by the bank holiday in March 1933. Harriman's sound judgment on credit risks, combined with the bank's reputation for probity and its sizeable capital cushion, saved the bank while, as one eyewitness put it, "the banking fabric of the entire nation was collapsing." Matters improved slowly over the 1930s, at the end of which decade the bank established its first branch outside of the city, in nearby Niagara Falls.

World War II brought the regional economy and the bank out of the Great Depression and into near euphoria as the entire Niagara peninsula became a key war munitions manufacturing corridor. Several hundred million federal dollars poured into the area to build new plants, enlarge existing ones and stock them full of machines and workers, who flooded in by the tens of thousands. The bank's deposits doubled, from $123.5 to $227 million in 1942 alone, while its number of employees plummeted as a result of military service. In 1945 the bank bought the First National Bank of Kenmore, the Citizen's National

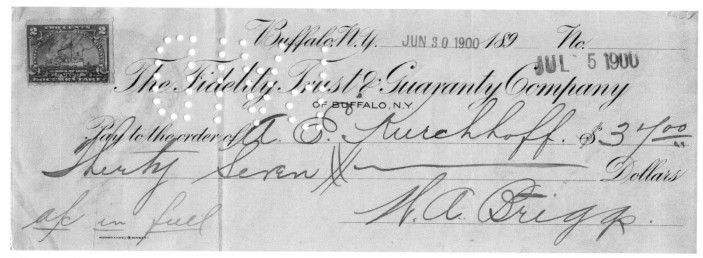

Fidelity Trust and Guaranty Company check, 1900.

Bank of Lancaster and the American Bank of Lackawanna. All three became branches.

The boom in the regional economy continued after the war. In 1941 $390 million worth of goods were produced in the region. That figure exceeded $1 billion in 1945 and was just shy of $1.7 billion a decade later. The bank continued to grow too, acquiring three more banks in 1946: one in Springville (Erie County), one in Dunkirk (Chautauqua County) and one in Corfu (Genesee County). That year and the next it also established de novo branches in Cheektowaga and Eggertsville, two thriving Buffalo suburbs. It moved into another thriving suburb, West Seneca, by purchasing the Ebenezer State Bank in 1948, and the following year it entered the Lockport market by purchasing the Lockport Exchange Trust Company.

More de novo branches followed, as did mergers with the First National Bank of Buffalo and the Bank of Clarence, both in 1955, and with Adam, Meldrum & Anderson State Bank the following year. Due to that growth, the bank at its centennial in 1956 had 36 offices in four counties, assets over $400 million and $32 million in capital, making it the 62nd largest of the 15,000 or so commercial banks in operation at that time.

By the middle of the first decade of the third millennium M&T's corporate culture was described as "sales-driven" and "entrepreneurial." In July 2006 M&T bought 21 Citibank branches in upstate New York, nine in Buffalo and 12 in Rochester. It subsequently shut down several of the branches that were located too close to existing M&T branches. By the end of 2006, when it entered the *Fortune* 500 (at #496), M&T had 672 branches in six states and Washington, DC, staffed by more than 13,300 workers, 1,500 ATMs and assets of $57 billion. These all helped to generate net income over $800 million. The bank provided consumers and businesses with retail and commercial banking services, as well as financial services like asset management, brokerage, discount brokerage, leasing, investment advisory services, mortgage banking and reinsurance.

In early 2007 the bank had exposure to Alt-A mortgages (below prime, but not as risky as subprime) that negatively impacted earnings. Other lenders experiencing difficulty selling their Alt-A loans at that time included WaMu, IndyMac and American Home Mortgage, all of which went bankrupt or had to be purchased during the ensuing financial crisis. The following year, the bank took a $78 million charge on some derivatives.

M&T made it through the 2008 financial crisis with its corporate life and independence, though it was in advanced merger discussions with Santander (#32) and received aid from Warren Buffett's Berkshire Hathaway. It initially resisted taking TARP funds but eventually received $600 million—the smallest amount it could have taken. The acquisition of TARP recipients Provident Bancshares in 2009 and Wilmington Trust in 2011, however, added to its TARP load. Unlike other banks, M&T proved in no rush to repay, holding onto the government's investment longer than any of its peers. It did not want to raise additional equity capital until after the markets stabilized, and its relatively low-paid executives were not threatened by salary caps imposed on banks that owed TARP monies.

In 2012 M&T began the process of acquiring Hudson City Bancorp (#43), a New Jersey based bank. By early 2014 the deal was still pending, with some analysts concerned that the deal would not close. On April 24, 2014, however, Deutsche Bank upgraded its recommendation for M&T from hold to buy, with analyst Matt O'Connor stating, "We continue to believe the deal will close. . . . Also, at a time when EPS estimates for most super regionals seem dependent on loan growth picking up and/or interest rates rising, [M&T]'s estimates seem achievable in a stable macro environment so long as the Hudson deal closes."

Sources

Alloway, Tracy. "M&T Bank Buys Hudson City for $3.7bn." *FT.com,* August 27, 2012.

Bajaj, Vikas. "M&T Sues Deutsche Bank Over $80 Million Loss." *The New York Times,* January 20, 2009, B1.

Crittenden, Michael R. "Global Finance: Anti-Laundering Effort Hit—Fed Finds Wide-Ranging Problems at M&T Bank, Delaying Acquisition Deal." *Wall Street Journal,* June 19, 2013, C3.

"Deutsche Bank Upgrades M&T Bank to Buy." *Wallstreetinsider.com,* April 24, 2014.

Eavis, Peter. "Real-Estate Loan Puzzle at M&T Bank." *Wall Street Journal,* October 21, 2009, C16.

Loosvelt, Derek, et al. *The Vault Guide to the Top 50 Banking Employers: 2008 Edition.* New York: Vault, 2007, 348–82.

"M&T Bank in Merger Talks Again." *Investor's Business Daily,* August 18, 2010, A2.

Newbury, George A. *A Story of Men, a Frontier City, and a Bank: Manufacturers and Traders Trust Company (1856–1956).* New York: Newcomen Society, 1956.

Peters, Andy. "M&T's Wilmers Scolds Big Banks, Empathizes with Working Class." *American Banker,* March 8, 2013.

Rieker, Matthias. "M&T Sues Deutsche Bank Over CDOs." *American Banker,* June 17, 2008, 2.

Reiker, Matthias and Eric Morah. "M&T Bank to Exit TARP, via Backdoor." *Wall Street Journal Online,* August 16, 2012.

Rizzo, Michael F. *Buffalo's Legacy of Power and Might.* Buffalo, NY: Michael F. Rizzo, 2011, 29–32.

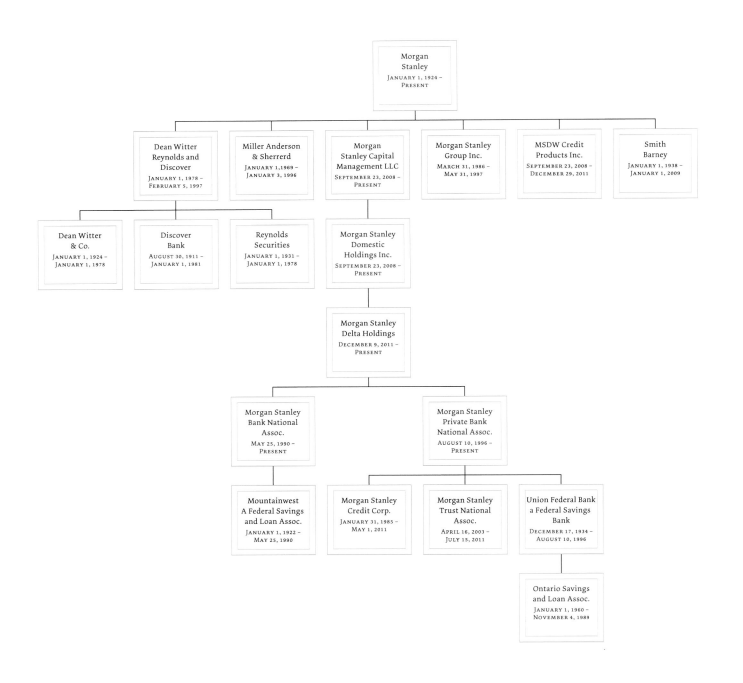

Morgan Stanley

RANK	HEADQUARTERS	TICKER	ASSETS	EARLIEST KNOWN ANCESTOR	INDUSTRY OF ORIGIN
6	New York, NY	MS	$803,000,000,000	1911	Investment Banking

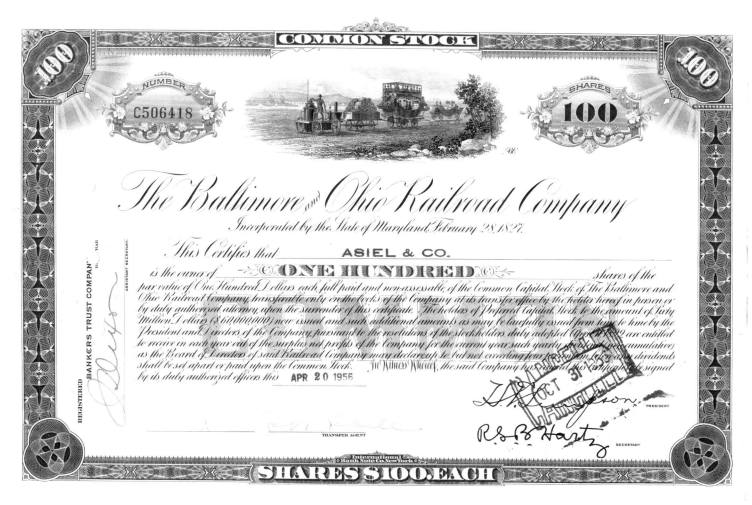

B&O Railroad Company stock certificate, 1956.

Morgan Stanley emerged during the Great Depression as a result of the passage of Glass-Steagall, which forced J.P. Morgan to choose between commercial and investment banking. Most partners chose the former and formed one the cores of the modern JPMorgan Chase (#1). Partners Henry Morgan and Harold Stanley demurred and formed a new, eponymous securities firm independent of J.P. Morgan, but still embodying its credo. According to Jack Morgan in 1933, that was to do "only first class business, and that in a first class way." Morgan Stanley remained psychologically close to J.P. Morgan in part because it was headquartered nearby on Wall Street, and in part because J.P. Morgan owned most of its preferred stock until the SEC forced Morgan Stanley to redeem J.P. Morgan's holdings in 1941.

Morgan Stanley managed initial public offerings (IPOs) and private placements of bonds, some $29.3 billion by the end of 1965. After a billion-dollar start in 1936, the pace of its offerings and placements declined and almost dipped below $100 million in 1943. After World War II, however, Morgan Stanley's book of business rapidly increased as it climbed the investment bank league tables, moving from 34th in corporate underwriting participations in 1942 to 12th a decade later. Morgan Stanley's ranking in the management of railroad and utility bonds also jumped over that period, from sixth to second place.

Between 1953 and 1965, its offerings dipped below $1 billion just once, in 1956, but more than doubled to over $2 billion in 1957. The company also participated in securities issues managed by other investment banks. Major clients prior to 1965 included American Can, Argentina, Bank of New York (#9), Borden's, Canada, Colgate-Palmolive, General Electric, General Motors Acceptance Corporation (#20), Italy, Merck, National Bank of Detroit (part of #36), Otis Elevator, Procter & Gamble, United Air Lines and the World Bank. Some of those clients were new, while others were holdovers from the old House of Morgan.

In 1941 the company became a partnership so that it could take a seat on the New York Stock Exchange. (It also became an associate member of the American Stock Exchange in 1959.) That allowed it to act as a broker in the purchase and sale of stocks and bonds on the exchanges, as well as in the over-the-counter market. Its principal clients were institutional investors like insurers, pension funds, commercial banks and investment funds.

Morgan Stanley also furnished financial advisory services to governments and corporations, both foreign and domestic. In addition to helping clients issue securities with the features investors desired, it helped corporations to finance mergers and acquisitions, to recapitalize, to purchase their own stock and to obtain stock exchange listings. The company also valued securities for banks, estates and individuals. Major clients on this side of its business included Aetna Life and Aetna Casualty, American Telephone and Telegraph (AT&T), Baltimore and Ohio Railroad (B&O), E. I. Du Pont De Nemours and Company, Eastman Kodak, H. J. Heinz Company, Johnson & Johnson, Minnesota Mining and Manufacturing Company (3M), Philip Morris, Shell Oil, United States Steel and Weyerhaeuser. In the 1970s the company also began offering advice on mergers and acquisitions as a separate service.

In 1965 four limited partners and 21 full partners owned Morgan Stanley. Stanley had died two years earlier, but Morgan remained

AT&T stock certificate, dated May 1, 1964.

and was aided by distinguished financiers like John M. Young and Walter W. Wilson. Over the decades, partners came and went, but the company remained respected, safe and secure under their collective watchful eye. That all began to change in the early 1970s when the company, which had been slipping from its perch atop the banking league tables under intense competition from Goldman Sachs (#5) and Salomon Brothers (now part of #3), opened a trading desk and began a bonus system.

Salomon CEO John Gutfreund argued that "the power to distribute securities would become the power to underwrite them," and Morgan Stanley's move to develop relationships with institutional investors proved him correct. The company had to sell shares to the public in order to raise its capital, which in 1970 stood at a paltry $7.5 million—far too little to support trading operations of any significance. Traders and the performance bonuses radically transformed the company's traditionally staid culture. Employees, the number of whom jumped from 200 to 1,700 over the 1970s, began to work the *entire* night when necessary, and the company's capital soared to $118 million.

In 1986 Morgan Stanley sold yet more shares to the public, increasing its capital to $1.5 billion. This enabled it to take other companies private in the leveraged buyout wave of the late 1980s. The idea was to borrow (the leverage) money to purchase controlling interests (the buyout) in underperforming companies, and then slash expenses (often through mass layoffs) and sell off unneeded assets. After several years of profitability, it would then take the company public again. The extra capital cushion was necessary in the event that a company could not

be turned around. In that case, the results were disastrous for everyone involved, including the LBO managers (like Kohlberg Kravis Roberts, or KKR) and their creditors (including Morgan Stanley).

By the early 1990s Morgan Stanley had transformed, according to Frank Partnoy. Now a law school professor, Partnoy in the early 1990s sold so many derivatives for Morgan Stanley, he claims, that the $1 billion his team earned "was enough to pay the salaries of most of the firm's 10,000 worldwide employees, with plenty left for us." Even the lowest-level employees, most in their 20s, earned six-figure incomes. Partnoy claimed the unit made so much money because it was composed of "rocket scientists" who had "mastered the complexities of modern finance."

In 1997 Morgan Stanley merged with Dean Witter, Discover & Co. Dean Witter was formed in San Francisco in 1924, went public in 1972 and became Dean Witter, Discover & Co. in 1992. The merged company called itself Morgan Stanley Dean Witter. On September 11, 2001, a fuel-laden commercial jetliner piloted by a terrorist struck Morgan Stanley's headquarters in the World Trade Center. Most of the 3,700 employees who worked in the building escaped the resulting inferno, but seven lost their lives.

Morgan Stanley got a big boost in 2005 when it replaced embattled Chairman and CEO Philip Purcell with John Mack, a veteran of three decades in the trenches at the storied investment bank. In 2006 Mack changed the company's name back to Morgan Stanley. The following year, in his biggest move, Mack spun off Discover (#33) after improving its lackluster financials. The move helped the company focus on

Borden's recipe book. Borden's was a major Morgan Stanley client in the postwar years.

its trading and money management divisions. Mack also bought real estate, including Hilton Hotels in Europe and office space in downtown San Francisco.

At the beginning of 2007 Mack delivered record revenues across all major divisions: institutional securities, equity sales, fixed income sales, commodities and derivatives trading, assessment management and advisory services. In the league banking tables, Morgan Stanley remained on the heels of Goldman Sachs (#5). Mack attributed the company's "outstanding results" to "effective, disciplined risk taking."

As the 2008 financial crisis developed, however, Morgan Stanley lost about 80% of its value. On September 18, 2008, Treasury Secretary Hank Paulson called Jamie Dimon, CEO of JPMorgan Chase (#1), to offer to give him Morgan Stanley for free. Having already been burned by the Bear Stearns buyout, when an initial price of $2 per share had been raised to $10, Dimon demurred. Reconstituting the House of Morgan was not worth the risk, as panic gripped the world's financial systems. As a result, Morgan Stanley had to become a BHC to tap emergency Federal Reserve loans. It also received significant TARP funds and took money from Japan's Mitsubishi Bank.

At the end of 2013 reporters still described the company as "bouncing back" after being "hit hard by the financial crisis" and compared it to giant life insurer MetLife because it had moved so heavily into the relatively staid field of asset management. Trading losses continued to hound it, however, as did lawsuits and potential lawsuits, including one by AIG (#7) regarding a variety of precrisis transactions.

Sources

Chernow, Ron. *The House of Morgan: An American Banking Dynasty and the Rise of Modern Finance*. New York: Grove Press, 1990.

Loosvelt, Derek, et al. *The Vault Guide to the Top 50 Banking Employers: 2008 Edition*. New York: Vault, 2007, 50–55.

McDonald, Duff. *Last Man Standing: The Ascent of Jamie Dimon and JPMorgan Chase*. New York: Simon and Schuster, 2009, ix–xi.

Morgan Stanley & Co.: A Summary of Financing, 1935–1965. New York: Morgan Stanley, 1965.

Partnoy, Frank. *Fiasco: The Inside Story of a Wall Street Trader*. New York: Norton, 1997.

Rogers, Ashleigh. "Which Is the Better Investment: Morgan Stanley or MetLife?" *LifeHealthPro*, November 8, 2013.

Warren, Zach. "AIG Could Sue Morgan Stanley Over Pre-Financial Crisis Deals." *Inside Counsel*, November 6, 2013.

Wetfeet. *25 Top Financial Services Firms*. San Francisco: Wetfeet. 2008, 69–72.

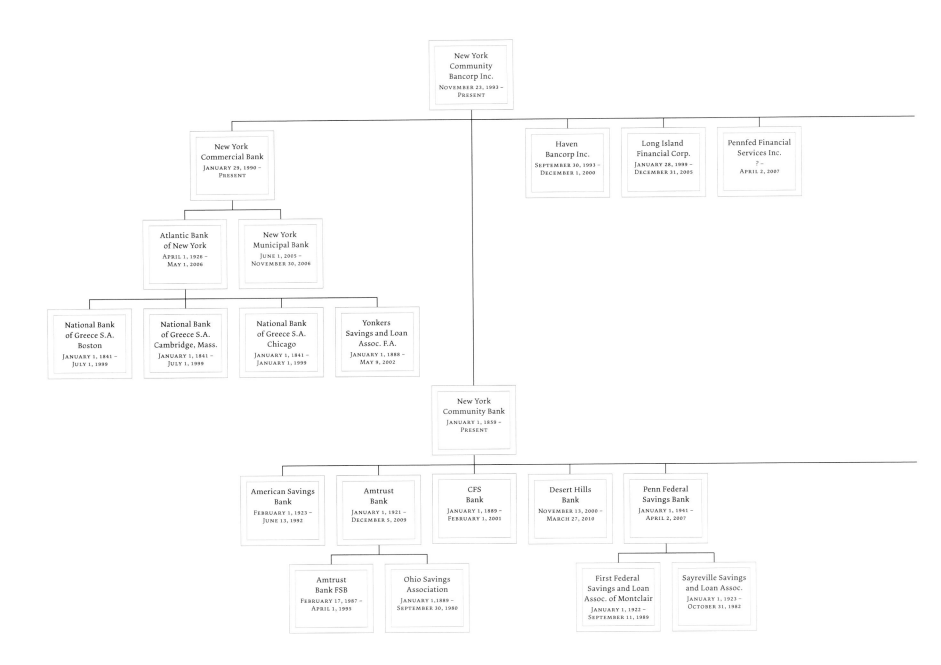

New York
Community
Bancorp Inc.
NOVEMBER 23, 1993 –
PRESENT

New York
Commercial Bank
JANUARY 29, 1990 –
PRESENT

Haven
Bancorp Inc.
SEPTEMBER 30, 1993 –
DECEMBER 1, 2000

Long Island
Financial Corp.
JANUARY 28, 1999 –
DECEMBER 31, 2005

Pennfed Financial
Services Inc.
? –
APRIL 2, 2007

Atlantic Bank
of New York
APRIL 1, 1926 –
MAY 1, 2006

New York
Municipal Bank
JUNE 1, 2005 –
NOVEMBER 30, 2006

National Bank
of Greece S.A.
Boston
JANUARY 1, 1841 –
JULY 1, 1999

National Bank
of Greece S.A.
Cambridge, Mass.
JANUARY 1, 1841 –
JULY 1, 1999

National Bank
of Greece S.A.
Chicago
JANUARY 1, 1841 –
JANUARY 1, 1999

Yonkers
Savings and Loan
Assoc. F.A.
JANUARY 1, 1888 –
MAY 9, 2002

New York
Community Bank
JANUARY 1, 1859 –
PRESENT

American Savings
Bank
FEBRUARY 1, 1923 –
JUNE 13, 1992

Amtrust
Bank
JANUARY 1, 1921 –
DECEMBER 5, 2009

CFS
Bank
JANUARY 1, 1889 –
FEBRUARY 1, 2001

Desert Hills
Bank
NOVEMBER 13, 2000 –
MARCH 27, 2010

Penn Federal
Savings Bank
JANUARY 1, 1941 –
APRIL 2, 2007

Amtrust
Bank FSB
FEBRUARY 17, 1987 –
APRIL 1, 1995

Ohio Savings
Association
JANUARY 1,1889 –
SEPTEMBER 30, 1980

First Federal
Savings and Loan
Assoc. of Montclair
JANUARY 1, 1922 –
SEPTEMBER 11, 1989

Sayreville Savings
and Loan Assoc.
JANUARY 1, 1923 –
OCTOBER 31, 1982

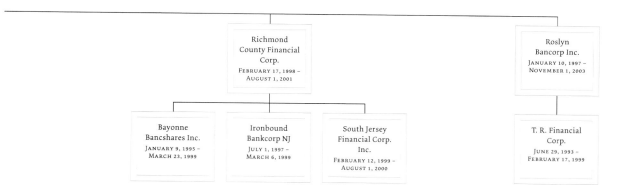

Richmond
County Financial
Corp.
FEBRUARY 17, 1998 –
AUGUST 1, 2001

Roslyn
Bancorp Inc.
JANUARY 10, 1997 –
NOVEMBER 1, 2003

Bayonne
Bancshares Inc.
JANUARY 9, 1995 –
MARCH 23, 1999

Ironbound
Bankcorp NJ
JULY 1, 1997 –
MARCH 6, 1999

South Jersey
Financial Corp.
Inc.
FEBRUARY 12, 1999 –
AUGUST 1, 2000

T. R. Financial
Corp.
JUNE 29, 1993 –
FEBRUARY 17, 1999

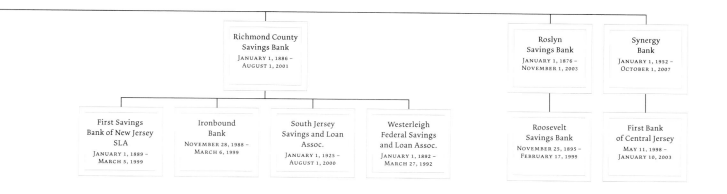

Richmond County
Savings Bank
JANUARY 1, 1886 –
AUGUST 1, 2001

Roslyn
Savings Bank
JANUARY 1, 1876 –
NOVEMBER 1, 2003

Synergy
Bank
JANUARY 1, 1952 –
OCTOBER 1, 2007

First Savings
Bank of New Jersey
SLA
JANUARY 1, 1889 –
MARCH 5, 1999

Ironbound
Bank
NOVEMBER 28, 1988 –
MARCH 6, 1999

South Jersey
Savings and Loan
Assoc.
JANUARY 1, 1925 –
AUGUST 1, 2000

Westerleigh
Federal Savings
and Loan Assoc.
JANUARY 1, 1892 –
MARCH 27, 1992

Roosevelt
Savings Bank
NOVEMBER 25, 1895 –
FEBRUARY 17, 1999

First Bank
of Central Jersey
MAY 11, 1998 –
JANUARY 10, 2003

New York Community Bancorp

RANK	HEADQUARTERS	TICKER	ASSETS	EARLIEST KNOWN ANCESTOR	INDUSTRY OF ORIGIN
42	Westbury, NY	NYCB	$44,000,000,000	1841	Commercial Banking

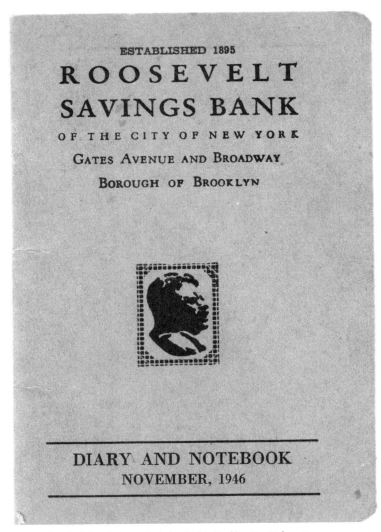

ESTABLISHED 1895

ROOSEVELT SAVINGS BANK

OF THE CITY OF NEW YORK

GATES AVENUE AND BROADWAY

BOROUGH OF BROOKLYN

DIARY AND NOTEBOOK
NOVEMBER, 1946

Diary and notebook from the Roosevelt Savings Bank in Brooklyn, New York, 1946.

Sandwiched between Garden City, Levittown, Mineola and Hicksville on Long Island is Westbury, New York, home of New York Community Bancorp. The bank began its existence in Flushing, Queens, in April 1859 as the Queens County Savings Bank. Chartered as a mutual, it had 40 trustees, all of whom had to be, by the terms of its charter, Queens County residents. Out of their number, the trustees elected a president and two vice presidents to manage the institution's daily affairs. Trustees were unpaid and could not borrow from the bank.

Like other antebellum savings institutions, the bank's main purpose was to encourage the poor to save. To attract the poor while deterring wealthy clientele, its charter capped deposits at $3,000 ($85,500 in 2012 dollars, using the consumer price index to adjust for inflation) and paid at least one percentage point lower interest on deposits exceeding $500 ($14,200 in 2012 dollars).

Despite such restrictions, deposits sat at $926,000 in 1899, when the bank had just over 3,000 depositors. They reached almost $2.2 million a decade later, when the number of depositors was nearly 6,000. Shortly after the Great War, in 1919, deposits exceeded $5.4 million and almost hit $21.5 million a decade after that. Despite 10 years of depression, the bank managed to grow its deposits to $32.7 million in 1939. By 1949 deposits had reached $90 million, and the number of depositors had reached almost 74,000.

In 1959 about 177,000 people had over $212 million on deposit in the bank. It prided itself on making homeownership easier with its mortgages, and on increasing employment with its loans to businesses and governments. By that time individual deposits could reach $10,000 and joint or trust accounts could be as high as $20,000. Individuals, as well as churches, societies and clubs, used the latter to safeguard their funds from theft or loss. Depositors also sought the 3.25% interest paid in 1959, as well as convenience. Deposits and withdrawals could be made via mail or at offices in Corona, Flushing, Kew Gardens Hills and Little Neck. Other services included savings bank life insurance, safe deposit boxes, money orders and travelers checks, as well as foreign remittance and school savings services.

After 1970 Queens County Bank began to specialize in low to moderate income apartment buildings in the greater New York area. Even during the Savings and Loan crisis in the 1980s, credit quality was not a problem at the bank. In 1993 it established a BHC called Queens County Bancorp. In 1996, two years after going public, it was one of the best performing thrifts in the country, with an efficiency ratio of just 30.45% in the first quarter of 2000, far below the national average of 57.24%.

Upon its acquisition of Haven Bancorp of Westbury for $196 million in stock in December 2000, its first acquisition after going public, the bank changed its name to New York Community Bank (and the name of its BHC to New York Community Bancorp) and moved to Westbury. "The case for the combination," Joseph R. Ficalora, the

Queens County Savings Bank metal calendar holder.

bank's chairman, president and CEO, told reporters, "is compelling" because the deal married "a proven deposit generator" (Haven) with "a proven generator of high-quality assets" (Queens County). With about $5 billion in assets at the time of the acquisition, the bank continued to grow in its niche. By the 2008 financial crisis, it had acquired four more BHCs and expanded its reach into New Jersey. "The whole idea," Ficalora said in 2001, "is to have a strong holding company that can operate community banks."

The "modest bank" found itself struggling in 2004, however, when it got caught holding mortgage-backed securities funded with short-term borrowings as interest rates rose, squeezing its net interest margin (the difference between the rate at which it borrowed and the rate at which it lent). Two years later, New York Community Bank continued to bump along, its long-term credit rating at BBB, even though a Standard & Poor's analyst admitted the bank had "essentially recovered from a misstep in 2004 in which it employed an unsuccessful wholesale leveraging strategy that incorporated a concentration of short-term funding of" mortgage-backed securities.

The errors committed in 2004, however, may have saved the bank from the worst of the subprime mortgage crisis because, by early 2007, it was sacrificing loan growth for credit quality. "While our balance of loans has shrunk somewhat over the past two quarters," Ficalora told investors in mid-2007, "the reduction not only reflects our commitment to maintaining our strong credit standing, but also our ability to refrain from lending in an environment that currently features irrational terms."

By 2013 the bank operated 278 branches in five states: New York, New Jersey, Ohio, Florida and Arizona. The final three came from its acquisition of AmTrust, which failed in 2009. In 2010 the bank added another small Arizona bank, Desert Hills, and folded it into AmTrust. The FDIC covered the bulk of AmTrust's many problems, but the bank's credit quality suffered somewhat as a result of the acquisitions and the recession. By 2011 it was on the mend with only 1.4% of loans classified as nonperforming. In 2012 the bank purchased the remnants of Aurora Bank, a subsidiary of the failed investment bank Lehman Brothers based in Delaware, but its credit quality continued to improve. By the end of 2013 charge-offs and loan loss provisions sank to trivial levels of just $5 million.

New York Community Bank hoped to avoid the problems encountered by other far-flung banks by using the distant branches as sources of funding, funneling their deposits to New York for investment in apartment mortgages. "We can easily grow this bank on the asset side

to two or three or four times," Ficalora told investors, while simultaneously suggesting that he was open to selling the bank if the right opportunity presented itself.

After carefully considering the trade-offs inherent in the Dodd-Frank Act, however, he instead went in search of a big acquisition—in the $15–$25 billion range—that would make the bank a "systematically important" institution, by catapulting it above the $50 billion threshold established in the new law. In early 2013 it was said to have courted OneWest Bank, which included remnants of the failed subprime monster IndyMac, but no deal had been announced by the end of 2013.

Sources

Barba, Robert. "New York Community, OneWest Would Make Smart Bedfellows." *American Banker*, March 14, 2013.

Eisinger, Jesse. "Long & Short: New York Community Bancorp Suffers Spread." *Wall Street Journal*, July 2, 2004, C1.

Epstein, Jonathan D. "Queens County Bancorp Rights Plan to Kick In If 10% Stake Is Bought." *American Banker*, February 2, 1996, 8.

Kline, Alan. "Queens County of NY Has $196M Deal to Buy Haven." *American Banker*, June 29, 2000, 24.

Mazzucca, Tim. "By Any Measure, Rates Hurt New York Community." *American Banker*, April 27, 2006, 20.

———. "In Brief: S&PConfirms New York Community Ratings." *American Banker*, December 19, 2006, 19.

Monks, Matthew. "New York Community's Next Deal Has to Be a Big One, CEO Says." *American Banker*, August 1, 2012.

———. "New York Community to Acquire $2.3B of Deposits from Former Lehman Unit Aurora." *American Banker*, April 2, 2012.

Rieker, Matthias. "New York Community Beefs Up: Issue of 60 Million Shares to Aid Expansion of AmTrust; 'We Have No Ego Stopping Us from Doing a Deal'." *Wall Street Journal*, December 8, 2009, C20.

———. "Queen County Gets Praise for In-Market Haven Deal." *American Banker*, August 1, 2000, 20.

Sorkin, Andrew Ross. "New York Community Bancorp to Acquire Bank." *The New York Times*, March 28, 2001, C4.

Stewart, Jackie. "New York Community's Earnings Hold Steady as Asset Quality Improves." *American Banker*, October 20, 2011.

Todd, Sarah. "New York Community's Profits Fall on Mortgage Banking." *American Banker*, October 24, 2013.

Wright, Robert E. *The First Wall Street: Chestnut Street, Philadelphia, and the Birth of American Finance.* Chicago: University of Chicago Press, 2005, 104–14.

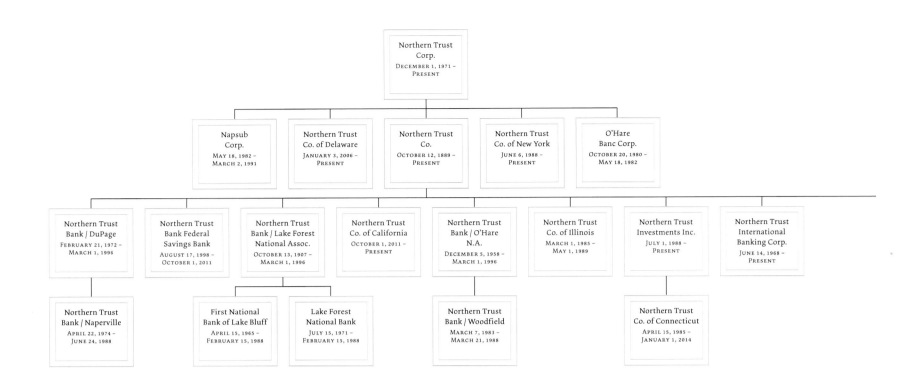

Northern Trust
Corp.
DECEMBER 1, 1971 –
PRESENT

Napsub
Corp.
MAY 18, 1982 –
MARCH 2, 1991

Northern Trust
Co. of Delaware
JANUARY 3, 2006 –
PRESENT

Northern Trust
Co.
OCTOBER 12, 1889 –
PRESENT

Northern Trust
Co. of New York
JUNE 6, 1988 –
PRESENT

O'Hare
Banc Corp.
OCTOBER 20, 1980 –
MAY 18, 1982

Northern Trust
Bank / DuPage
FEBRUARY 21, 1972 –
MARCH 1, 1996

Northern Trust
Bank Federal
Savings Bank
AUGUST 17, 1998 –
OCTOBER 1, 2011

Northern Trust
Bank / Lake Forest
National Assoc.
OCTOBER 13, 1907 –
MARCH 1, 1996

Northern Trust
Co. of California
OCTOBER 1, 2011 –
PRESENT

Northern Trust
Bank / O'Hare
N.A.
DECEMBER 5, 1958 –
MARCH 1, 1996

Northern Trust
Co. of Illinois
MARCH 1, 1985 –
MAY 1, 1989

Northern Trust
Investments Inc.
JULY 1, 1988 –
PRESENT

Northern Trust
International
Banking Corp.
JUNE 14, 1968 –
PRESENT

Northern Trust
Bank / Naperville
APRIL 22, 1974 –
JUNE 24, 1988

First National
Bank of Lake Bluff
APRIL 15, 1965 –
FEBRUARY 15, 1988

Lake Forest
National Bank
JULY 15, 1971 –
FEBRUARY 15, 1988

Northern Trust
Bank / Woodfield
MARCH 7, 1983 –
MARCH 21, 1988

Northern Trust
Co. of Connecticut
APRIL 15, 1985 –
JANUARY 1, 2014

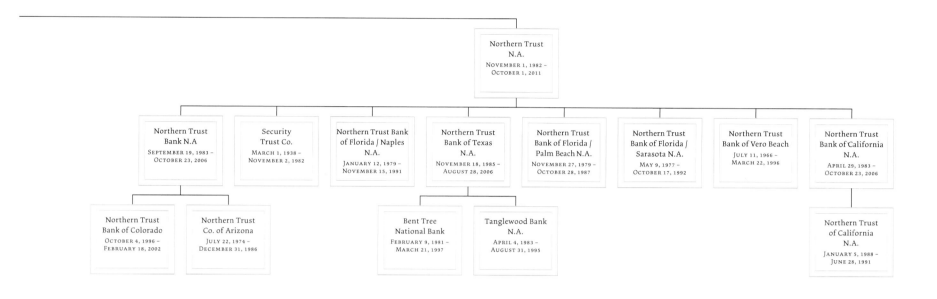

Northern Trust

RANK	HEADQUARTERS	TICKER	ASSETS	EARLIEST KNOWN ANCESTOR	INDUSTRY OF ORIGIN
28	Chicago, IL	NTRS	$97,000,000,000	1889	Commercial Banking

Retailer Marshall Field was among the Northern Trust's initial stockholders.

BANK BUILDING
OF
THE NORTHERN TRUST COMPANY—BANK
CHICAGO

N. W. CORNER LA SALLE AND MONROE STREETS
190 FEET FRONT ON LA SALLE STREET. 73 FEET ON MONROE
TO BE READY FOR OCCUPANCY IN NINETEEN HUNDRED AND SIX

| CAPITAL, | . . . . | $1,500,000 |
| SURPLUS, | . . . . | $1,000,000 |

DIRECTORS

A. C. BARTLETT	MARVIN HUGHITT	ALBERT A. SPRAGUE
J. HARLEY BRADLEY	C. L. HUTCHINSON	SOLOMON A. SMITH
WILLIAM A. FULLER	MARTIN A. RYERSON	BYRON L. SMITH

OFFICERS

BYRON L. SMITH, ... President
F. L. HANKEY, ... Vice-President
SOLOMON A. SMITH, . . 2D VICE-PRESIDENT   ARTHUR HEURTLEY, ... Secretary
THOMAS C. KING, ... CASHIER   HOWARD O. EDMONDS, . . . ASS'T SECRETARY
ROBERT McLEOD, ... ASS'T CASHIER   HAROLD H ROCKWELL, . . . ASS'T SECRETARY
G. J. MILLER, ... ASS'T CASHIER   EDWARD C. JARVIS, ... AUDITOR

PRESENT ADDRESS
S. E. CORNER LA SALLE AND ADAMS STREETS
CHICAGO

Early 20th century Northern Trust Company advertisement.

Byron L. Smith founded the Northern Trust because he believed Chicago area residents needed a safe savings bank and trust—an institution that would treat even the poorest widows and the most unfortunate orphans like clients instead of like mere depositors. As its first advertisement indicated, the trust transacted "a general banking business . . . under the new banking law" of the state. It made "loans on collateral security" and paid "interest on deposits," including the "daily balances . . . of corporations, merchants, individuals and others." It also did a trust business and kept "all investments of trust funds . . . separate and apart from the assets of the company." Its initial stockholders included industrialist Philip D. Armour, retailer Marshall Field, "capitalist" John DeKoven and sundry lawyers and bankers.

According to the trust's earliest chronicler, Byron Smith left an "indelible impress" on the organization, which developed "a deep sense of responsibility about the care of other people's money. "This feeling," the anonymous scribbler asserted, had "prevailed since the day the bank first opened its doors." And it appears to have persisted long after, thanks in part to Byron's son, Solomon Smith, who ran the trust until 1963, almost 50 years after assuming the presidency when his father died in 1914.

As Solomon put it, "the growth of the bank . . . kept pace with the growth" of Chicago, which was not an easy accomplishment in the heady late 19th century. With few corporate competitors at first and a strong reputation for prudent investment, the trust quickly accumulated assets—$35 million in its first three decades—from rich and poor alike. Quick to take advantage of organic growth opportunities, like the 1893 World's Fair in Chicago, the trust quickly ramped up its foreign office, which provided banking services to tourists, and its number of depositors, which hit 40,000 by 1919.

By the end of the Great War the trust had 20 officers and more than 300 employees who were "loyal" and "efficient" because management imbued them with "the spirit of being helpful . . . to the public," and because mangers took good care of them. The trust provided medical examinations, "a midday luncheon of light wholesome food suited to indoor occupation" and paid visits to employees "on the sick list." It offered elementary education for "younger employees of neglected schooling" and more advanced training in "the principles and practices of banking" for older, more educated employees. It also provided employees with a library, athletics and social gatherings, along with the increasingly obligatory life insurance and pension benefits. Unlike most banks, the trust also sent sales representatives to "call on people" and acquaint them with its services.

Like other well managed banks, the Northern Trust grew during the Great Depression, with deposits jumping from about $50 million in 1929 to $300 million in 1935. Desperate to grab some of that wealth for themselves, an unknown person or persons victimized Smith three times in 1933, first by mailing a bomb to his home in Chicago, then by threatening his life for $4,000 and finally by demanding that $5,000 be left at the gate of his home in the wealthy community of Lake Forest. The assassin-extortionists, however, did not appear for the package that police set out to trap them.

Deposits hit $1 billion in the 1960s, making the trust the fourth largest bank in Chicago, a position it maintained by moving aggressively into new technologies, like electronic check processing. By 1974, when it began to offer 24-hour foreign exchange service, it had 3,000 employees and a branch that it had opened in London in 1969, which made it the first Illinois-chartered financial institution to branch outside the United States. In 1982 the trust added a wealth management/private banking group and branches in Florida. Two years later it added discount brokerage to a repertoire that also included full-service brokerage in 1990. Institutional mutual funds followed two years later, and personal mutual funds followed two years after that, in 1994.

By the mid-1990s Northern Trust employed more than 6,400 people in Arizona, California, Florida, Illinois and Texas. It had $18.6 billion in assets and almost $500 billion under management. In addition to banking, it provided fiduciary, investment and financial consulting services for individuals, as well as credit, operating, trust and investment management services for corporations and other organizations. By that time Northern Trust's hallmark was "Signature Service," which it defined as "service of which the individual employee can be proud and with which the Northern client is more than satisfied."

That meant that "every person be treated with fairness, dignity and respect," which drove Northern Trust to implement equal employment opportunity and affirmative action policies. Those policies were largely successful, as the number of women in the senior vice president category and above increased from three in 1988 to 17 in 1995. The number of "people of color" in executive positions increased from 15 to 80 over that same timespan. Beginning in 1989, managers also took diversity training; nonmanagers began taking such training in 1993.

The trust's record on such matters, however, was not flawless: in 1995 it agreed to pay the Justice Department $700,000 for discriminating against minority loan applicants by asking them for higher levels of documentation than required of white applicants, and for turning down minority loan applicants with the same objective levels of credit as accepted white applicants. The severity of the problem, however, was insufficient to prevent the Federal Reserve from approving an acquisition while the case was adjudicated.

By the early 2000s Northern Trust had over $1 trillion in assets under custody and more than 9,300 employees worldwide, including about 6,000 in Chicago. It dipped into the hedge fund and private equity fund businesses too, as well as global real estate, without taking on too much risk. It did this by expanding via small acquisitions domestically, and with de novo operations abroad. By early 2008 it had 85 offices in 18 states, as well as 15 overseas offices and no urge to merge "just to get bigger for the sake of size," as its new CEO, 33-year Northern Trust veteran Rick Waddell, put it.

During the 2008 financial crisis, the trust actually turned a hefty profit and took no write-downs — one of the few big banks to do so — while fending off calls to bulk up on the cheap by buying a number of troubled businesses and toxic assets. "If there were more financial institutions like it," wrote Tom Sullivan in *Barron's* in early 2009, "neither the banking business nor the mutual fund business would have fared so badly last year." It took TARP money, but it returned it within a few months. By 2012 the bank had grown bloated and less profitable, prompting Waddell to cut more than 700 workers in a bid to reduce expenses by $250 million per year.

Named one of *Fortune's* "World's Most Admired Companies" for seven years in a row (2007–2013), Northern Trust also won a variety of other prestigious awards including *Global Finance Magazine's* "Top 50 Safest Global Banks in 2012" and *Financial Times's* "Best Private Bank in the US" award. Not surprisingly, it has also won accolades for corporate social responsibility, including one of the "Best Companies for Multicultural Women," "Best Places for Asians to Work" and one of the "100 Best Corporate Citizens." In 2011, for the sixth straight year, it received a perfect rating of 100 on LGBT equality issues on the *Corporate Equality Index*. It also won awards for workplace flexibility and green building design, as well as in areas related to its core business, like asset servicing, asset management and wealth management (e.g., named "Best Private Wealth Manager" by *Private Asset Management* in 2013 and "Best Trust Company" by *Family Office Review* in 2012). The Smiths would be proud.

Sources

Ackermann, Matt. "For New Northern Trust CEO, Megadeal Is Not an Option." *American Banker*, January 30, 2008, 11.

Chicago Area Partnerships. *Pathways and Progress: Corporate Best Practices to Shatter the Glass Ceiling*. Chicago: Women Employed, 1996, 42–44.

Kline, Alan. "Northern Trust 4Q Profit Falls 17%; More Layoffs Loom." *American Banker*, January 19, 2012.

Northern Trust. *Northern Trust History*. http://www.ntrs.com/. Accessed Oct. 29, 2013.

————. *Scenes of Old Chicago: Commemorating the Fiftieth Anniversary of the Northern Trust Company, 1889–1939*. Chicago: Northern Trust Company, 1939.

————. *Three Decades of Banking: 1889–1919*. Chicago: Northern Trust Company, 1919.

Sullivan, Tom. "Northern Trust Is on a Roll." *Barron's*, February 2009, 37.

Teitelbaum, David E. and Clarke D. Camper. "Developments in Fair Lending." *Business Lawyer* 51, 3 (May 1996): 843–59.

Van Sickle, Frederick. "A Special Place: Lake Forest and the Great Depression, 1929–1940." *Illinois Historical Journal* 79, 2 (Summer 1986): 113–26.

Weitzman, Hal. "Northern Trust Says the Party Is Over." *FT.com*, December 30, 2009.

Wilson, Mark R., Stephen R. Porter and Janice L. Reiff. "Northern Trust Co." *Dictionary of Leading Chicago Businesses (1820–2000)*. Chicago: Chicago Historical Society, 2005.

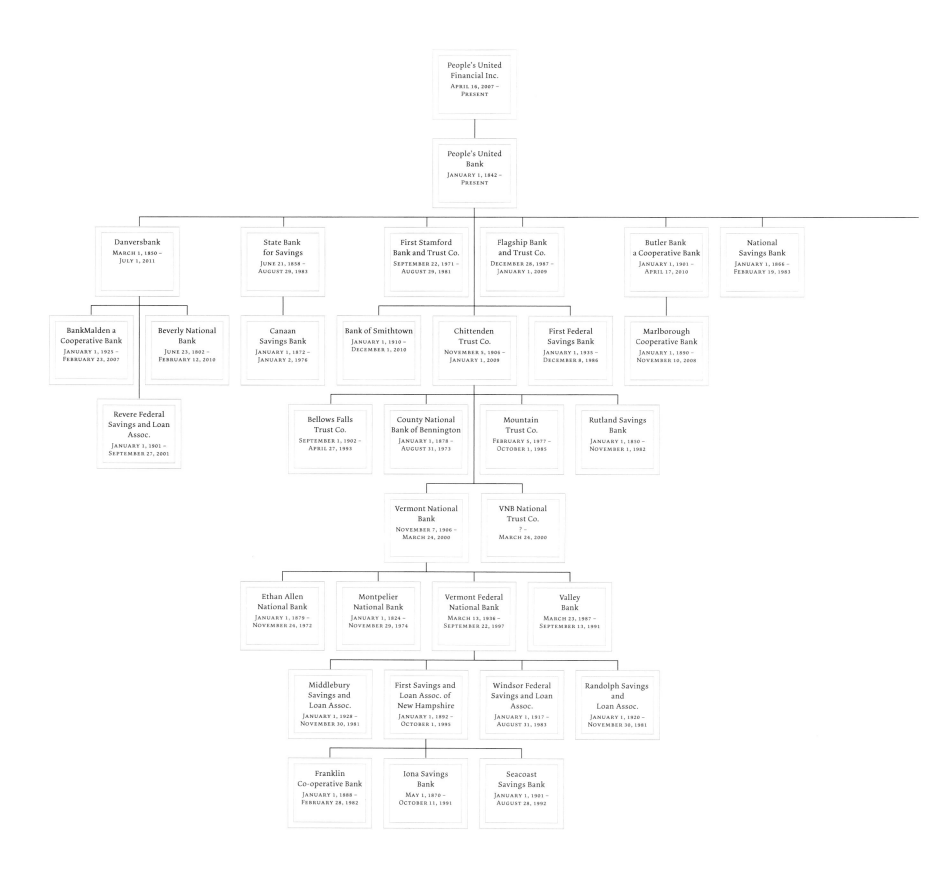

**People's United
Financial Inc.**
APRIL 16, 2007 –
PRESENT

**People's United
Bank**
JANUARY 1, 1842 –
PRESENT

Danversbank
MARCH 1, 1850 –
JULY 1, 2011

**State Bank
for Savings**
JUNE 21, 1858 –
AUGUST 29, 1983

**First Stamford
Bank and Trust Co.**
SEPTEMBER 22, 1971 –
AUGUST 29, 1981

**Flagship Bank
and Trust Co.**
DECEMBER 28, 1987 –
JANUARY 1, 2009

**Butler Bank
a Cooperative Bank**
JANUARY 1, 1901 –
APRIL 17, 2010

**National
Savings Bank**
JANUARY 1, 1866 –
FEBRUARY 19, 1983

**BankMalden a
Cooperative Bank**
JANUARY 1, 1925 –
FEBRUARY 23, 2007

**Beverly National
Bank**
JUNE 23, 1802 –
FEBRUARY 12, 2010

**Canaan
Savings Bank**
JANUARY 1, 1872 –
JANUARY 2, 1976

Bank of Smithtown
JANUARY 1, 1910 –
DECEMBER 1, 2010

**Chittenden
Trust Co.**
NOVEMBER 5, 1906 –
JANUARY 1, 2009

**First Federal
Savings Bank**
JANUARY 1, 1935 –
DECEMBER 8, 1986

**Marlborough
Cooperative Bank**
JANUARY 1, 1890 –
NOVEMBER 10, 2008

**Revere Federal
Savings and Loan
Assoc.**
JANUARY 1, 1901 –
SEPTEMBER 27, 2001

**Bellows Falls
Trust Co.**
SEPTEMBER 1, 1902 –
APRIL 27, 1993

**County National
Bank of Bennington**
JANUARY 1, 1878 –
AUGUST 31, 1973

**Mountain
Trust Co.**
FEBRUARY 5, 1977 –
OCTOBER 1, 1985

**Rutland Savings
Bank**
JANUARY 1, 1850 –
NOVEMBER 1, 1982

**Vermont National
Bank**
NOVEMBER 7, 1906 –
MARCH 24, 2000

**VNB National
Trust Co.**
? –
MARCH 24, 2000

**Ethan Allen
National Bank**
JANUARY 1, 1879 –
NOVEMBER 24, 1972

**Montpelier
National Bank**
JANUARY 1, 1824 –
NOVEMBER 29, 1974

**Vermont Federal
National Bank**
MARCH 13, 1936 –
SEPTEMBER 22, 1997

**Valley
Bank**
MARCH 23, 1987 –
SEPTEMBER 13, 1991

**Middlebury
Savings and
Loan Assoc.**
JANUARY 1, 1928 –
NOVEMBER 30, 1981

**First Savings and
Loan Assoc. of
New Hampshire**
JANUARY 1, 1892 –
OCTOBER 1, 1995

**Windsor Federal
Savings and Loan
Assoc.**
JANUARY 1, 1917 –
AUGUST 31, 1983

**Randolph Savings
and
Loan Assoc.**
JANUARY 1, 1920 –
NOVEMBER 30, 1981

**Franklin
Co-operative Bank**
JANUARY 1, 1888 –
FEBRUARY 28, 1982

**Iona Savings
Bank**
MAY 1, 1870 –
OCTOBER 11, 1991

**Seacoast
Savings Bank**
JANUARY 1, 1901 –
AUGUST 28, 1992

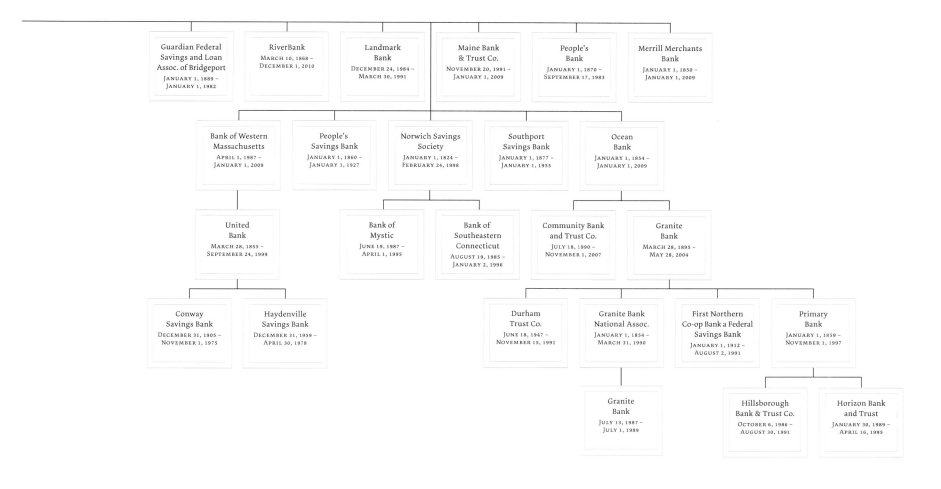

| | | Guardian Federal Savings and Loan Assoc. of Bridgeport
JANUARY 1, 1889 – JANUARY 1, 1982 | RiverBank
MARCH 10, 1868 – DECEMBER 1, 2010 | Landmark Bank
DECEMBER 24, 1984 – MARCH 30, 1991 | Maine Bank & Trust Co.
NOVEMBER 20, 1991 – JANUARY 1, 2009 | People's Bank
JANUARY 1, 1870 – SEPTEMBER 17, 1983 | Merrill Merchants Bank
JANUARY 1, 1850 – JANUARY 1, 2009 |

Bank of Western Massachusetts
APRIL 1, 1987 – JANUARY 1, 2009

People's Savings Bank
JANUARY 1, 1860 – JANUARY 1, 1927

Norwich Savings Society
JANUARY 1, 1824 – FEBRUARY 24, 1998

Southport Savings Bank
JANUARY 1, 1877 – JANUARY 1, 1955

Ocean Bank
JANUARY 1, 1854 – JANUARY 1, 2009

United Bank
MARCH 28, 1855 – SEPTEMBER 24, 1999

Bank of Mystic
JUNE 19, 1987 – APRIL 1, 1995

Bank of Southeastern Connecticut
AUGUST 19, 1985 – JANUARY 2, 1996

Community Bank and Trust Co.
JULY 18, 1990 – NOVEMBER 1, 2007

Granite Bank
MARCH 28, 1895 – MAY 28, 2004

Conway Savings Bank
DECEMBER 31, 1905 – NOVEMBER 1, 1975

Haydenville Savings Bank
DECEMBER 31, 1959 – APRIL 30, 1978

Durham Trust Co.
JUNE 18, 1947 – NOVEMBER 15, 1991

Granite Bank National Assoc.
JANUARY 1, 1854 – MARCH 31, 1990

First Northern Co-op Bank a Federal Savings Bank
JANUARY 1, 1912 – AUGUST 2, 1991

Primary Bank
JANUARY 1, 1859 – NOVEMBER 1, 1997

Granite Bank
JULY 13, 1987 – JULY 1, 1989

Hillsborough Bank & Trust Co.
OCTOBER 6, 1986 – AUGUST 30, 1991

Horizon Bank and Trust
JANUARY 30, 1989 – APRIL 16, 1995

People's United Financial   Bank

RANK	HEADQUARTERS	TICKER	ASSETS	EARLIEST KNOWN ANCESTOR	INDUSTRY OF ORIGIN
46	Bridgeport, CT	PBCT	$31,000,000,000	1802	Commercial Banking

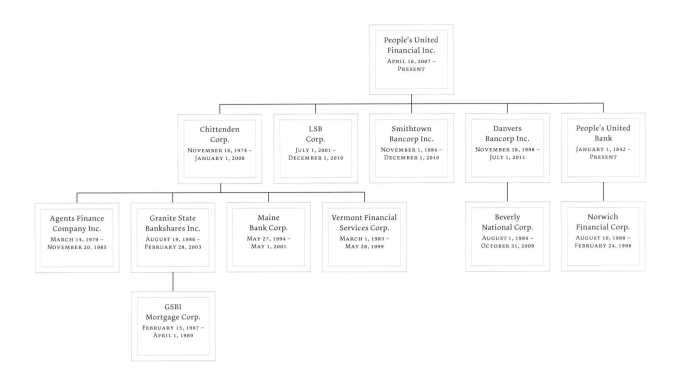

People's United Financial Inc.
APRIL 16, 2007 – PRESENT

Chittenden Corp.
NOVEMBER 18, 1974 – JANUARY 1, 2008

LSB Corp.
JULY 1, 2001 – DECEMBER 1, 2010

Smithtown Bancorp Inc.
NOVEMBER 1, 1984 – DECEMBER 1, 2010

Danvers Bancorp Inc.
NOVEMBER 18, 1998 – JULY 1, 2011

People's United Bank
JANUARY 1, 1842 – PRESENT

Agents Finance Company Inc.
MARCH 14, 1979 – NOVEMBER 20, 1985

Granite State Bankshares Inc.
AUGUST 19, 1986 – FEBRUARY 28, 2003

Maine Bank Corp.
MAY 27, 1994 – MAY 1, 2001

Vermont Financial Services Corp.
MARCH 1, 1983 – MAY 28, 1999

Beverly National Corp.
AUGUST 1, 1984 – OCTOBER 31, 2009

Norwich Financial Corp.
AUGUST 10, 1988 – FEBRUARY 24, 1998

GSBI Mortgage Corp.
FEBRUARY 15, 1987 – APRIL 1, 1989

People's United Financial

Holding Company

Bridgeport Savings Bank building postcard.

The bank at the core of this BHC began operations as the Bridgeport Savings Bank, chartered by Connecticut as a mutual savings bank in May 1842; Southport Savings Bank, chartered in the same fashion in May 1854; and the People's Savings Bank of Bridgeport, chartered in May 1860. All three banks were established by important businessmen and community leaders to help poor folks and professionals safeguard their savings and earn a little interest on them from pooled investments in mortgages, commercial bank stocks and railroad securities.

All three banks had a one vote per depositor rule in corporate elections, and all three thrived along with the city, the population of which increased from about 4,500 in 1840 to almost 50,000 in 1890. This dramatic growth was thanks in part to the efforts of famous showman P.T. Barnum, who served the city both as a booster and a real estate developer. In the latter half of the 19th century, Bridgeport was also home to Remington Arms, Singer and other important new corporations.

At the turn of the 20th century, Bridgeport Savings had assets of about $4 million and had made more than 4,000 mortgages. More organic growth occurred during the Great War, when 50,000 workers poured into the city to manufacture munitions and other war materiel. Over an 18-month period, the city's population increased 40%, and savings bank deposits increased 40%. After surviving runs associated with the recession of 1921, Bridgeport Savings thrived for the rest of the decade and merged with the People's Savings Bank in 1927 to form the Bridgeport-People's Savings Bank. Led by George Woods, the merged bank had 30 employees and assets of $32 million.

The bank survived the Great Depression because it backed its mortgage borrowers by paying their taxes for them when necessary, thus preventing tax auctions ruinous to both parties. According to Samuel

Bridgeport-People's Savings Bank advertising ink blotter.

Chittenden Trust Company calendar card, 1913.

Hawley, who assumed leadership of the bank in 1956, "this confidence in people was well repaid, as every dollar so advanced was eventually returned to the bank." The bank also used new forms of government assistance to help its borrowers make it through the rough times. For example, it was the first bank in Connecticut to make Federal Housing Administration (FHA) loans and, later, Veterans Administration (VA) loans. In the 1940s its assets doubled, surpassing the $100 million mark. It declared bonus dividends in 1942 to celebrate its centennial and in 1945 to celebrate victory in World War II.

In 1942 the bank also launched a life insurance product that by 1974 covered more than 20,000 people. (Unlike in most of the country, where banks could not offer insurance products, savings bank life insurance was legal in Massachusetts beginning in 1907 and in Connecticut and New York thereafter.) In the 1950s it began to follow its customers into the suburbs by opening branches, beginning with one in Stratford in 1953. Two years later, the bank merged with Southport Savings, changed its name to the People's Savings Bank-Bridgeport and continued opening new branches at the blazing rate of "better than one branch per year." The bank also computerized and added air conditioning, as well as a second $100 million in assets.

In the 1960s the bank increased the number of savings products it offered its depositors while simultaneously increasing dividend rates "frequently." After it began to pay interest on Christmas Club deposits, membership soared to more than 44,000, making it the largest such club in any savings bank in the nation. The bank hit $500 million in assets largely organically, while helping to revitalize downtown Bridgeport by building a new headquarters and financing major shopping and residential projects, including ones for low-income families.

The bank also made small loans to low-income entrepreneurs, well before Mohammad Yunnus made microfinance famous. "In this way," Hawley explained, "the bank has continued to adhere to its philosophy that those things which improve the prosperity and quality of life in Bridgeport will thereby benefit the depositors we serve."

Something worked, as by 1974 Bridgeport was Connecticut's largest city, its economy a mix of finance, higher education and commercial manufacturing ranging from helicopters to toasters.

To spread the good word about its services to the poor, who by the late 20th century were often wary of financial companies, the bank hired part-time sales representatives to call on people in their own neighborhoods on evenings and weekends. They explained to their

Southport Savings Bank, Southport, Connecticut, 1966.

potential clients how the bank could help them achieve their goals, and more than 12,000 families were aided by this "kitchen table banking" approach. Thanks to such innovations, by 1973 the bank had $1 billion in assets and 400 employees. It was New England's second largest savings bank and the largest home mortgage lender in the state.

In the early 1980s the bank merged with five other thrifts and changed its name to People's Bank. It added a sixth thrift, First Federal Savings of Norwalk, in 1986. Two years later, the bank demutualized but became part of a mutual holding company called People's Mutual Holdings. In the 1990s and 2000s it continued to grow organically and via a few acquisitions. In 2006 it gave up its state charter for a federal savings bank charter. The following year, the BHC demutualized and converted into an SLHC. Soon after, it bought Chittenden, a bank based in Burlington, Vermont, for $1.9 billion.

The acquisition added 130 branches in Maine, Massachusetts, New Hampshire and Vermont to People's 160-branch network in Connecticut and increased the bank's assets to $22 billion. The bank did not experience significant difficulties during the 2008 financial crisis, but it did not make another acquisition until 2010, when it purchased two small BHCs, one in New York and the other in Massachusetts, as well as

one small failed bank, Butler Bank of Lowell, Massachusetts. Early the following year, it also bought Danvers Bancorp of Massachusetts for $2.6 billion. Profits were up in 2012, thanks to improvement in credit quality and some cost-cutting measures.

Sources

"About People's Financial." *https://www.peoples.com/peoples/who-we-are.*Accessed December 19, 2013.

Browdie, Brian. "Cost Control, Fees Boost People's United Financial in 3Q." *American Banker*, October 22, 2012.

Hawley, Samuel W. *People's Savings Bank-Bridgeport: A Story of Private Thrift and Public Service.* New York: Newcomen Society, 1974.

"Hogan Lovells Advises Danvers Bancorp on Sale to People's United Financial, Inc." *Targeted News Service*, January 21, 2011.

"People's Bank (Bridgeport) (O) reports earnings for Qtr to June 30," *The New York Times*, July 21, 1989.

"People's United Bank, Bridgeport, Conn., Assumes All of Deposits of Butler Bank, Lowell, Mass." *US Fed News Service*, April 17, 2010.

"People's United Financial Inc.: Chittenden to Be Bought in Deal for $1.9 Billion." *Wall Street Journal*, June 28, 2007.

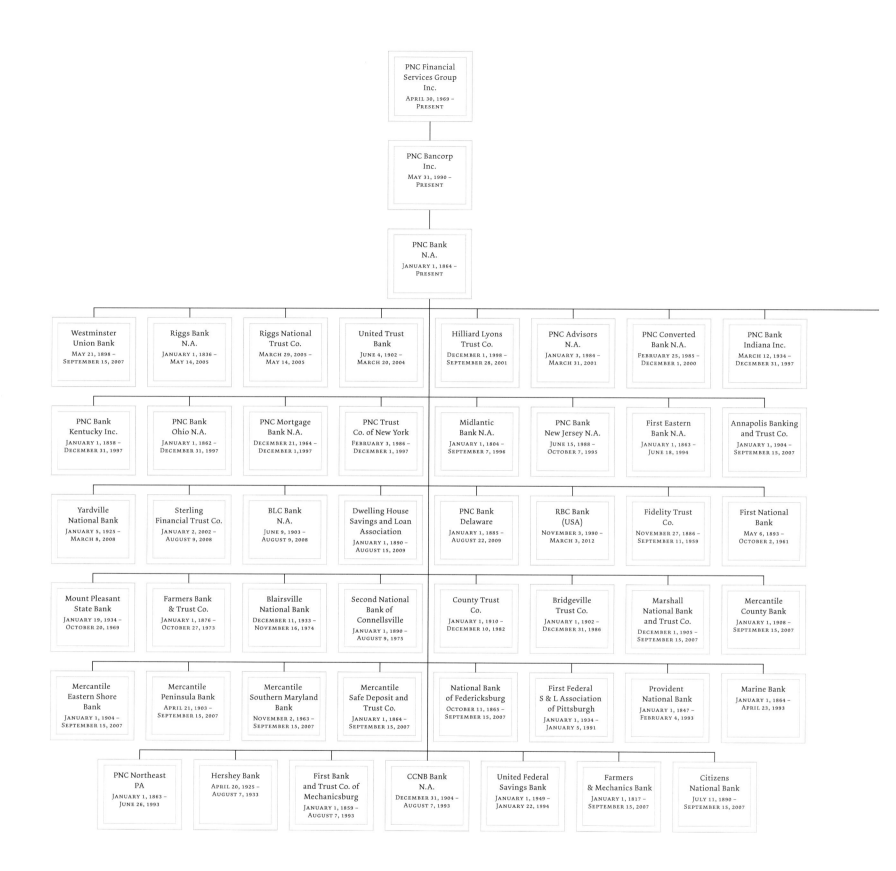

PNC Financial Services Group Inc.
APRIL 30, 1969 – PRESENT

PNC Bancorp Inc.
MAY 31, 1990 – PRESENT

PNC Bank N.A.
JANUARY 1, 1864 – PRESENT

Westminster Union Bank
MAY 21, 1898 – SEPTEMBER 15, 2007

Riggs Bank N.A.
JANUARY 1, 1836 – MAY 14, 2005

Riggs National Trust Co.
MARCH 29, 2005 – MAY 14, 2005

United Trust Bank
JUNE 4, 1902 – MARCH 20, 2004

Hilliard Lyons Trust Co.
DECEMBER 1, 1998 – SEPTEMBER 28, 2001

PNC Advisors N.A.
JANUARY 3, 1984 – MARCH 31, 2001

PNC Converted Bank N.A.
FEBRUARY 25, 1985 – DECEMBER 1, 2000

PNC Bank Indiana Inc.
MARCH 12, 1934 – DECEMBER 31, 1997

PNC Bank Kentucky Inc.
JANUARY 1, 1858 – DECEMBER 31, 1997

PNC Bank Ohio N.A.
JANUARY 1, 1862 – DECEMBER 31, 1997

PNC Mortgage Bank N.A.
DECEMBER 21, 1964 – DECEMBER 1,1997

PNC Trust Co. of New York
FEBRUARY 3, 1986 – DECEMBER 1, 1997

Midlantic Bank N.A.
JANUARY 1, 1804 – SEPTEMBER 7, 1996

PNC Bank New Jersey N.A.
JUNE 15, 1988 – OCTOBER 7, 1995

First Eastern Bank N.A.
JANUARY 1, 1863 – JUNE 18, 1994

Annapolis Banking and Trust Co.
JANUARY 1, 1904 – SEPTEMBER 15, 2007

Yardville National Bank
JANUARY 5, 1925 – MARCH 8, 2008

Sterling Financial Trust Co.
JANUARY 2, 2002 – AUGUST 9, 2008

BLC Bank N.A.
JUNE 9, 1903 – AUGUST 9, 2008

Dwelling House Savings and Loan Association
JANUARY 1, 1890 – AUGUST 15, 2009

PNC Bank Delaware
JANUARY 1, 1885 – AUGUST 22, 2009

RBC Bank (USA)
NOVEMBER 3, 1990 – MARCH 3, 2012

Fidelity Trust Co.
NOVEMBER 27, 1886 – SEPTEMBER 11, 1959

First National Bank
MAY 6, 1893 – OCTOBER 2, 1961

Mount Pleasant State Bank
JANUARY 19, 1934 – OCTOBER 20, 1969

Farmers Bank & Trust Co.
JANUARY 1, 1876 – OCTOBER 27, 1973

Blairsville National Bank
DECEMBER 11, 1933 – NOVEMBER 16, 1974

Second National Bank of Connellsville
JANUARY 1, 1890 – AUGUST 9, 1975

County Trust Co.
JANUARY 1, 1910 – DECEMBER 10, 1982

Bridgeville Trust Co.
JANUARY 1, 1902 – DECEMBER 31, 1986

Marshall National Bank and Trust Co.
DECEMBER 1, 1905 – SEPTEMBER 15, 2007

Mercantile County Bank
JANUARY 1, 1908 – SEPTEMBER 15, 2007

Mercantile Eastern Shore Bank
JANUARY 1, 1904 – SEPTEMBER 15, 2007

Mercantile Peninsula Bank
APRIL 21, 1903 – SEPTEMBER 15, 2007

Mercantile Southern Maryland Bank
NOVEMBER 2, 1963 – SEPTEMBER 15, 2007

Mercantile Safe Deposit and Trust Co.
JANUARY 1, 1864 – SEPTEMBER 15, 2007

National Bank of Federicksburg
OCTOBER 11, 1865 – SEPTEMBER 15, 2007

First Federal S & L Association of Pittsburgh
JANUARY 1, 1934 – JANUARY 5, 1991

Provident National Bank
JANUARY 1, 1847 – FEBRUARY 4, 1993

Marine Bank
JANUARY 1, 1864 – APRIL 23, 1993

PNC Northeast PA
JANUARY 1, 1863 – JUNE 26, 1993

Hershey Bank
APRIL 20, 1925 – AUGUST 7, 1933

First Bank and Trust Co. of Mechanicsburg
JANUARY 1, 1859 – AUGUST 7, 1993

CCNB Bank N.A.
DECEMBER 31, 1904 – AUGUST 7, 1993

United Federal Savings Bank
JANUARY 1, 1949 – JANUARY 22, 1994

Farmers & Mechanics Bank
JANUARY 1, 1817 – SEPTEMBER 15, 2007

Citizens National Bank
JULY 11, 1890 – SEPTEMBER 15, 2007

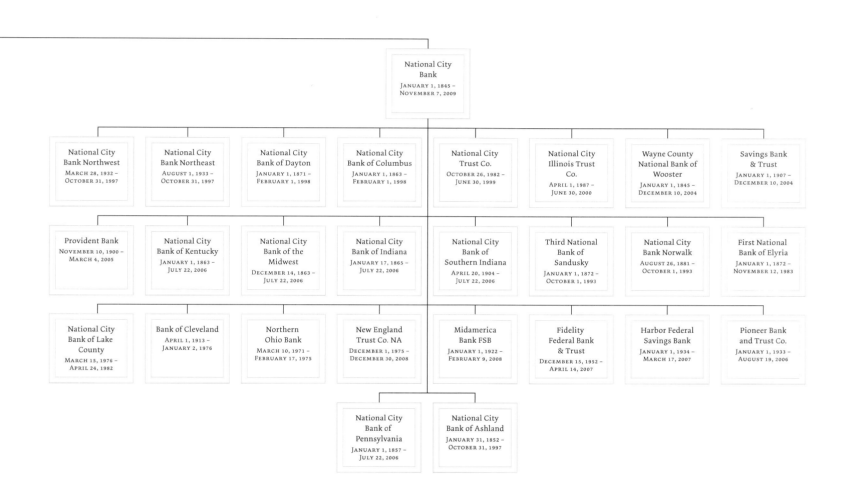

PNC Financial Services

Bank *(abridged)*

RANK	HEADQUARTERS	TICKER	ASSETS	EARLIEST KNOWN ANCESTOR	INDUSTRY OF ORIGIN
12	**Pittsburgh, PA**	**PNC**	**$305,000,000,000**	**1796**	**Commercial Banking**

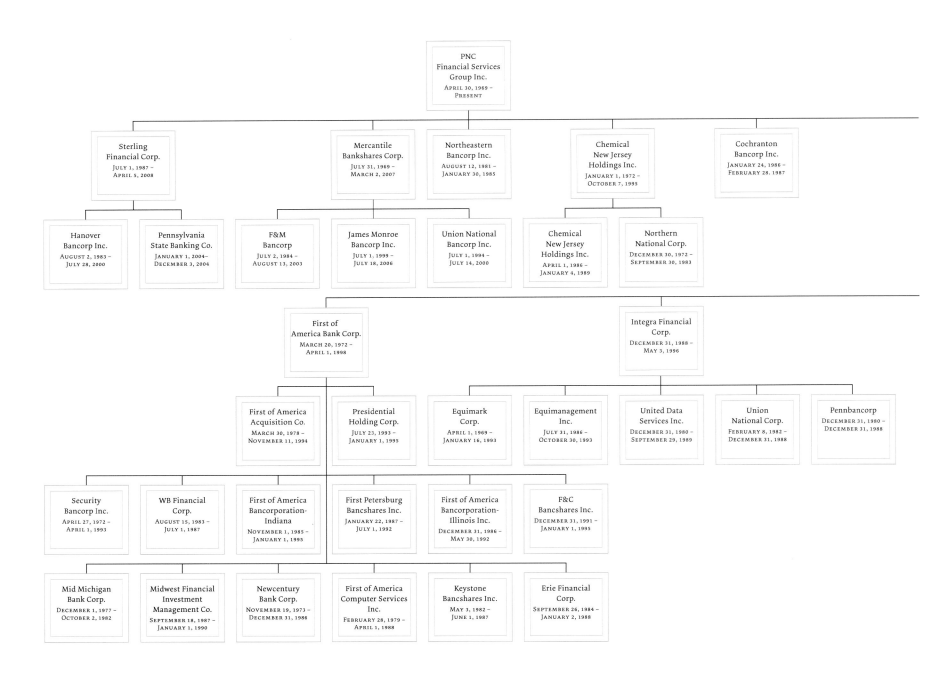

PNC
Financial Services
Group Inc.
APRIL 30, 1969 –
PRESENT

Sterling
Financial Corp.
JULY 1, 1987 –
APRIL 5, 2008

Mercantile
Bankshares Corp.
JULY 31, 1969 –
MARCH 2, 2007

Northeastern
Bancorp Inc.
AUGUST 12, 1981 –
JANUARY 30, 1985

Chemical
New Jersey
Holdings Inc.
JANUARY 1, 1972 –
OCTOBER 7, 1995

Cochranton
Bancorp Inc.
JANUARY 24, 1986 –
FEBRUARY 28. 1987

Hanover
Bancorp Inc.
AUGUST 2, 1983 –
JULY 28, 2000

Pennsylvania
State Banking Co.
JANUARY 1, 2004–
DECEMBER 3, 2004

F&M
Bancorp
JULY 2, 1984 –
AUGUST 13, 2003

James Monroe
Bancorp Inc.
JULY 1, 1999 –
JULY 18, 2006

Union National
Bancorp Inc.
JULY 1, 1994 –
JULY 14, 2000

Chemical
New Jersey
Holdings Inc.
APRIL 1, 1986 –
JANUARY 4, 1989

Northern
National Corp.
DECEMBER 30, 1972 –
SEPTEMBER 30, 1983

First of
America Bank Corp.
MARCH 20, 1972 –
APRIL 1, 1998

Integra Financial
Corp.
DECEMBER 31, 1988 –
MAY 3, 1996

First of America
Acquisition Co.
MARCH 30, 1978 –
NOVEMBER 11, 1994

Presidential
Holding Corp.
JULY 23, 1993 –
JANUARY 1, 1995

Equimark
Corp.
APRIL 1, 1969 –
JANUARY 16, 1993

Equimanagement
Inc.
JULY 31, 1986 –
OCTOBER 30, 1993

United Data
Services Inc.
DECEMBER 31, 1980 –
SEPTEMBER 29, 1989

Union
National Corp.
FEBRUARY 8, 1982 –
DECEMBER 31, 1988

Pennbancorp
DECEMBER 31, 1980 –
DECEMBER 31, 1988

Security
Bancorp Inc.
APRIL 27, 1972 –
APRIL 1, 1993

WB Financial
Corp.
AUGUST 15, 1983 –
JULY 1, 1987

First of America
Bancorporation-
Indiana
NOVEMBER 1, 1985 –
JANUARY 1, 1995

First Petersburg
Bancshares Inc.
JANUARY 22, 1987 –
JULY 1, 1992

First of America
Bancorporation-
Illinois Inc.
DECEMBER 31, 1986 –
MAY 30, 1992

F&C
Bancshares Inc.
DECEMBER 31, 1991 –
JANUARY 1, 1995

Mid Michigan
Bank Corp.
DECEMBER 1, 1977 –
OCTOBER 2, 1982

Midwest Financial
Investment
Management Co.
SEPTEMBER 18, 1987 –
JANUARY 1, 1990

Newcentury
Bank Corp.
NOVEMBER 19, 1973 –
DECEMBER 31, 1986

First of America
Computer Services
Inc.
FEBRUARY 28, 1979 –
APRIL 1, 1988

Keystone
Bancshares Inc.
MAY 3, 1982 –
JUNE 1, 1987

Erie Financial
Corp.
SEPTEMBER 26, 1984 –
JANUARY 2, 1988

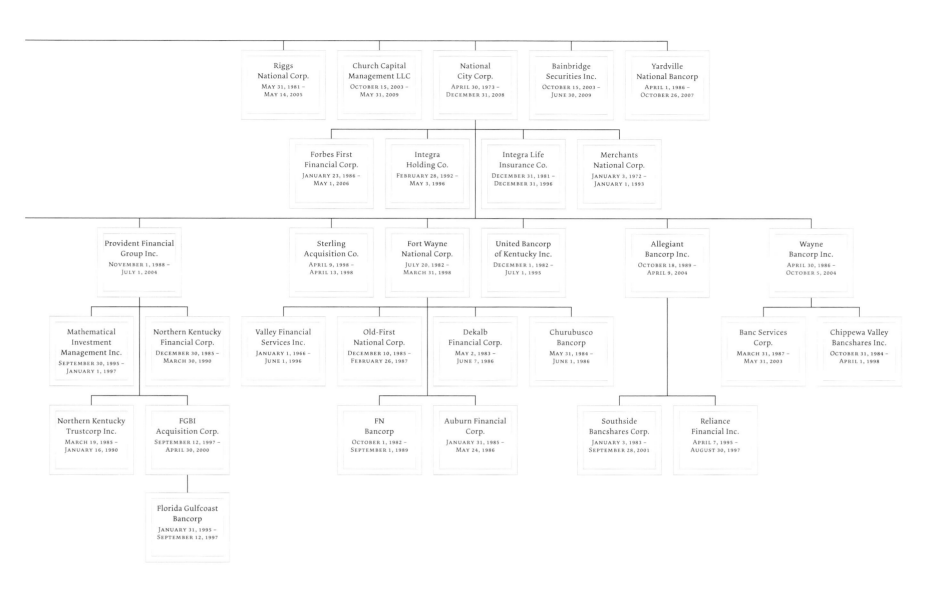

Riggs National Corp.
MAY 31, 1981 –
MAY 14, 2005

Church Capital Management LLC
OCTOBER 15, 2003 –
MAY 31, 2009

National City Corp.
APRIL 30, 1973 –
DECEMBER 31, 2008

Bainbridge Securities Inc.
OCTOBER 15, 2003 –
JUNE 30, 2009

Yardville National Bancorp
APRIL 1, 1986 –
OCTOBER 26, 2007

Forbes First Financial Corp.
JANUARY 23, 1986 –
MAY 1, 2006

Integra Holding Co.
FEBRUARY 28, 1992 –
MAY 3, 1996

Integra Life Insurance Co.
DECEMBER 31, 1981 –
DECEMBER 31, 1996

Merchants National Corp.
JANUARY 3, 1972 –
JANUARY 1, 1993

Provident Financial Group Inc.
NOVEMBER 1, 1988 –
JULY 1, 2004

Sterling Acquisition Co.
APRIL 9, 1998 –
APRIL 13, 1998

Fort Wayne National Corp.
JULY 20, 1982 –
MARCH 31, 1998

United Bancorp of Kentucky Inc.
DECEMBER 1, 1982 –
JULY 1, 1995

Allegiant Bancorp Inc.
OCTOBER 18, 1989 –
APRIL 9, 2004

Wayne Bancorp Inc.
APRIL 30, 1986 –
OCTOBER 5, 2004

Mathematical Investment Management Inc.
SEPTEMBER 30, 1995 –
JANUARY 1, 1997

Northern Kentucky Financial Corp.
DECEMBER 30, 1985 –
MARCH 30, 1990

Valley Financial Services Inc.
JANUARY 1, 1966 –
JUNE 1, 1996

Old-First National Corp.
DECEMBER 10, 1985 –
FEBRUARY 26, 1987

Dekalb Financial Corp.
MAY 2, 1983 –
JUNE 7, 1986

Churubusco Bancorp
MAY 31, 1984 –
JUNE 1, 1986

Banc Services Corp.
MARCH 31, 1987 –
MAY 31, 2003

Chippewa Valley Bancshares Inc.
OCTOBER 31, 1984 –
APRIL 1, 1998

Northern Kentucky Trustcorp Inc.
MARCH 19, 1985 –
JANUARY 16, 1990

FGBI Acquisition Corp.
SEPTEMBER 12, 1997 –
APRIL 30, 2000

FN Bancorp
OCTOBER 1, 1982 –
SEPTEMBER 1, 1989

Auburn Financial Corp.
JANUARY 31, 1985 –
MAY 24, 1986

Southside Bancshares Corp.
JANUARY 3, 1983 –
SEPTEMBER 28, 2001

Reliance Financial Inc.
APRIL 7, 1995 –
AUGUST 30, 1997

Florida Gulfcoast Bancorp
JANUARY 31, 1995 –
SEPTEMBER 12, 1997

PNC Financial Services

Holding Company *(abridged)*

Riggs National Bank, called the "Bank of the Presidents," ca. 1910-1926.

Ohio National Bank.

NC arose out of the merger of Pittsburgh National Corp. and Provident National Corp. in 1983, the largest US bank merger in history to that time. Pittsburgh National traced its roots to the formation of Pittsburgh Trust and Savings in 1852. It became the First National Bank of Pittsburgh in 1863 and the Peoples First National Bank and Trust in 1946, when it merged with the Peoples Pittsburgh Trust Company. The combined entity had $28 million in capital and about 275,000 customers. In 1959 it merged with Fidelity Trust to create Pittsburgh National, which had assets of $81 million and 52 offices in the Pittsburgh area. Philadelphia-based Provident began its corporate life in 1847 with the chartering of the Tradesmen's National Bank. It merged with Provident Trust Company, which Provident Life and Trust Company had spun off in 1922, to create Provident National in 1957.

In the first five years following the merger that created it, PNC more than doubled its assets, which reached $36 billion in 1988, by buying up banks in Pennsylvania and merging with Citizens Fidelity of Louisville, Kentucky. It continued growing thereafter, acquiring in 1989 the Bank of Delaware (chartered 1796) and a slew of small banks like Flagship Financial of Jenkintown, Pennsylvania. In 1993 it stepped up the pace and size of its acquisitions, which included banks in Massachusetts and Ohio, as well as Pennsylvania. It also bought Sears Mortgage Banking Group from retailing giant Sears, Roebuck that year.

By the end of 1994 PNC had assets of over $64 billion. The following year, it merged with Midlantic Corp. of Edison, New Jersey, for almost $3 billion in stock. Founded in the early 1980s with the merger of Midlantic and Continental of Pennsylvania, Midlantic had almost failed in the early 1990s, but a new CEO got it through by selling off about a third of the company's assets and reducing its efficiency ratio to 56%. Also in 1995, PNC bought Chemical Bank's (now part of #1) branches in New Jersey and suburban Philadelphia. Its main businesses at the time were mortgage banking, which operated through an origination network that spanned 33 states, managing proprietary mutual funds and student lending. About 47% of its earnings came from retail banking, 44% from corporate banking and the remaining 9% from investment management and trust services. About 35% of its loans were commercial, 29% mortgages, 26% consumer and the rest a potpourri.

By 1995 PNC operated about 550 branches in Delaware, Indiana, Kentucky, Ohio, New Jersey and Pennsylvania and owned small banks in West Virginia and Michigan. Its executives were able to manage that far-flung empire because PNC was recognized by bank scholar Alan Gart as "one of the most technologically advanced banks in the country." That allowed it to respond to customer queries and changing market conditions faster than most of its competitors, and at a lower cost, making it one of the most efficient superregional banks in the nation and one of the best capitalized as well.

Its ATMs, banking stations, back offices and telecom systems were all state-of-the-art, allowing it to shutter less productive branches without losing much in the way of deposits. Its CEO at the time, Thomas H. O'Brien, described PNC as "a hard-working, high-energy, no-nonsense bank, committed to operating at the highest levels of service and profitability."

Early in the first decade of the new millennium, regulators uncovered problems with PNC's balance sheet, causing the bank to restate its earnings and sending its stock spiraling downward. CEO Jim Rohr, who took over in 2000, quickly turned the bank around by streamlining its business units, cutting many jobs and implementing other cost-cutting measures.

In May 2005 PNC acquired Riggs Bank, the "bank of the presidents." Riggs Bank began its existence as a bank and brokerage formed in the nation's capital in 1836 or 1837 and was initially called Corcoran & Riggs after its two young principals, dry goods merchant-cum-capitalist William Wilson Corcoran and banker/adventurer George Washington Riggs. In 1841 the upstart company, with help from Riggs's wealthy father, Elisha, established a shrewd reputation by buying a $5 million US government bond offering at 101% of par and reselling it for a profit. Soon after, it began to attract the deposit and loan business of President John Tyler and other top government officials, including Secretary of State Daniel Webster.

In 1845 the bank purchased and moved its operations into the erstwhile Washington office of the Bank of the United States (1816–1836), thereby cementing its image as the federal government's primary fiscal agent. President James Polk also kept a personal account with the bank, which played a major role in the financing of the war with Mexico

Cashier handing out money at Riggs Bank, 1938.

Provident Life & Trust Company Bank, ca. 1888-1890.

Pittsburgh National Bank building.

(1846–1848). After the war, the bank continued to thrive and diversified into railroad securities.

Upon Corcoran's retirement in 1854, the bank continued operations as Riggs & Company. In addition to helping to fund the Union cause during the Civil War, it lent $7.2 million so the government could buy Alaska, the second greatest land deal in American history. The bank joined the national banking system in 1896 and continued to grow, thrive and help the US government to finance its many endeavors, including the Great War.

Riggs Bank also began providing foreign embassies and diplomats with various banking services, a business that eventually contributed to its acquisition by PNC. By 2000 Riggs had assets of some $5.5 billion and branches in Virginia and Maryland, as well as the nation's capital. During its long existence, 23 US presidents, or members of their families, banked at Riggs. The bank, however, was plagued by scandals in its final few years, leading to its eventual sale in 2005 after a post-September 11th terrorist money laundering probe revealed numerous disturbing transactions with a Saudi prince.

Rohr's reforms and the Riggs acquisition soon paid off. In 2006 *US Banker* named PNC the number one bank, and the following year

Fortune ranked it among the "most admired companies." The bank was also lauded for its employee training programs, its diverse workforce and its policies for working mothers. It was also widely considered one of the nation's most environmentally friendly banks, a sort of "green giant." It claimed that branches built to green standards saved overhead costs and also increased employee efficiency and loyalty. This is not to say that employee loyalty was a problem at the bank, which prided itself on a corporate culture described as "very conservative," "very nice" and focused on "producing exceptional work," but in a "low-stress environment."

Feeling good about business once again, in February 2007 PNC introduced a new slogan, "Leading the Way," during the Super Bowl. More substantively, the following month it acquired Mercantile Bankshares, an investment and wealth management bank with $17 billion in assets and 240 offices in Delaware, Maryland, Pennsylvania, Virginia and Washington, DC. By 2007 PNC's 27,500 employees operated 1,079 offices and served over 2.5 million clients on assets of almost $123 billion.

PNC avoided major problems during the 2008 financial crisis because approximately 60% of its revenue came from fees and because

PNC Park, home of Major League Baseball's Pittsburgh Pirates.

its lending standards were relatively stringent. Since it was one of the strongest of the bigger BHCs, PNC was able to acquire the troubled National City Corporation ("NatCity") in late October 2008, at the height of the panic.

Founded by businessmen in Cleveland in 1845 as the City Bank of Cleveland, NatCity switched from an Ohio free banking charter to a national charter in 1865. Initially capitalized at $200,000, National City Bank grew along with the economy of Cleveland in the second half of the 19th and the first half of the 20th centuries, dodging banking panics and making small fortunes during wars. Assets hit $5.7 million in May 1914, up from just $2.5 million two years earlier.

NatCity continued to grow during the Great War and the roaring 1920s, hitting about $40 million when the Great Depression struck. The bank's assets decreased some $11 million by the bank holiday of 1933, but it weathered the crisis because its loan and bond portfolios were solid. Deposits surged after the crisis, during the recovery and during the World War II, allowing assets to balloon to $475 million and capital and surplus to increase to $18 million by the end of 1944, when the bank's workforce stood at 475. In 1984 it became the largest bank in Ohio and the 26th largest bank in the nation when it merged with BancOhio Corporation. It continued to grow thereafter, always mindful to cut redundancies and streamline operations after acquisitions. It made its first interstate acquisition, First Kentucky National, in 1988. The following year it moved into the thrift business by purchasing a troubled mutual savings bank in Dayton called Gem Savings Association.

As interstate branching and other regulatory restrictions were lifted, NatCity began to increase the pace of its acquisitions. It made three deals between June 2003 and June 2004 alone. By March 2007 NatCity had assets of almost $139 billion, 31,000 employees, 2,100 ATMs and 1,300 branches, mostly in Florida, Indiana, Illinois, Kentucky, Michigan, Missouri, Ohio and Pennsylvania. Its retail banking unit provided a full range of loans, from education finance accounts to credit cards, as well as insurance. In addition, it provided financial services to small business owners and full-blown syndicated lending, treasury management and leasing to large corporate clients. It also operated Allegiant Asset Management Group and the core of its difficulties, National City Mortgage, which originated residential real estate loans throughout 47 states. It was avidly buying and selling banks right up to the end.

NatCity brought headaches and $7.6 billion in bailout money. Like other strong banks, however, PNC bounced back quickly from the 2008

financial crisis by shoring up costs and selling unneeded assets, like PNC Global Investment Services, a back office operation that went to the Bank of New York Mellon (#9) in 2010. By 2011 it was able to make another major acquisition, the Royal Bank of Canada's American retail banking business, for $3.62 billion. It also moved abroad, establishing Harris Williams and Company in 2010. By 2013 it had eight branches worldwide, including ones in London and Frankfurt, and 215 international employees.

Sources

"2 Pittsburgh Banks Name Merger Board." *The New York Times*, January 12, 1946, 20.

Benton, Elbert J. *A Century of Progress: Being a History of the National City Bank of Cleveland from 1845 to 1945.* Cleveland: National City Bank of Cleveland, 1945.

Carr, Roland T. *32 President's Square: Part I of a Two-Part Narrative of the Riggs Bank and Its Founders.* Washington, DC: Acropolis Books, 1980.

Cummings, James W. *Towards Modern Public Finance: The American War with Mexico, 1846–1848.* London: Pickering & Chatto, 2009.

Fraust, Bart. "Mergers, Acquisitions: New Bid Clinches BancOhio-National City Deal." *American Banker*, February 3, 1984, 3.

"Germany, United States: PNC Financial's Arm Opened Its Second Office in Europe in Germany's Frankfurt." *MENA Report*, June 16, 2013.

Loosvelt, Derek, et al. *The Vault Guide to the Top 50 Banking Employers: 2008 Edition.* New York: Vault, 2007, 364–68, 374–78.

Maturi, Richard J. "Buckeye Banker: National City Corp. Thrives in Ohio." *Barron's, National Business and Financial Weekly*, November 24, 1986, 54.

"National City Corp.: Acquisition of Wayne Bancorp Continues Consolidation Trend." *Wall Street Journal*, June 7, 2004, B4.

"National City Corp. Proposes to Acquire a Thrift in Ohio." *Wall Street Journal*, June 26, 1989, 1.

Newman, A. Joseph, Jr. "Pittsburgh National and Provident to Complete Merger Later Today." *American Banker*, January 19, 1983, 2.

O'Brien, Timothy. "At Riggs Bank, A Tangled Path Led to Scandal." *The New York Times*, July 19, 2004.

PNC. "Corporate History." http://pnclegacyproject.com. Accessed November 22, 2013.

Ringer, Richard. "National City Joins Superregional Ranks." *American Banker*, January 29, 1988, 2.

Spiegel, John, Alan Gart and Steven Gart. *Banking Redefined: How Superregional Powerhouses Are Reshaping Financial Services.* Chicago: Irwin Professional Publishing, 1996, 159–77.

Winkler, Rolfe and Jason Bush. "A Winning Deal for PNC Investors." *The New York Times*, February 3, 2010, B2.

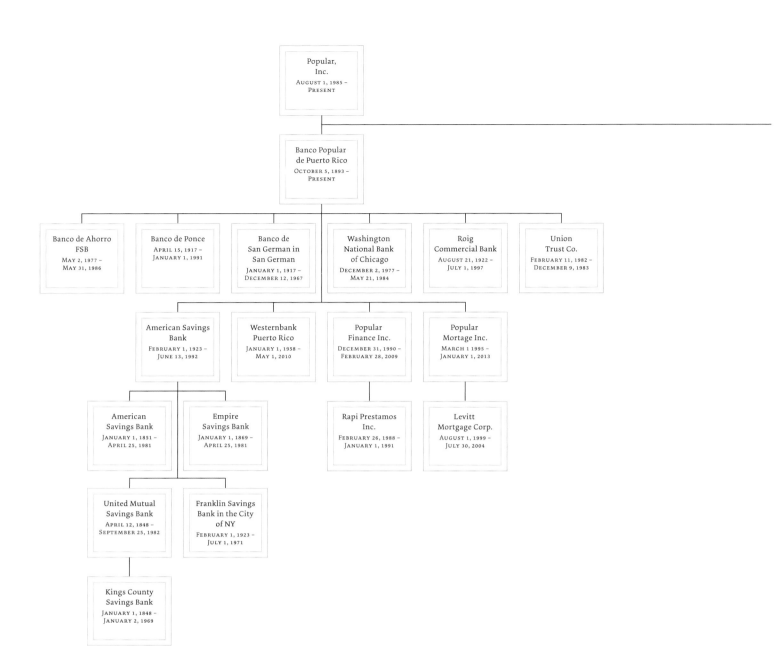

Popular,
Inc.
AUGUST 1, 1985 –
PRESENT

Banco Popular
de Puerto Rico
OCTOBER 5, 1893 –
PRESENT

Banco de Ahorro
FSB
MAY 2, 1977 –
MAY 31, 1986

Banco de Ponce
APRIL 15, 1917 –
JANUARY 1, 1991

Banco de
San German in
San German
JANUARY 1, 1917 –
DECEMBER 12, 1967

Washington
National Bank
of Chicago
DECEMBER 2, 1977 –
MAY 21, 1984

Roig
Commercial Bank
AUGUST 21, 1922 –
JULY 1, 1997

Union
Trust Co.
FEBRUARY 11, 1982 –
DECEMBER 9, 1983

American Savings
Bank
FEBRUARY 1, 1923 –
JUNE 13, 1992

Westernbank
Puerto Rico
JANUARY 1, 1958 –
MAY 1, 2010

Popular
Finance Inc.
DECEMBER 31, 1990 –
FEBRUARY 28, 2009

Popular
Mortage Inc.
MARCH 1 1995 –
JANUARY 1, 2013

American
Savings Bank
JANUARY 1, 1851 –
APRIL 25, 1981

Empire
Savings Bank
JANUARY 1, 1869 –
APRIL 25, 1981

Rapi Prestamos
Inc.
FEBRUARY 26, 1988 –
JANUARY 1, 1991

Levitt
Mortgage Corp.
AUGUST 1, 1999 –
JULY 30, 2004

United Mutual
Savings Bank
APRIL 12, 1848 –
SEPTEMBER 25, 1982

Franklin Savings
Bank in the City
of NY
FEBRUARY 1, 1923 –
JULY 1, 1971

Kings County
Savings Bank
JANUARY 1, 1848 –
JANUARY 2, 1969

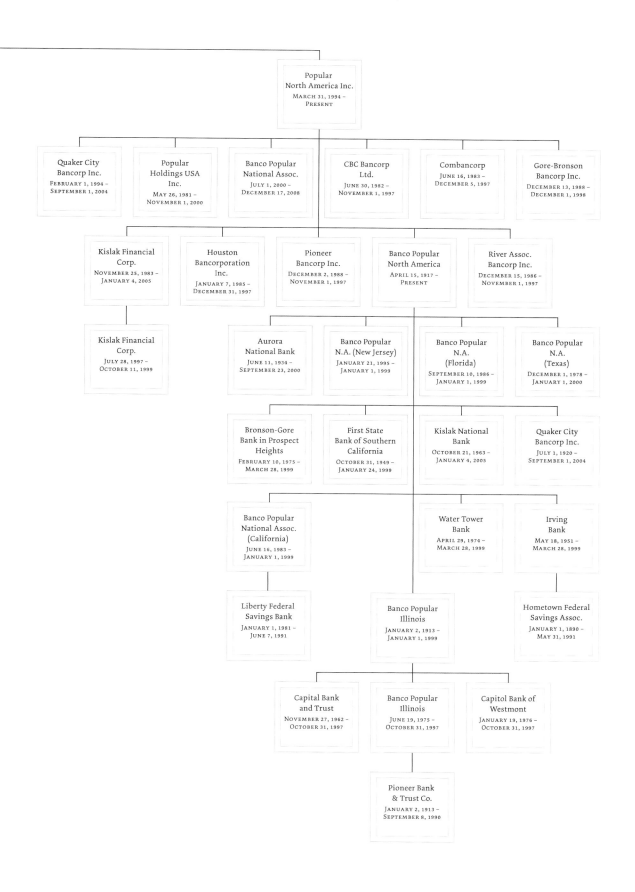

Popular

RANK	HEADQUARTERS	TICKER	ASSETS	EARLIEST KNOWN ANCESTOR	INDUSTRY OF ORIGIN
45	San Juan, PR	BPOP	$36,500,000,000	1848	Commercial Banking

Banco Popular's first branch, 1893.

Headquartered on the island of Puerto Rico, a US territory in the northeastern Caribbean, Popular traces its roots to 1893. That year, a group of businessmen led by Manuel Ferdandez Juncos formed La Caja de Economías y Prestamos Banco Popular in response to the global financial crisis that manifested itself in Spain (which controlled the island until 1898) as a monetary crisis and inflationary episode.

Born in Spain but raised in Puerto Rico, Juncos, with help from well-connected attorney Manuel F. Rossy Calderón and military leader Manuel Muñoz Barrios, wanted to develop a spirit of economy in all social classes, especially in the poor, by means of saving. More than 50 stockholders capitalized the bank; almost three-quarters held only one, two or three shares. The bank took deposits and made loans, paying at first 4% on the former and receiving up to 12% on the latter. It also discounted bills of exchange and other short-term business paper.

Most of the bank's stockholders, depositors and borrowers were from the capital city of San Juan. By 1897 the bank had 155 stockholders, and its capitalization had grown from 5,000 to 30,000 silver pesos. The Spanish-American War and the San Ciriaco hurricane pummeled the bank and the island in 1898, but both survived. The transition to American laws and the US dollar were also traumatic, but by 1903 the bank was again thriving along with the island's capital (which grew in population from 25,000 in 1901 to 170,000 in 1940) and its agricultural economy. Deposits reached nearly $162,000 by the end of 1906 and $922,000 by the end of 1913. Profitability was limited, however,

by the nature of the bank's business, which entailed numerous small transactions.

During the 1910s the bank's capital doubled from $50,000 to $100,000 in the face of stiff competition but a booming wartime economy. By 1926 an industrious salesman and entrepreneur, Rafael Carrión Pacheco, had purchased over half of the bank's shares. The bank survived the Great Depression in part because, unlike other Puerto Rican banks, it had not overspecialized in coffee loans. Nevertheless, its balance sheet shrank dramatically as sophisticated depositors sent their money to Canada for safekeeping. His wealth on the line, Carrión Pacheco negotiated a bailout package from the Reconstruction Finance Corporation, and soon after merged his bank with the Banco de Puerto Rico. The new institution, el Banco Popular de Puerto Rico, began business in 1936. Rebounding agricultural prices assured the new bank's success.

In 1942 Popular employed 243 people and over the years added many more as it slowly spread across the island. By 1956 it had 20 branches. It also employed a mobile branch run out of a bus to aid customers in almost two dozen tiny rural communities. It established a branch in the Bronx in 1961 to serve Puerto Ricans living and working in New York City, and in 1970 it became the first Puerto Rican bank to offer bilingual services.

By 1965 Popular had 37 branches at home and two in New York. Five years later, it operated 48 branches on the island, six in New York and one in Los Angeles. The bank's continued growth led it to become the first bank on the island, and the eighth in the United States, to computerize its operations. It also began to make automobile loans beginning

Banco Popular de Puerto Rico branch outside Old San Juan.

Gold weight from Banco Popular.

in 1957, and in 1968 it introduced a popular new La Reserva Popular account, which was a combination checking account and personal line of credit.

By 1972 deposits were $945 million, and Popular was one of the nation's 100 largest banks. By 1980 it operated 103 branches in Puerto Rico, as well as the six in New York and one in Los Angeles. A decade later it merged with La BanPonce Corporation, which added 173 branches to its network in Puerto Rico, 24 to its network in the United States proper and three in the Virgin Islands. Popular grew both larger and more efficient in the 1990s, as measured by the ratio between its book value and its market value. It did not grow as quickly as some of its competitors, however, because it remained focused on organic growth and profitability (ROE) instead of top line growth through acquisitions. Popular consciously engaged in personalized service so it could more effectively price discriminate and, hence, maximize profit from each transaction and customer relationship.

By 1998 Popular had $20 billion in assets and 476 financial service centers throughout the United States and Puerto Rico. One of the 40 largest banks in North America at the time, it was also one of America's leading Hispanic banks. In 2005 Popular bought E-Loan, an Internet lending site, for $300 million. Chairman Richard Carrion said he made the move in order to reenter the credit card business, which Popular had abandoned in 2000 by selling its portfolio to Metris, which HSBC (#11) acquired in 2005.

The 2008 financial crisis at first barely phased Popular, which cut its dividend in late 2008 but remained "well capitalized." The mortgage crisis, however, later hurt its balance sheet, requiring almost $1 billion in TARP funds. By 2010 its stock was in strong demand on rumors that it might sell its payment processor, Evertec, for $1 billion. It booked $325 million in profits when it took that business public in early 2013.

Popular was strong enough in 2010 to take advantage of a banking crisis that struck Puerto Rico by purchasing Westernbank, one of three distressed institutions the FDIC had to resolve there, but it had to sell off bad loans to raise cash. In October 2013 Popular finally sought permission to repay $935 million in TARP funds.

Sources

Bair, Sheila. *Bull by the Horns: Fighting to Save Main Street from Wall Street and Wall Street from Itself.* New York: Free Press, 2012, 281–82.

Baralt, Guillermo. *Tradición de Futuro: El Primer Siglo del Banco Popular de Puerto Rico, 1893–1993.* San Juan: Banco Popular de Puerto Rico, 1993.

Browdie, Brian. "Popular Strikes Deal to Liquidate Bad Loans." *American Banker*, March 4, 2013.

"Bullish Investors Flock to Popular, Inc. as Shares Reach a New 52-Week High." *Phil's Stock World*, April 13, 2010.

Johnson, Andrew R. "Popular Seeks to Repay TARP; Puerto Rico's Largest Bank Asks for Regulatory Approval to Repay $935 Million Bailout." *Wall Street Journal Online*, October 23, 2013.

Kase, Kimio and Tanguy Jacopin. *CEOs as Leaders and Strategy Designers: Explaining the Success of Spanish Banks.* New York: Palgrave Macmillan, 2008.

"Popular, Inc. Buying E-Loan." *Electronic Payments Week*, August 9, 2005, 1.

"Popular, Inc.: Popular Declares Cash Dividend." *Science Letter*, September 9, 2008, 3,989.

"Popular, Inc.: Strategic Expansion in the US, Puerto Rico, and Caribbean Basin." *Institutional Investor* 32, 10 (October 1998): D11.

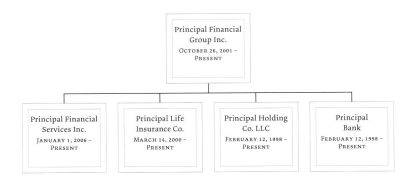

Principal Financial Group

RANK	HEADQUARTERS	TICKER	ASSETS	EARLIEST KNOWN ANCESTOR	INDUSTRY OF ORIGIN
16	Des Moines, IA	PFG	$197,000,000,000	1879	Insurance

Bankers Life ink blotter.

Throughout most of its existence, Principal Financial Group was principally an insurance company called Bankers Life. Established in 1879 in Des Moines, which at 22,408 people had just become the most populous place in Iowa, Bankers Life, as its name implied, provided life insurance for bank employees.

The brainchild of small town banker Edward Temple, the association used basic actuarial knowledge to improve upon the professional assessment plan whereby members paid benefits whenever a member died. Financed by refundable deposits, unrefundable initiation fees and quarterly assessments, the association could provide insurance even more cheaply than the best-run mutual company if its membership was healthy and grew quickly. To ensure that growth, the association decided to extend membership to people outside the state and the banking fraternity, as long as they were not intemperate, engaged in a dangerous occupation or from the South. By 1900 Bankers Life was open to the residents of 21 states, including New York, and its policies were sold primarily via some 2,400 small agent banks. Insurance in force was by then over $143 million.

In 1906 Bankers Life received a glowing recommendation from an insurance examiner who noted that the association's mortality and expense rates were both less than half the industry averages. The failure of other fraternal assessment life insurers, however, tainted its reputation. Soon after Temple died in 1909, the new leadership, under George Kuhns and Henry Nollen, decided to convert the association into a mutual insurer. In 1911, when the conversion was finally complete, the association became a company with nearly $500 million of insurance in force.

Expenses soared, but so too did the incentives of agents to push policies, and the company successfully innovated with "Life Paid Up at Seventy" and "Semi-Endowment" policies that proved extremely popular. The former policy provided that nobody who lived past age 70 had to continue to pay premiums; the latter paid half of the policy's face value at age 70, allowing consumption or reinvestment in an annuity product or other asset.

Meanwhile, Nollen, a 19th-century gentleman, and Kuhns, an upstart with an impoverished past, fought each other for control of the company. Kuhns triumphed because most of the agents were behind him and helped him to win an important proxy fight. He became president in 1916, a year after the fallout from the conversion had reduced insurance in force to $398 million. Thanks to a number of reforms, including raising the maximum policy payoff from $6,000 to $40,000,

new business streamed in from the states the association had already entered plus an additional 14 new ones and Washington, DC. By 1925 insurance in force had more than doubled to $844 million, and assets over that same span tripled, from $30 to $90 million.

Soon, the company had taken on all of the trappings of other big life insurers, including advertising campaigns, national conventions and colorful general agents like A.E. Nickelson, who drummed up business in central South Dakota by driving around with a keg of whiskey in his Model T (during Prohibition, no less). What better way to get the attention of a parched farmer trying to eke out a living on equally parched land? The company even ran a radio station, WHO, in the 1920s.

After Kuhns died in 1926, actuary Gerard Nollen, brother of the deposed Henry, became president. Nollen returned the company to many of its more conservative ways and saw it through the Great Depression, which did not strike the life insurance industry with anything like the force it hit the banking community. It did, however, lead to a spike in mortgage defaults and disability claims, as well as a dearth of new business. The company handled the many defaulted farm mortgages on its balance sheet by the mid-1930s by taking the titles, but then leasing the farms back to their former owners. Assets continued to grow every year of the Depression but amounted to only a $7 million increase in 1934.

Like many other insurers, the company scaled back its disability riders on new business as disability claims on existing policies soared. It also innovated yet again with a popular new "Family Protection Plan" that offered a bigger face value early in the policy's life to better protect minor dependents. Finally, it slashed expenses by cutting all salaries over $1,500 by 10%. Nollen also saw the company through a rash of lawsuits brought by disgruntled members of the old association. These were finally quashed by the US Supreme Court in 1931.

In 1941 Bankers Life made another monumental change in its business by entering the group life, accident, health, annuity and hospital insurance markets. Group insurance, which was sold to businesses rather than individuals and required different underwriting standards, called for the development of an entirely new sales force. By concentrating on small companies (25 or more employees) in the Midwest and taking advantage of the wage controls enacted during World War II (when companies competed for scarce workers by offering better fringe benefits) and new tax rules (allowing certain insurance costs to be written off as tax deductions), the company quickly developed a good book of group insurance business.

Marshall Field's store, Chicago, Illinois, ca. 1907-1910.

In 1943 an innovative new group product, "permanent group," sold well to companies like Marshall Field, Carrier Air Conditioning, the *Chicago Tribune*'s publishing company and other major employers. With that boost, insurance in force at Bankers hit $1 billion for the first time in 1945. The company's innovative policy form, however, was soon emulated by big, eastern life insurers, one in such a rush that it forgot to change Bankers Life to its own name at several spots in its contracts! Permanent group lost its momentum anyway when price controls were lifted after the war, but Bankers Life soon discovered a way to provide inexpensive but profitable group insurance to very small businesses, ones with just a handful of employees. By 1978, 80% of Banker Life's premiums stemmed from group insurance contracts.

Like other large mutual life insurance companies, Bankers Life in the postwar environment found it had to become a more sophisticated investor and more willing to take on risk where appropriate in order to maximize returns. The company that until the farm depression of the 1920s had prided itself on literally never losing a dollar on any investment had finally realized that ultraconservative investments meant ultralow returns. Its first move was to get out of farm mortgages and into urban ones. When the company hit the $1 billion asset mark in 1960, 41% of its invested assets were in urban mortgages and just 5% in farm loans. By 1969 farm loans had all but disappeared, and 7% of the company's assets were in common stocks, the asset class in which it had first invested less than a decade earlier.

In the late 1960s the company formed a slew of subsidiaries to handle new products like mutual funds, variable annuities and real estate investment trusts. It also updated its technology to keep up with the ever-increasing number of transactions it handled on behalf of its policyholders and clients. Computerization also transformed the work of actuaries, freeing their time and energy from the chains of laborious hand calculations. "We can do things now because we have the data that could never have been done in the past," actuary

1994 Lillehammer Winter Olympics pin featuring the Principal Financial Group logo.

C.L. Trowbridge explained. All the while the company continued to innovate with new policies and riders like Guaranteed Purchase Option, which allowed insureds to increase their coverage without the risk of being refused on medical grounds. Once again, however, other insurers soon copied its idea.

Even more frustrating to the company were the more than 50 upstart competitors that incorporated the word "Bankers" or even the phrase "Bankers Life" into their titles. Instead of chasing those companies with lawsuits, it at first decided to emphasize that it was "The" Bankers Life Company, which in 1978 had $27 billion of insurance in force and $5.8 billion in assets. In 1985, however, "The" company decided to jettison its old brand entirely and became Principal Financial Group (PFG).

By the early 1990s PFG had an extensive, mandatory in-house training program for new agents that sought to enhance their sales and general business skills, as well as their product knowledge and marketing prowess. The program was part of the company's broader "Network for Professional Studies," which included self and outside courses of study. A research study completed in 1994 concluded that training successfully increased trainee attitude, listening skills and ability to overcome objections by the same amount whether the training was conducted at agencies or in the home office.

PFG formed an online bank in 1998 that had about $2 billion in assets by June 2004. To form the bank, it adopted a mutual holding company organizational structure that also allowed it to make a major international push. Nevertheless, the company decided to demutualize in 2000 and, with help from demutualization specialist Goldman Sachs (#5), went public in the fall of 2001, shortly after the September 11 terrorist attacks. The attacks cost the company only about $6.5 million in direct claims, but the mood of the country made its IPO less successful than it might otherwise have been and decreased its share price.

By 2005 PFG employed nearly 14,000 people in 13 nations, including Australia, Brazil, Chile, China, Japan, Mexico and the UK, who serviced 4.7 million customers. By then it had $163 billion of insurance in force and serviced 49,000 employers' pension and 401(k) plans with about $170 billion of assets under management. It also had 800,000 mutual fund customers, making it one of the top 100 fund managers in the nation. In 2004 *Fortune* ranked it 211 on its "Largest 500 Corporations" list.

As a life and health insurer with a conservative balance sheet, PFG was more troubled by President Barack Obama's healthcare reforms in 2010 than the 2008 financial crisis. It did not need any bailouts because of the latter, but the former made it bail out of the health insurance market. It continued to grow organically nevertheless, and by early 2012 it was profitable and had $364 billion of assets under management. It also remained a great place to work, making *Working Mother's* "100 Best Companies" list for the 11th straight year.

Sources

Heinrich, Linda D. "A Corporate Training Evaluation Study at the Principal Financial Group." PhD diss., Drake University, 1994.

"J. Barry Griswell, Chief Executive Officer, Principal Financial Group (PFG)." *The IPO Reporter*, December 3, 2001, 6–7.

Loosvelt, Derek, et al. *The Vault Guide to the Top Financial Services Employers: 2006 Edition*. New York: Vault, 2005, 309–13.

"Making Mom's Life a Bit Easier: The Principal Financial Group Recognized." *Targeted News Service*, September 18, 2012.

"Principal Financial Group Drops on Weak 1Q Results." *LifeHealthPro*, April 30, 2012.

Wall, Joseph Frazier. *Policies and People: The First Hundred Years of the Bankers Life*. Englewood Cliffs, NJ: Prentice Hall, 1979.

Wright, Robert E. and George D. Smith. *Mutually Beneficial: The Guardian and Life Insurance in America*. New York: New York University Press, 2004.

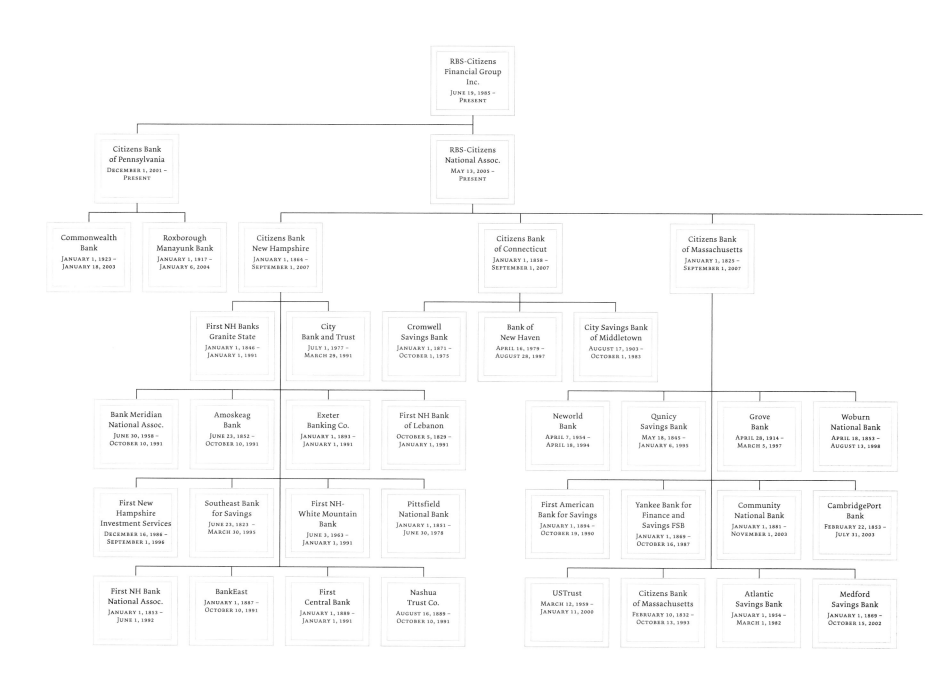

RBS-Citizens
Financial Group
Inc.
JUNE 19, 1985 –
PRESENT

Citizens Bank
of Pennsylvania
DECEMBER 1, 2001 –
PRESENT

RBS-Citizens
National Assoc.
MAY 13, 2005 –
PRESENT

Commonwealth
Bank
JANUARY 1, 1923 –
JANUARY 18, 2003

Roxborough
Manayunk Bank
JANUARY 1, 1917 –
JANUARY 6, 2004

Citizens Bank
New Hampshire
JANUARY 1, 1864 –
SEPTEMBER 1, 2007

Citizens Bank
of Connecticut
JANUARY 1, 1858 –
SEPTEMBER 1, 2007

Citizens Bank
of Massachusetts
JANUARY 1, 1825 –
SEPTEMBER 1, 2007

First NH Banks
Granite State
JANUARY 1, 1846 –
JANUARY 1, 1991

City
Bank and Trust
JULY 1, 1977 –
MARCH 29, 1991

Cromwell
Savings Bank
JANUARY 1, 1871 –
OCTOBER 1, 1975

Bank of
New Haven
APRIL 16, 1979 –
AUGUST 28, 1997

City Savings Bank
of Middletown
AUGUST 17, 1903 –
OCTOBER 1, 1983

Bank Meridian
National Assoc.
JUNE 30, 1958 –
OCTOBER 10, 1991

Amoskeag
Bank
JUNE 23, 1852 –
OCTOBER 10, 1991

Exeter
Banking Co.
JANUARY 1, 1893 –
JANUARY 1, 1991

First NH Bank
of Lebanon
OCTOBER 5, 1829 –
JANUARY 1, 1991

Neworld
Bank
APRIL 7, 1954 –
APRIL 18, 1994

Qunicy
Savings Bank
MAY 18, 1845 –
JANUARY 6, 1995

Grove
Bank
APRIL 28, 1914 –
MARCH 5, 1997

Woburn
National Bank
APRIL 18, 1853 –
AUGUST 13, 1998

First New
Hampshire
Investment Services
DECEMBER 16, 1986 –
SEPTEMBER 1, 1996

Southeast Bank
for Savings
JUNE 23, 1823 –
MARCH 30, 1995

First NH-
White Mountain
Bank
JUNE 3, 1963 –
JANUARY 1, 1991

Pittsfield
National Bank
JANUARY 1, 1851 –
JUNE 30, 1978

First American
Bank for Savings
JANUARY 1, 1894 –
OCTOBER 19, 1990

Yankee Bank for
Finance and
Savings FSB
JANUARY 1, 1869 –
OCTOBER 16, 1987

Community
National Bank
JANUARY 1, 1881 –
NOVEMBER 1, 2003

CambridgePort
Bank
FEBRUARY 22, 1853 –
JULY 31, 2003

First NH Bank
National Assoc.
JANUARY 1, 1853 –
JUNE 1, 1992

BankEast
JANUARY 1, 1887 –
OCTOBER 10, 1991

First
Central Bank
JANUARY 1, 1889 –
JANUARY 1, 1991

Nashua
Trust Co.
AUGUST 16, 1889 –
OCTOBER 10, 1991

USTrust
MARCH 12, 1959 –
JANUARY 11, 2000

Citizens Bank
of Massachusetts
FEBRUARY 10, 1832 –
OCTOBER 13, 1993

Atlantic
Savings Bank
JANUARY 1, 1954 –
MARCH 1, 1982

Medford
Savings Bank
JANUARY 1, 1869 –
OCTOBER 15, 2002

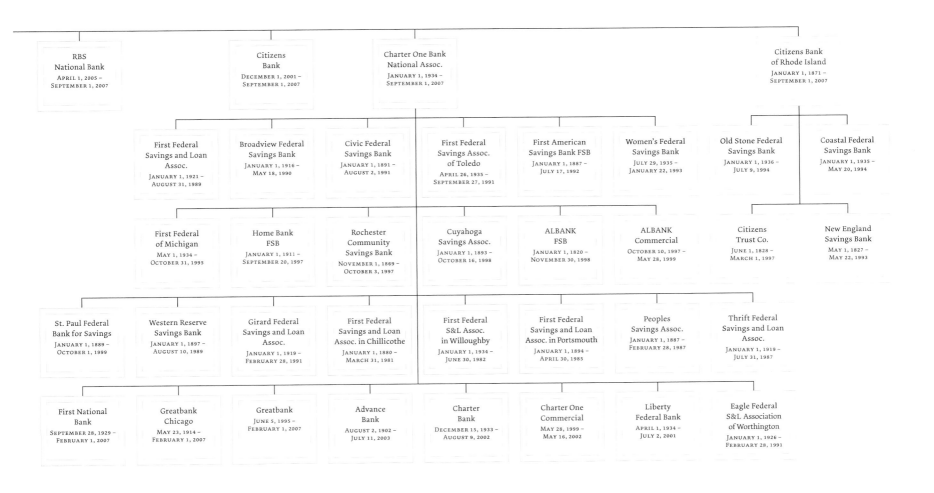

	RBS National Bank		Citizens Bank		Charter One Bank National Assoc.			Citizens Bank of Rhode Island
	APRIL 1, 2005 – SEPTEMBER 1, 2007		DECEMBER 1, 2001 – SEPTEMBER 1, 2007		JANUARY 1, 1934 – SEPTEMBER 1, 2007			JANUARY 1, 1871 – SEPTEMBER 1, 2007

First Federal Savings and Loan Assoc.
JANUARY 1, 1921 – AUGUST 31, 1989

Broadview Federal Savings Bank
JANUARY 1, 1916 – MAY 18, 1990

Civic Federal Savings Bank
JANUARY 1, 1891 – AUGUST 2, 1991

First Federal Savings Assoc. of Toledo
APRIL 26, 1935 – SEPTEMBER 27, 1991

First American Savings Bank FSB
JANUARY 1, 1887 – JULY 17, 1992

Women's Federal Savings Bank
JULY 29, 1935 – JANUARY 22, 1993

Old Stone Federal Savings Bank
JANUARY 1, 1936 – JULY 9, 1994

Coastal Federal Savings Bank
JANUARY 1, 1935 – MAY 20, 1994

First Federal of Michigan
MAY 1, 1934 – OCTOBER 31, 1995

Home Bank FSB
JANUARY 1, 1911 – SEPTEMBER 20, 1997

Rochester Community Savings Bank
NOVEMBER 1, 1869 – OCTOBER 3, 1997

Cuyahoga Savings Assoc.
JANUARY 1, 1893 – OCTOBER 16, 1998

ALBANK FSB
JANUARY 1, 1820 – NOVEMBER 30, 1998

ALBANK Commercial
OCTOBER 10, 1997 – MAY 28, 1999

Citizens Trust Co.
JUNE 1, 1828 – MARCH 1, 1997

New England Savings Bank
MAY 1, 1827 – MAY 22, 1993

St. Paul Federal Bank for Savings
JANUARY 1, 1889 – OCTOBER 1, 1999

Western Reserve Savings Bank
JANUARY 1, 1897 – AUGUST 10, 1989

Girard Federal Savings and Loan Assoc.
JANUARY 1, 1919 – FEBRUARY 28, 1991

First Federal Savings and Loan Assoc. in Chillicothe
JANUARY 1, 1880 – MARCH 31, 1981

First Federal S&L Assoc. in Willoughby
JANUARY 1, 1934 – JUNE 30, 1982

First Federal Savings and Loan Assoc. in Portsmouth
JANUARY 1, 1894 – APRIL 30, 1985

Peoples Savings Assoc.
JANUARY 1, 1887 – FEBRUARY 28, 1987

Thrift Federal Savings and Loan Assoc.
JANUARY 1, 1919 – JULY 31, 1987

First National Bank
SEPTEMBER 28, 1929 – FEBRUARY 1, 2007

Greatbank Chicago
MAY 23, 1914 – FEBRUARY 1, 2007

Greatbank
JUNE 5, 1995 – FEBRUARY 1, 2007

Advance Bank
AUGUST 2, 1902 – JULY 11, 2003

Charter Bank
DECEMBER 15, 1933 – AUGUST 9, 2002

Charter One Commercial
MAY 28, 1999 – MAY 16, 2002

Liberty Federal Bank
APRIL 1, 1934 – JULY 2, 2001

Eagle Federal S&L Association of Worthington
JANUARY 1, 1926 – FEBRUARY 28, 1991

RBS-Citizens Financial

Bank *(abridged)*

RANK	HEADQUARTERS	TICKER	ASSETS	EARLIEST KNOWN ANCESTOR	INDUSTRY OF ORIGIN
25	**Providence, RI**	**RBS**	**$122,500,000,000**	**1727**	**Commercial Banking**

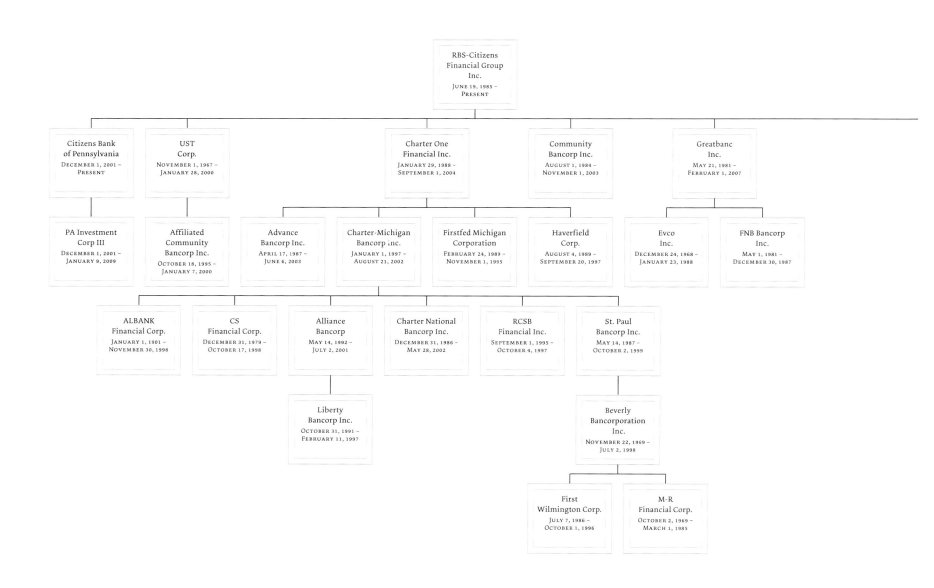

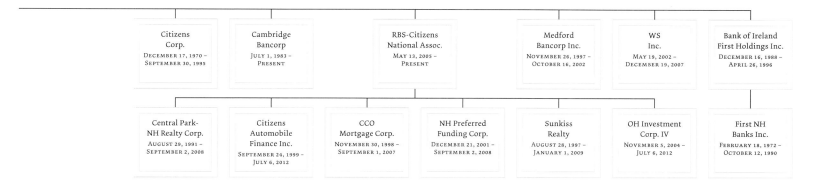

Citizens Corp.
DECEMBER 17, 1970 –
SEPTEMBER 30, 1995

Cambridge Bancorp
JULY 1, 1983 –
PRESENT

RBS-Citizens National Assoc.
MAY 13, 2005 –
PRESENT

Medford Bancorp Inc.
NOVEMBER 26, 1997 –
OCTOBER 16, 2002

WS Inc.
MAY 19, 2002 –
DECEMBER 19, 2007

Bank of Ireland First Holdings Inc.
DECEMBER 16, 1988 –
APRIL 26, 1996

Central Park-NH Realty Corp.
AUGUST 29, 1991 –
SEPTEMBER 2, 2008

Citizens Automobile Finance Inc.
SEPTEMBER 24, 1999 –
JULY 6, 2012

CCO Mortgage Corp.
NOVEMBER 30, 1998 –
SEPTEMBER 1, 2007

NH Preferred Funding Corp.
DECEMBER 21, 2001 –
SEPTEMBER 2, 2008

Sunkiss Realty
AUGUST 28, 1997 –
JANUARY 1, 2009

OH Investment Corp. IV
NOVEMBER 5, 2004 –
JULY 6, 2012

First NH Banks Inc.
FEBRUARY 18, 1972 –
OCTOBER 12, 1990

RBS-Citizens Financial   Holding Company *(abridged)*

18ᵗʰ century RBS note featuring the portrait of King George II.

Company of Scotland minute book title page, 1696.

The Royal Bank of Scotland, the RBS side of this BHC, received a charter from King George in 1727. It arose from the ashes of an international financial fiasco, the ill-fated Darien Scheme. In 1695 William Paterson and some 2,000 other Scots formed the Company of Scotland in an attempt to improve their own fortunes and those of their homeland. Three years later the company tried to colonize the Isthmus of Panama and, hence, monopolize the growing trade between the nations of the Atlantic and Pacific Oceans. The expedition had failed by early 1700, a victim of hubris, disease, Spanish raids and piracy. Eleven ships and 2,000 lives were lost, along with most of the stockholders' money.

The fiasco helped smooth the way for the creation of Great Britain, the Treaty of Union formed by England and Scotland in May 1707. As part of the deal, England paid the Scots almost £400,000, some of which was earmarked to compensate the victims of the Darien Scheme. Societies formed to protect the interests of those who were due money, and in 1724 one of them established the Equivalent Company and began lending out funds on behalf of former Company of Scotland shareholders. After the Bank of Scotland rebuffed its merger overture, the Equivalent Company decided to form its own bank. Thus, the Royal Bank of Scotland was born and headquartered in Edinburgh.

Both Scottish banks thrived along with Scotland's economy, which over the 18ᵗʰ century commercialized and then industrialized. The Royal Bank, in particular, developed a reputation for conservative innovation—inventing new products, such as overdrafts, without taking on excessive risks. As new banks, like the Ayr, arose and crashed, the Royal Bank moved ahead, through the age of steam and into that of electricity. It occasionally got into trouble, but its expanding network of branches helped it to recover. By the late 19ᵗʰ century it had a well-deserved reputation for probity. Its deposits grew, but slowly, from about £8.1 million in 1865 to £44.2 million in 1927, when profits were still under half a million pounds per year. That same year, the bank celebrated its bicentennial, and Sir Alexander K. Wright prophesized the bank would survive another century. It would not, at least not in a form recognizable to Wright or any of the bank's founders.

For the next six decades, the Royal Bank muddled along, through the Great Depression, World War II and Scotland's painful deindustrialization. It made a few acquisitions, opened an office in New York in 1960 and became Scotland's biggest bank when it bought National Commercial Bank of Scotland in 1969. But the bank was still not large by international standards and was decidedly not dynamic. Lloyds tried to buy it in 1979, and soon after so too did Standard Charter and Hong Kong and Shanghai Banking Corporation (now HSBC [#11]), but all of the deals faltered for one reason or another.

In 1987, in the wake of those close calls, George Mathewson, a Scottish nationalist trained as an engineer, joined the bank and encouraged it to purchase Citizens, a US bank, the following year. Formed as a mutual in Providence, Rhode Island, in 1828, Citizens had

NatWest piggy banks encouraging children to save.

Postcard featuring the Citizens Savings Bank building.

recently demutualized and formed a BHC in 1985. Royal Bank paid $440 million for the bank, which thrived under its new ownership.

Larry Fish ran Citizens for RBS, and he and his bank were focused on the three Cs: "customers, colleagues and community." For the most part RBS left Citizens alone, as long as it generated sufficient profits. A good part of that profit growth came from acquisitions, such as Mellon Financial and Charter One, which extended Citizens's reach into Mid-Atlantic and Midwestern markets.

Thanks to the successful Citizens acquisition, Mathewson took the inside track for the Royal Bank's top spot. As profits dwindled to almost nothing in the early 1990s, Mathewson and his allies radically reorganized the bank and significantly cut its staff in the process. The bank's share price and profitability improved considerably, from £265 million in 1993 to £695 million in 1997, but so too did its risk profile.

Mathewson was knighted in 1999 and allowed to handpick his successor. He chose Fred Goodwin, an accountant from Paisley, Scotland. Goodwin excelled at accounting because his brain was quick, methodical and logical. After a stint at Touche Ross, where he helped sort out the BCCI (Bank of Credit and Commerce International) scandal, the hypercompetitive Goodwin in 1995 took over the top post at the Clydesdale Bank, a Glasgow standard since the 1830s that had been recently acquired by National Australia Bank. Goodwin had a knack for making big deals. Under his leadership, RBS grew by leaps and bounds by acquiring banks, such as NatWest and ABN AMRO, that were several times its size. Along the way, RBS won a victory over its longtime rival, the Bank of Scotland, which also had tried to take over NatWest.

Goodwin and his team did a good job of integrating its early acquisitions, but as RBS itself grew, the sprawling institution became increasingly difficult to manage. After some flattering publicity about his achievements in *Forbes* and *Harvard Business Review*, as well as a knighthood, Goodwin moved to fulfill his promise to make RBS the world's largest bank. Investors took note and punished the bank's stock, but Goodwin persisted. Although its investment banking arm never became bulge bracket, RBS did become, briefly, the world's largest bank in terms of assets and a significant force in terms of employees (135,000) and worldwide offices (2,300).

The bank's executives and British regulators—the Bank of England, the Financial Services Authority and the Treasury—were blinded by their own seeming successes, giant bonuses and free market ideologies. Savvier investors realized the poor quality of much of RBS's

holdings, such as derivatives like CDOs (collateralized debt obligations) and CDSs (credit default swaps), the value of which depended on the continued buoyancy of real estate prices in America.

By the winter of 2007 the seemingly mighty Scottish financial empire began to unravel. RBS managed to raise additional capital, but depositors—big corporations with balances in the tens to hundreds of millions—began to pull their funds out of the bank. Other banks and big lenders also became increasingly hesitant to lend to RBS for more than a few days at a time.

After the meltdown of Lehman Brothers, Fannie Mae and other major financial institutions in the United States in August and September 2008, Goodwin said his bank faced a mere "liquidity" pinch, meaning it simply could not raise enough cash to operate in a difficult economic environment because of its large needs. Many realized, however, that the bank was insolvent, and that the value of its liabilities far exceeded the value of its assets.

Fearing a major financial collapse if RBS were allowed to go bankrupt, the British government finally interceded on October 8, 2008 by nationalizing the bank. Goodwin and most of the directors and top executives left with large severance packages, but stockholders did not see a dividend for years after the crisis.

In the end, to keep the bank going, the government had to inject over £45 billion of taxpayer money, for which it took an 80% ownership stake in the institution. The government could not keep the bank in line, as the LIBOR and other scandals revealed. However, it successfully reined in RBS's investment banking activities, and in early 2013 it announced plans to sell off Citizens Bank.

Sources

Colchester, Max and Patrick Margot. "RBS Heeds Call to Cede US Ground." *Wall Street Journal*, March 1, 2013, C1.

Loosvelt, Derek, et al. *The Vault Guide to the Top 50 Banking Employers: 2008 Edition.* New York: Vault, 2007, 178–81.

Martin, Iain. *Making It Happen: Fred Goodwin, RBS and the Men Who Blew Up the British Economy.* London: Simon & Schuster, 2013.

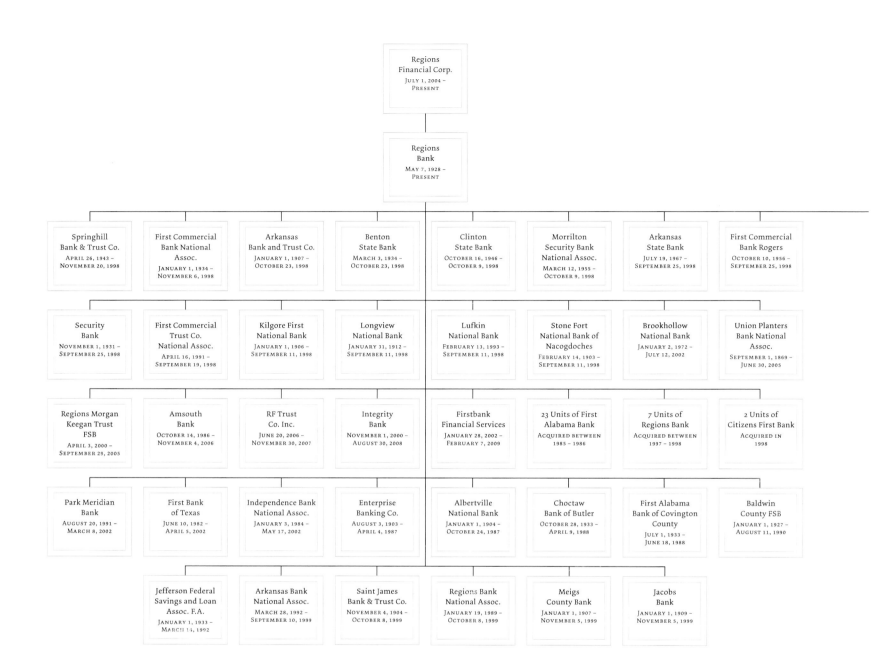

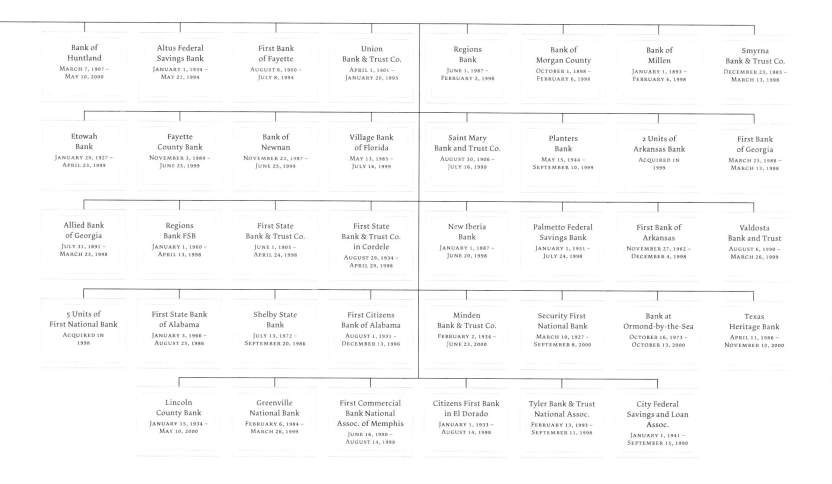

Bank of Huntland MARCH 7, 1907 – MAY 10, 2000	**Altus Federal Savings Bank** JANUARY 1, 1934 – MAY 21, 1994	**First Bank of Fayette** AUGUST 6, 1900 – JULY 8, 1994	**Union Bank & Trust Co.** APRIL 1, 1901 – JANUARY 20, 1995	**Regions Bank** JUNE 1, 1987 – FEBRUARY 2, 1998	**Bank of Morgan County** OCTOBER 1, 1898 – FEBRUARY 6, 1998	**Bank of Millen** JANUARY 1, 1893 – FEBRUARY 6, 1998	**Smyrna Bank & Trust Co.** DECEMBER 23, 1985 – MARCH 13, 1998
Etowah Bank JANUARY 29, 1927 – APRIL 23, 1999	**Fayette County Bank** NOVEMBER 3, 1989 – JUNE 25, 1999	**Bank of Newnan** NOVEMBER 23, 1987 – JUNE 25, 1999	**Village Bank of Florida** MAY 13, 1985 – JULY 16, 1999	**Saint Mary Bank and Trust Co.** AUGUST 30, 1906 – JULY 16, 1999	**Planters Bank** MAY 15, 1944 – SEPTEMBER 10, 1999	**2 Units of Arkansas Bank** ACQUIRED IN 1999	**First Bank of Georgia** MARCH 25, 1988 – MARCH 13, 1998
Allied Bank of Georgia JULY 31, 1891 – MARCH 23, 1998	**Regions Bank FSB** JANUARY 1, 1960 – APRIL 13, 1998	**First State Bank & Trust Co.** JUNE 1, 1905 – APRIL 24, 1998	**First State Bank & Trust Co. in Cordele** AUGUST 29, 1934 – APRIL 29, 1998	**New Iberia Bank** JANUARY 1, 1887 – JUNE 20, 1998	**Palmetto Federal Savings Bank** JANUARY 1, 1951 – JULY 24, 1998	**First Bank of Arkansas** NOVEMBER 27, 1962 – DECEMBER 4, 1998	**Valdosta Bank and Trust** AUGUST 6, 1990 – MARCH 26, 1999
5 Units of First National Bank ACQUIRED IN 1998	**First State Bank of Alabama** JANUARY 3, 1966 – AUGUST 25, 1986	**Shelby State Bank** JULY 13, 1972 – SEPTEMBER 20, 1986	**First Citizens Bank of Alabama** AUGUST 1, 1931 – DECEMBER 13, 1986	**Minden Bank & Trust Co.** FEBRUARY 2, 1934 – JUNE 23, 2000	**Security First National Bank** MARCH 10, 1927 – SEPTEMBER 8, 2000	**Bank at Ormond-by-the-Sea** OCTOBER 16, 1973 – OCTOBER 13, 2000	**Texas Heritage Bank** APRIL 11, 1986 – NOVEMBER 10, 2000
	Lincoln County Bank JANUARY 15, 1934 – MAY 10, 2000	**Greenville National Bank** FEBRUARY 6, 1984 – MARCH 26, 1999	**First Commercial Bank National Assoc. of Memphis** JUNE 16, 1990 – AUGUST 14, 1998	**Citizens First Bank in El Dorado** JANUARY 1, 1933 – AUGUST 14, 1998	**Tyler Bank & Trust National Assoc.** FEBRUARY 13, 1993 – SEPTEMBER 11, 1998	**City Federal Savings and Loan Assoc.** JANUARY 1, 1941 – SEPTEMBER 15, 1990	

Regions Financial

Bank *(abridged)*

RANK	HEADQUARTERS	TICKER	ASSETS	EARLIEST KNOWN ANCESTOR	INDUSTRY OF ORIGIN
24	**Birmingham, AL**	**NYCB**	**$119,000,000,000**	**1820**	**Commercial Banking**

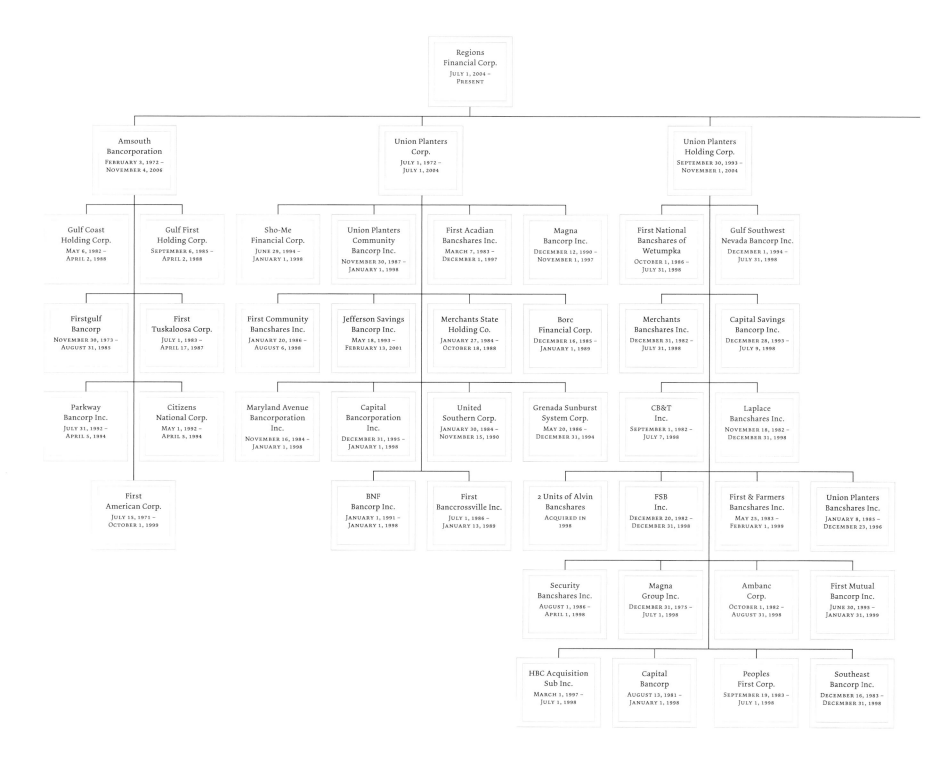

Regions Financial Corp.
JULY 1, 2004 –
PRESENT

Amsouth Bancorporation
FEBRUARY 3, 1972 –
NOVEMBER 4, 2006

Union Planters Corp.
JULY 1, 1972 –
JULY 1, 2004

Union Planters Holding Corp.
SEPTEMBER 30, 1993 –
NOVEMBER 1, 2004

Gulf Coast Holding Corp.
MAY 6, 1982 –
APRIL 2, 1988

Gulf First Holding Corp.
SEPTEMBER 6, 1985 –
APRIL 2, 1988

Sho-Me Financial Corp.
JUNE 29, 1994 –
JANUARY 1, 1998

Union Planters Community Bancorp Inc.
NOVEMBER 30, 1987 –
JANUARY 1, 1998

First Acadian Bancshares Inc.
MARCH 7, 1983 –
DECEMBER 1, 1997

Magna Bancorp Inc.
DECEMBER 12, 1990 –
NOVEMBER 1, 1997

First National Bancshares of Wetumpka
OCTOBER 1, 1986 –
JULY 31, 1998

Gulf Southwest Nevada Bancorp Inc.
DECEMBER 1, 1994 –
JULY 31, 1998

Firstgulf Bancorp
NOVEMBER 30, 1973 –
AUGUST 31, 1985

First Tuskaloosa Corp.
JULY 1, 1983 –
APRIL 17, 1987

First Community Bancshares Inc.
JANUARY 20, 1986 –
AUGUST 6, 1998

Jefferson Savings Bancorp Inc.
MAY 18, 1993 –
FEBRUARY 13, 2001

Merchants State Holding Co.
JANUARY 27, 1984 –
OCTOBER 18, 1988

Borc Financial Corp.
DECEMBER 16, 1985 –
JANUARY 1, 1989

Merchants Bancshares Inc.
DECEMBER 31, 1982 –
JULY 31, 1998

Capital Savings Bancorp Inc.
DECEMBER 28, 1993 –
JULY 9, 1998

Parkway Bancorp Inc.
JULY 31, 1992 –
APRIL 5, 1994

Citizens National Corp.
MAY 1, 1992 –
APRIL 5, 1994

Maryland Avenue Bancorporation Inc.
NOVEMBER 16, 1984 –
JANUARY 1, 1998

Capital Bancorporation Inc.
DECEMBER 31, 1995 –
JANUARY 1, 1998

United Southern Corp.
JANUARY 30, 1984 –
NOVEMBER 15, 1990

Grenada Sunburst System Corp.
MAY 20, 1986 –
DECEMBER 31, 1994

CB&T Inc.
SEPTEMBER 1, 1982 –
JULY 7, 1998

Laplace Bancshares Inc.
NOVEMBER 18, 1982 –
DECEMBER 31, 1998

First American Corp.
JULY 15, 1971 –
OCTOBER 1, 1999

BNF Bancorp Inc.
JANUARY 1, 1991 –
JANUARY 1, 1998

First Banccrossville Inc.
JULY 1, 1986 –
JANUARY 13, 1989

2 Units of Alvin Bancshares
ACQUIRED IN
1998

FSB Inc.
DECEMBER 20, 1982 –
DECEMBER 31, 1998

First & Farmers Bancshares Inc.
MAY 25, 1983 –
FEBRUARY 1, 1999

Union Planters Bancshares Inc.
JANUARY 8, 1985 –
DECEMBER 23, 1996

Security Bancshares Inc.
AUGUST 1, 1986 –
APRIL 1, 1998

Magna Group Inc.
DECEMBER 31, 1975 –
JULY 1, 1998

Ambanc Corp.
OCTOBER 1, 1982 –
AUGUST 31, 1998

First Mutual Bancorp Inc.
JUNE 30, 1995 –
JANUARY 31, 1999

HBC Acquisition Sub Inc.
MARCH 1, 1997 –
JULY 1, 1998

Capital Bancorp
AUGUST 13, 1981 –
JANUARY 1, 1998

Peoples First Corp.
SEPTEMBER 19, 1983 –
JULY 1, 1998

Southeast Bancorp Inc.
DECEMBER 16, 1983 –
DECEMBER 31, 1998

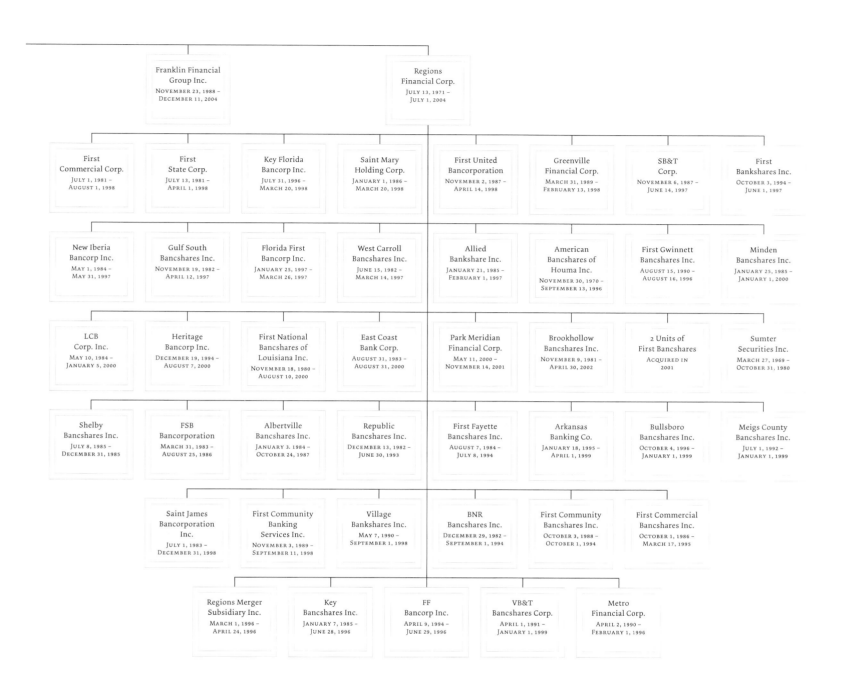

Franklin Financial
Group Inc.
NOVEMBER 23, 1988 –
DECEMBER 11, 2004

Regions
Financial Corp.
JULY 13, 1971 –
JULY 1, 2004

First
Commercial Corp.
JULY 1, 1981 –
AUGUST 1, 1998

First
State Corp.
JULY 13, 1981 –
APRIL 1, 1998

Key Florida
Bancorp Inc.
JULY 31, 1996 –
MARCH 20, 1998

Saint Mary
Holding Corp.
JANUARY 1, 1986 –
MARCH 20, 1998

First United
Bancorporation
NOVEMBER 2, 1987 –
APRIL 14, 1998

Greenville
Financial Corp.
MARCH 31, 1989 –
FEBRUARY 13, 1998

SB&T
Corp.
NOVEMBER 6, 1987 –
JUNE 14, 1997

First
Bankshares Inc.
OCTOBER 3, 1994 –
JUNE 1, 1997

New Iberia
Bancorp Inc.
MAY 1, 1984 –
MAY 31, 1997

Gulf South
Bancshares Inc.
NOVEMBER 19, 1982 –
APRIL 12, 1997

Florida First
Bancorp Inc.
JANUARY 25, 1997 –
MARCH 26, 1997

West Carroll
Bancshares Inc.
JUNE 15, 1982 –
MARCH 14, 1997

Allied
Bankshare Inc.
JANUARY 21, 1985 –
FEBRUARY 1, 1997

American
Bancshares of
Houma Inc.
NOVEMBER 30, 1970 –
SEPTEMBER 13, 1996

First Gwinnett
Bancshares Inc.
AUGUST 15, 1990 –
AUGUST 16, 1996

Minden
Bancshares Inc.
JANUARY 25, 1985 –
JANUARY 1, 2000

LCB
Corp. Inc.
MAY 10, 1984 –
JANUARY 5, 2000

Heritage
Bancorp Inc.
DECEMBER 19, 1994 –
AUGUST 7, 2000

First National
Bancshares of
Louisiana Inc.
NOVEMBER 18, 1980 –
AUGUST 10, 2000

East Coast
Bank Corp.
AUGUST 31, 1983 –
AUGUST 31, 2000

Park Meridian
Financial Corp.
MAY 11, 2000 –
NOVEMBER 14, 2001

Brookhollow
Bancshares Inc.
NOVEMBER 9, 1981 –
APRIL 30, 2002

2 Units of
First Bancshares
ACQUIRED IN
2001

Sumter
Securities Inc.
MARCH 27, 1969 –
OCTOBER 31, 1980

Shelby
Bancshares Inc.
JULY 8, 1985 –
DECEMBER 31, 1985

FSB
Bancorporation
MARCH 31, 1983 –
AUGUST 25, 1986

Albertville
Bancshares Inc.
JANUARY 3, 1984 –
OCTOBER 24, 1987

Republic
Bancshares Inc.
DECEMBER 13, 1982 –
JUNE 30, 1993

First Fayette
Bancshares Inc.
AUGUST 7, 1984 –
JULY 8, 1994

Arkansas
Banking Co.
JANUARY 18, 1995 –
APRIL 1, 1999

Bullsboro
Bancshares Inc.
OCTOBER 4, 1996 –
JANUARY 1, 1999

Meigs County
Bancshares Inc.
JULY 1, 1992 –
JANUARY 1, 1999

Saint James
Bancorporation
Inc.
JULY 1, 1983 –
DECEMBER 31, 1998

First Community
Banking
Services Inc.
NOVEMBER 3, 1989 –
SEPTEMBER 11, 1998

Village
Bankshares Inc.
MAY 7, 1990 –
SEPTEMBER 1, 1998

BNR
Bancshares Inc.
DECEMBER 29, 1982 –
SEPTEMBER 1, 1994

First Community
Bancshares Inc.
OCTOBER 3, 1988 –
OCTOBER 1, 1994

First Commercial
Bancshares Inc.
OCTOBER 1, 1986 –
MARCH 17, 1995

Regions Merger
Subsidiary Inc.
MARCH 1, 1996 –
APRIL 24, 1996

Key
Bancshares Inc.
JANUARY 7, 1985 –
JUNE 28, 1996

FF
Bancorp Inc.
APRIL 9, 1994 –
JUNE 29, 1996

VB&T
Bancshares Corp.
APRIL 1, 1991 –
JANUARY 1, 1999

Metro
Financial Corp.
APRIL 2, 1990 –
FEBRUARY 1, 1996

Regions Financial

Holding Company *(abridged)*

First National Bank building in Huntsville, Alabama, 1934.

Regions Financial has a long and winding history that begins with the chartering of the Bank of the State of Alabama in 1820. That bank, which had an authorized capitalization of $2 million, had difficulty raising capital. In late 1823 the state government amended the charter and became the sole subscriber by selling its bonds in New York for cash. Thus, the bank did not begin operations until 1824.

Initially headquartered in Cahaba, it moved to the new state capital of Tuscaloosa two years later. The bank, which was staffed solely by political appointees, was doomed from the beginning, but not before it created a statewide branch network, including an office in Huntsville established in 1835. The Bank of the State died in the early 1840s, but in 1852 the remainder of its Huntsville branch was chartered as the Northern Bank of Alabama. It became the National Bank of Huntsville in 1865. During the Civil War, its cashier saved its assets from marauding Union troops by hiding them in the chimney and refusing to disclose their location even under the threat of hanging. Apparently there was not much to hide, as the bank was initially capitalized at $100,000; in 1870 it had assets of only $275,000, and its asset base actually shrank to $267,400 by 1875. The institution changed its name to the First National Bank of Huntsville in 1889.

The second Regions lineage began in 1871 as the First National Bank of Montgomery, which by 1875 already had assets of over $521,000. By 1910 it was the state's second largest national bank with assets of $4.2 million. At the end of World War I, it organized the First Joint Stock Land Bank to make real estate loans under a 1916 federal law. (All such institutions stopped making loans in 1933 and were liquidated completely by 1951.)

From its inception until 1931, the First National was run by just three men: Dr. William Owen Baldwin (1871–1886), an early president of the American Medical Association; his son, Abram Martin Baldwin (1898–1931); and Henry Clay Tompkins (1886–1898), an in-law of the Baldwins. Along the way, they bought up a half dozen banks in the city and did not even miss a dividend payment during the Great Depression, making it one of the few banks in the country so well-situated. They even foreclosed on another bank, the Fourth National. After the war, the bank opened Montgomery's first military-based and hospital-based bank branches, as well as its first ATM.

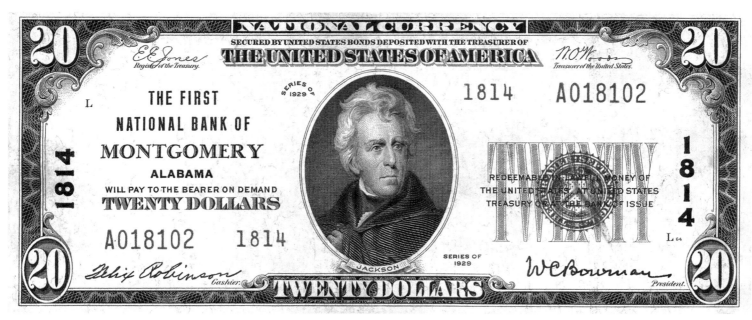

First National Bank of Montgomery $20 note.

The third Regions lineage began in 1928 with Birmingham's Exchange Bank. Established to serve the city's bankless but tony south side, it was one of the first three Alabama banks allowed to reopen after the bank holiday of 1933. In 1947 it became the first bank in Birmingham to offer a parking lot and a drive-in teller window. It became Exchange Security in 1957 when it merged with Security Commercial. In 1959 it added American Bank and Trust Company of Bessemer, just west of Birmingham.

The three lineages came together during the "credit crunch" of the late 1960s. Frank Plummer, president of the First National Bank of Montgomery, couldn't lend to Blount Brothers Construction because it needed more cash than the bank could provide, not because it was a bad credit risk. Plummer, a former New Yorker who worked as a clerk at Marine Midland (now part of #11) during the Great Depression, also thought that by growing larger, the bank could tap scale economies, attract better talent and spur a more liquid market for its stock.

Robert Lowry of First National Bank of Huntsville and Norman Pless of Exchange Security Bank were thinking along the same lines as Plummer, so in 1970 the three moved to create a multibank holding company called First Alabama Bancshares. They sold their banks to it in 1971, after the Federal Reserve approved its application to become the state's first BHC. (By the end of the decade the number of Alabama BHCs had grown to six.)

Plummer became president and CEO, Lowry board chairman and Pless vice chairman. The BHC began with assets of approximately $550 million, but by the middle of the first decade of the third millennium that figure had grown to $93.5 billion.

Growth started in 1972 with the acquisition of Real Estate Financing. Over the next decade, First Alabama purchased almost two dozen small banks throughout Alabama, culminating in 1981 with the acquisition of Merchants National, the largest bank in Mobile. It was the only major market in the state where the bank had previously lacked a presence. Along with the deal came Carl E. Jones, a future Regions CEO.

Thanks to the merger, assets hit $2 billion in 1980 and $3 billion just 18 months later, which was good news for profits when return on assets hit 1.3%, the highest of any bank in the sunbelt. Its return on equity was second best in the Southeast for BHCs with more than $1 billion in assets. Such performance allowed it to increase dividends every year for an entire decade, which put it on Moody's "Dividend Achievers" list. An investor of $100 would have had $348 in 1983 if she went with First Alabama, but only $250 if she opted instead for a Dow Jones Industrial Average index fund.

By 1983 First Alabama had 3,500 employees and 124 offices that serviced areas containing 70% of the state's population. It also owned five nonbanking subsidiaries: a mortgage company that operated in Alabama, Florida, Georgia and Texas; a leasing company; a credit card issuer; an insurer; and an investment advisor, all of which were profitable. The bank was looking forward to legislation allowing it to branch across state lines, but Plummer warned that it would "stay with fundamentals." Prudence, profit, customer service and employee motivation were his mantras.

In 1987 the bank's attorney, R.E. Steiner III, developed a device that allowed the formation of de novo branches across county lines, which was still illegal in Alabama. That same year, after a regional interstate branching accord was reached, the bank jumped into the Florida Panhandle by acquiring a bank in Milton. In 1990 First Alabama opened 38 new branches, several of which stemmed from the acquisition of defunct federal savings and loans from the Resolution Trust Corporation.

In 1993 the bank operated in seven states, and its assets surpassed $10 billion. It discovered, however, that people outside Alabama did not want to do business with a bank that had the same name as their hated football rival (The Alabama Crimson Tide). So it changed its name to Regions and continued growing.

In 1996 Regions added FNB and its $3.2 billion in assets and branches in central Florida and Georgia. Two years later, it bought up First Commercial and its network of branches in Arkansas, Texas and Tennessee for $7.3 billion. In 2001 it purchased Rebsamen, the sixth largest bank-owned insurance agency in the country. It also bought Memphis-based investment firm Morgan Keegan that year for $789 million.

In 2004 Jones noted that Regions had increased dividends every year since its inception, a streak of 33 years, and credited the bank's success to "solid finances." He also lauded the bank's employees as "people who will make the difference" and who "clearly articulate the values and vision that bind them together as societal pressures seek to rip them apart."

The "Regions Vision," he said, was to "help our customers and communities realize their dreams by anticipating, understanding and meeting financial needs through responsive associates — who have the ability to build effective solutions." That vision could be achieved, Jones stated, by optimizing shareholder value, thinking collaboratively, continuously increasing service quality, building human capital in employees, respecting employees and customers, creating a work-life balance and "doing the right thing."

In 2004 Regions joined the top 15 rankings by merging with Union Planters Corporation of Memphis, expanding its footprint to 15 states and five million customers and its assets to $85 billion. Two years later, Regions merged with AmSouth Bancorporation to create a top-10 bank with assets in excess of $140 billion. By 2007 Regions had almost 36,000 employees in some 2,000 offices spread across the Midwest and South. That year it sold EquiFirst Corporation, its subprime mortgage origination business, to Barclays Bank for a mere $76 million, a reflection, no doubt, of the first tremors of the financial earthquake to follow.

Like many other banks, Regions was impacted by the 2008 financial crisis with large losses on real estate loans that led to hundreds of millions in losses through 2011. As a result, Regions needed to access $3.5 billion in government TARP funds. By early 2012, however, its credit quality had improved enough to drive its stock price up dramatically.

Sources

Curtis, Wayne C. *Establishing and Preserving Confidence: The Role of Banking Alabama, 1816–1994.* Troy, AL: Troy State University, 1994.

Fitzpatrick, Dan. "Bank's Reporting Under Fire: SEC, Others Examining Whether Regions Financial Improperly Classified Bad Loans." *Wall Street Journal*, December 24, 2012, C1.

Jones, Carl E., Jr. *Regions Financial Corporation: Strength, Stability and Growth in Financial Services.* Exton, PA: Newcomen Society, 2004.

Loosvelt, Derek, et al. *The Vault Guide to the Top 50 Banking Employers: 2008 Edition.* New York: Vault, 2007, 379–82.

Peters, Andy. "Lingering Legal Exposure Hangs Over Regions Financial's Revival." *American Banker*, September 9, 2013, 3.

Plummer, Frank A. *First Alabama Bancshares: An Outstanding Record of Performance.* New York: Newcomen Society, 1984.

Rieker, Matthias. "Regions Financial's Profit Triples." *Wall Street Journal Online*, July 24, 2012.

Rieker, Matthias and Saabira Chaudhuri. "Regions Financial Swings to Profit." *Wall Street Journal Online*, January 22, 2013.

Merchants National Bank sign displaying the time and temperature, 1955.

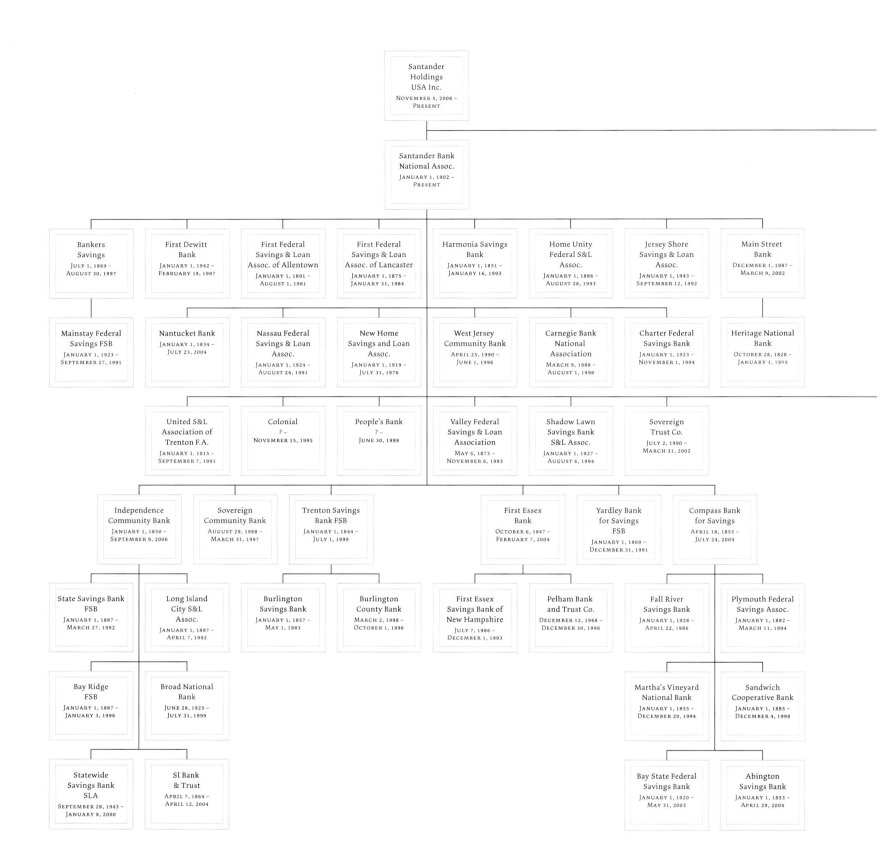

Santander
Holdings
USA Inc.
NOVEMBER 5, 2008 –
PRESENT

Santander Bank
National Assoc.
JANUARY 1, 1902 –
PRESENT

Bankers
Savings
JULY 1, 1869 –
AUGUST 30, 1997

First Dewitt
Bank
JANUARY 1, 1942 –
FEBRUARY 19, 1997

First Federal
Savings & Loan
Assoc. of Allentown
JANUARY 1, 1891 –
AUGUST 1, 1981

First Federal
Savings & Loan
Assoc. of Lancaster
JANUARY 1, 1875 –
JANUARY 31, 1984

Harmonia Savings
Bank
JANUARY 1, 1851 –
JANUARY 16, 1993

Home Unity
Federal S&L
Assoc.
JANUARY 1, 1886 –
AUGUST 28, 1993

Jersey Shore
Savings & Loan
Assoc.
JANUARY 1, 1943 –
SEPTEMBER 12, 1992

Main Street
Bank
DECEMBER 1, 1987 –
MARCH 9, 2002

Mainstay Federal
Savings FSB
JANUARY 1, 1923 –
SEPTEMBER 27, 1991

Nantucket Bank
JANUARY 1, 1834 –
JULY 23, 2004

Nassau Federal
Savings & Loan
Assoc.
JANUARY 1, 1924 –
AUGUST 24, 1991

New Home
Savings and Loan
Assoc.
JANUARY 1, 1919 –
JULY 31, 1976

West Jersey
Community Bank
APRIL 25, 1990 –
JUNE 1, 1996

Carnegie Bank
National
Association
MARCH 9, 1988 –
AUGUST 1, 1998

Charter Federal
Savings Bank
JANUARY 1, 1923 –
NOVEMBER 1, 1994

Heritage National
Bank
OCTOBER 28, 1828 –
JANUARY 1, 1999

United S&L
Association of
Trenton F.A.
JANUARY 1, 1915 –
SEPTEMBER 7, 1991

Colonial
? –
NOVEMBER 15, 1995

People's Bank
? –
JUNE 30, 1999

Valley Federal
Savings & Loan
Association
MAY 6, 1873 –
NOVEMBER 6, 1993

Shadow Lawn
Savings Bank
S&L Assoc.
JANUARY 1, 1927 –
AUGUST 6, 1994

Sovereign
Trust Co.
JULY 2, 1990 –
MARCH 31, 2002

Independence
Community Bank
JANUARY 1, 1850 –
SEPTEMBER 9, 2006

Sovereign
Community Bank
AUGUST 29, 1988 –
MARCH 31, 1997

Trenton Savings
Bank FSB
JANUARY 1, 1844 –
JULY 1, 1999

First Essex
Bank
OCTOBER 6, 1847 –
FEBRUARY 7, 2004

Yardley Bank
for Savings
FSB
JANUARY 1, 1869 –
DECEMBER 31, 1991

Compass Bank
for Savings
APRIL 18, 1855 –
JULY 24, 2004

State Savings Bank
FSB
JANUARY 1, 1887 –
MARCH 27, 1992

Long Island
City S&L
Assoc.
JANUARY 1, 1887 –
APRIL 7, 1992

Burlington
Savings Bank
JANUARY 1, 1857 –
MAY 1, 1983

Burlington
County Bank
MARCH 2, 1998 –
OCTOBER 1, 1996

First Essex
Savings Bank of
New Hampshire
JULY 7, 1986 –
DECEMBER 1, 1993

Pelham Bank
and Trust Co.
DECEMBER 12, 1968 –
DECEMBER 30, 1996

Fall River
Savings Bank
JANUARY 1, 1928 –
APRIL 22, 1986

Plymouth Federal
Savings Assoc.
JANUARY 1, 1882 –
MARCH 11, 1994

Bay Ridge
FSB
JANUARY 1, 1887 –
JANUARY 3, 1996

Broad National
Bank
JUNE 28, 1925 –
JULY 31, 1999

Martha's Vineyard
National Bank
JANUARY 1, 1855 –
DECEMBER 29, 1994

Sandwich
Cooperative Bank
JANUARY 1, 1885 –
DECEMBER 4, 1998

Statewide
Savings Bank
SLA
SEPTEMBER 28, 1943 –
JANUARY 8, 2000

SI Bank
& Trust
APRIL 7, 1864 –
APRIL 12, 2004

Bay State Federal
Savings Bank
JANUARY 1, 1920 –
MAY 31, 2003

Abington
Savings Bank
JANUARY 1, 1853 –
APRIL 29, 2004

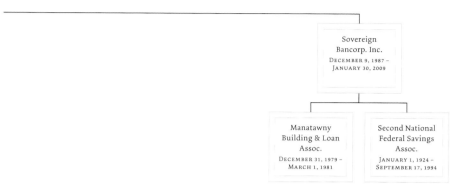

Sovereign
Bancorp. Inc.
DECEMBER 9, 1987 –
JANUARY 30, 2009

Manatawny
Building & Loan
Assoc.
DECEMBER 31, 1979 –
MARCH 1, 1981

Second National
Federal Savings
Assoc.
JANUARY 1, 1924 –
SEPTEMBER 17, 1994

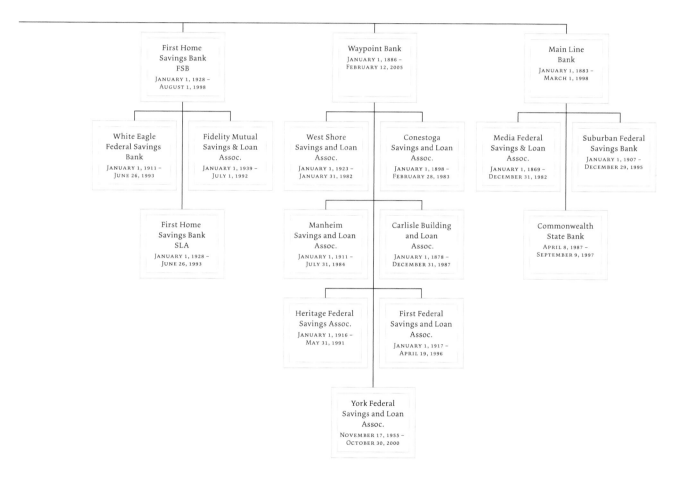

First Home
Savings Bank
FSB
JANUARY 1, 1928 –
AUGUST 1, 1998

Waypoint Bank
JANUARY 1, 1886 –
FEBRUARY 12, 2005

Main Line
Bank
JANUARY 1, 1883 –
MARCH 1, 1998

White Eagle
Federal Savings
Bank
JANUARY 1, 1911 –
JUNE 26, 1993

Fidelity Mutual
Savings & Loan
Assoc.
JANUARY 1, 1939 –
JULY 1, 1992

West Shore
Savings and Loan
Assoc.
JANUARY 1, 1923 –
JANUARY 31, 1982

Conestoga
Savings and Loan
Assoc.
JANUARY 1, 1898 –
FEBRUARY 28, 1983

Media Federal
Savings & Loan
Assoc.
JANUARY 1, 1869 –
DECEMBER 31, 1982

Suburban Federal
Savings Bank
JANUARY 1, 1907 –
DECEMBER 29, 1995

First Home
Savings Bank
SLA
JANUARY 1, 1928 –
JUNE 26, 1993

Manheim
Savings and Loan
Assoc.
JANUARY 1, 1911 –
JULY 31, 1984

Carlisle Building
and Loan
Assoc.
JANUARY 1, 1878 –
DECEMBER 31, 1987

Commonwealth
State Bank
APRIL 8, 1987 –
SEPTEMBER 9, 1997

Heritage Federal
Savings Assoc.
JANUARY 1, 1916 –
MAY 31, 1991

First Federal
Savings and Loan
Assoc.
JANUARY 1, 1917 –
APRIL 19, 1996

York Federal
Savings and Loan
Assoc.
NOVEMBER 17, 1955 –
OCTOBER 30, 2000

Santander Holdings USA

Bank *(abridged)*

RANK	HEADQUARTERS	TICKER	ASSETS	EARLIEST KNOWN ANCESTOR	INDUSTRY OF ORIGIN
32	**Boston, MA**	**SOV-PC**	**$79,000,000,000**	**1828**	**Commercial Banking**

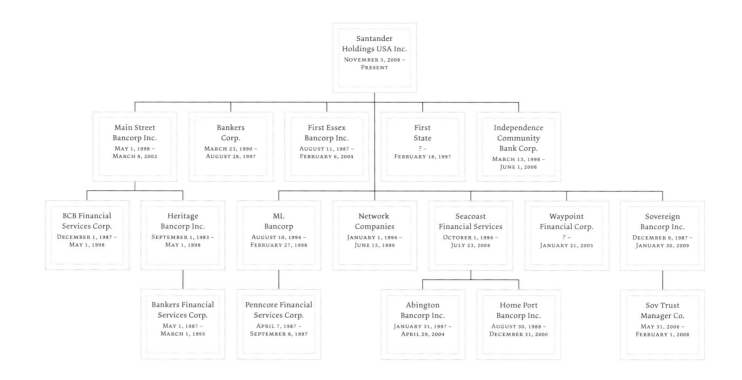

Santander Holdings USA

Holding Company

Banco Crédito y Ahorro Ponceño stock certificate, 1974.

Santander Holdings is the US subsidiary of Santander Group, one of the world's largest and most sophisticated banks with more than 180,000 employees and 102 million customers served by more than 14,000 branches worldwide, as of 2013. Just two decades ago, Banco Santander, the original entity of the group, was a second-tier retail bank in Spain. It has been controlled by the same family, which owns a 2.5% stake in the bank, for three generations. It succeeded because it gained international experience in Latin America before going head-to-head with top-rate European banks, first at home in Spain and then on their own turf. Santander Holdings USA represents its foray into English-speaking America.

Six businessmen, aided by about fourscore stockholders, founded Banco de Santander in the port city of Santander on Spain's north central coast in 1857. For the next century, the bank managed, despite its relatively small size, to survive the vicissitudes of Spain's volatile political system and boom-and-bust economy, largely because it remained tightly focused on retail banking. In 1922 it was not among Spain's 50 largest banks, and its local rival, Banco Mercantil, was three times its size. Like other Spanish banks, its profits sank during the civil war (1936–1939) and World War II. It did not grow again until the second half of the 1940s, when it fell under the control of the Botín family, which had long and deep roots in Santander's business community.

Under the Botín family, the bank grew through acquisition, including the 1946 purchase of archrival Banco Mercantil, as well as organically, though the latter was stymied by de novo branching restrictions.

Nevertheless, Banco de Santander operated 129 branches in 28 of the country's 50 provinces by its centenary in 1957. It also operated representative offices in Caracas, Havana and Mexico City, as well as one in London. It expanded further in the 1960s when it bought stakes in a few Brazilian and Argentine banks. The bank's main activities, however, remained centered in northern Spain and big Spanish cities like Barcelona and Madrid. Its investments remained small-scale and conservative, allowing the bank to emerge from the crises of the 1970s in better shape than its peers, which had taken large equity stakes in industrial firms.

When Emilio Botín II passed the bank's leadership to his namesake son in 1986, Banco Santander had nearly 1,500 domestic and 150 foreign branches and about 10,000 employees. Its name was prestigious, but it was still a small bank, even by domestic standards. Emilio Botín III was determined to change that and succeeded by focusing on retail banking while making some remarkable equity trades, including the over €700 million it made by selling its Royal Bank of Scotland (#25) position in 2005, three years before that institution had to be nationalized by the British government. The sale, however, did not end Santander's long-standing relationship with the Scottish bank, as evidenced by their joint takeover of the Dutch giant ABN AMRO in 2007.

Those and other acquisitions funded rapid expansion in the bank's core business, retail banking, at both home and abroad. Botín III thought rapid growth essential to his bank's survival in light of the deregulation of the domestic financial system that came as a result of

Banco Crédito y Ahorro Ponceño checks.

Spain's democratic turn in 1977 and its membership in the European Union in 1986. Innovation followed on the heels of the intense deregulatory wave of the late 1980s and early 1990s.

One such innovation was Santander's *supercuenta* account, which paid 11% annual interest on balances of 500,000 pesetas ($4,000) or more at a time when domestic inflation ran at less than 7%. A war of deposits ensued that nearly destroyed Banesto, one of Santander's rivals and later a key acquisition. In the early 1990s Santander also introduced a successful investment fund and the *superhipoteca*, a mortgage with interest rates two full percentage points below those of its rivals. It also sold its products in a way new to Spanish banking, with massive marketing and advertising campaigns.

Meanwhile, Botín III bided his time, awaiting opportunities while the bank's capital grew "peseta by peseta, patiently, prudently." In 1994 it finally acquired its weakened rival Banesto, outbidding Banco Bilbao Vizcaya (the parent of BBVA Compass [#35]) by 14%, and in the process became Spain's second largest bank. But it was still small by international standards, so Botín III pressed on, merging with Banco Hispano Central in 1999. After a three-year power struggle, Botín III reasserted complete control of the institution, dubbed Santander Central Hispano, which was by then Spain's largest bank and, thanks to aggressive overseas expansion, one of the world's biggest as well (13th in 2006).

Santander also expanded aggressively in Latin America in the 1990s, building on its earlier incursions into the Portuguese- and Spanish-speaking New World. Despite much competition fostered by the deregulation of the financial systems of most Latin American nations, it managed to become the region's largest retail bank in terms of deposits and loans by buying, among others, Argentine banks Banco de Venezuela and Banco Rio, Brazilian banks Bancos Geral de Comercio y Noroeste and Banespa, and Banco Santiago in Chile.

Santander's entry into the United States came via Puerto Rico, America's Spanish-speaking territory in the Caribbean. Santander purchased First National Bank of Puerto Rico in 1976 and the Banco Crédito y Ahorro Ponceño, which had 14 branches, including one in New York, in 1978. Other acquisitions soon followed, and by 1990 Santander was the second largest bank on the island. Six years later, it had 18% of the market and more than 70 branches. In 1977 and 1979 Santander branches also opened in New York and Miami.

Santander Holdings USA was composed of several businesses, including First Fidelity, in which it took a 13.5% stake in 1991. By June 1995 it owned almost a third of First Fidelity, but the following year, after First Fidelity's merger with First Union, Santander sold out, earning a capital gain of over $1.5 billion in the process.

By far its most important US holding in 2013 was Sovereign Bank, a savings and loan with 750 branches and a strong customer base

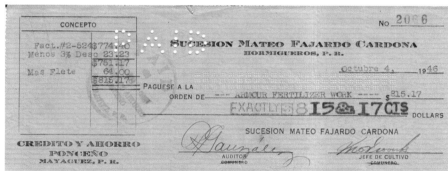

along the northern I-95 corridor. Later headquartered in Boston, Sovereign began business as a building and loan association in Wyomissing, Pennsylvania, in 1902. It changed its name to Sovereign in 1986 and formed an HC, Sovereign Bancorp, the next year. Between 1990 and 2008, Sovereign acquired 28 financial institutions, including Independence Community Bank, the high loan losses of which caused Sovereign to take a $1.6 billion write-down in early 2008. It also purchased more than 280 branches and 550 ATMs from FleetBoston Financial in 2000, the largest branch acquisition in US history to that time.

In its typical fashion, Santander purchased a 20% stake in Sovereign in 2005 and upped it to 25% the following year. When the American bank was weakened by poor investments made during the US housing bubble, Santander acquired the rest of it in 2009. Sovereign, which boasted more than 700 branches and more than 8,500 employees and at one point was one of the biggest 20 banks in America, was completely rebranded as Santander by the end of 2013.

According to Spanish business school professors Kimio Kase and Tanguy Jacopin, Santander's success can be largely attributed to its IT systems, which allowed it to tap scale economies wherever they appeared. With the bank's relentless growth, therefore, came increased operational efficiency — its ratio of personnel and general expenses over net operating revenue improved annually and

dramatically after 1998 — and hence both the means and the desire to expand yet further. Great IT also allowed it to expand quickly into new niche markets, like auto dealership finance in Western Europe, without undue cost or pressure.

Sources

Aceña, Pablo Martin. *Banco Santander: 150 Years of History, 1857–2007.* Alcalá de Henares: University of Alcalá, 2007.

Guillen, Mauro F. and Adrian Tschoegl. *Building a Global Bank: The Transformation of Banco Santander.* Princeton: Princeton University Press, 2008.

Kase, Kimio and Tanguy Jacopin. *CEOs as Leaders and Strategy Designers: Explaining the Success of Spanish Banks.* New York: Palgrave Macmillan, 2008.

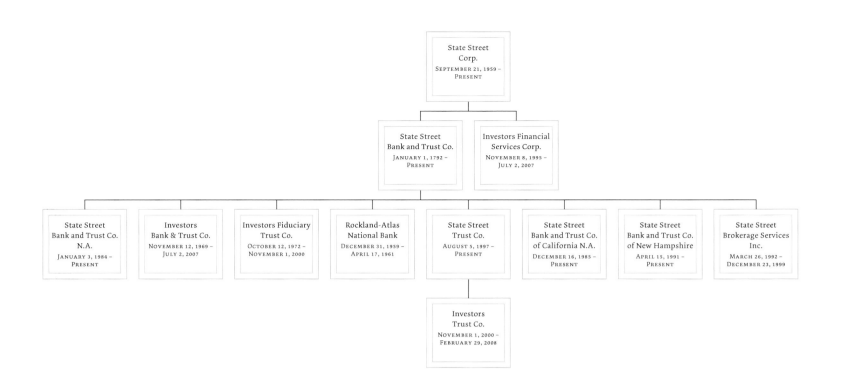

State Street

RANK	HEADQUARTERS	TICKER	ASSETS	EARLIEST KNOWN ANCESTOR	INDUSTRY OF ORIGIN
15	Boston, MA	STT	$227,000,000,000	1792	Commercial Banking

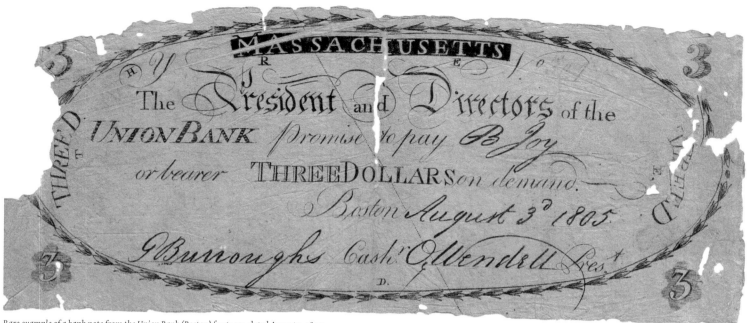

Rare example of a bank note from the Union Bank (Boston) for $3.00, dated August 3, 1805.

State Street Corporation weathered the 2008 financial crisis, and by June 2009 the company had a robust $16.4 *trillion* in assets under custody and administration and another $1.6 *trillion* under management. These numbers were up from $6.1 trillion and $.7 trillion, respectively, at the end of 2000, when it employed 17,600 workers in 23 countries and 90 markets. By 2009 it operated in 27 countries and more than 100 markets globally, making it the world's leading provider of financial services to institutional investors, including mutual funds, pension funds and sovereign wealth funds (SWFs), or huge pools of capital owned by sovereign governments such as China, Kuwait, Singapore and Russia. The relatively trivial $227 billion listed on its genealogy refers only to State Street's own assets, money it has invested in some 20 entrepreneurial businesses charged with creating new financial products for institutional clients under broad units such as Investment Research and Management, Trading and Brokerage Services, Fund Accounting and Custodial Services.

In 1998 Dearborn Financial ranked State Street the 24th best stock to own in America. Like other successful BHCs, State Street made "taking care of existing clients" its "first priority." Although it offered traditional banking services, most of its revenues sprang from the management or servicing of investment funds. It also earned fees from accounting, recordkeeping, securities custody, information services and management, foreign exchange trading and cash management.

It also sought to expand its client base, particularly outside the United States. The key to both goals was to ramp up its IT reach and expertise. E-business, it early realized, would allow it to provide better service and more choice, which would ultimately lead to more revenues and, hopefully, more profits. Of course, the company's high-tech gadgetry—which ranged from information delivery systems like State Street Global Link to electronic trading platforms like FX Connect—cost a fortune, some 20%–25% of operating expenses. IT was so important to the company in the late 1990s that *Computerworld* regularly ranked it one of the top 20 places to work in the field. Former CEO Marshall Carter often referred to State Street as more of a tech company than a financial institution.

It had not always been so. State Street's corporate existence began in 1792, with the chartering of the Union Bank of Boston, the city's third commercial bank. Capitalized at $400,000 and led by Boston notables like Stephen Higginson and Oliver Wendell (great grandfather of Oliver Wendell Holmes), it opened for business at the corner of State Street and Exchange Lane soon after, despite wagers at two-to-one that the bank would never issue a single note. It quickly thrived, its stock price reaching $250 by late 1793. It dropped to about $120 in 1795 as a result of the equivalent of a stock split. Thanks to a strong dividend record, the stock price remained well above par ($100) through 1810, when its deposits totaled about $562,000.

In late 1811, however, its stock price dipped when it encountered difficulties not rectified until after the outbreak of the War of 1812. That war's end saw the bank's stock price plummet below par, to a low of $82 in late August 1816. Its stock price rebounded to $106 by late 1818, however, and the bank weathered the Panic of 1819 with little difficulty, although the cashier accepted a $200 reduction in his $2,000 annual salary to help keep costs down.

By 1822 Union Bank's stock traded at $109. The price fluctuated but stayed above par throughout the entire 1820s and the first half of the 1830s, dropping to a low of $95 in late 1836. The Panics of 1837 and 1839 reduced the price still further, to a low of $90.25 in late 1839, but the bank held on and its stock briefly touched $104 in March 1841. It remained within $10 of par throughout the rest of the decade and into the 1850s, when it began to regularly exceed $110 per share, in which range it stayed (except for a brief dip during the Panic of 1857) until at least the Civil War, when extant stock data breaks off. As its dividends averaged more than 6% over its 133-year corporate existence, however, it is safe to say that the stock of the bank, which became the National Union Bank of Boston in 1865, remained around par until State Street purchased it in 1925.

In 1891 the State Street Safe Deposit and Trust Company was chartered and began business. Named after a famous commercial avenue in Boston, the company shortened its name to State Street Trust Company in 1897 and moved to the corner of State and Exchange Streets in 1900, when its deposits totaled about $2 million. By 1911 deposits had risen to $13 million, thanks in part to the opening of a

40, 44 State Street, Union Bank building lunch club.

State Street Bank at 225 Franklin Street, ca. 1970.

branch in the Back Bay section of Massachusetts Avenue in 1902. In 1916 the company bought the Paul Revere Trust Company, which provided it with additional deposits, valuable customers, some leadership and a location in Copley Square.

In 1925 State Street purchased the National Union Bank, which increased its aggregate deposits to over $57 million. From a dozen employees in 1900, State Street in a quarter of a century had grown to a staff of 350. Many of these employees worked in a new headquarters building, made of granite in the colonial style explicitly to create "an air of solidity" on the outside and a feeling of simplicity and homey-ness on the inside.

"I have seen a remarkable thing," a banker from Salem wrote upon visiting the company's new building for the first time, "a homelike bank." Like many chain family restaurants in the late 20th century, the company plastered its interior with a variety of memorabilia from the good old days. It had so many interesting items, in fact, that it published a book or "log" about many of the pieces, which included a large collection of models of famous ships.

In 1970 State Street opened its first foreign office, in Munich, Germany. By the end of the century it had added 15 more. Between 1990 and 1998, its foreign assets under management and foreign assets under custody increased from $3 billion to $26 billion and $30 billion to $186 billion, respectively. It had about 11,000 employees in the latter year. A person who had purchased $10,000 of its stock in 1987 and reinvested the dividends in yet more shares would have owned $61,000 worth of State Street stock a decade later.

Sources

Log of the State Street Trust Company. Boston: State Street Trust Company, 1926.

Nugée, John, Andrew Rozanov and George Hoguet. *Vision: Sovereign Wealth Funds Emerging from the Financial Crisis.* Boston: State Street, 2009.

Sylla, Richard E., Jack Wilson and Robert E. Wright, "Early U.S. Securities Prices." *EH.Net* (2006): *http://eh.net/databases/early-us-securities-prices.*

Walden, Gene. *The 100 Best Stocks to Own in America* 5th ed. Chicago: Dearborn Financial Publishing, 1998, 86–89.

Weill, Peter and Richard Woodham. "State Street Corporation: Evolving IT Governance." MIT Sloan School of Management Working Paper No. 4236–02. April 2002.

Yogg, Michael R. *Passion for Reality: Paul Cabot and the Boston Mutual Fund.* New York: Xlibris Corporation, 2006.

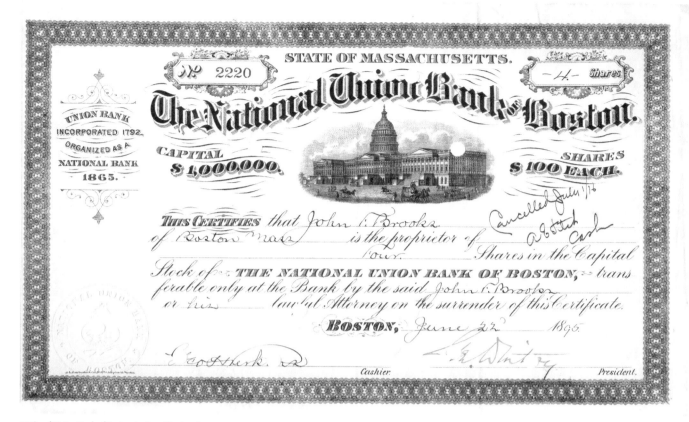

National Union Bank of Boston stock certificate, 1895.

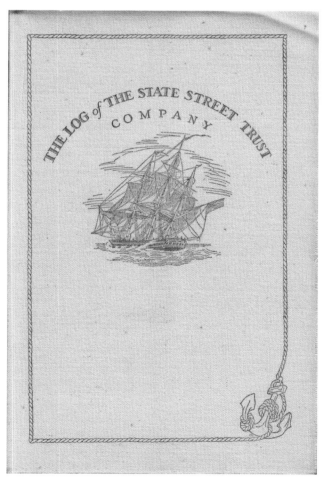

Log of the State Street Trust Co., 1926 (cover).

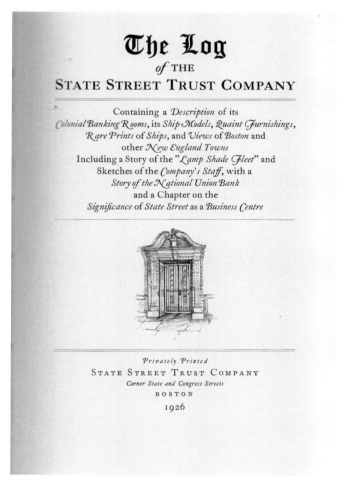

Log of the State Street Trust Co., 1926 (title page).

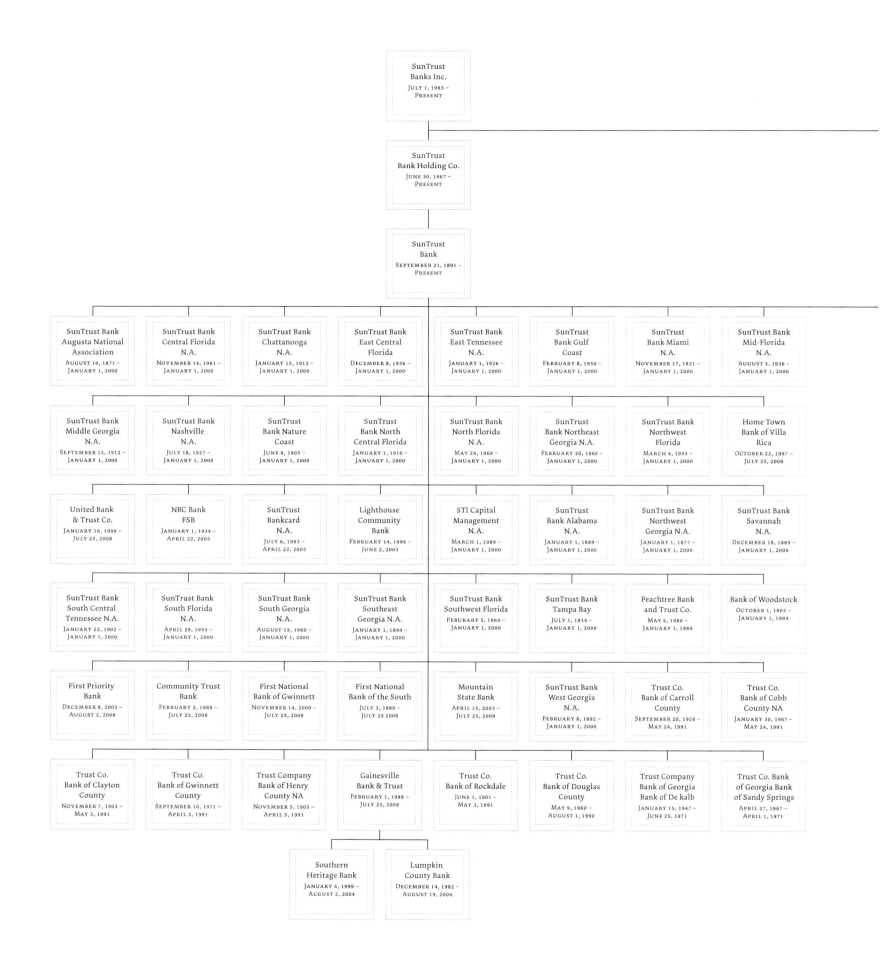

SunTrust Banks Inc.
JULY 1, 1985 –
PRESENT

SunTrust Bank Holding Co.
JUNE 30, 1967 –
PRESENT

SunTrust Bank
SEPTEMBER 21, 1891 –
PRESENT

SunTrust Bank Augusta National Association
AUGUST 10, 1871 –
JANUARY 1, 2000

SunTrust Bank Central Florida N.A.
NOVEMBER 14, 1961 –
JANUARY 1, 2000

SunTrust Bank Chattanooga N.A.
JANUARY 15, 1912 –
JANUARY 1, 2000

SunTrust Bank East Central Florida
DECEMBER 8, 1936 –
JANUARY 1, 2000

SunTrust Bank East Tennessee N.A.
JANUARY 1, 1926 –
JANUARY 1, 2000

SunTrust Bank Gulf Coast
FEBRUARY 8, 1950 –
JANUARY 1, 2000

SunTrust Bank Miami N.A.
NOVEMBER 17, 1921 –
JANUARY 1, 2000

SunTrust Bank Mid-Florida N.A.
AUGUST 5, 1936 –
JANUARY 1, 2000

SunTrust Bank Middle Georgia N.A.
SEPTEMBER 12, 1912 –
JANUARY 1, 2000

SunTrust Bank Nashville N.A.
JULY 18, 1927 –
JANUARY 1, 2000

SunTrust Bank Nature Coast
JUNE 8, 1905 –
JANUARY 1, 2000

SunTrust Bank North Central Florida
JANUARY 1, 1910 –
JANUARY 1, 2000

SunTrust Bank North Florida N.A.
MAY 24, 1968 –
JANUARY 1, 2000

SunTrust Bank Northeast Georgia N.A.
FEBRUARY 20, 1866 –
JANUARY 1, 2000

SunTrust Bank Northwest Florida
MARCH 4, 1955 –
JANUARY 1, 2000

Home Town Bank of Villa Rica
OCTOBER 22, 1997 –
JULY 25, 2008

United Bank & Trust Co.
JANUARY 16, 1990 –
JULY 25, 2008

NBC Bank FSB
JANUARY 1, 1934 –
APRIL 22, 2005

SunTrust Bankcard N.A.
JULY 6, 1993 –
APRIL 22, 2005

Lighthouse Community Bank
FEBRUARY 14, 1996 –
JUNE 2, 2003

STI Capital Management N.A.
MARCH 1, 1989 –
JANUARY 1, 2000

SunTrust Bank Alabama N.A.
JANUARY 1, 1889 –
JANUARY 1, 2000

SunTrust Bank Northwest Georgia N.A.
JANUARY 1, 1877 –
JANUARY 1, 2000

SunTrust Bank Savannah N.A.
DECEMBER 18, 1889 –
JANUARY 1, 2000

SunTrust Bank South Central Tennessee N.A.
JANUARY 22, 1902 –
JANUARY 1, 2000

SunTrust Bank South Florida N.A.
APRIL 29, 1955 –
JANUARY 1, 2000

SunTrust Bank South Georgia N.A.
AUGUST 15, 1960 –
JANUARY 1, 2000

SunTrust Bank Southeast Georgia N.A.
JANUARY 1, 1894 –
JANUARY 1, 2000

SunTrust Bank Southwest Florida
FEBURARY 5, 1964 –
JANUARY 1, 2000

SunTrust Bank Tampa Bay
JULY 1, 1914 –
JANUARY 1, 2000

Peachtree Bank and Trust Co.
MAY 6, 1960 –
JANUARY 1, 1984

Bank of Woodstock
OCTOBER 1, 1905 –
JANUARY 1, 1984

First Priority Bank
DECEMBER 8, 2003 –
AUGUST 2, 2008

Community Trust Bank
FEBRUARY 2, 1988 –
JULY 25, 2008

First National Bank of Gwinnett
NOVEMBER 14, 2000 –
JULY 25, 2008

First National Bank of the South
JULY 3, 1989 –
JULY 25 2008

Mountain State Bank
APRIL 15, 2003 –
JULY 25, 2008

SunTrust Bank West Georgia N.A.
FEBRUARY 8, 1892 –
JANUARY 1, 2000

Trust Co. Bank of Carroll County
SEPTEMBER 20, 1926 –
MAY 24, 1991

Trust Co. Bank of Cobb County NA
JANUARY 30, 1967 –
MAY 24, 1991

Trust Co. Bank of Clayton County
NOVEMBER 7, 1903 –
MAY 3, 1991

Trust Co. Bank of Gwinnett County
SEPTEMBER 16, 1971 –
APRIL 5, 1991

Trust Company Bank of Henry County NA
NOVEMBER 5, 1905 –
APRIL 5, 1991

Gainesville Bank & Trust
FEBRUARY 1, 1988 –
JULY 25, 2008

Trust Co. Bank of Rockdale
JUNE 1, 1901 –
MAY 3, 1991

Trust Co. Bank of Douglas County
MAY 9, 1960 –
AUGUST 1, 1990

Trust Company Bank of Georgia Bank of De kalb
JANUARY 15, 1947 –
JUNE 25, 1971

Trust Co. Bank of Georgia Bank of Sandy Springs
APRIL 27, 1967 –
APRIL 1, 1971

Southern Heritage Bank
JANUARY 4, 1999 –
AUGUST 2, 2004

Lumpkin County Bank
DECEMBER 14, 1982 –
AUGUST 19, 2004

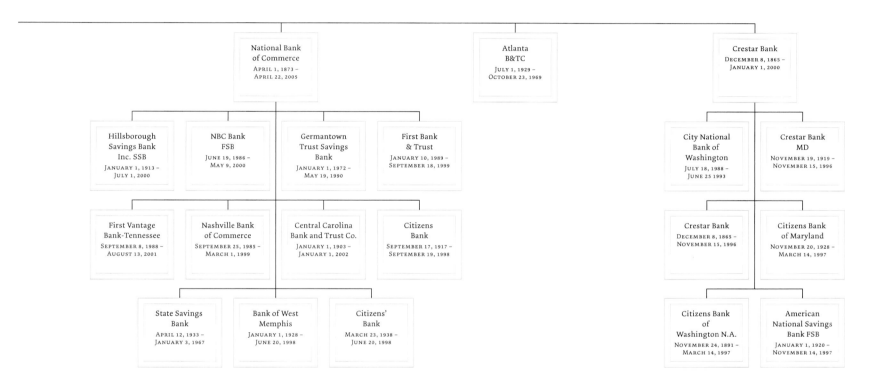

SunTrust Banks

Bank *(abridged)*

RANK	HEADQUARTERS	TICKER	ASSETS	EARLIEST KNOWN ANCESTOR	INDUSTRY OF ORIGIN
18	Atlanta, GA	STI	$172,000,000,000	1811	Commercial Banking

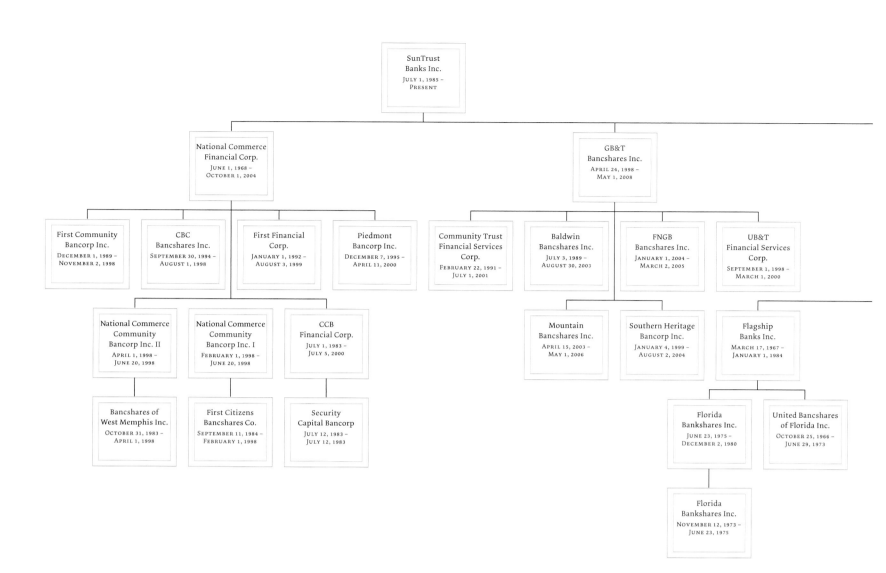

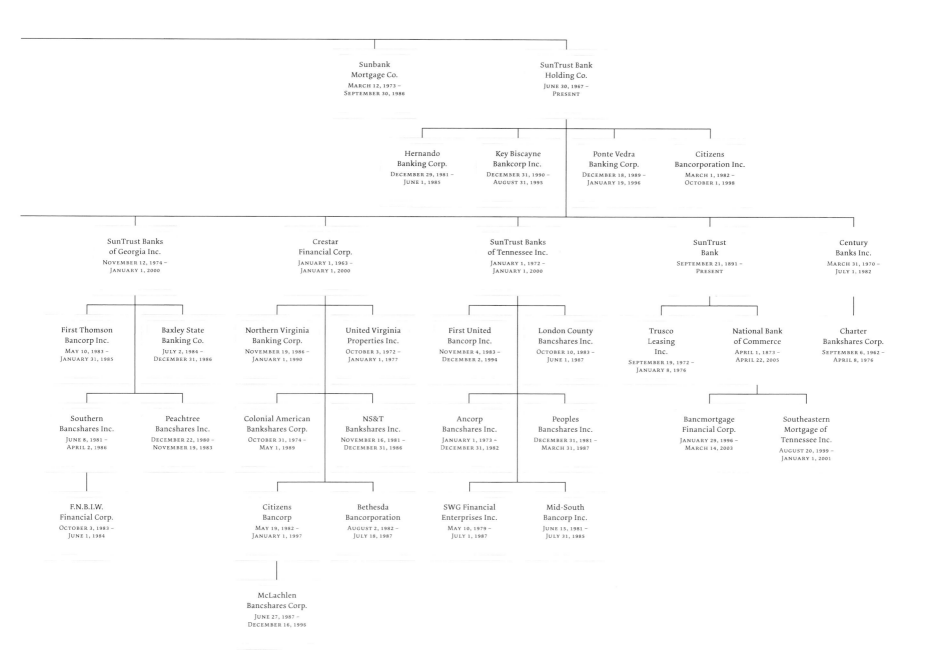

Sunbank
Mortgage Co.
MARCH 12, 1973 –
SEPTEMBER 30, 1986

SunTrust Bank
Holding Co.
JUNE 30, 1967 –
PRESENT

Hernando
Banking Corp.
DECEMBER 29, 1981 –
JUNE 1, 1985

Key Biscayne
Bankcorp Inc.
DECEMBER 31, 1990 –
AUGUST 31, 1995

Ponte Vedra
Banking Corp.
DECEMBER 18, 1989 –
JANUARY 19, 1996

Citizens
Bancorporation Inc.
MARCH 1, 1982 –
OCTOBER 1, 1998

SunTrust Banks
of Georgia Inc.
NOVEMBER 12, 1974 –
JANUARY 1, 2000

Crestar
Financial Corp.
JANUARY 1, 1963 –
JANUARY 1, 2000

SunTrust Banks
of Tennessee Inc.
JANUARY 1, 1972 –
JANUARY 1, 2000

SunTrust
Bank
SEPTEMBER 21, 1891 –
PRESENT

Century
Banks Inc.
MARCH 31, 1970 –
JULY 1, 1982

First Thomson
Bancorp Inc.
MAY 10, 1983 –
JANUARY 31, 1985

Baxley State
Banking Co.
JULY 2, 1984 –
DECEMBER 31, 1986

Northern Virginia
Banking Corp.
NOVEMBER 19, 1986 –
JANUARY 1, 1990

United Virginia
Properties Inc.
OCTOBER 3, 1972 –
JANUARY 1, 1977

First United
Bancorp Inc.
NOVEMBER 4, 1983 –
DECEMBER 2, 1994

London County
Bancshares Inc.
OCTOBER 10, 1983 –
JUNE 1, 1987

Trusco
Leasing
Inc.
SEPTEMBER 19, 1972 –
JANUARY 8, 1976

National Bank
of Commerce
APRIL 1, 1873 –
APRIL 22, 2005

Charter
Bankshares Corp.
SEPTEMBER 6, 1962 –
APRIL 8, 1976

Southern
Bancshares Inc.
JUNE 8, 1981 –
APRIL 2, 1986

Peachtree
Bancshares Inc.
DECEMBER 22, 1980 –
NOVEMBER 19, 1983

Colonial American
Bankshares Corp.
OCTOBER 31, 1974 –
MAY 1, 1989

NS&T
Bankshares Inc.
NOVEMBER 16, 1981 –
DECEMBER 31, 1986

Ancorp
Bancshares Inc.
JANUARY 1, 1973 –
DECEMBER 31, 1982

Peoples
Bancshares Inc.
DECEMBER 31, 1981 –
MARCH 31, 1987

Bancmortgage
Financial Corp.
JANUARY 29, 1996 –
MARCH 14, 2003

Southeastern
Mortgage of
Tennessee Inc.
AUGUST 20, 1999 –
JANUARY 1, 2001

F.N.B.I.W.
Financial Corp.
OCTOBER 3, 1983 –
JUNE 1, 1984

Citizens
Bancorp
MAY 19, 1982 –
JANUARY 1, 1997

Bethesda
Bancorporation
AUGUST 2, 1982 –
JULY 18, 1987

SWG Financial
Enterprises Inc.
MAY 10, 1979 –
JULY 1, 1987

Mid-South
Bancorp Inc.
JUNE 15, 1981 –
JULY 31, 1985

McLachlen
Bancshares Corp.
JUNE 27, 1987 –
DECEMBER 16, 1996

SunTrust Banks

Holding Company *(abridged)*

Coca-Cola sign in San Francisco, California, 2012.

SunTrust formed in 1985 from the merger of Sun Banks of Florida and Trust Company of Georgia. Trust Company of Georgia began business in Atlanta in 1891 under the name Commercial Travelers' Saving Bank. It changed its name and business model the following year to fulfill its goal — as one of the company's chroniclers asserted — of making the New South a reality. With New England transplant Ernest Woodruff at the helm, the Trust Company of Georgia helped to do just that by financing companies like Atlantic Ice and Coal, Atlantic Steel, Continental Gin and Coca-Cola.

Some deals brought immediate fees, while others brought long-term gains. In 1919, for example, the company helped J.P. Morgan (#1) underwrite the IPO of an Atlanta-based beverage company of middling size. J.P. Morgan sold its stock, but the Trust Company of Georgia held onto its $110,000 worth of shares. It then watched them blossom into $3 billion as that local company — Coca-Cola — grew very large and famous indeed.

When it came to company expenses, Woodruff was notoriously tightfisted. Instead of paying 25 cents extra per line to enjoy new continental-type telephones, he made everyone keep their old-fashioned upright phones. To save $1,000 on insurance, Woodruff and his eventual successor, Thomas K. Glenn, once stuffed $1 million of bonds into their clothes to transport them safely from a New York bank to Atlanta via taxicab and the Crescent Limited. Glenn was a good businessman too, and also full, as the company's chronicler claimed, of "the gentler qualities of kindness and Christian charity that were a reflection of his own deep religious faith." Even as Atlanta awoke from its long, smoldering economic slumber, Glenn knew everybody and everybody knew him. Under his leadership, the company during the 1920s became the head of a group bank by acquiring, through the agency of a BHC

called the Trust Company of Georgia Associates, the following institutions: National Exchange Bank of Augusta (chartered 1871), Fourth National Bank of Columbus (chartered 1892), First National Bank and Trust Company in Macon (formed by merger in 1930), First National Bank of Rome (chartered 1877) and the Liberty National Bank and Trust Company of Savannah (chartered 1889).

The group bank also established Motor Contract Company in 1935 to finance automobile purchases. It changed Motor Contract's name to Trusco Finance Company in 1945. The subsidiary, which had offices in Albany, Athens, Augusta, Columbus, Macon, Rome and Savannah in Georgia as well as Montgomery in Alabama, had accumulated over $1.8 million in profits by the end of 1954. The company sold it for $2.7 million in 1959.

Woodruff and Glenn saw the Great Depression approaching and got the company ready, which enabled it to save many customers while the rest of the financial system crumbled around it. In 1937, as the Depression was in its last throes, Georgian Robert Strickland took the helm of the bank. Within two years, he started a factoring division charged with financing small businesses through the collateralization of their accounts receivable. The company also began advising Southern banks on bond purchases and bond portfolio development.

Disaster struck in 1946 when both Strickland and Glenn fell deathly ill. As Woodruff had died in 1944, the bank was bereft of top leaders until attorney John Sibley answered the call to serve as board chairman. Aided by an able executive team, Sibley kept the company healthy. By 1951 the company, which called itself "The Bank for Business in the Southeast," had four departments — commercial banking, trust, investment and factoring — with over $225 million in combined assets.

A Suntrust Bank building in Washington, DC, 2010.

Not content to rest on its prior achievements, the company in 1950 began, with the help of outside consultants, a system of self-analysis and improvement that held it in good stead over the coming decades. In 1952 it doubled its official capital from $2 to $4 million and still had $6 million in a surplus account. That same year it lent half a million dollars to the Kingdom of Belgium, its first loan to a foreign sovereign government, and it began to lend to big companies like Delta Air Line and Lockheed. Deposits poured in as Georgia's economy boomed and its residents' total income increased from just shy of $1 billion in 1940 to almost $4.25 billion in 1953. The state's economy also industrialized and diversified in the postwar decades, buffering the company and other banks from droughts and agricultural price volatility.

In 1959 Sibley bowed out, and a new leadership team assumed control of the bank, which would soon have assets north of $260 million. They established new education and training and industrial development departments and embarked on a long-overdue automation program that included a machine to read and sort checks and a computerized accounting system. The modernization program cost $900,000 and was completed in 1964.

In 1962 the company had a spate of new but unwelcomed business when a chartered airplane crashed at Orly Airfield outside Paris, France. More than 100 prominent Atlanta residents died in the disaster, and many had named the company as executor. Orphaned minor children relied on the company to find them guardians and to manage the assets their parents had left them. One client happy that he did business with the bank noted that "a trust company . . . follows a policy, not a sentiment; it is more enduring than personal friends, because it does not sicken, change or die; it will never forget you; its memory, in a correspondence file, is imperishable; its goodwill toward you, entrusted

to a succession of experts in the creation and preservation of goodwill, persists on and on throughout good conduct unworn by use, undried by time; it is conversant with all the laws, not afraid of 'red tape.' While I am living it helps build my estate, and when I pass on it will keep the record straight for my loved ones."

The trust business generated stable fees, not interest income. While other banks drifted downriver as a result of the turbulent undercurrent created by interest rate volatility, Trust Company of Georgia was chained to the bedrock of $1.4 billion in assets under management. Yet it realized that it needed to attract traditional depositors as well, so it grew its branch network from nine in 1964 to 33 (most strategically located in new shopping centers) by the end of 1973. It started calling itself Trust Company Bank without officially changing its legal status. One branch was even established in Nassau, Bahamas, in 1970, the company's first overseas office, so that it could enter the Eurodollar market.

By 1973 deposits, including those of the affiliated banks, exceeded $1 billion and loans hit $995 million, up from $90 million in 1958. The company's factoring and lock-box services also expanded, the former to $320 million. It could not take advantage of the Bank Holding Company Act of 1969, however, because it already owned a BHC, the Trust Company of Georgia Associates, and because it guarded its Coca-Cola investment, an asset it could hold because it was chartered as a trust, not a bank.

Meanwhile, in Florida, the First National Bank at Orlando had formed in 1934 to fill the void left by the waves of bank failures that had destroyed all but one of Orlando's banks. Capitalized at a mere $240,000, the bank was not big, but it was friendly. According to an early customer (who later wrote its 50th anniversary history), its first president, Linton Allen, "made you glad you had come into the bank, just by the way he greeted you" even though he knew that you "didn't have two nickels to rub together." He stopped a run on his previous bank, in nearby Sanford, simply by talking to depositors a la Jimmy Stewart in the seminal scene in the movie *It's a Wonderful Life*.

Allen's congenial way of doing business lingered, as half a century after the bank's founding (and 20 years after his death), there was "scarcely a meeting of local Sun Bank officials but that Linton Allen's name or his philosophy isn't referred to." Another early customer recalled, "He was loyal to his community as well as his bank." Allen himself often claimed, "Build your community and you build your bank." And that was not just rhetoric: Disney World, Epcot, Interstate 4, Florida's Turnpike, Martin-Marietta and the University of Central Florida all ended up in or near Orlando due in part to his influence.

Thanks to Allen and his carefully picked team of employees, First National soon became the leading bank in the leading city of rapidly growing central Florida. It did so by specializing in consumer lending and implementing a management training program that in 1983 became Sun Bank University. To work around Florida's stringent branching restrictions, the bank went the chain bank route, setting up affiliates that were tied to it solely by interlocking directorates and stockholdings. For example, 76.2% of the stockholders of First National owed 61% of its first affiliate, College Park Bank, which connected its drive-through facility to its walk-in office by a tunnel to comply with an antiquated state branching law. First National's first drive-up teller was actually stationed below street level, right at the curb, and interacted with customers via mirrors and a dumbwaiter.

The state's branching restrictions were eventually weakened, however, by the formation of BHCs. The bank formed a BHC, called First at Orlando Corp., in 1967 and made its affiliated banks true subsidiaries. By 1969 the BHC's assets exceeded $400 million. Two years later, it changed its name to Sun Banks to stress its connection to all of Florida, and not just Orlando, while reinforcing its friendly image.

In 1977, when branching restrictions were further eased, Sun Banks owned 21 banks and assets of $2.1 billion. In addition to allowing it to turn subsidiaries into branches, the new legislation allowed the bank to form de novo branches, which it immediately set about doing, establishing 22 in 1977 alone. By the end of 1978 it had 84 branches and 83 ATMs. More changes in 1979 helped growth, and the bank's assets topped $3.3 billion by the end of 1980. In August 1981 Sun Banks's stock began to trade on the New York Stock Exchange. At the end of 1982, the bank had 162 offices in 25 market areas in Florida, and assets hit $5 billion.

The biggest purchase up until that time took place in 1983, when the bank acquired Flagship Banks for $334 million. It immediately sold some of Flagship's banks, as well as a few of its own branches that were made redundant by the deal. When the dust cleared in early 1984, Sun Banks had 260 offices, even more than its biggest competitor, Barnett Banks.

Effective July 1, 1985, Florida allowed banks from 11 states in the Southeast to merge with Florida banks. Sun Banks of Florida and Trust Company of Georgia, which had been Sun's correspondent bank for decades, jumped at the opportunity. The combined institution had assets of almost $20 billion by year's end. The next year the bank merged with Third National Corporation of Nashville, which added another $5 billion in assets.

By 1994 SunTrust, as the merged institution was called, provided corporate finance, credit cards, credit-related insurance, data processing and information services, discount brokerage, factoring, investment banking, mortgage banking and trust services. Its CEO, James B. Williams, said that "we have never believed nor do we believe now that bigness, in and of itself, is a virtue, and we do not measure our success in terms of size." Rather, he encouraged bank employees to "think like a shareholder," meaning to stay focused on "quality, profitability and performance."

The bank's loan portfolio that year consisted of $9.6 billion of commercial loans, $12.9 billion in home mortgages and other real estate loans, $1.2 billion of construction loans, $3.8 billion in consumer loans and $.7 billion of credit card loans. Bank scholar Alan Gart praised its "strong balance sheet . . . excellent customer service . . . good control of operating costs . . . [and] consistent financial ratios."

In 1998 Dearborn Financial ranked SunTrust the 26th best company to own in America, and that included both financial and nonfinancial stocks. It lauded the bank for "adding innovative new services for its customers," including a home banking service called "PC Banking." The bank also opened convenience branches in Publix and Winn-Dixie supermarkets. All told, it employed about 19,400 people in 650 offices spread over Florida, Georgia, Tennessee and Alabama. Most importantly from Dearborn Financial's perspective was its stock growth—334% over the previous decade—with 17 consecutive years of increased earnings per share.

By 2006 SunTrust Banks had assets of almost $179 billion, about 34,000 employees and almost 1,700 branches in 11 Southeastern and Mid-Atlantic states, as well as Washington, DC. The plural "Banks" in its name was intentional, to signal that its more than 50 banks maintained significant autonomy to generate revenue in their geographical areas and niche specialties, which included asset management, brokerage, consumer banking, commercial leasing, credit-related insurance, investment banking services and mortgage lending. That same year, J.D. Power and Associates ranked SunTrust mortgage highest in customer satisfaction on first mortgage loans. The next year, 10 SunTrust private financial advisors made *Bank Investment Consultant* magazine's "50 Best" list.

By then SunTrust Banks was one of the leading corporate advocates in the nation for hiring persons with disabilities (PWDs). It all began with a single customer service representative who attracted customers to her branch by being able to communicate with sign language. Seeing a potentially profitable niche, managers responded enthusiastically and began offering services to people with other sorts of disabilities. Soon, the bank began to seek to hire PWDs to interact with customers with different disabilities and develop tailored products for them (e.g., Braille statements), but also to fill general staffing gaps. It discovered that PWDs were typically outstanding employees and began to spread the word to other businesses via Business Leadership Networks in Florida, Maryland, Tennessee, Virginia and nationwide. Internally, as the number of its PWD employees grew, it established a Disability Resource Center to identify and meet any special needs they might have and began a Disability Mentoring Day in 2001.

In 2007 the bank took a hit from the mortgage sector. It had begun offering "shortcut mortgages," which featured an expedited loan approval and closing process, in 1995. During the height of the housing boom, from 2005 to 2007, it originated numerous doomed subprime mortgages. When the mortgage crisis hit in 2008, SunTrust needed more capital, so it sold its coveted holdings in Coca-Cola. When the $2 billion in proceeds proved insufficient, it ended up taking its maximum allotment of TARP funds, $4.85 billion.

"Given the increasingly uncertain economic outlook," CEO James M. Wells III told *American Banker*, "we have concluded that further augmenting our capital at this point is a prudent step, especially if the current recession proves to be longer and more severe than previously expected." It was a shrewd move because the bank had a difficult time

Trust Company of Georgia stock certificate.

rebounding from the crisis, losing $2 billion over five consecutive quarters. As reporter Paul Davis quipped, in 2005 SunTrust "was a low-profile, mortgage-heavy underperformer that seemed primed for takeover by a bigger competitor," but by 2010, after a new CEO and "considerable cost-cutting," the bank "was a low-profile, mortgage-heavy underperformer that seemed primed for takeover by a bigger competitor."

In early 2011 the bank was still on shaky ground, as it had not repaid its TARP money and still had tens of thousands of mortgages in foreclosure. The bank responded to the crisis by cutting costs with its "excellence in execution" initiative. That meant shrinking employment, compensation, office space and the number of branches. The bank was still slicing expenses in 2013 in an attempt to achieve a 60% efficiency ratio, a big drop from its 81.5% score in 2011.

Sources

Bauerlein, Valerie and Andrew Edwards. "Loans Gone Bad Hit SunTrust." *Wall Street Journal*, January 24, 2008, C5.

Bereman, Nancy and Stephanie J. Hargrave. "SunTrust Banks." In *Hidden Talent: How Leading Companies Hire, Retain, and Benefit from People with Disabilities*, edited by Mark L. Lengnick-Hall, 55–60. Westport, CT: Praeger, 2007.

Cumming, Chris. "SunTrust to Close 40 Branches." *American Banker*, March 6, 2013.

Davis, Paul. "Mortgage Woes Deal SunTrust an Efficiency Setback." *American Banker*, October 21, 2013.

———. "SunTrust Pays a Second Call on Treasury." *American Banker*, December 10, 2008, 1.

———. "Turnaround Is Proving Elusive for SunTrust." *American Banker*, April 13, 2010, 1.

Lepro, Sara. "SunTrust to Refile Loads of Documents." *American Banker*, February 28, 2011, 4.

Loosvelt, Derek, et al. *The Vault Guide to the Top 50 Banking Employers: 2008 Edition*. New York: Vault, 2007, 406–11.

Martin, Harold H. *Three Strong Pillars: The Story of the Trust Company of Georgia*. Atlanta: Trust Company of Georgia, 1974.

Peters, Andy. "SunTrust Aims to Cut Salary, Compensation Costs." *American Banker*, January 22, 2013.

Powers, Ormund. *Fifty Years: The Sun Bank Story, 1934–1984*. Orlando, FL: Sun Bank, 1984.

Scholtes, Saskia. "SunTrust Sells Stake in Coke." *FT.com*, July 22, 2008.

Spiegel, John, Alan Gart and Steven Gart. *Banking Redefined: How Superregional Powerhouses Are Reshaping Financial Services*. Chicago: Irwin Professional Publishing, 1996, 259–69.

Story of the Trust Company of Georgia On Its 60th Anniversary. Atlanta: Trust Company of Georgia, 1951.

Walden, Gene. *The 100 Best Stocks to Own in America* 5th ed. Chicago: Dearborn Financial Publishing, 1998, 94–97.

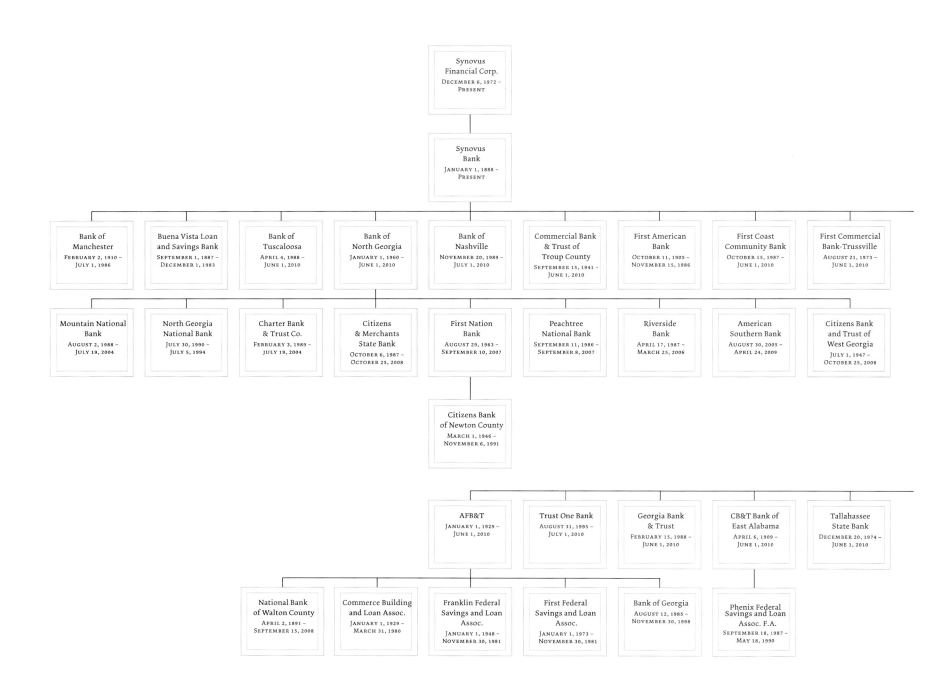

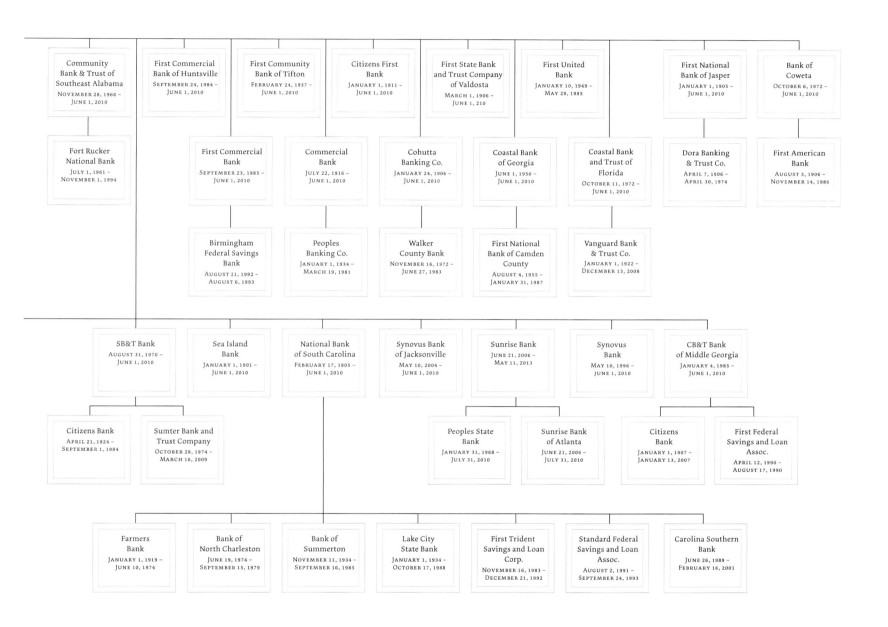

Community Bank & Trust of Southeast Alabama NOVEMBER 28, 1966 – JUNE 1, 2010	First Commercial Bank of Huntsville SEPTEMBER 24, 1984 – JUNE 1, 2010	First Community Bank of Tifton FEBRUARY 24, 1937 – JUNE 1, 2010	Citizens First Bank JANUARY 1, 1911 – JUNE 1, 2010	First State Bank and Trust Company of Valdosta MARCH 1, 1906 – JUNE 1, 210	First United Bank JANUARY 10, 1949 – MAY 29, 1985	First National Bank of Jasper JANUARY 1, 1905 – JUNE 1, 2010	Bank of Coweta OCTOBER 6, 1972 – JUNE 1, 2010

Fort Rucker National Bank
JULY 1, 1961 – NOVEMBER 1, 1994

First Commercial Bank
SEPTEMBER 23, 1985 – JUNE 1, 2010

Commercial Bank
JULY 22, 1916 – JUNE 1, 2010

Cohutta Banking Co.
JANUARY 24, 1906 – JUNE 1, 2010

Coastal Bank of Georgia
JUNE 1, 1950 – JUNE 1, 2010

Coastal Bank and Trust of Florida
OCTOBER 11, 1972 – JUNE 1, 2010

Dora Banking & Trust Co.
APRIL 7, 1906 – APRIL 30, 1974

First American Bank
AUGUST 3, 1906 – NOVEMBER 14, 1986

Birmingham Federal Savings Bank
AUGUST 21, 1992 – AUGUST 6, 1993

Peoples Banking Co.
JANUARY 1, 1934 – MARCH 19, 1981

Walker County Bank
NOVEMBER 16, 1972 – JUNE 27, 1983

First National Bank of Camden County
AUGUST 4, 1955 – JANUARY 31, 1987

Vanguard Bank & Trust Co.
JANUARY 1, 1922 – DECEMBER 13, 2008

SB&T Bank
AUGUST 31, 1970 – JUNE 1, 2010

Sea Island Bank
JANUARY 1, 1901 – JUNE 1, 2010

National Bank of South Carolina
FEBRUARY 17, 1905 – JUNE 1, 2010

Synovus Bank of Jacksonville
MAY 10, 2004 – JUNE 1, 2010

Sunrise Bank
JUNE 21, 2006 – MAY 11, 2013

Synovus Bank
MAY 10, 1996 – JUNE 1, 2010

CB&T Bank of Middle Georgia
JANUARY 4, 1985 – JUNE 1, 2010

Citizens Bank
APRIL 21, 1924 – SEPTEMBER 1, 1984

Sumter Bank and Trust Company
OCTOBER 28, 1974 – MARCH 16, 2009

Peoples State Bank
JANUARY 31, 1968 – JULY 31, 2010

Sunrise Bank of Atlanta
JUNE 21, 2006 – JULY 31, 2010

Citizens Bank
JANUARY 1, 1907 – JANUARY 13, 2007

First Federal Savings and Loan Assoc.
APRIL 12, 1990 – AUGUST 17, 1990

Farmers Bank
JANUARY 1, 1919 – JUNE 10, 1974

Bank of North Charleston
JUNE 19, 1974 – SEPTEMBER 15, 1979

Bank of Summerton
NOVEMBER 11, 1934 – SEPTEMBER 16, 1985

Lake City State Bank
JANUARY 1, 1934 – OCTOBER 17, 1988

First Trident Savings and Loan Corp.
NOVEMBER 16, 1983 – DECEMBER 21, 1992

Standard Federal Savings and Loan Assoc.
AUGUST 2, 1991 – SEPTEMBER 24, 1993

Carolina Southern Bank
JUNE 26, 1989 – FEBRUARY 16, 2001

Synovus Financial

Bank

RANK	HEADQUARTERS	TICKER	ASSETS	EARLIEST KNOWN ANCESTOR	INDUSTRY OF ORIGIN
50	**Columbus, GA**	**SNV**	**$26,500,000,000**	**1887**	**Commercial Banking**

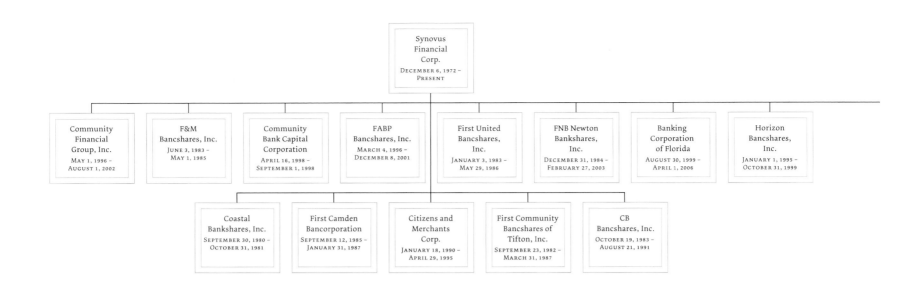

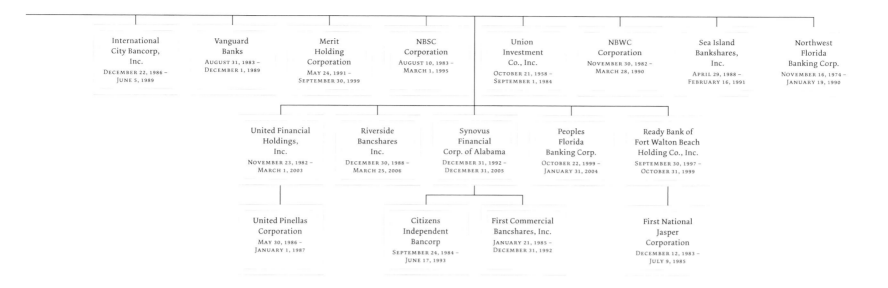

International
City Bancorp,
Inc.
DECEMBER 22, 1986 –
JUNE 5, 1989

Vanguard
Banks
AUGUST 31, 1983 –
DECEMBER 1, 1989

Merit
Holding
Corporation
MAY 24, 1991 –
SEPTEMBER 30, 1999

NBSC
Corporation
AUGUST 10, 1983 –
MARCH 1, 1995

Union
Investment
Co., Inc.
OCTOBER 21, 1958 –
SEPTEMBER 1, 1984

NBWC
Corporation
NOVEMBER 30, 1982 –
MARCH 28, 1990

Sea Island
Bankshares,
Inc.
APRIL 29, 1988 –
FEBRUARY 16, 1991

Northwest
Florida
Banking Corp.
NOVEMBER 16, 1974 –
JANUARY 19, 1990

United Financial
Holdings,
Inc.
NOVEMBER 23, 1982 –
MARCH 1, 2003

Riverside
Bancshares
Inc.
DECEMBER 30, 1988 –
MARCH 25, 2006

Synovus
Financial
Corp. of Alabama
DECEMBER 31, 1992 –
DECEMBER 31, 2005

Peoples
Florida
Banking Corp.
OCTOBER 22, 1999 –
JANUARY 31, 2004

Ready Bank of
Fort Walton Beach
Holding Co., Inc.
SEPTEMBER 30, 1997 –
OCTOBER 31, 1999

United Pinellas
Corporation
MAY 30, 1986 –
JANUARY 1, 1987

Citizens
Independent
Bancorp
SEPTEMBER 24, 1984 –
JUNE 17, 1993

First Commercial
Bancshares, Inc.
JANUARY 21, 1985 –
DECEMBER 31, 1992

First National
Jasper
Corporation
DECEMBER 12, 1983 –
JULY 9, 1985

Synovus Financial

Holding Company *(abridged)*

According to Michael Novosel, a retired Army officer and Congressional Medal of Honor recipient, "seeing the Synovus sign is like seeing the international Red Cross symbol—you know that behind it is an organization of dedicated people who are there to help." How many other big banks have been favorably compared to the Red Cross recently? Probably none. The difference is that Synovus is not led by people per se; it is led by values. Not stock market valuations, but core beliefs about right and wrong.

At Synovus, the Golden Rule mixes with market sensibility: do unto others as they want to be done unto. That means listening to what customers want and developing products that meet those needs as efficiently as possible. It also means learning the ABCS: Always the Best Customer Service. Senior executives talk about values among themselves and with employees and customers as much as they talk about strategies. Values, they believe, lead to practices, and practices to outcomes. So good values lead to good outcomes—numerically, morally and even spiritually. These values have suffused the company's history since its founding four generations ago.

In the Eagle and Phenix textile mill in Columbus, Georgia, in the late 1870s a female factory operative was discovered to have $60 in bank notes sewn into her dress when the garment was destroyed after getting caught in a textile machine. Thankfully unhurt, the woman explained she knew of no safer place for her savings. The factory owner responded by founding the Eagle and Phenix Savings Bank, and he put the mill's treasurer, George Gunby Jordan, in charge of it.

In 1888 Jordan leveraged his experience at the Eagle and Phenix by founding two banks of his own, the Third National Bank and the Columbus Savings Bank. Working closely with Vice President William Clark Bradley, Jordan and his banks helped fund the construction of a hydroelectric dam and other important projects while continuing to pay dividends even in the aftermath of the Panics of 1893 and 1907.

The two institutions merged to form the Columbus Bank and Trust (CB&T) in 1930, with $9 million in assets, just as the Great Depression deepened. Not only didn't CB&T close during the ensuing economic and financial fiasco, but it did not even reduce employment. Jordan died during the Depression, but Bradley carried on until after World War II. He was succeeded by his son-in-law, D. Abbott Turner, who maintained the high standard of personal integrity of the founders. Like many community bankers, Turner by all accounts was loved by both his employees and customers alike.

James W. "Jim" Blanchard ran the bank from 1957 until his death in 1969 and slowly but surely modernized its operations without losing the traditional focus on the customer or the community. He also nearly tripled the bank's assets, from $33 to $94 million. Bill Curry, the retired president of a local competitor, then took over until Jim's son, James H. "Jimmy" Blanchard, was ready to take the reins in 1970. Jimmy created a one-bank holding company in 1972 and immediately began to lobby for the passage of legislation allowing the formation of multibank holding companies in Georgia. CB&T Bankshares, as the new entity was called, applied to acquire another bank on the very day in 1976 that Georgia passed the legislation Jimmy sought.

Blanchard ran the bank for more than 30 years; Jordan, Bradley and Turner family members were still involved as advisors, investors and board members. Under Blanchard, the bank grew rapidly through acquisition, but never for the sake of growth alone. "We're looking for targets," Blanchard explained, "where there's economic opportunity, where people mix and are compatible." The numbers must be right, but so too must the "feel." Acquisitions must entail "good banks, good markets and good people. . . . We wouldn't want to acquire any bank," Blanchard stated, "where we wouldn't want to take the folks home to momma."

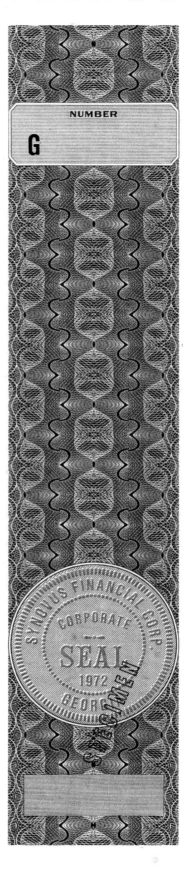

Specimen Synovus stock certificate, 1990.

7-　　13623-210　　-90

SM

'US
CORP.

E STATE OF GEORGIA

UMBUS, GEORGIA OR NEW YORK, NEW YORK.

SEE REVERSE FOR
RIGHTS LEGEND

CUSIP 87161C 10 5
SEE REVERSE FOR CERTAIN DEFINITIONS

SPECIMEN

ND NON-ASSESSABLE SHARES OF THE COMMON STOCK OF

transferable on the books of the Corporation by the holder hereof in person or by duly

f this certificate properly endorsed.

t until countersigned and registered by the Transfer Agent and Registrar.

F the Corporation and the facsimile signatures of its duly authorized officers.

DATED:

COUNTERSIGNED AND REGISTERED:
COLUMBUS BANK AND TRUST COMPANY
(COLUMBUS, GA.)
TRANSFER AGENT
AND REGISTRAR,

BY

DENT

ETARY

AUTHORIZED SIGNATURE.

SHARES

American Bank Note Company

Eagle & Phenix Mill No. 1.

Third National Bank building in Atlanta, Georgia.

Rather than ruthlessly integrate them into their system, in the 1980s the bank allowed the companies it took over, almost invariably small community banks, to retain some of their autonomy. It sought to maintain employee morale and customer loyalty, relying on the absence of other big banks in its markets, and not dramatic cuts, to earn its profits. By the late 1990s, however, it had pressured affiliates into switching computer systems and making other reforms consonant with what Blanchard called the "New Bank." Despite some resistance to change from the executives of acquired businesses, the bank, which changed its name to Synovus in 1989, was very profitable, earning the *Wall Street Journal*'s praise as the "No. 1 Bank in the South" for its shareholder returns over 1993–1998. It subsequently ranked highly on profitability lists compiled by *Forbes* and *Business Week* as well. Return on assets and return on equity were both substantially higher than its peer group average throughout the 1990s, and its efficiency ratio was better too.

Despite some evidence that its corporate culture was slowly degenerating over the 1990s, Synovus executives weren't paying lip service when they said that the organization's strength ultimately rested on its employees. Synovus, a neologism meaning "new synergy," truly treated them well and was consistently ranked by *Fortune* magazine as one of the "Top 10 Best Companies to Work For

in America." That same magazine also listed it as one of the country's most admired companies.

The words most often used to describe the company's culture included appreciation, camaraderie, caring, empathy, fairness, healing, honesty, humility, integrity, modeling, respect, service and trust. When hiring, the bank looked for those attributes in its employees, but it also sought to foster them, and to help turn good values into good behaviors after the initial hire. Managers were expected to "live the values," "share the vision," "make others successful" and "manage the business." So along with all the soft skills, its Center for People Development also helped employees to develop the analytical business and computer skills the bank needed to thrive.

"Sure, we're sensitive, gentle and kind in our leadership style," Blanchard recently told researcher Francis Hamilton, "but that does not mean that it's an excuse for average or mediocre. It doesn't mean we cannot apply discipline. It doesn't mean we're not going to hold people accountable for excellence." In addition to being good listeners who created an atmosphere of trust, the bank's leaders were supposed to foster rational risk-taking and creativity.

One area where Synovus excelled was in back office operations. In recent decades about a third of Synovus's profits came from Total System Services (TSYS), a credit card processor the bank launched along with its own credit card offering in 1959. In 1973 TSYS began processing card information and billing electronically and soon was processing paperwork for other banks' credit cards. Synovus decided to grow the business, which it correctly identified as recession-proof. It spun off 20% of TSYS in 1983 but kept the rest for itself.

In 1998 Dearborn Financial ranked Synovus as the 10th best company to own in America. At that time, it operated a group of 34 banks scattered across five states in the Southeast, but what made it stand out to analysts was TSYS. By 2003 the subsidiary was the second largest credit and debit card processor in the nation, with revenues of over $1 billion and clients including JPMorgan Chase (#1), Bank of America (#2), Capital One (#13) and numerous large global financial companies in Canada, Great Britain, Japan and Mexico. By 2004 banking generated about 70% of Synovus's profits, while TSYS pitched in about 30%, making it a true "source of strength" for its BHC, which was the original rationale for allowing banks to own nonbank subsidiaries like it in the first place.

The Synovus culture stayed strong for so long because of selection, not because the company was small in any absolute sense of the word. By 1989 Synovus operated in four states, Mexico, Puerto Rico and Canada. A decade later it was the parent of 48 companies, including 36 community banks, and it had more than $12.5 billion in assets and 10,000 "team members." In addition to banks, Synovus by the turn of the century owned a trust company, a securities affiliate, a mortgage lender and an insurer.

In 2003 Synovus's vice chairman, Richard Anthony, described the bank as "a mid-sized regional network of decentralized community banks." It was big enough to service substantial corporate borrowers, he noted, but because of its decentralized decision making still presented a local face to its retail customers. "'One size fits all' is not in the Synovus vocabulary," he said, asserting that the bank was a shapeshifter or chameleon that adapted to local circumstances no matter where it spread—urban, rural or in betwixt.

Customers acquired from takeovers were not jarred, but rather received the same good service they always had, plus all of the new services available through the Synovus suite. But the company was not resting on past successes, realizing that, as Anthony put it, "continuous improvement is necessary if the company is to excel in the future." That meant adding a sales orientation to the bank's already strong customer service culture without going overboard by engaging in "product pushing just for the sake of creating revenues. . . . Every salesperson," Anthony explained, "is expected to sell products based on customer needs," not the bank's wants. Carefully constructed bonus plans were key to striking the right balance, but headquarters did not force specific incentives on its subsidiaries.

By 2005 Synovus employed more than 12,000 team members (two-thirds of whom were women and one-quarter of whom were minorities) in 40 affiliate banks spread over 400 locations in the United States and abroad. The culture easily attracted team players. Those with more egoistical goals who sneaked or blundered past the company's screening process soon discovered it was best to move on because the do-gooder culture was just too strong, entrenched and ubiquitous to buck.

And that extends right to the top, where "Servant Leadership" is the norm. "The boss," the bank's leaders say, echoing beliefs widely held in corporate America in the 19th century, "is there to serve the organization and its people, not the other way around." That was the same concept of stewardship—of serving others, including future generations—that permeated BB&T (#17) and many smaller banks across the nation, but that was largely absent at the biggest banks by the turn of

the millennium. The Cultural Trust Committee, which every month put representatives from every level and business in the bank in front of the CEO, was charged with maintaining the health of the corporate culture, which has been described as a "culture of the heart."

In 2003 Anthony wrote that Synovus's vision was "to be the finest financial services company in the world." Continuing with its strategy of buying small banks and allowing them to continue to run mostly on their own, the bank's financial position remained stronger than that of most of its peers until late 2007, when it spun off the rest of TSYS and began to feel the pinch of deteriorating credit quality. It responded by selling off troubled assets at discounts in the range of 20%.

Despite its decisive action and initially strong capital base, however, the bank was in serious trouble by late 2009 after five straight quarters of major losses. TARP funds amounting to nearly $968 million kept it going, but its stock price plummeted and rumors swirled that TD (#14), BB&T (#17), SunTrust (#18) or Regions (#24) would soon buy it. Almost three years later, in August 2012, Synovus, which had returned to profitability in 2011, held the dubious distinction of owing more TARP funds than any other bank in the country. Yet it retained its independence, and in May 2013 was allowed to buy a failed bank even though it still had not repaid the government.

"It's another signal that the recovery of Synovus is not complete," claimed Jeff Davis of Mercer Capital, "but certainly in the late eighth inning or maybe even top of the ninth."

Sources

Anthony, Richard. "The Future of Banking at Synovus Financial Corporation." In *The Future of Banking*, edited by Benton E. Gup, 265–69. Westport, CT: Quorum Books, 2003.

Boraks, David. "Hybrid Synovus' Plan: Evolve But Don't Budge." *American Banker*, March 30, 2004, 1.

Davis, Paul. "At Synovus, a Wholesale Exit from Bad Assets: Quicker Disposals Eyed as a Way to Clear Decks for Acquisitions." *American Banker*, June 20, 2008, 1.

_____. "Withering Capital at Synovus as Losses Grow." *American Banker*, November 17, 2009, 1.

Dobbs, Kevin. "Spinoff May Give TSYS, Synovus Deal Options." *American Banker*, October 26, 2007, 1.

Drazin, Robert, Edward D. Hess and Farah Mihoubi. "Synovus Financial Corporation: 'Just take care of your people'." In *Leading with Values: Positivity, Virtue, and High Performance*, edited by Edward D. Hess and Kim S. Cameron, 9–28. New York: Cambridge University Press, 2006.

Hamilton, Francis. "Developing a Shared Mental Model: Operationalizing Servant-Leadership at Synovus Financial." PhD diss., University of South Florida, 2005.

Kulikowski, Laurie. "A Downgrade for Synovus, But Prospects Called Good." *American Banker*, May 6, 2005, 23.

Militello, Frederick C. and Michael D. Schwalberg. *Leverage Competencies: The Key to Financial Leadership Success*. Morristown, NJ: Financial Executives Research Foundation, 2000, 147–66.

Reiker, Matthias and Eric Morah. "M&T Bank to Exit TARP, via Backdoor." *Wall Street Journal Online*, August 16, 2012.

Skinner, Tara. "The Empiricist Paradox: Fostering Internal Stability While Pursuing Change at Synovus Financial Corp." MA thesis, Stonier Graduate School of Banking, 1999.

Stewart, Jackie. "Surprising Synovus Deal Shows TARP Banks Can Do M&A, Too." *American Banker*, May 17, 2013, 1.

Walden, Gene. *The 100 Best Stocks to Own in America* 5th ed. Chicago: Dearborn Financial Publishing, 1998, 35–38.

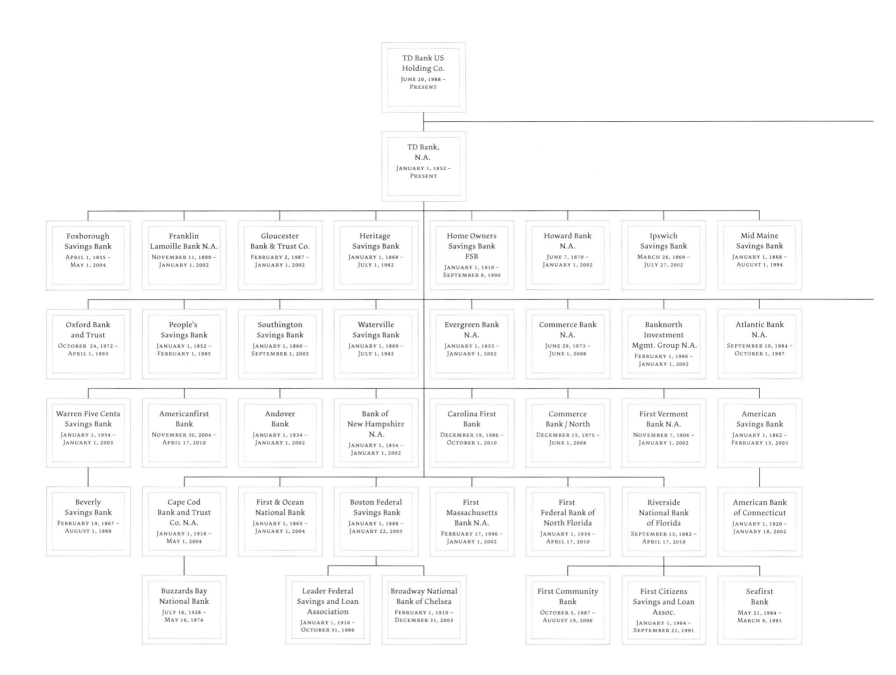

TD Bank US
Holding Co.
June 20, 1988 –
Present

TD Bank,
N.A.
January 1, 1852 –
Present

Foxborough
Savings Bank
April 1, 1855 –
May 1, 2004

Franklin
Lamoille Bank N.A.
November 11, 1899 –
January 1, 2002

Gloucester
Bank & Trust Co.
February 2, 1987 –
January 1, 2002

Heritage
Savings Bank
January 1, 1868 –
July 1, 1982

Home Owners
Savings Bank
FSB
January 1, 1910 –
September 8, 1990

Howard Bank
N.A.
June 7, 1870 –
January 1, 2002

Ipswich
Savings Bank
March 26, 1869 –
July 27, 2002

Mid Maine
Savings Bank
January 1, 1868 –
August 1, 1994

Oxford Bank
and Trust
October 24, 1972 –
April 1, 1993

People's
Savings Bank
January 1, 1852 –
February 1, 1985

Southington
Savings Bank
January 1, 1860 –
September 1, 2002

Waterville
Savings Bank
January 1, 1869 –
July 1, 1982

Evergreen Bank
N.A.
January 1, 1853 –
January 1, 2002

Commerce Bank
N.A.
June 29, 1973 –
June 1, 2008

Banknorth
Investment
Mgmt. Group N.A.
February 1, 1996 –
January 1, 2002

Atlantic Bank
N.A.
September 10, 1984 –
October 1, 1997

Warren Five Cents
Savings Bank
January 1, 1954 –
January 1, 2003

Americanfirst
Bank
November 30, 2004 –
April 17, 2010

Andover
Bank
January 1, 1934 –
January 1, 2002

Bank of
New Hampshire
N.A.
January 1, 1854 –
January 1, 2002

Carolina First
Bank
December 19, 1986 –
October 1, 2010

Commerce
Bank / North
December 15, 1975 –
June 1, 2008

First Vermont
Bank N.A.
November 7, 1906 –
January 1, 2002

American
Savings Bank
January 1, 1862 –
February 15, 2003

Beverly
Savings Bank
February 19, 1867 –
August 1, 1988

Cape Cod
Bank and Trust
Co. N.A.
January 1, 1916 –
May 1, 2004

First & Ocean
National Bank
January 1, 1865 –
January 1, 2004

Boston Federal
Savings Bank
January 1, 1888 –
January 22, 2005

First
Massachusetts
Bank N.A.
February 17, 1996 –
January 1, 2002

First
Federal Bank of
North Florida
January 1, 1934 –
April 17, 2010

Riverside
National Bank
of Florida
September 15, 1882 –
April 17, 2010

American Bank
of Connecticut
January 1, 1920 –
January 18, 2002

Buzzards Bay
National Bank
July 16, 1928 –
May 16, 1974

Leader Federal
Savings and Loan
Association
January 1, 1916 –
October 31, 1986

Broadway National
Bank of Chelsea
February 1, 1910 –
December 31, 2003

First Community
Bank
October 5, 1987 –
August 19, 2006

First Citizens
Savings and Loan
Assoc.
January 1, 1964 –
September 21, 1991

Seafirst
Bank
May 21, 1984 –
March 9, 1991

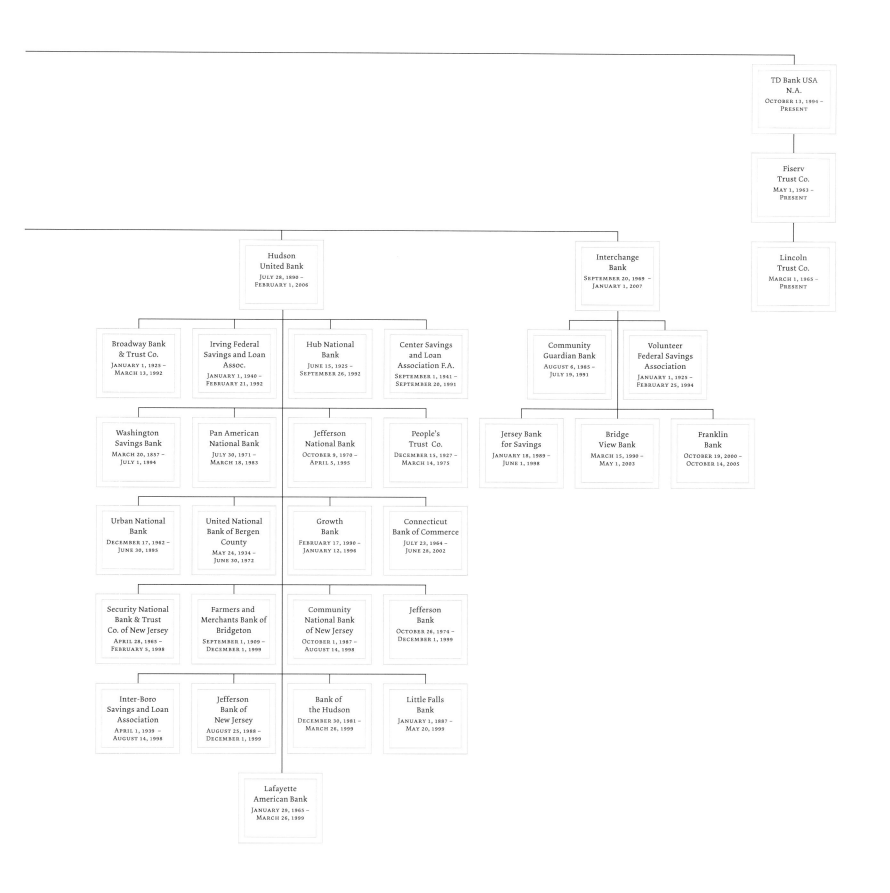

TD Bank US Holding

Bank *(abridged)*

RANK	HEADQUARTERS	TICKER	ASSETS	EARLIEST KNOWN ANCESTOR	INDUSTRY OF ORIGIN
14	**Portland, ME**	**TD**	**$229,000,000,000**	**1803**	**Commercial Banking**

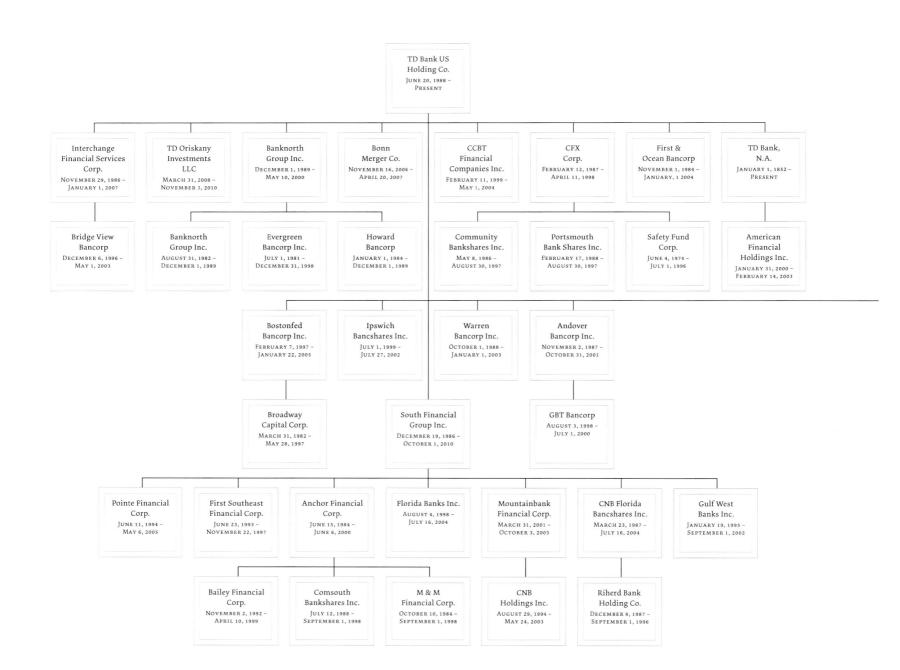

TD Bank US Holding Co.
JUNE 20, 1988 – PRESENT

Interchange Financial Services Corp.
NOVEMBER 29, 1986 – JANUARY 1, 2007

TD Oriskany Investments LLC
MARCH 31, 2008 – NOVEMBER 3, 2010

Banknorth Group Inc.
DECEMBER 1, 1989 – MAY 10, 2000

Bonn Merger Co.
NOVEMBER 16, 2006 – APRIL 20, 2007

CCBT Financial Companies Inc.
FEBRUARY 11, 1999 – MAY 1, 2004

CFX Corp.
FEBRUARY 12, 1987 – APRIL 11, 1998

First & Ocean Bancorp
NOVEMBER 1, 1984 – JANUARY, 1 2004

TD Bank, N.A.
JANUARY 1, 1852 – PRESENT

Bridge View Bancorp
DECEMBER 6, 1996 – MAY 1, 2003

Banknorth Group Inc.
AUGUST 31, 1982 – DECEMBER 1, 1989

Evergreen Bancorp Inc.
JULY 1, 1981 – DECEMBER 31, 1998

Howard Bancorp
JANUARY 1, 1984 – DECEMBER 1, 1989

Community Bankshares Inc.
MAY 8, 1986 – AUGUST 30, 1997

Portsmouth Bank Shares Inc.
FEBRUARY 17, 1988 – AUGUST 30, 1997

Safety Fund Corp.
JUNE 4, 1974 – JULY 1, 1996

American Financial Holdings Inc.
JANUARY 31, 2000 – FEBRUARY 14, 2003

Bostonfed Bancorp Inc.
FEBRUARY 7, 1997 – JANUARY 22, 2005

Ipswich Bancshares Inc.
JULY 1, 1999 – JULY 27, 2002

Warren Bancorp Inc.
OCTOBER 1, 1988 – JANUARY 1, 2003

Andover Bancorp Inc.
NOVEMBER 2, 1987 – OCTOBER 31, 2001

Broadway Capital Corp.
MARCH 31, 1982 – MAY 28, 1997

South Financial Group Inc.
DECEMBER 19, 1986 – OCTOBER 1, 2010

GBT Bancorp
AUGUST 3, 1998 – JULY 1, 2000

Pointe Financial Corp.
JUNE 11, 1994 – MAY 6, 2005

First Southeast Financial Corp.
JUNE 23, 1993 – NOVEMBER 22, 1997

Anchor Financial Corp.
JUNE 15, 1984 – JUNE 6, 2000

Florida Banks Inc.
AUGUST 4, 1998 – JULY 16, 2004

Mountainbank Financial Corp.
MARCH 31, 2001 – OCTOBER 3, 2003

CNB Florida Bancshares Inc.
MARCH 23, 1987 – JULY 16, 2004

Gulf West Banks Inc.
JANUARY 19, 1995 – SEPTEMBER 1, 2002

Bailey Financial Corp.
NOVEMBER 2, 1992 – APRIL 10, 1999

Comsouth Bankshares Inc.
JULY 12, 1988 – SEPTEMBER 1, 1998

M & M Financial Corp.
OCTOBER 10, 1984 – SEPTEMBER 1, 1998

CNB Holdings Inc.
AUGUST 29, 1994 – MAY 24, 2003

Riherd Bank Holding Co.
DECEMBER 9, 1987 – SEPTEMBER 1, 1996

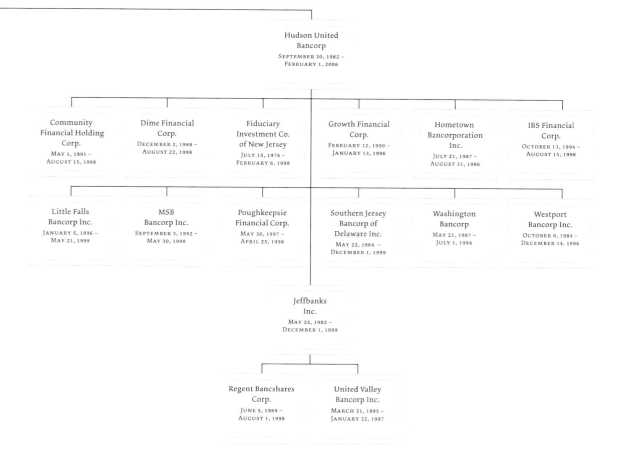

Hudson United
Bancorp
SEPTEMBER 30, 1982 –
FEBRUARY 1, 2006

Community
Financial Holding
Corp.
MAY 1, 1991 –
AUGUST 15, 1998

Dime Financial
Corp.
DECEMBER 2, 1988 –
AUGUST 22, 1998

Fiduciary
Investment Co.
of New Jersey
JULY 15, 1976 –
FEBRUARY 6, 1998

Growth Financial
Corp.
FEBRUARY 12, 1990 –
JANUARY 13, 1996

Hometown
Bancorporation
Inc.
JULY 21, 1987 –
AUGUST 31, 1996

IBS Financial
Corp.
OCTOBER 13, 1994 –
AUGUST 15, 1998

Little Falls
Bancorp Inc.
JANUARY 5, 1996 –
MAY 21, 1999

MSB
Bancorp Inc.
SEPTEMBER 3, 1992 –
MAY 30, 1998

Poughkeepsie
Financial Corp.
MAY 30, 1997 –
APRIL 25, 1998

Southern Jersey
Bancorp of
Delaware Inc.
MAY 22, 1984 –
DECEMBER 1, 1999

Washington
Bancorp
MAY 21, 1987 –
JULY 1, 1994

Westport
Bancorp Inc.
OCTOBER 9, 1984 –
DECEMBER 14. 1996

Jeffbanks
Inc.
MAY 25, 1982 –
DECEMBER 1, 1999

Regent Bancshares
Corp.
JUNE 5, 1989 –
AUGUST 1, 1998

United Valley
Bancorp Inc.
MARCH 31, 1995 –
JANUARY 22, 1997

TD Bank US Holding

Holding Company (abridged)

Reverse side of a $10 Bank of Toronto note, ca. 1890s, American Bank Note Company, New York. This beautiful medallion-ruling portrait of Victoria and Albert was used on the back of Bank of Toronto bank notes for approximately 80 years.

TD Bank, which stands for Toronto-Dominion, was formed in 1955 out of the merger of the Bank of Toronto and the Dominion Bank. It is aptly named, as it has been spreading its dominion over the United States, via its Maine-based BHC, since 2003.

The Bank of Toronto was established in 1855 by a group of Ontario millers who needed liquidity loans to run their capital-intensive businesses efficiently. Its charter mandated that £CA 200,000 be subscribed before business could commence, and at first the bank's subscription agent collected more vague promises than actual signatures and earnest payments on shares. The bank's opening was therefore delayed until July 1856.

While obtaining stockholders had been an arduous task that eventually involved tapping some English and American investors, finding depositors and borrowers proved relatively easy, so the bank rapidly grew organically at first. Lumbermen joined millers in the discount teller's line, while area farmers queued up to make deposits. The Panic of 1857 and a crop failure, however, prostrated the bank along with the Canadian economy in 1858 and 1859. In response, the bank cut back on lending and shuttered three branches.

In July 1867 Canada gained independence from Great Britain and unified most provinces under a single government that soon fell under the sway of the Bank of Montreal, giving it monetary powers that allowed it to dominate weaker institutions. "The Bank of Montreal has the government in its power," the Guelph *Mercury* reported in 1867, "and is disposed to play the tyrant." A long, costly and politicized war over Canadian banking and monetary policies ensued, but the result was a positive one: the Bank Act of 1871, which gave banks extensive branching powers and other salutary regulations. That year, the bank had only five branches, all in Ontario. By 1878 it had seven branches, a number that grew to 14 by 1896, when its capital and reserves amounted to $3.8 million.

The Bank of Toronto grew along with the Canadian economy and was also highly profitable. By 1873, before yet another banking panic wracked the bank and the economy, its capital was increased to $1.5 million, its reserve to $785,000 and it was paying 12% dividends. Not surprisingly, its stock, which traded on the exchanges in both Toronto and Montreal, generally stayed in the $185 to $194 range, higher than any other bank in the land. Its profitability, however,

spurred competitors, including its future merger partner, the Dominion Bank.

Formed by a group of Toronto businessmen and professionals in 1869 and chartered the same year, Dominion did not open for business until February 1871 because the incorporators found it difficult to secure the minimum capitalization required by its charter — $400,000 in subscriptions and $100,000 in cash. At that date, so soon after independence and confederation, the Canadian economy was still poor, backward and localized, especially compared to that of its precocious neighbor to the south. The Canadian financial system was much smaller and less stable than it would soon become, and Dominion stepped into the void left by the failure of several fairly important early Canadian banks. Despite its initial difficulty raising capital, Dominion hit the ground running. As its stock price soared above par, it actually considered two mergers among its first order of business. After inspection of the troubled banks' balance sheets, however, it demurred, and for the rest of its first half-century it never again sought "to absorb or unite with any other bank."

With organic growth the only route open to it, Dominion eagerly established de novo branches in its first year of operation, including branches in Toronto, Oshawa, Orillia, Whitby and Uxbridge. Branches in various neighborhoods of Toronto, as well as in Belleville and Lindsay, soon followed. With little industry or stock market activity yet evident, Dominion concentrated on financing the operations of wholesale exporters, companies that sold commodities like lumber and barley to the United States and further abroad. Thanks to prudent lending standards, the bank was, according to its historian, "never . . . involved in the financial worries of any moment." Its steady dividend, never below 8%, put its stock, in the words of Canadian banking historian Adam Shortt, "in the first rank of Canadian banks, a position which it has always maintained." By 1896 Dominion had grown slightly larger than the Bank of Toronto and would remain so until the two banks merged almost six decades later.

Despite shocks that ruined some of its competitors, Dominion continued to pay high dividends and increase its capital and surplus, in part because it remained an Ontario-only institution until 1897, when it finally opened a branch in Winnipeg, and 1898, when it moved into Montreal. Unusually rapid growth followed. Between 1885

Dominion Bank building, Quebec.

TD Canada Trust Tower in Toronto, 2008.

and 1900, Dominion doubled its number of branches from 11 to 22. Between then and 1905, it doubled the number again.

In 1906 Dominion's capital and reserves stood at only $6.8 million compared to $8.4 million at the Bank of Toronto. However, at almost $50 million its total assets were $11 million greater than those of its rival, which ushered in the 20th century by opening 39 branches in Ontario and four in Quebec. Some of the Bank of Toronto's new branches tapped into areas just opening up to new mining, timber and hydroelectric projects. Others back-filled agricultural areas that had matured in the final years of the 20th century owing to increased demand for Canadian beef and dairy products. Others attended to the needs of newer manufacturing centers, such as Kitchener and Waterloo, while still others were needed to service expanding urban centers like Toronto and London (Ontario). Not surprisingly, deposits swelled from $9.2 million in 1900 to $24.7 million in 1906. Although the growth spurt was dramatic and unprecedented, it was well planned and timed, as only four of the branches were subsequently shuttered.

From about 1905 until the Great War, the emphasis of both banks shifted from the East to the Canadian prairie. By 1915 Dominion had 95 branches in operation, including ones in Manitoba, the Territories, Calgary, Edmonton, Regina and Vancouver. It also established a branch in London in 1911. By 1914 its capital stood at $6 million and its reserve fund at $1 million, defending assets of some $80 million.

The Bank of Toronto moved into the region by buying some well-established but small local banks, some private and some chartered, and in the Canadian style turned them into branches. Then it moved to create its own de novo branches, being careful to follow the railroads and wheat farmers. By the end of 1913 it had eight branches in Alberta, nine in Manitoba and 25 in Saskatchewan. Both banks, however, found it difficult to make their western branches, which were often little more than a few employees and a counter, stick.

Unlike the United States, Canada entered the Great War in 1914 and hence felt its full effects, including inflation, well before its southern neighbor did. Its relatively large, well-regulated banks adapted well to the shocks and prospered by lending to the government, industry and agriculture. In 1918 the Bank of Toronto's assets exceeded $100 million, and Dominion's topped $153 million. The following year, the Bank of Toronto's annual profits exceeded $1 million for the first time, but its leaders, like those of the Dominion, were concerned about postwar deflation, higher taxes, decreased demand for Canadian exports and a banking overexpansion (between 1917 and 1920, Canadian banks had added 1,661 branches, an increase of over 50%). The two banks participated in the boom, but not as largely as their competitors. That was a good thing, as the attrition rate was high: 27 of 44 branches opened by the Bank of Toronto between 1919 and 1922 were gone within a decade. The Dominion Bank's record was almost as bad: 23 of its 47 new branches had to be shuttered.

Most of the closures were in agricultural areas, especially on the prairies, which were wracked by low prices (wheat went from $2.37 a bushel in 1919 to below $1 in 1922), drought and livestock die-offs. Some of the damage, though, was self-inflicted. In October 1923 a run ensued on Dominion when one of its tellers tried to explain to a non-English speaking immigrant that he could not cash the check the immigrant had presented because the check's maker had insufficient funds in the bank by saying in a loud voice "no money in the bank."

The nation's other banks knew Dominion was solid, however, so they did not add to the pressure and even refrained from taking advantage of the situation by advising large depositors not to bother switching banks solely on account of misguided rumors. Like the final scene from *It's a Wonderful Life*, National City Bank of New York (#3) wired "our facilities are at your disposal." The run by small depositors proceeded anyway, but most of the deposits soon returned as confidence was restored by the alacrity and speed with which the bank's tellers cashed out and a $1.5 million deposit by the Ontario government. Nevertheless, the run proved costly. By 1926 Dominion had assets of $127 million versus $115 million at the Bank of Toronto, a significant reduction from 1918. Also, the Bank of Toronto had 168 branches by 1926, and the Dominion only 118.

The late 1920s were good times in Canada. The Great Depression was not as severe in Canada as in the United States, although it too suffered from the effects of drought, dust and deflation. Branches in troubled areas, like the infamously arid Palliser Triangle in southern Alberta and Saskatchewan, were shuttered or ran at a loss while branches in less affected areas kept both banks afloat. Nevertheless, Canada emerged from the Depression with the Bank of Canada, a central bank charged with conducting monetary policy, regulating banks and acting as a lender of last resort.

Canada was well clear of the Depression in 1939, when it joined the war effort against Nazi Germany. As two decades earlier, a major war stimulated its economy, covering up the remaining cracks. The nation's banks could not help but make money, even though burdened by the administration of ration coupons, high employee turnover and capital and loan controls. By the war's end the Bank of Toronto's total capital stood at almost $20 million and Dominion's was over $15 million. Dominion had more than $300 million in assets, while the Bank of Toronto had more than $350 million.

Despite postwar labor unrest and inflation, the decade after World War II proved equally lucrative for both banks, as they decreased their holdings of government bonds and again began lending large sums to businesses to finance agricultural and industrial production, as well as international trade. By 1954 the Bank of Toronto operated 256 branches, and Dominion 193. The former had assets of $593.6 million, the latter $538.5 million. They came to the negotiating table in May 1954 as equals, and some referred to their union as a "marriage."

When the merger was finalized in early 1955, TD became one of Canada's famed "Big Six" banks along with BMO (#26), Royal Bank of Canada, Scotiabank, Canadian Imperial Bank of Commerce and National Bank. For decades it was stuck in the fifth spot, ahead of the relatively diminutive and ironically named National Bank (which was mostly based in Quebec), but sat nowhere near the top. It was well-run and a major lender to the cable television industry, but not the market leader. Early foreign forays ended quickly, as in the case of merger talks with Chase Manhattan (#1) in the early 1960s; eventually, as in the case of an early 1970s California foray which was sold to Japanese investors in 1983; or disastrously, as in the case of branches in Lebanon being robbed by a bazooka-toting employee.

TD Bank's growth spurt began late in the 20th century, with its acquisition of American discount broker Waterhouse Investor Services in 1996. It spun off the business, rechristened online broker TD Waterhouse, in 1999 but reprivatized it (bought up all the outstanding shares) in 2001. In 2005 it sold the business to Ameritrade Holding Corporation, retaining about a 40% stake in the new company, called TD Ameritrade, which it increased to 45% in 2010. That was all done through TD Securities, the wholesale banking arm of TD. With 20 offices in 18 cities worldwide and 3,000 employees, TD Securities topped many of the Canadian league banking tables in securities underwriting, equities research, M&A advice, foreign exchange and, via TD Capital, private equity investments.

In 2000 TD Bank grew again, by buying Canada Trust for $8 billion in cash. Established in London, Ontario in 1864, Canada Trust (née Huron & Erie Savings and Loan Society) started as an agricultural bank. It was highly profitable and grew to be Canada's sixth largest financial institution after some 18 mergers, including its purchase

of Canada Permanent in 1989. It was Canada Trust that introduced Canadians, and TD Bank, to extended hours, advertising in 1976 its clever new schedule as "Eight to Eight, Six Days Straight." (Banking on Sunday was then unthinkable.) "Canada Trust was a marketing department with a bank attached to it," joked W. Edmund "Ed" Clark, a Canada Trust holdover who took the helm at TD Bank in 2002. He later made the motto of its US BHC "America's Most Convenient Bank," opened it seven days a week, and staffed it with helpful, smiling employees.

Clark, a Harvard economics PhD, realized after Ottawa officials blocked the merger of the Royal Bank of Canada and BMO in 1998 that the days of domestic acquisitions were over for Canadian banks like TD. To grow, TD would have to expand to America. In a decade, TD established more branches in the United States (1,300) than it had put up in its home country in a century in a half (1,150), and the bank had grown from $278 billion in assets in 2002 to $806 billion at the end of the third quarter of 2012. That made TD Canada's second largest bank, behind Royal, and the sixth largest bank in North America by assets, deposits and market value. (Of course, those figures refer to the entire bank, not just its American BHC.) At the end of 2012 it was the only bank traded on the NYSE with a triple-A credit rating, and it actually earned a billion more dollars than Royal did.

Some of the growth was organic, good old-fashioned taking market share away from its competitors by providing better service. As Clark explained to CNBC's Maria Bartiromo and countless other reporters, "when people find out we're open longer, have better service, roll their pennies for free and have treats for their dogs, they'll come." But for Clark, whose strategic acumen was once compared to that of a "3-D chess player," acquisitions were key.

They began in 2005 and accelerated during the 2008 financial crisis, which barely touched TD or the Canadian financial system. TD remained profitable throughout the downturn and was even able to raise new capital. In 2007, for example, Clark swooped in to buy Commerce Bank and suddenly the bank was almost as ubiquitous in New York City as Starbucks. As the crisis deepened, other acquisitions followed, many on the I-95 corridor from Maine to Florida.

In another major transaction, TD Bank bought Chrysler Financial from a private equity company, Cerberus Management, for about $6.3 billion in December 2010. But don't let all the acquisitions fool you, Clark reminded investors. TD Bank remained a Canadian bank at heart, and that meant it favored stability above all else. Indeed, Clark, who was still leading the bank at the end of 2013, endorsed Basel III capital standards and called for the industry to return to traditional banking.

Sources

Adubato, Steve. *You Are the Brand*. New Brunswick, NJ: Rutgers University Press, 2011, 60–64.

Bair, Sheila. *Bull by the Horns: Fighting to Save Main Street from Wall Street and Wall Street from Itself*. New York: Free Press, 2012, 357.

Green, Howard. *Banking on America: How TD Bank Rose to the Top and Took on the U.S.A.* Toronto: HarperCollins 2013.

Loosvelt, Derek, et al. *The Vault Guide to the Top 50 Banking Employers: 2008 Edition*. New York: Vault, 2007, 417–21.

Schull, Joseph. *100 Years of Banking in Canada: A History of the Toronto-Dominion Bank*. Toronto: Copp Clark, 1958.

Skelton, Oscar. *The Dominion Bank: Fifty Years of Banking Service, 1871–1921*. Toronto: The Dominion Bank, 1922.

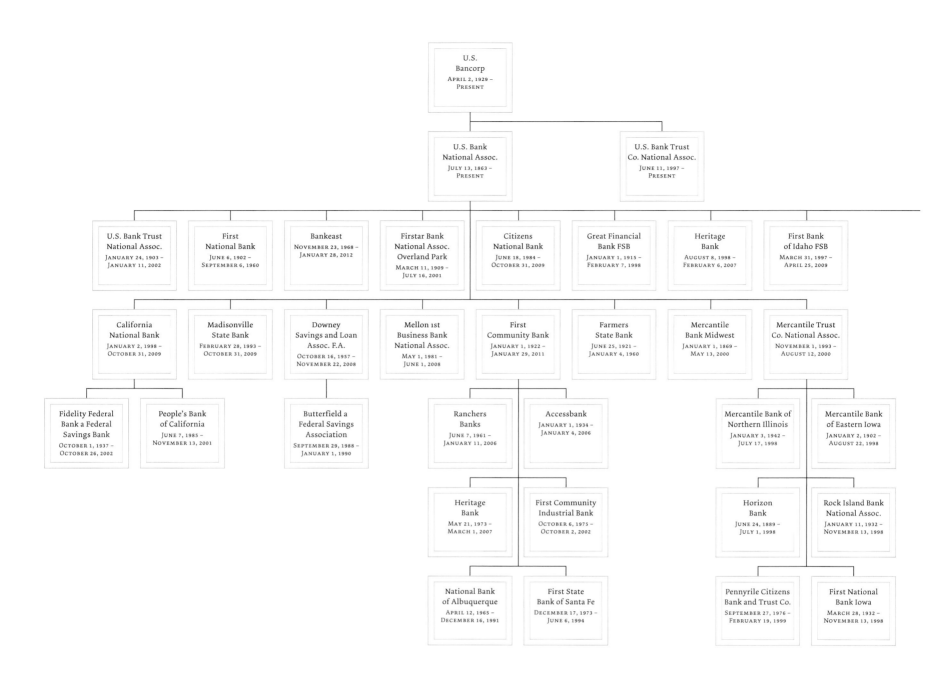

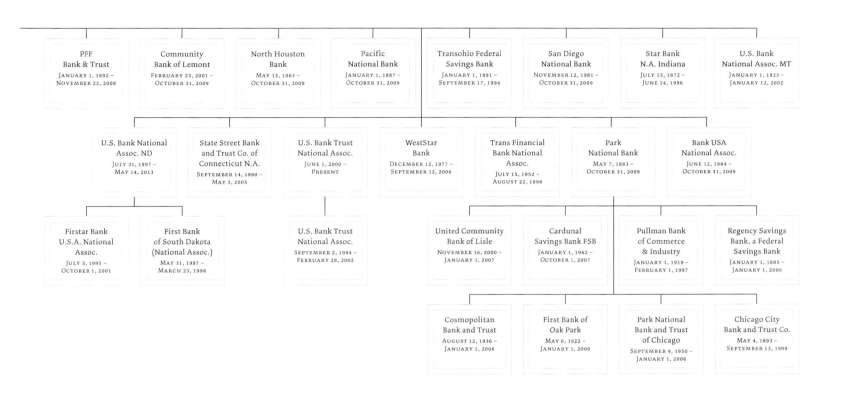

| | PFF Bank & Trust JANUARY 1, 1892 – NOVEMBER 22, 2008 | Community Bank of Lemont FEBRUARY 23, 2001 – OCTOBER 31, 2009 | North Houston Bank MAY 15, 1963 – OCTOBER 31, 2009 | Pacific National Bank JANUARY 1, 1887 – OCTOBER 31, 2009 | Transohio Federal Savings Bank JANUARY 1, 1891 – SEPTEMBER 17, 1994 | San Diego National Bank NOVEMBER 12, 1981 – OCTOBER 31, 2009 | Star Bank N.A. Indiana JULY 15, 1872 – JUNE 14, 1996 | U.S. Bank National Assoc. MT JANUARY 1, 1923 – JANUARY 12, 2002 |

| | U.S. Bank National Assoc. ND JULY 31, 1997 – MAY 14, 2013 | State Street Bank and Trust Co. of Connecticut N.A. SEPTEMBER 14, 1990 – MAY 3, 2005 | U.S. Bank Trust National Assoc. JUNE 1, 2000 – PRESENT | WestStar Bank DECEMBER 12, 1977 – SEPTEMBER 12, 2006 | Trans Financial Bank National Assoc. JULY 15, 1952 – AUGUST 22, 1998 | Park National Bank MAY 7, 1883 – OCTOBER 31, 2009 | Bank USA National Assoc. JUNE 12, 1984 – OCTOBER 31, 2009 |

| | Firstar Bank U.S.A. National Assoc. JULY 3, 1995 – OCTOBER 1, 2001 | First Bank of South Dakota (National Assoc.) MAY 31, 1997 – MARCH 23, 1998 | U.S. Bank Trust National Assoc. SEPTEMBER 2, 1994 – FEBRUARY 28, 2002 | United Community Bank of Lisle NOVEMBER 16, 2000 – JANUARY 1, 2007 | Cardunal Savings Bank FSB JANUARY 1, 1962 – OCTOBER 1, 2007 | Pullman Bank of Commerce & Industry JANUARY 1, 1919 – FEBRUARY 1, 1997 | Regency Savings Bank, a Federal Savings Bank JANUARY 1, 1885 – JANUARY 1, 2006 |

| | Cosmopolitan Bank and Trust AUGUST 12, 1936 – JANUARY 1, 2006 | First Bank of Oak Park MAY 6, 1922 – JANUARY 1, 2006 | Park National Bank and Trust of Chicago SEPTEMBER 9, 1950 – JANUARY 1, 2006 | Chicago City Bank and Trust Co. MAY 4, 1893 – SEPTEMBER 13, 1999 |

U.S. Bancorp

Bank *(abridged)*

RANK	HEADQUARTERS	TICKER	ASSETS	EARLIEST KNOWN ANCESTOR	INDUSTRY OF ORIGIN
10	**Minneapolis, MN**	**USB**	**$353,000,000,000**	**1853**	**Commercial Banking**

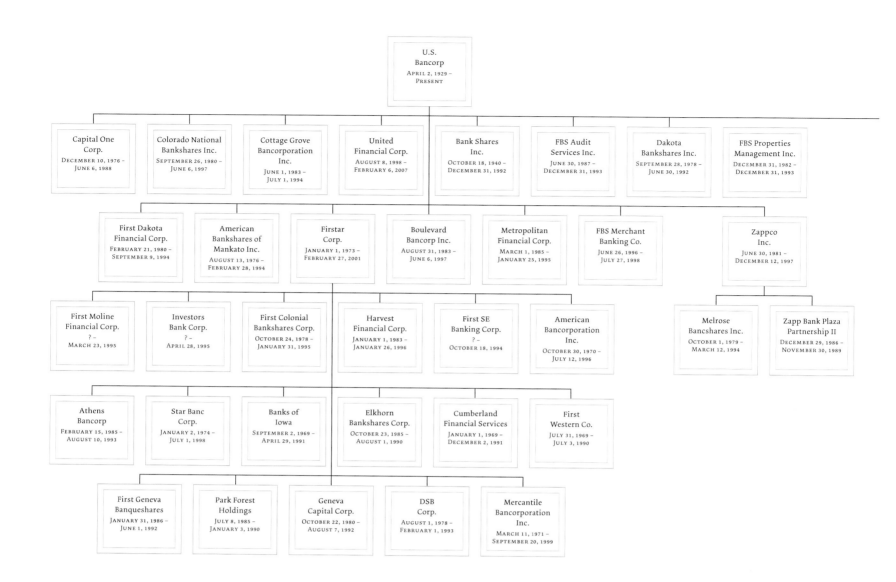

U.S.
Bancorp
APRIL 2, 1929 –
PRESENT

Capital One
Corp.
DECEMBER 10, 1976 –
JUNE 6, 1988

Colorado National
Bankshares Inc.
SEPTEMBER 26, 1980 –
JUNE 6, 1997

Cottage Grove
Bancorporation
Inc.
JUNE 1, 1983 –
JULY 1, 1994

United
Financial Corp.
AUGUST 8, 1998 –
FEBRUARY 6, 2007

Bank Shares
Inc.
OCTOBER 18, 1940 –
DECEMBER 31, 1992

FBS Audit
Services Inc.
JUNE 30, 1987 –
DECEMBER 31, 1993

Dakota
Bankshares Inc.
SEPTEMBER 28, 1978 –
JUNE 30, 1992

FBS Properties
Management Inc.
DECEMBER 31, 1982 –
DECEMBER 31, 1993

First Dakota
Financial Corp.
FEBRUARY 21, 1980 –
SEPTEMBER 9, 1994

American
Bankshares of
Mankato Inc.
AUGUST 13, 1976 –
FEBRUARY 28, 1994

Firstar
Corp.
JANUARY 1, 1973 –
FEBRUARY 27, 2001

Boulevard
Bancorp Inc.
AUGUST 31, 1983 –
JUNE 6, 1997

Metropolitan
Financial Corp.
MARCH 1, 1985 –
JANUARY 25, 1995

FBS Merchant
Banking Co.
JUNE 26, 1996 –
JULY 27, 1998

Zappco
Inc.
JUNE 30, 1981 –
DECEMBER 12, 1997

First Moline
Financial Corp.
? –
MARCH 23, 1995

Investors
Bank Corp.
? –
APRIL 28, 1995

First Colonial
Bankshares Corp.
OCTOBER 24, 1978 –
JANUARY 31, 1995

Harvest
Financial Corp.
JANUARY 1, 1983 –
JANUARY 26, 1996

First SE
Banking Corp.
? –
OCTOBER 18, 1994

American
Bancorporation
Inc.
OCTOBER 30, 1970 –
JULY 12, 1996

Melrose
Bancshares Inc.
OCTOBER 1, 1979 –
MARCH 12, 1994

Zapp Bank Plaza
Partnership II
DECEMBER 29, 1986 –
NOVEMBER 30, 1989

Athens
Bancorp
FEBRUARY 15, 1985 –
AUGUST 10, 1993

Star Banc
Corp.
JANUARY 2, 1974 –
JULY 1, 1998

Banks of
Iowa
SEPTEMBER 2, 1969 –
APRIL 29, 1991

Elkhorn
Bankshares Corp.
OCTOBER 23, 1985 –
AUGUST 1, 1990

Cumberland
Financial Services
JANUARY 1, 1969 –
DECEMBER 2, 1991

First
Western Co.
JULY 31, 1969 –
JULY 3, 1990

First Geneva
Banqueshares
JANUARY 31, 1986 –
JUNE 1, 1992

Park Forest
Holdings
JULY 8, 1985 –
JANUARY 3, 1990

Geneva
Capital Corp.
OCTOBER 22, 1980 –
AUGUST 7, 1992

DSB
Corp.
AUGUST 1, 1978 –
FEBRUARY 1, 1993

Mercantile
Bancorporation
Inc.
MARCH 11, 1971 –
SEPTEMBER 20, 1999

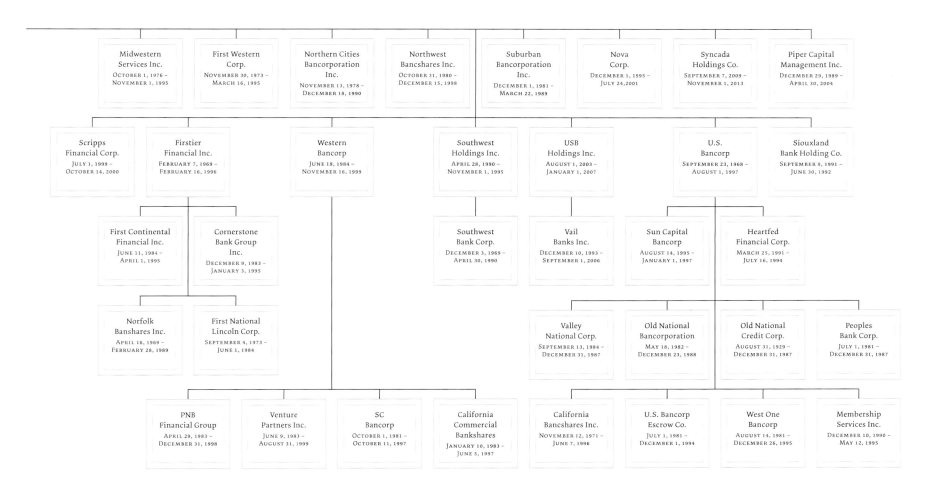

Midwestern Services Inc.	First Western Corp.	Northern Cities Bancorporation Inc.	Northwest Bancshares Inc.	Suburban Bancorporation Inc.	Nova Corp.	Syncada Holdings Co.	Piper Capital Management Inc.
OCTOBER 1, 1976 – NOVEMBER 1, 1995	NOVEMBER 30, 1973 – MARCH 16, 1995	NOVEMBER 13, 1978 – DECEMBER 18, 1990	OCTOBER 31, 1980 – DECEMBER 15, 1998	DECEMBER 1, 1981 – MARCH 22, 1989	DECEMBER 1, 1995 – JULY 24, 2001	SEPTEMBER 7, 2009 – NOVEMBER 1, 2013	DECEMBER 29, 1989 – APRIL 30, 2004

Scripps Financial Corp.
JULY 1, 1999 – OCTOBER 14, 2000

Firstier Financial Inc.
FEBRUARY 7, 1969 – FEBRUARY 16, 1996

Western Bancorp
JUNE 19, 1984 – NOVEMBER 16, 1999

Southwest Holdings Inc.
APRIL 28, 1990 – NOVEMBER 1, 1995

USB Holdings Inc.
AUGUST 1, 2003 – JANUARY 1, 2007

U.S. Bancorp
SEPTEMBER 23, 1968 – AUGUST 1, 1997

Siouxland Bank Holding Co.
SEPTEMBER 9, 1991 – JUNE 30, 1992

First Continental Financial Inc.
JUNE 11, 1984 – APRIL 1, 1995

Cornerstone Bank Group Inc.
DECEMBER 9, 1983 – JANUARY 3, 1995

Southwest Bank Corp.
DECEMBER 3, 1969 – APRIL 30, 1990

Vail Banks Inc.
DECEMBER 10, 1993 – SEPTEMBER 1, 2006

Sun Capital Bancorp
AUGUST 14, 1995 – JANUARY 1, 1997

Heartfed Financial Corp.
MARCH 25, 1991 – JULY 16, 1994

Norfolk Banshares Inc.
APRIL 16, 1969 – FEBRUARY 28, 1989

First National Lincoln Corp.
SEPTEMBER 4, 1973 – JUNE 1, 1984

Valley National Corp.
SEPTEMBER 13, 1984 – DECEMBER 31, 1987

Old National Bancorporation
MAY 18, 1982 – DECEMBER 23, 1988

Old National Credit Corp.
AUGUST 31, 1929 – DECEMBER 31, 1987

Peoples Bank Corp.
JULY 1, 1981 – DECEMBER 31, 1987

PNB Financial Group
APRIL 29, 1983 – DECEMBER 31, 1998

Venture Partners Inc.
JUNE 9, 1983 – AUGUST 31, 1999

SC Bancorp
OCTOBER 1, 1981 – OCTOBER 11, 1997

California Commercial Bankshares
JANUARY 10, 1983 – JUNE 5, 1997

California Bancshares Inc.
NOVEMBER 12, 1971 – JUNE 7, 1996

U.S. Bancorp Escrow Co.
JULY 1, 1981 – DECEMBER 1, 1994

West One Bancorp
AUGUST 14, 1981 – DECEMBER 26, 1995

Membership Services Inc.
DECEMBER 10, 1990 – MAY 12, 1995

U.S. Bancorp

Holding Company (abridged)

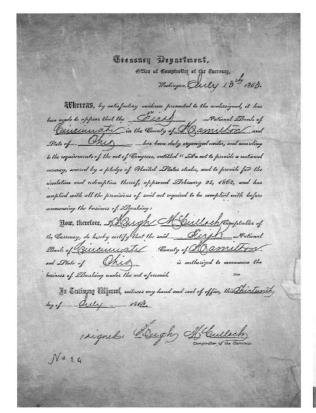

United States National Bank of Oregon, 1893.

First National Bank of Cincinnati opened as the Civil War raged across the Ohio River. The national charter was signed 10 days after the Battle of Gettysburg and just after Union General Ambrose Burnside declared martial law in Cincinnati. The bank later became part of today's U.S. Bancorp by way of Star Bancorporation. This is the charter under which U.S. Bancorp operates today.

Wisconsin National Bank advertisement, 1894.

The U.S. Bancorp BHC was formed when Firstar acquired U.S. Bancorp in 2001. It offers a wide range of financial services to businesses and consumers and also provides payment processing via its Elavon subsidiary. U.S. Bancorp — the original bank — began its existence in Oregon in 1891 styled as the United States National Bank of Portland. Headed by Donald Macleay, a Scot well-versed in business and banking, and other influential businessmen, the U.S. National started small but was able to survive the bank runs that ruined half of Portland's other banks during the Panic of 1893. It did so thanks to the bank's conservative lending and dividend policies, as well as timely injections of Macleay's personal fortune. It took much of the rest of the decade for the bank to recover. Macleay never did recover, dying in 1897 at age 63 after a trip to his native Scotland failed to restore his health.

In 1902 U.S. National merged with Ainsworth National, an older but smaller bank that came with a large and solid book of loans and a stable of ambitious young bankers, including the merged institution's president, John C. Ainsworth. The new U.S. National grew quickly in the first three decades of the new century. It absorbed Wells Fargo's (#4) Portland bank in 1905, and even the Panic of 1907 barely touched the state's booming economy or its banks. During the Great War, farm profits increased dramatically, as did the profits of the lumber and shipbuilding industries. Not surprisingly, the bank grew by leaps and bounds, from $12 million in assets in 1914 to $41 million in 1919, and dividends soared. It also used some of its profits to form a trust department in 1919.

The postwar recession caused some consternation and cutbacks, but Ainsworth kept the bank off the rocks, and by 1925 an examiner considered it to be "in a flourishing condition." Soon thereafter, the bank bought Ladd & Tilton for $700,000 and transferred the private bank's assets to U.S. National's headquarters over a single hectic weekend. The transaction increased the number of the bank's depositors to 75,000 and its assets to $64.6 million, making U.S. National the largest bank in the country — north of San Francisco and west of Minneapolis, that is. The bank grew again in 1927 when it split the remaining assets and deposits of the failed Northwestern National with First National, another large Portland bank.

Stymied by branching restrictions from growing further, and fearful of being subsumed by A.P. Giannini's growing empire (eventually Bank of America [#2]), the bank in 1928 formed the United States National Corporation. That new entity, which was controlled by the bank's officers, purchased West Coast National Bank in 1930, which was soon followed by the acquisition of eight additional banks, making it one of the nation's largest group banks.

Portland, considered one of the strongest banking cities in America at the time, did not suffer from the Great Depression at first. Eventually, however, high unemployment and business failures led the almost 40-year-old Hibernia Commercial and Savings Bank to close its doors in December 1931, an event that touched off Portland's first major bank run just months after Ainsworth had turned control of the bank over to Paul Dick. Working with the State Superintendent of Banks, Dick announced withdrawal restrictions effective until the "unreasonable hysteria" gripping depositors had passed.

Almost $10 million flowed out of the bank in the last quarter of 1931 and the first half of 1932. In early 1933 the Portland Clearinghouse Association, an institution that cleared checks for Portland's banks,

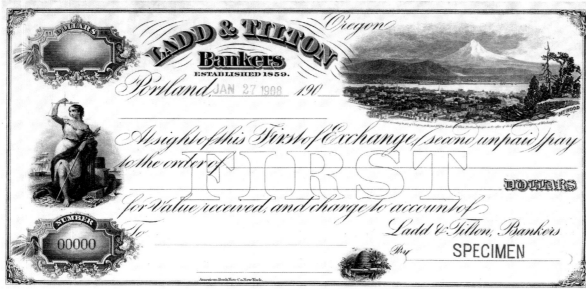

Ladd & Tilton specimen sight draft, 1908.

First Bank building sign and bank officials.

took the extreme step of drawing up special certificates backed by collateral, including warehouse receipts for canned food, just in case cash became unavailable. They were never put into circulation because the flow of deposits reversed after implementation of President Roosevelt's bank holiday reforms, but the bank felt it prudent to cut its dividends, salaries and loan book nonetheless. Unwilling to lend to shaky businesses or individuals with limited prospects, the bank, like many of its peers, became more of a government bond mutual fund than a traditional lender.

The Depression brought about the relaxation of branching restrictions in Oregon by highlighting the vulnerability of small unit banks to economic shocks, and also by denuding many rural communities of all their banks. Legislation enacted in early 1933 allowed U.S. National to turn some of its holding company's independent banks into branches. The passage of Glass-Steagall later that same year loosened yet more restrictions. U.S. National was the first bank to establish a branch under its reforms, which made it possible for the bank to shutter its BHC, for the time being anyway.

The Depression made rapid growth impossible, but by 1940 the economy had revived enough to induce the bank to make a few acquisitions, including the Farmers and Fruitgrowers Bank of Medford, First National of Corvallis and the Ladd & Bush Bank of Salem. War again brought prosperity to the nation, the state, the city and the bank. It eagerly participated in the financing of local war industries, including shipbuilders. Aided by a massive influx of some 128,000 workers paid by the bank, newly completed Liberty cargo ships and tankers slid off their racks and into the sea at rates thought impossible just a few years earlier. The bank also purchased huge sums of federal government bonds on its own account and helped the government to sell bonds to its customers. In one 10-day period in late 1943 alone, the bank sold $21 million of war bonds throughout the state.

Dick died in early 1945 and was succeeded by Edward Sammons, who within months made the bank's 29th acquisition, the First National Bank of Madras. Sammons was far from done. At the war's end, the bank had deposits of $581 million and more than 1,000 employees. Under his leadership, the bank grew in both size and sophistication. Between 1945 and 1955, it added 35 branches, six de novo and 29 through purchase. The acquisition of the Commercial Bank of Oregon in 1954,

which added 11 branches and $32 million in deposits, was the largest and most important of the era. In case of war or other catastrophe, the bank designated branches as backup headquarters, created a line of succession to the presidency and backed up the bank's records, something made easier by the adoption of computerized recordkeeping in the 1950s and 1960s.

In 1960 Sammons assumed the board chairmanship, and the presidency was awarded to E.J. Kolar, who came to the bank in the merger with West Coast National in 1930. A wave of de novo branch formation soon followed, along with a handful of new acquisitions. The bank hit the 100-branch mark in 1965 and decided to enlarge its name to the United States National Bank of Oregon to reflect its growing geographical reach. It also reorganized itself into six divisions, each headed by a regional manager. LeRoy Staver, a lifer at the bank, assumed the presidency in 1966, just in time for the infamous nationwide "credit crunch" and the formation of the BankAmericard network, of which the bank was a charter member.

The following year, Staver bought Commerce Mortgage Company, then a major mortgage banker in the West, to gain entry into Washington State and to further diversify the bank's portfolio. In 1968 the bank spread yet further by incorporating the United States National Bank International Corporation, an Edge Act corporation that made international loans and equity investments.

To make further geographical and sectoral diversification possible, Staver in 1968 formed a BHC called U.S. Bancorp and made U.S. National its first subsidiary. Over the next few years, it turned the bank's subsidiaries, like Commerce Mortgage, into subsidiaries of the BHC. Starting in 1970 the bank began expanding aggressively across the nation and the globe, buying a share of Allied Bank International with 17 other regional banks, establishing a branch in the Bahamas, starting up U.S. Datacorp, which offered computerized payroll and other services, and creating Bancorp Leasing, which financed ships, computer systems and other big ticket assets.

In 1974 John A. Elorriaga took the helm of U.S. Bancorp and continued its vigorous growth into credit life insurance, mortgages, commercial financing and the other niches regulators allowed. Elorriaga's parents had emigrated during the Great War from the Basque region of Spain to eastern Oregon, where John was born and raised. During

Proof department of the First National Bank of Cincinnati, 1954.

World War II, he worked hard making bombers for Boeing and saving his pennies at Washington Mutual Savings Bank (later WaMu and now part of JPMorgan Chase [#1]). He later served as a glider mechanic in the European theater. After the war, he attended college on the GI Bill. Friendships he made at the University of Oregon led him to U.S. National, and he joined its executive training program in 1951.

Elorriaga worked hard, learned on the job and studied bank management at the Pacific Coast Banking School. Sammons took a liking to him and the bank policy papers and other special assignments he wrote, so he moved up. In 1966, however, he left the bank to earn more money at Evans Product and Columbia Corporation. When he returned to the bank in 1972, he brought with him several ideas he picked up at those companies, including employee incentive plans. But Elorriaga himself took a pay cut to return and explained it to his wife this way: "When I die, and I look in that mirror, I don't want to see a person who didn't do all he could for his friends and for his community. I don't want to see someone who stayed where he was because he could make more money.... The satisfaction I get in life is doing the best I can for others."

Under pressure from regulators, the bank sold U.S. Datacorp in 1978. Sensing that regulators were going to limit permissible activities, Elorriaga decided to concentrate on traditional banking, but in new geographical areas. So in 1980 it began to establish banks in other states, including Wisconsin, Idaho, Utah, Montana, California, Texas and Colorado. It kept costs down, in part, by making extensive use of part-time staff.

In 1981 the *Wall Street Transcript* named Elorriaga the best CEO of a regional bank in the western United States. But the honor did not go to his head, and the bank's leadership continued to stress that "banking is people." That meant serving the interests of customers, of course, but also employees, who after 1975 enjoyed college-level training opportunities in the bank's General Banking Education program.

By the late 1980s, however, the bank was struggling, and rumors swirled that it would cut 700 of its 6,000 employees spread over nearly 200 branches. Elorriaga had to fend off talk that the bank was for sale and did so by making acquisitions of his own. When Elorriaga left in 1987, the bank was strong and independent, but half a continent away its eventual parent was waxing ever larger.

Firstar did its first business in 1853 as the Farmers' and Millers' Bank. A decade later it became the First National Bank of Milwaukee. After surviving a major embezzlement scandal in 1905, in 1919 it merged with the Wisconsin National Bank, which had been founded in 1892. The new institution, styled the First National Wisconsin Bank, was capitalized at $6 million. Meanwhile, in 1894, the Milwaukee Trust Company formed under the leadership of its founder, a 72-year-old banker named Hoel H. Camp, who had helped to form the Farmers' and Millers'. Described as "a dean of the banking profession" and a "pioneer banker in Milwaukee" who "always stood unflinchingly against visionary schemes for swelling the bank's dividends," Camp retired in 1901. Thereafter, the trust grew quickly and after several name changes and a 1919 merger, it became the state's largest trust, the First Wisconsin Trust Company. A former assistant to the Secretary of the Treasury, Catherine B. Cleary, ran the trust from 1969 until 1976, one of the few women ever to head up a major financial institution.

First National Wisconsin Bank, First Wisconsin Trust and other institutions eventually wound up under the same BHC, which in 1989 became Firstar after expanding beyond Wisconsin into Arizona, Florida, Illinois, Iowa and Minnesota. The trust side of the business remained relatively small—in 1993 it had $30 billion under administration, 6,000 accounts, 600 corporate clients, 1,500 employee benefit plans and 500 employees. Firstar also owned a consumer finance company, an investment research and management company and other businesses. But the real power was in its banking—if the bank, which was often spoken of as an acquisition target, could remain independent.

In the 1990s Firstar went on a bank acquisition rampage during which it purchased 18 banks and bulked up from $7.6 billion in assets in 1993 to almost $38.5 billion by the end of 1998. After it merged with Star Banc in 1998, it operated 720 offices in nine states. The following year, in a $10.6 billion deal, it merged with Mercantile Bank, which had about 500 locations in six states, three of which were new territory for Firstar. The Mercantile Bank dated back to the State Savings Institution (formed in 1855) and the Mercantile Trust Company (formed in 1899). By 1971 it was a BHC, and by the late 1980s it was, like Firstar, snapping up other banks as quickly as possible in order to maintain its independence.

The Mercantile merger made Firstar the 13th largest bank in the nation by assets ($76 billion) and seventh by territorial reach. The splurge followed a decade of 28.5% average annual growth in stock price and 27 consecutive years of dividend growth, numbers which got it named to Dearborn Financial's "100 Best Stocks to Own" list in 2000. Firstar had won the race with Mercantile, but it was not yet finished growing.

REGISTERED · REGISTERED

NUMBER
OR

BN 56283

12.50% DEBENTURE
DUE MAY 1, 2010

DOLLARS

CUSIP 911596 AD 6

U.S. BANCORP

U.S. Bancorp, a corporation duly organized and existing under the laws of the State of Oregon (herein called the "Company," which term includes any successor corporation under the Indenture hereinafter referred to), for value received, hereby promises to pay to

SEE REVERSE FOR CERTAIN DEFINITIONS

12.50%
DUE
2010

12.50%
DUE
2010

or registered assigns,
the principal sum of

DOLLARS

on May 1, 2010, and pay interest thereon from May 1, 1980 or from the most recent Interest Payment Date to which interest has been paid or duly provided for, semi-annually on May 1 and November 1 in each year, commencing November 1, 1980, at the rate of 12.50% per annum, until the principal hereof is paid or duly provided for. The interest so payable, and punctually paid or duly provided for, on any Interest Payment Date will, as provided in such Indenture, be paid to the Person in whose name this Debenture (or one or more Predecessor Debentures) is registered at the close of business on the Regular Record Date for such interest, which shall be the April 15 or October 15 (whether or not a Business Day), as the case may be, next preceding such Interest Payment Date. Any such interest not so punctually paid or duly provided for will forthwith cease to be payable to the Holder on such Regular Record Date and may either be paid to the Person in whose name this Debenture (or one or more Predecessor Debentures) is registered at the close of business on a Special Record Date for the payment of such Defaulted Interest to be fixed by the Trustee, notice whereof shall be given to Holders of Debentures not less than 10 days prior to such Special Record Date, or be paid at any time in any other lawful manner not inconsistent with the requirements of any securities exchange on which the Debentures may be listed, and upon such notice as may be required by such exchange, all as more fully provided in said Indenture. Payment of the principal of (and premium, if any) and interest on this Debenture will be made at the office or agency of the Company maintained for that purpose in the City of Portland, Oregon, in such coin or currency of the United States of America as at the time of payment is legal tender for payment of public and private debts; provided, however, that at the option of the Company, interest may be paid by check mailed to the address of the Person entitled thereto as such address shall appear in the Debenture Register.

Reference is hereby made to the further provisions of this Debenture set forth on the reverse hereof, which further provisions shall for all purposes have the same effect as if set forth at this place.

Unless this certificate of authentication hereon has been executed by the Trustee under the Indenture or its successor thereunder, or by the Authenticating Bank, by manual signature, this Debenture shall not be entitled to any benefit under the Indenture or be valid or obligatory for any purpose.

In Witness Whereof, the company has caused this Debenture to be duly executed under its corporate seal.

U.S. Bancorp

DATED:

CERTIFICATE OF AUTHENTICATION
THIS IS ONE OF THE DEBENTURES REFERRED TO IN THE WITHIN-MENTIONED INDENTURE.
UNITED STATES NATIONAL BANK OF OREGON
AS AUTHENTICATING BANK
BY

SPECIMEN
AUTHORIZED OFFICER

CORPORATE SEAL
U.S. BANCORP
OREGON

BY
John Elorriaga
CHAIRMAN OF THE BOARD

ATTEST:

Robert H. Hurt
SECRETARY

BY
Carl W. Mays Jr.
PRESIDENT

© SECURITY-COLUMBIAN UNITED STATES BANKNOTE CORPORATION

U.S. Bancorp specimen bond certificate.

The 2001 merger with U.S. Bank made good sense because Firstar also had a culture of service. As its mission statement said, "we will serve the interests of our clients, employees and the shareholders . . . through adherence to high standards of service, profitability and community involvement." After the merger, U.S. Bank continued to stress customer service, opening branches in Walgreens, Safeway and other stores and focusing on its "Five Star Service Guarantee." In 2006 it purchased 23 new branches in Colorado. By 2011 the bank operated more than 3,000 branches and 5,300 ATMs to aid its 16 million customers spread over 25 states, the gratifying result of over 50 business-savvy mergers since 1988.

Unlike many other large BHCs, it allowed its branch managers considerable discretion in order to better meet customers' needs. After it acquired United Financial Corporation of Montana in 2007, for example, it allowed its main bank, Heritage, to continue operating under its own brand and did not change staffing. Promotion within its ranks was on the basis of merit, not seniority, and it promoted good people quickly in order to retain them. In 2006 *U.S. Banker* ranked it number one in the nation for its women in executive positions. That same year *LATINA Style* named it one of the "Top 50 Best Places for Latinas to Work."

Most importantly, perhaps, U.S. Bancorp delivered top results without sipping subprime poison. When other banks were stumbling over themselves to get to the subprime pie, U.S. Bancorp was buying up the municipal and corporate bond trustee businesses of SunTrust (#18) and ABN AMRO. Although its earnings per share dropped in 2008–2009, the bank avoided the acute problems that struck most of its peers during the 2008 financial crisis. FDIC Chairman Sheila Bair called it "a very good, well-run bank." Warren Buffett found value too, and by 2011 had bought up 4.1% of the bank's shares.

Sources

Bair, Sheila. *Bull by the Horns: Fighting to Save Main Street from Wall Street and Wall Street from Itself*. New York: Free Press, 2012, 286–87, 331.

Buffett, Mary and David Clark. *The Warren Buffett Stock Portfolio: Warren Buffett Stock Picks: Why and When He Is Investing in Them*. New York: Scribner, 2011, 171–76.

Carey, Timothy A. "Examining Alternatives to Evaluate Merger Success at Firstar." MBA thesis, Cardinal Stritch University, 2000.

Firstar Trust Company. *Celebrating a Century of Service, 1894–1994*. (1994).

Law, Adair. *Abundantly Blessed: The John Elorriaga Story*. John and Lois Elorriaga Family Trust, 2007.

Loosvelt, Derek, et al. *The Vault Guide to the Top 50 Banking Employers: 2008 Edition*. New York: Vault, 2007, 278–81.

Singer, Claude. *U.S. National Bank of Oregon and U.S. Bancorp, 1891–1984*. Portland: U.S. Bancorp, 1984.

Walden, Gene. *The 100 Best Stocks to Own in America* 7th ed. Chicago: Dearborn Financial Publishing, 2000, 5-8.

Wetfeet. *25 Top Financial Services Firms*. San Francisco: Wetfeet. 2008, 83-85.

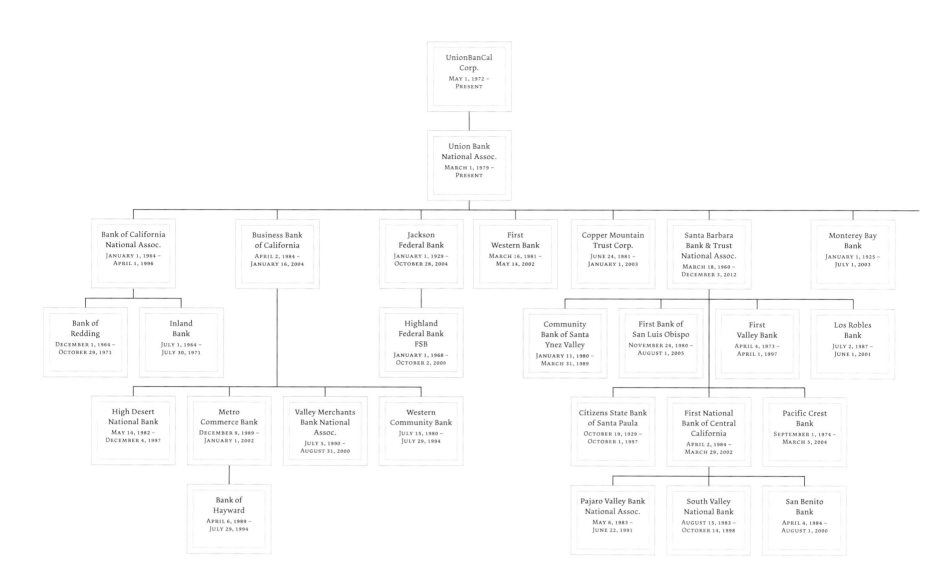

UnionBanCal
Corp.
MAY 1, 1972 –
PRESENT

Union Bank
National Assoc.
MARCH 1, 1979 –
PRESENT

Bank of California
National Assoc.
JANUARY 1, 1964 –
APRIL 1, 1996

Business Bank
of California
APRIL 2, 1984 –
JANUARY 16, 2004

Jackson
Federal Bank
JANUARY 1, 1929 –
OCTOBER 28, 2004

First
Western Bank
MARCH 16, 1981 –
MAY 14, 2002

Copper Mountain
Trust Corp.
JUNE 24, 1981 –
JANUARY 1, 2003

Santa Barbara
Bank & Trust
National Assoc.
MARCH 18, 1960 –
DECEMBER 3, 2012

Monterey Bay
Bank
JANUARY 1, 1925 –
JULY 1, 2003

Bank of
Redding
DECEMBER 1, 1964 –
OCTOBER 29, 1971

Inland
Bank
JULY 1, 1964 –
JULY 30, 1971

Highland
Federal Bank
FSB
JANUARY 1, 1968 –
OCTOBER 2, 2000

Community
Bank of Santa
Ynez Valley
JANUARY 11, 1980 –
MARCH 31, 1989

First Bank of
San Luis Obispo
NOVEMBER 24, 1980 –
AUGUST 1, 2005

First
Valley Bank
APRIL 4, 1973 –
APRIL 1, 1997

Los Robles
Bank
JULY 2, 1987 –
JUNE 1, 2001

High Desert
National Bank
MAY 14, 1982 –
DECEMBER 4, 1997

Metro
Commerce Bank
DECEMBER 8, 1989 –
JANUARY 1, 2002

Valley Merchants
Bank National
Assoc.
JULY 5, 1990 –
AUGUST 31, 2000

Western
Community Bank
JULY 15, 1980 –
JULY 29, 1994

Citizens State Bank
of Santa Paula
OCTOBER 19, 1929 –
OCTOBER 1, 1997

First National
Bank of Central
California
APRIL 2, 1984 –
MARCH 29, 2002

Pacific Crest
Bank
SEPTEMBER 1, 1974 –
MARCH 5, 2004

Bank of
Hayward
APRIL 6, 1989 –
JULY 29, 1994

Pajaro Valley Bank
National Assoc.
MAY 6, 1983 –
JUNE 22, 1991

South Valley
National Bank
AUGUST 15, 1983 –
OCTOBER 14, 1998

San Benito
Bank
APRIL 4, 1984 –
AUGUST 1, 2000

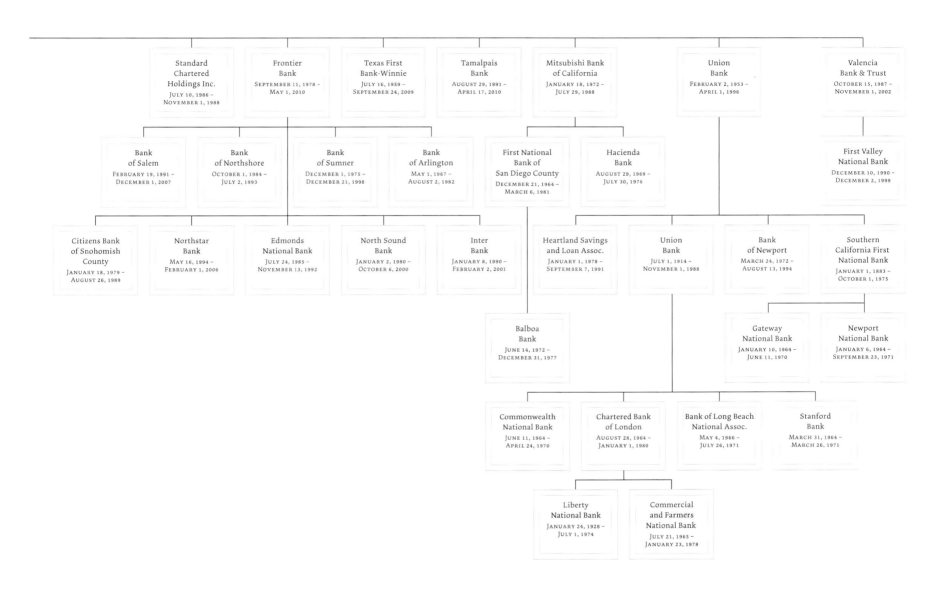

	Standard Chartered Holdings Inc.	Frontier Bank	Texas First Bank-Winnie	Tamalpais Bank	Mitsubishi Bank of California		Union Bank	Valencia Bank & Trust

Standard Chartered Holdings Inc.
JULY 10, 1986 – NOVEMBER 1, 1988

Frontier Bank
SEPTEMBER 11, 1978 – MAY 1, 2010

Texas First Bank-Winnie
JULY 16, 1959 – SEPTEMBER 24, 2009

Tamalpais Bank
AUGUST 29, 1991 – APRIL 17, 2010

Mitsubishi Bank of California
JANUARY 18, 1972 – JULY 29, 1988

Union Bank
FEBRUARY 2, 1953 – APRIL 1, 1996

Valencia Bank & Trust
OCTOBER 15, 1987 – NOVEMBER 1, 2002

Bank of Salem
FEBRUARY 19, 1991 – DECEMBER 1, 2007

Bank of Northshore
OCTOBER 1, 1984 – JULY 2, 1993

Bank of Sumner
DECEMBER 1, 1975 – DECEMBER 21, 1998

Bank of Arlington
MAY 1, 1967 – AUGUST 2, 1982

First National Bank of San Diego County
DECEMBER 21, 1964 – MARCH 6, 1981

Hacienda Bank
AUGUST 29, 1969 – JULY 30, 1976

First Valley National Bank
DECEMBER 10, 1990 – DECEMBER 2, 1999

Citizens Bank of Snohomish County
JANUARY 18, 1979 – AUGUST 26, 1989

Northstar Bank
MAY 16, 1994 – FEBRUARY 1, 2006

Edmonds National Bank
JULY 24, 1985 – NOVEMBER 13, 1992

North Sound Bank
JANUARY 2, 1980 – OCTOBER 6, 2000

Inter Bank
JANUARY 8, 1990 – FEBRUARY 2, 2001

Heartland Savings and Loan Assoc.
JANUARY 1, 1978 – SEPTEMBER 7, 1991

Union Bank
JULY 1, 1914 – NOVEMBER 1, 1988

Bank of Newport
MARCH 24, 1972 – AUGUST 13, 1994

Southern California First National Bank
JANUARY 1, 1883 – OCTOBER 1, 1975

Balboa Bank
JUNE 14, 1972 – DECEMBER 31, 1977

Gateway National Bank
JANUARY 10, 1964 – JUNE 11, 1970

Newport National Bank
JANUARY 6, 1964 – SEPTEMBER 23, 1971

Commonwealth National Bank
JUNE 11, 1964 – APRIL 24, 1970

Chartered Bank of London
AUGUST 28, 1964 – JANUARY 1, 1980

Bank of Long Beach National Assoc.
MAY 4, 1966 – JULY 26, 1971

Stanford Bank
MARCH 31, 1964 – MARCH 26, 1971

Liberty National Bank
JANUARY 24, 1928 – JULY 1, 1974

Commercial and Farmers National Bank
JULY 21, 1965 – JANUARY 23, 1978

UnionBanCal

Bank

RANK	HEADQUARTERS	TICKER	ASSETS	EARLIEST KNOWN ANCESTOR	INDUSTRY OF ORIGIN
27	San Francisco, CA	UB	$102,000,000,000	1864	Commercial Banking

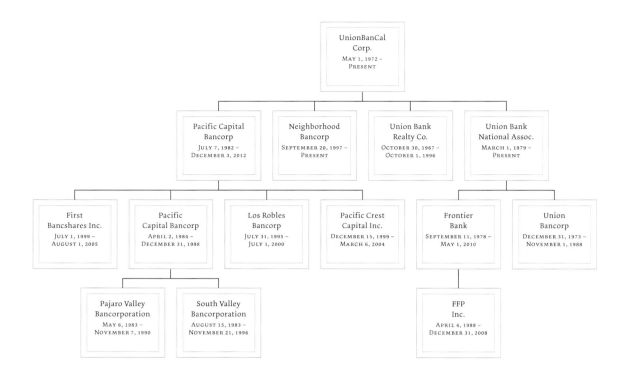

UnionBanCal Corp.
MAY 1, 1972 – PRESENT

Pacific Capital Bancorp
JULY 7, 1982 – DECEMBER 3, 2012

Neighborhood Bancorp
SEPTEMBER 20, 1997 – PRESENT

Union Bank Realty Co.
OCTOBER 30, 1967 – OCTOBER 1, 1996

Union Bank National Assoc.
MARCH 1, 1979 – PRESENT

First Bancshares Inc.
JULY 1, 1999 – AUGUST 1, 2005

Pacific Capital Bancorp
APRIL 2, 1984 – DECEMBER 31, 1998

Los Robles Bancorp
JULY 31, 1995 – JULY 1, 2000

Pacific Crest Capital Inc.
DECEMBER 15, 1999 – MARCH 6, 2004

Frontier Bank
SEPTEMBER 11, 1978 – MAY 1, 2010

Union Bancorp
DECEMBER 31, 1973 – NOVEMBER 1, 1988

Pajaro Valley Bancorporation
MAY 6, 1983 – NOVEMBER 7, 1990

South Valley Bancorporation
AUGUST 15, 1983 – NOVEMBER 21, 1996

FFP Inc.
APRIL 4, 1988 – DECEMBER 31, 2008

UnionBanCal

Holding Company

Early Bank of California stock certificate, ca. 1860s-1870s.

UnionBanCal is a member of Mitsubishi UFJ Financial Group, which is part of the Mitsubishi keiretsu and the only significant Japanese presence in America's "Big 50." Headquartered in Tokyo, the giant financial holding company formed from the merger of Mitsubishi Bank and the Bank of Tokyo in 1999, and the merger of that entity with UFJ Bank in 2006. It held assets of about $2.5 trillion in early 2013, making it the second largest BHC in the world. Its American presence, however, was limited to UnionBanCal, the BHC of Union Bank, N.A., which was formerly known as the Union Bank of California. The Union Bank of California traces its origins to The Bank of California, which opened for business in 1864, and Union Bank and Trust of Los Angeles, which began operations in 1914.

The Bank of California received a charter from the state of California in 1864. As its first act of business it acquired a private bank that had been in operation, under various partners, since 1856. Organized by the private bankers as well as a long list of the state's most prominent business leaders, including its first president, financier Darius Ogden Mills, The Bank of California began life with a paid-up capital of $2 million and many friends in government, industry and media.

So like Minerva, who sprang full-armed from the head of Jove, the bank was a powerhouse at its very inception and with its deep coffers soon attracted the best bankers, bank buildings and vaults in the entire tramontane West. Some of its many important early projects included increasing commercial activity with Russian Alaska, financing the transcontinental railroad and exploiting Nevada's Comstock Lode. Within two months of opening, it operated an "agency" in Virginia City, the boomtown associated with that lode. Due to the bank's extensive reach, California Street, where the main entrance of its San Francisco headquarters was located, came to be known as the "Wall Street of the West."

The Bank of California's success drove its dividends so high that its stock price hit $150 above par. As the profits increased in its first decade, the bank increased its capital to $5 million. In 1872, a portent of things to come, the bank signed an agreement with the Japanese government to refine old Japanese coins via its San Francisco Assaying and Refining subsidiary. It also lent it $500,000 in gold so the Japanese could begin minting new coins in Osaka.

The following year, William C. Ralston, one of the private bankers who helped found the bank, and its cashier since its incorporation, replaced Mills and became the second of only eight presidents to run the bank in its first 85 years. Ralston averted a run on the bank by exchanging gold bars for gold and silver coins at the US Subtreasury under cover of darkness and a cloak of secrecy. By the time crazed depositors appeared demanding their money, Ralston and his tellers were able to make such a conspicuous showing of the bank's riches that the run was stopped in its tracks.

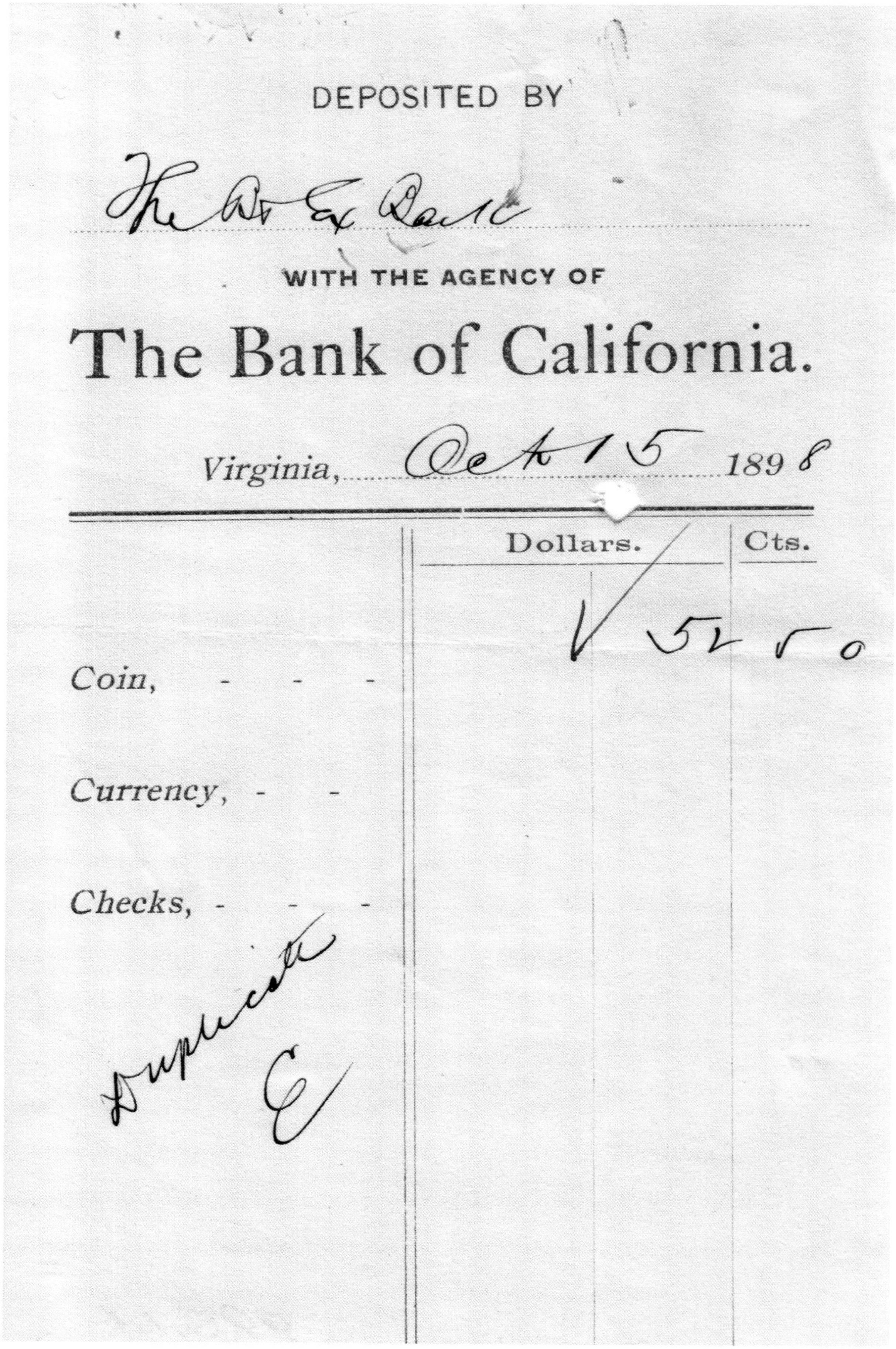

DEPOSITED BY

[handwritten signature]

WITH THE AGENCY OF

The Bank of California.

Virginia, *Oct 15* 189 8

	Dollars.	Cts.
	52	50
Coin, - - -		
Currency, - -		
Checks, - - -		

[handwritten: Duplicate]

Bank of California deposit slip, 1898.

BANK OF CALIFORNIA, SAN FRANCISCO.

Bank of California building in San Francisco, 1875.

Ruins after the San Francisco earthquake, 1906.

Due to a run in 1875, however, the bank had to shut down for over a month. Ralston resigned and apparently committed suicide in San Francisco Bay. Mills returned to the presidency and righted the bank by raising $7.8 million in new capital from stockholders, to which Mills himself also contributed $1 million. The infusion of capital increased confidence so much that when the bank reopened people competed for the honor of being the first to make a deposit.

After its brush with death, The Bank of California grew along with San Francisco and the entire state, the population of which increased from 864,694 in 1880 to 1,485,953 in 1900. In 1889, after a quarter century of business, its assets were just under $15 million. By 1903 its resources totaled more than $21 million on capital of $2 million and reserves of $4 million. That same year, The Bank of California purchased a controlling interest in the National Bank of D.O. Mills and Company of Sacramento (which it would sell in 1925) and opened the Mission Bank to service San Francisco's Mission District, which then was a rough, immigrant neighborhood. For 20 years Mission was an unofficial, affiliated institution, but the bank bought it outright in 1927.

It was not the bank's first outright acquisition, as in 1905 it bought the London and San Francisco Bank, Limited (LSFBL). Organized in 1865 by British and German bankers to finance the export trade, LSFBL purchased John Parrott and Company, a pioneer San Francisco banking house, in 1871. In 1882, 1889 and 1901, unencumbered by the branching restrictions that handcuffed domestic banks, it established branches in Portland, Oregon, as well as in Tacoma and Seattle, Washington. After the sale, regulators allowed the bank to keep LSFBL's out-of-state branches, which later became strategic assets for the bank. Also in 1905, Homer S. King left the presidency of Wells Fargo & Company Bank (#4) and assumed the bank's presidency.

After the 1906 earthquake, the bank's vault was encased in the fire that destroyed the financial district and most of San Francisco. When finally cool enough to be opened three weeks after the conflagration, the vault proved itself worthy, its contents shaken but not destroyed. In the meantime, tellers paid out on the basis of their recollection of customer balances. An emergency branch operated while the bank built a

"handsome new building" replete with a new vault.

In 1910, after receiving assurances it could keep its branches in Nevada, Oregon and Washington, the bank switched to a national charter and thereby became The Bank of California, National Association. It purchased the San Francisco National Bank that same year. Like The Bank of California, San Francisco National traced its roots to an antebellum banking partnership that incorporated as the Sather Banking Company in 1887 before switching to a national charter and taking its new name a decade later. In 1917 the bank shuttered its Virginia City agency, which had become unprofitable as the Comstock ran dry of silver. Two years later, the Tacoma branch purchased the Fidelity Trust Company, which had deposits in excess of $7 million. The following year, 1920, the bank opened a trust department. Thanks to such moves and the wartime economy, assets jumped from $80.7 million in 1917 to over $112 million by the end of 1921, when 25 officers directed the activities of more than 350 employees.

The bank, which apparently had adopted more conservative lending practices after its near failure in 1875, weathered the Great Depression well enough to lend what the bank's president, James J. Hunter (1938–1950), called "liberal support" to other institutions. A Canadian with experience at the Bank of Montreal (#26), Hunter increased the bank's resources threefold in just a decade.

By 1950 it boasted a capital and surplus of $17 million, assets in excess of $330 million, "and depositors number many thousands." After rejecting merger overtures in the late 1950s, "The Bank," as it literally called itself, spread aggressively into Southern California in the 1960s and became the first bank with branches in every major port from San Diego to Seattle. It also established an Edge Act corporation that allowed it to establish branches overseas, including the Philippines, Taiwan, Tokyo and Guatemala. The Bank of California hit $1 billion in assets in 1964, and it listed on the New York Stock Exchange under the ticker BNC in early 1970.

In 1905 an old-timer had claimed The Bank of California was "a good old bank and the people have confidence in it. It'll be here as long as there is a San Francisco." That pronouncement turned out

Darius Ogden Mills, ca. 1903.

THE

BANK OF CALIFORNIA,

SAN FRANCISCO.

Capital Paid Up - - - - - $5,000,000.

D. O. MILLS, President.   W. C. RALSTON, Cashier.

AGENTS:

In NEW YORK, Messrs. LEES & WALLER; in BOSTON, TREMONT NATIONAL
BANK; in LONDON, ORIENTAL BANK CORPORATION.

Letters of Credit issued available for the purchase of Merchandise throughout the
United States, Europe, India, China, Japan, and Australia.

EXCHANGE FOR SALE ON THE ATLANTIC CITIES,

DRAWN DIRECT ON

London, Dublin, Paris, St. Petersburg, Amsterdam, Hamburg,
Bremen, Frankfort-on-the-Main, Vienna, Leipsic, Sydney,
Melbourne, Yokohama, Shanghai, Hongkong.

Advertisement for the Bank of California published in The Overland Monthly, *1870.*

to be premature, as in 1983 the bank was acquired by the Mitsubishi Bank of California, which was the 1972 spin-off of an agency of the Mitsubishi Bank established in Los Angeles in 1962. In 1996 BankCal, the holding company of The Bank of California/Mitsubishi, and Union Bank merged their businesses and names to form the Union Bank of California, the main subsidiary of the UnionBanCal BHC.

As its name implies, Union Bank was itself an amalgam of banks. These included the First National Bank of San Diego, which had been established in 1883; the Bank of Tokyo of California, the postwar reincarnation of the Yokohama Specie Bank that established a branch in San Francisco in 1886; and Kaspare Cohn Commercial and Savings Bank, established in 1914 by a German wool fleece entrepreneur who decided during the Great War that the bank would fare better under the name Union Bank and Trust Company of Los Angeles.

Initially capitalized at $50,000 and led by cattle rancher and store owner Jacob Gruendike, First National Bank of San Diego was aptly named, as it was the first bank in southern California to finance the construction and operation of a commercial fishing fleet and the first on the Pacific Coast to finance automobiles. It was also the first to open a branch office in San Diego County and made the first private aircraft loans in the region. It stayed open late on Saturdays to accommodate depositors traditionally paid after work that day.

In 1922, when regulators prevented First National from providing real estate loans and trust services to its customers, the bank established an independent entity just for those purposes. It merged with its offspring five years later to form the First National Trust and Savings Bank of San Diego.

During the Great Depression, the bank's directors bought distressed loans that regulators insisted it write off. The directors were right; all the loans were eventually repaid, with interest. In 1967 the bank changed its name to Southern California First National Bank. The following year, it formed a holding company called Southern California First National Corporation. It converted to a one-bank holding company the following year and went on an acquisition spree.

Cohn/Union offered personalized service to businesses, including sheep ranchers, wool merchants and other regional industries. In 1928 it became the first bank in the West to offer "Banking at Home" service conducted exclusively by mail. Like other conservatively run banks, it actually increased its deposit base during the dark days of the Depression.

It started to calculate interest on savings deposits daily in 1960 and eliminated the old passbook system. Later, it was the first major bank in California to offer free checking accounts and interest on checking deposits. In 1962 it reached the billion-dollar asset mark, and five years later it set up a one-bank holding company, Union Bancorp. The next day, the BHC bought Western Mortgage, the largest mortgage company in the nation, founded in 1933. In 1968 it created two new subsidiaries, Unionamerica Capital Corporation and Unionamerica Computer Corporation. The following year, the BHC bought insurance broker Swett & Crawford and property and casualty insurer Harbor Insurance, changed its name to Unionamerica, Inc. and listed on the New York Stock Exchange under the ticker UNI. In 1990 Union became the first major bank on the West Coast to offer seven-day-a-week banking via its supermarket branches.

The Bank of Tokyo of California catered at first to Japanese-Americans and Japanese citizens residing in California. It later financed Japanese corporations trading with the United States. In the 1960s it established branches in San Jose, Fresno, Crenshaw and Los Angeles, in part to counteract the new Mitsubishi Bank agency in L.A. and other incursions from the Far East. Most Japanese banks eventually withdrew from the US market, but Mitsubishi held on, establishing a full-blown state-chartered subsidiary in L.A. in 1972.

By the early 1970s Bank of Tokyo of California was one of the largest banks in the state. In 1975 it showed its heft by purchasing the increasingly troubled Southern California First National, which admitted it had grown too quickly: "We didn't have the depth of staff. We didn't have the organization." The new bank, California First Bank, had 104 branches in the state and three overseas and 3,000 employees. At the time, it was the eighth largest bank in the state and the 50th largest in the nation.

Over the next 13 years it grew organically while maintaining its competitive edge. This allowed it in 1988 to acquire Union Bank, which in 1979 had fallen to Standard Chartered Bank Limited Group of Great Britain. When the British bank fell on hard times in 1988, it sold off Union Bank to raise cash. Union Bank kept its name in the merger with California First, which proceeded at a leisurely pace compared to the Wells Fargo model, but now answered to managers in Tokyo instead of London.

Meanwhile, Mitsubishi was also thriving by combining de novo branch expansion with acquisitions, like the 1976 purchase of Hacienda Bank and its four branches and the 1981 purchase of First National Bank of San Diego County (which shouldn't be confused with the bank that became part of California First). Two years later, it beat out a late competitive bid from Wells Fargo (#4) to acquire The Bank of California, the state's eighth largest bank with $2.5 billion in deposits, for $50 per share. Although under new leadership, The Bank of California's operations were initially kept separate from that of its parent, which valued rapid growth over slashing expenses. BanCal, as it called itself, hit $10 billion in assets in 1990.

BanCal and Union merged to create the Union Bank of California in 1996 when their parents, the Bank of Tokyo and Mitsubishi Bank, also merged. The new bank was the 25th largest in the United States and the third largest in California. It had 238 full service and 31 limited service branches in California, 17 overseas offices and the old Bank of California holdover branches in Washington and Oregon. Not surprisingly given both banks' prior history, the merger process took a decade to complete. UnionBanCal stock did not list on the New York Stock Exchange, under the ticker UB, until 1999, the year that "Mission Excel" launched an effort to cut costs by eliminating redundancies. (It stopped trading in 2008 when its Japanese management took it private.) The bank's efficiency ratio improved over the next few years at the expense of 1,400 jobs, credit cards, indirect auto lending and branches in Guam and Saipan, but it still needed to launch "Project UB" (unified bank) in 2005 to clean up residual "silos."

By 2002 UnionBanCal began buying up California community banks like Valencia, First Western and Monterey Bay, to fill in its retail branch network. It stopped once it realized it had difficulty retaining their loan portfolios. In 2005 it sold off its entire international banking group to Wachovia (now part of #4). In May 2007 Masaaki Tanaka took control of the bank, which was struggling to bring its retail banking up to the level of its commercial banking unit, from Takashi Morimura. As deposits continued to leak out, the bank cut its workforce of about 10,000 and looked for other ways of increasing efficiency, like making its recruiting process paperless.

Despite the cuts, Union Bank of California was considered by many a good company to work for because it valued "continuous learning" and backed it up with "comprehensive training and development programs." *Fortune* named the bank one of "America's 50 Best Companies for Diversity" and ranked it higher on that list than any other bank. The bank also prided itself on being "very community-focused" and philanthropic.

In 2007 Union Bank of California had assets of almost $55 billion and operated 323 branches in California, Oregon, Washington and two foreign countries. Just two years later, its assets had hit $70 billion, and its branch network had grown to 335, making it one of the few big banks that expanded during the 2008 financial crisis. It concentrated on the consumer, correspondent, middle market, real estate, small business and trade finance markets, but it also provided business insurance, investment and financial management, private banking and global custody and trust services. It lent mainly in the communications, energy, entertainment, media, public utilities and retail sectors and was barely touched by the crisis because it had the smallest percentage of nonperforming mortgage loans (.4%) of any large bank, while bigger rivals like Bank of America and Wells Fargo had nonperforming percentages of 5.9 and 7.6, respectively. But as those banks rebounded in 2012, UnionBanCal suffered from lower earnings because of higher loan losses and expenses related to the acquisition of Pacific Capital Bancorp of Santa Barbara.

Sources

Browdie, Brian. "UnionBanCal Earnings Fell in 4Q on Higher Spending." *American Banker*, January 29, 2013.

_____. "UnionBanCal Profits Drop 28% on Higher Provision." *American Banker*, October 29, 2012.

Buechse, Oliver, Penny Maines and Bruce Corbin. *Union Bank: A California History of 145 Years*. San Francisco: Union Bank, 2009.

Hunter, James J. *Partners in Progress, 1864–1950: A Brief History of the Bank of California, N.A., and of the Region It Has Served for 85 Years*. New York: Newcomen Society, 1950).

Loosvelt, Derek, et al. *The Vault Guide to the Top 50 Banking Employers: 2008 Edition*. New York: Vault, 2007, 422–25.

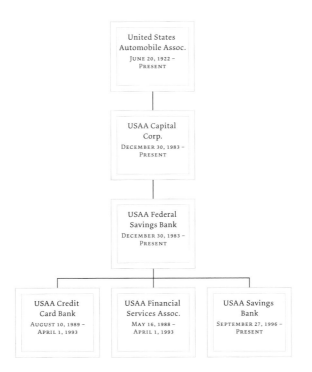

United States
Automobile Assoc.
JUNE 20, 1922 –
PRESENT

USAA Capital
Corp.
DECEMBER 30, 1983 –
PRESENT

USAA Federal
Savings Bank
DECEMBER 30, 1983 –
PRESENT

USAA Credit
Card Bank
AUGUST 10, 1989 –
APRIL 1, 1993

USAA Financial
Services Assoc.
MAY 16, 1988 –
APRIL 1, 1993

USAA Savings
Bank
SEPTEMBER 27, 1996 –
PRESENT

USAA

RANK	HEADQUARTERS	TICKER	ASSETS	EARLIEST KNOWN ANCESTOR	INDUSTRY OF ORIGIN
23	San Antonio, TX	Not listed	$120,000,000,000	1922	Insurance

President Warren Harding, ca. 1915-1923.

USAA's current tag line, "We know what it means to serve," is a double entendre: the organization serves its members and most of its members serve the nation, in the armed forces. USAA is not listed on a stock exchange because it is not a joint-stock corporation. Rather, it is a "reciprocal-type interinsurance exchange," an entity akin to a mutual corporation. According to a handwritten note scratched onto the frontispiece of the author's copy of its most recent history, a note to "Aldo" penned by author Paul Ringenbach in August 1997, "USAA has been successful because all of us do the best we can." That sentiment holds water over the entire history of this unique BHC.

In 1922 some Army officers stationed in Texas who had grown tired of trying to find automobile insurance adequate to their mobile lifestyles decided to do something about it. They formed the United States Army Automobile Insurance Association and had the gumption to ask President Warren Harding, an automobile enthusiast and the nation's commander-in-chief, to join them. He refused, but most could not resist the offer of inexpensive insurance backed not by a distant for-profit corporation but by fellow members of the military, the same people who had each other's backs on the field of battle.

Over the years, USAA extended its membership to include officers from the other armed services, retired and reserve officers, widows and widowers and finally, beginning in 1996, enlisted personnel and their families. It had to become more inclusive because by the late 1990s it enjoyed an incredible 95% share of its original market of active military officers. In 2013 it ran television commercials where USAA families proudly announced when they became eligible for USAA membership. They were all beaming, as well they should because USAA offered arguably the best insurance deals in the entire nation. Eligibility for its insurance was among the best perks for military personnel aside from perhaps the GI Bill. Its cut rates started at its inception in the 1920s, when it set its premiums at the official average or "manual" rate minus 20%. Despite the low premiums, the organization achieved a top rating from insurance rating agency A.M. Best owing to its conservative investment, accounting and claims policies.

The number of USAA members, and policies in force, grew steadily in the 1920s and 1930s and began to soar in the late 1940s. The number of members even dropped, for the only time in the organization's history, in 1946, before turning upward again as the postwar economy boomed. By licensing in additional states (eventually all) and underwriting a wider range of products, including multiline casualty and life insurance, the company's membership hit 200,000 around 1954 and 400,000 around 1960. In 1968 the organization had more than 600,000 members and over 1.2 million policies in force.

By 1970 USAA was a global organization with assets greater than $250 million owned jointly by its more than 725,000 members. To better meet the needs of this growing, sprawling group, USAA established service centers in Colorado, Florida, New York, Virginia

Sherry Conquest, a general adjuster with USAA, takes photos of a damaged house for a claim in Moore, Oklahoma, May 23, 2013.

and elsewhere and was one of the first insurers to switch to electronic data processing in the 1950s. Subsequent upgrades allowed it to issue policies in a single day, down from the 55 steps and six weeks it took in 1969.

In the 1970s, 1980s and 1990s, USAA spread beyond insurance into banking and brokerage. Two-thirds of its members held a USAA credit card, and many others had a car loan, annuity, mutual fund, discount brokerage account or savings deposit with the organization via one of its subsidiaries, all of which lived up to its parent's high standards. In June 1995, for example, *Money* magazine called USAA Federal Savings Bank the "Best Bank in America" for its outstanding customer service, generous rates, minimal fees and financial safety. To fund the formation and expansion of that and other new product subsidiaries, the company in 1987 established the USAA Capital Corporation (CAPCO). In 1985 the company had diversified enough to move away from Statutory Accounting Principles (SAP) for insurers to the Generally Accepted Accounting Principles (GAAP) used by most companies.

The key to USAA's success in its core business, as well as its new endeavors, was service so good that it was accused of almost making "a religion" out of it. In 2007, for example, *BusinessWeek* ranked it the top customer service organization in the nation. Good service started with the CEO, who used regular meetings with employees to discover problems or inefficiencies that he could then fix, and moved all the way down the management chain.

"We intimately understand exactly who most of our member-customers are," Bill Cooney, president of the property and casualty group, explained. So when a typhoon named Pamela wrecked the military base on Guam in 1976, USAA responded within days with a crack team that worked 15-hour days for almost two weeks, mostly without electricity, to process more than 1,100 claims. After that tour de force, an Air Force captain wrote that "not one other company responds as you do."

Another member called USAA "the best insurance company in the world" even after it *denied* his claim for losses incurred during the Iranian Revolution. (The company provided policyholders with ample warning that their property in Iran was at risk.) To ensure that they kept the company on the right path, executives regularly read member letters and, after 1992, important comments made over the telephone to staff members via the computerized ECHO (Every Contact Has Opportunity) system. "I've got a list as long as my arm of changes implemented due to the system," Cooney claimed. The organization prided itself on its use of technology. In 2006 *Computerworld* ranked it the 17th best place in the country to work in IT.

To ensure the perpetuation of its customer service-oriented culture, USAA screened its employees carefully. "If you don't like helping people," Cooney told applicants, "don't come to work here. This is not the right place for you."

Once it found people dedicated to making members' lives better,

USAA office in Colorado Springs, 2008.

USAA was very good to them, even allowing those who had not served in the armed forces to purchase USAA products. And it trained them extensively, in formal classrooms for up to 10 weeks and 65 hours annually thereafter, in addition to elective courses and on-the-job training via telephone conversation monitoring and analysis. It also developed a one-week executive management course at Darden, the University of Virginia's graduate business school.

Year after year, USAA was selected as one of the best employers in the country, a "safe harbor where employees have incredible opportunities" according to one author that Cooney liked to quote. Its workers showed that they agreed with all the praise by sticking around, giving the business a turnover rate of only 6% or 7% a year, half the industry average.

By the late 20th century USAA had some 18,500 employees, a worldwide membership of more than 3 million and 54 subsidiaries and affiliates. By 2006, when its net worth was estimated at $13.12 billion, it had about six million members, six domestic offices and offices in London and Frankfurt. Of every 100 insurance accounts, customers retained 98 of them annually, a very high rate attributed to the organization's superior customer service. "Our membership trusts us," Cooney explained, and well they should.

USAA was not directly involved in the 2008 financial crisis. According to banking consultant Steven Reider, it did not load up on "speculative real estate development loans or any of the other high-risk instruments that afflicted so many large banks." USAA's organic growth prospects remained good as well. According to Roger Adams, its chief marketing officer, "Millions of people who are eligible for USAA haven't yet joined . . . Many don't even know they are eligible or understand what USAA can do for them."

Sources

Cooney, Bill. "United Services Automobile Association: Hardwire Service Information." In *Customer Service: Extraordinary Results at Southwest Airlines, Charles Schwab, Lands' End, American Express, Staples, and USAA*, edited by Fred Wiersema, 183–218. New York: HarperBusiness, 1998.

Dunn, Edward C. *USAA: Life Story of a Business Cooperative.* New York: McGraw-Hill, 1970.

Loosvelt, Derek, et al. *The Vault Guide to the Top Financial Services Employers: 2008 Edition.* New York: Vault, 2007, 323–28.

Peters, Andy. "USAA, Military-Focused Credit Unions Rev Up Advertising." *American Banker*, November 7, 2013.

Ringenbach, Paul T. *USAA: A Tradition of Service, 1922–1997.* San Antonio, TX: Donning Company Publishers, 1997.

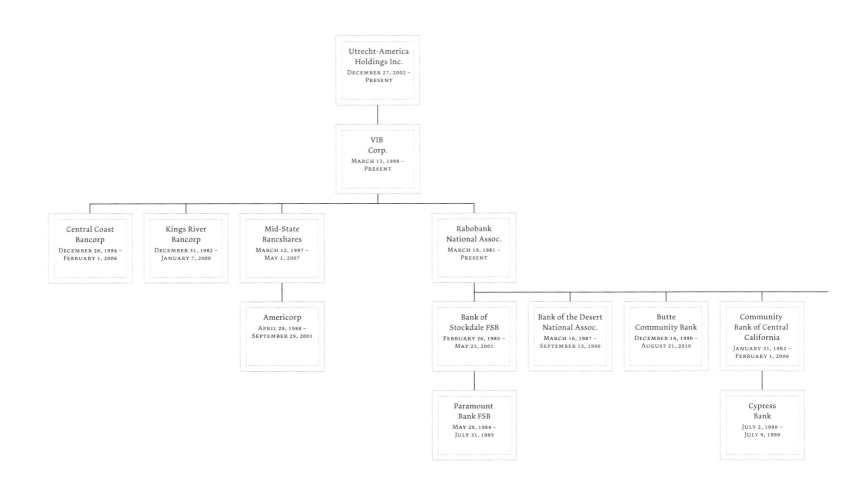

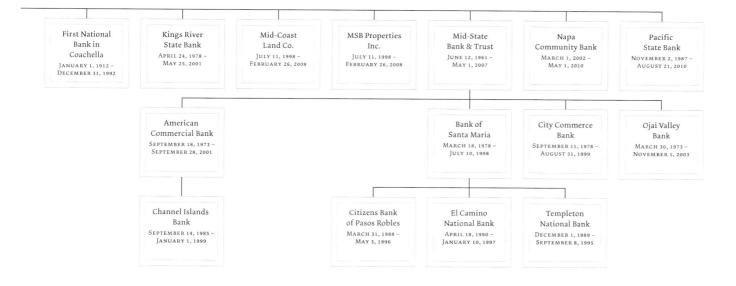

First National
Bank in
Coachella
JANUARY 1, 1912 –
DECEMBER 31, 1992

Kings River
State Bank
APRIL 24, 1978 –
MAY 25, 2001

Mid-Coast
Land Co.
JULY 11, 1998 –
FEBRUARY 26, 2008

MSB Properties
Inc.
JULY 11, 1998 –
FEBRUARY 26, 2008

Mid-State
Bank & Trust
JUNE 12, 1961 –
MAY 1, 2007

Napa
Community Bank
MARCH 1, 2002 –
MAY 1, 2010

Pacific
State Bank
NOVEMBER 2, 1987 –
AUGUST 21, 2010

American
Commercial Bank
SEPTEMBER 18, 1973 –
SEPTEMBER 28, 2001

Bank of
Santa Maria
MARCH 18, 1978 –
JULY 10, 1998

City Commerce
Bank
SEPTEMBER 11, 1978 –
AUGUST 31, 1999

Ojai Valley
Bank
MARCH 30, 1973 –
NOVEMBER 1, 2003

Channel Islands
Bank
SEPTEMBER 14, 1985 –
JANUARY 1, 1999

Citizens Bank
of Pasos Robles
MARCH 31, 1988 –
MAY 3, 1996

El Camino
National Bank
APRIL 18, 1990 –
JANUARY 10, 1997

Templeton
National Bank
DECEMBER 1, 1989 –
SEPTEMBER 8, 1995

Utrecht-America Holdings

RANK	HEADQUARTERS	TICKER	ASSETS	EARLIEST KNOWN ANCESTOR	INDUSTRY OF ORIGIN
39	New York, NY	Not listed	$49,000,000,000	1898	Commercial Banking

Friedrich Wilhelm Raiffeisen, founder of the cooperative movement of credit unions in Germany and inspiration for Rabobank.

Two windmills in Holland, ca. 1890-1899.

This unlisted entity is part of the Rabobank Group, the BHC of the Netherlands's largest cooperative bank, Coöperatieve Centrale Raiffeisen-Boerenleenbank B.A., which is headquartered in the ancient city of Utrecht about a half hour southeast of Amsterdam by rail. Its primary US holding is Rabobank, N.A., composed of several California financial institutions, including Valley Independent Bank (acquired in 2002); Lend Lease Agribusiness and Ag Services of America (acquired in 2003); Community Bank of Central California (acquired in 2006); Mid-State Bank and Trust (acquired in 2007); and Butte Community Bank, Napa Community Bank and the failed Pacific State Bank (all acquired in 2010).

In addition to being the world's first major commercial powerhouse, the Netherlands was also a major exporter of foodstuffs, especially dairy products, and other agricultural goods, like flowers, because of intensive growing techniques like greenhouses and a canal system that provided both cheap irrigation and transportation. In the late 19th century, agriculturalists eager for more credit facilities than traditional Dutch banks were willing or able to provide started a number of farmers' credit cooperatives. The new institutions, which included the precursors to the Rabobank, increased the quantity and decreased the price of credit so substantially that by 1910 there were 600 of them, with 50,000 members in total. Like US credit unions, the Dutch credit cooperatives were initially community-oriented intermediaries that used local deposits to fund local loans.

In 1972 Coöperatieve Centrale Raiffeisen-Bank in Utrecht merged with Coöperatieve Centrale Boerenleenbank in Eindhoven. Its new style was Rabobank, a portmanteau created from **Ra**iffeisen, **Bo**erenleen and **bank**. Both banks had formed in 1898 as part of the cooperative banking wave described above, and both were technically subsidiaries of the member banks that founded them. The Utrecht bank acted as a central bank for the Protestant cooperative association banks of the North; the

Eindhoven bank served the network of typically formally incorporated banks in the more Catholic South. Both supplied their member banks with loans and assisted them with more complex transactions. By 1925, when the cooperative movement peaked, 710 banks composed the Utrecht network and 537 that of Eindhoven.

Members were at first liable for the debts of their local cooperatives, but that was relaxed in 1980 and entirely eliminated in 2000 by a unique cross-guarantee structure and the accumulation of surpluses in a general fund large enough to merit a triple-A credit rating for the bank. Liability was an important concern during the Great War, during which the Netherlands's economy suffered greatly as a neutral abutting blockaded Germany, and the Great Depression, when the Netherlands Bank feared that bank runs would ruin the entire system.

The cooperative banking system survived despite much privation among farmers, but then the Nazis arrived. Unlike many commercial banks, the cooperative banks refused to cooperate with the occupiers and suffered for it. After World War II ended, Marshall Plan aid and the Dutch National Agriculture Recovery Service helped the sector immensely as the country's farmers struggled first to feed their fellow countrymen and then to reestablish their considerable export markets.

Another big boost came from monetary reforms that forced Dutch citizens to establish bank accounts; many chose their local cooperative bank over distant, aloof commercial banks. The credit cooperatives thereby came to control the bulk of the nation's savings, a position they built upon during the rest of the century. In 1958 the cooperatives held 1.7 million accounts; by 1967 that number hit four million (out of a population of less than 13 million). With more on deposit than good agricultural risks, the cooperatives began to look for other borrowers.

In the 1950s Dutch financial institutions of all types began to break out of their traditional molds to offer a wider range of services to broader groups of people. Commercial banks began making loans to consumers, farmers and small businesses while credit cooperatives, flush with cash, started to lend to big, distant businesses. The cooperatives also grew increasingly formal and complex, moving out of the living rooms of part-time cashiers and into offices with multiple full-time employees. The increasing size, complexity and professionalization of the cooperatives led to the merger of their two central banks, which increasingly had found themselves in competition with each other as well as with commercial banks, owing to pressure exerted not by their executives but rather by their members, as expressed through their respective general assemblies.

Throughout the 20th century and into the 21st, Rabobank provided services to its member banks, which were its owners, not its branches. Each local cooperative bank, especially those in the Utrecht network, was autonomous. Members elected a local board of directors and a local supervisory board, which then selected delegates to regional assemblies of 20 banks. Each regional assembly then elected six people to represent it in the central delegates assembly, an advisory body for the general assembly that selected the board of directors, supervisory board and executive board for Rabobank.

In the 1980s, after finally fully integrating its two rather disparate banking cultures and dealing with the economic disruptions of the 1970s, Rabobank developed into a universal bank by providing "Allfinanz," all types of finance (commercial and investment banking and insurance), via wholly owned subsidiaries like Rabo Mortgage Bank; De Lage Landen, an international leasing and trade finance specialist; and Robeco, an asset manager (which it sold to the Japanese financial services group Orix in 2013). It offered its customers everything from the largest ATM network in the country to private banking and asset management services.

After the merger, Rabobank emerged as one of the Netherland's "Big Three" banks, along with ABN AMRO and ING. (Its assets in 1980 amounted to NLG100 billion [Dutch guilders].) With little room for domestic growth, Rabobank began to stretch its cooperative model overseas, at first in 1973 in a joint currency trading venture called London and Continental Bank; then with Bank of America (now part of #2) as part of a short-lived experiment (1975–1976); then via Unico Banking Group, a cooperative venture with five European counterparts started in 1977; and finally, in 1980, with de novo branches in Curacao and Frankfurt. New York followed the next year, and it set up offices in Dallas (1988), San Francisco (1988) and Chicago (1994) as well.

By 1990 Rabobank operated 35 foreign branches, mostly in port cities, and employed 915 people, both far fewer than its Dutch rival, ABN Bank. By 1998 it ran 85 branches in 36 countries; by 2005 it operated 267 foreign branches and employed almost 7,500 people outside of the Netherlands. Branches, as opposed to member banks, were new to Rabobank but did not change the bank's traditional focus on agribusiness, though it did nudge the institution toward a new niche, the healthcare sector.

Internationalization also did not change its cooperative essence. "What has not changed," wrote Rabobank CEO Herman Wijffels and Rabobank International Chairman R. Arthur Arnold in 1998, "is the inherent customer focus which Rabobank and its subsidiaries bring to a new global community . . . clients can be assured of our dedication and commitment to their interests rather than those of anonymous shareholders."

Rabobank's purchase of California retail banks was part of its new internationalization strategy, one that sought geographical diversification on both sides of the balance sheet and increased focus on its agribusiness niche. California was attractive because it was the largest agricultural economy in the world, yet its agricultural banking system was still highly fragmented. In 2004 Rabobank failed to take over Farm Credit Services of America, part of the US Farm Credit system.

By 2012 Rabobank N.A. operated 120 retail branches and was ranked highest in customer satisfaction in California retail banks in 2011 and 2012 by J.D. Power and Associates. Although it had some exposure to "toxic" subprime assets and suffered losses, it was the only large bank in the Netherlands that did not require any government aid. After the 2008-2011 financial crises (including the Eurozone troubles), Rabobank also continued to grow at home, purchasing the stressed Friesland Bank in 2012 and the custom of its 300,000 depositors in the northern part of the country.

In October 2013 Rabobank agreed to pay about $1 billion in penalties to four regulators for its role in the LIBOR price fixing scandal, but the bank's culture remained strong enough to save its reputation. By 2013 Rabobank had spread across 42 countries and employed about 60,000 people, only 30 of whom were implicated in the wrongdoing. The bank cooperated with regulators as soon as the rate-fixing scheme was brought to its attention, and Piet Moerland, its chairman, apologized for the bank's role in the international scandal and stepped down. Thanks to the way it handled the scandal, and the careful, qualitative way that it continued to screen borrowers, Rabobank retained its triple-A rating.

Sources

Birchall, Johnston. *Finance in an Age of Austerity: The Power of Customer-Owned Banks*. Northampton, MA: Edward Elgar, 2013, 28–29, 107.

Lavelle, Anne. *The Art of Cooperation: The Netherlands and Its Rabobank*. Amsterdam: Inmerc, 1998.

Maslinski, Michael. "Start by Looking at Rabobank Model." *FT.com*, June 14, 2012.

Mazzucca, Tim. "Rabobank, Calif. Strategy Stresses Branches for Now." *American Banker*, March 8, 2007.

McLannahan, Ben. "Orix Set to Buy Robeco from Rabobank." *FT.com*, February 15, 2013.

"Netherlands: Rabobank Settles Libor and Euribor Investigations." *MENA Report*, October 30, 2103.

Steinglass, Matt. "Dutch Lender to Merge with Rabobank." *FT.com*, April 2, 2012.

"United States: Deanna Blaise Appointed Retail Banking Regional Manager For Rabobank In The Central Valley." *MENA Report*, September 13, 2012.

Westerhuis, Gerarda. *Conquering the American Market: ABN AMRO, Rabobank, and Nationale-Nederlande Working in a Different Business Environment, 1965–2005*. Amsterdam: Boom, 2008.

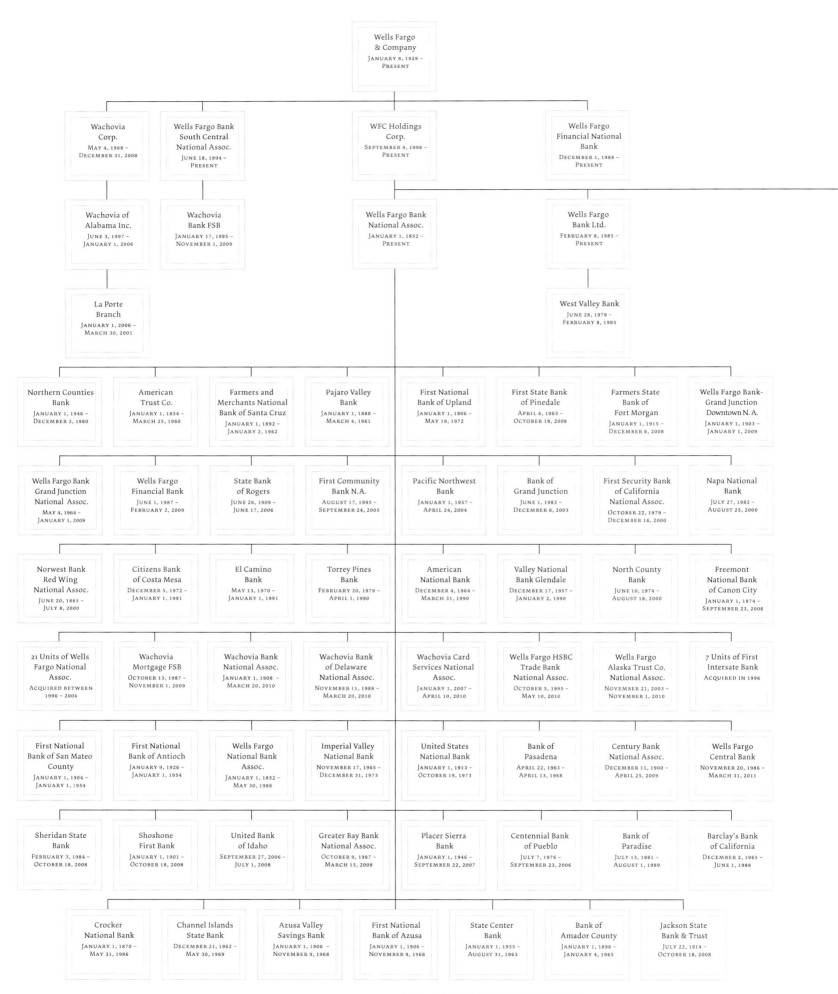

Wells Fargo
& Company
JANUARY 8, 1929 –
PRESENT

Wachovia
Corp.
MAY 4, 1968 –
DECEMBER 31, 2008

Wells Fargo Bank
South Central
National Assoc.
JUNE 18, 1894 –
PRESENT

WFC Holdings
Corp.
SEPTEMBER 9, 1998 –
PRESENT

Wells Fargo
Financial National
Bank
DECEMBER 1, 1988 –
PRESENT

Wachovia of
Alabama Inc.
JUNE 3, 1997 –
JANUARY 1, 2006

Wachovia
Bank FSB
JANUARY 17, 1995 –
NOVEMBER 1, 2009

Wells Fargo Bank
National Assoc.
JANUARY 1, 1852 –
PRESENT

Wells Fargo
Bank Ltd.
FEBRUARY 8, 1985 –
PRESENT

La Porte
Branch
JANUARY 1, 2006 –
MARCH 30, 2001

West Valley Bank
JUNE 28, 1978 –
FEBRUARY 8, 1985

Northern Counties
Bank
JANUARY 1, 1946 –
DECEMBER 2, 1960

American
Trust Co.
JANUARY 1, 1854 –
MARCH 25, 1960

Farmers and
Merchants National
Bank of Santa Cruz
JANUARY 1, 1892 –
JANUARY 2, 1962

Pajaro Valley
Bank
JANUARY 1, 1888 –
MARCH 4, 1961

First National
Bank of Upland
JANUARY 1, 1906 –
MAY 19, 1972

First State Bank
of Pinedale
APRIL 6, 1963 –
OCTOBER 18, 2008

Farmers State
Bank of
Fort Morgan
JANUARY 1, 1915 –
DECEMBER 6, 2008

Wells Fargo Bank-
Grand Junction
Downtown N. A.
JANUARY 1, 1903 –
JANUARY 1, 2009

Wells Fargo Bank
Grand Junction
National Assoc.
MAY 4, 1964 –
JANUARY 1, 2009

Wells Fargo
Financial Bank
JUNE 1, 1987 –
FEBRUARY 2, 2009

State Bank
of Rogers
JUNE 26, 1909 –
JUNE 17, 2006

First Community
Bank N.A.
AUGUST 17, 1995 –
SEPTEMBER 24, 2005

Pacific Northwest
Bank
JANUARY 1, 1957 –
APRIL 24, 2004

Bank of
Grand Junction
JUNE 1, 1983 –
DECEMBER 6, 2003

First Security Bank
of California
National Assoc.
OCTOBER 22, 1979 –
DECEMBER 16, 2000

Napa National
Bank
JULY 27, 1982 –
AUGUST 25, 2000

Norwest Bank
Red Wing
National Assoc.
JUNE 20, 1865 –
JULY 8, 2000

Citizens Bank
of Costa Mesa
DECEMBER 5, 1972 –
JANUARY 1, 1991

El Camino
Bank
MAY 13, 1970 –
JANUARY 1, 1991

Torrey Pines
Bank
FEBRUARY 20, 1979 –
APRIL 1, 1990

American
National Bank
DECEMBER 4, 1964 –
MARCH 31, 1990

Valley National
Bank Glendale
DECEMBER 17, 1957 –
JANUARY 2, 1990

North County
Bank
JUNE 10, 1974 –
AUGUST 18, 2000

Freemont
National Bank
of Canon City
JANUARY 1, 1874 –
SEPTEMBER 23, 2006

21 Units of Wells
Fargo National
Assoc.
ACQUIRED BETWEEN
1996 – 2004

Wachovia
Mortgage FSB
OCTOBER 13, 1987 –
NOVEMBER 1, 2009

Wachovia Bank
National Assoc.
JANUARY 1, 1908 –
MARCH 20, 2010

Wachovia Bank
of Delaware
National Assoc.
NOVEMBER 11, 1988 –
MARCH 20, 2010

Wachovia Card
Services National
Assoc.
JANUARY 1, 2007 –
APRIL 10, 2010

Wells Fargo HSBC
Trade Bank
National Assoc.
OCTOBER 5, 1995 –
MAY 10, 2010

Wells Fargo
Alaska Trust Co.
National Assoc.
NOVEMBER 21, 2003 –
NOVEMBER 1, 2010

7 Units of First
Intersate Bank
ACQUIRED IN 1996

First National
Bank of San Mateo
County
JANUARY 1, 1904 –
JANUARY 1, 1954

First National
Bank of Antioch
JANUARY 9, 1926 –
JANUARY 1, 1954

Wells Fargo
National Bank
Assoc.
JANUARY 1, 1852 –
MAY 30, 1986

Imperial Valley
National Bank
NOVEMBER 17, 1965 –
DECEMBER 31, 1973

United States
National Bank
JANUARY 1, 1913 –
OCTOBER 19, 1973

Bank of
Pasadena
APRIL 22, 1963 –
APRIL 13, 1968

Century Bank
National Assoc.
DECEMBER 11, 1900 –
APRIL 25, 2009

Wells Fargo
Central Bank
NOVEMBER 20, 1986 –
MARCH 31, 2011

Sheridan State
Bank
FEBRUARY 3, 1984 –
OCTOBER 18, 2008

Shoshone
First Bank
JANUARY 1, 1901 –
OCTOBER 18, 2008

United Bank
of Idaho
SEPTEMBER 27, 2006 –
JULY 1, 2008

Greater Bay Bank
National Assoc.
OCTOBER 9, 1987 –
MARCH 15, 2008

Placer Sierra
Bank
JANUARY 1, 1946 –
SEPTEMBER 22, 2007

Centennial Bank
of Pueblo
JULY 7, 1976 –
SEPTEMBER 23, 2006

Bank of
Paradise
JULY 13, 1981 –
AUGUST 1, 1989

Barclay's Bank
of California
DECEMBER 2, 1965 –
JUNE 1, 1988

Crocker
National Bank
JANUARY 1, 1870 –
MAY 31, 1986

Channel Islands
State Bank
DECEMBER 21, 1962 –
MAY 30, 1969

Azusa Valley
Savings Bank
JANUARY 1, 1906 –
NOVEMBER 9, 1968

First National
Bank of Azusa
JANUARY 1, 1906 –
NOVEMBER 9, 1968

State Center
Bank
JANUARY 1, 1955 –
AUGUST 31, 1963

Bank of
Amador County
JANUARY 1, 1896 –
JANUARY 4, 1965

Jackson State
Bank & Trust
JULY 22, 1914 –
OCTOBER 18, 2008

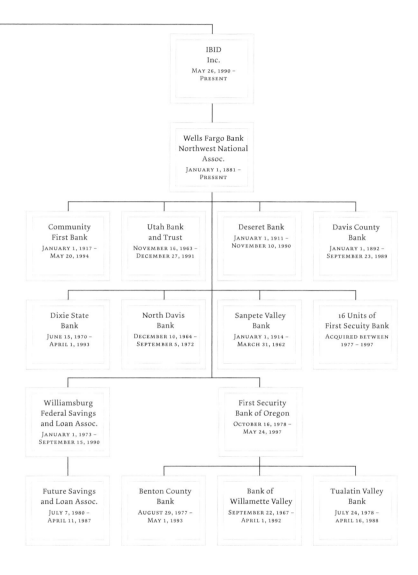

IBID
Inc.
MAY 26, 1990 –
PRESENT

Wells Fargo Bank
Northwest National
Assoc.
JANUARY 1, 1881 –
PRESENT

Community
First Bank
JANUARY 1, 1917 –
MAY 20, 1994

Utah Bank
and Trust
NOVEMBER 16, 1963 –
DECEMBER 27, 1991

Deseret Bank
JANUARY 1, 1911 –
NOVEMBER 10, 1990

Davis County
Bank
JANUARY 1, 1892 –
SEPTEMBER 23, 1989

Dixie State
Bank
JUNE 15, 1970 –
APRIL 1, 1993

North Davis
Bank
DECEMBER 10, 1964 –
SEPTEMBER 5, 1972

Sanpete Valley
Bank
JANUARY 1, 1914 –
MARCH 31, 1962

16 Units of
First Secuity Bank
ACQUIRED BETWEEN
1977 – 1997

Williamsburg
Federal Savings
and Loan Assoc.
JANUARY 1, 1973 –
SEPTEMBER 15, 1990

First Security
Bank of Oregon
OCTOBER 16, 1978 –
MAY 24, 1997

Future Savings
and Loan Assoc.
JULY 7, 1980 –
APRIL 11, 1987

Benton County
Bank
AUGUST 29, 1977 –
MAY 1, 1993

Bank of
Willamette Valley
SEPTEMBER 22, 1967 –
APRIL 1, 1992

Tualatin Valley
Bank
JULY 24, 1978 –
APRIL 16, 1988

Wells Fargo

Bank *(abridged)*

RANK	HEADQUARTERS	TICKER	ASSETS	EARLIEST KNOWN ANCESTOR	INDUSTRY OF ORIGIN
4	San Francisco, CA	WFC	$1,400,000,000	1782	Freight

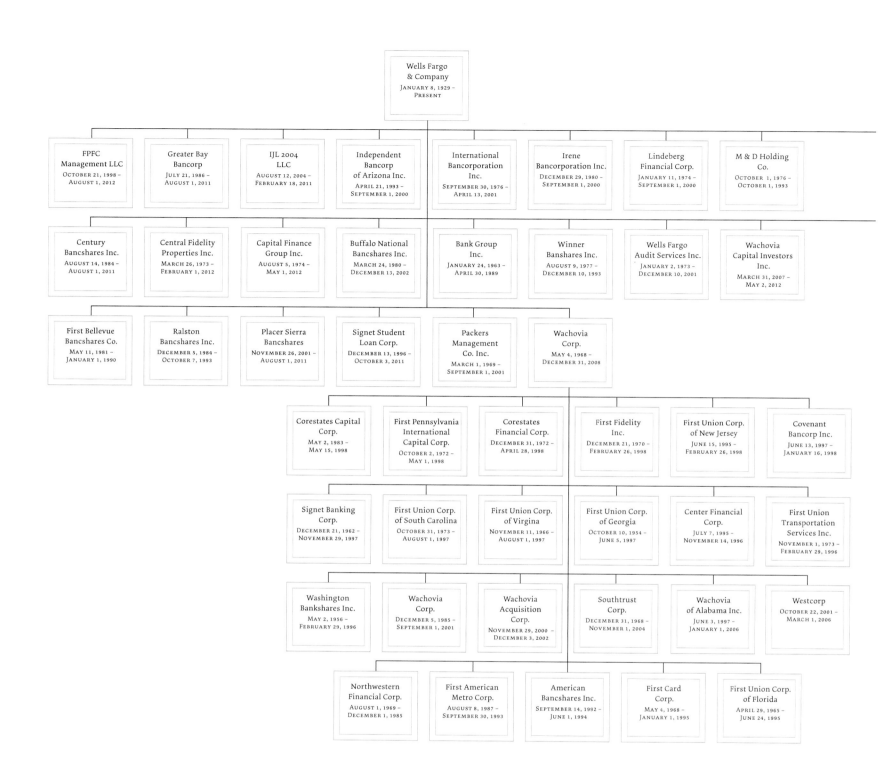

Wells Fargo & Company
January 8, 1929 – Present

FPFC Management LLC
October 21, 1998 – August 1, 2012

Greater Bay Bancorp
July 21, 1986 – August 1, 2011

IJL 2004 LLC
August 12, 2004 – February 18, 2011

Independent Bancorp of Arizona Inc.
April 21, 1993 – September 1, 2000

International Bancorporation Inc.
September 30, 1976 – April 13, 2001

Irene Bancorporation Inc.
December 29, 1980 – September 1, 2000

Lindeberg Financial Corp.
January 11, 1974 – September 1, 2000

M & D Holding Co.
October 1, 1976 – October 1, 1993

Century Bancshares Inc.
August 14, 1984 – August 1, 2011

Central Fidelity Properties Inc.
March 26, 1973 – February 1, 2012

Capital Finance Group Inc.
August 5, 1974 – May 1, 2012

Buffalo National Bancshares Inc.
March 24, 1980 – December 13, 2002

Bank Group Inc.
January 24, 1963 – April 30, 1989

Winner Banshares Inc.
August 9, 1977 – December 10, 1993

Wells Fargo Audit Services Inc.
January 2, 1973 – December 10, 2001

Wachovia Capital Investors Inc.
March 31, 2007 – May 2, 2012

First Bellevue Bancshares Co.
May 11, 1981 – January 1, 1990

Ralston Bancshares Inc.
December 5, 1984 – October 7, 1993

Placer Sierra Bancshares
November 26, 2001 – August 1, 2011

Signet Student Loan Corp.
December 13, 1996 – October 3, 2011

Packers Management Co. Inc.
March 1, 1969 – September 1, 2001

Wachovia Corp.
May 4, 1968 – December 31, 2008

Corestates Capital Corp.
May 2, 1983 – May 15, 1998

First Pennsylvania International Capital Corp.
October 2, 1972 – May 1, 1998

Corestates Financial Corp.
December 31, 1972 – April 28, 1998

First Fidelity Inc.
December 21, 1970 – February 26, 1998

First Union Corp. of New Jersey
June 15, 1995 – February 26, 1998

Covenant Bancorp Inc.
June 13, 1997 – January 16, 1998

Signet Banking Corp.
December 21, 1962 – November 29, 1997

First Union Corp. of South Carolina
October 31, 1973 – August 1, 1997

First Union Corp. of Virgina
November 11, 1966 – August 1, 1997

First Union Corp. of Georgia
October 10, 1954 – June 5, 1997

Center Financial Corp.
July 7, 1995 – November 14, 1996

First Union Transportation Services Inc.
November 1, 1973 – February 29, 1996

Washington Bankshares Inc.
May 2, 1956 – February 29, 1996

Wachovia Corp.
December 5, 1985 – September 1, 2001

Wachovia Acquisition Corp.
November 29, 2000 – December 3, 2002

Southtrust Corp.
December 31, 1968 – November 1, 2004

Wachovia of Alabama Inc.
June 3, 1997 – January 1, 2006

Westcorp
October 22, 2001 – March 1, 2006

Northwestern Financial Corp.
August 1, 1969 – December 1, 1985

First American Metro Corp.
August 8, 1987 – September 30, 1993

American Bancshares Inc.
September 14, 1992 – June 1, 1994

First Card Corp.
May 4, 1968 – January 1, 1995

First Union Corp. of Florida
April 29, 1965 – June 24, 1995

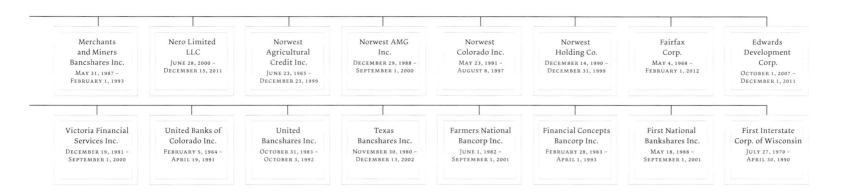

Merchants and Miners Bancshares Inc.	Nero Limited LLC	Norwest Agricultural Credit Inc.	Norwest AMG Inc.	Norwest Colorado Inc.	Norwest Holding Co.	Fairfax Corp.	Edwards Development Corp.
MAY 31, 1987 – FEBRUARY 1, 1993	JUNE 28, 2000 – DECEMBER 15, 2011	JUNE 23, 1965 – DECEMBER 23, 1999	DECEMBER 29, 1988 – SEPTEMBER 1, 2000	MAY 23, 1991 – AUGUST 8, 1997	DECEMBER 14, 1990 – DECEMBER 31, 1999	MAY 4, 1968 – FEBRUARY 1, 2012	OCTOBER 1, 2007 – DECEMBER 1, 2011

Victoria Financial Services Inc.	United Banks of Colorado Inc.	United Bancshares Inc.	Texas Bancshares Inc.	Farmers National Bancorp Inc.	Financial Concepts Bancorp Inc.	First National Bankshares Inc.	First Interstate Corp. of Wisconsin
DECEMBER 19, 1991 – SEPTEMBER 1, 2000	FEBRUARY 5, 1964 – APRIL 19, 1991	OCTOBER 31, 1983 – OCTOBER 3, 1992	NOVEMBER 30, 1980 – DECEMBER 13, 2002	JUNE 1, 1982 – SEPTEMBER 1, 2001	FEBRUARY 28, 1983 – APRIL 1, 1993	MAY 18, 1988 – SEPTEMBER 1, 2001	JULY 27, 1970 – APRIL 30, 1990

Wells Fargo

Holding Company *(abridged)*

Wells Fargo Express Co. Deadwood Treasure Wagon and guards with $250,000 gold bullion from the Great Homestake Mine, Deadwood, South Dakota, 1890.

Wells Fargo began life in California during the infamous gold rush and was named for its founders, Henry Wells and William G. Fargo, who were seasoned express men and partners in American Express (#19). The company made money by delivering mail, packages and people to mining camps and hauling away gold, which gave it entree into banking.

People in California who needed to make payments in distant cities paid Wells, Fargo and Company in gold in California in exchange for a piece of paper, called a bill of exchange, that entitled the holder of the bill to draw gold (or its equivalent) from Wells, Fargo accounts in any of the distant cities in which it held deposits. That economized on shipping costs and allowed miners to move their profits across the nation, and indeed the world, relatively quickly and safely. Soon after forming, the company also began accepting deposits and making loans and collections throughout northern California.

Profits poured in from both sides of the business—the stagecoach express and the bank—thanks in large part to the legendary customer service provided by the company's employees, who soon developed a reputation for both honesty and punctuality. Both businesses expanded rapidly, as did the company's capital and dividends. Nevertheless, during a banking panic in February 1855, having run out of both gold dust and coin, it had to suspend payments for a few days. The company claimed to have a net worth of almost $400,000 and begged the public to allow it "a few days to convert some" of its assets into cash. Its depositors, many of whom were Chinese laborers loyal to the company, complied and left their deposits in the bank. The company survived the crisis and by the end of the year had 55 agencies throughout California and Oregon.

Wells, Fargo quickly recovered and continued to grow, both organically and by acquisition, in both of its major fields of operation as the business spread throughout the West and into Canada, Alaska and Mexico. In the early 1860s it ran several "Pony Express" lines that sped messages across the vast western expanses until telegraph lines were run. In 1864 the company completed a "Grand Consolidation" of all the major stage lines west of the Missouri River. It also expanded its reach overseas, to Australia, Hong Kong, Europe, Japan and Latin America.

Not everything was rosy, however. Between 1870 and 1884, outlaws attempted to rob 355 of the company's gold shipments, the vast majority consisting of attacks on stagecoaches. It lost some gold, but with the help of posses and detectives, it was able to secure 226 criminal convictions. The company's detectives eventually managed to capture and convict "Black Bart," a mining engineer named Charles Boles who successfully robbed 27 stagecoaches between 1875 and 1883 before finally being betrayed by a laundry mark on a handkerchief he left at the scene of a thwarted heist.

Meanwhile, the banking side of the business was thriving and innovating. In 1864 it began to offer telegraphic transfers, basically bills of exchange or checks sent electronically instead of the old-fashioned way. It added money orders to its repertoire in 1885 and in the 20th century offered travelers checks and foreign postal remittances.

By the early 20th century, the express business, which had grown to over 100,000 miles of routes and 35,000 workers employed in some 10,000 offices, was earning 10% per year at best, while the bank department was earning 30%–40%. When in 1918 the government suggested an alliance of the major express companies as a wartime measure, the company acceded and the new American Railway Express Company took over its domestic routes. As a member of an informal holding

A Wells Fargo log building in Tanana, Alaska, ca. 1900-1916.

Wells Fargo Express Co., 1905-1945.

company known as American Express Company (a predecessor to #19), Wells Fargo and Company Express continued operating shipping routes in Mexico and Cuba and an armored car service in the United States until the 1960s, but it never regained its previous splendor. Its former banking department, by contrast, achieved ever-higher levels of success.

At first organized as an unincorporated joint-stock company, Wells, Fargo later incorporated in New York and, in 1866, in Colorado as part of a complicated merger deal. In 1905 its banking department finally split off and obtained a banking charter through its merger with the Nevada National Bank of San Francisco. Organized in 1875 by James Fair, James Flood, William O'Brien and John Mackay, the so-called Silver Kings made rich by Nevada's famous Comstock Lode, the Nevada had converted to a national charter in 1897. About that time the bank's president, I.W. Hellman, proclaimed that its goal was "not to be the largest bank in San Francisco, but to be the soundest and the best."

Despite selling off its branches at first, the new entity, called Wells Fargo Nevada National Bank, was the second largest commercial bank in San Francisco. It suffered terribly during the earthquake and resultant fires in April 1906, but it managed to wire its correspondents: "Building Destroyed. Vaults Intact. Credit Unaffected." It operated out of the US Mint for a month afterwards while Hellman tried to convince people that the bank was "in an exceedingly strong position" and that the city's businessmen were "filled with energy and with the determination, in rebuilding our city, to make it stronger and more beautiful than ever."

The bank also survived the Panic of 1907, which some scholars believe was touched off by the earthquake, as well as the Great War. In the 1920s the bank grew conservatively, increasing its asset base from $86.4 million in 1920 to $94 million by early 1924, when it merged with the Union Trust Company. Established by Hellman in 1893, Union Trust was the West's oldest trust company. Due to the merger, it began handling savings accounts, under the name Wells Fargo Bank and Union Trust Company, for the first time.

Frederick L. Lipman took charge of Wells and ran it as conservatively as Hellman had, which largely explains why the bank survived the Great Depression. The bank could not help but thrive during World War II, and at the end of 1947 it boasted assets of half a billion

dollars. It decided it needed to increase its retail banking presence in the 1950s, so it set up a small network of branches in the Bay Area. In 1954 it went back to calling itself Wells Fargo Bank and continued its acquisitive ways.

A decade and a notable merger (with American Trust Company) later, Wells Fargo was the 18th largest bank in the nation with assets of almost $3.8 billion and over 100 branches. Established in 1854 as the San Francisco Accumulating Fund (and later called the San Francisco Savings and Loan Society), American Trust had been California's oldest bank, besides Wells. After merging with the San Francisco Savings Union in 1910, the Mercantile Trust Company in 1920 and the American Bank of San Francisco in 1927, it established in Northern California one of the nation's best retail bank networks.

Called the Wells Fargo American Trust Company until it shortened its name to Wells Fargo Bank in 1962, the bank spread into both Southern California and the credit card market in 1967. The following year it chartered a one-bank holding company called Wells Fargo and Company so that it could expand outside of California and into new areas of finance. In 1987 it incorporated again, this time in Delaware.

In the 1970s the bank began offering its customers ATM services. Over the next several decades, it also leveraged the personal computer, Internet and telecom revolutions to increase automation and reduce paperwork throughout its business. In 1986 Wells Fargo almost doubled in size by merging with the Crocker Bank, a California financial institution that formed in 1870 and was named after its founder, Charles Crocker. Crocker's son, William H., was one of the most respected financiers in San Francisco and ran the bank until 1937. In 1926 Crocker merged with First National Gold Bank, which also began business in 1870.

In 1956 Crocker First National Bank merged with Anglo-California National to form Crocker-Anglo National Bank. Anglo-California dated from 1873 and was an early proponent of branch banking. The bank then merged with Citizens National Bank of Los Angeles in 1963 to create a statewide behemoth. In 1971 it shortened its name to The Crocker Bank and adopted a jewel-like logo that jived nicely with Wells Fargo's traditional diamond logo.

By the end of 1994 Wells Fargo had assets of about $54 billion and was one of the largest retail banks in the nation, with 600 branches,

Wells, Fargo & Co.'s express office, C Street, Virginia City, 1866.

Advertisement from Budweiser's "Great Contributions to Good Taste" relates the story of Wells Fargo.

1,900 ATMs and a 24-hour telephone banking service. Its efficiency ratio was 56.6%, one of the best in its class, and its noninterest income was growing nicely. It continued to interact with customers well via new technology and one-employee mini-branches set up in most California supermarket chains.

In 1996 Wells Fargo acquired First Interstate Bancorp of Los Angeles, a western superregional that traced its origins to A.P. Giannini's Transamerica (which was affiliated with #2). After passage of the BHCA of 1956, Transamerica was broken up into several pieces, including FirstAmerica Corporation. That BHC changed its name to Western Bancorporation in 1961 and First Interstate in 1981.

Over the years, the BHC made numerous acquisitions small and large, including Pacifica National Bank, United California Bank, IntraWest Bank of Denver and Alex Brown Financial Group. By 1994 First Interstate was the nation's 14th largest BHC, with assets of almost $56 billion and 1,100 branches spread over 13 western states stretching from Alaska to Texas. At 21.6%, its return on equity that year was among the best of the superregionals, on net income of $733.5 million. In October 1995 Wells Fargo moved on First Interstate, only to have its initial offer rejected in favor of that of First Bank System of Minneapolis (now U.S. Bancorp [#10]). When that deal fell through, Wells Fargo pounced and won its prize for $11.6 billion, the largest bank acquisition in US history to that time.

In 1998 Wells Fargo took over Norwest, a superregional bank headquartered in Minneapolis. Initially organized in 1929, by the mid-1990s Norwest owned 88 commercial banks serving 16 states, including remote ones like the Dakotas, Montana and Wyoming. Its 45,000 employees provided banking, insurance, investments and other financial services to people in all 50 states and 10 Canadian provinces via more than 3,000 branches, including a network of 781 mortgage stores located in all 50 states. It also operated a consumer finance company, Norwest Financial, which had more than 1,000 stores in 46 states and throughout Canada. It was one of the nation's largest and most profitable banks, thanks to what observers called its "superb financial ratios." CEO Richard Kovacevich said its goal was to "be regarded as one of America's great companies," a bank able to "out-local" the big banks and outsize the locals.

Besides adding a lot of heft, Norwest brought to Wells Fargo considerable expertise, including knowledge of "how to sell and cross-sell." With that help, Wells Fargo showed that cross-selling financial products can work; its average retail customer used more than five of its products, and its average business customer more than six. However, what Wells was really good at, some analysts concluded, was managing its employees well and providing them with incentives to promote the bank's products.

Wells also treated its workers well. Employees reported being pleased with their bosses and colleagues, and *Business Ethics* called it one of the nation's top 10 "Best Corporate Citizens." In 2006 the Human Rights Campaign awarded it a perfect 100 on its corporate equality index; that same year *DiversityInc.* ranked it 17th out of 50 large American companies for diversity. In addition to fair hiring practices, which included recruiting at public universities as well as the usual elite schools, the bank often lent to small businesses, including those owned and operated by women and ethnic minorities.

In 2008 Wells Fargo acquired the troubled Wachovia, then the fourth largest BHC in the country with $720 billion in assets (but by

Wells Fargo received in San Francisco a check drawn on Bullion & Exchange Bank in Carson, and it returned the check along with this "invoice" to the bank in Carson for "collection and credit" to a Wells account there. The document is dated October 28, 1892, and the stamp shows the funds were paid three days later.

year's end almost as much in liabilities). The acquisition gave it a first-time presence in 16 eastern states. Wachovia was the product of a series of mergers between Wachovia National Bank (chartered 1879) of North Carolina and First Atlanta Mortgage Corporation, Southern First Federal Savings and Loan Association, First National Bank of Atlanta and South Carolina National that occurred between 1985 and 1991. Like most other financial giants, it had grown quickly in the 1990s and early 2000s through an aggressive merger and acquisitions strategy.

First Union, a North Carolina-based bank that traced its lineage back through CoreStates to one of the nation's first banks (Philadelphia National Bank, chartered in 1803), bought long-time rival Wachovia in 2001 and assumed its name. First Union achieved dominant status because in 1995, in one of the biggest bank mergers to that time, it had acquired New Jersey's First Fidelity Bancorp, an institution that traced its roots back to the State Bank of Newark chartered by Revolutionary War heroes in 1812. The merger made First Union a superregional, the sixth largest BHC in the nation with almost 2,000 branches and 10.5 million customers spread across 14 states from Connecticut to Florida, assets of $123 billion and a market cap around $13 billion.

The new Wachovia then went on to acquire AmNet Mortgage, Golden West Financial, Ameriprise Financial, A.G. Edwards and other coveted institutions that gave it 13 million customers serviced by 3,400 "financial centers" spread over 21 states and Washington, DC, as well as 770 retail brokerage offices in 48 states. At its height, it employed more than 100,000 people and operated almost 3,900 offices worldwide. But with more banks came bigger problems. Golden West was one source of trouble, as it was so over-exposed to "toxic mortgages" that even some regulators like FDIC Chairman Sheila Bair noticed its delirium. Another cause of Wachovia's issues was its commercial real estate lending business, which experienced heavy losses.

The final blow to Wachovia came when the SEC insisted it buy back $9 billion of "auction rate securities" it had sold to unsuspecting small businesses and charities. The $7 billion in new capital it was able to raise turned out to be insufficient to cover $32 billion in losses, so it entered into merger negotiations with Citigroup and Wells Fargo. The former turned out to be in no condition to take on a bank as big as Wachovia, but instead was angling for government assistance. Citigroup won its initial bid ($1 per share plus government guarantees) but did not finalize the deal quickly enough, allowing Wells Fargo to counter ($7 per share and no guarantees) and purchase Wachovia and its huge presence on the East Coast. With Wachovia under its belt,

Wells Fargo had a branch or ATM within two miles of more than 150 million Americans.

Over its long history, Wells Fargo has made more than 12,000 acquisitions, but never one as large in absolute or relative terms as Wachovia, the assets of which were much larger than Wells Fargo's $486 billion. As a result, Wells Fargo integrated Wachovia slowly, careful not to injure the fallen giant's brand, which remained remarkably strong despite its demise.

Wells Fargo was well-positioned to take on such a burden because it exited the subprime business in 2007 and actively pursued mortgage defaulters. It lost its triple-A S&P credit rating during the crisis, but dropped only to AA-. By 2013 The Economist heralded the bank as "the big winner from the financial crisis" because after a brief dip in 2009, its profits surged from less than $3 billion to over $5 billion by 2013.

Warren Buffett saw it all coming, as usual. During and following the panic, when all bank stocks were depressed, he added more Wells Fargo shares to his portfolio, which had contained some since 1989. By 2011 Buffett owned 6.8% of the bank, which represented his second largest investment, behind Coca-Cola.

Sources

Adubato, Steve. *You Are the Brand*. New Brunswick, NJ: Rutgers University Press, 2011, 210–14.

Bair, Sheila. *Bull by the Horns: Fighting to Save Main Street from Wall Street and Wall Street from Itself*. New York: Free Press, 2012, 95–105.

Buffett, Mary and David Clark. *The Warren Buffett Stock Portfolio: Warren Buffett Stock Picks: Why and When He Is Investing in Them*. New York: Scribner, 2011, 193–202.

Hatch, Alden. *American Express: A Century of Service*. Garden City, NY: Doubleday, 1950.

Loosvelt, Derek, et al. *The Vault Guide to the Top 50 Banking Employers: 2008 Edition*. New York: Vault, 2007, 142–47, 172–77, 296–99.

Loomis, Noel M. *Wells Fargo*. New York: Clarkson No. Potter, 1968.

Spiegel, John, Alan Gart and Steven Gart. *Banking Redefined: How Superregional Powerhouses Are Reshaping Financial Services*. Chicago: Irwin Professional Publishing, 1996, 179–96, 223–58, 271–81, 361–82, 421–57.

Wainwright, Nicholas B. *History of the Philadelphia National Bank: A Century and a Half of Philadelphia Banking, 1803–1953*. Philadelphia: Philadelphia National Bank, 1953.

"Wells Fargo: Riding High." *The Economist*, September 14, 2013, 77-78.

Wells Fargo Since 1852. San Francisco: Wells Fargo, 1988.

Wetfeet. *25 Top Financial Services Firms*. San Francisco: Wetfeet. 2008, 89–95.

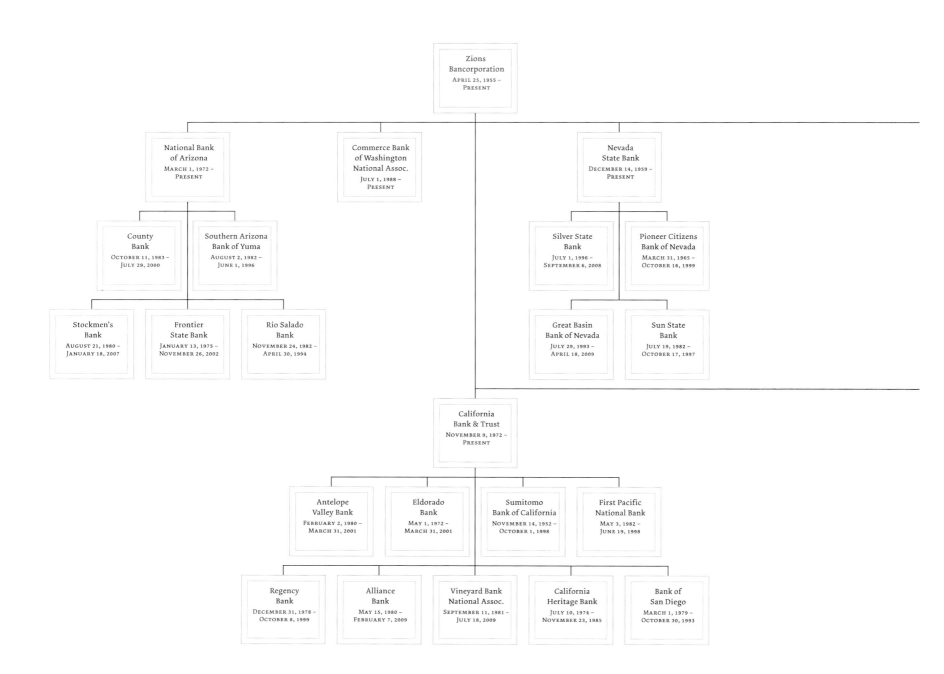

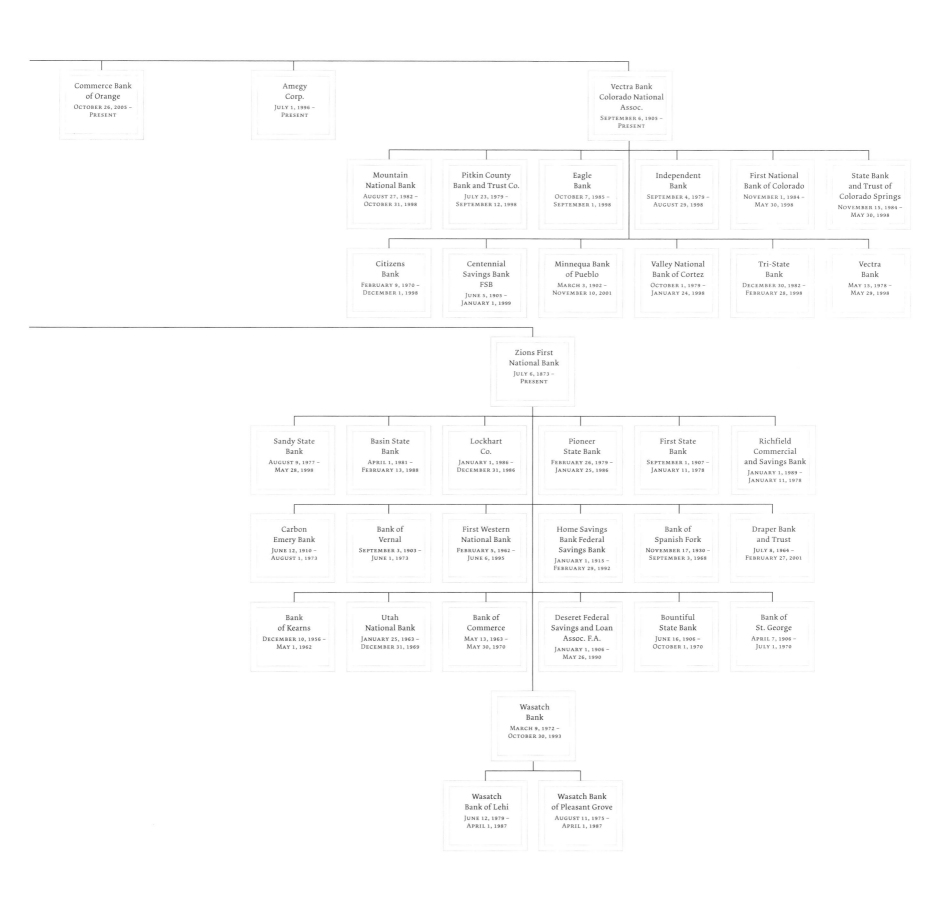

Zions Bancorporation

Bank *(abridged)*

RANK	HEADQUARTERS	TICKER	ASSETS	EARLIEST KNOWN ANCESTOR	INDUSTRY OF ORIGIN
38	**Salt Lake City, UT**	**ZION**	**$55,000,000,000**	**1873**	**Commercial Banking**

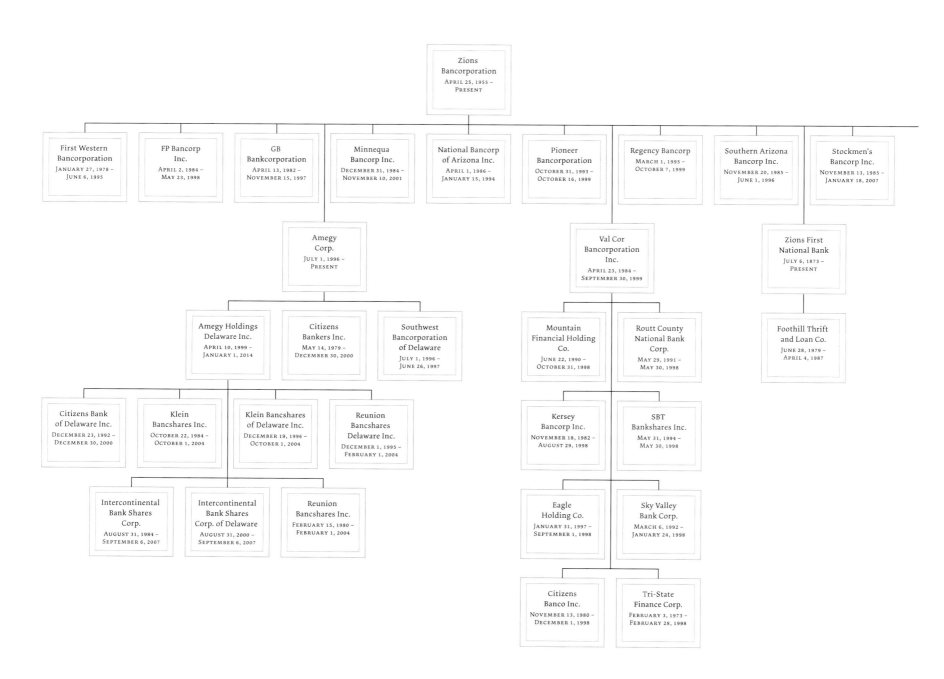

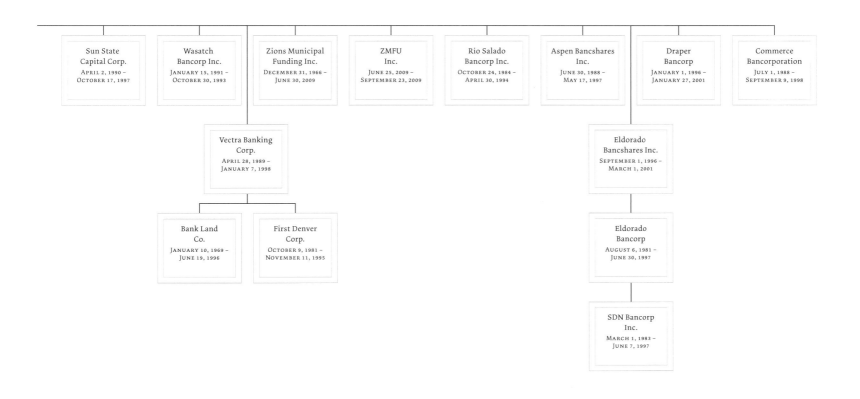

Zions Bancorporation   Holding Company *(abridged)*

Photograph of Mormon leader Brigham Young, founder of Zion's Savings Bank and Trust Company, ca. 1855-1865.

Mormon leader Brigham Young established Zion's Savings Bank and Trust Company in Salt Lake City in 1873 and capitalized it at $200,000. The Mormon Church owned the bank until 1960, when business interests purchased it. It may sound strange for a religious organization to own a bank, but Mormons were unafraid of Mammon. Young himself believed that savings and investment were next to Godliness. "If you wish to get rich, save what you get," he beseeched his co-religionists. "A fool can earn money, but it takes a wise man to save and dispose of it to his own advantage."

Due to Young's encouragement and 10% interest paid on deposits, the bank's coffers filled even as a financial panic stunned other banks throughout the nation. A few weeks later, the bank bought the savings deposits of the Deseret National Bank. It later cut its deposit interest to 8% per year while charging borrowers from 1.25%–2% per month, a nice gross spread. When panic again seized the financial system in 1893, Wilford Woodruff, the bank's president, was also head of the Mormon Church. He asserted that "the bank will stand," and it did, some claim by divine intervention.

It did seem rather miraculous that Heber J. Grant (a future president of the bank) was able to raise $336,000 at 6% when the going interest rate during the panic hit 182.5% per year. But a more likely explanation was that savvy New York investors knew that the mighty Mormon Church backed the institution and that a sure 6% was better than a

small chance of actually being repaid the principal of a debt burdened with such a monstrous interest charge. Of course the bank also backed the church, for example, in 1899 by purchasing $200,000 of its bonds and lending it $20,000 to purchase temple lots in Missouri.

The bank grew along with Salt Lake City and Utah, which finally achieved statehood in 1896. By its 50th anniversary it had assets of $12 million. It survived the Great Depression because of "carefully made loans, conservative policies and strict attention to good banking principles." Being backed by the church was again important, too. After suffering $1.5 million of withdrawals in February 1932 as a result of the collapse of Deseret Savings Bank, the bank's Orval Adams made a conspicuous display of $1 million in cash borrowed from New York's Irving Trust (now part of #9) and Grant, now president, posted a notice reminding depositors that "the church is the largest stockholder in Zion's Bank. Back of that ownership is the pledge of the strength, integrity and resources of the church. It will not let this bank fail. . . . There is no safer bank in the state or the nation." Those tactics worked, as the run ended and deposits began to flow back in.

Zion's Savings Bank and Trust merged with the First National Bank of Salt Lake City and Utah Savings and Trust Company in 1957. Adams became president of the new institution, which boasted deposits of $109.5 million and was styled Zions First National Bank. First National had been chartered as the Utah National Bank in 1890 and

Temple Square headquarters of the Mormon Church, Salt Late City, Utah, ca. 1898-1905.

was also owned by the church. The third entity in the merger, Utah Savings, dated from 1889, and the church bought a majority interest in it circa 1915.

Just three years after the big merger, businessmen headed by Leland B. Flint and Roy W. Simmons bought Zions First from the church. Even after the sale, the Mormon Church continued to keep its sizeable deposits in the institution, as did many thrifty individual Mormons. Zions First used those deposits, capital raised during its 1966 IPO and assets of almost $154 million to quickly increase its top and bottom lines. In 1962 it purchased the Bank of Kearns and its $3 million of assets. Soon after, it established branches in Taylorsville and several in Salt Lake City. When Simmons became president upon Flint's death in 1964, the bank had assets just under $200 million and nine offices. Growth continued both organically and through acquisitions, including the purchase of the Bank of Spanish Fork in 1968. By the end of the decade, Zions had 15 offices and assets of $316 million. Ten new offices were added in 1970 alone, seven through acquisition and three through de novo expansion.

Thanks to yet more acquisitions, by the end of 1974 Zions was Utah's second largest bank, with $566 million in assets, 35 branches and 900 employees. Moreover, Zions Utah Bancorporation (ZUB), a one-bank holding company, had spread outside of its original Utah stronghold into Colorado, Idaho and Oregon with "financial offices" that offered insurance, money orders, mortgages and lucrative consumer loans.

In addition, ZUB's leasing company, which specialized in the lease of commercial equipment in the middling range (then $30,000), was authorized to do business in six states, the core four plus Arizona and California. Management had its eyes set on the West Coast, particularly California, for future expansion and was also contemplating entering the commercial finance and factoring businesses. Thanks

to relaxation of interstate branching restrictions, it entered Arizona as a full-fledged bank in 1986. Simmons used his connections with Kennecott Copper Corporation, Utah Portland Cement, Beneficial Life, Denver & Rio Grande Western Railroad and other corporations to aid his bank's development.

Despite hitting a rough patch in the mid-1980s, ZUB, redubbed Zions Bancorporation in 1987, grew along with Utah's energy sector, Salt Lake City and its high-tech center and the greater West. By 1995, with founder Roy Simmons chairman of the board and his son, Harris, in the president/CEO chair, it had 126 offices, including 10 in Arizona and 24 in Nevada. That same year, Zions had $5.6 billion in assets and superior earnings growth driven by sharp gains in net interest income and noninterest revenues (fees), as well as expert expense control. It was the 26th most efficient bank in the nation, and its nonperforming asset ratio was among the top 10 best. Return on equity exceeded 18%, and the balance sheet was described as "very clean" and with "strong reserves." Between 1993 and 2007, Zions made 32 acquisitions. By the end of 2007 it operated 508 branches in 10 states plus nine nonbank subsidiaries.

Despite being depicted in the media as a "sapling among sequoias," Zions maintained enough strength, thanks to growth in the regional economy and its conservative credit policies, to continue growing fast enough to maintain its independence. It did a large volume of repurchase agreements and municipal bonds, and its Zions Capital Market Group—which formed from the 1993 acquisition of Discount Corp. of New York—was the only primary dealer in government securities located between Chicago and the West Coast. It was also a significant underwriter and distributor of municipal and government agency securities, including those of the Small Business Administration and Farmer Mac. Zions was also an early leader in consumer loan

IMPORTANT

Zion's Savings Bank and Trust Company was in no way affiliated with the Deseret Savings Bank The Church had no financial or stock interest in the Deseret Savings Bank

The Church is the largest stockholder in this Bank. Back of that ownership is the pledge of the strength, integrity and resources of the Church **IT WILL NOT LET THIS BANK FAIL**

Fortunately, this bank needs no help from the Church. It is in a strong, clean, liquid condition. It can pay off every depositor in full. Fear of its failure is not only without foundation, but positively foolish. There is no safer bank in the State or the Nation.

Heber J. Grant.
Anthony W. Ivins.

This sign was posted by the LDS Church during the Great Depression to substantiate the stability of Zion's Bank.

securitization—the purchasing, packaging and resale of home equity, credit cards and automobile loans—to institutional investors for a fee.

Despite its early entry into the loan securitization business, Zions did not find itself embroiled in the subprime mortgage crisis of the 2000s because the Simmons family, other officers and employees owned about a third of its stock, so the institution remained relatively conservative. Growth for growth's sake was unlikely in a bank where the CEO had studied economies of scale in banking at the master's level and found "precious few" of them.

Nevertheless, the bank's performance slid as loan growth stagnated during the recession, and it accepted $1.4 billion in TARP funds to "help jump-start the economy" in the words of the *Washington Post*. It subsequently slashed dividends and repaid the TARP money completely, with stipulated dividends, in 2012.

While carefully maintaining the quality of its assets, Zions also took care to ensure a steady stream of deposits by leveraging the skills of Utah's technology sector. It was the first bank, for example, to allow business customers to deposit checks remotely by computer, and in 2012 one of its executives endorsed the use of social media, including Facebook and Twitter, to engage with customers. By 2013 Zions had almost 500 branches and 10,000 employees, but the spirit of Brigham Young and Roy Simmons was apparently still strong.

"It's still all about the value we work to create for our clients, and for our communities," executive John Seaman told *The Enterprise* magazine. "We do that by helping families save for their futures, through philanthropy that invests in our communities, and through supporting the local industries and businesses that fuel our economy. We recognize that our success has been, and will continue to be, tied to the success of those we serve."

Sources

Appelbaum, Binyamin and David Cho. "Treasury Moves to Invest in More Banks." *Washington Post*, October 24, 2008, D1.

Douglas, Norman E. "Zions Utah Bancorporation Revisited." *Burroughs Clearing House* 58, 7 (1974): 20–21, 57–58.

Lamiman, Kevin. "Zions Bancorporation." *Better Investing* 58, 2 (October 2008): 33–34.

Marshall, Jeffery. "A High Climber from Utah." *US Banker* (April 1996), 33.

Simmons, Roy W. *Zions First National Bank: Growing Into Its Second Hundred Years*. New York: Newcomen Society, 1974.

Stewart, Jackie. "Zions Shareholders Back Say-On-Pay Plan, Reject Clawback." *American Banker*, May 29, 2012.

"The Mormon Way of Business." *The Economist*, May 5, 2012, 68.

"United States: Zions Bancorporation Repays in Full its Remaining $700 Million in TARP Funds, Overall Positive Return on Tarp Bank Programs Now Totals More than $21 Billion." *MENA Report*, September 27, 2012.

"Utah's Banking Pioneer Turns 140." *The Enterprise*, August 19, 2013, F1.

"Utah Parent Is Breaking Up Discount Corp.: A Wall Street Trading Loss Brings a Move to Salt Lake City." *The New York Times*, February 14, 1995, D5.

Wack, Kevin. "Tech Talk Rules ABA Convention." *American Banker*, October 17, 2012.

Zions First National Bank clock, Salt Lake City, Utah.

Conclusion

This study focuses on the genealogies of the nation's 50 largest financial institutions as of the early 21st century. A quick look at the family trees of these institutions indicates an explosive growth in American banking. From just three banks in the 1780s, the American banking system expanded to nearly 30,000 independent banks at the peak in numbers in the early 1920s. Almost all of those banks were so-called unit banks, or banks with only one office. Such a system is prone to bank failures and financial crises, as it makes it difficult for banks to diversify their assets and liabilities.

Bank failures during the Great Depression of the 1930s cut the peak number of banks roughly in half, where the number remained until the 1980s. Since the 1980s, the number of independent banks has again been reduced by half or more by mergers, acquisitions, failures and other types of disappearances. To a great extent, the giant financial holding companies that now dominate the US financial system, and whose genealogies are featured here, have been creations of recent decades.

When it comes to creating megabanks, the United States is a latecomer. The leading nations of Europe, as well as Canada, have had banking systems with a relatively small number of large banks with extensive, often nationwide, branch systems since the late 19th century. Some, such as Germany and France, have long featured "universal" banking, meaning large institutions that combine commercial banking with investment banking, trading and other financial services. Why, until recently, was the United States different?

Financial historians Charles Calomiris and Steven Haber in a recent book provide some answers to this interesting question.[1] They argue that banking is, and always has been, intimately intertwined with politics. Therefore, differences in political structures have resulted in different banking structures. What made American banking so different from that of other leading nations was the US political system, which for most of US history resulted in the states rather than the federal government controlling banking development. In many states, unit bankers sought protection from competition. To that end, they forged political alliances with populist politicians fearful of any concentrated power, especially financial power, and worked together to prevent branch banking. The unit banker-populist political coalition was quite successful at both the state and federal levels in staving off nearly all attempts to allow branch banking within states or across state lines. This is why the nation historically had so many unit banks and so few branch banks.

US banking development did not begin that way, however. Its initial phase was instituted mostly by members of the Federalist political party and their leader, Treasury Secretary Alexander Hamilton. The Bank of the United States (BUS), chartered by Congress in 1791 at Hamilton's behest, was by far the largest financial institution in the country, and it operated a nationwide branch banking system. Hamilton's bank, as he intended (see the Introduction to this volume), inspired state governments to create more banks. The economy was overwhelmingly agricultural, but its most dynamic and modern sector was the financial one. By 1795 there were two dozen banks, causing

Hamilton's successor at the Treasury Department, Oliver Wolcott Jr., to declare that "Banks are multiplying like mushrooms."[2] This was only the beginning. Soon many, but not all, in the rival Jeffersonian political party also liked banks, as long as they could control them. So the states chartered more and more banks.

By the early 19th century, the state unit banker-populist political coalition was already forming, and it won a victory in 1811 when Congress narrowly refused to renew the charter of the BUS. During the ensuing War of 1812, federal finances were crippled by the absence of the national bank, so an item high on the postwar agenda was the chartering of a second BUS with nationwide branching powers in 1816. It proved to be no more durable than the first BUS: after Congress voted to renew its charter in 1832, Andrew Jackson, the populist president, vetoed the bill. The United States would not have another central bank until 1914, and the unit banker-populist political coalition would stifle branch banking, interstate banking and universal banking for a century and a half, until the 1980s.

Ironically, Hamilton's BUS model of a bank with nationwide branching powers migrated north to Canada. Canada's first banks simply copied Hamilton's charter, and they stuck with that model from the early 19th century to the present. That was possible because in Canada, unlike the United States, banking was controlled at the federal level and not by the provinces (akin to US states) of the country.

In the United States, the long era of unit banker-populist political control of banking had its shortcomings. It was "inherently unstable, noncompetitive and inefficient in its allocation of credit."[3] Regulatory laws such as Regulation Q, which specified what banks could pay in interest on checking accounts (zero) and savings accounts (low), were designed to protect banks. However, by the 1970s with the advent of retail money market funds and cash management sweep accounts at brokerages, they were simply causing disintermediation and a loss of financial market share for banks.

At the same time, technological changes, such as the ATM (which the unit banks fought as "branches," but lost on that), undermined protected local bank monopolies. The Savings & Loan Crisis of the 1980s drove further changes when laws allowed failed savings & loans to be absorbed by larger financial institutions, even ones from other states. The final nail in the coffin of the old unit banker-populist political alliance came in 1994, when Congress passed a law allowing nationwide branch banking, and the United States returned to a nationwide branch banking system.

The collapse of the old unit banker-populist political alliance in the 1980s and 1990s made possible the emergence of megabanks and gigantic bank holding companies (BHCs) in the United States. Although a majority of the 50 largest BHCs have their roots in traditional commercial banking, there is also a wide variety of antecedents, from brokerage houses and investment banks to manufacturers and insurance companies. We also see a wider geographical dispersal of these institutions. When US banking began, most banks formed in the northeastern states, and primarily in the large port cities. Now some 225 years later, the locations of the large BHC headquarters reflect the

FOUNDED A.D. MDCCXCV.

Drawn under the Direction of the Author, and Engraved by M. Mériget.

The Bank of the United States of America.

Bank of the United States building on South Third Street in Philadelphia.

expansion of the country and its economy. While that should not be surprising, what may be unexpected is that 11 of the BHCs are owned by foreign BHCs that are headquartered outside the United States, with three in Spain, two each in Canada and Great Britain, and one each in France, Germany, Japan and the Netherlands. Finance has truly become global.

The growth of the American economy is intertwined with the growth of the banking sector. When that sector is healthy, the nation has benefited. And, as the 2008 financial crisis demonstrated, when banks become unhealthy, the entire economy suffers. If the collapse of the old unit banker-populist political coalition that prevented a more rational banking development in the United States for 150 years should have improved the safety, soundness and efficiency of our financial institutions, why then did we have the recent crisis?

That is still a large and much-debated issue. Calomiris and Haber suggest it might be rooted in a new coalition of bankers and politicians, where the political deal was that banks could grow large and become megabanks only if they agreed to direct credit to politically favored constituencies — some communities and some sectors such as housing — that would not have received as much credit on purely economic grounds.[4]

Will the financial consolidations traced in this volume continue? Or have they reached, and maybe even exceeded, their economically rational limits? The next chapters of the banks' histories should be interesting to follow as they are written in the years and decades ahead.

Notes

1. Charles W. Calomiris and Stephen H. Haber, *Fragile by Design: The Political Origins of Banking Crises & Scarce Credit* (Princeton: Princeton University Press, 2014).
2. Oliver Wolcott Jr. to Alexander Hamilton, September 25, 1795.
3. Calomiris and Haber, *Fragile by Design*, 154.
4. Calomiris and Haber, *Fragile by Design*, Chapters 7 and 8.

Illustration Credits

Museum of American Finance (xii)*
Prints & Photographs Division, Library of Congress, LC-USZ62-9583 (3)*
Museum of American Finance (11, left)
Harris & Ewing Collection, Prints & Photographs Division, Library of Congress,
    LC-DIG-hec-21551 (11, right)
Museum of American Finance (12)*
Prints & Photographs Division, Library of Congress, HABS VA-1413-2 (13, top)
National Photo Company Collection, Prints & Photographs Division, Library of Congress,
    LC-USZ62-97758 (13, bottom left)
Museum of American Finance (13, bottom right)*
Museum of American Finance (14)
Museum of American Finance (15)
Prints & Photographs Division, Library of Congress, LC-DIG-pga-004472 (18, left)*
Prints & Photographs Division, Library of Congress, LC-DIG-pga-02405 (18, right)
Prints & Photographs Division, Library of Congress, LC-DIG-ggbain-19886 (19)
Museum of American Finance (21)*
Museum of American Finance (22)
Museum of American Finance (23, top)
Museum of American Finance (23, center)*
Museum of American Finance (23, bottom)
Bain Collection, Prints & Photographs Division, Library of Congress,
    LC-DIG-ggbain-09939 (25)
Collection of Mark D. Tomasko (27)*
Prints & Photographs Divison, Library of Congress, LC-USZC2-3834 (32, left)
Prints & Photographs Division, Library of Congress, LC-USZC2-3895 (32, right)
Frank and Frances Carpenter Collection, Prints & Photographs Division, Library of
    Congress, LC-USZ62-108295 (33)
Collection of Mark D. Tomasko (34)
    © C Bettmann/CORBIS (41, left)
Library of Congress, Prints & Photographs Division, FSA/OWI Collection,
LC-DIG-fsa-8d28753 (41, right)*
Library of Congress, Prints & Photographs Division, FSA/OWI Collection,
LC-DIG-fsa-8d28748 (43)*
Museum of American Finance (44)*
Museum of American Finance (45,top)
Museum of American Finance (45, bottom)
Prints & Photographs Division, Library of Congress, LC-DIG-ppmsca-17523 (49, left)*
Museum of American Finance (49, right)
Museum of American Finance (50)
Museum of American Finance (51, left)
Museum of American Finance (51, right)
Museum of American Finance (52)*
Prints & Photographs Division, Library of Congress, LC-USZ62-122678 (53)
Library of Congress, Geography and Map Division, g3904w pm006700 (58)
Courtesy of BB&T Corporation (59, left)
Courtesy of BB&T Corporation (59, right)
Courtesy of BB&T Corporation (60)*
Courtesy of Mark Anderson (66)
Courtesy of Heritage Auctions (67)*
Florence-Lauderdale Public Library Digital Archive (68)
Detroit Publishing Company Photograph Collection, Prints & Photographs Division,
    Library of Congress, LC-DIG-det-4a13392 (69)*
Courtesy of BMO Corporate Archives (73)*
Courtesy of BMO Corporate Archives (75, left)
Courtesy of BMO Corporate Archives (75, right)
Museum of American Finance (79)
Museum of American Finance (84, left)
Museum of American Finance (84, right)
Museum of American Finance (85)
Museum of American Finance (86-87)*
Courtesy of Charles Schwab (89)
Courtesy of Charles Schwab (91)
National Photo Company Collection, Prints & Photographs Division, Library of Congress,
    LC-DIG-npcc-23165 (93)*
Museum of American Finance (94, left)
Museum of American Finance (94, right)

Museum of American Finance (95, left)
Museum of American Finance (95, right)*
Museum of American Finance (96, left)*
Museum of American Finance (96, right)
Museum of American Finance (97)
Museum of American Finance (100)
Museum of American Finance (101)
Museum of American Finance (103, left) *
Museum of American Finance (103, right)*
The Jon B. Lovelace Collection of California Photographs in Carol M. Highsmith's America
    Project, Library of Congress, Prints and Photographs Division, LC-DIG-highsm-21194
    (106)*
Museum of American Finance (107)
Detroit Publishing Company Photograph Collection, Prints & Photographs Division,
    Library of Congress, LC-DIG-det-4a27659 (112)*
G. Eric and Edith Matson Photograph Collection, Prints & Photographs Division, Library
    of Congress, LC-DIG-matpc-04670 (115, left)
Bain Collection, Prints & Photographs Division, Library of Congress,
    LC-DIG-ggbain-10624 (115, right)
Bain Collection, Prints & Photographs Division, Library of Congress,
    LC-DIG-ggbain-17819 (116, left)
Museum of American Finance (116, right)*
Courtesy of Carsten Frenzl, Flickr user: "cfaobam" (117)
The Cooper Collections (119)
Library of Congress, Prints & Photographs Division, FSA/OWI Collection,
    LC-DIG-fsa-8c33414 (121)
Museum of American Finance (123, left)
Museum of American Finance (123, right)
Museum of American Finance (124-125)
Museum of American Finance (131, top)*
Collection of Mark D. Tomasko (131, center)
Museum of American Finance (131, bottom)
Museum of American Finance (132)
Harris & Ewing Collection, Prints & Photographs Division, Library of Congress,
    LC-DIG-hec-13912 (133)*
Courtesy of First Niagara Financial Group (136, top)
Panoramic Photographs, Prints & Photographs Division, Library of Congress, pan 6a11798
    (136, bottom)
Courtesy of First Niagara Financial Group (137, left)
Courtesy of First Niagara Financial Group (137, right)
Museum of American Finance (139, left)
Museum of American Finance (139, right)
Museum of American Finance (141)
Museum of American Finance (144, left)*
Museum of American Finance (144, right)
Museum of American Finance (146-147)*
© Copyright HSBC Holdings pl (HSBC Group Archives) 2005 All Rights Reserved (150-151)*
© Copyright HSBC Holdings pl (HSBC Group Archives) 2005 All Rights Reserved (150,
    bottom)
Museum of American Finance (152)
© Copyright HSBC Holdings pl (HSBC Group Archives) 2005 All Rights Reserved (153)
Jersey City Free Public Library, the New Jersey Room (155, left)
Jersey City Free Public Library, the New Jersey Room (155, right)
Jersey City Free Public Library, the New Jersey Room (156)
Courtesy of the Newark Public Library (157)
Courtesy of the Columbus Metropolitan Library (162, left)*
Courtesy of the Columbus Metropolitan Library (162, right)
Library of Congress, Prints & Photographs Division, HABS, HABS MO,110-MARVI,1—1
    (165, left)
Library of Congress, Prints & Photographs Division, Balthazar Korab Archive at the
    Library of Congress, LC-DIG-krb-00627 (165, right)
Collection of Mark D. Tomasko (166-167)*
Museum of American Finance (173)*
Museum of American Finance (174)
Museum of American Finance (177)
Museum of American Finance (178-179)
Collection of Mark D. Tomasko (184)Frank and Frances Carpenter Collection, Prints &
    Photographs Division, Library of Congress, LC-DIG-ppmsc-02045 (185)

Library of Congress, Prints & Photographs Division, HABS, HABS OHIO,18-CLEV,14—1 (186, left)*

Collection of Mark D. Tomasko (186, right)

Collection of Mark D. Tomasko (187)

Prints & Photographs Division, Library of Congress, LC-USZ62-111698 (192, left)*

Museum of American Finance (192, right)

Museum of American Finance (193)

Museum of American Finance (195)

Museum of American Finance (196)*

Museum of American Finance (197)

Museum of American Finance (200)*

Museum of American Finance (201)

Bain Collection, Prints & Photographs Division, Library of Congress, LC-DIG-ggbain-30683 (204, left)

Collection of Mark D. Tomasko (204, right)*

Museum of American Finance (209)

Museum of American Finance (210, top)

Museum of American Finance (210, bottom)

Library of Congress, Prints & Photographs Division, HABS, HABS CONN,1-SOUPO,24—1 (211)

Library of Congress, Prints & Photographs Division, LC-DIG-npcc-32070 (216, left)

Courtesy of the Columbus Metropolitan Library (216, right)

Library of Congress, Prints & Photographs Division, photograph by Harris & Ewing, LC-DIG-hec-24186 (217)*

Library of Congress, Prints & Photographs Division, HABS, HABS PA,51-PHILA,256A—1 (218, left)*

Detre Library and Archives, Sen. John Heinz History Center (218, right)*

Courtesy of Chris Connelly (219)

Courtesy of Popular, Inc. (222)

Courtesy of Popular, Inc. (223, left)

Courtesy of Popular, Inc. (223, right)

Museum of American Finance (225)

Detroit Publishing Company Collection, Prints & Photographs Division, Library of Congress, LC-DIG-det-4a18132 (226)

Museum of American Finance (227)

The Royal Bank of Scotland Group plc ©2015 (232, left)

The Royal Bank of Scotland Group plc ©2015 (232, right)

The Royal Bank of Scotland Group plc ©2015 (233, left)*

Citizens Savings Bank, Providence, Rhode Island. PC6447. Rhode Island Postcard Collection, Providence Public Library, Providence, RI. (233, right)

Library of Congress, Prints & Photographs Division, HABS, HABS ALA,45-HUVI,3—1 (238)*

Courtesy of Heritage Auctions (239)

S-3497B: Merchants National Bank. Erik Overbey Collection, The Doy Leale McCall Rare Book and Manuscript Library, University of South Alabama (240-241)

Museum of American Finance (245)*

Museum of American Finance (246-247)*

Museum of American Finance (249)

Courtesy of the Bostonian Society (250, left)

Courtesy of the Bostonian Society (250, right)

Museum of American Finance (251, top)

Museum of American Finance (251, bottom left)

Museum of American Finance (251, bottom right)

The Jon B. Lovelace Collection of California Photographs in Carol M. Highsmith's America Project, Library of Congress, Prints and Photographs Division, LC-DIG-highsm-20807 (256)

The George F. Landegger Collection of District of Columbia Photographs in Carol M. Highsmith's America, Library of Congress, Prints and Photographs Division, LC-DIG-highsm-09773 (257)

Collection of Mark D. Tomasko (259)

Collection of Mark D. Tomasko (264-265)

Library of Congress, Prints & Photographs Division, HAER, HAER GA,108-COLM,17—4 (266, left)

Kenan Research Center at the Atlanta History Center (266, right)*

Collection of Mark D. Tomasko (272)*

City of Toronto Archives, Fonds 1568, Item 368 (273)

Courtesy of Kenny Louie, Flickr user: "kennymatic" (274)

Courtesy of US Bank (280, left)

Collection of Mark D. Tomasko (280, center)

Courtesy of US Bank (280, right)

Collection of Mark D. Tomasko (281)

Courtesy of US Bank (281, right)*

Courtesy of US Bank (282)

Collection of Mark D. Tomasko (283)

Collection of Mark D. Tomasko (287)

Museum of American Finance (288)

Scribner's Monthly, July, 1875, Vol. X, No. 3, p. 271 (289, left)

Prints & Photographs Division, Library of Congress, LC-USZ62-26279 (289, right)

Prints & Photographs Division, Library of Congress, LC-USZ62-55552 (290, left)*

The Cooper Collections of U.S. History (290, right)*

Harris & Ewing Collection, Prints & Photographs Division, Library of Congress, LC-DIG-hec-30082 (293)

© ADREES LATIF/Corbis (294)

Courtesy of David Shankbone, Creative Commons Attribution-Share Alike 3.0 Unported License (295)

Courtesy of Rabobank (298, left)*

Photocrom Prints, Prints & Photographs Division, Library of Congress, LC-DIG-ppmsc-05874 (298, right)

John C. H. Grabill Collection, Prints & Photographs Division, Library of Congress, LC-DIG-ppmsc-02598 (304)

Frank and Frances Carpenter Collection, Prints & Photographs Division, Library of Congress, LC-DIG-ppmsc-02266 (305, left)

Harris & Ewing Collection, Prints & Photographs Division, Library of Congress, LC-DIG-hec-20622 (305, right)

Lawrence & Houseworth Collection, Prints & Photographs Division, Library of Congress, LC-USZ62-11055 (306, left)

Museum of American Finance (306, right)

Museum of American Finance (307)

Brady-Handy Photograph Collection, Prints & Photographs Division, Library of Congress, LC-DIG-cwpbh-01671 (312)*

Photocrom Prints, Prints & Photographs Division, Library of Congress, LC-DIG-ppmsca-17879 (313)

Used by permission, Utah State Historical Society, all rights reserved (314)

Library of Congress, Prints & Photographs Division, HABS, HABS UTAH,18-SALCI,12A—1 (315)

Museum of American Finance (317)*

Additional images featured on cover:

Mountain Climber from Diners Club Advertisement, Museum of American Finance*

Huntington National Bank Building, Courtesy of the Columbus Metropolitan Library*

Index

Gonzalez, Francisco, 68
Goodwin, Fred, 233
Gorman, John, 136–37
government bailouts: AIG, 25, 26–27; BoA, 44; GMAC/Ally, 12. *See also* Reconstruction Finance Corporation; "too big to fail" policy; Troubled Asset Relief Program (TARP)
Grant, Heber J., 312, 314
Grant, Steven, 21
Great Britain, holding companies in, *ix*, 232–33, 317. *See also* HSBC North America; RBS-Citizens Financial
Great Depression: American Express and, 20; bank failures during, 316; The Bank of California and, 289; Bank of Lumberton and, 58; Bank of Montreal and, 74; Bank of Oklahoma and, 78; Bankers Life and, 225; BB&T and, 59–61, *60*; BONY and, 49; Bridgeport-People's Savings Bank and, 209–10; in Canada, 274–75; Chase and, 172; Chemical Bank during, 176; CIT Group and, 94–95; City Company (Citigroup) and, 102; Deere & Co. and, 165; Detroit Savings Bank and, 112–13; and First Hawaiian Bank, 34–35; First National Bank of Montgomery and, 238; J.P. Morgan during, 175; M&T Bank and, 192; Mellon and, 51; Merrill Lynch and, 42; National City Bank (Cleveland) and, 219; Netherlands during, 298; Northern Trust during, 205; and Oregon branching regulations, 281; Paribas and, 32; Popular and, 222; in Portland, Or., 280–81; Queens County Savings Bank and, 200; Tennessee Valley Bank and, 67; Trust Company of Georgia and, 256; Wells Fargo and, 305; Zions Bank and, 312, *314*
Greenberg, Maurice R. (Hank), 26
GreenPoint Mortgage Funding, 85
Greenwood Trust, 119, 120
Guaranty Trust, 172, 175
Gudelski, Leonard, 155
Gulliver, Stuart, 152
Gutfreund, John, 196

H

Haber, Steven, 316, 317
Hadley, Thomas Jefferson, 58
Hales, Jacob Cecil, 59
Hamel, Gary, 89, 90, 140
Hamilton, Alexander, *xii*, 1, 49, *49*, 172, 316
Hamilton, Francis, 266
Harding, Warren, *293*, 293
Harriman, Lewis G., 192
Harrison, William B., Jr., 176
Haven Bancorp, *198*, 200. *See also* New York Community Bancorp
Hawaii, *33*, *34*, 34–35. *See also* First Hawaiian Bank
Hawaii Thrift and Loan, 35
Hawley, Samuel, 209–10
Hayden-Clinton National Bank, 162
Hellman, I.W., 305
Hepburn, Alonzo Barton, 172
Hermance, Ronald E., 155–56
Herzog, Lester, 184
Hibernia National Bank, *84*, 85, *85*
history of banking, 1–3
Hoaglin, Thomas E., 163
Hoffman, Claire (née Giannini), 40
HongKong and Shanghai Banking Corporation (HSBC), 150–51, 151–52, *152*, 153, 232. *See also* HSBC North America
HongKong Bank, 151–52
Hope, C.C., 42
Household International, 152
Howard, Fred, 113
HSBC. *See* Hong Kong and Shanghai Banking Corporation
HSBC North America, *viii*, *ix*, x, xi, 6, **148–53**; and the AIG bailout, 26; CIT Group and, 97; credit cards, 86; and Discover, 120; Metris purchased, 223
Hudson City Bancorp, *viii*, *ix*, x, xi, **154–57**, 193
Hunter, James J., 289
Huntington, B.G., 162
Huntington, Francis, 162
Huntington, Peletiah Webster, 162, *162*
Huntington, Theodore, 162
Huntington Bancshares, *viii*, *ix*, x, xi, **158–63**

I

IDS. *See* Investor Diversified Services
Immelt, Jeffrey, 140
incorporation of banks and BHCs, 1–2
industrial loan corporations (ILCs), 2. *See also* Ally Financial; General Electric Capital; John Deere Capital
IndyMac, 193, 201
ING, 86, 299
insurance, as industry of origin, xi. *See also* American International Group; Principal Financial Group; United Services Automobile Association
investment banking, 1, 4; as industry of origin, xi (*see also* Goldman Sachs; JPMorgan Chase; Morgan Stanley)
Investor Diversified Services (IDS), 17, 21
Irving Trust, 47, 50, 312
Isaac, William, 130
Ittleson, Anthony, 96
Ittleson, Henry, 93, 94, 96
Ittleson, Henry, Jr., 96

J

Jackson, Andrew, 316
Japan: American banks in, 25; GE Capital and, 140; holding companies in, *ix*, 287, 317 (*see also* UnionBanCal)
Jennings, Henry B., 59
John Deere Capital, *viii*, *ix*, x, xi, **164–67**
John Parrott and Company, 289
joint-stock companies, 1, 2, 4
Jones, Carl E., 239
Jordan, George Gunby, 264
J.P. Morgan, 101, 174–75. *See also* JPMorgan Chase; Morgan Stanley
JPMorgan Chase, *viii*, *ix*, x, xi, **168–79**; and the AIG bailout, 26; and Morgan Stanley, 175, 177, 195, 197; subsidiaries, 6; and Synovus' TSYS, 267
J.S. Morgan, 174–75. *See also* Morgan Grenfell
Juncos, Manuel Fernandez, 222

K

Kador, John, 91
Kaiser, George B., 78
Kaufman, Henry, 103
Key Banks, 185. *See also* KeyCorp
KeyCorp, *viii*, *ix*, x, xi, **180–87**
Kidder, Peabody, 1, 139
King, Frank, 152
King, Homer S., 289
King, Kelly, 61
Kingston Trust, 184
Kirtz, E. Keith, 130
Kleinberg, Brian, 21
Kluge, John, 140
Koelmel, John, 136–137
Kolar, E.J., 281
Kovacevich, Richard, 306
Kuhn Loeb. *See* Lehman Brothers [Kuhn Loeb]
Kuhns, George, 225

L

Ladd & Tilton, 280, *281*
Lamont, Thomas W., 175
Lane, Robert W., 166
large, complex financial institutions (LCFIs), 6–7
Leffingwell, Russell, 175
Legg Mason, 103
Lehman Brothers [Kuhn Loeb], *16*, 21, 61, 103, 201
Leith-Ross, Sir Frederick, 151
leveraged buyouts, 196
Lewis, Ken, 42, 44
LIBOR price fixing scandal, 299
Lipman, Frederick L., 305
Lloyds, 232
Lockport Savings Bank, 136
Logan, James, 74
London and San Francisco Bank, Ltd., 289
Lowe, L. Vincent, Jr., 61
Lowry, Robert, 239
Lundell, Walter, 96
Lybarger, Stanley, 78
Lynch, Edmund C., 42. *See also* Merrill Lynch

M

M&T Bank, *viii*, *ix*, x, xi, 156, **188–93**
Mack, John, 119, 120, 196–97
Mackay, John, 305
MacLean, Hector, 59
Macleay, Donald, 280
Manhattan Company (Manhattan Bank), 172, 174. *See also* JPMorgan Chase
Manufacturers Hanover, 97, 169, 171, 175
Manufacturers National Corporation, 113
Manufactures and Traders [National] Bank, 192, 192–93. *See also* M&T Bank
manufacturing, as industry of origin, xi. *See also* Ally Financial; General Electric Capital; John Deere Capital
Marine Midland, 151
Marshall, Gerald R., 78
Marshall Field's department store, 226, *226*
Martin, Henry, 192
Martin, Paul, 74
Mason, John, 175–76
Mathewson, George, 232, 233
Mayer, Harold, 177
McCabe, Frank Wells, 184
McCloy, John, 172
McColl, Hugh, 41, 42
McCoy, John, 176, 177
McDermott, James J., 176
McFadden Act (1927), 2
McLean, Wilton Angus, 58, 59
Meadow Brook National Bank, 96
Melick, Baltus, 175
Mellon, Andrew, 51–52
Mellon, Richard, 51
Mellon, Richard King (R.K.), 51
Mellon, Thomas, 51
Mellon Financial Corporation, 48, 50–52, 233. *See also* Bank of New York Mellon
Mercantile Bank, 151, *276*, 282. *See also* Firstar
Mercantile Bankshares, 218
Mercantile Trust Company, 305
merchant banks and merchant banking, 4, 7n1
Merchants Bank (New York), 172, 177
Merchants Bank of Canada, 74
Merchants National Bank (Mobile), 239, 240–41
Merchants Union Express, 18, 21
mergers, 4–6. *See also specific institutions*
Merrill, Charles, 42. *See also* Merrill Lynch
Merrill, Edwin G., 49
Merrill Lynch: and the AIG bailout, 26; in Bank of America organization, 36, 38, 44; competitors, 89, 90, 91, 103, 123; fees, 89; stock certificate, *45*. *See also* Bank of America (BoA)
MetLife, 103, 140, 197
Meyer, Henry, 187
Michigan Bank, 96
Midland Bank (Britain), 150, 151
Midlantic Corp., 216. *See also* PNC Financial Services
Mid-State Bank and Trust, *297*, 298
Miller, Eugene, 113
Mills, Darius Ogden, 287, 289, 290
Milwaukee Trust Company, 282. *See also* Firstar
Mission Bank, 289
Mitchell, Charles E., 101–102
Mitsubishi Bank, 197, 287, 290, 291. *See also* UnionBanCal
Moerland, Piet, 299
Molson, John, 73
Molsons Bank, 74, *75*
money orders, 18, 19
Money Trust, 175
Monsanto Company, 93, 97
Monterey Bay Bank, 284, 291
Moore, Gilpin, 165
Morgan, Henry, 195
Morgan, J. P., Jr. ("Jack"), 175, 195
Morgan, J. Pierpont, 174, 175
Morgan, Junius S., 175
Morgan Grenfell, 116, 175
Morgan Guaranty, 175. *See also* Guaranty Trust; J.P. Morgan; JPMorgan Chase
Morgan Keegan, 234, 239

Acknowledgments

Without exaggeration, this book would not, and could not, have been completed without Charles Royce, who both inspired the project and supported it financially from start to finish with no strings attached. If more successful financiers were as enlightened as Mr. Royce, Americans' perceptions of the financial system would be more sophisticated and accurate and hence our nation's financial policies would be much more efficacious than they currently are.

Our heartfelt thanks, too, go to David Cowen, president of the Museum of American Finance, for his support of the project and his help during the editorial process.

The authors can claim no credit for this book's stunning visual imagery. Sarah Buonacore, the Museum's collections manager, conducted the image research and when she could not find an appropriate illustration in the Museum's collection or elsewhere, Mark Tomasko generously made available items from his own collection, including the lathework certificate design on the inside cover and first and last pages. And Maura Ferguson, the Museum's director of exhibits and educational programs, magically transformed Excel files containing merger and acquisition data into a visual form that the book designer, Luke Bulman of Thumb, could turn into the genealogical charts found herein.

We thank Becky Folkerts, the interlibrary loan coordinator at Augustana College, for acquiring dozens of obscure bank histories for us. We also recognize and thank Gary Richardson (Federal Reserve Bank of Richmond), Jesse Stiller (Office of the Comptroller of the Currency) and Eugene White (Rutgers University) for providing us with data, direction and encouragement early in the project.

The enthusiasm of publisher Myles Thompson at Columbia Business School Publishing was also immensely helpful as it suggested that we were not, in fact, crazy for committing to this enormous undertaking. And the editorial guidance from editor Bridget Flannery-McCoy was invaluable in translating mountains of research into book form. Finally, Kristin Aguilera, the Museum's deputy director, adroitly managed the project and coordinated all the moving parts, from the cover art to the index, so the authors could concentrate on research and writing.

— Robert E. Wright, Sioux Falls, SD
   Richard Sylla, New York, NY
   October 2014